JOHN CATT'S

Which School? 2018

Published in 2017 by
John Catt Educational Ltd,
12 Deben Mill Business Centre, Old Maltings Approach,
Melton, Woodbridge, Suffolk IP12 1BL UK
Tel: 01394 389850
Fax: 01394 386893
Email: enquiries@johncatt.com
Website: www.johncatt.com

Designed and typeset by Theoria Design. www.theoriadesign.com

A CIP catalogue record for this book is available from the British Library.

ISBN: 978 1 911382423

Contacts

Editor
Jonathan Barnes
Email: jonathanbarnes@johncatt.com

Advertising & School Profiles
Tel: +44 (0) 1394 389850
Email: sales@johncatt.com

Distribution/Book Sales
Tel: +44 (0) 1394 389863
Email: booksales@johncatt.com

Website: www.schoolsearch.co.uk

Contents

Editorial

School profiles

Directory

Appendices

How to use this guide

Which School? has been specifically designed with the reader in mind. There are clearly defined sections providing information for anyone looking at independent education in the UK today.

Are you looking for help and advice? Take a look at our editorial section (pages 5-40). Here you will find articles written by experts in their field covering a wide variety of issues you are likely to come across when choosing a school for your child. Each year we try to find a differing range of topics to interest and inform you about the uniqueness of independent education.

Perhaps you are looking for a school or college in a certain geographical region? Then you need to look first in the directories, which begin on page D295. Here you will find basic information about all the schools in each region complete with contact details. From this section you will be directed to more detailed information in the guide where this is available. An example of a typical directory entry is given below.

Are you looking for a certain type of school or college in your local area? Then you will need to look in the directories for your local area (see page D295 for a list of all regions). Underneath each school you will find icons that denote the different types of schools or the qualifications that they offer.

Some of you may already be looking for a specific school or college. In which case, if you know the name of the school or college but are unsure of its location, simply go to the index at the back of the guide where you will find all the schools listed alphabetically. Page numbers prefixed with the letter D denote the directory section; those without, a detailed profile.

If, however, you need to find out more information on relevant educational organisations and examinations, then you can look in the appendices where you will find up-to-date information about the examinations and qualifications available (page 407).

There is also a section giving basic details about the many varied and useful organisations in the education field (page 423).

The profile and directory information in this guide is also featured on **www.schoolsearch.co.uk**, which also includes social media links, and latest school news.

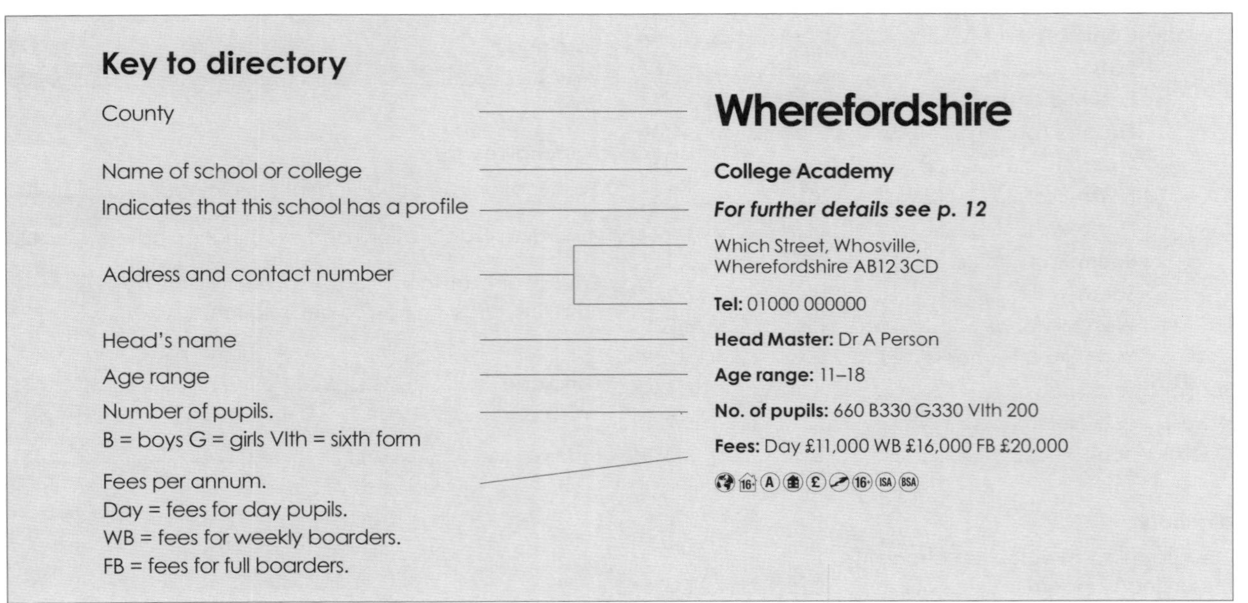

Key to directory icons

Key to symbols:

- Boys' school
- Girls' school
- International school
- Tutorial or sixth form college

Schools offering:

- A levels
- Boarding accommodation
- Bursaries
- Entrance at 16+
- International Baccalaureate
- Learning support
- Vocational qualifications

The questions you should ask

However much a school may appeal on first sight, you still need sound information to form your judgement

Schools attract pupils by their reputations, so most go to considerable lengths to ensure that parents are presented with an attractive image.

Modern marketing techniques try to promote good points and play down (without totally obscuring) bad ones. But every Head knows that, however good the school prospectus is, it only serves to attract parents through the school gates. Thereafter the decision depends on what they see and hear.

When you choose a school for your son or daughter, the key factor is that it will suit them. Many children and their parents are instinctively attracted (or otherwise) to a school on first sight. But even if it passes this test, and 'conforms' to what you are looking for in terms of location and academic, pastoral and extracurricular aspects, you will need to satisfy yourself that the school does measure up to what your instincts tell you.

Research we have carried out over the years suggests that in many cases the most important factor in choosing a school is the impression given by the Head. As well as finding out what goes on in a school, parents need to be reassured by the aura of confidence which they expect from a Head. How they discover the former may help them form their opinion of the latter.

So how a Head answers your questions is important. Based on our research, we have drawn up a list of 24 points on which you may need to be satisfied. The order in which they appear below does not necessarily reflect their degree of importance to each parent, but how the Head answers them may help you draw your own conclusions:

- How accessible is the Head, whose personality is seen by most parents as setting the 'tone' of the school?
- Will your child fit in? What is the overall atmosphere?
- To which organisations does the school belong? How has it been accredited?
- What is the ratio of teachers to pupils?
- What are the qualifications of the teaching staff?
- How often does the school communicate with parents through reports, parent/teacher meetings or other visits?
- What is the school's retention rate? Do larger lower classes and smaller upper classes reflect a school's inability to hang on to pupils?
- What are the school's exam results? What are the criteria for presenting them? Are they consistent over the years?
- How does the school cope with pupils' problems?
- What sort of academic and pastoral advice is available?
- What is the school's attitude to discipline?
- Have there been problems with drugs or sex? How have they been dealt with?
- What positive steps are taken to encourage good manners, behaviour and sportsmanship?
- Is progress accelerated for the academically bright?
- How does the school cope with pupils who do not work?
- What is the attitude to religion?
- What is the attitude to physical fitness and games?
- What sports are offered and what are the facilities?
- What are the extracurricular activities? What cultural or other visits are arranged away from the school?
- What steps are taken to encourage specific talent in music, the arts or sport?
- Where do pupils go when they leave – are they channelled to a few selected destinations?
- What is the uniform? What steps are taken to ensure that pupils take pride in their personal appearance?
- What are the timetable and term dates?
- Is it possible to speak to parents with children at the school to ask them for an opinion?

Are independent schools good value for money?

Barnaby Lenon, Chairman of the Independent Schools Council, tackles the question that every parent should ask

What are independent schools like these days? Are they good value for money?

Some rich families send their children to independent schools but the typical independent school parent is an upper-middle income family where both mother and father work and they make sacrifices to pay school fees.

In recent years independent schools have raised money to subsidise the fees of lower and middle income families. Today a third of pupils at private schools are on reduced fees and in many independent schools over 10% of pupils are on a means-tested bursary. At Manchester Grammar School, for example, over 200 pupils have a means-tested bursary which averages 93% of the fee.

Independent schools have increased their fees faster than the rise in average incomes. This has priced some middle-income parents out of the market. The average day fee of a private school in the UK is £13,500 a year. Nevertheless, independent school numbers have continued to grow and there are 600,000 pupils at independent schools

Why are they so successful?

Independent schools provide a very good education. Research by the Centre for Evaluation and Monitoring at the University of Durham in 2016 found that pupils in independent schools were two years ahead of state school pupils of similar ability. In 2016 82 of the top 100 schools in terms of A-level results were ISC schools, despite the fact that a high proportion of children at the most academic state schools receive private tutoring and these schools are more selective than most independent schools. These good A-level results are the reason that so many independently educated pupils go to top universities and thus on to good jobs.

According to the OECD international tests, 15-year old pupils in UK independent schools score on average at least 50 test points (around one and a half years of schooling) more than the average score of their peers in most other school types and perform as strongly as the average pupil within the top performing East Asian countries. A significant proportion of independent school pupils in England are amongst the highest-performing 15-year-olds in science anywhere in the world.

For more information about the Independent Schools Council, see page 34

The main reason that independent schools do well is that they have very high expectations of their pupils and everything that happens follows from this. Their independence from government gives them the scope to gear the education to the individual child, relatively free of government's curriculum constraints. Subjects which have withered in state schools, such as modern languages, classics, music and science, are popular in independent schools.

Independent schools also place a far greater emphasis on activities outside the classroom than most state schools. Art, music, drama and sport are very strong – which is why people complain that there are 'too many' independent school pupils dominating acting and sport, for example. But is not a coincidence: they have been trained at school.

Whereas in the state sector there has been a drive to make schools similar to each other (comprehensives in the 1970s and 1980s, Academisation since 2010), independent schools tend to have specialisations and are different from each other. There are, for example:

- Schools for pupils with special needs
- Schools for pupils of high ability
- Boarding schools, which are so important for parents who have to work abroad or move around a great deal.
- Single-sex schools
- Cathedral choir schools
- Music and dance schools
- Schools with a religious foundation, including Catholic schools.
- Nursery schools, so important in some areas where state provision is weak.

Independent schools are continuing to grow and thrive. They are making a big effort to hold down fee increases and increase the number of bursaries. They are the most successful type of school in the UK.

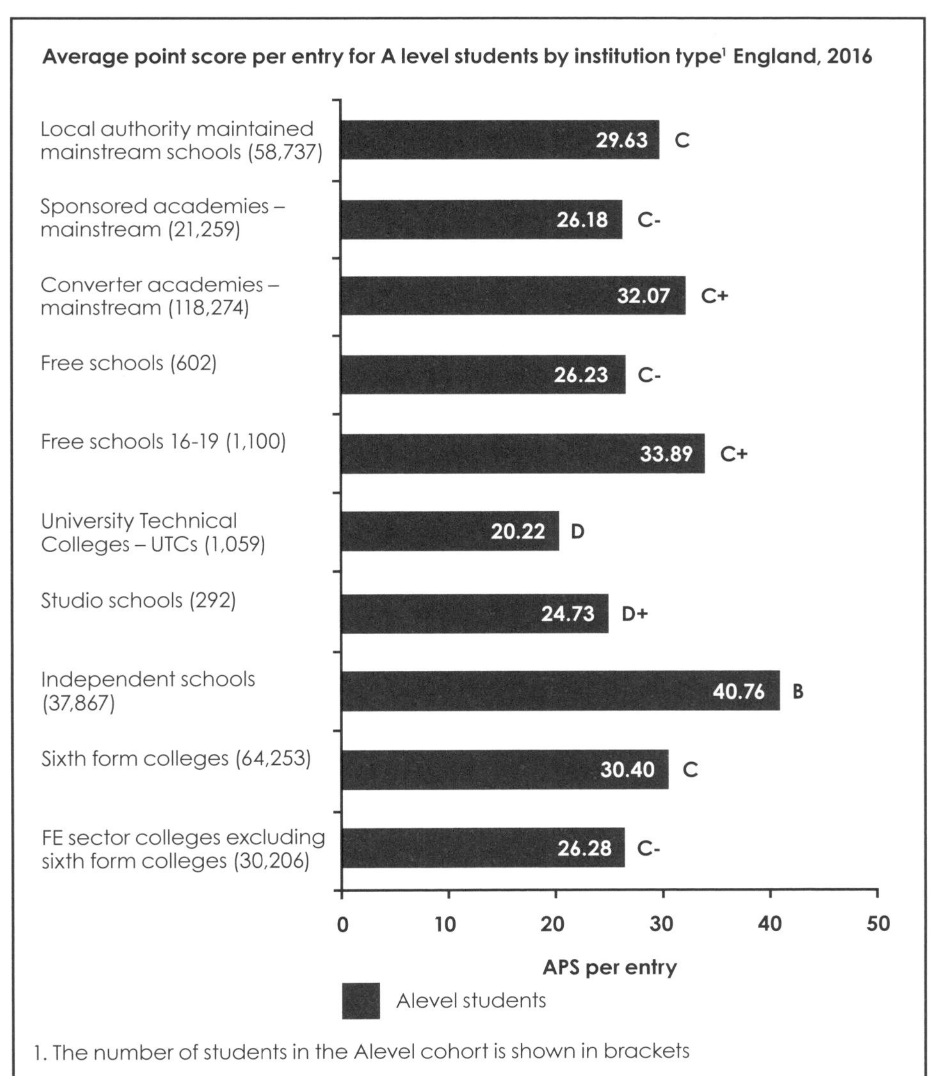

Source: DfE, 2017, Revised A level and other 16-18 results in England, 2015/2016, DfE

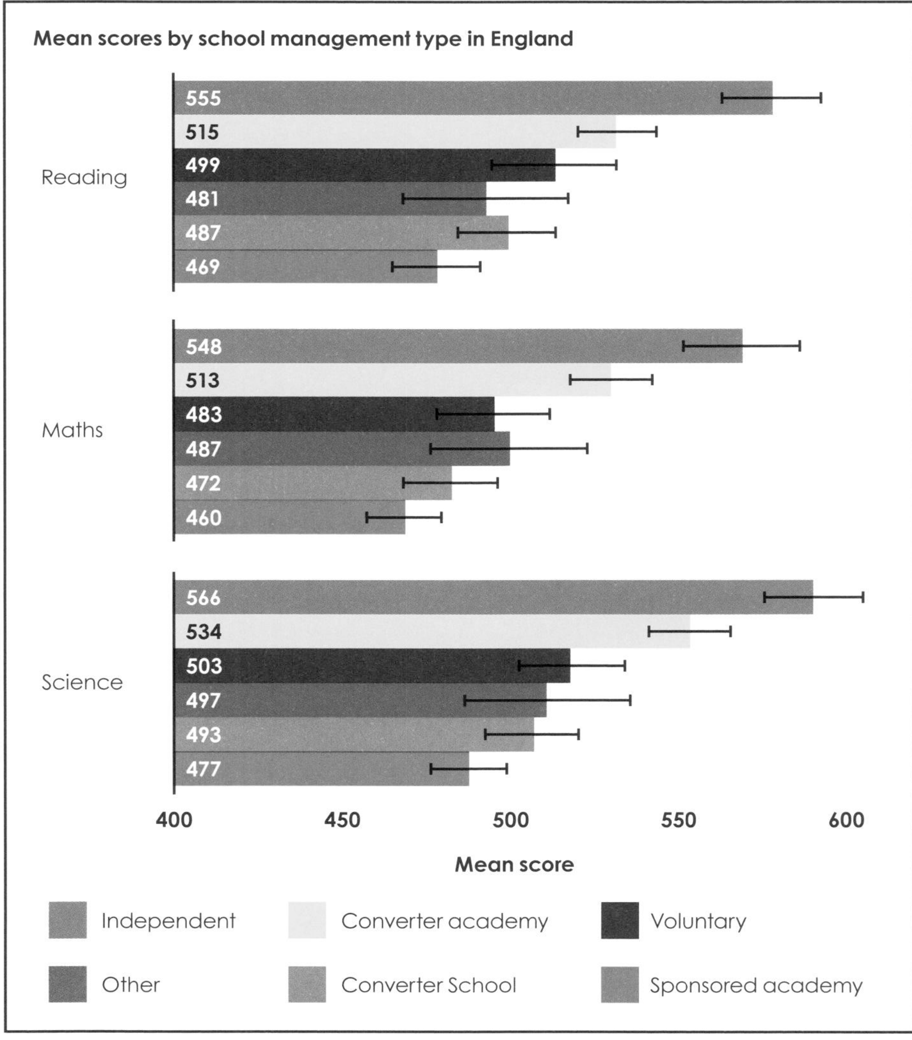

Source: Achievement of 15-year olds in England: PISA 2015, John Jerrim and Nikki Shure, UCL Institute of Education

How single sex schools are tackling gender imbalance

Charlotte Avery, 2017 President of the Girls' Schools Association, considers the impact of environment on schooling

It seems not a week goes by without something in the news about the gender imbalance in our schoolchildren's achievement. If it's not the lack of girls taking up physics and a career in engineering, it's the fact that the UK's gender imbalance in maths is one of the most pronounced in the developed world.

Across most developed countries, according to the OECD (Organisation for Economic Co-operation and Development), boys are better than girls at maths. The fact that you may think no surprise there may well be part of the problem. According to the OECD's Andreas Schleicher, the difference doesn't exemplify innate differences but is driven by girls' lack of confidence in their maths skills, alongside lower expectations that they will need maths in future careers. There is, Schleicher says, a close correlation between expectation and achievement.

What does this mean for parents looking for the right school for their children? Simply that, if you want your son or daughter to feel completely free to pursue their natural interests, unfettered by gender stereotypes or the gender-weighted expectations of either themselves or others, then you must do everything you can to make sure that both your child's home and school environment, and the people in them, place as few gender-weighted expectations on your child as is humanly possible.

You'd be forgiven for assuming that educating girls alongside boys would eradicate stereotypes and result in girls every bit as likely to study maths and boys every bit as likely to study English. Unfortunately – at least in the UK – the facts trounce this hypothesis.

Closing Doors is the most recent research on the subject by the Institute of Physics. It looks at six subjects with big gender disparities, three with a male bias and three a female bias: English, maths, biology, physics, psychology and economics. The findings show that the majority of co-educational schools fail to counter whatever drives young people to make gender-weighted choices when picking A Level subjects. The study does find co-educational schools that achieve, or at least approach, gender parity. However, the proportions are relatively low, ie 3.9 per cent of state-funded and 22.5 per cent of independent co-educational schools. What this does show is that it is possible to counteract gender imbalance, but clearly it's not something that comes easily to most co-educational schools.

Taking the opposite sex out of the equation for the few hours when young people are in the classroom can relieve significant pressure. In my opinion, it allows for focus, and experience shows that it gives pupils the space to study what they want to study – instead of what they and/or others believe they should study.

More research by the Institute of Physics, It's Different for Girls, points to the greater propensity of girls in single sex schools to study physics at A Level. The study finds that girls who attend girls' schools – in both the maintained and independent sectors – are more likely to continue physics beyond GCSE. In independent schools, the percentage of boys taking A Level physics is almost the same whether they are educated in a single sex or co-ed setting, but there is a marked difference with girls. Girls who attend independent girls' schools are almost 1.5 (1.46) times more likely to take A Level physics than girls who attend independent co-ed schools.

All this reflects what anyone who cares to peruse the exam results published by the Department for Education (DfE) can find for themselves. If you compare A Level results of girls in Girls' Schools Association (GSA) schools with those of all girls in England, you will see that girls at GSA schools are significantly more likely to take maths, chemistry and physics A level and over twice as likely to take most languages at A level.

But, I hear you cry, isn't single sex teaching falling out of fashion? In fact, despite a decline in the number of schools that are exclusively single sex, teaching in single sex groups – for girls and boys – is thriving. The Independent Schools Council's annual census shows that as many as 40 per cent of all the schools in its membership teach either all girls or all boys between years seven and 11; even at sixth form 36 per cent are single sex. Girls' schools today come in many different shapes and sizes. Some are exclusively all-girls, others are predominantly girls-only with boys in the nursery and/or sixth form. However, year after year, they fare disproportionately well in exam performance and sending students to Oxbridge and other Russell Group universities..

All of this is powerful data which demonstrates that being educated in an all-girls or all-boys environment can enable children – particularly girls – to counter stereotypical choices and expectations in their education. The Institute of Physics research is difficult to ignore because the sample sizes are so large.

If you are concerned about gender imbalance and you want your daughter to continue to enjoy her interest in tinkering with machinery or your son to pursue his love of poetry, my advice is to consider carefully their school environment. Whatever you decide, we are fortunate that the UK independent sector provides such a great choice. As well as co-educational schools, we have the alternative of all-girls, all-boys, predominantly girls or boys, and even diamond model schools, where girls and boys are taught together in the early years, separately from age 11 to 16, and together again in the sixth form. It's a wealth of parental choice which is undoubtedly worthy of celebration.

MUM

How to choose a secondary school

Nigel Williams, Head of Leighton Park School, asks you to consider what you really want for your children

The days of knowing, from the moment your children are born, which schools they are likely to attend have, for the great majority of us, long gone. Since the beginning of the 21st century the vast array of different options and choice has made parenting even more difficult and even more stressful, especially when it comes to choosing a secondary school. Sometimes the postcode lottery will mean that choosing where to live will be a direct consequence of deciding which school you want your child to attend. If you don't want to move house, parents looking for a day place should not rule out boarding as there is so much more flexibility on offer now with weekly and occasional boarding options gaining in popularity.

There are so many factors to consider but ultimately what should matter most is whether a school will reflect the educational philosophy that most appeals to you? Information is available in inspection reports, which can be very helpful. But perhaps more insightful, is talking to parents of students already attending the schools you are considering; they are usually more than willing to share their experiences. Sometimes you will be surprised by the findings of your research and may even alter your preconceptions.

The desire for academic success is a given and all schools will do their best to develop the academic potential of the children. That criteria does not therefore do much to help the decision making process, particularly with the tricky and misleading league tables to wade through. Arguably of more importance is the approach that a school uses to achieve academic success. From an academic 'hot house' at one end of the spectrum to a school that inspires a lifelong love of learning and treats each student as an individual at the other end. The debates will continue to rage over academic performance in single sex schools, but the social advantages and life lessons of living and learning with both sexes, as we all do throughout the rest of our lives, must also be considered. It is worth asking in which academic areas the school excels to enable you to match with your child's academic strengths.

Similarly the school's co-curricular programme should offer a breadth and depth of activities that match your child's interests. Does the range of clubs seem dominated by music, sport, art, drama or technology? You might consider a leaning in one direction to be positive if your child is especially gifted in one area, or you may prefer a wider range of opportunities that allow your child to develop new skills such film making or the Duke of Edinburgh Award scheme.

> We have a vision for our children; to see them laugh through life, to be successful in their chosen and considered careers, to realise their potential and to be surrounded by friends in their busy and caring social lives. Choosing the secondary school to realise this vision is a key decision.

Pastoral and welfare care has become of vital importance. There has been a massive increase in the number of mental health issues affecting young people as they learn to deal with the pressures of the digital age. To achieve happiness, success and progress the child needs to feel safe and secure in a school that regards their well-being of central importance. Does it provide wraparound care for all pupils, with early arrival provision and late stay? With both parents working, this flexibility can be a very important consideration; children sense when their parents are stressed and it can affect their wellbeing and success.

The real question is; what do we really want for our children? We want them to be happy, successful, comfortable in their own skin and comfortable in the company of others. We have a vision for our children; to see them laugh through life, to be successful in their chosen and considered careers, to realise their potential and to be surrounded by friends in their busy and caring social lives. Choosing the secondary school to realise this vision is a key decision.

One of the biggest decisions to be made is how confident are we that the school we choose will meet the individual needs of our child. Ultimately, the journey of discovery should enable parents to shortlist two or three schools. Entering a child for nine or ten entrance tests certainly keeps options open but puts huge pressure on the child. Parents know their own children and know what will be in their best interests. It is an important part of the selection process for parents to be strong and be prepared to make key decisions, even in the face of 'pester power'.

Choosing a secondary school today is not just about teaching and learning, it is about preparing your child for life in an ever changing environment. Matching the right school to the right child has never been more important.

Nigel Williams is Head of Leighton Park School in Berkshire, a co-ed day and boarding senior school grounded in the Quaker testimonies of truth, integrity, simplicity, peace, equality, sustainability and respect. *For more information see page 204*

ighton Park
School

The advantages of boarding

Mike Brewer, Deputy Head at EF Academy Torbay, outlines the benefits of the boarding experience

Boarding schools are rightly the subject of a lot of public interest. They are unique institutions that have a rich history, going back many hundreds of years in the UK, and yet they are not always easily understood. Perhaps the simplest explanation is that they are a combination of excellent schooling and a supportive home setting. This enables a boarding school to establish a very prominent community for its students through the shared experience of living in a home away from home, shared goals of academic and co-curricular success, the support of peers and, in many cases, an identity as a 'family'. The majority of modern boarding schools have excellent international profiles, taking pride in an exchange of cultures and ideas that thoroughly prepares students for life in the 21st Century. It is as true now as ever that friends made at boarding school are friends for life.

A great feature of life in a boarding school is that there is always somebody to talk to. In addition to qualified boarding staff, because students have a great deal in common and quickly recognize the importance of having goals shared by the community, they enjoy an atmosphere in which being successful is 'cool'. Students are proud to study and work hard and they applaud one another when they see their fellow students succeed.

Further, the reach of the school is such that it allows for a complete investment in the students' journey, day and night. Boarding schools are perfectly placed for direct intervention, with teachers and boarding staff in close liaison responding to student seamlessly needs as they arise. Boarding schools are widely recognised for producing significant academic advantages. A major reason for that is the overlap between school and 'home'. For example, in many residence buildings students have in-house support from qualified teaching staff.

It also helps that the school day doesn't abruptly end and boarding staff will make sure that the school knows which students are doing well and which ones are in need of further support, from additional revision to additional scrutiny during study time. Students are also a good source of support for one another, being easily able to form study groups and spurring each other on through friendly academic competition.

Teachers in boarding schools understand how much time and support is available, they also know that our students are often competing for places at universities that are highly selective. Our teachers are always keen to ensure that students have plenty to do that will push them beyond the minimum requirements of their courses. The independent school sector, which includes the majority of boarding schools, has a hugely impressive success rate in terms of access to top universities.

Through the carefully constructed routines of a boarding school, students learn to become independent in a safe and supportive setting. For many young people, their first taste of independence is when they leave home for university and, unfortunately, each year universities see students that are unprepared for the challenges and opportunities that life brings. Boarding school students have the advantage of having been taught how to motivate themselves, having been guided how to develop personal and professional relationships and having had experience of looking after themselves.

Of course, this independence is balanced with highly individualised levels of care that are made possible through holistic approach that boarding lends itself so readily to. Boarding schools recognise the need to have dedicated and highly qualified staff in place 24/7, often including the availability of professional medical and counselling services.

At the heart of every great boarding school is a thriving co-curricular programme. This helps to build a good work/life balance, enabling students to stay active and healthy, engaging them in sport and developing a portfolio of skills that will help them become successful in life beyond school. Many boarding schools have incredible facilities, from fully-equipped science laboratories to athletics tracks and even their own theatres. Students at boarding schools are usually able to take advantage of these incredible resources during evenings and at weekends, giving them time to familiarise themselves with environments that will inspire future university and even career choices.

Arguably the greatest feature of a boarding school education is that it creates lasting memories that often help positively and permanently shape a young person's life. The bonds of friendship forged in boarding school are that much stronger, easily transcending national boundaries; the inclusive ethos and committed work ethic helps create future leaders in all walks of life.

Michael Brewer is Deputy Head of EF Academy Torbay, Michael has worked in boarding schools for the past eleven years, including a very happy time as a residential Head of Boarding. He inspects boarding schools for the Independent Schools Inspectorate and recently completed his MA dissertation on the experiences of Victorian and Native American boarders.

For more information about EF Academy Torbay, see page 228

The rise of the Prep School Baccalaureate

James Barnes on why more than 50 senior schools are recognising a fresh approach to assessment

In 2012 the founding PSB schools recognised an opportunity to do things a bit differently which was created by senior schools pre-testing and offering places earlier and earlier. Initially this was with the caveat of 'subject to Common Entrance' but it has moved inexorably towards CE being used not as a qualifying examination but in most cases purely for setting purposes.

This is allied to the increasing range of entrance routes to senior schools – although it is the pre-test that rules the roost. Closely related to this has been the shift in ISI framework criteria, clearly identifying and emphasising the need for the development of skills alongside knowledge, in order for schools to be recognised as excellent when reflecting pupils' academic and other achievements. Recent ISI reports on PSB schools have emphasised this with report comments stating, for example: '(There are) many excellent examples of teachers setting clear and specific targets for pupils to improve where PSB criteria are used effectively' and 'Older pupils develop a substantial awareness of how to develop their own study skills such as hypothesizing, reflecting, analyzing and selecting, as a result of staff's excellent use of the Prep School Baccalaureate which targets such skills with precision.'

In recent years more junior schools have stepped away from strictly adhering to ISEB syllabus content, dropping this, trimming that or simply stating that they are going to do their own thing. Where the PSB has a clear advantage, is in creating and monitoring a framework for study, within which schools operate independently. There are clear expectations about embedding key skills – communication, collaboration, leadership, etc – within schemes of work and all aspects of school life, and staff participating fully in subject meetings that enable sharing and promoting of good practice.

The active assessment of skills with pupils is unique; whilst this is initially driven by teachers in the lower school, by Year 5 the emphasis is on self-assessment by pupils, with the support of a strong tutorial system. What the PSB doesn't do is sell courses or demand the use of a prescribed syllabus. The expectation is that schools will follow a broad and balanced curriculum and that what they do will be reflected by strong ISI reports; if a report is glowing the PSB will work well in a school – if it isn't, it is unlikely that a school will match expectations for membership.

So what makes us believe that the PSB approach is the right one? Put simply, the sheer weight of educational research that emphasises the crucial need for developing skills alongside knowledge. The Pearson Report Making Education Work emphasised that non-cognitive skills and attributes such as team working, emotional maturity, empathy and other interpersonal skills are important as proficiency in English or mathematics in ensuring young people's employment prospects. A technique being trialled in a number of maintained sector schools, that focuses on thinking skills, has seen results improve dramatically. In developing a framework for study the PSB trustees endorsed a focus that drew schools away from potentially slavish assessment to better developed skills.

The proof, inevitably, is in the pudding; the growth of schools in membership, and continuing interest from schools seeking membership, shows that the PSB is the right idea at the right time. With a philosophy that extends from Early Years, and the development of a whole school approach to teaching and learning, the PSB is a powerful vehicle for excellence.

As things stand over 50 senior schools welcome the PSB as a valid course of study and recognise the PSB certificate – reflecting assessment across subjects studied and the core skills – as proof of standards achieved across the curriculum. Most schools additionally accept pupils via their own entrance tests and some use core CE – with a growing number not requiring MFL. Crucially the greater flexibility of entrance requirements enables PSB schools to offer broad, exciting and educationally enriching courses; in a PSB school children will participate in an engaging curriculum that inspires independent thinking and intellectual curiosity. The breadth of courses reflected on the PSB certificate is a reflection of what individual schools promote for study and the commitment to shared good practice within the PSB enriches what our schools offer.

As a growing group of junior and senior schools, set within the context of the fragmentation of a common entrance route, the PSB has an increasingly important role to play in ensuring that individuality does not simply become splintered isolation. The PSB continues to evolve as its membership grows. The original skills matrix has been transformed by fresh input, a wellbeing grid is being trialled and a Skills Curriculum developed in conjunction with our senior school membership – this is all driven by teachers in our schools rather than 'dropped in' from an outside body without being worked through in practical circumstances. The greatest strength of the PSB is the fact that change is driven by staff within schools which gives it exceptionally powerful ownership and overseen by a committee of PSB Heads and trustees from the wider education community.

Member schools have no doubt that the PSB has been hugely beneficial, not simply in raising academic standards but crucially in preparing their pupils for the challenges of life and work in senior schools and beyond.

James Barnes is The Communications Director of the PSB.

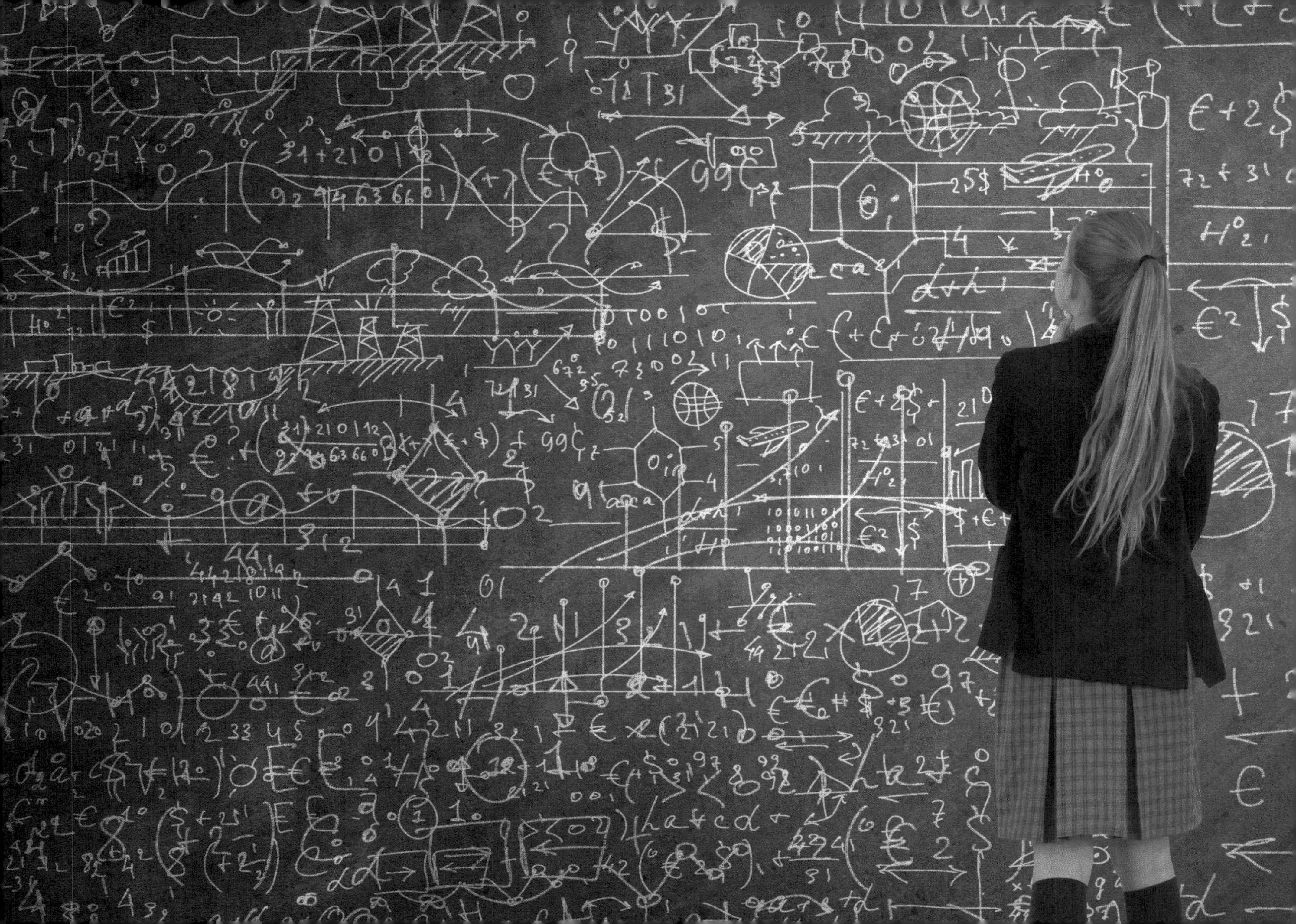

It is questions, not answers, that truly matter

Adam Williams, Headmaster of Lord Wandsworth College, believes that '+2' students are the future...

In February 2017, it was widely reported that geologists claimed to have discovered a new continent to the East of Australia: Zealandia. At 4.9 million km2 of land mass, 94% of which is underwater, Zealandia would be the world's smallest (and 8th) continent. It broke away from Australia 60 to 85 million years ago and then slowly sank back into the Pacific ocean. It is bold statements such as these, statements based on years of detailed research, curiosity and a creative approach by our scientists that sets our minds racing with more questions than answers. Maps and projected images entice us further to think, to postulate and to become embroiled in the what ifs...

The same can be said of recent archaeological discoveries on the Ness of Brodgar, Orkney, which uncovered a thriving civilisation 5000 years ago (potentially Britain's first Ancient Capital), whose stone circles pre-dated and potentially inspired those of Stonehenge and countless others, and which through painstaking research revealed its secrets of art, engineering, architecture, and navigation in some of the most treacherous waters in the UK, even by today's standards. For 1000 years, this society thrived before (it is thought) relinquishing their Neolithic way of life, enticed by the modern technologies of the Bronze age on the mainland.

One could choose many a reference point, but in this world of the more mundane and predictable passage of passing exams, it is an absolute pre-requisite for us, as teachers, to seek out the inspirational, stretching and bending our exam courses well beyond the specification and into the realms of research. We must aspire for our pupils to greet our teaching with a chiming chorus of "but why?" "but how?" or "sir, I've been thinking." We call this our '+2' at Lord Wandsworth College, encouraging pupils to stretch themselves to an academic level two years ahead of where they currently are and providing staff with a mandate to do the same. Embedding such behaviour at schools means all become role models and all can aspire for the +2 at their level. One only draws the line at the Upper 6th, who in looking at the years ahead often ask if they can lie in until 12pm and miss lectures...

Schools are becoming ever better at engendering relationships with University research, business, and professional networks – just in time too, for "we'll all be obsolete in 20 years"' is often a tongue-in-cheek response to a September morning INSET on technology and the future. And yet, for all these changes, education will never disappear – in fact one might argue that the pupils of today who sit eagerly in front of us with iPad and skinny latte in hand have never needed us more. But how can we prepare our pupils for this brave new world?

> It is an absolute pre-requisite for us, as teachers, to seek out the inspirational, stretching and bending our exam courses well beyond the specification and into the realms of research. We must aspire for our pupils to greet our teaching with a chiming chorus of "but why?" "but how?" or "sir, I've been thinking..."

Pupils can 'plug in' and be taught A level Film Studies from California as part of the MOOC world for example, and it will be this diversity of time and place for learning that will take us onwards. Recently, our pupils joined up for joint Biology lessons with a school in Ghana as they compared and contrasted experiments in differing biomes; teaching walls will allow their debates to flourish across time zones and virtual worlds will be commonplace. However exciting these new technologies are though, our tech-savvy pupils require us, as educators, to ensure learning is collaborative and inspires creativity and curiosity. Lord Wandsworth College's inaugural coding competition, sponsored by the world-renowned Red Hat organisation, was testament to this. One cannot overstate the importance of inspiring curiosity and creativity in the generations to come: it is non-negotiable.

We seek learning that brings real-world problems into the classroom as we cast off the shackles of a Victorian education system, rather, be inspired by schools such as High Tech High in San Diego. Project-based learning and a clear understanding of data interpretation still require lashings of emotional intelligence, a strong moral compass and a need to be both a mentor and coach.

It is an exciting future for us all and even though we, as a school, sit nestled in 1200 acres of rolling countryside on the edge of London with tractors and ploughs keeping our landscape in check (tracked by satellite, of course), the future shines bright for our +2 pupils.

For more information about Lord Wandsworth College, see page 206

Preparing your child for 7+ Entrance Exams

Lorrae Jaderberg and Katie Krais, Joint Founders and Managing Directors of JK Educate, offer some leading advice

The 7+

As the competition for secondary school places continues to intensify, 7+ entrance to independent preparatory schools (especially those with a senior department) is becoming increasingly popular. This means that the competition at 7+ is becoming increasingly fierce for academically selective independent schools across the country.

Is the 7+ the right choice for your child?

As for the 11+, a child should be academically assessed before embarking on this journey. If their academic potential doesn't match up to the school's expectations, then applying there might be setting them up to fail, even if they can be prepared well enough to secure a place there. Children should not be intensively tutored to get into a school for which they lack the innate aptitude to succeed and thrive once they are there.

The 7+ might facilitate entry to independent prep schools designed to prepare children for entry to academically selective senior schools, or for admission to academically selective independent schools with their own senior school. Once a child is in such a school, they still need to meet the school's required standards, and may still be examined at 11+, but they often effectively by-pass Common Entrance pressures.

How can you prepare your child for the 7+?

Although there are age-related differences to the 11+, it's still unfair to send a child into this unprepared. They would be at a disadvantage and might find it a demoralising experience with a long-term negative impact. Children need to understand what they will face and how best to prepare themselves for it, so a knowledgeable tutor's help can often be the most effective tool.

If the child is at a pre-prep, the school may be able to offer help, although this isn't always the case as they might prefer the child to progress to their prep school if they have one. State primary schools cannot and do not offer extra teaching for 7+ candidates.

Parents don't need to panic if their child is young in her year. At such a young age, a child born in September will still have a clear developmental advantage over one born the following August, but consideration will be given to relative ages. If tested, verbal and non-verbal reasoning scores are generally weighted against birth date.

How is the 7+ assessed?

Written exam content will be primarily English and maths based, whilst spelling, memory, mental arithmetic and creative skills may sometimes be assessed verbally on a one-to-one basis. In addition, group exercises are also sometimes used to look at a child's initiative and creativity, and their ability to work with others.

The English written paper will usually focus on comprehension of text and story writing. The expectation will be for a good use of vocabulary and a reading level well above average, with good structure and close attention to the precise questions being asked. Good handwriting should be practised as it is a real asset. Prepared and memorised answers will rarely be of use; candidates need to demonstrate the ability to meet the questions set for them on the day.

The written maths exam may include questions on any part of the Year 2 syllabus and sometimes questions will be pitched beyond that level. Mental arithmetic is very important, but be aware that quite complex word problems can also be included.

More schools are starting to include verbal reasoning and non-verbal reasoning; a lot of children really enjoy these puzzles and challenges, but they should still be practised.

Will there be an interview?

Most schools will call back for interview those children who have done well in the exams, but others may interview every candidate on the exam day. Interviews may comprise a one-to-one conversation with the headteacher and group tasks with other candidates. The interview will reveal the child's social skills, confidence and focus, whilst the group tasks will show their ability to follow direction and cooperate with other children. Schools will be on the look-out for children who have been told what to say, and what not to say, by parents.

What are schools looking for?

Children aged six and seven are obviously less established in school life and less capable of academic focus than those tested at 11+, but the schools are very aware of this. They will place value on social skills demonstrated in interview and group tasks, and on creative and verbal or listening skills. Schools will be looking for well-rounded children, but it's a fact that academic performance in a written exam remains the main measure.

Parents should avoid placing pressure on their children and encourage them to see the assessment process as an opportunity to show what they can do, rather than a test they must pass. This will allow them to relax, do their best and be themselves, which can only make a school want them more!

For more information visit jkeducate.co.uk

Opening doors through a specialist music education

Bryony Bell, of Chetham's School of Music, on the sound of success

Chetham's, in the heart of Manchester, is the largest of nine specialist Music and Dance schools across Britain, offering a world-class music education to 8-18 year olds with means-tested funding for 90% of students through the DfE's Music and Dance scheme. The school's musical accolades range from 5 star reviews in The Times to major competition successes – in recent years, Chetham's students have claimed prizes in the BBC Young Musician competition, the BBC Proms Inspire composers' competition, and the BBC Radio 2 Young Brass Awards, to name but a few. With that in mind, visitors to the school may be unsurprised to discover that its bespoke new building contains two floors of individual, acoustically-designed practice rooms, over 100 pianos, or an £8.7m award-winning concert hall; nor that every one of its 300 students enjoys an individualised timetable, including time for individual instrumental lessons, chamber and ensemble rehearsals, supported practice and music theory. What sometimes they forget, is that the top two floors of this unique building comprise classrooms, computer suites and science labs, where a dedicated team of teachers support students to achieve the strongest exam results of any non-academically selective school in Greater Manchester.

That level of success begins, says the school's Head Alun Jones, with a simple question: what should an 18-year old musician look like? The answer, of course, includes the careful nurturing of prodigious talent – but it's also crucial that students are socially aware, eloquent and informed. For many, the choice to study at Chetham's marks the start of a journey to the professional concert platform, via conservatoires and orchestras throughout the world; for others, music remains a lifelong passion alongside careers in law, medicine, politics or academia. The key is in ensuring that doors are opened, and not closed; that by choosing music at what may be a very young age, students do not lose sight of other interests or talents.

Students joining Chetham's quickly grow accustomed to packed school days and an ever-changing timetable, with music lesson times changing each week to avoid impacting unduly on any single subject. Practice before school and at lunchtime, and rehearsals continuing until early evening, can create what looks like a daunting schedule. For most students here, though, playing is as vital as breathing, and many have struggled to find a home in mainstream education, where their commitment to music set the apart from their peers. Chetham's provides a space where they belong, and where their commitment is supported by their fellow students as well as by music, academic and pastoral staff. The three are closely connected, and in the weekly concerts meeting – where students are assigned to upcoming performance opportunities – the workload and wellbeing of each young musician is as important a factor in each decision as the quality of their playing. A reduced concert schedule throughout May and June allows students to focus on public exams, and academic visits to study French in Paris, or geography in Iceland, are planned alongside musical tours to Poland, Italy and across the UK.

> "It's essential that we ensure that students have a chance to grow as young people, as well as young musicians."
> Alun Jones, Head

Since joining Chetham's in 2016, Mr Jones has prioritised students' welfare, increasing non-musical activities for boarders, opening up new channels of communication between students, staff and parents, and expanding already strong links between the school and Manchester's professional music sector. Chetham's First Scouts now meet weekly, and have held their first camping trip; prefects and school council members come together regularly to talk through elements of school life from uniform to catering. "It's essential that we ensure that students have a chance to grow as young people, as well as young musicians," Mr Jones explains. "They come to Chetham's from such a wide range of backgrounds, from different cultures and social groups, and find a common language through music. It's our job to help them use that language as a starting point to discover who they are as adults, to choose careers, and to build the skills they need to succeed – whatever path they choose to take."

A careful balancing act – but no more so than for a student in mainstream school who is also involved in youth orchestras or sports. Bringing these elements together within one organisation – in which students live, study and play across a single site – ensures a symbiotic relationship across departments to form a single, supportive community. A recent conversation with students asked them to sum up Chetham's in three words. Music came surprisingly low on the list – so central to their lives, it barely needed to be mentioned. They talked instead about family, inspiration, professionalism, fun – a space where they are free to follow their passions, a base from which to start whichever journey they may choose.

For more information about Chetham's School of Music, see page 164

Preparing for tomorrow's world

James O'Hanlon, Head of Careers at Dauntsey's, explains the importance of careful guidance

Just as the world of work has transformed in the last few decades so, I am pleased to say, has the world of careers guidance. Today, developing the right skills for employers is no longer just subject-specific. Of far greater importance is guiding pupils towards the development of aptitudes and skills which are transferable to a range of different roles. Achieving excellent grades is often a given and other factors are now equally, if not more, important; how well you interview, whether you can show an aptitude for what you want to do and are genuinely excited by it, whether you can cope when things get tough, how quickly you learn and apply what you learn and how you can make yourself stand out from a crowd.

Interestingly, up to 70% of roles offered by companies are 'degree-blind' (according to Highflyers Recruitment) – ie it's a case of meeting the employers' criteria, regardless of the specifics of your degree. The first step for many job opportunities is made on-line, meaning you don't have the luxury of selling yourself through a CV and face-to-face interview when embarking on an application. The NHS, one of the UK's largest graduate employers, is one organisation to adopt this recruitment strategy for non-medical roles. Developing strong numeracy and verbal reasoning skills and having an ability to navigate these screening procedures is crucial to moving to the interview stage with the chance to engage on a face-to-face basis.

In short, as careers counsellors, we need to be much smarter about the world of work and how we guide young people to work towards the best openings. Here at Dauntsey's, my role as careers advisor focuses on getting to know the pupils, their strengths and weaknesses and guiding them towards the best opportunities available here which will take them on to the next stage.

We run a programme of events where we highlight a particular sector. For example, a recent event focused on agri-business. A range of roles were represented by experts; biotech, food retailing, disease control in livestock, drone development, commodities trading and marketing. Sixth form pupils had the opportunity to explore the multi-faceted aspects of this industry and the roles therein.

Another event focused on sport. Many pupils here have a great love of sport – both viewing and participating in it. Twelve individuals representing different roles highlighted that behind every professional sportsperson lies a team of physiotherapists, sponsorship managers, marketing executives, nutritionists and agents.

We also run evenings based on the Speed Dating format where pupils have multiple mini meetings with a wide range of professionals. All career events that we run include an aspect of networking where pupils are encouraged to "work the room" and recognise the importance of building contacts and being able to open up opportunities. We have a network of contacts across a wide range of industries, drawn from the community, Old Dauntseians and existing parents. They are very generous with their time and keen to share their knowledge and experiences. This is enormously beneficial for the pupils to hear.

We encourage pupils to look at developing skills outside their areas of strength and competence. Many future roles will place them outside their comfort zone and being prepared to operate in such situations is an attractive attribute to display to a prospective employer. Bringing something extra always enhances an application and pupils are encouraged to have this in mind as they decide what to take up and what to drop during their school career. Can they keep up one language – so critical in today's global economy? Would drama improve their presentation skills? Would involvement in team sports show they are a team player?

We help pupils find work experience, although there is increasing competition from university students seeking the same opportunities in the first years of their degree. There is a wider understanding that the sooner you can secure relationships in the world of work the better, it's not a case of leaving it until you graduate. Work experience can often come through contacts and connections which are crucial and it's never too early to start building them. We have a mentoring programme which gives pupils the opportunity to learn from Old Dauntseians and parents, pick their brains, explore options and discover new possibilities.

A new – and growing – option is the world of apprenticeships where work is combined with study. They present a great opportunity for some and can be a lot more cost-effective than the university route. Certainly, they move you onto the employment track sooner, although they can't replicate the life-enriching opportunity University presents to study a subject at the very highest level.

I am pleased to say that pupils leaving Dauntsey's go on to pursue a wide and varied range of careers. Looking back at school class lists and photographs, it's fascinating to reflect on what they have gone on to be – barristers and solicitors, doctors and nurses, journalists and press secretaries, chemical engineers and F1 design engineers, biotechnologists and AI designers, architects and museum curators, NGO officers and social workers and, I am pleased to say, teachers and lecturers.

All of them, I hope, would acknowledge that the route to their chosen career has not always been straightforward and that in most cases it is the attributes beyond academic results which have made the difference to their journey.

For more information about Dauntsey's see page 48

It takes a ~~village~~ school to raise a child

Regan Schreiber on the importance of pastoral care and how schools are taking on a greater responsibility

An African proverb says, "It takes a village to raise a child". In our ever-changing world, it now takes a school to raise a child. With the alarming statistics of children being diagnosed with depression at a young age, and resilience and well-being becoming the new "watch words" in schools, there is an ever-greater need for schools to be aware of the roles that they are to play in raising a child. When looking at 'which school' to choose, I urge you to look beyond the outstanding facilities, the superbly equipped classrooms and the extensive playing fields. What really matters is the school's interpretation of the exceptional pastoral care it promises to deliver and to discover what this really means for the children in its care.

John Newman once said that teaching requires a moral dimension otherwise it is cold and arctic. Well, never has this been more relevant than today. Teachers have always been story-tellers, carers, educators, coaches and a myriad of other roles (too many to mention), but one which has to be a priority is that of being a parent and role-model to the children.

My philosophy, which has always guided me in teaching and indeed boarding, is that every child should be "parented" each and every day. Allow me to expand on this notion: children should not be allowed to get through a day without an adult asking them how they are feeling and digging a little below the surface in order to get to know the child better and help the child feel appreciated, loved and cared for. This is even more pressing in today's times, where life has bombarded and stolen that precious time that parents and their children were able to enjoy in the past.

This is where schools come in. And by schools I mean the staff – the men and women who work with your children day and night. This includes the administrative staff, the domestic staff, the grounds men, the matrons and the teachers. We all have a role to play in the lives of the children in our care.

Communication is key. Schools need to ensure that they have created an environment that encourages adults to talk freely and warmly about children, to discuss their concerns and there should be a philosophy of believing that childhood is precious. The bottom line is that children need good role models entwined in their lives.

> Teachers have always had an enormous responsibility in looking after children and that level of responsibility has increased further to include making sure that a child is learning valuable life lessons.

This healthy communication needs to exist between the children and the adults too. The children need to believe that they have a voice and that we are the ears! Children at school will be looking to the adults for guidance, support, advice and dare I say, love and a sense of belonging.

Teachers have always had an enormous responsibility in looking after children and that level of responsibility has increased further to include making sure that a child is learning valuable life lessons. From being able to tie shoes to ride a bicycle and to learn to read – these are many of the skills that children were taught by parents. For whatever reason, the responsibility for some of these skills has fallen on the shoulders of schools. And we teachers are ready for this. Teachers have always believed that there is more to merely teaching lessons. Only now is it becoming clearer for all to see. Teachers need to help children build self-confidence, instil a sense of self-belief, foster an appreciation and tolerance for others, facilitate friendships, help discover new talent and that which makes a child's tail wag, as well as to reinforce the importance of self-control and self-respect. Teachers and parents need to work together.

It is no longer the job of the village. The village has shut its doors and moved on. The village people are struggling to survive themselves. Schools need to now carry the banner for raising children. Schools need to shoulder even more responsibility in helping children to become well-balanced individuals. Schools need to shift the focus from grades to a holistic focus on the well-being of the child. So yes, we are no longer teaching children, we are raising children.

School and parents need to embrace the challenge and work together for the sake of our children. Teachers and parents must become partners. They can no longer wave to each other from the car park or the street, they need to meet face to face and celebrate their children and talk. They need to become active partners in the rearing of children.

So, when choosing which school, make sure you meet the staff who will be those all-important role-models for your children and who will be responsible for the delivery of that exceptional pastoral care.

Let's start raising our children together!

Regan Schreiber is Head of Boarding at Hazlegrove Prep School in Somerset.
For more information about Hazlegrove Prep School see page 232

YOKOHAMA
TYRES

Traditional values recognised alongside modern ambition

Kirkham Grammar School Headmaster Daniel Berry ended his first year as head with an excellent inspection report

The rigour, volume and attention to detail of an Independent School Inspection means that every area of Kirkham Grammar School was under scrutiny. Of the last three inspections, the earlier two have been deemed 'very good' with the most recent recognising the school as 'excellent across all areas', the highest grading possible within the independent sector. During the inspection over 60 lessons were observed, meetings undertaken and every aspect of the school's infrastructure and life scrutinised.

The inspection found that the quality of the pupils' academic and other achievements is excellent, saying: "Pupils are articulate and display excellent verbal and communication skills." The report adds: "Pupils are ambitious learners, eager to respond to challenging opportunities in lessons and clear target setting in marking." The quality of the pupils' personal development was also deemed excellent: "Pupils reflect the strong family ethos of the school and demonstrate excellent collaboration in and out of lessons." The recent inspection confirmed what was already known; Kirkham Grammar School is the best kept educational secret in Lancashire. However, it was pleasing for everyone that it has been officially acknowledged against national criteria that we are working hard to ensure our pupils get the finest education.

It has certainly been one of my proudest and clearly rewarding professional decisions to join such an historic school as Kirkham Grammar School. The start of the new academic year 2016-17 was a significant one for me personally as I entered my first full academic year as Headmaster. In these challenging times, where other independent schools are opting to be free schools or become part of a multi-academy trust, we have strengthened our 'Truly Independent' status. It is heartening to stress that we welcomed a large cohort into the first year and retained the largest number into the sixth form for a number of years. I have become convinced that central to our success going forward is maintaining the principle of independence. We are a school that is well equipped to move forward and to ensure that pupils, who only travel through this school once, receive the very best. We can reflect proudly on our achievements from last year to prepare us well for the future.

> We are proud of our school and the lifelong memories that clutch at our hearts and are full of opportunity; memories of muddy rugby fields, laughing friends and sunbathed cricket pitches.

Kirkham Grammar School aims to give pupils the widest possible perspective on the available opportunities before they leave us. In light of this, we were delighted to support National Careers Week this year in the drive to improve the life chances and social mobility of our young people. Celebrating careers provides them with a real motivational boost, raises their aspirations and encourages them to pursue their full potential. In support of our initiative, it was a privilege to welcome local businesses to Kirkham as they brought real career examples to life. Alongside our new programme of bespoke Career Workshops, the result was truly inspiring. Set over four separate evenings during the week, the Career Workshops were a departure from our usual Annual Careers Fair. They looked at opportunities within STEM, medicine, commerce, wealth management and law, as well as interactive skills development taster sessions. Strategically, KGS adopts a core value of 'educating the whole person'. Our Career Workshops were designed to support this ethos alongside our young people as they begin to navigate their career and higher education journey.

However, it is the tradition and long history of KGS that remains strong and underpins our ethos. People, buildings and the world around us are constantly changing. However, the core of KGS remains. We will ensure the traditional values are recognised alongside modern ambition. The longer I spend at Kirkham Grammar School, the more I understand what clearly makes it such a unique school. The following is still relevant to our fine school today: The virtue of a school does not depend entirely on its classrooms, the equipment in its laboratories, the number of its pupils, nor even the success of its exam results. There is an unseen influence that is exerted by buildings and surroundings that are beautiful and dignified and in keeping with fine honourable traditions and high ideals embedded at KGS. We are proud of our school and the lifelong memories that clutch at our hearts and are full of opportunity; memories of muddy rugby fields, laughing friends and sunbathed cricket pitches. There is something at KGS that is intangible but very real, the atmosphere in which we dwell, that pervasive spirit which surrounds us and influences all of which we strive to achieve. It is a great heritage at KGS and one which will stay with you for life. As we enter a new chapter in the school's long and successful history, we look forward to even more from our wonderful pupils.

For more information about Kirkham Grammar School see page 168

Navigating the new landscape of A level reform

David Shah, Director of Studies at MPW Cambridge, offers some advice to students and their families

The planning of a prospective sixth-form student's A levels has always required the utmost consideration. Building on successful GCSEs – the results of which are not even known when the 'What A levels?' conversation usually starts – and projecting towards potential university or vocational goals are important parts of this process. If truth be told it is often a very stressful time for students and parents alike.

So the last thing needed is the added complication of the on-going A level reform. Although this has been a reality in the sixth-form landscape for the past two years, it reaches its culmination in 2017/2018. Whether you are a student who is just about to embark on two-year A levels, one who is looking to change your educational setting between Years 12 and 13, or one who is looking to improve on already achieved A level grades as an alternative to UCAS Clearing, seeking expert advice has never been more strongly recommended.

Many of the young people and parents who approach us for A level guidance do come remarkably well-informed. Indeed, most of them have often started their research by going on line or even started important conversations with Admissions Officers. Many know specific detail on which subjects are required for a particular university course. Others realise that there is little advantage in taking courses too similar in content, and understand that demonstrating a breadth of knowledge can be very valuable. Some are sufficiently wise and appreciate that it is better to take three A levels and get great results in all three than to take on more and risk lower grades and potentially fewer UCAS points. The best informed student may even ask about which exam board a given A level subject is taught in. On this latter point, knowing the difference between OCR A and OCR B (Salters) Chemistry is vital in planning an End of Year 12 Transfer which includes this subject. The A level reform, however, has added a whole new dimension of complexity (and confusion) to the exercise.

Beyond the government's guiding principles in setting down the reform – a political response to perceived A level inflation, as identified by Michael Gove in his previous role as Education Secretary – one of the most visible changes has been the 'decoupling' of AS and A levels. Whereas before, AS level exams taken at the end of the lower-sixth year would count for 50% of the A level, now their value is significantly diminished. They form a self-contained qualification and a full A level's marks are now only available in the final upper-sixth exams. The move from a modular system to a more linear one which places much greater emphasis on the final exam will very likely lead to tougher end of year examinations, increasing the stress on all. Perhaps this is balanced by a system where there is now less coursework and fewer practicals. However, if you then add to the mix the phased transition from the older (or 'legacy') to the new ('reformed') A levels which have been introduced in three distinct 'waves', between September 2015 and September 2017, you will begin to appreciate the average sixth form aspirant actually has a lot to think about.

Of the young people approaching MPW over the coming months, we could have a Year 13 student who – even before their summer exams – is not confident about achieving their target grades or has reassessed their university goals or even both. In other words, they need a 'Plan B'. If this student, for instance, is looking to revisit A levels in a year in Economics, Geography and Mathematics, the first would have to be undertaken in its entirety as a 'reformed' subject, the last would still be examined in 'legacy' units in Summer 2018, while the Geography could be either. How this is then framed in a universities application also requires a knowledgeable educator's insight.

All sixth form colleges worth their salt should be offering prospective students and their parents the expert advice needed to navigate their way through the changing A level landscape. Different schools will have different policies – some, for instance, may elect not to enter any students for AS exams, perhaps arguing that this will increase actual teaching time.

We must now just hope that the politicians who have an influence allow these changes to embed properly and do not decide to reset the compass again anytime soon.

For more information on MPW Cambridge, see page 80

Whether you are a student who is just about to embark on two-year A levels, one who is looking to change your educational setting between Years 12 and 13, or one who is looking to improve on already achieved A level grades as an alternative to UCAS Clearing, seeking expert advice has never been more strongly recommended.

An outstanding education is more than mere training

Guy Ayling, Warden of Llandovery College, says a little deviation from the syllabus is no bad thing

The definition of *education* is wide ranging and depends to a large degree on who you ask. The wonderful diversity of the independent sector – surely its greatest strength – reflects varying interpretations and offers something for just about everyone. Broadly speaking however we might reach a consensus that education is systematic learning that develops a sense of analysis, judgment and reasoning; there can be little doubt that our schools address that challenge to great effect. More than occasionally however we hear the word *training* pop up in discussions on education and school provisions might appear to be simply a loose confederation of training opportunities. Training, imparting a special skill or behaviour, is certainly part of the educational process but it can never express in itself the breadth and richness of a good education and must be seen within a wider more coherent whole.

At Llandovery College in Carmarthenshire, Wales, we embrace passionately an all-round education. Everything that we do must sit on at least one of our three pillars of learning: *making better decisions, good citizenship* and *intellectual rigour and curiosity*, through which our pupils learn to tackle a rapidly evolving world with confidence and cheerfulness. These pillars are merely an updating of the great Thomas Arnold's maxim that education is about 'first religious and moral principle, second gentlemanly conduct, third academic ability.'

The College's Combined Cadet Force and Duke of Edinburgh's Award scheme of which we are so proud, train our young in specific skills such as weapon handling, map reading and climbing; but learning to approach challenges confidently and positively, to see a project through to completion and overcoming fear when doing something new is the more valuable sum gain of these activities and so much greater than the training parts. Through the training therefore a deeper educational value is nurtured.

Likewise, the training pupils receive in Llandovery College's vegetable gardens certainly develops the skills to put fresh food on the table, but it is part of a wider curriculum-based experience aimed at developing an appreciation for the harmony of nature and humankind's responsibility to it, a pressing issue on which I wrote in this publication in 2015. The seven Principles of Harmony – Geometry, Interdependence, Cycles, Diversity, Health, Beauty and Oneness – are now fully embedded in our Prep School curriculum, pupils engage enthusiastically with the work of the Sustainable Food Trust and Llandovery College boasts an internship programme for young adults set on a career in sustainability. Recently hosting an international conference on Harmony in Food and Farming, at which HRH the Prince of Wales (pictured) spoke passionately on issues close to his heart, has provided further encouragement to our efforts to engrain a new way of thinking at the College. Our training in this area then reveals deeper more important truths.

Training is part of the collective educational process and often in itself forgotten but remains relevant for a lifetime in its contribution to the broader experience that develops more profoundly valuable skills and attitudes. If it was all about training, there would be courses on how to leave Europe smoothly, but there are not.

Where training has its greatest and potentially most dangerous impact is in the classroom. League tables and hothouses have produced a pernicious and frenzied atmosphere in education where careers, of staff rather than students, can be broken on a set of results. The temptation then to train our pupils to perform in the examination hall is almost irresistible, a reality all the more curious for the entirely contrived context of these tests. Teachers are forgiven now for discarding all the really 'interesting stuff' they might want to share with curious minds and keeping strictly to the examination specification. Our pupils are aware of it too: 'is this on the syllabus?' and 'do we need to know this?' are telling questions pupils never asked when I started teaching many years ago.

Mark Twain is reputed to have said something along the lines that history does not repeat itself but it often rhymes. If we simply train our young for specific tasks then they will do a job well once but lack adaptability; the exact repeat will not come round again and they will lack the skills to notice the rhyme. The examinations we train for will never happen again, they are fixed both in time and space, but they can be of lifelong use if we do not lose sight of what they should really be teaching us.

I am confident however that the independent sector recognises that this training is not really an education and mitigates against it by allowing, indeed encouraging, occasional deviation from the syllabus, as well as offering a myriad of societies and other enrichment activities and opportunities that lie at the heart of a true education.

Our schools therefore keep the true flame of education burning brightly.

For more information on Llandovery College see page 280

Llandovery
College

Help in finding the fees

Chris Procter, joint managing director of SFIA, outlines a planned approach to funding your child's school fees

Average school fee increases in the last year were 3.5% which is the lowest since 1994, however this is still significantly higher than inflation. Recent analysis shows that school fees have increased by 553% in the last 25 years, compared to a rise in consumer prices of 201% and wage rises of 217%.

The latest Independent Schools Council (ISC) survey, completed by 1,259 of the 1,301 schools in UK membership indicate that there are now 522,879 pupils being educated privately, the highest number since records began in 1974. 86.6% of these were day school pupils, 13.4% were boarders. The share of girls and boys at ISC schools is very nearly equal, with boys representing 51% of all pupils.

The overall average boarding fee is £10,753 per term and the overall average day fee is £4,702 per term. However, fees charged by schools vary by region – for example the average boarding fee ranges from £8,505 per term in the North East to £12,121 per term in Greater London; the average day fee ranges from £3,445 per term in the North West to £5,524 per term in Greater London.

The overall cost (including university fees) might seem daunting: the cost of educating one child privately could well be very similar to that of buying a house but, as with house buying, the school fees commitment for the majority of parents can be made possible by spreading it over a long period rather than funding it all from current resources.

It is vital that parents do their financial homework, plan ahead, start to save early and regularly. Grandparents who have access to capital could help out; by contributing to school fees they could also help to reduce any potential future inheritance tax liability.

Parents would be well-advised to consult a specialist financial adviser as early as possible, since a long-term plan for the payment of fees – possibly university as well – can prove very advantageous from a financial point of view and offer greater peace of mind. Funding fees is neither science, nor magic, nor is there any panacea. It is quite simply a question of planning and using whatever resources are available, such as income, capital, or tax reduction opportunities.

The fundamental point to recognise is that you, your circumstances and your wishes or ambitions, for your children or grandchildren are unique. They might well be similar to those of other people but they will still be uniquely different. There will be no single solution to your problem. In fact, after a review of all your circumstances, there might not be a problem at all.

So, what are the reasons for seeking advice about education expenses?

- To reduce the overall cost?
- To get some tax benefit?
- To reduce your cash outflow?
- To invest capital to ensure that future fees are paid?
- To set aside money now for future fees?
- To provide protection for school fees?
- Or just to make sure that, as well as educating your children, you can still have a life?!

Any, some, or all of the above – or others not listed – could be on your agenda, the important thing is to develop a strategy.

At this stage, it really does not help to get hung up on which financial 'product' is the most suitable. The composition of a school fees plan will differ for each family depending on a number of factors. That is why there is no one school fees plan on offer.

The simplest strategy but in most cases, the most expensive option, is to write out a cheque for the whole bill when it arrives and post it back to the school. Like most simple plans, that can work well, if you have the money. Even if you do have the money, is that really the best way of doing things? Do you know that to fund £1,000 of school fees as a higher rate taxpayer paying 40% income tax, you currently need to earn £1,667, this rises to £1,818 if you are an additional rate taxpayer where the rate is 45%.

How then do you start to develop your strategy? As with most things in life, if you can define your objective, then you will know what you are aiming at. Your objective in this case will be to determine how much money is needed and when.

You need to draw up a school fees schedule or what others may term a cash flow forecast. So, you need to identify:

- How many children?
- Which schools and therefore what are the fees? (or you could use an average school fee)
- When are they due?
- Any special educational needs?
- Inflation estimate
- Include university costs?

With this basic information, the school fees schedule/cash flow forecast can be prepared and you will have defined what it is you are trying to achieve.

Remember though, that senior school fees are typically more than prep school fees – this needs to be factored in.

Also be aware that the cost of university is not restricted to the fees alone; there are a lot of maintenance and other costs involved: accommodation, books, food, to name a few. Don't forget to build in inflation, I refer you back to the data at the beginning of this article.

You now have one element of the equation, the relatively simple element. The other side is the resources you have available to achieve the objective. This also needs to be identified, but this is a much more difficult exercise. The reason that it is more difficult, of course, is that school fees are not the only drain on your resources. You probably have a mortgage, you want to have holidays, you need to buy food and clothes, you may be concerned that you should be funding a pension.

This is a key area of expertise, since your financial commitments are unique. A specialist in the area of school fees planning can help identify these commitments, to record them and help you to distribute your resources according to your priorities.

The options open to you as parents depend completely upon your adviser's knowledge of these complex personal financial issues. (Did I forget to mention your tax position, capital gains tax allowance, other tax allowances, including those of your children and a lower or zero rate tax paying spouse or partner? These could well be used to your advantage.)

A typical school fees plan can incorporate many elements to fund short, medium and long-term fees. Each plan is designed according to individual circumstances and usually there is a special emphasis on what parents are looking to achieve, for example, to maximise overall savings and to minimise the outflow of cash.

Additionally it is possible to protect the payment of the fees in the event of unforeseen circumstances that could lead to a significant or total loss of earnings.

Short-term fees

Short-term fees are typically the termly amounts needed within five years: these are usually funded from such things as guaranteed investments, liquid capital, loan plans (if no savings are available) or maturing insurance policies, investments etc. Alternatively they can be funded from disposable income.

Medium-term fees

Once the short-term plan expires, the medium-term funding is invoked to fund the education costs for a further five to ten years. Monthly amounts can be invested in a low-risk, regular premium investment ranging from a building society account to a friendly society savings plan to equity ISAs. It is important to understand the pattern of the future fees and to be aware of the timing of withdrawals.

Long-term fees

Longer term funding can incorporate a higher element of risk (as long as this is acceptable to the investor), which will offer higher potential returns. Investing in UK and overseas equities could be considered. Solutions may be the same as those for medium-term fees, but will have the flexibility to utilise investments that may have an increased 'equity based' content.

Finally, it is important to remember that most investments, or financial products either mature with a single payment, or provide for regular withdrawals; rarely do they provide timed termly payments. Additionally, the overall risk profile of the portfolio should lean towards the side of caution (for obvious reasons).

There are any number of advisers in the country, but few who specialise in the area of planning to meet school and university fees. SFIA is the largest organisation specialising in school fees planning in the UK.

This article has been contributed by SFIA and edited by Chris Procter, Managing Director.

Chris can be contacted at: SFIA, 29 High Street, Marlow, Buckinghamshire, SL7 1AU
Tel: 01628 566777
Fax: 0333 444 1550
Email: enquiries@sfia.co.uk
Web: www.schoolfeesadvice.org

The Independent Schools Council

The Independent Schools Council (ISC) works with its members to promote and preserve the quality, diversity and excellence of UK independent education both at home and abroad

What is the ISC?

ISC brings together seven associations of independent schools, their heads, bursars and governors. Through our member associations we represent over 1,300 independent schools in the UK and overseas. These schools are ranked among the best in the world and educate more than half a million children each year.

ISC's work is carried out by a small number of dedicated professionals in our offices in Central London. We are assisted by the contributions from expert advisory groups in specialist areas. Our priorities are set by the board of directors led by our Chairman, Barnaby Lenon. We are tasked by our members to protect and promote the sector in everything we do.

ISC schools

ISC schools are at the forefront of educational achievement in every way. They are the most academically successful schools and offer excellent teaching, extensive facilities and an astonishing breadth of co-curricular activities. There are schools to suit every need, whether you want a day or boarding school, single sex or co-education, a large or a small school, or schools offering specialisms, such as in the Arts.

Our schools are very diverse: some of our schools are selective and highly academic, offering a chance to stretch the bright child. Others have very strong drama or music departments full of creative opportunities in plays, orchestras and choirs. For children with special needs such as dyslexia or autism there are many outstanding independent schools that offer the best provision in the country.

And of course, our schools have very strong track records of high achievement at sport, offering superb facilities, excellent coaches and a full fixture list. Independent schools excel at the traditional sports like football and rugby, but also offer more unusual sports like rowing, fencing and even rock climbing.

There is also a wealth of co-curricular opportunity available. Whether your child is into debating, sailing, the Model United Nations or is interested in army training in the Combined Cadet Force, most schools offer numerous clubs and activities. It all adds up to an exciting, broad and stimulating all-round education.

Academic results

In 2017 47.9% of A-level subjects taken at independent schools were graded A*/A - this is almost double the national average of 26.3%. This year also saw nearly two thirds of independent school GCSE entries being awarded an A*/A or 9/8/7, three times the national average. This is especially impressive given many fee-charging schools are not academically selective. In 2017, there was an increase in Year 13 candidates taking Extended Project, Pre-U, and BTEC qualifications. The average points score for pupils taking the IB Diploma was 37, roughly equivalent to 4.5 As at A-level. In the International Baccalaureate, 3.7% of pupils obtained 45 points, the highest mark, which is only achieved by 0.1% of candidates worldwide.

Fee Assistance

ISC schools are sympathetic to the financial challenges facing many parents and the amount of bursaries and scholarships available has grown to reflect this. A third of pupils receive fee assistance, the value of this help totals over £900m.

ISC Associations

There are seven member associations of ISC each with its own distinctive ethos:

Girls' Schools Association (GSA) **– see page 36**

Headmasters' and Headmistresses' Conference (HMC) **– see page 37**

Independent Association of Prep Schools (IAPS) **– see page 38**

Independent Schools Association (ISA) **– see page 39**

The Society of Heads **– see page 40**

Association of Governing Bodies of Independent Schools (AGBIS) – www.agbis.org

Independent Schools' Bursars Association (ISBA) –www.isba.org.uk

Further organisations who are affiliated to ISC: Boarding Schools Association (BSA), Council of British International Schools (COBIS), Scottish Council of Independent Schools (SCIS) and Welsh Independent Schools Council (WISC).

The Independent Schools Council can be contacted at:
First Floor,
27 Queen Anne's Gate,
London,
SW1H 9BU
Telephone: 020 7766 7070
Fax: 020 7766 7071
Website: www.isc.co.uk

Choosing a school initially

Educational institutions often belong to organisations that guarantee their standards. Here we give a brief alphabetical guide to what the initials mean

BSA

The Boarding Schools' Association

Since its foundation in 1966, the Boarding Schools' Association (BSA) has had the twin objectives of the promotion of boarding education and the development of quality boarding through high standards of pastoral care and boarding accommodation. Parents and prospective pupils choosing a boarding school can, therefore, be assured that the 550+ schools in membership of the BSA are committed to providing the best possible boarding environment for their pupils.

A school can only join the BSA if it is in membership of one of the ISC (Independent Schools Council) constituent associations or in membership of SBSA (State Boarding Schools' Association). These two bodies require member schools to be regularly inspected by the Independent Schools' Inspectorate (ISI) or Ofsted. Between April 2007 and August 2011, all boarding inspections, in both independent and state schools, were carried out by Ofsted, whose reports can be found on their website. Boarding inspection of independent schools has been conducted by ISI since September 2012. Ofsted retains responsibility for the inspection of boarding in state schools. Boarding inspections must be conducted every three years. Boarding is judged against the National Minimum Standards for Boarding Schools (revised 2011) with considerable input from the BSA.

Relationship with government

The BSA is in regular communication with the Department for Education (DfE) on all boarding matters. The Children Act (1989) and the Care Standards Act (2001) require boarding schools to conform to national legislation and the promotion of this legislation and the training required to carry it out are matters on which the DfE and the BSA work closely. The key area is in training.

Boarding training

The programme of training for boarding staff whose schools are in membership of the BSA has been supported and sponsored in the past by the DfE. The BSA maintains the high standards expected as a consequence of that support. The Utting Report on the Safeguards for Children Living Away from Home highlighted the importance of the development of 'policy, practice and training for services for children who live away from home'. It focuses on the right of parents to expect that staff looking after children are competent to do so, and points out the responsibility of central government to secure consistent national standards in promoting the welfare of children away from home. The Singleton Review (March 2009) reiterated the importance of rigorous safeguarding of such children.

In addition the BSA organises five conferences and more than 50 seminars a year for governors, Heads, deputies, housemasters and housemistresses, and matrons and medical staff where further training takes place in formal sessions and in sharing good practice. The BSA provides the following range of training and information:

- Professional qualifications for both teaching and non-teaching staff in boarding schools. The BSA has been responsible for the development of courses leading to university validated Certificates of Professional Practice in Boarding Education. These certificates, the result of at least two years' study, are awarded by the University of Roehampton.
- A rolling programme of day seminars on current boarding legislation and good practice.

State Boarding Schools Association

The BSA issues information on the 38 state boarding schools in England and Wales and the BSA should be contacted for details of these schools. In these schools parents pay for boarding but not for education, so fees are substantially lower than in an independent boarding school.

National Director: Robin Fletcher MBA, MPhil, FRSA
Director of Training: Alex Thomson OBE, BSc(Hons), PGCE, DipEd, FCIPD
Boarding Schools' Association
4th Floor
134-136 Buckingham Palace Road
London SWIW 9SA
Tel: 020 7798 1580
Fax: 020 7798 1581
Email: bsa@boarding.org.uk
Website: www.boarding.org.uk

GSA

The Girls' Schools Association, to which Heads of leading girls' schools belong

The Girls' Schools Association represents the heads of many of the top performing day and boarding schools in the UK independent schools sector and is a member of the Independent Schools Council.

The GSA encourages high standards of education for girls and promotes the benefits of being taught in a largely girls-only environment. GSA schools are internationally respected and have a global reputation for excellence. Their innovative practice and academic rigour attract pupils from around the world. As a whole, students at GSA schools tend to achieve disproportionately high results and are more likely to study and do well in STEM (science, technology, engineering, maths) subjects than girls in other schools. A high percentage – 96% – progress to higher education.

Twenty first century girls' schools come in many different shapes and sizes. Some cater for 100% girls, others provide a predominantly girls-only environment with boys in the nursery and/or sixth form. Some follow a diamond model, with equal numbers of boys but separate classrooms between the ages of 11 to 16. Educational provision across the Association offers a choice of day, boarding, weekly, and flexi-boarding education. Schools range in type from large urban schools of 1000 pupils to small rural schools of around 200. Many schools have junior and pre-prep departments, and can offer a complete education from 3/4 to 18. A significant proportion of schools also have religious affiliations. Heads of schools in the Girls' Day School Trust (GDST) are members of the GSA.

The Association aims to inform and influence national educational debate and is a powerful and well-respected voice within the educational establishment, advising and lobbying educational policy makers on core education issues as well as those relating to girls' schools and the education of girls. The Association liaises with the Department for Education, the Office for Standards in Education, the Qualifications and Curriculum Authority and other bodies.

The GSA also provides its members and their staff with professional development courses, conferences, advice and opportunities to debate and share best practice, ensuring that they have every opportunity to remain fully up-to-date with all aspects of their profession.

As the GSA is one of the constituent bodies of the Independent Schools' Council (ISC), its schools are required to undergo a regular cycle of inspections to ensure that these rigorous standards are being maintained. GSA schools must also belong to the Association of Governing Bodies of Independent Schools, and Heads must be in membership of the Association of School and College Leaders (ASCL).

The Association's secretariat is based in Leicester.

Suite 105, 108 New Walk, Leicester LE1 7EA
Tel: 0116 254 1619
Email: office@gsa.uk.com
Website: www.gsa.uk.com
Twitter: @GSAUK

President 2018: Gwen Byrom, Loughborough High School
President 2017: Charlotte Avery, St Mary's Cambridge
Chief Executive: Vivienne Durham.

gsa

Photo: Roedean School

HMC

The Headmasters' and Headmistresses' Conference, to which the Heads of leading independent schools belong

Founded in 1869 the HMC exists to enable members to discuss matters of common interest and to influence important developments in education. It looks after the professional interests of members, central to which is their wish to provide the best possible educational opportunities for their pupils.

The Heads of some 289 leading independent schools are members of The Headmasters' and Headmistresses' Conference, whose membership now includes Heads of boys', girls' and coeducational schools. International membership includes the Heads of around 53 schools throughout the world.

The great variety of these schools is one of the strengths of HMC but all must exhibit high quality in the education provided. While day schools are the largest group, about a quarter of HMC schools consist mainly of boarders and others have a smaller boarding element including weekly and flexible boarders.

All schools are noted for their academic excellence and achieve good results, including those with pupils from a broad ability band. Members believe that good education consists of more than academic results and schools provide pupils with a wide range of educational co-curricular activities and with strong pastoral support.

Only those schools that meet with the rigorous membership criteria are admitted and this helps ensure that HMC is synonymous with high quality in education. There is a set of membership requirements and a Code of Practice to which members must subscribe. Those who want the intimate atmosphere of a small school will find some with around 350 pupils. Others who want a wide range of facilities and specialisations will find these offered in large day or boarding schools. Many have over 1000 pupils. About 30 schools are for boys only, others are coeducational throughout or only in the sixth form. The first girls-only schools joined HMC in 2006. There are now about 25 girls-only schools.

Within HMC there are schools with continuous histories as long as any in the world and many others trace their origins to Tudor times, but HMC continues to admit to membership recently-founded schools that have achieved great success. The facilities in all HMC schools will be good but some have magnificent buildings and grounds that are the result of the generosity of benefactors over many years. Some have attractive rural settings, others are sited in the centres of cities.

Pupils come from all sorts of backgrounds. Bursaries and scholarships provided by the schools give about a third of the 220,000 pupils in HMC schools help with their fees. These average about £30,000 per annum for boarding schools and £13,000 for day schools. About 170,000 are day pupils and 43,000 boarders.

Entry into some schools is highly selective but others are well-suited to a wide ability range. Senior boarding schools usually admit pupils after the Common Entrance examination taken when they are 13.

Most day schools select their pupils by 11+ examination. Many HMC schools have junior schools, some with nursery and pre-prep departments. The growing number of boarders from overseas is evidence of the high reputation of the schools worldwide.

The independent sector has always been fortunate in attracting very good teachers. Higher salary scales, excellent conditions of employment, exciting educational opportunities and good pupil/teacher ratios bring rewards commensurate with the demanding expectations. Schools expect teachers to have a good education culminating in a good honours degree and a professional qualification, though some do not insist on the latter especially if relevant experience is offered. Willingness to participate in the whole life of the school is essential.

Parents expect the school to provide not only good teaching that helps their children achieve the best possible examination results, but also the dedicated pastoral care and valuable educational experiences outside the classroom in music, drama, games, outdoor pursuits and community service. Over 90% of pupils go on to higher education, many of them winning places on the most highly-subscribed university courses.

All members attend the Annual Conference, usually held in a large conference centre in September/October. There are ten divisions covering England, Wales, Scotland and Ireland where members meet once a term on a regional basis, and a distinctive international division.

The chairman and committee, with the advice of the general secretary and membership secretary, make decisions on matters referred by membership-led sub-committees, steering groups and working parties. Close links are maintained with other professional associations in membership of the Independent Schools Council and with the Association of School and College Leaders.

Membership Secretary: Ian Power.
Tel: 01858 465260
General Secretary: Dr William Richardson.
Tel: 01858 469059
12 The Point
Rockingham Road
Market Harborough
Leicestershire LE16 7QU
Email: gensec@hmc.org.uk
Website: www.hmc.org.uk

Leading Independent Schools

IAPS

The Independent Association of Prep Schools (IAPS) is a membership association representing leading headteachers and their prep schools in the UK and overseas

With more than 650 members, IAPS schools represent a multi-billion pound enterprise, educating more than 160,000 children and employing more than 20,000 staff.

Schools are spread throughout cities, towns and the countryside and offer pupils the choice of day, boarding, weekly and flexible boarding, in both single sex and coeducational settings. Sizes vary from 100 to more than 800 per school, with the majority between 150 and 400. Most schools are charitable trusts, some are limited companies and a few are proprietary. There are also junior schools attached to senior schools, choir schools, those with a particular religious affiliation and those that offer specialist provision as well as some schools with an age range extending to age 16 or above.

IAPS only accredits those schools that can demonstrate that they provide the highest standards of education and care. Member schools offer an all-round, values-led, broad education, which produces confident, adaptable, motivated children with a lifelong passion for learning. In order to be elected to membership, a Head must be suitably qualified and schools must be accredited through a satisfactory inspection. IAPS offers its members and their staff a comprehensive and up-to-date programme of professional development courses to ensure that high professional standards are maintained.

Pupils are offered a rich and varied school life. The targets of the National Curriculum are regarded as a basic foundation, which is greatly extended by the wider programmes of study offered. Specialist subject teaching begins at an early age and pupils are offered a range of cultural and sporting opportunities. Together with more than 30 recreational games, music, art and drama form part of curricular and extracurricular activities. In addition, IAPS organises holiday and term-time sporting competitions for pupils to take part in, including skiing, sailing, judo, swimming, golf, fencing and squash, amongst many others.

IAPS has well-established links with senior independent schools, and experience in methods of transfer and entry to them. As the voice of independent prep school education, it has national influence and actively defends and promotes the interests of its members. It lobbies the government on their behalf and promotes prep school issues on a national and international stage. IAPS works directly with ministers and national policy advisers to ensure that the needs of the prep school sector are met.

IAPS
11 Waterloo Place, Leamington Spa,
Warwickshire CV32 5LA
Tel: 01926 887833
Email: iaps@iaps.uk
Website: iaps.uk

Excellence in Education

The Independent Association of Prep Schools

ISA

The Independent Schools Association, with membership across all types of school

The Independent Schools Association (ISA), established in 1879, is one of the oldest of the Headteachers' associations of independent schools that make up the Independent Schools' Council (ISC). It began life as the Association of Principals of Private Schools, which was created to encourage high standards and foster friendliness and cooperation among Heads who had previously worked in isolation. In 1895 it was incorporated as The Private Schools Association and in 1927 the word 'private' was replaced by 'independent'. The recently published history of the association, *Pro Liberis*, demonstrates the strong links ISA has with proprietorial schools, which is still the case today, even though boards of governors now run the majority of schools.

Membership is open to any Head or Proprietor, provided they meet the necessary accreditation criteria, including inspection of their school by a government-approved inspectorate. ISA's Executive Council is elected by members and supports all developments of the Association through its committee structure and the strong regional network of co-ordinators and area committees. Each of ISA's seven areas in turn supports members through regular training events and meetings.

ISA celebrates a wide-ranging membership, not confined to any one type of school, but including all: nursery, pre-preparatory, junior and senior, all-through schools, coeducational, single-sex, boarding, day and performing arts and special schools.

Promoting best practice and fellowship remains at the core of the ISA, as it did when it began 140 years ago. The association is growing, and its 431 members and their schools enjoy high quality national conferences and courses that foster excellence in independent education. ISA's central office also supports members and provides advice, and represents the views of its membership at national and governmental levels. Pupils in ISA schools enjoy a wide variety of competitions, in particular the wealth of sporting, artistic and academic activities at area and national level.

President : Lord Lexden
Chief Executive: Neil Roskilly, BA PGCE NPQH FRSA FRGS

ISA House, 5-7 Great Chesterford Court, Great Chesterford, Essex CB10 1PF
Tel: 01799 523619
Email: isa@isaschools.org.uk
Website: www.isaschools.org.uk

ISA celebrates a wide ranging membership, not confined to any one type of school, but including all: nursery, pre-preparatory, junior and senior, all-through schools, coeducational, single-sex, boarding, day and performing arts and special schools

The Society of Heads

The Society of Heads represents the interests of independent secondary schools

The Society of Heads represents the interests of the smaller, independent, secondary schools. The Society celebrated its 50th Anniversary in 2011. The Society has as its members over 110 Heads of well-established secondary schools, many with a boarding element, meeting a wide range of educational needs. All member schools provide education up to 18, with sixth forms offering both A and AS levels and/or the International Baccalaureate. Also some offer vocational courses. Many have junior schools attached to their foundation. A number cater for pupils with special educational needs, whilst others offer places to gifted dancers and musicians. All the schools provide education appropriate to their pupils' individual requirements together with the best in pastoral care.

The average size of the schools is about 350, and all aim to provide small classes ensuring favourable pupil:teacher ratios. The majority are coeducational and offer facilities for both boarding and day pupils. Many of the schools are non-denominational, whilst others have specific religious foundations.

The Society believes that independent schools are an important part of Britain's national education system. Given their independence, the schools can either introduce new developments ahead of the maintained sector or offer certain courses specifically appropriate to the pupils in their schools. They are able to respond quickly to the needs of parents and pupils alike.

Schools are admitted to membership of the Society only after a strict inspection procedure carried out by the Independent Schools Inspectorate. Regular inspection visits thereafter ensure that standards are maintained.

The Society is a constituent member of the Independent Schools Council and every full member in the Society has been accredited to it. All the Society's Heads belong to the Association of School and College Leaders (ASCL) (or another recognised union for school leaders) and their schools are members of AGBIS.

The Society's policy is: to maintain high standards of education, acting as a guarantee of quality to parents who choose a Society school for their children; to ensure the genuine independence of member schools; to provide an opportunity for Heads to share ideas and common concerns for the benefit of the children in their care; to provide training opportunities for Heads and staff in order to keep them abreast of new educational initiatives; to promote links with higher and further education and the professions, so that pupils leaving the Society's schools are given the best advice and opportunities for their future careers; and to help Heads strengthen relations with their local communities.

The Society of Heads' Office,
12 The Point, Rockingham Road, Market Harborough,
Leicestershire LE16 7QU
Tel: 01858 433760
Email: gensec@thesocietyofheads.org.uk
Website: www.thesocietyofheads.org.uk

The average size of the schools is about 350, and all aim to provide small classes ensuring favourable pupil: teacher ratios. The majority are coeducational and offer facilities for both boarding and day pupils. Many of the schools are non-denominational, whilst others have specific religious foundations

School profiles

Channel Islands

St Michael's Preparatory School

St. Michael's Preparatory School is situated in a unique educational setting on Jersey in the Channel Islands. A forward thinking IAPS prep school preparing pupils for the rigours of secondary school education both on and off island. We place great emphasis upon the traditional values of care, consideration and courtesy.

The staff and pupils are justifiably proud of the School, and work together to create and maintain a high-achieving, well-organised and friendly environment in which every child is encouraged to do 'a little bit better' than anyone thought possible.

The curriculum is designed to give all children a broad, balanced and relevant education, which enables them to develop as enthusiastic, active and competent learners acquiring the knowledge, skills and understanding to allow them to grow up in today's world leading a full and active life. The school's ethos places emphasis on the individual and aims to encourage development in academic, physical, spiritual, moral and cultural aspects of the 'whole child'.

The teaching is multi-sensory, allowing children of all abilities and learning styles to be able to make progress in their learning. Differentiation is integral to the curriculum and children with special needs are well supported, as are the gifted and talented, who go on to achieve scholarship success.

The schemes of work are based upon the National Curriculum, the Jersey Curriculum and the requirements of the ISEB Common Entrance and Scholarship syllabuses. The curriculum is enriched and enhanced by numerous trips and visits as Jersey has an array of museums, cultural sites of interest and environmental locations.

The school prepares children for Common Entrance and Scholarships to English boarding secondary schools as well as entry to local Jersey establishments. We also offer a shell year (Year 9) specifically to provide a bridging opportunity for Year 10 entry to our island state schools. Classes are small and there is a very low pupil to teacher ratio. All expected subjects are taught and there are flourishing and well-equipped Art, Music, Science, Design Technology and ICT departments as well as a custom built Sports Hall, Dance/Drama Studio, Gymnasium and indoor Swimming Pool.

As well as providing a wide range of academic subjects, the school seeks to introduce each child to a large variety of sports, performing arts, activities and challenges enabling him or her to discover, through experience, hidden talents and preferences with a view to future specialisation.

I hope St. Michael's pupils will leave us having achieved the very best they are capable of, having found out what it is that they love and are good at, having learned to challenge themselves and to value other people.

"St Michael's makes ordinary children special, and special children extra-ordinary." A parent quote.

ST MICHAEL'S
PREPARATORY SCHOOL

(Founded 1949)

La Rue de la Houguette, St Saviour, Jersey JE2 7UG UK

Tel: 01534 856904

Fax: 01534 856620

Email: office@stmichaels.je

Website: www.stmichaels.je

Head of School: Mr Mike Rees

Appointed: 2014

School type: Coeducational Day

Age range of pupils: 3–14

No. of pupils enrolled as at 01/09/2017: 309

Boys: 171 ***Girls:*** 138

Fees per annum as at 01/09/2017:

Day: £9,375–£14,475

Average class size: 18 max

Teacher/pupil ratio: 1:9

Central & West

Dauntsey's School

Dauntsey's is a leading co-educational boarding and day school for 11-18 year olds. The school sits in an estate of one hundred and fifty acres of idyllic countryside in Wiltshire and offers some 800 pupils challenge and inspiration both inside and outside the classroom.

The Dauntsey's Experience

Academic excellence is at the heart of all that we do. However, education is much more than grades on a piece of paper. It's about developing the skills and characteristics, such as resilience, flexibility and a willingness to have a go, which we all need to have a successful, happy life. That's where our adventure, enrichment and extra-curricular activities have a crucial role to play. From drama, dance, music, sport and a huge range of clubs and societies, to our lecture series, adventure programmes and volunteering initiatives – there are opportunities to suit everyone.

The Dauntsey's Community

Community and collaboration underpin many aspects of Dauntsey's; it is a happy place with a strong family atmosphere, where friendship matters and where courteous informality between staff and pupils is highly valued.

Our pupils are expected to give of their best and to have a spirit of adventure. We aim to push them out of their comfort zone, both inside and outside the classroom, and we want them to arrive at the end of their time in the School saying: 'I did not think that I could do that, but I did.'

Our pupils, both boarding and day, come from many different schools and so arrive at Dauntsey's eager to make new friends. Both communities are fully integrated and boarding houses rapidly become home-from-home and fellow boarders become extended family. All pupils attend School six days a week with Saturday school compulsory for day and boarders alike, with a full academic programme for all year groups and sports matches every Saturday afternoon. A range of activities on Saturday evening and Sunday encourage friendship and a sense of community.

Houses in the Upper School (for pupils aged 14-18 years) are single sex. Lower School pupils (aged 11-14 years) board at the co-educational Manor, a fabulous Victorian mansion in extensive grounds, a short walk away from the main School campus.

"Coming back to the Manor at the end of the day feels like coming home. There is so much to do and so many people I like – I've certainly never felt lonely!" – Richard, Second Form Boarder at The Manor

Entry Requirements

At all stages, admission to Dauntsey's is via examination and interview. Pupils can join Dauntsey's aged 11, 13 or 16. We recommend that potential applicants and their families attend one of our open mornings, which offer an opportunity to see the School on a normal working day, to meet current pupils and talk to both teaching and admissions staff. We hold two open mornings a year in May and October. Individual appointments can be organised by contacting the Admissions Office at admissions@dauntseys.org.

For more information please visit our website which gives a real flavour of life at Dauntsey's – www.dauntseys.org

"We ask our pupils and staff to be ambitious and to pursue excellence in all areas of school life." – Head Master, Mark Lascelles

"Dauntsey's is... fab!" – Good Schools Guide

(Founded 1542)

High Street, West Lavington, Devizes, Wiltshire SN10 4HE UK

Tel: 01380 814500

Fax: 01380 814501

Email: admissions@dauntseys.org

Website: www.dauntseys.org

Head Master: Mr Mark Lascelles

Appointed: September 2012

School type: Coeducational Boarding & Day

Age range of pupils: 11–18

No. of pupils enrolled as at 01/09/2017: 820

Boys: 416 ***Girls:*** 404 ***Sixth Form:*** 270

No. of boarders: 300

Fees per annum as at 01/09/2017:

Day: £18,450

Full Boarding: £30,540

Average class size: 18; 12 in Sixth Form

Teacher/pupil ratio: 1:8

EF Academy Oxford

EF Academy International Boarding Schools prepares students for a global future with a superior secondary school education in the U.S. or UK. At EF Academy, we believe in every student's ability to succeed. We empower them to do so through our renowned curricula, as well as quality one-on-one relationships with teachers and mentors alike. With a student body made up of 75 different nationalities, multilingualism and intercultural exchange are built into every course, which helps distinguish our students' academic credentials to both university admissions officers and future employers.

The School

Our private boarding school is situated in the city of Oxford, renowned for its scholastic tradition and rich cultural and architectural heritage. EF Academy students join Oxford's vibrant academic community, which attracts leading scholars from around the world. Ten minutes from Oxford's center, the campus has spacious classrooms, modern science labs and inviting lounges. Students have access to the library and sports center of nearby Oxford Brookes University. In the international environment at EF Academy Oxford, students aged 16 to 19 live and learn together.

Students live in on-campus residences with their classmates and house parents. House parents look after the students and ensure that they are safe and comfortable when they are not in class.

Academics

Education at EF Academy Oxford is highly individualized. Students follow the IB Diploma or A-Level program and take intensive English language courses. They benefit from an enrichment program that includes visits to University of Oxford and they regularly attend lectures in a variety of subjects. Our teachers with links to the university often arrange visits to its math department and science laboratories, ensuring students at EF Academy receive the ultimate pre-university experience.

University Placement

EF Academy Oxford graduates have gone on to attend universities such as Imperial, St. Andrews and Durham. All of our students receive acceptance to university degree programs, many for highly competitive courses such as Economics, Engineering or Medicine. Dedicated university advisors work together with students to help them prepare the best applications possible. This involves giving them feedback on their personal statements, holding mock interviews and exploring program options with them. Our university advisors can also support students who are interested in applying to universities in the U.S. or in their home country.

Pastoral Care

At EF Academy Oxford, each student is assigned a personal tutor whose role is to monitor the student's academic progress and general welfare. They can turn to their tutor whenever they need support with homework and courses, or when they are experiencing homesickness.

Co-curricular Activities

Universities look for well-rounded students who get involved and extend their learning beyond the classroom. Students at EF Academy Oxford have access to a wide range of co-curricular activities. From subject-specific academic groups and competitions to sports and arts, there is an option for every student. The school's activities coordinator also arranges excursions for students on the weekends so they have the opportunity to experience the culture in and around Oxford.

Pullens Lane, Headington, Oxfordshire OX3 0DT UK

Tel: +41 (0) 43 430 4095

Email: iaeurope@ef.com

Website: www.ef.com/academy

Head of School: Dr. Paul Ellis

School type: Coeducational Boarding

Age range of pupils: 16–19

No. of pupils enrolled as at 01/09/2017: 160

Fees per annum as at 01/09/2017:

IB Diploma/A-Levels: £28,800

King Edward's Senior School

As the city's former grammar school, founded in 1552, KES has a very healthy tradition of nurturing academic excellence and ambition, reflected in the School's outstanding results which consistently place us in the top five independent schools in the South West. The ethos of the School is one that encourages all pupils to play as hard as they work and to make the most of all the wonderful opportunities available, both in and out of the classroom, that enable them to grow and thrive within a supportive and caring framework. We set the bar high, but we also give our pupils all the tools that they need to reach those ambitious standards. We aim to foster talent in all its forms and to open doors to enquiry and discovery. Independent-mindedness and creative spirit are strong suits, but so too is the sense of community that seeks to respect and value all its members.

As a family of three schools, the Pre-Prep, Junior and Senior sections of King Edward's offer an inspiring and supportive environment for children age 3 to 18. Some join us just for the Sixth Form, many stay for their entire school career. All pupils are encouraged to be the best they can be and all are nurtured along the pathway to leading happy, fulfilled and successful lives at school and beyond.

In 2015 the School was inspected by the ISI and was judged as 'excellent' across all eight aspects of school life under review including governance and pastoral care provision. The report noted that *"The success of the school lies in the strength of the ethos which permeates it from the EYFS to the sixth form. All three sections of the school encourage the pupils to strive for excellence and to achieve to the best of their ability in a stimulating environment so that they acquire a love of learning which goes beyond the formal curriculum."*

The ISI report also rated the school's co-curricular programme as 'excellent', with over 100 clubs and activities taking place on a weekly basis. The programme has been designed to support the school's aim to encourage pupils to acquire a lifelong passion for knowledge, discovery and adventure. From Lego Robotics to Yoga and Fencing to Photography, life outside of the classroom enables each pupil to explore their own sporting, creative and cultural potential.

Described by a current parent as *"a little piece of school heaven"* our Pre-Prep and Nursery offers an exciting and stimulating start to school life. A desire to make learning irresistible in a nurturing environment is at the heart of everything we do. Weekly Forest School lessons, trips, specialist teachers and inspiring projects all help to enrich our broad and creative curriculum. With school days full of magical discovery and excitement, our children play, make friends and explore the world together.

"KES feels like a happy school" noted The Good Schools Guide after its recent visit to our Junior School. With unrivalled facilities including specialist teaching rooms for Science, Art, Design Technology and Music, and a state of the art ICT Suite and Technology Centre, all housed around a lovely central library, not to mention an adventure playground, dipping ponds and meadow outside, our Junior School children flourish and grow as they take advantage of all that the school has to offer.

(Founded 1552)

North Road, Bath, Bath & North-East Somerset BA2 6HU UK

Tel: 01225 464313

Fax: 01225 481363

Email: reception@kesbath.com

Website: www.kesbath.com

Head: Mr MJ Boden MA

Appointed: 2008

School type: Coeducational Day

Age range of pupils: 11–18

No. of pupils enrolled as at 01/09/2017: 1085

Fees per term as at 01/09/2017:

Pre-Prep: £3,270 per term

Junior: £3,625 per term

Senior: £4,585 – £4,660 per term

Monkton Combe School

Setting standards for life
Monkton Combe School, just a mile from the World Heritage City of Bath, is an independent, co-educational boarding and day school for pupils aged 2-18. We pride ourselves on our lively Christian ethos, excellent exam results and our strong pastoral care. At Monkton, we are setting standards for life; giving young people the qualities of character they need to become trusted employees, inspiring leaders, valued friends and loving parents. Boarding is at the very heart of Monkton, and the unique atmosphere of the School is enjoyed by boarders and day pupils alike. All the houses reflect the spirit and ethos of the School, but each exudes its own personality generated by its pupils, houseparent's and staff.

A broad and varied curriculum
As shown by Monkton's outstanding exam results over the last five years fulfilling academic potential is one of our key priorities. However Monkton thinks differently, we start with a proactive pastoral environment to develop academically strong enthusiastic learners within a living Christian ethos. Our students work hard and are well motivated, being supported and encouraged through the care and enthusiasm of our gifted teachers, who are committed to delivering lessons that are lively and enjoyable, as well as being rigorous and demanding. Strategies for supporting gifted and talented students are well established and are continually updated and extended.

Busy days and full weekends
One of Monkton's strengths is the breadth of activities available to pupils at weekends – in fact, many of our day pupils will spend all weekend at school just so they can join in the Monkton social life. Every Saturday afternoon there is a full programme of sporting activities which follow on after morning lessons. There are some brilliant social events hosted by the houses throughout the year – a bonfire party, a summer fete, a barbecue, to name but a few – and these, together with the music, drama and sporting competitions, keep the students extremely busy. They can also enjoy the School productions, DVD nights, sixth form centre parties, junior discos and informal concerts – there is almost too much to choose from!

Transforming lives
Our outstanding pastoral care, strong moral framework and culture of service to others make us an ideal choice for parents looking for a school that will nurture and challenge their child spiritually, emotionally and socially as well as developing their academic potential to the full. We aim to instil our values of confidence, integrity, humility and service in all of our pupils.

Come and visit
To find out more, please visit www.monktoncombeschool.com or to arrange a visit, please contact the Registrar, on +44 (0)1225 721133 or e-mail: admissions@monkton.org.uk.

(Founded 1868)

Monkton Combe, Bath,
Bath & North-East Somerset BA2 7HG UK

Tel: 01225 721133

Email: admissions@monkton.org.uk

Website: www.monkton.org.uk

Principal: Mr Chris Wheeler

Appointed: January 2016

School type: Coeducational Day & Boarding

Age range of pupils: 2–18

Average class size: 22

Teacher/pupil ratio: 1:9

Oxford Tutorial College

Oxford Tutorial College is a highly successful independent college specialising in A-level, BTEC and GCSE courses for students 15+ in the heart of Oxford.

Established in 1988, the college has gained an excellent reputation for providing effective preparation for public examinations and university entry, achieved by thorough, exam-specific teaching and close attention to the needs of each individual student. We strongly believe that one size really does not fit all. We have a fantastic track record in helping students achieve their best, with many of our students being offered places at Russell Group and top 20 universities.

The OTC Experience

The college offers an environment quite different from that of a traditional school. The teaching approach is refreshingly interactive and informal. The emphasis on small group work and one-to-one tutorials enables a clear focus on individual needs and learning styles and a variation of pace and emphasis, which helps students to approach their work calmly and objectively. This 'tutorial method' is an extremely flexible teaching approach, which provides a dialogue between tutor and students' and thus enables reinforcement of understanding and careful attention to areas of weakness.

The support provided by both subject tutors and each student's Personal Tutor is thoughtful and creative and students are encouraged at every stage to take an active part in the learning process through self-motivation, involvement, personal study and research. This is an important preparation for higher education. Various extra-curricular activities are offered enabling students to explore and develop the skills they will need in later life.

"I have found the quality of the teaching to be great and the enthusiasm teachers have tfor the subject inspiring." – Lisha, A Level Student

The college has an inclusive ethos and a culture which encourages industry and a growing sense of responsibility. Students are encouraged at every stage to take an active part in the learning process.

There are no restrictions as to the choice of subjects or subject combinations, although students are advised to make choices appropriate to their degree course or vocational aim and to take subjects which engage their interest and fit in with their abilities and aptitudes.

The College

Our campus is a friendly, welcoming place and a home away from home for young people of many different cultures. There are plenty of social events throughout the year to let you get to know your fellow students better. We are very proud of what our students accomplish every year.

Our graduates go on to study at some of the UK's most prestigious universities and have stellar careers ahead of them thanks to the skills they learnt and choices they made while studying with us. They leave us equipped with essential qualifications, valuable life experience and English language skills that help them communicate confidently. But more than that, they also take away happy memories and lasting friendships.

Academic scholarships are available, please ask the College for further details.

Entry Requirements:

OTC accepts students throughout the year. We recommend that potential applicants visit our college by booking an individual appointment with the Admissions Office at admissions@oxfordtutorialcollege.com.

(Founded 1988)

12-13 King Edward Street, Oxford,
Oxfordshire OX1 4HT UK

Tel: +44 (0)1865 793333

Email: admissions@oxfordtutorialcollege.com

Website: www.oxfordtutorialcollege.com

Principal: Mr Mark Love

Appointed: 2017

School type: Co-educational Day & Boarding

Age range of pupils: 15+

No. of pupils enrolled as at 01/01/2017: 288

Average class size: Av 4-8, Max 6-10

Shiplake College

Shiplake College is a thriving boarding and day school for boys aged 11-18, with girls joining in the Sixth Form. In September 2017 it welcomed a record 475 pupils to the school, a rise from 400 in September 2014. Overlooking the River Thames, two miles upstream of the famous Henley Royal Regatta stretch, students enjoy an inspirational 45-acre rural site. Flexi, weekly and full boarding is available from Year 7 (age 11).

Shiplake provides a friendly, supportive and structured environment to bring out the best in each and every pupil. Renowned for outstanding pastoral care and personal development, the College welcomes pupils with wide-ranging skills and talents, who will make the most of the many opportunities we offer them. We provide an education that is tailored to the individual and we do this through engaging and inspirational teaching, delivered in small classes where our teachers can know and understand each pupil's method of learning.

With a greater focus on academic rigour in recent years, it is no surprise that the College continues to achieve a year-on-year improvement in GCSE and A Level examination results. There is a wide range of A Level and BTEC subjects available, with all Sixth Formers also undertaking either the EPQ or CoPE as part of a bespoke PULSE (Personal Understanding, Learning Skills and Enrichment) programme. Leavers secure places at a variety of leading institutions, including Oxbridge, Russell Group and Ivy League universities.

In addition to a strong academic foundation, the College offers excellent sporting, artistic and co-curricular opportunities. Two afternoons are reserved for an array of clubs and activities, including a comprehensive outdoor education programme, with pupils encouraged to extend their horizons and experience new challenges and responsibilities. A newly opened Art, Music and contemporary Thinking Space, complete with lecture theatre and recording studio, offers pupils state-of-the-art facilities.

Academic lessons take place within the five day working week and each day ends with an hour of academic support during which pupils undertake independent study or seek help with homework from teachers. Sports training takes place on three afternoons a week, with the majority of fixtures scheduled for Saturday mornings. Full boarders take part in a vibrant weekend programme of trips and activities on Saturday afternoons and Sundays, with day pupils and weekly boarders able to enjoy additional family and down time at home.

A full ISI inspection in 2015 judged Shiplake as 'excellent' – the highest accolade – across all nine inspection categories. Commendation of this magnitude is rare in education, placing Shiplake amongst the leading schools in the country.

Entry points are normally at Year 7 (11+), Year 9 (13+) and Year 12 (16+). Prospective families are encouraged to arrange an individual visit or attend an open morning, which take place in October and March each year. Please go to www.shiplake.org.uk to book your attendance, register your child, or request our prospectus, as well as explore the whole site, which contains a wealth of information relating to all aspects of life at Shiplake. This is the first port of call for details of admissions processes, fees, bus routes and answers to most academic, co-curricular and pastoral questions that prospective parents may have. News articles are posted every day during term time, showcasing a wide variety of activities and celebrating the many successes of our pupils.

Academic, Art, Music, Drama and Sport Scholarships, and means-tested bursaries, are available. Please contact the Registrar for further details.

SHIPLAKE COLLEGE
HENLEY-ON-THAMES

(Founded 1959)

Henley-on-Thames, Oxfordshire RG9 4BW UK

Tel: +44 (0)1189 402455

Fax: +44 (0)1189 405204

Email: registrar@shiplake.org.uk

Website: www.shiplake.org.uk

Headmaster: Mr A G S Davies BSc(St Andrews)

Appointed: 2004

School type: Boys' Boarding & Day

Religious Denomination: Church of England

Age range of boys: 11–18

Age range of girls: 16–18

No. of pupils enrolled as at 01/09/2017: 475

Boys: 420 ***Girls:*** 55 ***Sixth Form:*** 192

No. of boarders: 140

Fees per annum as at 01/09/2017:

Day: £17,100–£21,480

Weekly Boarding: £23,970–£29,970

Full Boarding: £31,950

Flexi Boarding (2 nights per week): £20,190 – £24,570

Average class size: 18

Teacher/pupil ratio: 1:6

The Unicorn School

The Unicorn School is a specialist, independent day school for girls and boys aged 6 to 16 years who have Specific Learning Difficulties: dyslexia, dyspraxia, dyscalculia and Speech, Language and Communication Needs (SLCN). Pupils can join us at any age from Year 2 upwards, and now have the opportunity to complete both their primary and their secondary education at our school.

The Unicorn School provides a nurturing environment in which every pupil is helped to build self-confidence, appreciate their learning difficulties and develop their own personal learning style. Our goal is for every child to flourish at The Unicorn School, leaving with the confidence to learn, the appetite for study, and the desire to continue to succeed in their education and beyond.

Our bespoke approach integrates all aspects of learning under one roof: Highly qualified teachers with a passion for special educational needs, small class sizes, an adapted National Curriculum made accessible to those with learning difficulties, specialist teaching techniques, one-to-one tuition for every pupil, focused study sessions to support GCSE preparation, and for those who need it, in-house Speech and Language Therapy and Occupational Therapy.

Providing a cherishing environment and specialist teaching, The Unicorn School bridges the gap between our pupils' current performance and their potential achievement.

GCSE Provision

The Unicorn School has undergone ground breaking developments, becoming the only dyslexia-specialist day school in Oxfordshire to provide GCSE education. We also offer one-year GCSE re-sit courses.

We have carefully selected a GCSE programme which will enable our pupils to achieve a sound bank of essential qualifications. By focussing on a small number of key subjects, we give our pupils the best opportunity to succeed. Our GCSE courses have been chosen to play to our pupils' many strengths, avoiding those subjects with a heavy bias towards writing, spelling and punctuation; or with an extensive research element. Our GCSE teachers are highly qualified professionals. Specialist teaching makes the GCSE syllabus accessible to pupils with dyslexia and related learning difficulties.

A Quarter-Century of Achievement

In 2016 we celebrated our school's 25-year anniversary. Founded in 1991, The Unicorn School has supported over 500 pupils with our specialist teaching. We begin our second quarter-century with pride in our achievements and excitement for the future development of our school.

A Warm Welcome

We warmly welcome you to visit us at The Unicorn School to discuss how we can support your child's needs. To join us at our upcoming open mornings, or to book an individual visit please contact our Registrar on 01235 530222, or registrar@unicornoxford.co.uk.

(Founded 1991)

20 Marcham Road, Abingdon,
Oxfordshire OX14 1AA UK

Tel: 01235 530222

Email: info@unicornoxford.co.uk

Website: www.unicornoxford.co.uk

Headteacher:
Mr. Andrew Day BEd (Hons)University of Wales (Cardiff)

Appointed: April 2015

School type: Coeducational Day

Age range of pupils: 6–16 years

No. of pupils enrolled as at 01/09/2017: 74

Boys: 50 ***Girls:*** 24

Fees per annum as at 01/09/2017:

Day: £19,500

Average class size: 9

air
THE GREAT KAPOK TREE

Westonbirt School

Westonbirt School offers exceptional senior education for girls in small classes with expert teachers dedicated to ensuring each girl reaches her full potential. Housed in a Victorian mansion set in 210 acres of beautiful parkland, Westonbirt is coupled with a very successful co-ed Prep school for children aged 3-11 on the same site. Students can be carefree, feel secure in their inspiring surroundings and enjoy fresh air and extensive space.

Individuality and success is celebrated at Westonbirt, while development is nourished. As an inclusive school of just over 200 girls, achievements are competitive with many larger schools. Girls are regularly selected to play lacrosse for England and Wales, Drama productions have aired at the Edinburgh Fringe to high acclaim and over two-thirds of girls play at least one musical instrument. Over 90% of Sixth Form students go on to their first choice universities including Cambridge, Durham, Cardiff, Bristol, UCL and Central St. Martins.

Westonbirt has undergone a significant fee re-structure with day fees reducing by up to 30% from September 2017. With 29% A*-A grades and 56% A*-B grades at A level in 2017, Westonbirt delivers strong results for its non-selective intake and great value for an excellent education.

Westonbirt offers modern teaching and sporting facilities including a £3 million sports centre, 25m indoor swimming pool, state of the art music technology suite and a nine-hole golf course.

An innovative Skills for Life program is designed to complement academic success and prepare students for the challenges facing them in a global society. The robust scheme explores the diversity of the workplace, promotes career achievement and offers practical and financial training for life beyond school.

(Founded 1928)

Westonbirt, Tetbury, Gloucestershire GL8 8QG UK

Tel: 01666 881333

Fax: 01666 880364

Email: enquiries@westonbirt.org

Website: www.westonbirt.org

Headmistress: Mrs Natasha Dangerfield

Appointed: 2012

School type: Girls' Boarding & Day

Age range of girls: 11–18 years

Fees per term as at 01/09/2017:

Day: £4,995 per term

Full Boarding: £9,750 per term

Average class size: 15-20

Teacher/pupil ratio: 1:7

Wycombe Abbey

Wycombe Abbey is a global leader in outstanding education and modern boarding. The School is committed to creating tomorrow's women leaders and has a long tradition of academic excellence, it is consistently one of the country's top performing schools.

Our learning environment is supportive, yet challenging, with a sense that pupils and their teachers are on an educational journey together. We pride ourselves on the outstanding teaching provided by our specialists who communicate a genuine love of their subject and serve to inspire the girls they teach.

We believe that education should not simply be about delivering a curriculum and examination syllabus, but that real learning stems from stimulating intellectual curiosity and nurturing a love for the subjects being taught, which will stay with our girls throughout their lives.

In all we do, boarding is the key to our continued success. The School has a culture that inspires throughout the day, seven days a week, empowering girls to achieve their best, academically and socially. In our happy and close community, each girl is known, and cherished, as an individual. Consequently, every girl's potential, whatever that might be, is explored and fulfilled.

Girls learn to be independent, to value and support others, and to develop the skills needed for future challenges in a global workplace. Given the nature of boarding life, girls are able to enjoy a wealth of co-curricular opportunities. Each and every girl carves out a unique learning path according to her interests and has the space to thrive within our magnificent grounds. Our approach to boarding is also sympathetic to the needs of today's families and pupils have the opportunity to go home regularly and parents are actively involved in the numerous School events and activities.

The School is an oasis of calm, set in 170 acres of magnificent, conservation-listed grounds and woodland. Modern, state-of-the-art facilities include the Sports Centre, with a 25-metre indoor pool, the Performing Arts Centre with a theatre and recital hall, an atrium café, dance and fitness studios, and extensive sports pitches. Two brand new Boarding Houses will open in September 2017 and a refurbishment of all the boarding accommodation will follow.

Wycombe Abbey is easily accessible with excellent transport links. It is about 35 miles west of London and 30 miles east of Oxford. It is a 30-minute journey from Heathrow Airport and a 90-minute journey from Gatwick Airport by road.

To find out more about gaining a place at Wycombe Abbey, please visit our website at www.wycombeabbey.com or contact our Admissions Team on (+44) (0) 1494 897008 or by emailing registrar@wycombeabbey.com.

(Founded 1896)

High Wycombe, Buckinghamshire HP11 1PE UK

Tel: +44 (0)1494 897008

Email: registrar@wycombeabbey.com

Website: www.wycombeabbey.com

Headmistress: Mrs Rhiannon J Wilkinson MA (Oxon) MEd

Appointed: September 2013

School type: Girls' Day & Boarding

Religious Denomination: Church of England

Age range of girls: 11–18

No. of pupils enrolled as at 01/09/2017: 611

Fees per annum as at 01/09/2017:

Day: £28,350

Full Boarding: £37,800

East

Bedford School

Bedford School is an independent boarding and day school that offers boys aged 7-18 a complete and balanced education. We aim to teach boys to think intelligently, act wisely and be fully engaged in a challenging and changing world.

Situated on an extensive parkland estate of 50 acres in the heart of Bedford, the school is a lively community of day boys, weekly and full boarders.

Our highly qualified teaching staff are selected on their ability to communicate and inspire. The result is a vibrant, stimulating environment, were boys can be happy, grow in self-confidence, thrive academically and make the most of the wide range of opportunities on offer. Our broad curriculum offers boys a varied choice of subjects, and our academic success is demonstrated by a long history of impressive examination results at GCSE, A level, and in the International Baccalaureate Diploma, and university entrances: in 2016 77% of boys went on to Russell Group universities, including Oxford and Cambridge.

In addition to our established reputation for academic excellence, we are renowned for our strengths in sport, music and the arts.

Throughout each boy's time at the school, we aim to inspire a lifelong interest in sport, promoting teamwork, wellbeing, fitness and, most of all, enjoyment. The School's sporting resources are outstanding – a floodlit twin Astroturf complex, indoor swimming pool, tennis and squash courts, playing fields, fitness centre and recreation centre combine to provide first-class facilities from which many international players have emerged.

With our state-of-the-art music school, Bedford has one of the largest music departments in the country and a high proportion of students learn to play one or more instruments. In fact many parents choose Bedford School in preference to a specialist music school to provide excellent music tuition within a strong academic environment.

Drama and theatre studies continue to thrive, and our commitment to the arts is demonstrated through our stunning new 290-seat theatre, The Quarry Theatre at St Luke's, which officially opened in July 2015. Our first-rate art studios are available to everyone to explore sculpture, photography, fine art and design.

We offer an extensive and diverse programme of extracurricular activities to all boys; including the CCF (Combined Cadet Force), Duke of Edinburgh's Award Scheme, community service, fundraising charity groups, and more than 50 other clubs and societies from astronomy to young enterprise.

Whilst committed to the benefits of single sex teaching, we also work closely with our sister school Bedford Girls' School to provide a wide ranging programme of co-educational extracurricular and social activities.

Scholarships worth up to 35% of annual school fees are available to boys who excel academically, or show outstanding talent in art, drama, music or sport. Families can also apply for additional funding through our means-tested bursary scheme.

We warmly invite you to join us at one of our open mornings or for a private visit to see the school in action, meet the boys and staff, and get a flavour of life here at Bedford School. Please contact Anna Steiger, Director of Admissions, for further information on 01234 362216 or email admissions@bedfordschool.org.uk.

Bedford School is part of The Harpur Trust. Company No. 3475202/Charity no. 1066861.

(Founded 1552)

De Parys Avenue, Bedford, Bedfordshire MK40 2TU UK

Tel: +44 (0)1234 362216

Email: admissions@bedfordschool.org.uk

Website: www.bedfordschool.org.uk

Head Master: Mr James Hodgson BA

Appointed: 2014

School type: Boys' Day & Boarding

Religious Denomination: Anglican

Age range of boys: 7–18 years

No. of pupils enrolled as at 01/09/2017: 1061

Fees per annum as at 01/09/2017:

Day: £11,973–£18,477

Weekly Boarding: £20,310–£30,219

Full Boarding: £21,309–£31,251

Average class size: 15-20

Teacher/pupil ratio: 1:10

Berkhamsted School

Berkhamsted School offers much to make it worthy of closer consideration: a long established reputation for excellent educational provision, high quality facilities and the extensive choice of co-educational experiences enjoyed by its pupils; an attractive location in a thriving market town with easy access to London; and a range of services that support the lives of busy families.

It is also one of only a small number of schools in the country to offer a 'diamond' structure that combines the best of both single-sex and co-educational teaching. Boys and girls are taught together until the age of 11 (Berkhamsted Pre-Prep and Berkhamsted Prep), separately from 11-16 (Berkhamsted Boys and Berkhamsted Girls), before coming back together again in a joint Sixth Form (Berkhamsted Sixth).

Pupils across the School enjoy the benefits of being part of a small, caring community based in an environment appropriate to their specific educational needs, yet with access to the state-of-the-art facilities of a large school; a 550-seat theatre, a six-lane 25m swimming pool and sports centre, spacious, modern dining facilities and one of the best art departments in the country.

Another feature of Berkhamsted is the provision of a range of services that make life easier for parents who are juggling busy schedules; from flexible boarding options that include occasional, weekly or full boarding in high quality accommodation to a range of coach routes, 'extended day' support, day nursery provision (five months to three years) and wrap-around care 50 weeks of the year.

Academic results are consistently strong with an average of over 70% A*-B grades at A level and more than 30% of pupils having an A* in their results. In 2017, GCSE students achieved 68.5% of grades at A* to A. On average 98% of Sixth Form leavers go on to a degree course (20% after gap year) at Oxford, Cambridge, Russell Group and other highly ranked universities for their chosen subjects. In the last six years 42 students have accepted a place at Oxford or Cambridge.

Berkhamsted offers all the key components of a traditional independent school education: small class sizes, specialist staff and excellent standards of teaching throughout the school. Alongside this, an outstanding co-curricular programme seeks to foster and develop a wide range of interests and hobbies – music, sport, drama, public speaking and adventure training. An extended co-curricular programme has seen the timetable of the school day adapted to accommodate a wide selection of clubs and societies within core school hours. Berkhamsted also has a strong tradition of undertaking service within the local community from Year 9 (13+) onwards.

The School prides itself on offering outstanding levels of pastoral care and, in another echo of its boarding roots, the House system is a key feature of Berkhamsted. Senior School pupils are allocated to Houses and the Head of House, supported by House Tutors, has the primary responsibility for the academic and pastoral progress of each student in their House. Over and above the close academic supervision and support, this structure provides an excellent social base for pupils, allowing them to mix and get to know others across the year groups.

Berkhamsted offers scholarships – academic, art, drama, music and sport – and means-tested bursaries to talented pupils on entry to the school.

Parents are welcome to visit the School at any time: please call 01442 358001 for an appointment and a tour to appreciate what Berkhamsted can offer your family.

BERKHAMSTED
SCHOOL

(Founded 1541)

Overton House, 131 High Street, Berkhamsted, Hertfordshire HP4 2DJ UK

Tel: 01442 358001

Email: admissions@berkhamstedschool.org

Website: www.berkhamstedschool.org

Principal: Mr Richard Backhouse MA(Cantab)

Appointed: January 2016

School type:
Co-educational & single-sex, day & boarding

Age range of pupils: 3–18

No. of pupils enrolled as at 01/09/2017:

Sixth Form: 405

Pre-Prep/Prep: 547

Senior Boys: 439

Senior Girls: 375

Fees per annum as at 01/09/2017:

Day: £10,365–£20,250

Weekly Boarding: £27,115

Full Boarding: £32,255

Average class size: 20

Brentwood School

Brentwood School shines out as a beacon of excellence. Academically, we sit comfortably alongside the best day and boarding schools in the country, and we enjoy an unparalleled local reputation.

Our students are happy individuals who thrive on the high standards which are expected of them. They benefit from state-of-the-art facilities, set in the heart of Brentwood in Essex, and surrounded by 75 acres of green playing fields and gardens.

We celebrate a 461-year history and take our heritage seriously. We are a Christian School with a chapel and a chaplain, and our School values, encapsulated in our motto "Virtue, Learning and Manners", have as much resonance today as they did when written by English poet John Donne in 1622. Our pupils are expected to have self-respect, to exhibit pride in their appearance and embrace values such as courtesy, consideration for others, kindness, looking after each other, honour, courage, sportsmanship, duty and selflessness.

Brentwood School pupils achieve excellent academic standards that rank among some of the best in the country. Our track record of exam results shows consistent high grades are achieved by all our pupils. They work exceptionally hard and are supported by highly professional and inspiring teachers to achieve excellent results at both GCSE level and in Sixth Form, whether studying A levels or the IB Diploma. An average of seven students per year are offered places at Oxford or Cambridge and over 80% of offers are from Russell Group universities.

We use the freedom of independence wisely to innovate and develop a truly creative curriculum – one that really is best for our pupils.

We offer both GCSEs and IGCSEs; A levels and IB Diploma, and Global Perspectives from age 12. More recent curriculum developments include the introduction of a Human Universe course in the Fourth and Fifth Year, which examines critical thinking and global issues.

Brentwood was the first school in Essex, and one of the first in the country, to adopt the Diamond Model: single-sex classes from the age of 11-16 within an overall mixed gender environment. We believe this model helps our teachers to tailor their teaching to the different learning styles of boys and girls and provides the best of single gender teaching within a coeducational environment.

From an early age, we encourage pupils to aim high, think creatively and develop independence, so by the time they leave Sixth Form, they are well prepared for the expected, but can also tackle the unknowns. A flourishing Old Brentwoods community keeps thousands of alumni connected across the globe.

Our vast and exciting co-curricular programme enjoys national prominence, and we focus on providing opportunities for all to participate, as well as the pursuit of excellence for the most able.

Our Combined Cadet Force is one of the oldest and largest in the country, we offer The Duke of Edinburgh's Award to pupils who want to satisfy their taste for adventure, and a Community Service Unit which raises tens of thousands of pounds every year to help specific charitable organisations.

Our sports centre houses a 25-metre swimming pool, glass-backed squash courts, fencing salle and dance studio and pupils achieve top sporting honours both nationally and internationally.

Our musicians have played in the National Youth Orchestra, and our actors have gained places in the National Youth Theatre, RADA and other top Drama schools.

The lessons pupils learn at Brentwood will last for a lifetime. Integrity, initiative, a spirit of enterprise and an international mind-set help our pupils to thrive in the twenty-first century.

Brentwood School

(Founded 1557)

Middleton Hall Lane, Brentwood, Essex CM15 8EE UK

Tel: 01277 243243

Fax: 01277 243299

Email: headmaster@brentwood.essex.sch.uk

Website: www.brentwoodschool.co.uk

Headmaster: Mr Ian Davies

Appointed: September 2004

School type: Coeducational Day & Boarding

Religious Denomination: Church of England

Age range of pupils: 3–18

No. of pupils enrolled as at 01/09/2017: 1529

Boys: 837 ***Girls:*** 692

Fees per annum as at 01/09/2017:

Day: £18,216

Full Boarding: £35,700

Average class size:

18 in Preparatory and Senior School; 8 in Sixth Form

Teacher/pupil ratio: 1:9

125
Service of Celebration

Haileybury

Haileybury is an independent co-educational boarding school, located between London and Cambridge, in 500 acres of beautiful Hertfordshire countryside. Our spectacular grounds are home to outstanding facilities, excellent teaching and superb pastoral care for our community of boarding and day pupils.

Founded in 1862, Haileybury is proud of its history, tradition and values, taking the best from the past whilst also looking to the future. Academic rigour and outstanding co-curricular provision are at the heart of the college, providing exceptional opportunities and a truly all-round education, which enables our pupils to discover enduring passions and talents. Haileyburians leave as confident, tolerant and ambitious individuals, who are leaders and life-long learners and who can make a difference in the world beyond school.

Academic opportunity

We offer a dedicated Lower School for Years 7 and 8, a wide range of GCSEs and IGCSEs and the choice of the IB Diploma or A Levels in the Sixth Form. Haileybury is one of the leading IB schools in the UK as ranked by The Times' IB League Table and in the Top 100 Independent Schools for A Levels.

Boarding and day

More than two thirds of pupils are boarders and school life is centred around the 12 different boarding houses and Lower School. Children may join at 11+, 13+ or 16+. Flexi-boarding is available in Lower School (Years 7 and 8), allowing families this option without committing to full boarding early in a child's senior school career. From Year 9 onwards, full boarding is offered with the additional flexibility of pupils being able (if they so wish) to return home after sports commitments on Saturday afternoons.

Exceptional opportunities

A key part of our philosophy is about empowering each child to follow their passions and to build their self-confidence.

We therefore provide an enormous range of co-curricular opportunities, spanning everything from music and drama to sport and physical activities. There are a huge number of clubs and societies to cater for all interests including sailing, rowing, rugby, lacrosse, netball, swimming, Combined Cadet Force, Duke of Edinburgh Award, Model United Nations, charity and community action and much more.

Pupils benefit from professional sports coaches and the college regularly hosts speakers and performers from the arts, sporting and academic worlds. Music at Haileybury is exceptional, with an abundance of concerts, recitals and public performances each year and more than 30 visiting specialists teaching hundreds of instrumental lessons every week.

Supportive environment

A caring environment is crucial to happiness and fulfilment. For those who join us, Haileybury is like a home-from-home. Warm and friendly, we give each and every child the confidence to find their identity, embracing failings as much as successes in their personal journey of discovery.

A warm welcome

We have a busy programme of Open Days and taster events which take place throughout the year. We warmly invite you to visit to discover what life at Haileybury has to offer and why your child will flourish here. For further information, please contact the Head of Admissions, Mrs Michele Metcalfe, at admissions@haileybury.com.

Haileybury

(Founded 1862)

Haileybury, Hertford, Hertfordshire SG13 7NU UK

Tel: +44 (0)1992 706200

Email: admissions@haileybury.com

Website: www.haileybury.com

The Master: Mr Martin Collier MA BA PGCE

Appointed: September 2017

School type: Coeducational Boarding & Day

Age range of pupils: 11–18

(entry at 11+, 13+ and 16+)

No. of pupils enrolled as at 01/09/2017: 804

Boys: 466 ***Girls:*** 338 ***Sixth Form:*** 323

No. of boarders: 515

Fees per annum as at 01/09/2017:

Day: £16,455–£24,753

Full Boarding: £20,796–£32,784

Teacher/pupil ratio: 1:7

King's Ely

We know that if we could bottle the spirit of King's Ely we would be onto a real winner, but we would like you to come and experience it for yourself.

Nestled in the heart of the beautiful cathedral city of Ely, King's Ely is an inspiringly visionary independent co-educational day and boarding school, yet one that is built on a fascinating history stretching back over 1,000 years.

We serve the academic and pastoral needs of around 1,000 boys and girls from the age of one right the way through to 18, with boarders from seven years old. King's Ely is located just 15 minutes north of Cambridge and a short walk from Ely train station, with school buses stopping at key locations around the area.

The adventure of a King's Ely education enables pupils of all ages to flourish, from the toddlers in King's Ely Acremont and Nursery to the young men and women in our Sixth Form; and whether a student shines in a classroom or lab, on a stage, on a pitch or on a mountainside, our school promises an abundance of opportunity for personal development, both academically and socially.

We empower our young people to challenge themselves, to push beyond the boundaries of their own expectations and to achieve more than they ever believed possible. King's Ely students achieve excellent GCSE and A Level results, with 98% gaining places in their first or insurance choice university. But our school is about much more than league tables.

Innovative approaches to teaching and learning are the hallmark of every section of King's Ely. Through a broad and balanced curriculum, pupils develop the self-knowledge and inner resilience that will enable them to face the challenges of an ever-changing world.

Music, drama, art and textiles are each embedded in the culture of King's Ely, with vast opportunities for pupils of all abilities and aspirations.

All major sports are offered, along with an impressive array of other activities, helping every pupil to realise their sporting potential. Rowing, athletics, golf, cricket, hockey, tennis, rugby, netball, equestrian and football – the choices are endless. The working week, which no longer includes formal lessons on Saturdays, also enables pupils to participate fully in regional and national events.

King's Ely boasts some of the region's most historic buildings yet teaching facilities are modern and purpose-built. Our close links with Ely Cathedral make the perfect setting for concerts and performances, a daily extension to the school's workspace, the school chapel, and a place of outstanding beauty and spirituality.

Boarders, including the Ely Cathedral Boy and Girl Choristers, live in picturesque boarding houses, well led by caring housemasters and housemistresses. A strong pastoral structure where childhood is respected and cherished is a key feature.

From the high peaks of the Himalayas to the gushing torrents of the rivers in the Alps, our unique Ely Scheme also offers boundless opportunities for pupils to learn through outdoor education. We also give students the chance to undertake their Duke of Edinburgh Award at all three levels.

King's Ely is a family – a community that is vibrant, nurturing and inclusive. We are a school that can take each child on a seamless journey, travelling from one section to the next, whilst welcoming newcomers at key transition stages. Only by visiting King's Ely can you feel the energy and warmth of our community.

(Founded 973)

Ely, Cambridgeshire CB7 4DB UK

Tel: 01353 660700

Fax: 01353 667485

Email: enquiries@kingsely.org

Website: www.kingsely.org

Principal:

Mrs Susan Freestone MEd, GRSM, LRAM, ARCM, FRSA

Appointed: 2004

School type: Coeducational Boarding & Day

Age range of pupils: 1–18

No. of pupils enrolled as at 01/09/2017: 1025

Boys: 564 ***Girls:*** 461 ***Sixth Form:*** 185

No. of boarders: 205

Fees per annum as at 01/09/2017:

Day: £13,830–£20,853

Full Boarding: £22,053–£30,189

Average class size: Max 20

Teacher/pupil ratio: 1:9

Lockers Park

Lockers Park is a day and boarding school where pupils receive a first class education that is balanced and happy. Set in 23 acres of beautiful Hertfordshire countryside, just outside London, the school has been educating boys aged 7 to 13 for over 140 years while a recently launched Pre-Prep supports boys and girls aged 4 to 7.

Academia, The Arts, Music, Sport and Co-Curricular success are celebrated in equal measure at Lockers Park. The school prides itself on treating pupils as individuals, utilising a practical approach to learning that helps them discover hidden talents and initiate lifelong passions along the way. The school believes engaging in outdoor activities and playing structured sport every day is intrinsic to good schooling, leading to increased concentration and success during academic lessons.

Central to a Lockers Park education is the upholding of traditional values. Respect, honesty, tolerance and compassion still remain just as, if not more, important in today's ever-changing, 24-hour world. Charged with educating the men of the future, the school aims to develop pupils' self-confidence, resilience and self-esteem, ensuring Lockers Park boys leave as well-rounded individuals, fully equipped for the excitement and challenges of senior school life.

Academic Excellence

Treating boys as individuals is at the very heart of Lockers Park's approach. Allowing boys to be themselves, comfortable within their school environment, encourages them to gain confidence and flourish academically.

This strategy continues to reap dividends, securing strong academic results for the school year-on-year, preparing boys for the country's leading public and independent schools via Common Entrance and Scholarships. Recent graduates have moved on to Eton College, Harrow School, Bedford School and Rugby School to name but a few.

Co-Curricular Opportunities

A rich palette of opportunities is accessible to each and every boy. Whether it's Sport, Science & Technology, Music, Art and Drama, pupils are encouraged to enrich and broaden their Lockers Park experience in many ways.

A full sporting programme and excellent facilities see pupils enjoy team games of rugby, football and cricket alongside individual sports such as tennis, squash, athletics, swimming, rifle shooting, cross-country and skiing at the local Snow Centre.

It is widely recognised that music at Lockers Park is outstanding. Over 95% of pupils learn a musical instrument with many learning two or three. A thriving String Orchestra and Chapel Choir are just some of the options on offer to pupils. Autumn 2017 will see the exciting addition of a Recording Studio with sequencing software to further enhance the school's music provision.

Other recent highlights have included a successful tour to South Africa, Chess Club continuing to go from strength-to-strength, securing 2nd place at the IAPS National Chess Championships (in only the second year of taking part), and the School Chapel Choir's 10th appearance at the Children's Trust Concert in St John's, Smith Square, London.

Encouraging Environment

Social and emotional growth is just as important as academic progression, and a highly-regarded team of staff work to ensure pupils are happy and well-motivated. A warm, family orientated and inclusive approach gives the care, comfort and support that is vital for the boys' well-being and success.

Come and find out what life at Lockers Park is all about; please contact the Marketing & Admissions Manager, Mrs Susan Johnson at sjohnson@lockerspark.herts.sch.uk.

(Founded 1874)

Lockers Park Lane, Hemel Hempstead, Hertfordshire HP1 1TL UK

Tel: 01442 251712

Fax: 01442 234150

Email: secretary@lockerspark.herts.sch.uk

Website: www.lockerspark.herts.sch.uk

Headmaster: Mr C R Wilson

Appointed: September 2013

School type:
Boys' Boarding, Flexible Boarding & Day, Co-Ed Pre-Prep

Age range of boys: 4–13

Age range of girls: 4–7

No. of pupils enrolled as at 01/09/2017: 170

Fees per annum as at 01/09/2017:

Day: £10,050–£16,530

Full Boarding: £23,160

Average class size: Av 14

Teacher/pupil ratio: 1:8

Mander Portman Woodward – Cambridge

Cambridge is where the MPW success story began. Some 44 years ago, three Cambridge graduates – Messieurs Mander, Portman and Woodward came together with an ambition to create a unique secondary education experience. They focused on several elements, based on their great Alma Mater, which they considered significant to the overall learning experience. Amongst these were the following: small class sizes, a strong tutorial system and superb teaching – and all of these within an informal atmosphere, which would allow creative minds to flourish.

Move the clock forward to the present day and these elements are still very much the hallmark of an MPW education. With fewer than 10 students per class for GCSE and A level, (though in fact the college average is closer to 5 in a class), the learning experience is truly personalised. As well as simulating the small class size at Oxbridge our students experience the privilege of being treated as an individual and not a number. Small classes mean our students know their questions will be answered and that they will have genuine contact time with their tutors in every lesson. With more than 30 A level subjects on offer and no restrictions on combinations, our students can choose subjects that suit them. Whilst Maths, Business, Economics and of course the Sciences remain popular choices, less well known subjects such as Ancient History and Classical Civilisation are also available.

With a current cohort of 60% British and 40% International, MPW Cambridge offers a world-class education to all. Education, however, is much more than what happens in the classroom. The preparation for life after secondary education is important too. Students need to be especially well-informed when they begin their UCAS application. The daily help by the personal tutors to each tutee is immense. From initial, informal discussion on determining the most suitable university course, through several drafts of the personal statement, often through BMAT or other entrance tests, for some even through daunting interview prospects, the MPW Personal Tutor is there. Their mandate is to 'hold the student's hand' throughout, providing encouragement and support.

We're also proud to assist those who might not have done so well the first time around. Our weekly assessments provide diagnostics where we can see which elements require further support. They also ensure that all of our students are fully prepared for the actual exam and properly understand critical success factors such as timing and weighting.

Last but not least, what others say. '*The college provides an outstanding quality of education. An outstanding curriculum supported by very well informed teaching enables students to reach standards of work that are well above average. The provision for the students' spiritual, moral, social and cultural development and their welfare, health and safety are outstanding. By the time the students leave they have developed into mature, thoughtful and responsible young people.*' Ofsted 2016.

Mander Portman Woodward

(Founded 1987)

3-4 Brookside, Cambridge CB2 1JE UK

Tel: 01223 350158

Fax: 01223 366429

Email: cambridge@mpw.ac.uk

Website: www.mpw.ac.uk

Principal: Dr Markus Bernhardt

Appointed: September 2017

School type: Coeducational Day & Boarding

Age range of pupils: 15–19

Average class size: 10 max

Teacher/pupil ratio: 1:5

M|P|W

Manor Lodge School

Manor Lodge enjoys an excellent reputation for modern facilities, beautiful grounds, a creative curriculum, well qualified and caring teachers, high academic standards, innovative and exciting expressive arts, wide-ranging sporting opportunities for all and confident, articulate children who are a joy to share time with. We pride ourselves in maintaining a warm, supportive atmosphere in which every individual child is allowed to blossom academically, artistically and socially at an appropriate pace as part of an inclusive family. Whatever their talents, and every child has unique gifts, we will find and nurture them and everyone's success is celebrated.

The school works in close partnership with parents where open dialogue is encouraged and regular meetings take place to review every aspect of a child's development. Our belief is that if a child is happy, valued and supported, they will learn and grow in all respects and thus be suitably prepared for life beyond Manor Lodge. A typical MLS child, as described by local secondary school heads, is articulate, confident, with good study habits and skills and is quick to involve themselves in all aspects of school life.

Our sports teams have achieved considerable success locally as well as at county and national level. We host our own annual tournaments as well as competing in many local and national events on top of an active fixture list with all the South Herts/North London Prep Schools. Manor Lodge children also regularly enter art, prose and science exhibitions and competitions winning many awards.

Manor Lodge children are highly active in raising money for local, national and international charities. They also love to share their talents with senior citizens in retirement homes at Christmas.

We organise over 60 clubs and activities for the children. The music department runs three choirs, plus a community choir, a full orchestra, a jazz band and ensembles, performing in concerts and musical theatre productions. Manor Lodge is proud of its tradition of children performing and it is our belief that it complements and enriches the academic side of school life.

The school is proud of its record in achieving over twenty scholarships to local secondary schools in each of the past fifteen years with our current record standing at 50 in one year. On average over 95% of parents obtain their first choice of school on secondary transfer.

Always seeking to enhance our facilities and improve the experience for our children, we have recently completed an impressive new performing arts/sports hall and teaching block which is now providing a 400 seater theatre/sports hall, dance studio, drama workshop, music teaching rooms, music practice rooms and three Year 6 classrooms. Right alongside is an all-weather artificial grass pitch which provides a suitable surface for netball, hockey and football as well as a large space for playtimes. These new facilities complement the long established listed building, modern teaching block, dining room, extensive playing fields and sports pavilion.

If you are looking for a school with a true family atmosphere where children feel loved, safe and appreciated for who they are, where there are high academic standards and wonderful opportunities to develop artistic and sporting interests to last a lifetime, then Manor Lodge might just be the school for you.

Manor Lodge

(Founded 1991)

Rectory Lane, Ridge Hill, Shenley, Hertfordshire WD7 9BG UK

Tel: 01707 642424

Fax: 01707 645206

Email: enquiries@manorlodgeschool.com

Website: www.manorlodgeschool.com

Headmaster: Mr G Dunn CertEd

Appointed: June 2011

School type: Coeducational Day

Age range of pupils: 3–11

No. of pupils enrolled as at 01/09/2017: 430

Boys: 214 ***Girls:*** 216

Fees per annum as at 01/09/2017:

Day: £10,650–£11,910

Average class size: 19

Teacher/pupil ratio: 1:13

Orwell Park School

Set in more than 100 acres of parkland overlooking the River Orwell in Suffolk, Orwell Park provides a broad and balanced education for boys and girls, boarders and day pupils, between the ages of 3 and 13. A modern, caring and flexible approach to boarding sets Orwell Park apart as a forward thinking school, which continues to instil traditional values such as commitment, compassion and courtesy in its pupils.

At Orwell Park, we have worked with all staff, all pupils and had discussions with and feedback from many parents in order to identify the values upon which we want to base our school. It is essential for everyone to 'buy in' to the ethos if they are to feel part of it. This is key because success depends on the values being modelled by adults (staff and parents), who should work together, so embedding the values as far as possible at home as well as at school. "Becoming the best that we can be" is in keeping with our focus on the principles of Growth Mindset. It is a phrase that we hope will remind us that we are on a journey to grow and develop in all areas of our lives, in the classroom, on the sports field and in our interactions with one another and the wider world. It also reminds us that this is a journey we are on together as a community. Our overarching value is 'Integrity', which we define as strength of character and strong moral principles, and we aspire for this to underpin everything that we do. We have five core values, each with supplementary values, which provide a common moral framework within which we aim to conduct ourselves: Kindness, Collaboration, Courage, Spirit and Respect.

As a school, we seek to explore these values, deepen our understanding, improving our application of them and to weave them through the fabric of the School. We aim to embed them in various ways including displays around the school, assemblies, through our rewards and sanctions and, perhaps most importantly of all, through staff and parents modelling our chosen values.

Academically, Orwell Park prides itself on successfully preparing children for entry to senior school at 13+, in 2017, 24 leavers won scholarships: for academic excellence or for music, art, sport, design and technology – all to a wide range of senior independent schools. Orwell Park offers academic challenge to all children and learning support to those who need it. In the classroom, a traditional curriculum (including classics) is taught, using the most modern methods.

Whilst we value greatly the past, we also embrace technology and, as such, every child in Years 3-8 has their own iPad in order to enhance learning in the classroom and beyond. The iPads allow pupils to learn in a way that they are used to, fostering collaboration between pupils, whilst providing portability.

In addition to the traditional curricular subjects, Orwell Park pupils are involved in a comprehensive activity programme, including: orchestra and various ensembles, chess, community service, skiing, equestrianism, climbing on the bouldering wall, OPS Challenge (a two-year mini DofE course), camping and campfire fun in the school's woodlands, Art and DT clubs, Brownies and Blueys (boys' club), as well as numerous large-scale theatrical productions.

Music plays a great part in the life of Orwell Park, with 80% of the children learning an instrument. The school boasts over 40 practice rooms, three concert grand pianos, and a modern, well equipped music technology suite. Art, design and technology are an important part of the curriculum and are a focus for creative talent.

The recently opened Pre-Prep has its own landscaped area and forms part of the 110 acre site, which includes the main Prep School.

For further details about Orwell Park, please call 01473 659225 and speak to our Registrar or visit www.orwellpark.co.uk

ORWELL PARK SCHOOL

(Founded 1867)

Nacton, Ipswich, Suffolk IP10 0ER UK

Tel: 01473 659225

Fax: 01473 659822

Email: admissions@orwellpark.org

Website: www.orwellpark.co.uk

Headmaster: Mr Adrian Brown MA(Cantab)

Appointed: September 2011

School type: Coeducational Boarding & Day

Religious Denomination: Interdenominational

Age range of pupils: 2½–13

No. of pupils enrolled as at 01/09/2017: 301

Boys: 174 ***Girls:*** 127

No. of boarders: 116

Fees per term as at 01/09/2017:

Pre-Prep Day: £2,634 – £3,746 per term

Prep Day: £5,484 – £6,078 per term

Prep Boarding: £7,032 – £8,374 per term

Average class size: 12-14

Teacher/pupil ratio: 1:12

St Cedd's School

St Cedd's School is a coeducational 3-11 IAPS Charitable Trust School offering pupils the opportunity to aspire and achieve in a caring environment that nurtures talent and supports individual endeavour. This is a school in which every child matters. We value and celebrate their many diverse talents and qualities and the grounded confidence the pupils develop results in great personal achievement.

Individual Pupil Progress

Most children exceed the Early Learning Goals by age 5 and the progress of pupils, of all abilities, throughout the school is rapid. Our internal SATs assessment results and 11+ scores far exceed national averages and annually we celebrate an unrivalled success rate to selective grammar and independent senior schools with an impressive track record of scholarship awards. This level of achievement is significant given that we are academically non-selective. Assessments on entry are designed to capture the strengths, weaknesses and areas for development of each child so that the education is tailored to individual needs.

Centre of Excellence

The Independent Schools Inspectorate (ISI) placed St Cedd's School at the top level in every category of inspection in February 2013 which places the school amongst the very best 3-11 preparatory schools in the country. The accolade confirms what we witness every day; high academic achievement, outstanding records of attainment in music, an inclusive sporting ethos and successes at national tournaments, a sense of purpose and ambition that shows itself in the attitude and actions of the pupils and staff, and a very effective pastoral care system.

Broad and Balanced Curriculum

With over 70 after-school activities to choose from, extra study opportunities are balanced with a firm focus on academic work. This synergy supports the development of confident self-assured pupils ready for the challenges ahead. PE, music, art, French and science are taught by specialists with the teaching of PE, music and French starting in Nursery. Acknowledging the breadth of talents of pupils is an important aspect of life at St Cedd's School. To this end, our baccalaureate-style Year 6 curriculum, HOLDFAST, leads to awards in recognition of 'Holistic Opportunities to Learn and Develop, Furthering Achievement, Service and Talent'.

As a member of the Choir Schools Association our Choristers sing in the Cathedral Choir and the Junior and Senior Chamber Choirs sing at Evensong.

Nurturing the Future

For 85 years, boys and girls at St Cedd's School have been enjoying a quality of education that is among the very best you will find. We provide the best start in our Nursery where the boys and girls thrive in a colourful and nurturing environment that widens their horizons and instils in them a love of learning.

Breakfast Club operates from 7:30am-8:00am and a wrap-around care programme is open until 6pm. Fees include curriculum-linked extra-curricular activities, 1-1 learning support, lunch and the majority of after-school clubs.

To attend an open day, request a prospectus or to arrange an individual tour, please contact Mrs Abbott on 01245 392810 or email admissions@stcedds.org.uk.

St Cedd's School

(Founded 1931)

178a New London Road, Chelmsford, Essex CM2 0AR UK

Tel: 01245 392810

Email: info@stcedds.org.uk

Website: www.stcedds.org.uk

Head: Dr Pamela Edmonds

Appointed: January 2011

School type: Coeducational Day

Age range of pupils: 3–11

No. of pupils enrolled as at 01/09/2017: 400

Boys: 200 ***Girls:*** 200

Fees per annum as at 01/09/2017:

Day: £8,550–£10,110

Average class size: 24

St Faith's

Bright Beginnings, Exciting Futures

A world of future-thinking academic teaching, personal and social development, competitive sport and artistic appreciation is opened up to children as they enter St Faith's. Donning our iconic striped blazer and stepping into our school, rich in heritage and ambitious for the future, instils a sense of pride and eagerness in every child. Opportunities to learn, explore, create and think abound in every classroom from art to engineering, science to history.

At St Faith's each child is taught, developed and nurtured, to equip them well for life, whatever path they choose to take. Our teachers are passionate about sharing their knowledge, exploring new ideas, challenging the status quo and instilling a life-long passion for learning. Teaching styles are tailored to meet each individual child's needs. Lessons are accessible, engaging and challenging for all pupils. Top-down excellence in all lessons ensures we continually stretch our pupils to achieve more than they thought possible. Our academic curriculum is ground-breaking in its innovative content and has been commended by institutions including the Royal Society, Cambridge University, the James Dyson Foundation and the Spanish Embassy.

Exemplary, innovative and forward-facing academic subjects are interspersed each day with sporting endeavors, musical experiences, artistic creations and dramatic performances. Assemblies, tutor time and plenty of play-time ensure children have a chance to express themselves away from the classroom. Our curriculum covers all National Curriculum subjects and more. Owing to small class sizes, exceptional teachers and the above average ability of our children all subjects follow an accelerated curriculum and the vast majority of pupils work at a higher level commensurate with their age.

Our green and spacious 9-acre site, located in the heart of Cambridge, together with extensive playing fields a two-minute walk away, provide some of the best facilities of any prep school in the UK. Every classroom is equipped with modern teaching technology. Crucially, teachers are trained how and when to use this technology to enhance learning. The shelves in our library are crowded with over 11,000 works of fiction and non-fiction with relevance to our youngest and most mature of pupils. Engineering suites provide access to tools and equipment beyond many inventor's wildest dreams. Fully-equipped science laboratories and computer suites are used by all year groups. Our current £2M investment to expand our STEAM facilities will include flexible large indoor spaces for inter-disciplinary projects, a roof-top greenhouse and a night sky viewing platform.

Our broad sporting education is not simply a focus for sporting glory and trophy collection. At St Faith's we believe sport is a conduit for developing mental as well as physical fitness. The losing as well as winning of sporting fixtures builds mental resilience and is an emotive demonstration of getting out of life what you put in. Of course team work is omnipresent in many sporting events and as such our pupils learn to revel in team as well as individual accolades, better preparing them for their futures. Drama and the performing arts are tools not only for teaching children a life-long love of the arts but for promoting self-belief and confidence.

St Faith's pupils stand out as confident, articulate, grounded and courteous, attributes which will stand them in good stead for their futures.

St Faith's
CAMBRIDGE

(Founded 1884)

Trumpington Road, Cambridge, Cambridgeshire CB2 8AG UK

Tel: 01223 352073

Fax: 01223 314757

Email: admissions@stfaiths.co.uk

Website: www.stfaiths.co.uk

Headmaster: Mr N L Helliwell

Appointed: September 2011

School type: Coeducational Day

Age range of pupils: 4–13

No. of pupils enrolled as at 01/09/2011: 540

Boys: 318 ***Girls:*** 222

Fees per annum as at 01/09/2011:

Day: £11,865–£14,955

Average class size: 16-18

St Margaret's Preparatory School

St. Margaret's Prep School is a happy, co-ed, independent school for children aged 2 – 11.

Our lovely school, formerly the Coach House and Stable block for Gosfield Hall before becoming a school in 1946, is situated in 7 acres of beautiful parkland in the heart of rural North Essex, within easy reach of Halstead, Braintree, Sudbury, Colchester, Chelmsford, Felsted and Gt. Dunmow.

Parents who send their children to St Margaret's know they can trust us to make education fun and stimulating, they know our reputation for developing exceptionally well-rounded pupils with a love of learning.

Our aim is to ensure that every child is engaged in their learning and given as many opportunities as possible for intellectual, physical and social growth. We do this within a structured, disciplined yet enjoyable, environment, where each child is helped to fulfil their potential, in class, in the arts, in music and on the sports field.

We believe in celebrating the achievements of every child, encouraging them to learn, recognising their strengths and supporting them as they try new things. From the moment a child enters St. Margaret's, they become part of our School family. Pupils are taught by specialist teachers in a broad range of lessons and extra-curricular subjects. Our Nursery children share the same specialist teachers for French, PE and Music as the rest of the school. This is reflected in the superb scholarship results we see year after year in Academia, Sport, Music and Art.

Music is a particular speciality of the school; with thirteen visiting peripatetic teachers supporting our own music teachers we offer lessons in a range of instruments from cello to harp, trumpet to drums and everything in between. With a vast array of ensembles and choirs every child is encouraged to join in. Over 80% of our Prep children have an individual lesson in at least one instrument.

St. Margaret's Early Years was awarded 'Outstanding' in all areas in our most recent Ofsted inspection, and the whole school was judged 'Excellent' by the Independent Schools Inspectorate with achievement for many found to be 'Exceptional'.

We are extremely proud of the range of activities we offer our pupils, with many extra-curricular before and after school clubs, directed by individuals qualified in that subject, and carefully designed with academic and social development of children fully in mind.

At St. Margaret's, each individual has the opportunity to develop their strengths and to discover new talents and interests. From the very youngest child, our pupils are polite and kind, and grow to develop into mature and independent individuals.

Our children are our greatest achievement, and we are very proud to be a part of their lives.

Every day's an Open Day – come and see for yourself why we're so proud of our School.

(Founded 1946)

Gosfield Hall Park, Gosfield, Halstead, Essex CO9 1SE UK

Tel: 01787 472134

Fax: 01787 478207

Email: admin@stmargaretsprep.com

Website: www.stmargaretsprep.com

Headmaster: Mr. Callum Douglas

School type: Coeducational Day

Age range of pupils: 2–11

Fees per annum as at 01/09/2017:

Day: £9,315–£11,280 (excluding the nursery)

Average class size: Max 18

The Leys School

The School – to inspire
Located in the heart of the historic university city of Cambridge, The Leys' leafy 50 acre campus offers pupils the very best of both worlds; a traditional Cambridge education making the most of the School's links with the University, balanced with some of the most envied facilities in the country. The School's ethos centres around its aim to give every child a rounded and holistic education.

Academic life – to learn
Through the provision of a broad and balanced curriculum, pupils at The Leys develop into articulate, creative and culturally-aware individuals. Whether at GCSE or A Level stage the School's reputation for academic success is well-earned with high-ranking results and almost all pupils going to their first choice university. The School frequently calls upon its Cambridge University connections, bringing in a range of distinguished guest speakers such as Professor Stephen Hawking (who's own son is indeed an Old Leysian), running alongside The Leys' own Lecture Series. Each pupil's timetable is tailored to suit their needs, interests and aptitudes while encouraging them to succeed and develop their own, individual talents.

Outstanding facilities – to motivate
The School is not all about academia; the opportunities for broadening horizons are endless. Recent developments at The Leys include: Great Hall – a world-class, state-of-the-art theatre, dance studio and drama centre combining contemporary performance spaces with brand new science facilities. The Boathouse – situated along the banks of the River Cam and shared with Kings, Selwyn and Churchill Colleges, this £4M redeveloped facility offers pupils an unrivalled opportunity to become involved in a true 'Cambridge' sport. In addition to this there are over 40 acres of dedicated sports fields and astro-turf allowing every pupil, irrespective of ability, to enjoy a huge range of sporting activities.

Extra-curricular activities – to achieve
All pupils at The Leys take part in either Duke of Edinburgh awards or CCF (Combined Cadet Force) and this plays a valuable part in their wider education. There are also endless opportunities for debating, community service, leadership, fundraising, music and numerous clubs and societies to join.

Pastoral care – to support
The Leys is, primarily, a boarding school and places much importance on providing a caring, friendly and secure environment for all its pupils. Each child, whether a full boarder, home boarder or day pupil, is attached to one of 11 houses. Housemasters, Housemistresses and Matrons with support from a number of assistant staff are on hand 24/7 to ensure each child is given a real home from home. The feeling of 'Community' lies at the heart of the School, so while they may live in one House, they mix with their peers across the whole campus.

Scholarships – to encourage
While it is true that all children are in some way gifted, The Leys is keen to encourage those with sporting, academic, artistic or musical talents and offers a range of scholarships across all year groups.

Visiting The Leys
The School's prospectus and website will give a good overview of the opportunities available but prospective parents and pupils are encouraged to visit the School. To arrange this please contact the Admissions Team on 01223 508904 or email admissions@theleys.net

THE Leys
CAMBRIDGE

(Founded 1875)

Trumpington Road, Cambridge, Cambridgeshire CB2 7AD UK

Tel: 01223 508900

Fax: 01223 505303

Email: admissions@theleys.net

Website: www.theleys.net

Headmaster: Mr Martin Priestley

Appointed: September 2014

School type: Coeducational Boarding & Day

Age range of pupils: 11–18

No. of pupils enrolled as at 01/09/2017: 565

Fees per annum as at 01/09/2017:

Day: £15,435–£21,390

Full Boarding: £23,295–£31,965

Average class size: 15-20

Teacher/pupil ratio: 1:8

H·M·KING·GEORGE·THE·FIFTHS·GATEWAY

Tring Park School for the Performing Arts

Tring Park School for the Performing Arts stands at the forefront of specialist performing arts education in the UK. Tring Park also offers a full and rounded education to GCSE, BTEC and A level (up to 23 A level subjects), in an atmosphere of high academic performance. At Tring Park talented young people from 8–19 specialise in Dance, Acting, Musical Theatre or Commercial Music, whilst gaining excellent academic qualifications. Entrance is via audition and scholarships are available for Dance via the Government's Music and Dance Scheme. School scholarships and bursaries are available for Drama and Musical Theatre.

Pupils perform regularly both in Tring Park's Markova Theatre as well as in London, throughout the UK and Europe. Musical Theatre productions include: *Calamity Jane*, *Jesus Christ Superstar*, Rodgers & Hart's *Babes in Arms*, *Guys and Dolls* and *Cabaret*. Tring Park provides 25 young ballet dancers to perform annually in the Christmas production of *Nutcracker* and *Le Corsaire* with English National Ballet at the London Coliseum. It also provides dancers for English National Ballet productions at the Royal Albert Hall. Six pupils have played the part of Billy in *Billy Elliot* in the West End and on tour, another joined the cast of *Matilda* in the role of Lavender and current pupils Harley Bird is the voice of the famous cartoon character *Peppa Pig*. In 2016 the Tring Park choir "The Sixteen" won the BBC Songs of Praise Senior School Choir of the Year.

Alumni success

Daisy Ridley – Rey in *Star Wars* and *Murder on the Orient Express*
Lily James – *Cinderella*, the BBC adaptation of *War and Peace* and *Romeo and Juliet*
Lily James and Jessica Brown Findlay – ITV's *Downton Abbey*
Bryony Hannah and Helen George – BBC1's *Call the Midwife*
Nafisa Baba – winner BBC Young Dancer of the Year 2017
Drew McOnie – 2016 Olivier Award winner and director of the Musical King Kong on Broadway

Dance companies including:

Birmingham Royal Ballet
Danish Royal Ballet
English National Ballet
New Adventures
Scottish Ballet
Random Dance
See www.tringpark.com/alumni for further information.

Tring Park also has considerable academic success with students entering Russell Group universities and another who was awarded a Scholarship to study English at Churchill College, Cambridge. Other students have left to read Medicine, Law and and Engineering whilst others are working in stage management and in other performance-related industries.

Please check the website for upcoming Open Days
To apply online: www.tringpark.com/opendays
Registrar: Adélia Wood-Smith
registrar@tringpark.com
Registered charity No. 1040330

(Founded 1919)

Tring Park, Tring, Hertfordshire HP23 5LX UK

Tel: 01442 824255

Fax: 01442 891069

Email: info@tringpark.com

Website: www.tringpark.com

Principal: Mr Stefan Anderson MA, ARCM, ARCT

Appointed: September 2002

School type: Coeducational Boarding & Day

Religious Denomination: Non-denominational

Age range of pupils: 8–19

No. of pupils enrolled as at 01/09/2017: 335

Boys: 97 ***Girls:*** 243 ***Sixth Form:*** 217

No. of boarders: 205

Fees per annum as at 01/09/2017:

Day: £14,070–£22,410

Full Boarding: £23,715–£33,540

East Midlands

Mount St Mary's College

Mount St Mary's College is an independent Catholic day and boarding school for boys and girls, founded in the Jesuit tradition. Located on a beautiful campus in the heart of the Derbyshire countryside, the school offers high quality teaching facilities, outstanding sporting resources alongside broad and engaging extra-curricular opportunities. Students aged 11 to 18 are taught by highly qualified and dedicated teachers who ensure that care of the individual and the pursuit of excellence are at the heart of everyday life. Each student is taught that in order to achieve their very best, they must always strive harder, higher and with the service of others at the heart of what they do. Excellent examination results each year support this approach.

We proudly embrace the guiding principles of the Catholic faith and the Jesuit approach to teaching and learning. These core values have stood the test of time: they are simple, effective and universal.

Mount St Mary's College in 2017 is a vibrant and growing school. Although much has changed in its remarkable history the Mount preserves and cherishes its Jesuit identity. It is true to its founding principles of developing 'Men and Women for Others' whilst ensuring they are prepared for the modern world they will soon take their place in. Whilst the majority of the students at the school are from the local area, travelling daily from Sheffield, Chesterfield, Rotherham, Doncaster, Mansfield and beyond, many using the fleet of school minibuses, students also come from many countries around the world. Students come to live alongside the British students from many European countries as well as many from further afield including Mexico, Chile, Fiji, the Middle East, Hong Kong, China and Nigeria to name a few. This creates a diverse, cosmopolitan environment, reflective of the wider world, where students learn to live and work alongside one another, preparing for all that comes next.

Sport has been a long standing area of strength at the Mount. And whilst rugby and hockey remain strong and successful sports, the Mount has moved with the times and offers a broad range of sporting opportunities in athletics, cricket, swimming, fencing, shooting, pentathlon, biathlon, fitness and much more. The investment in facilities and staff means the Mount offers a sports program that ensures that all students are able to access sport throughout their week, whether as a novice or at the elite level that a notable number achieve.

The reputation for excellence in Music is well established. Throughout the year the various choirs, individuals and ensembles create highlights for all to enjoy. Over 75% of students at the preparatory school Barlborough Hall play at least one instrument and more than 40% at the senior school do so. Concerts are performed each term and whilst the showcase Academy Concert tops the bill at the end of May, many other opportunities to perform are offered. Friends of the school and members of the wider community are always welcome to attend.

We warmly invite you to come and see what a Mount education could mean for your family at one of our open mornings, or for a private visit to see the school in action, meet staff and students and get an insight into life at Mount St Mary's College. Please contact Victoria McAllister, Head of Admissions for further information on 01246 433 388 or email admissions@msmcollege.com

(Founded 1842)

College Road, Spinkhill, Derbyshire S21 3YL UK

Tel: 01246 433388

Email: admissions@msmcollege.com

Website: www.msmcollege.com

Headmaster: Dr Nicholas Cuddihy

Appointed: 2014

School type: Coeducational Day & Boarding

Age range of pupils: 11–18

No. of pupils enrolled as at 01/09/2017: 360

Fees per annum as at 01/09/2017:

Day: £11,669–£13,406

Weekly Boarding: £18,202–£23,431

Full Boarding: £22,128–£29,046

Average class size: 15-20

Teacher/pupil ratio: 1:10

Greater London

Avon House Preparatory School

"Avon House is a family, concerned for the happiness and general well-being of all. Celebrating and supporting every pupil begins with self-esteem, honesty, fairness, integrity, respect for oneself and respect for others. In our happy, secure environment the emphasis is placed on each child being recognised as a valued individual. We hope our pupils will develop their full potential in both academic and non-academic fields, with a strong moral understanding of truth, equality and humanity. We aim to give our pupils life-enhancing strategies to build on as they progress towards the adult world."

Avon House is an independent, co-educational prep school in Essex offering a happy, stable and disciplined environment for children aged from three to eleven.

Our preparatory school aims to provide a happy, supportive and disciplined environment where emphasis is placed on the development of each child as an individual, allowing each one to realise their potential and to thrive in other areas such as sport, music, dance and drama.

Avon House School offers a broad and balanced curriculum delivered by a highly capable team of professional staff.

Situated on the High Road in Woodford Green, Essex, our convenient location and caring environment offer all children a secure start to an educational life that will be rich in opportunity and experience.

We aim to provide our children with an appetite for learning, a thirst for knowledge and a curiosity for the wider world.

We strive to achieve academic excellence beginning with firm foundations and to present children with occasions to create memorable experiences during these important years.

Avon House is a school community where children are valued as individuals and encouraged to demonstrate their own unique personalities both in class and beyond.

The energy and imagination of the staff provide children with the enthusiasm to go the extra mile creating opportunities within our unique learning environment.

We welcome visits from prospective parents during the school day.

CELEBRATING & SUPPORTING EVERY CHILD

AVON HOUSE
PREPARATORY SCHOOL

490 High Road, Woodford Green, Essex IG8 0PN UK

Tel: 020 8504 1749

Email: office@ahsprep.co.uk

Website: www.avonhouseschool.co.uk

Headteacher: Mrs Amanda Campbell

Appointed: September 2011

School type: Coeducational Day

Religious Denomination: Christian

Age range of pupils: 3–11

No. of pupils enrolled as at 01/09/2017: 230

Fees per annum as at 01/09/2017:

Day: £9,375–£10,290

AVON HOUSE
DYSLEXIA AND EDUCATION CENTRE
Tel: 020 8559 0708
AVON HOUSE
PREPARATORY SCHOOL
Co-education for 2½ to 11 years
SCHOOL
KEEP

Breaside Preparatory School

Breaside Preparatory School, located in Bromley, Kent, prepares pupils from 2.5 to 11 years for both Grammar and Independent Senior Schools in a caring and nurturing environment.

Once again, SATs and 11+ entry results for 2017 were outstanding, with 100% of Year 6 pupils gaining their first choice at Senior School.

Parents are given guidance on the schools that we recommend for their children throughout their time at Breaside and we pride ourselves on getting the children into the right school for them as individuals.

Should I choose Breaside Preparatory School for my child?

Do they really offer more than a local primary school? The answer to both of these questions is a resounding 'Yes'.

As their name suggests, the role of preparatory schools is to prepare your child for their entrance into senior education, so don't be surprised to see a plethora of subjects on the curriculum. Your child will experience a well rounded education albeit in a nurturing environment. Classes are significantly smaller, allowing all pupils to progress. At the same time, this allows all staff to know their pupils and therefore offer a bespoke curriculum. Preparatory schools provide a wealth of opportunity for your child both academically and pastorally. Self confidence is encouraged and children are constantly motivated to enjoy and embrace all the opportunities that arise within this positive learning environment.

The academic curriculum within a preparatory school is clearly of the utmost importance. Throughout your child's time at their preparatory school, they will be prepared for the common entrance and scholarship tests and preparatory schools' academic credentials are renowned. Parents evidently send their child to a preparatory school in the hope that they will reach their optimum level. However, paying fees does not automatically ensure your child's place at a top grammar or independent senior school. Nevertheless, as a parent, you do have the right to have high expectations and preparatory schools clearly recognise this and deliver a high quality education.

If the above isn't enough to tempt you, consider the other aspects of a stimulating, all-round education. Your child will have the opportunity to experience a wide range of music, playing in an orchestra or participating in the choir. Peripatetic teachers within a preparatory school can introduce your child to a wealth of instruments, regardless of ability. Drama is also extensive with children as young as 3 taking part in plays. Within the encouraging atmosphere of a preparatory school, this can only help to aid your child's confidence. Let's not forget the range of sporting events that your child can take part in. Children in a preparatory school experience a range of sports, including rugby, hockey, swimming and cricket.

Should you choose a preparatory school for your child? Well, if you want to give them the best possible start in life, then the answer has to be yes. The investment will pay off as you see your child blossom into a well rounded, self confident, individual, ready to face the world!

For more information or a personal tour of the School and Kindergarten please call 020 8460 0916, info@breaside.co.uk, www.breaside.co.uk

(Founded 1950)

41-43 Orchard Road, Bromley, Kent BR1 2PR UK

Tel: 020 8460 0916

Fax: 020 8466 5664

Email: info@breaside.co.uk

Website: www.breaside.co.uk

Executive Principal:

Mrs Karen A Nicholson B.Ed, NPQH, Dip EYs

Appointed: 2008

School type: Coeducational Day

Age range of pupils: 2.5–11

No. of pupils enrolled as at 01/09/2017: 365

Boys: 181 ***Girls:*** 184

Fees per annum as at 01/09/2017:

Day: £10,545–£12,285

Farringtons School

Aims

Our aims are numerous, but very clear: to provide the best in education for every child in our care within a happy, safe, supportive Christian environment; to offer a wide variety of extracurricular pursuits to all age groups in order to promote the healthy development of the whole child; and to produce confident, self-reliant, compassionate and responsible young men and women, who, when they leave us at 18, will be equipped to take up the challenges of the 21st century.

Location

Farringtons occupies 25 acres of parkland in picturesque Kent, yet it is only 12 miles from central London. Chislehurst is five minutes from the M25, 45 minutes from Gatwick Airport, 1.5 hours from Heathrow International Airport and 20 minutes by train from Charing Cross and Waterloo stations.

Academic Achievement

With most pupils proceeding to higher education, academic standards are high; each pupil is encouraged to strive to reach his or her full potential. Our academic success is due to small classes, dedicated staff and supportive teaching, which ensures each pupil receives the individual attention needed. Academic achievement, as well as the all-round development of the individual, is of prime importance at Farringtons.

Sixth Form

The Sixth Form should be a bridge between school and university, and our Sixth Form leavers regularly go on to degree courses in their chosen subjects, including medicine, law and engineering, as well as courses at prestigious universities.

There is a wide choice of A Level subjects on offer, and staff are always on hand to offer advice on the correct combination of subjects to suit the aspirations and abilities of each student.

Sixth Formers are given a greater degree of freedom than pupils in other years and are encouraged to take a responsible and independent approach to their studies, albeit with the guidance and help of their tutor.

Boarding

At Farringtons we provide happy, warm and friendly surroundings for our boarders, and different living areas for each age group.

When parents are unable to be nearby, we know we must create and maintain a homely and secure living environment in which the pupils feel safe, confident and cared for, whatever their age. Boarders are cared for by house staff, who liaise with parents, guardians, form tutors and other staff to ensure the wellbeing of each student.

Weekly boarding provides a happy solution for those parents who wish to prioritise schoolwork and activities during the week. It also enables attendance for those whose daily travel is difficult and ad hoc. Boarding is also available for pupils who need to board for short periods when parents are away.

A debating society, football club, tae kwon do, a maths club and maths clinic, The Duke of Edinburgh's Award, a textiles club, drama club, jazz dance, fencing, Business Enterprise, ballet, trampolining, a choir, concert band and an orchestra are just some of the many interests available to pupils at lunch times and after school.

At weekends there are regular sporting fixtures and also supervised outings to the theatre, cinema, ice rink, shopping centre, museums, roller skating rink, waxworks and local places of interest, as well as to London, of course, which remains a firm favourite.

(Founded 1911)

Perry Street, Chislehurst, Kent BR7 6LR UK

Tel: 020 8467 0256

Email: admissions@farringtons.kent.sch.uk

Website: www.farringtons.org.uk

Head: Mrs Dorothy Nancekievill

Appointed: January 2015

School type: Co-educational Day & Boarding

Religious Denomination: Methodist

Age range of pupils: 3–18

No. of pupils enrolled as at 01/09/2017: 681

Boys: 340 ***Girls:*** 341 ***Sixth Form:*** 94

No. of boarders: 70

Fees per annum as at 01/09/2017:

Day: £14,610

Weekly Boarding: £28,830

Full Boarding: £30,600

Average class size: 15-20

Kew College

Set in leafy South-West London, Kew College is a gem of a school. In terms of education, it is a centre of excellence providing a rich, relevant and varied curriculum, but it is much more than that.

The minute you walk through the door, the ethos of the school is apparent; it is a friendly and caring environment which is relaxed but purposeful. The relationship between staff and pupils is warm and open and there is a tangible buzz of creativity in the air. The children are respectful, responsible, hard-working, and fun-loving individuals who thrive given opportunities to take risks in their learning and set challenges for themselves.

The results of entrance exams to secondary schools at Year 6 are excellent year on year, with numerous scholarships attained. Set this against the school's non-selective background and it is testimony to the quality of education that it provides. The children display an overwhelming desire to achieve and are inspired by staff who work with boundless energy, dedication and determination. No stone is left unturned as they strive to support and nurture every child to achieve to their full potential.

Education at Kew College is also about helping the pupils to develop their intellectual character. The children have a concrete sense of their own strengths and a confidence that goes hand in hand with that self-belief. This is coupled with a gracious sense of humility and open-mindedness, the realisation that the way forward in tomorrow's world is through co-operation and team work. This strong moral value system is embedded from an early age so that, by the time the pupils leave Kew College, they are able to think independently and critically. They are inquisitive, reflective and well-rounded; true individuals who are prepared for the rigours of secondary school and for the changing world in which they live.

"Both of our boys joined the school in the Nursery and have flourished in the nurturing and caring environment the school provides. The children are all confident, articulate, well-mannered, and thoroughly nice kids who are comfortable in the company of adults. Our boys have thrived at Kew College and always raced enthusiastically into school each day. The teaching and school philosophy is very much focused on helping each child to achieve their best in a happy environment. As parents, we really couldn't ask for more." **The Stewart family**

"We chose Kew College for our four daughters for its warm atmosphere and its happy, friendly, and well-mannered pupils. We feel fortunate to have also found a school which fulfils its promise of educating our children to their highest potential. We have children with differing abilities and personalities but Kew College has provided support and education for all of them. Every child at this school is unique, but one thing that every child here has in common is that they will leave strengthened by their experience." **The Ahmed Family**

Registrar: Mwarburton@kewcollege.com

(Founded 1953)

24-26 Cumberland Road, Kew, Surrey TW9 3HQ UK

Tel: 020 8940 2039

Fax: 020 8332 9945

Email: enquiries@kewcollege.com

Website: www.kewcollege.com

Headteacher:
Mrs Marianne Austin BSc(Hons) MA(Hons) ACA PGCE

School type: Coeducational Day

Age range of pupils: 3–11

No. of pupils enrolled as at 01/09/2017: 296

Boys: 146 ***Girls:*** 150

Fees per annum as at 01/09/2017:

Nursery: £7,050

Kindergarten – Year 6: £11,550

Average class size: 20

King's House School

'An excellent, all-round, happy prep school that brings out the best in all its children.' King's House Parent

King's House is a lively, busy, happy School and one where we feel that the boys (and girls in our wonderful nursery) thrive. Our aim is to offer a broad education to all our pupils, enabling them to develop their academic, social, sporting and artistic attributes. This breadth and balance on offer is we believe one of the strengths of the School.

King's House is a friendly, caring and supportive School. We have a strong sense of community both within the School and with our parents but we are also keen to play a role in the local and global community and to develop our pupils' sense of awareness of the world around them.

King's House is non-selective at our two main entry points, Nursery and Reception. We believe that boys benefit from staying in the prep environment until they are 13 years old before moving on. Their final two years here allow them to flourish, grow up and develop their sense of responsibility, taking on roles around the School. The boys are well-prepared for the transition to senior schools and we are justifiably proud of our 100% pass rate at Common Entrance into some of the most academic schools in the country. The emphasis though is always on finding the right school for the right child.

King's House believes in the importance of developing its pupils physically through PE and Games taught from Nursery upwards. From Year 1, the boys take advantage of our 35-acre sports ground in Chiswick for games with plenty of teams enabling as many boys as possible the opportunity to experience competitive fixtures. The main sports are football, rugby and cricket but athletics, swimming and tennis also feature. In recent years the School has enjoyed considerable sporting success particularly with its rugby teams and successful sports tours. At the School we have a fully equipped gym and AstroTurf which offers variety for weekly PE sessions.

King's House prides itself in a strong tradition of excellence in the Arts recognising that by giving our children the opportunity to express themselves we are helping them to develop self-confidence and awareness. With a large, fully equipped theatre we can be ambitious in our choice of productions.

Art and Design Technology are central to the creative arts teaching and the boys are encouraged to express themselves using a variety of media with work being displayed all around the School.

Computing and programming are playing an increasingly important role in the children's education from Nursery upwards. The Junior and Senior departments have computer suites and all classrooms have interactive whiteboards. There is also a Mac suite.

The School takes advantage of the opportunity our proximity to London affords us with regular trips to museums, galleries and theatres as well as Richmond Park and Kew Gardens. There are annual and bi-annual trips such as the Classics trip to Italy, French trip to Brittany and ski trip as well as sports tours.

King's House is proud of its 70 year history. Its principles and standards are founded on Christian values although the School is not aligned to any particular religion, and welcomes pupils of all religions and backgrounds.

(Founded 1946)

68 King's Road, Richmond, Surrey TW10 6ES UK

Tel: 020 8940 1878

Fax: 020 8939 2501

Email: schooloffice@kingshouseschool.org

Website: www.kingshouseschool.org

Head: Mr Mark Turner BA, PGCE, NPQH

Appointed: September 2012

School type: Boys' Day

Age range of boys: 3–13

Age range of girls: 3–4

No. of pupils enrolled as at 01/09/2017: 460

Fees per annum as at 01/09/2017:

Day: £2,165–£5,120 per term

Average class size: 24

Lyonsdown School

Situated in the leafy suburb of New Barnet, Lyonsdown School provides a happy, secure environment in which children can thrive and achieve personal excellence.

Lyonsdown has the facilities for high quality teaching and learning, yet is small enough for each child to be nurtured as an individual. Class sizes allow the caring, well qualified staff to help pupils achieve high standards, not only academically, but creatively and physically in an atmosphere of relaxed purposefulness.

Founded in 1906, the school has built on traditional values to create a curriculum and environment to prepare children to take their place in the 21st century.

Our philosophy is that a child's education is a shared responsibility between school and home. We positively encourage the support of parents, offering a partnership that embraces regular contact and communication.

The Early Years Foundation Stage creates the basis on which future building blocks of learning can be developed. Great care is given to the development of social skills, confidence and enthusiasm for learning, both in the classroom and in the outdoor learning areas. Children are encouraged to progress and develop their skills, knowledge and understanding across seven areas of learning. Reception children are introduced to specialist teachers for computing, music, French, PE, art and science.

Pupils continue their learning in the Lower School under the pastoral care of their class teachers. Specialist teaching extends to include design and technology.

Lyonsdown education continues for girls in the Upper School. Throughout years 3 to 6, 8 to 11-year-olds extend their knowledge of subjects, studying them in greater depth. They develop the disposition needed to become self-motivated learners. Pupils are encouraged to become critical thinkers, to express thoughts and feelings, to write creatively and use their imagination. They enjoy using their numeracy skills, interpreting and using data and applying their knowledge to problem solving situations. Computing, including coding, is an integral part of work across the curriculum and specialist teaching extends to Maths and English from Year 4.

Pupils' education is supplemented through a wide variety of educational visits and visitors from the community, such as theatre groups and interactive workshops. Year 5 and 6 participate in residential trips during the Summer Term.

During Year 6, many girls sit entrance examinations for leading independent and selective maintained schools. External test results continue to be excellent.

We place a high priority on personal development. Growth in moral, spiritual and cultural values is encouraged as part of the everyday ethos of the school. Daily collective worship is broadly Christian in character in accordance with the school's foundation, but actively includes learning from other faiths. Assemblies provide an opportunity for the school community to gather together to consider spiritual and moral issues. Pupils are encouraged to develop their physical skills through a variety of activities. PE is considered to be an important ingredient in the development of confidence and team work, and is taught in a large purpose built gymnasium from an early age. The Upper School girls also use off site facilities for sport and games. Healthy competition is embraced and children's achievements – in and out of school – are celebrated. As pupils move through the school, foundations are laid in the sports of netball, hockey, football, athletics, rounders and tennis.

Lyonsdown School Trust Ltd, a registered charity (No. 312591), aims to keep fees low in order to make independent education available to a wider community.

(Founded 1906)

3 Richmond Road, New Barnet, Barnet, Hertfordshire EN5 1SA UK

Tel: 020 8449 0225

Email: enquiries@lyonsdownschool.co.uk

Website: www.lyonsdownschool.co.uk

Head: Mr C Hammond BA (Hons) PGCE

Appointed: September 2017

School type: Independent Coeducational Day

Age range of boys: 3–7

Age range of girls: 3–11

No. of pupils enrolled as at 01/09/2017: 185

Boys: 17 ***Girls:*** 168

Fees per annum as at 01/09/2017:

Day: £4,080–£10,200

Average class size: 16-22

Teacher/pupil ratio: 1:10

enjoy

St Catherine's School

St. Catherine's combines over 100 years' experience of Independent education with a modern curriculum that prepares girls for success in the 21st Century. It is a Catholic school with pupils from many different faith and ethnic backgrounds. Everyone is a member of a vibrant, caring and supportive community in which pupils are happy, confident and inspired to meet challenges. Inspectors from the Diocese of Westminster reported that 'pupils flourish because of the secure, caring ethos of the School.' 'Teaching at St. Catherine's is more than the sum of its classroom parts. Pupils have a wrap-around experience that leads them to learn exceptionally well.' A recent inspection by the Independent Schools Inspectorate endorsed this, giving St. Catherine's the highest accolade possible, judging the pupils' academic and other achievements as well as their personal development to be excellent.

It is in the Prep Department, which takes girls from 3 to 11 years of age, that the firm foundations are laid to prepare pupils for the challenges and opportunities available in the Senior School.

The girls certainly rise to the challenges posed by public examinations. The school is proud of the value that is added to their achievements as they progress through the school and that their academic predictions are consistently exceeded. This is borne out in their excellent GCSE and A level results.

With the present A level system it is important for pupils to have continuity and stability from GCSE into A level. The teaching staff are passionate about giving the girls at St. Catherine's the opportunity to build on their outstanding GCSE results in the environment where they feel confident that their teachers know them and will both support and challenge them. This gives them the optimum chance of obtaining the best possible results in order to achieve a place at the University of their choice.

In partnership with parents, the Headmistress and her staff strive to produce well educated, confident, balanced young people who are outward looking and are able to meet the challenges of adult life with common sense, integrity and resilience.

Those who visit St. Catherine's often remark on the warm, caring and friendly atmosphere and the self-confidence and enthusiasm of its pupils.

A school can never stand still and St. Catherine's is no exception. In the last nine years major building projects have enhanced the facilities at the school, added new subjects to the curriculum and changed syllabi and schemes of work to make them even more challenging and interesting. The Sixth Form offers further opportunities to the girls in both curricular and extra-curricular programmes, as well as supporting them and helping them to prepare for university and beyond.

Information about public examination results, extra-curricular opportunities, wrap-around care facilities can all be found on the school website: www.stcatherineschool.co.uk

With recent changes to the National Curriculum and public examinations at both GCSE and A level, the Senior Management Team and Governors remain ever vigilant and will ensure all staff are fully prepared to continue to provide the best education possible for the pupils they teach.

(Founded 1914)

Cross Deep, Twickenham, Middlesex TW1 4QJ UK

Tel: 020 8891 2898

Fax: 020 8744 9629

Email: info@stcatherineschool.co.uk

Website: www.stcatherineschool.co.uk

Headmistress: Sister Paula Thomas BEd(Hons), MA

Appointed: September 2007

School type: Girls' Day

Age range of girls: 3–18

No. of pupils enrolled as at 01/09/2017: 430

Fees per annum as at 01/09/2017:

Day: £10,509–£14,517

Average class size: 15-20

Teacher/pupil ratio: 1:11

St. Catherine's
Sixth Form Centre

Staines Preparatory School

Founded in 1935, Staines Preparatory School has been delivering high quality education to the children of Surrey for over 80 years. We are a happy, welcoming and non-selective school that prides itself on creating a genuine family atmosphere allied to a first rate educational experience.

We have a strong track record of our pupils going on to competitive grammar and independent schools and a visit to us will reveal all our children are confident, well-adjusted, global citizens. Our educational experience is both challenging and fun, giving our pupils the tools to achieve well above the national average.

This supportive and nurturing environment enables children to fulfil their potential and become confident, independent lifelong learners across all areas of the curriculum. This year there has been a successful whole school approach to embedding a 'Growth Mindset' culture at Staines Preparatory School. This has had a positive impact on different approaches to learning. There have been various parental workshops and seminars on how parents can support their child's learning across the curriculum, delivered by staff and external speakers. The pupils at Staines Prep learn the value of commitment to successful learning. In addition to this, our pupils develop discipline and a sense of responsibility.

Beyond the original school façade, we have multi-million pound developments of new classrooms, a science lab which many secondary schools would be envious of, a large sports hall and theatre space which all pupils take advantage of. We are committed to delivering the highest quality educational experience and our independent status allows us to provide a bespoke learning opportunity alongside the National Curriculum.

Our newly constructed Environmental Area 'The Sanctuary' allows the children to bring science to life. They can pond dip, bird watch and even experience a barefoot walk whilst learning to safely explore the great outdoors. We use Forest School principles to teach skills that can be used in the classroom and beyond, encouraging team work, responsibility and communication as well as building self-esteem and independence. The children are not limited in what they can do but instead are taught how to access and manage the risks in nature.

We provide wraparound care from 7.30am until 6pm and are less than 5 minutes' walk from Staines railway station, making pick-up and drop-off that little bit easier. We understand how hard our parents work, and we aim to support them to provide the best start in life with a Staines Prep education.

To come and experience the school first hand, you can arrange a private tour to fit in around your commitments, or visit us at one of our popular Open Morning which run throughout the year. Details of these can be found on our website.

(Founded 1935)

3 Gresham Road, Staines upon Thames,
Surrey TW18 2BT UK

Tel: 01784 450909

Email: admissions@stainesprep.co.uk

Website: www.stainesprep.co.uk

Head of School:
Ms Samantha Sawyer B.Ed (Hons), M.Ed, NPQH

Appointed: September 2014

School type: Coeducational Day

Age range of pupils: 3–11

No. of pupils enrolled as at 01/09/2017: 377

Boys: 200 ***Girls:*** 177

Fees per annum as at 01/09/2017:

Day: £9,510–£11,055

Average class size: 16 (max 20)

Exceptional

London

Bassett House School

At Bassett House, 2017 marks 70 years of educating young children to achieve their very best. The school's founder, Sylvia Rentoul, recognised children as individuals, and encouraged them to express themselves, helping to grow their achievements and self-confidence.

Focused attention remains our hallmark. We believe tailor-made teaching opens up young minds to endless possibilities, encouraging them to think creatively. We start by ensuring high staff-to-pupil ratios and many specialist teaching staff. Our teachers know every child in their care inside out and use great teaching supported by our excellent equipment (including cutting-edge IT) to bring lessons to life for each child. Our 'sport for all' ethos encourages all our children to think of themselves as athletes, while allowing our sporting stars to shine. We offer football, netball, tag rugby, hockey, tennis, rounders, athletics, gymnastics and eurhythmics as part of the core curriculum and clubs in swimming, fencing, yoga and dance.

We don't stop there. Vibrant music and drama give our children a passion for participation and performance, fostering a sense of achievement and boosting self-confidence. Our children first take to the stage from age 3 and have many opportunities to shine throughout life at Bassett House, whether in whole-school assemblies, stage shows or concerts. We have choirs, musical ensembles and an orchestra and provide individual instrumental music lessons from specialist music teachers.

Our extra-curricular clubs, together with our weekly enrichment hour, expand our children's horizons beyond the core curriculum. Each term children can choose to add a variety of activities to the school day, be it Lego modelling, computer coding, Scottish dancing, origami, chess, geography, cookery, arts and crafts or Zumba.

Residential trips from year 3 onwards create a sense of adventure and build self-reliance. The glow of a 7 year-old's face recounting a nighttime bug-hunting expedition, a 9 year-old's thrill at working with a friend to sail a dinghy, or a 10 year-old embracing the challenge of sleeping out under a self-made shelter: we create these memorable moments, knowing that their positive effects will last a lifetime.

All of this makes not only for well-rounded individuals, it translates into excellent academic results. When they leave aged 11, Bassett House children are ready to thrive at London's best senior schools. And they do: our children win places to the cream of London's senior schools. For those who want to board, Bassett House prepares them well for life at leading boarding schools.

We collaborate closely with our sister schools, Orchard House and Prospect House, sparking off new ideas to promote ever more successful teaching practices. The three schools share a common ethos but each retains its unique personality.

The schools (brought together under the umbrella of House Schools Group) are proudly non-selective. True to our belief, children are not tested and judged at the tender age of 3 or 4 years. Our outstanding results repeatedly show all children can fulfil their potential, regardless of early learning ability. We encourage our high fliers to skyrocket, whilst children who need a little extra help are given the support they need to reach their fullest potential.

Our last full ISI inspection awarded us 'excellent' and 'outstanding' in all areas and we flew through our 2016 compliance inspection.

This year, as we celebrate our 70th birthday, we look forward to another year of stellar success in education.

(Founded 1947)

60 Bassett Road, London, W10 6JP UK

Tel: 020 8969 0313

Email: info@bassetths.org.uk

Website: www.bassetths.org.uk

Headmistress:
Mrs Philippa Cawthorne MA (Soton) PGCE Mont Cert

Appointed: January 2014

School type: Co-educational Day

Age range of pupils: 3–11

No. of pupils enrolled as at 01/09/2017: 190

Fees per annum as at 01/09/2017:

Day: £8,520–£17,760

Average class size: 20

Teacher/pupil ratio: 1:7

Cameron House

The curriculum

'An excellent curriculum provides all pupils... with opportunities to achieve high standards in a wide range of subjects and activities... within a creative, stimulating environment where all pupils are treated as individuals and encouraged to do their best. The quality of the pupils' achievements and learning is excellent.' (ISI Inspection 2016) Pupils of all abilities are prepared broadly and deeply for the full gamut of 11+ examinations within a rich and dynamic academic curriculum, using high quality resources and a broad range of ICT. We encourage children to research, reflect, ask questions, listen well and problem-solve – and to develop positive learning habits for life around the 'Five Cs of Cameron House': curiosity, collaboration, creativity, critical thinking and courage.

Setup and atmosphere

'Across the school the quality of the pupils' personal development is excellent... All pupils display excellent moral development, have a firm sense of right and wrong, and are extremely courteous.' (ISI Inspection 2016) We aim to be a vibrant, warm and high-energy school, to which pupils are proud to belong and to which they contribute by growing their own skills, character and personal relationships. Our dedicated and highly qualified teachers know every pupil and every family, aiming to care for each with wisdom, professionalism and kindness.

Games and the arts

'Pupils develop excellent physical skills at all ages through the busy and demanding range of activities and... achieve significant success in competitive sports in relation to the size of the school.' (ISI Inspection 2016) Sport is integral to the rhythm of school life both within the timetable, and within the extra-curricular programme, with our team sports including touch rugby, netball, football and hockey, and individual sports such as fencing and karate offered as well. We are passionate about the arts, and provide a wealth of creative activities in art, design and technology, music and drama – through timetabled specialist teaching, after-school clubs, themed days, cultural visits and opportunities to train and perform in the school's arts programme, as well as local and national events.

Pastoral care

'Pastoral care makes an excellent contribution to pupils' personal development. Strong personal relationships reflect the friendly, family atmosphere. Staff know their pupils very well and... the school maintains very close links with parents.' (ISI Inspection 2016) We are a relaxed but respectful community, working together for the common good within a culture of praise and mutual respect, aiming to develop self-respect, self-discipline and empathy in our relationships, strong spiritual awareness and a deep appreciation of the beauty of the natural world. We want to embody our motto – 'Da Mihi Sapientiam' (Give Me Wisdom) – by growing wisdom in our pupils in thought, word and deed.

Outstanding characteristics

Cameron House has been led by the same Director-Principal for 37 years, providing seamless, detailed and passionate oversight and care. 'The quality of governance is excellent. Dynamic and energetic leadership across the school is highly effective in enabling the school to successfully fulfil its aim to create a happy and warm family atmosphere in which pupils are treated as individuals and are motivated to work and play to the best of their ability. Senior and middle managers provide clear educational direction and this is demonstrated in the excellent quality of pupils' achievements and in their outstanding personal development' (ISI Inspection 2016)

(Founded 1980)

4 The Vale, Chelsea, London, SW3 6AH UK

Tel: 020 7352 4040

Fax: 020 7352 2349

Email: izzy@cameronhouseschool.org

Website: www.cameronhouseschool.org

Acting Headmistress: Miss Mary-Anne Malloy BE (HDE)

Principal:
Miss Josie Cameron Ashcroft BSc(Hons), DipEd, CertT

School type: Coeducational Day

Religious Denomination:
Church of England, all denominations welcome

Age range of pupils: 4–11

No. of pupils enrolled as at 01/09/2017: 118

Boys: 58 ***Girls:*** 60

Fees per annum as at 01/09/2017:

Day: £17,925

City of London School

A rounded education in the Square Mile

'There is no such thing as a typical City boy. What characterises the education offered is a true preparation for life.'

City of London is a truly unique independent school, not least because of its unrivalled location on the banks of the Thames, between St. Paul's Cathedral and the Tate Modern. We are at the heart of the capital and our pupils benefit enormously from all that is on offer on our doorstep. Our location allows us to attract the very best outside speakers, offer top-class work shadowing placements and visit the many places of interest in this world-class city.

We are a modern and forward-looking institution drawing on clever boys from all social, economic and ethnic backgrounds and, in so doing, truly reflect the diversity of the capital in the 21st century. Boys come from a huge number of both state primary and independent preparatory schools and, once here, receive an academic yet liberal education. Our central location allows boys to travel to City from all over London, encouraging resourcefulness and self-reliance in their journey to school, and in their wider life.

Our examination results are excellent, but, more importantly, boys leave us with a sense of identity and an independence of thought and action which are rare among leavers from private schools; it is significant that the vast majority of boys go on to their first choice of university, with a large number attending Oxford and Cambridge universities, and various medical schools.

Facilities are outstanding (the school moved downstream to its new buildings in 1986) and are continually updated. The state-of-the-art Winterflood Theatre and refurbished Science laboratories provide a first-rate environment in which our pupils learn and thrive. A new Creative Learning Centre and Library opened to pupils in September 2016, further enhancing our facilities.

We are generously endowed with academic, music and sports Scholarships and in addition, the bursary campaign has raised significant funding for a number of full-fee places to be awarded each year to those who could not otherwise afford even a proportion of fees. In this way, the school seeks to maintain the socio-economic mix which has always been its tradition and strength.

Admission at 10+, 11+ and 13+ is by entrance examinations, followed by interviews for those candidates who complete their examination papers to a satisfactory standard.

For a prospectus and to book on to one of our numerous parental visits, please contact:
The Admissions Department
Tel: 020 3680 6300
Email: admissions@cityoflondonschool.org.uk

CITY OF LONDON SCHOOL

(Founded 1442)

Queen Victoria Street, London, EC4V 3AL UK

Tel: 020 3680 6300

Fax: 020 7329 6887

Email: admissions@cityoflondonschool.org.uk

Website: www.cityoflondonschool.org.uk

Head: Mr A R Bird MSc

Appointed: January 2018

School type: Boys' Day

Age range of boys: 10–18

No. of pupils enrolled as at 01/09/2017: 930

Sixth Form: 250

Fees per annum as at 01/09/2017:

Day: £16,731

CITY OF LONDON
SCHOOL

Devonshire House Preparatory School

Academic and leisure facilities
The school is situated in fine premises in the heart of Hampstead with its own walled grounds. The aim is to achieve high academic standards whilst developing enthusiasm and initiative throughout a wide range of interests. It is considered essential to encourage pupils to develop their own individual interests and a good sense of personal responsibility.

Curriculum
Early literacy and numeracy are very important and the traditional academic subjects form the core curriculum. The younger children all have a class teacher and classroom assistant and their day consists of a mixture of formal lessons and learning through play. Whilst children of all ages continue to have a form teacher, as they grow older an increasing part of the curriculum is delivered by subject specialists. The combined sciences form an increasingly important part of the timetable as the children mature. The use of computers is introduced from an early stage, both as its own skill and as an integrated part of the pupils' education.

Expression in all forms of communication is encouraged, with classes having lessons in art, music and drama, and French. Physical exercise and games also play a key part of the curriculum. Much encouragement is given to pupils to help widen their horizons and broaden their interests. The school fosters a sense of responsibility amongst the pupils, and individuality and personal attention for each pupil is considered essential to make progress in the modern world.

The principal areas of the National Curriculum are covered, though subjects may be taken at a higher level, or at a quicker pace. For the girls approaching the 11+ senior schools' entry examinations, special emphasis is given to the requirements for these, and in the top two years for the boys, Common Entrance curriculum is taught. The pupils achieve great success in these examinations and a number also sit successfully for senior school scholarships.

The school has its own nursery, The Oak Tree Nursery, which takes children from two-and-a-half years of age.

Entry requirements
The Oak Tree Nursery: For children entering the Oak Tree Nursery, places are offered on the basis on an informal assessment made at the nursery. Children in The Oak Tree Nursery transfer directly to the Junior School.

The Junior School: For children entering the junior school from the ages of three to five, places are offered on the basis of assessment made at the school. From the age of six, places are usually subject to a written test taken at school. At eight, children transfer directly into the upper school. Parents and their children are welcome to visit for interview and to see around the school.

The Upper School: Entry to the upper school is principally from the junior school. For pupils seeking to join the school from elsewhere places are normally subject to a written entrance test.

(Founded 1989)

2 Arkwright Road, Hampstead, London, NW3 6AE UK

Tel: 020 7435 1916

Email: enquiries@devonshirehouseprepschool.co.uk

Website: www.devonshirehouseschool.co.uk

Headmistress: Mrs S. Piper BA(Hons)

School type:
Preparatory, Pre-preparatory & Nursery Day School

Religious Denomination: Non-denominational

Age range of boys: 2½–13

Age range of girls: 2½–11

No. of pupils enrolled as at 01/09/2017: 650

Boys: 350 ***Girls:*** 300

Fees per annum as at 01/09/2017:

Day: £9,750–£17,865

Francis Holland School, Regent's Park, NW1

Academic Curriculum

Girls on arrival are placed in one of three parallel forms and taught a broad curriculum. In the second year they start a second language – Italian, German or Spanish. Girls usually take nine or ten subjects for GCSE, 11 in some cases. All girls choose four subjects and complete at least three full A levels by the end of the Upper Sixth. All proceed to higher education including leading universities in the UK, such as Oxford and Cambridge, as well as to top global institutions such as those in the US. Applications are also made to art, drama or music colleges. The curriculum is kept under constant review, and there is regular consultation with parents about each girl's programme of study. Option blocks are built around girls' choices for GCSE and A level rather than forcing them to conform to a more limited structure. Many sixth formers successfully complete the Extended Project, a qualification designed to challenge the most able students beyond A level. Results are consistently high with many achieving A*s in their project. The ISI Inspection Report in February 2014 reported Francis Holland as 'Excellent' in all key areas of school life.

Pastoral

The school fosters a happy atmosphere in which pupils thrive as individuals whilst appreciating the importance of courtesy and altruistic behaviour. Girls are encouraged to extend their intellectual curiosity and creativity, both in the classroom and through the lively extra-curricular schedule of clubs, activities and excursions.

Entry requirements

Entry at 11 is by means of written tests in English and mathematics, together with an interview. A few girls are accepted into the sixth form each year and into other years as vacancies occur.

Examinations offered

GCSE subjects offered: Art, Classical Civilisation, Computer Science, English, English Literature, French, German, Geography, Greek, History, Italian, Latin, Mathematics, Music, PE, Religious Studies, Spanish, Physics, Chemistry and Biology. Additional subjects at A level include History of Art, Economics, Politics, Psychology and Drama and Theatre.

Academic & leisure facilities

The school has its own new swimming pool and gymnasium and uses Regent's Park for tennis, hockey, rounders and netball. The Gloucester Wing, opened by HRH The Duke of Gloucester, provides additional classrooms and seminar rooms, a fourth art studio and a performance area for music, drama and theatre studies. There are two school orchestras, several choirs and a jazz band. Music, drama, art and sport play an important part in the school. Individual instrumental lessons and lessons in speech and drama are popular. The central London location provides excellent opportunities to support the curriculum with visits to art exhibitions and museums. With almost 100 extra-curricular clubs and activities on offer, including British Sign Language, fencing, ceramics and Mandarin Chinese, there is a genuine opportunity for girls to explore their individual interests and extend their learning beyond the classroom.

Scholarships and bursaries

Academic, music and art scholarships available at Year 7 and sixth form. Entry bursaries up to 100% of fees.

Contact

For details of all open events please contact the Admissions Registrar, Mrs Danielle Hesketh, on 020 7723 0176 or email registrar@fhs-nw1.org.uk

(Founded 1878)

Clarence Gate, Ivor Place, Regent's Park, London, NW1 6XR UK

Tel: 020 7723 0176

Fax: 020 7706 1522

Email: registrar@fhs-nw1.org.uk

Website: www.fhs-nw1.org.uk

Head: Mr C B Fillingham MA (King's College London)

School type: Independent Girls' Day

Age range of girls: 11–18

No. of pupils enrolled as at 01/09/2017: 495

Sixth Form: 120

Fees per annum as at 01/09/2017:

Day: £19,260

Average class size: 15 (GCSE) and 8 (Sixth Form)

Francis Holland School, Sloane Square, SW1

Academic Curriculum
Girls throughout the school follow a strong academic curriculum including a compulsory modern language, Latin, separate sciences and drama. At GCSE three subjects are added to a core of six or seven subjects and in the sixth form four subjects leading to three or four A levels is the norm. Many pupils study for the Extended Project Qualification which develops independent research skills. On leaving school all girls proceed to higher education, sometimes following a gap year. Destinations include Oxford, Cambridge and other leading universities in the UK and abroad, particularly to the United States. Applications to art, music and drama colleges are also strong. A level and GCSE results are consistently high. The April 2017 ISI inspection reported Francis Holland as 'Excellent' for Educational Quality in terms of pupil's academic and other achievements and pupil's personal development.

Pastoral
A distinctive feature is the school's nurturing and caring ethos. Girls are known as individuals and encouraged and supported in a happy and purposeful environment. Great emphasis is placed on building emotional resilience and character. Innovative PSHE, mindfulness, enrichment, skills and leadership programmes contribute to this focus.

Entry requirements
Entry at 4+ is by means of a school-based assessment and at 11+ there are written tests in English and mathematics, and a further half-day school assessment including an interview. A few girls are accepted into the sixth form each year and into other years if vacancies occur.

Examinations offered
GCSE subjects offered: Art, Classical Civilisation, Computing, English, English Literature, French, German, Geography, Classical Greek, History, Drama, Latin, Mathematics, Music, PE, Religious Studies, Spanish, Physics, Chemistry and Biology. Additional subjects at A level include History of Art, Economics, Psychology, Further Maths, Government and Politics and photography.

Co-curriculum
The extensive co-curricular programme, comprising music, drama, art and sport, has been further strengthened by Carmel Hall, the specialist performing arts centre. The most recent drama production was 'A Midsummer Night's Dream'. The school also has strong links with local London theatres such as The Royal Court and the Donmar Warehouse in Covent Garden. Charitable activities are strongly encouraged and girls undertake ambitious projects that not only raise thousands of pounds, but also develop leadership and team working skills including The Duke of Edinburgh's Award. Survival skills and resilience are developed through The Exploration Society. Ballet, drama and instrumental lessons are popular and all girls have numerous opportunities to go on day and residential trips at home and abroad.

Scholarships and bursaries
Academic scholarships, music scholarships and art awards are available at Year 7 and the same range is available on entry to the sixth form, with the addition of a drama scholarship. Entry bursaries up to 100% of fees.

Contact
For details of all open events please contact the Registrar, Mrs Fiona Holland, on 020 7730 2971 or email registrar@fhs-sw1.org.uk

(Founded 1881)
39 Graham Terrace, London, SW1W 8JF UK
Tel: 020 7730 2971
Fax: 020 7823 4066
Email: registrar@fhs-sw1.org.uk
Website: www.fhs-sw1.org.uk
Head: Mrs Lucy Elphinstone MA(Cantab)
Appointed: September 2012
School type: Independent Girls' Day
Age range of girls: 4–18
No. of pupils enrolled as at 01/09/2017: 520
Sixth Form: 70
Fees per annum as at 01/09/2017:
Day: £17,760–£20,085
Average class size: 12 (GCSE) and 6 (Sixth Form)

Heathside Preparatory School

Heathside is a small and friendly day school, housed in three historic buildings a few minutes' walk from a beautiful meadow on Hampstead Heath, where the children play every lunchtime.

The school is a unique and highly successful learning environment, rated 'Outstanding' in all seven areas by Ofsted. With talented and inspirational teachers and a strong focus on individual learning and pastoral care, our students flourish:

"One of the most significant features of the school is the happy atmosphere evident in all classes… From a very young age, children develop a real thirst and enthusiasm for learning and this continues throughout the school… Pupils are kind and courteous to one another and relate to adults extremely well… They are highly motivated to learn, enjoy school and embrace all aspects of school life… They have high levels of confidence and self-esteem… The quality of pupils' work is exceptional."

We encourage the development of the whole person and, as a result, Heathside is a relaxed and happy place and academic standards are high. We have a proud tradition of tailoring our teaching so that every child gets the best from each lesson – a high staff-to-student ratio, a focus on small-group work and individual attention allow us to offer challenge and support as appropriate:

"The headteacher is an inspirational leader… who leads a dynamic team of highly qualified staff, all of whom share her vision in providing education of the highest standard… The quality of teaching is outstanding… Teachers have exceptional subject knowledge and are keen and enthusiastic in their approach to teaching… Lessons are extremely well planned… Teaching is adapted to meet the differing learning needs and styles of all pupils… Pupils consistently remain engaged, enthused and interested…"

The curriculum builds strong foundations in literacy and numeracy, scientific understanding and creative thinking:

"The quality of the curriculum is outstanding and this results in pupils' outstanding levels of achievement. The richness, breadth and diversity of the curriculum enable pupils to develop an extensive range of knowledge and skills… The school's extra-curricular activities are strengths of the school and the programme has an exceptional impact in supporting pupils' learning."

We produce highly able mathematicians and lifelong readers and writers. We playfully bring out the artist in everyone. Every child in the school learns French from a native speaker, and we offer lessons in Spanish, Mandarin, German and Italian. Music and drama are particular strengths, and everyone performs several times a year. We play a wide range of sports to high standards. Everyone from Reception up plays chess, and we have been national chess champions many times. Extra-curricular activities range from Capoeira and Chinese to our popular Write-and-Recite and Philosophy Clubs.

We teach outdoors when we can. We have lots of inspirational visitors and enriching trips. We look after each other. We live and learn well. When it snows, we build snowmen and go tobogganing on Hampstead Heath.

"The success of the current Year 6 pupils in gaining scholarships and entry into a range of highly respected London independent schools reflects the outstanding achievements pupils make within the school."

Most children join us in the Nursery, which can take children from two years of age. We do have occasional places in other years. It is never too early to register for a place, which you can do from our website. At the right time, your child will be invited to spend a morning with us. We do have waiting lists and we give priority to Heathside siblings; we strive to keep you well informed about the availability of places.

If you would like to find out more, please arrange a visit to get to know the school.

(Founded 1993)

16 New End, Hampstead, London, NW3 1JA UK

Tel: +44 (0)20 7794 5857

Fax: +44 (0)20 7435 6434

Email: admissions@heathside.net

Website: www.heathside.net

Headteacher: Ms Melissa Remus MSc

School type: Coeducational Day

Age range of pupils: 2–14

No. of pupils enrolled as at 01/09/2017: 550

Fees per annum as at 01/09/2017:

Day: £15,000–£18,300 (Nursery PT £10,000)

GRATITUDE
OUTSTANDING

James Allen's Girls' School

Including James Allen's Preparatory School

'When you begin your life as a JAGS girl you join a community which combines extraordinary tradition with a forward-looking approach. The oldest girls' school in London, we strive for excellence in all we do, developing scholarly young women who gain top academic results and places at top institutions. But there is nothing pompous or old fashioned about a JAGS education.

Come and visit us and you will meet future doctors and engineers in our labs, Oxbridge scholars in our library and the next generation of politicians and diplomats in our lecture theatre. But these same girls will also be volunteers in charity placements at the weekends, will sing loudly in the gospel choir or tap dance across our stage. The portrait of our founder, James Allen, hangs on the main school corridor. The same man who had the vision to educate young women back in 1741, proudly declares beneath the painting that he was 'Six feet high, skilful as a Skaiter, a Jumper, athletic and humane'. We love the fact that James could skate – a true advocate of a full extra-curricular programme. But it's his humanity we most admire and most seek to uphold.

Celebrating a grounded approach and founded on a long standing tradition of diversity and access, JAGS is a genuine reflection of modern, south London life.'

Sally-Anne Huang, Headmistress

James Allen's Girls' School welcomes girls from 4 – 18 years. Admission is primarily at 4+, 7+, 11+ and 16+ and is based upon assessment. There are occasionally chance vacancies available. Full bursaries are available at 11+ and 16+ as well as academic scholarships alongside sports, art and music scholarships. For information on admissions please visit our website www.jags.org.uk

Our facilities are excellent; 22 acres of fields and astro pitches, a state-of-the-art swimming pool, dance studios, a climbing wall, a professionally designed theatre, extensive well-stocked libraries and, opening Spring 2018, a brand new music centre with dedicated practice rooms and ICT suites.

Every girl is encouraged to explore a wide range of subjects at the beginning of their school career, covering all key areas and including several language options and creative disciplines. As they mature and choose to focus on subject specialisms, the inspirational teaching we offer allows them not only to gain qualifications at the highest level but also to develop research skills and become independent learners.

At JAGS we care that your daughter is happy. Most of the time things will go really well. Girls will build good relationships with each other and their teachers and thrive at JAGS. Ensuring consistency of care, every pupil's Form Tutor remains with them through each Key Stage. The school has two School Nurses who are available to deal with medical and personal problems. Students can also talk to a CAMHS counsellor who visits twice a week or one of our two Youth Workers. Sometimes it is felt that a pupil will benefit from a having a staff or Sixth Form mentor.

JAGS is consistently ranked in the top 20 of UK secondary schools for A-level results. JAGS students go on to study at wide range of universities and colleges across the globe including Oxbridge colleges. For the most up to date list of university places offered to JAGS students, please see our website.

(Founded 1741)

144 East Dulwich Grove, Dulwich, London, SE22 8TE UK

Tel: 020 8693 1181

Email: enquiries@jags.org.uk

Website: www.jags.org.uk

Head of School: Mrs Sally-Anne Huang MA, MSc

Appointed: September 2015

School type: Girls' Day

Religious Denomination: Church of England

Age range of girls: 4–18

No. of pupils enrolled as at 01/09/2017: 1075

Fees per annum as at 01/09/2017:

Pre-Prep & Prep: £5,215 per term

Senior School: £5,755 per term

Average class size: 18-28

Teacher/pupil ratio: 1:9

Kensington Park School

Academic excellence in the heart of London

Kensington Park School is a new academically rigorous independent school for boys and girls aged 11-18. It boasts some of the country's most experienced teachers and offers excellent cultural and sporting opportunities, all in the heart of London.

While the school is new, its leadership and teachers have long, successful track-records at some of the best independent schools in the UK. A large contingent come from St Paul's School, including Dick Jaine, the former acting High Master, and senior teachers, along with Heads of Department, for subjects such as Mathematics, Chemistry and Economics. These superb teachers bring to KPS more than 25 years' experience of helping pupils achieve outstanding grades at GCSE and A Level as well as entry into the world's top universities.

Day and boarding school with a dedicated Sixth Form Centre

KPS operates from two buildings either side of Kensington Gardens:

- KPS Sixth Form, in Queen's Gate, which opened in September 2017 for pupils aged 16-18
- KPS Seniors, in Bark Place, opening in September 2018 for pupils aged 11-16

This configuration enables KPS to have a dedicated Sixth Form Centre where A Levels and preparation for university entrance can be taught in a specialist environment. Our sixth formers have specifically tailored timetables conducive to A Level study and our Sixth Form teachers are a team of true experts, with several A Level chief examiners and textbook authors among their number.

The school also has excellent boarding facilities in South Kensington, welcoming pupils from all over the UK and from around the world.

Superb sporting and cultural opportunities

KPS is committed to academic rigour and the highest standards of achievement. However, life at KPS is about much more than academics. The school offers its pupils opportunities to become proficient at many different sports and to develop a wide range of social and cultural interests, giving them a much broader and more enriching experience as a result.

KPS has partnered with providers of exceptional sports facilities in and around its West London home. These include Imperial College's Ethos Sports Centre with its state-of-the-art gym, pool and climbing wall; expert coaches, including former Olympians, in fencing and riding; and Fulham Reach Boat Club, a superbly equipped new rowing facility on the Thames. There will be an exciting outdoor education programme, including the Duke of Edinburgh award scheme. Similar partnerships are in place for music and drama.

How to apply

As a new school, whilst being selective, KPS does not yet have the same extreme competition for places present at some of the other top independent schools. Pupils will be able to access the same quality of teaching, without the stressful and complex application procedures.

KPS is now accepting applications for 11+, 13+ and sixth form entry in September 2018. If you would like to find out more information about KPS or wish to make an application, please contact Jane Lovell, Registrar at j.lovell@kps.co.uk.

Kensington Park
SCHOOL

Kensington Park School Sixth Form
59 Queen's Gate, South Kensington,
London, SW7 5JP UK

Kensington Park School Seniors
40-44 Bark Place, London, W2 4AT

Tel: +44 (0)20 7225 0577

Email: admissions@kps.co.uk

Website: www.kps.co.uk

Director of Education: Mr. Dick Jaine MA

Executive Principal: Mr. Marwan Mikdadi MSc

School type: Coeducational Boarding & Day

Age range of pupils: 11–18

Fees per term as at 01/09/2017:

Day (UK): £7,500 per term

Day (International): £8,500 per term

Boarding (UK): £12,800 per term

Boarding (International): £13,800 per term

Kensington Park
SCHOOL
59
59

Newton Prep

In a London landscape crowded with prep schools, Newton Prep stands out for its unbeatable combination of vibrant size and eclecticism, its senior school level of facilities and outside spaces and its position at the heart of Central London's most burgeoning community.

We are constantly inspired by our location. On our doorstep is the grand vision that is the rapidly growing Battersea Power Station development; up the road is the new US embassy, soon to be joined by the Dutch embassy, all amid the massive regeneration of Nine Elms. There's an electricity in the air and it's important that we are a part of that buzz. It is also key to our ethos: to ensure that Newton children are well-educated, curious, kind and articulate but, above all, in this modern world (and equipped with the best of British values), to encourage them to think for, and be, themselves.

Last year, we celebrated Newton@25, our programme of events across the whole of the academic year to celebrate where we have come in the 25 years since our foundation in 1991. It was a Silver Jubilee with a shiny splash of something different: we raised over £25,000 for our four chosen charities (and a massive £83,000 for our Newton Bursary Fund, thereby enabling bright local children to access a Newton education) and we found 25 new in-school talents with the wildly successful Newton's Got Talent competition. We premiered the Silver Symphony, written by our very own Director of Music and played in tandem with the London Mozart Players at our end of year celebration and treated over a thousand people to a Silver Splash party across the site of the school. Our aim in doing so was to ensure that each child and every parent felt that they had contributed personally to this milestone in the school's life, putting us in good shape for the next 25 years!

At Newton Prep, we provide a liberal environment in which children are equipped with a sense of self, resilience and hopefulness, beyond the obvious need to excel academically. We encourage children to think beyond the curriculum and they hoover it up. Whether it's piano lessons, judo or archery, children need ways of engaging. We aim for our Newton Prep children to enter adolescence feeling that they already have more to contribute than just academic achievements. Yes, we need to get them into the right schools but not at the expense of their well-being and character.

Luckily, our extensive resources enable such intellectual inquisitiveness. With a huge all-weather pitch, an 120-seat recital hall, a music technology suite, recording studio, 300seat auditorium, three gymnasiums, bustling art studios, dance studios, a library and science labs, children are encouraged to "do" as well as "learn". We even have a well-loved garden: where our children practise circus skills, hunt for mini-beasts and conduct scientific experiments: like when Year 8 students lit up the London skies with their own explosion.

Despite the excellence of their education, Newton Prep children are notable for their lack of arrogance and entitlement. The kindness and generosity shown by the pupils towards their peers is remarkable and we are particularly proud of the engagement between the older children and the little ones.

We are not a blazers-and-boaters kind of school. We don't have to look to the past and can focus all our energies on ensuring a bright future for our children. As one current parent has commented, "Newton combines a quirky nature and knowledge of families with great space and facilities… All the teachers understand my (very different) children, the management is open to fresh ideas and the school is large enough to accommodate variety."

Admission to the Nursery is by registration; to the Lower School (Reception to Y2) by registration, with a gentle and informal assessment; to the Upper School (Y3-8) by registration and competitive testing..

(Founded 1991)

149 Battersea Park Road, London, SW8 4BX UK

Tel: 020 7720 4091

Fax: 020 7498 9052

Email: admin@newtonprep.co.uk

Website: www.newtonprepschool.co.uk

Headmistress: Mrs Alison Fleming BA, MA Ed, PGCE

Appointed: September 2013

School type:
Coeducational Pre-Preparatory & Preparatory Day

Age range of pupils: 3–13

No. of pupils enrolled as at 01/09/2017: 647

Boys: 358 ***Girls:*** 289

Fees per annum as at 01/09/2017:

Day: £6,840–£18,930

Average class size: 20 (smaller in Years 7&8)

Newton @ 25
Newton @ 25
Newton @ 25

North Bridge House

North Bridge House prides itself on providing an individually tailored education for boys and girls, aged from 2 years 9 months to 18 years. We know, support and inspire every pupil to achieve their full potential and provide a solid foundation for a successful academic career and adult life.

Pupils can join us from Nursery and stay until Sixth Form without the added pressure of entrance exams, or we can prepare them for other top senior schools. To ensure each individual flourishes, we work closely with parents to choose the right educational environment for their child and help many win much sought after scholarships. In turn, our high-achieving Senior and Sixth Form schools prepare pupils for university life and the world of work through careers events, industry speakers, job experience and mock interviews.

At the heart of each school is a highly qualified and inspirational team of teachers who deliver a rich and varied range of academic and extra-curricular activities, tailor-made to challenge, stimulate and reward our pupils. This, together with our outstanding pastoral support, allows them to grow in confidence and independence. At our Senior and Sixth Form, the progressive teaching team also refer to research into teen development to further understand and maximize the potential of their pupils. For example, Sixth Formers start their lessons later in the day as studies have shown that their sleeping patterns make them less likely to absorb teaching early in the morning.

Through PE and games we develop the individual's physical and emotional wellbeing, as well as essential team working skills. The latter are then further enhanced in the senior years through the Duke of Edinburgh Awards, civic engagements and leadership programmes.

At North Bridge House we nurture each individual to exceed their expectations – and pave the way to success and the top universities.

To find out more, please do join us at an open day or book a private tour at northbridgehouse.com/open.

School locations:
North Bridge House Nursery School
33 Fitzjohn's Avenue, Hampstead, London NW3 5JY
North Bridge House Pre-Preparatory School
8 Netherhall Gardens, Hampstead, London NW3 5RR
North Bridge House Preparatory School
1 Gloucester Avenue, Regent's Park, London NW1 7AB
North Bridge House Senior School Hampstead
65 Rosslyn Hill, Hampstead, London NW3 5UD
North Bridge House Senior School & Sixth Form Canonbury
6-9 Canonbury Place, Islington, London N1 2NQ

North Bridge House

(Founded 1939)

Main Address
65 Rosslyn Hill, London, NW3 5UD UK

Tel: 020 7428 1520

Email: admissionsenquiries@northbridgehouse.com

Website: www.northbridgehouse.com

Head of Nursery & Pre-Prep Schools:
Mrs. Christine McLelland

Head of Prep School: Mr. Brodie Bibby

Head of Senior School Hampstead: Mr. Brendan Pavey

Head of Senior School & Sixth Form Canonbury:
Mr. Jonathan Taylor

School type: Co-educational Day

Age range of pupils: 2 years 9 months–18 years

No. of pupils enrolled as at 01/09/2017: 1350

Fees per annum as at 01/09/2017:

Day: £13,680–£18,555

Average class size: 20

Orchard House School

At Orchard House School, children are loved first and taught second. Our Pupil Pastoral Plan monitors the well-being of each child and was recently shortlisted for a TES (Times Educational Supplement) national award for educational innovation. This emphasis on a nurturing environment is not, however, at the cost of academic excellence. In fact, our outstanding results show how creating the right environment enables every child to thrive academically and emotionally. We believe learning should be exciting and fun, and the children should positively want to come to Orchard House every day. And they do: we harness the exuberance and energy of every child in our care, and instil within them a lifelong love of learning.

Orchard House's diverse curriculum creates a sense of adventure, developing the children's appetite for risk. This feeds into greater academic and creative achievements. Whether it's a whole-school skipping day, a project with Jaguar to enable our 10- and 11-year-old mathematicians to engineer performance cars or learning archery in Normandy (taught solely in French), Orchard House children embrace novel tasks throughout their time with us. By the time they sit 11+ exams, they are past masters at tackling new challenges with verve: this shows in our stellar results.

Sport at Orchard House encourages a respectful, competitive attitude, teaching children the value of camaraderie and the buzz of going for gold, or goal. We offer football, netball, rugby, hockey, lacrosse, cross country, tennis, athletics, triathlon, cricket, rounders, swimming and gymnastics and arrange regular team-sport fixtures against other schools, often lifting the trophy and always relishing the match.

Similarly, music and drama build confidence and self-esteem, as well as many opportunities for every child to perform. Visiting music teachers offer individual instrumental tuition on a variety of instruments. We have a school orchestra, Pippin choir, chamber choir, senior and junior choir and a parent and staff choir. There are many other instrumental groups including a pupil-led rock band.

We collaborate closely with our sister schools, Bassett House and Prospect House, sparking off new ideas to promote ever more successful teaching practices. The three schools share a common ethos but each retains its unique personality. The schools (brought together under the umbrella of House Schools Group) are proudly non-selective. True to our belief, children are not tested and judged at the tender age of 3 or 4 years. Our educational success shows all children can fulfil their potential, regardless of early learning ability.

The Independent Schools Inspectorate recently awarded Orchard House the highest accolades of 'excellent' in all areas and 'exceptional' in achievements and learning. These are mirrored in our first-class academic results and the scholarships our pupils win to their next schools.

(Founded 1993)

16 Newton Grove, Bedford Park, London, W4 1LB UK

Tel: 020 8742 8544

Email: info@orchardhs.org.uk

Website: www.orchardhs.org.uk

Headmistress:
Mrs Maria Edwards BEd(Beds) PGCE(Man) Mont Cert

Appointed: September 2015

School type: Co-educational Day

Age range of pupils: 3–11

No. of pupils enrolled as at 01/09/2017: 290

Fees per annum as at 01/09/2017:

Day: £8,520–£17,760

Average class size: 20

Teacher/pupil ratio: 1:7

Prospect House School

At Prospect House School, we focus on making each child feel valued and secure and on making their educational experience both challenging and fun. This allows us to develop every child to their fullest potential, as our outstanding results demonstrate. Our most recent full Independent Schools Inspectorate inspection, in 2013, rated us 'excellent' against all the inspectors' criteria and we flew through our 2017 regulatory compliance inspection.

Prospect House's superb teachers provide a supportive and encouraging academic environment in which children excel. The sound of laughter is never far away, as Prospect House children discover their aptitude for sport, music, art, computing, drama or a whole host of other opportunities both within the curriculum or before or after school. Whether taking up the trombone, building a go-cart or orienteering on Putney Heath, our children relish each new challenge and emerge better able to face the next challenge that comes their way.

Music is an important part of life at Prospect House. We have over 200 individual music lessons taking place each week and a school orchestra, chamber choir and senior and junior choirs, as well as a number of ensembles. All children act in assemblies, school plays, musical productions and concerts throughout the year. Children in Years 1 to 6 enjoy drama lessons and our high-quality staging, lighting, sound and props give every production a professional feel.

Physical activity promotes wellbeing, so we offer a busy sports programme. This includes football, netball, hockey, running, cross country, tennis, athletics, cricket, rounders, swimming, dance and gymnastics. Our approach to fixtures and tournaments successfully balances participation for everyone with letting our sports stars shine.

Residential trips thrill the children with the sense of adventure, encouraging risk-taking and building self-reliance, whether on a history expedition, a bushcraft adventure or a week in Normandy immersed in the French language and culture.

We encourage our children to think for themselves, to be confident and to develop a sense of responsibility for the world in which they live. By the time they leave us aged 11, Prospect House children are ready to thrive at London's best senior schools. This is reflected in our impressive 11+ results. In 2017, academic, sports or music scholarships made up over 12% of our overall senior school offers.

We collaborate closely with our sister schools, Bassett House and Orchard House, sparking off new ideas to promote ever more successful teaching practices. The three schools share a common ethos but each retains its unique personality.

The schools (brought together under the umbrella of House Schools Group) are proudly non-selective. True to our belief, children are not tested and judged at the tender age of 3 or 4 years. Our stellar results repeatedly show all children can fulfil their potential, regardless of early learning ability. We encourage our high-flyers to soar, whilst children who need a little extra help are given the support they need to reach their fullest potential. At Prospect House, every child is helped to achieve a personal best.

(Founded 1991)

75 Putney Hill, London, SW15 3NT UK

Tel: 020 8246 4897

Email: info@prospecths.org.uk

Website: www.prospecths.org.uk

Headmaster: Mr Michael Hodge BPED(Rhodes) QTS

Appointed: September 2017

School type: Co-educational Day

Age range of pupils: 3–11

No. of pupils enrolled as at 01/09/2017: 300

Fees per annum as at 01/09/2017:

Day: £8,520–£17,760

Average class size: 20

Teacher/pupil ratio: 1:7

Queen's Gate School

Queen's Gate School is an independent day school for girls between the ages of 4 and 18 years. Established in 1891, the school is an Educational Trust situated in five large Victorian Houses within easy walking distance of Kensington Gardens, Hyde Park, and many of the main London museums.

The School offers an education for life in a challenging environment where sound values and individuality are nurtured within a supportive atmosphere. Our aim is to create a secure and happy environment in which the girls can realise their academic potential and make full use of individual interests and talents. We encourage the development of self-discipline and create an atmosphere where freedom of thought and ideas can flourish.

Girls follow as wide a curriculum as possible and generally take GCSEs in ten subjects that must include English, Mathematics, a science and a modern language. A full range of A level subjects is offered. In the Lower Sixth girls normally take four subjects, reducing to three in the Upper Sixth.

Sport is highly valued at Queen's Gate with two compulsory sessions for all girls each week. We have many sports available at other times during the school day including netball, athletics, basketball, hockey, fencing, swimming, rowing, horse riding, cross-country, biathlon and dance.

The Principal, Mrs Rosalynd Kamaryc, has been in post since 2006 and has built on the existing strengths of the school, whilst enabling girls to enjoy new opportunities in and out of the classroom.

In September 2007, the School entered an exciting new period in our long history when the Junior School moved into splendid new buildings at 125 and 126 Queen's Gate, just a few yards down the road from the Senior School. The new buildings, beautifully restored, boast spacious form rooms, three fully equipped laboratories, a state of the art ICT Room, a separate Art and DT studio and an elegant Assembly Hall. Junior pupils also use some of the Senior School facilities and benefit from specialist subject teaching from Senior School staff. Senior girls often visit the Junior School to assist with activities, thus reinforcing the continuity of education from 4-18 available at Queen's Gate.

Admission is by test and interview in the Junior School. Entrance to the Senior School is by the North London Independent Girls' Schools' Consortium entrance examination at 11+, and the school's own entrance examinations to other years in the Senior School. Applicants for the Sixth Form must achieve six GCSEs at Grade 8 or above with Grade 8 or 9 required in those subjects they wish to pursue at A level.

In addition to the Open Events that are run by the Senior and Junior Schools throughout the year, parents are always welcome to make a private visit to see the schools at work. Appointments can be made by contacting the Registrar on 0207 594 4982 or by email registrar@queensgate.org.uk.

Queen's Gate

(Founded 1891)

133 Queen's Gate, London, SW7 5LE UK

Tel: 020 7589 3587

Fax: 020 7584 7691

Email: registrar@queensgate.org.uk

Website: www.queensgate.org.uk

Principal: Mrs R M Kamaryc BA, MSc, PGCE

Appointed: January 2006

School type: Girls' Day

Age range of girls: 4–18

No. of pupils enrolled as at 01/01/2017: 533

Junior School: 159

Senior School: 373

Fees per annum as at 01/09/2017:

Junior School: £17,550

Senior School: £19,575

Average class size: 23

Teacher/pupil ratio: 1:10

St Paul's Cathedral School

Governed by the Dean and Chapter and seven lay governors, the original residential choir school, which can date its history back to the 12th century, has, since the 1980s, included non-chorister day boys and girls aged 4-13. The number of pupils is currently 250.

In its 2017 inspection, the ISI awarded the School its highest accolade of 'Excellent' in both educational attainment and pupil progress.

A broad curriculum prepares all pupils for 11+ and 13+ examinations including scholarship and Common Entrance examinations. The school has an excellent record in placing pupils in outstanding senior schools, many with scholarships. With its unique and central location, the school is able to make the most of what London can offer culturally and artistically in particular. A wide variety of sports and musical instrument tuition is offered: the school has an exceptional record in preparing pupils for ABRSM exams. Choristers receive an outstanding choral training as members of the renowned St Paul's Cathedral Choir.

The life of the school is based on the following aims and principles:

St Paul's Cathedral School is a Christian, co-educational community which holds to the values of love, justice, tolerance, respect, honesty, service and trust in its life and practice, to promote positive relationships throughout the school community and where the safety, welfare and emotional well-being of each child is of the utmost importance.

The school aims to instil a love of learning through a broad curriculum. It aims to give each pupil the opportunity to develop intellectually, socially, personally, physically, culturally and spiritually. All pupils are encouraged to work to the best of their ability and to achieve standards of excellence in all of their endeavours.

Through the corporate life of the school, and through good pastoral care, the school encourages the independence of the individual as well as mutual responsibility. It aims to make its pupils aware of the wider community, espouses the democratic process and encourages a close working relationship with parents and guardians.

Facilities: the school is situated on one site to the east of St Paul's Cathedral. It has a separate Pre-Prep department, excellent Science lab and ICT room. It has two outside play areas and a hall. There are plans to provide new boarding facilities for the choristers.

Entry is at 4+ and 7+ years. 4+ entry is held in the November preceding the September a child will enter the school and 7+ entry is held in the January preceding the September a child will enter the school. At 7+, pupils are given a short test and spend a day in school. Chorister voice trials are held throughout the year for boys between 6 and 8 years old. Further information can be found on the school's website www.spcslondon.com

St Paul's Cathedral School is a registered charity (No. 312718), which exists to provide education for the choristers of St Paul's Cathedral and for children living in the local area.

ST PAUL'S CATHEDRAL SCHOOL

(Founded 12th Century or earlier)

2 New Change, London, EC4M 9AD UK

Tel: 020 7248 5156

Fax: 020 7329 6568

Email: admissions@spcs.london.sch.uk

Website: www.spcslondon.com

Headmaster:
Mr Simon Larter-Evans BA (Hons), PGCE, FRSA

Appointed: September 2016

School type: Coeducational Pre-Prep, Day Prep & Boarding Choir School

Religious Denomination: Church of England, admits pupils of all faiths

Age range of pupils: 4–13

No. of pupils enrolled as at 01/09/2017: 248

Boys: 144 ***Girls:*** 104

Fees per term as at 01/09/2017:

Day: £4,501–£4,855 per term

Full Boarding: £2,808 per term

Average class size: 15-20

Teacher/pupil ratio: 1:10

The Lloyd Williamson School

Introduction

The Lloyd Williamson Schools have grown in both size and reputation to become the established schools they are today. The main departments are: three Nurseries, a Transition School for 5-7 year olds, a Senior School for 7-11 year olds and an Upper School for 11-14-year-olds. We plan to expand age range to 18 taking one extra year group per year from 2019.

The names *Lloyd* and *Williamson* are family names that belong to the proprietor. We believe they convey one of the main points of ethos at the school: that we are a *family* – and a strong one at that!

We have built an excellent reputation for strong academic standards and personalised, holistic learning for individual children.

We are based in W10 and W8 in the Borough of Kensington and Chelsea, with small classes to a maximum of sixteen. The schools have extended opening hours, competitive, realistic fees and all-year-round provision, including Holiday Clubs.

Mission Statement and Ethos:

- We celebrate childhood and nurture each child to be the best they can be in a challenging and inspiring environment that ignites a passion for life and learning – we are not a one-size-fits-all school
- Teachers build positive relationships, working with each child to be curious, intellectual and creative – we all like to think outside the box – fear of failure is banished!
- Equality and diversity permeate the fabric of our school – we are a family where everyone belongs, based on empathy and respect
- We encourage partnership and dialogue with parents and children thrive academically without losing their childhood – we cherish each child's self-esteem
- A blend of traditional and forward thinking teaching prepares our children for their next school and for life

Admissions

Parents are invited to meet the Co-Principals for personal and individual tours of the school during school hours in order to gain a real flavour of how the school operates on a daily basis.

The school supports requests for places from families with a diverse range of backgrounds; the binding quality is motivation! We do not compare children with one another; we challenge them against their own goals and next steps. This allows children to feel safe, be creative and curious instead of managing anxiety about 'not keeping up'! Our children are happy, confident students available to learn – they develop a rich and positive sense of who they are and can be.

The school is open from 7:30am-6:00pm (main school hours from 8:30am-3:30pm). This means that working parents can drop off their children and get to work knowing their children are safe and without the additional cost of nannies.

As a small school, everyone knows everyone from the babies up to our oldest member of staff!

We cherish individuality and self-confidence and our aim is that every child will develop an organic and strong positive sense of self. We enable this through the development of positive relationships so that all our children can learn to be strong and independent.

Contact Information

www.lws.org.uk
Admissions: admin@lws.org.uk
Main School and W10 Nursery: 020 8962 0345
W8 Nurseries: 020 7243 3331

LLOYD WILLIAMSON
SCHOOLS

(Founded 1999)

12 Telford Road, London, W10 5SH UK

Tel: 020 8962 0345

Fax: 020 8962 0345

Email: admin@lws.org.uk

Website: www.lloydwilliamson.co.uk

Co-Principals: Ms Lucy Meyer & Mr Aaron Williams

Appointed: December 1999

School type: Coeducational Day

Age range of pupils: 4 months–14 years (18 in 2019)

Fees per annum as at 01/09/2017:

Day: £13,560

Average class size: 12-16

Teacher/pupil ratio: 1:12

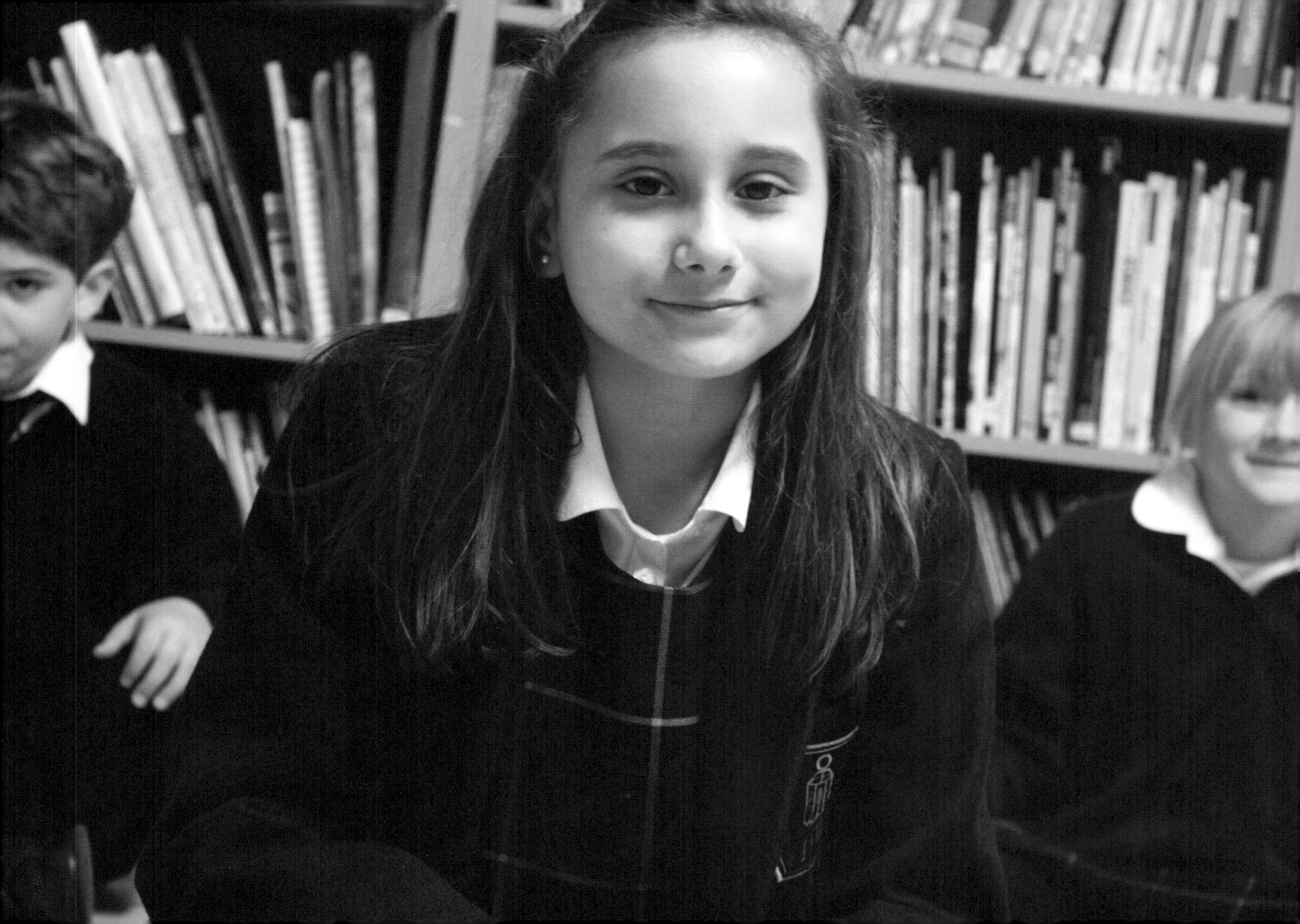

The White House Preparatory School & Woodentops Kindergarten

The White House Prep School recently celebrated its 30 year anniversary and is continuing to go from strength to strength, most recently being named by the Sunday Times in their top ten "Best Prep Schools in London" and 54th nationally. Family run for 30 years, the co-educational prep school located in leafy Clapham, is still helmed by Founder and Principal Mary McCahery. Mary is still deeply involved with the school and the development of the school's pupils along with the long-standing, enthusiastic and brilliant teaching staff. Their motto 'Curo et Consocio' and ethos "Our Family School, Your Family School" set the tone of daily life at The White House and show the great importance placed on the family nature and approach, so often absent in schools these days.

The White House Prep prides itself on choosing to be deliberately small in size and this commitment, together with excellent teachers, inspires and encourages individuality in all pupils. Children are nurtured throughout their school career so that when they leave at 11+ they are confident, well-mannered and armed with an excellent education. Children go on to a selection of the best schools in London and surrounding boarding schools, with over 40% of children receiving scholarships year on year. This excellence was commended in the school's recent ISI (Independent Schools Inspectorate) inspection where they were awarded Outstanding in every area for the whole school.

The extensive curriculum is enriched with French, Spanish, Latin, Music, Drama, Sports, IT and more. The recent IT suite upgrade has seen the adoption of a cloud-based curriculum, which places cyber security and coding at the forefront, giving the children essential tools in the evolving technology landscape. Teachers keep children invigorated and inspired by taking them out of the classroom on trips to the latest exhibitions and museums and the school has recently introduced reading The Week Junior in class to broaden pupils knowledge and understanding of current events. After-school clubs are popular and pupils can enjoy a wide variety including Football, Car Club, Golf, Karate, Netball, Swimming, Choir, Ballet, Computing, Chess, Badminton, Science, Cooking and Fashion.

Pastoral care and ensuring children are happy at school is paramount. Pupils are known by teachers throughout the school and this means they can visit any of them if they have a problem. They enjoy a close relationship with their form teacher and the school works closely with parents as partners in the child's education.

The White House offers its pupils the ability to have a complete education and a developmental journey that can start from Woodentops Nurseries from 6 months if needed (Part of The White House Family) and Woodentops Kindergarten (from 2.5 yrs old) all the way through to leaving at 11+. A large number of siblings and a very supportive parental body means that the school has an exceptionally nurturing atmosphere. They, like the school are focused on creating happy, caring and confident young children who have a real sense of curiosity and love of learning. This develops children that stand out from their peers. Confident but without arrogance, self-assured but not pushy with a strong moral compass and unbounded enthusiasm who have good manners and respect for each other.

(Founded 1985)

24 Thornton Road, London, SW12 0LF UK

Tel: 020 8674 9514

Email: office@whitehouseschool.com

Website: www.whitehouseschool.com

Principal: Mrs. Mary McCahery

Headmaster: Mr. Tony Lewis

School type: Coeducational Day

Age range of pupils: 2–11

No. of pupils enrolled as at 01/09/2017:

Boys: 62 ***Girls:*** 55

Fees per term as at 01/09/2017:

Day: £4,436 (Reception – Yr 2)–£4,740 (Yr 3 – Yr 6) per term

Average class size: 16

Teacher/pupil ratio: 1:8

10X

Westminster School

Westminster School: the Key to a World-Class Education
Inquisitive minds deserve the most inspiring teachers. At Westminster the secret of our teaching is not only in the skilled and enthusiastic imparting of knowledge but, more importantly, to show students how to reveal a deeper understanding of the world for themselves. Lessons at Westminster are founded on the principle of Socratic dialogue, where our pupils are encouraged to question and challenge ideas, to test them out for themselves in experiment, discussion and plenty of creative opportunities. Equipped with superb subject knowledge and the best pedagogical practice, teachers at Westminster enjoy responding to the enthusiasms of their pupils and guiding them carefully in their discoveries.

When independent initiative is so highly valued, it's no surprise, then, that well over half of Westminster pupils are offered places at Oxford, Cambridge and the leading Ivy League universities each year, and that they win so many prizes in national competitions, from Space Design to Chamber Music, Poetry and Cryptography. But it's the quieter, day-to-day enthusiasm for learning buzzing within our central London haven of Dean's Yard which makes life at Westminster so special. On any day, you will find students giving a huge variety of lunchtime talks well attended by their peers from all years: Growing your own Heart, Behavioural Finance, The Spanish Film Revolution, Post-Structuralist Theory and The Geography of the Sugar Trade, are all recent examples.

Our pupils are outward looking. Exceptional opportunities to listen to visiting speakers at the top of their fields inspire and encourage them to engage meaningfully in real world events. In the first week this term, we welcomed Sarah Fane Founder of Afghan Connect; Professor John Watts from Corpus Christi College, Oxford; the Entomologist Dr George McGavin; the activist Dr Nina Ansary, and Zanny Minton Beddoes, the Editor in Chief of the Economist – and we work hard to provide such a range of talks every week. This wealth of experience spurs our pupils on to become politically engaged so that they, in turn, are inspired to shape history and to influence the world for the better.

The enjoyment of learning how to do things really well is infectious. It is a lesser known fact that Westminster regularly beats schools with a strong sporting reputation at Football, Cricket and a wide-range of other sports including Fencing (Independent Schools Senior Epée Champion 2017), Climbing (Independent Schools Best Senior Climber 2017) and Cross Country (National Schools Championships). This year, our pupils have been awarded the England Independent Schools Cap for Girls' Football and have rowed to gold in the GB Junior Eight. It is no coincidence that three of the Boat Race teams were coxed by Old Westminsters, or that eight of our current pupils have represented the school in the National Youth Orchestra.

We believe that happiness is all about loving what we do and celebrating each other's efforts. When the ISI inspectors visited in November 2016 they noted that 'kindness is a key characteristic of the school's ethos' and that 'pupils are passionate about sharing their interests'. When our pupils do exceptionally well, it's because they are supported by a busy and vibrant community with superb teachers and a real love of learning- in all fields – for its own sake. Success is a happy by-product of a Westminster Education.

(Refounded 1560)

Little Dean's Yard, Westminster, London, SW1P 3PF UK

Tel: 020 7963 1003

Fax: 020 7963 1002

Email: registrar@westminster.org.uk

Website: www.westminster.org.uk

Headmaster: Mr Patrick Derham

Appointed: September 2014

School type:
Boys' Boarding & Day, Coeducational Sixth Form

Religious Denomination: Church of England

Age range of boys: 13–18

Age range of girls: 16–18

No. of pupils enrolled as at 01/09/2017: 744

Boys: 613 ***Girls:*** 131

No. of boarders: 184

Fees per annum as at 01/09/2017:

Day: £26,130–£28,566

Full Boarding: £37,740

Average class size: 20 up to GCSE

North-East

Durham School

Durham School provides an excellent education for 3 to 18-year-old girls and boys, in the heart of the impressive City of Durham. Our School, which is over 600 years old, has a strong sense of tradition and pupils are encouraged to value the experiences and lessons learnt of those who came before. However, it is a School that relishes the challenge of preparing pupils for the modern day world and the speed at which it changes. Our mission is to provide our students with a complete education; one which instils in them an aspiration for achievement, a respect for others whilst instilling a confidence for life.

The three pillars of Durham School which support this mission and so provide an environment where pupils can explore, make mistakes, learn and grow are:

- Academic challenge which gives students a lifelong appetite for learning.
- Pastoral care to provide our students with emotional, moral and spiritual strength.
- Co-curricular opportunities which enrich and develop the individual, and foster leadership, collaboration and teamwork.

We do this by nurturing and supporting our students to become:

- Thinkers who can understand, research, evaluate and create, both collaboratively and independently.
- Individuals who are morally sound, emotionally resilient, reflective and effective communicators.
- Adults who act with responsibility, humility and kindness and are ready to make a positive contribution to society.

Our Facilities – At the Senior School (11-18 years) we have five Houses, four of which cater for boarders be they full, weekly or flexi boarders. We have well equipped classrooms to facilitate a high standard of academic education to all our pupils. Our Prep School (3-11 years) offers fantastic facilities to all its day pupils; from an outdoor adventure playground to a fully equipped science laboratory. Our extensive grounds, of some 35 acres, overlook the World Heritage Site of Durham Cathedral and are home to numerous rugby pitches, cricket greens, a swimming pool, an all-weather pitch, a gym and a boat club to mention just a few of our sporting facilities. We also have a dedicated sixth form centre, careers office, theatre, music studio and practice rooms.

Chapel – The Senior School's Chapel is a pivotal part of the School's daily life and ethos and is where the pupils meet four times a week, it also hosts many musical concerts. Although the Chapel is of a strong Anglican heritage we welcome pupils from all faiths and beliefs and value the contribution that they bring to the School. The School always ends its week with a Chapel Service where pupils gather to hear and celebrate about each other's achievements.

Academic Life – We offer an education that aims to add value and inspire the individual pupil nurturing and encouraging them as individuals to aim high and to achieve to the best of their abilities. We believe that the supportive nature of the whole Durham School community and house system provide the pastoral care that facilitates pupils having the confidence to pursue their academic studies with vigour and enthusiasm, leading them to achieve the highest results. Our pupils are well rounded and have shown to be able to excel in the classroom, on the sports field and in the concert hall as well in social situations, leadership tasks and preparation for life beyond school at university and the world of work. Indeed our Alumni include a long list of distinguished and eminent professionals working in such disciplines as medicine, law, business and the arts.

(Founded 1414)

Durham City, Durham DH1 4SZ UK

Tel: +44 (0)191 386 4783

Fax: +44 (0)191 383 1025

Email: admissions@durhamschool.co.uk

Website: www.durhamschool.co.uk

Headmaster: Mr K McLaughlin

Appointed: September 2014

School type: Coeducational Day & Boarding

Religious Denomination: Church of England

Age range of pupils: 3–18

No. of pupils enrolled as at 01/09/2017: 560

Boys: 383 ***Girls:*** 177 ***Sixth Form:*** 156

Fees per term as at 01/09/2017:

Day: £2,756–£5,331 per term

Weekly Boarding: £7,347–£8,786 per term

Full Boarding: £8,460–£9,846 per term

Overseas Boarders (Years 7-13): £9,182 – £10,589 per term

Average class size: 15-20

Teacher/pupil ratio: 1:10

Royal Grammar School

The Royal Grammar School is a special place, proud of its heritage, known and respected throughout the country as well as the North East. We inspire and nurture our students to be the best they can be, creating a deep sense of belonging and forging connections that will last a lifetime.

Our students go on to study highly selective courses at the most sought-after universities, but also leave realising that life outside the classroom has been equally rewarding.

Excellence and success are built on the freedom our students are given to explore and the desire to push boundaries both in and outside the classroom. By exploring their passions in a happy environment we encourage self-expression and truly nurture their academic promise.

All students, from the lowest age of seven through to the top end of the senior school at 18, are encouraged to get involved with a wide range of activities, challenging and stretching their minds to evolve new ways of thinking and discover future opportunities.

Student well-being is at the heart of everything we do. Our warm and caring culture helps nurture confidence and develop all the skills needed for a successful and happy life. Adopting a team around the child approach, we bring together a number of associated partners including, teachers, parents, counsellors and school nurses, to offer support to students, doing all we can to ensure they feel happy, supported and valued on their journey through school.

We are able to combine all of this on one site, based in the heart of Jesmond, just a stone's throw from Newcastle city centre. The school has been in its present location since 1906 and has some fine Edwardian buildings, yet we continue to invest to ensure we have first class facilities with the latest technologies. Our sports facility opened its doors in September 2015 and has a 25m pool, free-weights gym, fitness studio and a second sports hall. This sits alongside an impressive Performing Arts Centre which features a 300-seater theatre, recording studio, dance studio, individual teaching rooms and a keyboard lab, and we are about to commence our next building development project which will create more inspiring spaces for learning.

For more information about the RGS and for information on visiting, please go to www.rgs.newcastle.sch.uk

(Founded 1545)

Eskdale Terrace, Newcastle upon Tyne, Tyne & Wear NE2 4DX UK

Tel: 0191 281 5711

Email: hm@rgs.newcastle.sch.uk

Website: www.rgs.newcastle.sch.uk

Headmaster: Mr John Fern

School type: Coeducational Day

Age range of pupils: 7–18

No. of pupils enrolled as at 01/09/2017: 1325

Boys: *769* ***Girls:*** 556 ***Sixth Form:*** 341

Fees per annum as at 01/09/2017:

Day: £10,662–£12,657

Average class size: 24

Teacher/pupil ratio: 1:12

RGS Sport

North-West

Chetham's School of Music

The thriving creative community at Chetham's includes around 300 students aged 8-18, whose common passion is music. Entry to the School is based solely on musical ability and potential, never on background or ability to pay, thanks to bursaries up to full fees through the Government's Music and Dance Scheme, which are provided for 90% of students. This common bond of musical passion makes for a truly inspirational place which transforms the lives of all who are part of it.

This magic is the result of many different qualities that permeate the fabric of Chetham's: the warm and welcoming atmosphere, the daily creative buzz, admirable academic standards, Chetham's history and heritage, our superb teaching and performance spaces, the city of Manchester as a cosmopolitan location, our many different backgrounds and personalities – and of course, the music. Chetham's is the largest specialist Music School in the UK and is the only one based in the north of England. The School is also a national and international resource for music education – welcoming teachers, professional players, composers and conductors, community groups, school children and other young musicians, both experienced and novices, to come together and make music. Our network of partnerships with professional orchestras and organisations extends across the music industry, and our alumni populate orchestras and ensembles across the world.

Based in the heart of Manchester, Chetham's is housed in a state-of-the-art new School building, with its onsite concert hall, The Stoller Hall, offering a world-class acoustic for student performances and visiting artists from around the world. The concert hall, and the School's vibrant Outreach programme, continue to develop strong links between Chetham's students and the professional musical community, building on the School's already strong position within Manchester's cultural sector.

All students follow a full academic programme alongside their musical studies, in which excellent results are achieved through small class sizes, a dedicated teaching team, and a community which values success. In 2016, Chetham's was the highest achieving non academically-selective school in Manchester, and every year students progress to leading music conservatoires and universities across the world. We take as much pride in those who move on to careers in engineering, medicine or law as in those playing leading roles on the concert platform; in DJs, jazz pianists and folk singers as in classical conductors and soloists. What unites every member of the Chetham's community is their passion for music; a passion that, whatever their future direction, will forever enrich their lives.

Admissions to Chetham's

Open Days:
Saturday 14 October 2017
Saturday 20 January 2018

Chetham's holds regular Open Days in October and January each year, when prospective students can meet staff and students, hear ensembles in rehearsals, and discover more about a specialist music education.

Admission is by audition only, where music tutors will look for a student's musical potential. There are no academic requirements, and means-tested Government funding through the Music and Dance scheme means that 90% of students receive up to full support with school fees. Many students benefit from Advice Auditions, a chance to play for School tutors and to receive guidance on your musical progression before making a full application to the School. Auditions and Advice Auditions run throughout the year.

(Founded 1969)

Long Millgate, Manchester,
Greater Manchester M3 1SB UK

Tel: 0161 834 9644

Fax: 0161 839 3609

Email: hello@chethams.com

Website: www.chethams.com

Head of School: Mr Alun Jones

Appointed: September 2016

Chair of Governors: Dame Sandra Burslem

School type: Coeducational Boarding & Day

Age range of pupils: 8–18

No. of pupils enrolled as at 01/09/2017: 299

Fees per annum as at 01/09/2017:

Day: £24,819

Full Boarding: £32,031

Average class size: av 20

Teacher/pupil ratio: 1:10

Green Meadow Independent Primary School

Green Meadow Independent Primary School was established in September 2009. It is a purpose built school with state of the art facilities which include interactive whiteboards, a computer suite, large all weather pitch used for a variety of sports and an excellent adventure playground area. The school also has two covered play areas available to all age groups, with safety flooring that are used for Physical Education as well as play.

Our vision is to develop an outstanding school to enable all children who attend to fulfil their full potential. Through nurturing our children, both academically and spiritually, we aim to provide them with secure foundations for life, so that when they leave Green Meadow they have an excellent all round education and a positive disposition to learning.

Philosophy and Academic Aims

- To provide a happy and stimulating environment for study
- To provide a safe and secure environment, in which pupils can thrive
- To treat all pupils as individuals
- To encourage pupils to strive for academic excellence.
- To develop knowledge, skills and understanding.
- To offer all pupils a broad and balanced curriculum.
- To foster a spirit of enquiry.
- To develop every individual's potential.
- To equip pupils with technological expertise.
- To prepare pupils for future educational and working environments.
- To promote community and global awareness.
- To encourage self-discipline and a high standard of behaviour.
- To develop positive relationships.
- To promote self-confidence and independence, but also co-operation.
- To foster and promote caring for others and spiritual development.
- To promote healthy choices.
- To encourage physical and mental fitness.

Green Meadow welcomes children from the age of three to eleven from families of all faiths and beliefs. With a small and friendly atmosphere, the school aims to inspire its pupils both academically and morally. We offer an affordable option in independent education with fees starting from only £3900 per annum for Reception Class. Please see our website for further details on fees.

We are committed to ensuring that the class sizes are never greater than 24 which is a 1:12 adult-child ratio with a teaching assistant. In small classes the children learn faster, they quickly develop confidence to express their ideas and opinions and small classes also help create a climate for learning.

We have dedicated specialist teachers that ensure the needs of all pupils are met, from high achievers to those experiencing difficulties.

We encourage children with independent thought, and a curiosity and love of learning, which will help them grow in self worth and confidence within a caring, safe and supportive environment. We believe that praise is important and that every child should feel valued. We aim to impart the shared values of respect for others and the environment, personal responsibility, tolerance and understanding of right and wrong, so that our pupils may become valued members of the community in which they live.

As Head teacher, I feel privileged to be leading this school and to be working with such a motivated and talented group of staff. We are very fortunate to have supportive and engaged parents who enjoy getting involved in our extra curriculum activities such as the Christmas concerts, assemblies and charity events etc.

Sandra Green, Proprietor/Headteacher

Robson Way, Lowton, Warrington, Cheshire WA3 2RD UK

Tel: 01942 671138

Email: greenmeadowteachers@gmail.com

Website: www.greenmeadowindependentprimaryschool.co.uk

Head: Mrs S Green

School type: Coeducational Day

Age range of pupils: 4–11

Fees per annum as at 01/09/2017:

Kindergarten: from £110 a week

Reception: £3,900

Key Stage 1: £4,500

Key Stage 2: £4,995

READ WITH
Biff, Chip & Kipper
Baby Gold Stars
Five

Kirkham Grammar School

At Kirkham Grammar School, we believe in the values of a traditional education alongside a drive towards modern ambition. It is our intention to continue to build upon our 460 year history as a recognised centre of excellence for academic attainment and the holistic development of the learner. We believe everyone has a place in our community including our parents, pupils, staff, governors and alumni alike; we all have a part to play in the drive for continued excellence.

Kirkham Grammar School is an Independent Co-educational Day and Boarding School for pupils aged 3-18. The school prides itself on its warm family atmosphere. Whilst academic success is at the heart of the school's aims, it has recently enjoyed record-breaking GCSE and A-level results. In its last ISI Inspection the school was described as "a friendly, supportive community based on mutual regard, which provides a caring, inclusive environment, in which all pupils are helped to grow in self confidence and self-esteem and develop their individual talents". This balance is achieved through the provision of a wide array of co-curricular activity to complement the pupils' learning within the classroom. The school therefore provides a breadth of activity for all, encouraged and supported by a dedicated team of staff.

The Senior School has undergone a transformation over the last decade and boasts a host of magnificent new facilities. The teaching provision includes a completely new block of twelve interactive classrooms and a science block designed to meet the needs of the large number of pupils who pursue studies in this area. Sporting facilities are outstanding with a new floodlit all weather surface and Lawrence House Pavilion. Drama provision has been enhanced by the fine studio dedicated to Theatre Studies. Most recently the school has developed its Sixth Form Centre, titled "Six Degrees", affording our students cafeteria facilities alongside new ICT provision and a modern recreation area. A new Music Centre was officially opened in January 2013 by International Soprano Lynne Dawson. A new Sports Hall, Fitness Facility and Changing Areas were also completed in January 2013. During 2017 we will be enhancing the Senior School campus with the addition of a new classroom and further sporting facilities.

The Junior School, founded in 1990, is situated opposite the Senior School and has a roll of 250 pupils aged from 3-11 years. As well as enjoying its own on site state of the art facilities, it also has access to Senior School facilities, including an Astroturf pitch and multi-purpose Hall.

The Pre-School is designed to the highest specification for children aged three and four years old. The facilities include a fully equipped playroom where children are able to access a range of resources and materials to support play and learning. Some children exhibit obvious ability in academic, sporting or creative endeavours from an early age; others do not, and may lack confidence as a result. We strive to discover the aptitudes, build the self-esteem and develop the potential of every one of our children. High levels of individual attention are central to achieving this aim, with the school's excellent staff being the key resource. We see co-curricular opportunities easily accessed and essential to every child's full development. Girls' and boys' sport flourishes at all ages, a full musical scheme is in place and every child has the opportunity to appear in a number of performance related activities each year.

Kirkham Grammar School Headmaster, Daniel Berry, ended his first year as Head with an excellent inspection report. The report recognised the school as 'excellent across all areas', the highest grading possible within the independent sector.

We believe Kirkham Grammar School exists for our children and therefore they must have the best!

(Founded 1549)

Ribby Road, Kirkham, Preston, Lancashire PR4 2BH UK

Tel: 01772 684264

Fax: 01772 672747

Email: info@kirkhamgrammar.co.uk

Website: www.kirkhamgrammar.co.uk

Headmaster: Mr. Daniel Berry

Appointed: 2016

Head of Junior School: Mrs. Annette Roberts

School type: Co-educational Boarding & Day

Age range of pupils: 3–18

No. of pupils enrolled as at 01/09/2017: 860

Boys: 450 ***Girls:*** 410 ***Sixth Form:*** 180

No. of boarders: 60

Fees per annum as at 01/09/2017:

Senior School (11-18 years): £3,743 (Day) – £7,105 (Boarding) per term

Junior School (4–11 years): £2,798 (Day) per term

Pre-School (3-4 years): £242 (Full week)– £49.25 (Full day)

Average class size: 12

Teacher/pupil ratio: 1:9

Rossall School

For many, a childhood by the sea is a dream; at Rossall, that dream becomes a reality. Rossall is an exceptional school, rooted in its heritage yet innately dynamic, brimming with personality and excited about the future.

We are shaped by our coastal location and somehow infused with the sense of anticipation, curiosity and adventure that early explorers must have felt – where can we go? What will we find? How can we get there?

We are shaped by the wonderful architecture which creates a safe haven within its Cambridge-like quads, by the vast dining hall, atmospheric Chapel and beautiful rooms.

We are shaped by our expansive site and make full use of our 160 acres, particularly for outdoor activities and sport, from cross country running and CCF field exercises to golf practice and Ross-hockey on the beach. Our ponds, trees, marsh, grassland and dunes also provide unending scope for outdoor learning and discovery.

But above all, we are shaped by the great people, both staff and students, who live and work at Rossall. There is an indelible Rossall spirit that is cultivated here – warmth, courage, humour, empathy, resilience, curiosity and the ability to talk to anyone are some of its most prominent features! It is a compelling mix.

Our teachers provide a brilliant balance of inspiration, care and deep subject knowledge to fire the imagination and ensure that our students have all the building blocks they need for success, not only at school and not only in the classroom, but also later on in life. We are proud of our students' academic achievements and delighted that they achieve consistently above national and world averages in their examinations.

We deliver a broad and balanced curriculum with the principles of the International Baccalaureate learner profile at its heart. In the Nursery, we follow the Early Years Foundation Stage (EYFS) learning goals. From the age of 2 to 11, we offer the IB Primary Years Programme (PYP). At age 16, students sit GCSE and iGCSE examinations, then students choose between the IB or A Level route in the Sixth Form. The IB principles run through our teaching and learning in every phase of the school and underpin a dynamic and enjoyable yet rigorous learning experience.

With nearly fifty different nationalities living and learning together at Rossall, we truly are a global village. The combination of UK day students and students from right across the world creates an exciting international dimension and an appreciation of diverse culture, religions and politics.

Whether joining Rossall as a day or boarding pupil, you will be coming to a vibrant and happy community. All the basic needs are catered for, but in a most generous way – food is plentiful and delicious, we have an on-site Medical Centre, our houses are beautifully appointed and our houseparents and tutors are amazing – adept, knowledgeable and attuned to the needs of the young people in their care.

To come and experience the School first hand, you can arrange a private tour to fit in with your commitments.

Scholarships: To enable a wide range of children to join Rossall, we offer a number of scholarships each year. We offer academic, music, drama and sports scholarships to children in Years 3, 5, 7, 9 and 12.

(Founded 1844)

Broadway, Fleetwood, Lancashire FY7 8JW UK

Tel: +44 (0)1253 774201

Fax: +44 (0)1253 772052

Email: admissions@rossall.org.uk

Website: www.rossallschool.org.uk

Head: Ms Elaine Purves

Appointed: September 2013

School type: Co-educational Boarding & Day

Religious Denomination:
Church of England but accept all religions

Age range of pupils: 2–18

No. of pupils enrolled as at 01/09/2017: 600

Boys: 321 ***Girls:*** 279 ***Sixth Form:*** 170

No. of boarders: 270

Fees per annum as at 01/09/2017:

Day: £7,830–£12,750

Full Boarding: £20,100–£36,450

Average class size: Max 22

Teacher/pupil ratio: 1:6

Stonyhurst College

Stonyhurst is Britain's leading Catholic boarding and day school, with over 400 years of history, set in a magnificent Grade I listed building in a beautiful setting. The oldest Jesuit school in the world, Stonyhurst is part of a well-proven educational tradition, with global links to other Jesuit schools and colleges in every continent. We achieve high academic results, have exceptional pastoral care, and offer an enormous range of extra-curricular opportunities.

The pupils in our care are given the individual attention, resources and space in which to grow intellectually, spiritually and emotionally. Stonyhurst has an outstanding academic record, with many pupils going on to top universities in the UK, Europe and around the world; Stonyhurst pupils will attend Oxbridge in September 2017, with others attending the Russell Group and International universities of their choice.

Teaching at Stonyhurst centres on the individual and encourages pupils to study independently, and to think for themselves. Small classes and exceptionally good teacher-pupil relationships enable pupils to achieve their full academic potential. All pupils have a personal tutor. A strong learning support department enables those with special educational needs to achieve their best. In the sixth form we offer the International Baccalaureate alongside A levels. Pupils have a wealth of support to guide them through their chosen courses and to assist them with their application to university.

The creative life of the College is rich and varied, offering many opportunities in music, art, drama and dance. Standards are high, with prestigious choral and organ scholarships frequently awarded to Stonyhurst pupils, as well as places on National Youth Theatre courses. Sport plays an important part in the life of Stonyhurst; we are represented in local and national fixtures, and international tours take our pupils all over the world. The main team games are rugby, hockey, cricket, netball, athletics and football. Additional sports include cross-country running, squash, tennis, gymnastics, basketball, fencing and swimming. Facilities include a heated swimming pool, state-of-the-art tennis dome, a 9 hole golf course, all weather pitch, squash and tennis court.

Ethos

As a Jesuit school, Stonyhurst seeks to enable each individual pupil to thrive, by enabling them to find, develop and use their unique talents. We believe the distinctive nature of Stonyhurst, informed also by an extensive volunteering programme, helps to ensure that the strong leadership qualities many pupils develop are tempered with a thoughtful compassion and awareness of others.

Boarding at Stonyhurst is centred upon excellent pastoral care in a happy, well-ordered environment, in high quality accommodation. Boys board in year-groups (called playrooms) and are cared for by their playroom master and his team. For girls, there are two boarding houses: one for Lower Line (years 9 to 11) and another for Higher Line (the sixth form). Each is run by a housemistress and her team. Stonyhurst is very much a 7-day-a-week boarding school with a busy weekend activity programme: this includes visits to the cinema, theatre or sports events, or cultural excursions to places such as York or Liverpool.

Everyone attends Whole School Mass in St Peter's Church on Sunday morning. About 65% of our pupils are Catholic, we also have young people who belong to other Christian traditions, and other faiths; all are encouraged to play a full part in the spiritual life of the school. Special celebrations are held to mark the major feast days of the year.

STONYHURST

(Founded 1593)

Stonyhurst, Clitheroe, Lancashire BB7 9PZ UK

Tel: 01254 827073

Fax: 01254 827131

Email: UKadmissions@stonyhurst.ac.uk
SMHadmissions@stonyhurst.ac.uk
Internationaladmissions@stonyhurst.ac.uk

Website: www.stonyhurst.ac.uk

Headmaster: John Browne MA

Appointed: 2016

School type: Coeducational Boarding & Day

Age range of pupils: 13–18

No. of pupils enrolled as at 01/09/2017: 480

Sixth Form: 240

No. of boarders: 330

Day: £19,560

Weekly Boarding: £29,250

Full Boarding: £34,110

Full Boarding (IB): £35,610

Average class size: 15

Teacher/pupil ratio: 1:8

Windermere School

Windermere School is situated in the heart of the Lake District National Park. The rugged beauty of the landscape not only makes for an inspiring educational setting but enables students to make use of what surrounds them.

The curriculum offered at Windermere School reflects the belief that students should be exposed to as many opportunities as possible and leave the School as well-rounded individuals. We have offered the International Baccalaureate Diploma programme (DP) since 2009.

Windermere School is not academically selective and we aim to help each student find the pathway most suitable for their ambitions. We believe that it is essential that students have access to high quality careers advice and are given the opportunity to explore an extensive range of career options. We are committed to finding what is right for each student, whether it be the DP or Certificate programme.

Over the past few years, leavers have gone onto a variety of universities, including Oxford, Cambridge, Imperial College and Durham.

We are a Round Square School and this blends perfectly with the IB philosophy and the two intersect with Service at their cores and we support many Service initiatives. Each year a group of students travel to South Africa to support the Tiger Kloof Service project. We also support worldwide humanitarian appeals and, locally, provide support in residential care homes and with conservation projects.

There is a vast array of academic and extra-curricular opportunities available to students: School musical, sports and adventurous expeditions. The School boasts its very own RYA accredited watersports centre and in 2014 it was the first school in the UK to be awarded Champion Club status for its race training.

The Sixth Form boarding house is designed to promote the successful transition between School and Higher Education. It is laid out in apartments with twin and single bedrooms, a bathroom, common room and kitchen. There is also a large communal space for socialising and numerous socials events are held throughout the year.

We offer a challenging and enriching education from the age of three, at our junior campus, Elleray and up to the age of 18 at our senior campus, Browhead. Windermere School has a modern and innovative approach that encourages young people to strive for excellence in all things.

(Founded 1863)

Patterdale Road, Windermere, Cumbria LA23 1NW UK

Tel: 015394 46164

Fax: 015394 88414

Email: ws@windermereschool.co.uk

Website: www.windermereschool.co.uk

Head of School: Ian Lavender

School type: Coeducational Boarding & Day

Age range of pupils: 3–18

No. of pupils enrolled as at 01/09/2017: 340

Fees per annum as at 01/09/2017:

Day: £17,250

Weekly Boarding: £29,265

Full Boarding: £30,420

South-East

Aberdour School

Founded in 1933, Aberdour is an award-winning and extremely successful preparatory school where boys and girls aged 2-13 benefit from learning, playing and growing together in a caring and safe environment. Set in 12 acres of parkland and with a wide range of specialist facilities and specialist staff, we are large enough to offer the breadth of opportunity you would wish for your child but small classes ensure that each pupil is individually supported. At Aberdour, every child has the opportunity to shine. Children are encouraged to achieve their potential and it is our belief that every child who walks through our door has brilliance within them. It is our aim to find and nurture that brilliance and celebrate, as a whole community, the success of every child.

Personalised Achievement Learning (PAL) is our own system for maximising individual achievement and learning. Parents send their children to Aberdour because they want them to get the most that they possibly can from their primary education. PAL enables us to build a bespoke education for each and every child. The guiding principle is that we place the child at the centre of everything we do. At Aberdour we manage their educational process, in its most holistic sense, focusing on the individual child.

- We recognise the aspirations of each child
- We understand each child's personal learning style
- We provide truly flexible learning programmes, truly flexible teaching and access to a broad range of academic, sporting and extra-curricular activities
- We actively manage each child's goals and progress, adapting their education so that it stretches and flexes as the child develops
- At Aberdour, we follow our own three elements of educational development – academic, pastoral and aspirational.

Children can join Aberdour at age 2 in the Pre-Preparatory department and then transfer to the Preparatory school at age 7. Pupils are prepared for all the major Senior Schools and many scholarships have been won, including Academic, Music, Dance, Information Technology, Drama and All-rounder awards.

The School enjoys excellent facilities and has extensive grounds with adventure play areas, a large tree house, woodlands and acres of sports field. As well as the ample playing fields there are two all-weather areas, a large sports hall and an indoor heated swimming pool. These facilities enable the children to participate in a wide range of sporting activities. There is a comprehensive range of after-school clubs which include amongst others, fencing, gymnastics, dance and drama, chess and orchestra. Language lessons include French, Spanish and Mandarin. Drama, Art and Music have a major role in the school curriculum. There is a wide range of specialist music lessons in all instruments and the opportunity to join either the orchestra or choir.

Aberdour has two science laboratories, a design technology classroom and an impressive brand new Arts & Innovation Centre comprising a STEM Room, classrooms, Language Studio, Music rooms and Dance studio. The school has also just opened a brand new Digital Creativity Room incorporating augmented and virtual reality learning.

Aberdour offers a uniquely personalised education and was rated 'outstanding' in all areas in its most recent ISI Inspection.

Aberdour floret qui laborat

(Founded 1933)

Brighton Road, Burgh Heath, Tadworth, Surrey KT20 6AJ UK

Tel: 01737 354119

Fax: 01737 363044

Email: enquiries@aberdourschool.co.uk

Website: www.aberdourschool.co.uk

Headmaster: Mr S. D. Collins

Appointed: September 2006

School type: Coeducational Day

Age range of pupils: 2–13 years

No. of pupils enrolled as at 01/09/2017: 357

Fees per term as at 01/09/2017:

Day: £1,350–£4,650 per term

Bethany School

Set on a 60 acre rural campus in the beautiful Kent countryside, Bethany School is a flourishing co-educational day and boarding school that provides a welcoming and caring environment for pupils between the ages of 11 and 18.

Bethany enjoys a reputation as a particularly friendly and happy community. It is a strong, thriving school with an enviable building programme, including recent and regular upgrading of boarding school facilities; a fantastic new six lane 25m indoor swimming pool, state-of-the-art fitness suite and a new Sixth Form centre with excellent facilities.

Location

Situated in Kent's 'Garden of England', Bethany has an idyllic location with easy accessibility. London is less than an hour by train, Gatwick Airport one hour by taxi and Heathrow an hour and a half. The Eurostar terminal at Ashford International is just 30 minutes away.

The curriculum and information technology

As a mainstream school, Bethany prides itself on nurturing academic excellence while catering for pupils with a broad range of abilities. The School offers a wide variety of subjects in modern classrooms with specialist facilities, including our Science Centre with modern laboratories.

The entire campus is served by a wireless network and the new Year 7 and 8s are given an iPad to use in lessons. From Year 9, all pupils have their own laptop and much of the curriculum is delivered through ICT. Almost all of our Sixth Formers progress on to university courses, leaving Bethany with a mature self-confidence and clear direction.

CReSTeD registered since 1994, Bethany's Learning Support department enjoys an international reputation for its success in giving specialist help to dyslexic pupils within the mainstream curriculum. In addition, for those pupils who require it, we offer support for English as an Additional Language.

Boarding life and overseas pupils

We offer boarding in full, weekly and flexi arrangements across five boarding houses, and our boarding community brings great diversity to Bethany. We are a small school and yet we have boarders coming from 22 different countries, enriching our education with a variety of experiences and backgrounds.

"Education for life in a changing world" underlies everything we do at Bethany and its success is evidenced by the excellent transition from School to University made by our pupils each year. Sixth Form boarders benefit from single bedrooms with en suite bathrooms, all with easy access to kitchens and laundry rooms. This experience, combined with our Body for Life programme, is designed to be a stepping stone to life at university, all within the supportive environment of the School.

Outside the classroom

At Bethany, we believe that pursuits outside the classroom are very important in developing pupils' personalities. Everyone takes part in sport at least three times a week, and additionally chooses from a huge array of extra-curricular activities including horse riding, chef school, golf, fishing, clay pigeon shooting, archery, orchestra and country pursuits. The Duke of Edinburgh's Award is hugely popular and very successful at Bethany.

Throughout the School there are opportunities to perform in drama, music and dance. Our Art department is particularly strong and many pupils join us to take advantage of our 'mini art college'.

The Headmaster firmly believes that school should be enjoyed rather than endured and it is the atmosphere of positive nurturing and encouragement, focused on the potential of each individual, that helps makes Bethany 'refreshingly different'.

Bethany
since 1866

(Founded 1866)

Curtisden Green, Goudhurst, Cranbrook, Kent TN17 1LB UK

Tel: 01580 211273

Fax: 01580 211151

Email: registrar@bethanyschool.org.uk

Website: www.bethanyschool.org.uk

Headmaster: Mr Francie Healy BSc, HDipEd, NPQH

Appointed: 2010

School type: Co-educational Boarding & Day

Age range of pupils: 11–18 years

No. of pupils enrolled as at 01/09/2017: 313

Boys: 203 ***Girls:*** 110 ***Sixth Form:*** 98

No. of boarders: 106

Fees per annum as at 01/09/2017:

Day: £16,245–£17,925

Weekly Boarding: £25,185–£27,825

Full Boarding: £27,165–£30,585

Average class size: 15-17

Teacher/pupil ratio: 1:8

Christ's Hospital

If you want a school with the 'wow' factor in abundance, look no further than Christ's Hospital.

Magnificent sprawling red-brick campus and historic works of art to take your breath away – and if that isn't enough, the continuing academic success is bound to impress.

Christ's Hospital has been rated 'excellent' in every aspect by the Independent Schools' Inspectorate.

Headmaster, Simon Reid is clear what makes the school unique: "Many ask why Christ's Hospital calls itself A School Like No Other.

It is because of our roots, what the school is, what we do, where we come from and what we strive to be.

Christ's Hospital offers its pupils something very distinctive in UK independent education. As the forerunner in the field of social mobility, Christ's Hospital is the leading charitable School in the country and an inspiration for other schools wanting to offer bursary assisted places.

Our pupils come from a wide range and diverse mix of backgrounds. We are one of the oldest boarding schools and one of only four coeducational full boarding schools in the country. Before the School moved to Horsham, Christ's Hospital was originally a London school (1552 – 1902).

We are unashamedly academic – with 98% of pupils moving on to the leading universities in this country and abroad. However, we know that many key lessons are learnt beyond the classroom and Christ's Hospital's broader curriculum opportunities are remarkable.

The pupils at Christ's Hospital receive much of the very best an independent education can provide – the journey they make from the time they arrive to when they leave is often profoundly rewarding, and along the way we support their growing resilience and success as they move on to university and beyond. We delight in their achievements and welcome them back to inspire and encourage current pupils.

Visit our website – uncover the secrets of our School – see our results, our pupils, their historic uniform and, of course, our fascinating history which dates back to King Edward VI and Tudor England."

Christ's Hospital is able to offer an unrivalled number of means-tested bursaries. These bursaries range from 5% remission of fees up to and including 100% remission. Pupils' fees are assessed according to family income, so it's a child's ability and potential to benefit from a Christ's Hospital education that determines their selection.

The school hasn't been afraid to develop; modern facilities have been built in sympathetic style. Those changes are echoed in the challenging and varied curriculum. A levels are offered alongside the demanding Pre-U qualification and the globally respected International Baccalaureate Diploma Programme.

One student says:

"I fell in love with Christ's Hospital when I visited during an Open Day and knew it was where I wanted to be. There was such an amazing atmosphere.

Before coming here, I didn't really enjoy any particular subject; I just did okay at everything. At Christ's Hospital, I have discovered what I enjoy the most. Drama has been a highlight and I enjoy English, and creative writing.

The school slogan is 'a school like no other' and I certainly haven't seen anywhere else that is quite so beautiful in terms of the grounds and its traditions."

A SCHOOL LIKE NO OTHER

(Founded 1552)

Horsham, West Sussex RH13 0LJ UK

Tel: 01403 211293

Fax: 01403 211580

Email: enquiries@christs-hospital.org.uk

Website: www.christs-hospital.org.uk

Headmaster: Mr Simon Reid

Appointed: September 2017

School type: Coeducational Day & Boarding

Religious Denomination: Church of England

Age range of pupils: 11–18

No. of pupils enrolled as at 01/09/2017: 900

Fees per annum as at 01/09/2017:

Day: £16,950–£21,330

Full Boarding: £32,790

CHRIST'S HOSPITAL WAS FOUNDED ON THE
SITE OF THE GREYFRIARS IN THE CITY OF
LONDON BY KING EDWARD

Churcher's College

Churcher's College is an Independent day school for boys and girls from 3-18 years of age offering Nursery, Junior, Senior and Sixth Form education. With around 865 pupils in the Senior School and 225 pupils in the Junior School (not including the Nursery) of approximately equal numbers of boys and girls, Churcher's College enjoys recognition as one of the most accomplished independent, co-educational day schools in the country.

The school is hosted on two sites in Hampshire which enables the Junior School and Nursery pupils to flourish in their own beautiful grounds in Liphook, whilst maintaining close links to the Senior School and Sixth Form located in nearby Petersfield. Both sites offer extensive on-site playing fields and unrivalled facilities, providing the comfort and opportunities of an open, healthy environment.

Churcher's College offers the widest range of experiences and the opportunity to be the best. The school has received independent acknowledgement for its academic success, creative and performing arts, adventurous activities and sporting achievements. Churcher's is an inclusive school where parents, children, staff and friends all contribute to the rich and broad education provided. We aim to nurture children into educated informed, socially responsible and respectful citizens ready to succeed in life.

"I am hugely impressed with the number of opportunities that have been made available to me throughout my time at Churcher's. I have taken part in the Biology, Chemistry, and Physics Olympiads and completed an EPQ on human evolution. I have also been very fortunate to receive an offer to study Natural Sciences at Cambridge where I hope to continue my education in Chemistry, Cell Biology and Maths. As for extra-curricular opportunities I have thoroughly enjoyed the adventurous activities available. These have included the 2016 Devizes to Westminster kayak marathon and completions of the Ten Tors and the Welsh 3000's events. However, my highlight has been going on expedition to the Galapagos for 5 weeks. The last seven years have been incredibly busy and even more enjoyable due to the huge array of opportunities available in all areas of school life." **Pupil**

"Thank you … we are very proud of her … she is absolutely over the moon to be going to her first choice of university. We wanted to say what a wonderful two years she has had at Churcher's – she has never been so happy at school and has done amazingly well in all areas as well as creating a great friendship group – we couldn't have asked for more!"
Sixth form parent

"Our family feel hugely privileged to have discovered Churcher's and its team."
Senior school parent

"By the time the pupils leave the school they are well balanced, thoughtful and considerate individuals with an excellent standard of personal development."
"Teachers have strong knowledge which they present enthusiastically to their pupils; this acts as a stimulus for increasingly sophisticated thinking."
"The extra-curricular provision is excellent."
ISI Inspection 2015

"Value added is impressive: one whole grade at A level higher than ALIS value added expectation."
"The school achieves balance very well … those happy keeping busy in a lively environment will enjoy life at Churcher's College."
The Good Schools Guide Inspection 2017

(Founded 1722)

Petersfield, Hampshire GU31 4AS UK

Tel: 01730 263033

Fax: 01730 231437

Email: admissions@churcherscollege.com

Website: www.churcherscollege.com

Headmaster: Mr Simon Williams MA, BSc

Appointed: September 2004

School type: Coeducational Independent Day

Age range of pupils: 3–18 years

No. of pupils enrolled as at 01/09/2017:

Senior School: 865

Junior School: 225

Fees per annum as at 01/09/2017:

Day: £9,675–£14,220

Average class size: 24

Teacher/pupil ratio: 1:12

Cranleigh School

Cranleigh is Surrey's leading co-educational independent school offering both day and boarding education for children aged 7-18, enabling siblings to be educated together.

Set on adjacent hills, the Preparatory School and the Senior School enjoy a spectacular 280-acre rural setting on the Surrey/West Sussex border, by the Surrey Hills, an Area of Outstanding Natural Beauty; yet they are conveniently situated close to the mainline city of Guildford, roughly equidistant between Gatwick and Heathrow, and only an hour's drive from London, where Cranleigh pupils regularly visit professional exhibitions and performances.

Both the Prep and the Senior Schools are proud of their excellent academic track records, culminating in outstanding performances at Common Entrance, GCSE and A-level. 99% of pupils go on to Higher Education, and Cranleigh also has a consistently strong Oxbridge contingent.

Such academic excellence does not come at the expense of co-curricular success at Cranleigh and the Schools currently boast national and county level representatives in a wide range of sports, including kayaking, cricket, riding, hockey, rugby and swimming. The School is currently rated third best school in the country for sports.

Pupil participation in sport, music and drama is actively encouraged at all levels; most Saturdays see every pupil playing sport for the school. More than 10 dramatic productions each academic year provide acting opportunities for all and the hugely popular Technical Theatre encourages the development of backstage skills.

Around 40 per cent of pupils play at least one musical instrument. Many take the opportunity to perform in more than 30 concerts a year, with over 10 musical groups, including symphony orchestra, wind band, chapel choir, big band, strings, trios, quartets and several other choirs.

The Schools offer outstanding facilities alongside new academic blocks. Sports facilities enjoyed by both the Prep and the Senior School include a double-sized indoor sports centre, four artificial playing surfaces, full equestrian centre, two expansive hard court areas for netball and tennis, a generous array of rugby and cricket pitches, a three-par, nine-hole golf course and an indoor pool. Equally outstanding sports staff includes former England players, a former Davis Cup player, an England national coach and an Olympic Gold Medallist (Hockey).

The Schools also boast professional-standard theatre facilities, rehearsal rooms, beautiful art studio spaces and a modern design centre fully equipped with 3D printers. The students have the opportunity to showcase their work in professional exhibitions several times a year.

Most importantly, Cranleigh prides itself on providing a happy, nurturing environment, founded upon an extremely supportive pastoral system (every pupil has their own tutor) and a high staff to pupil ratio, underscored by an invariably passionate House spirit. In such an environment, pupils can flourish into the well-rounded, self-motivated and confident individuals Cranleighans are famed for becoming, well prepared for life after school and invariably blessed with a circle of lifelong friends.

Pupils enter Cranleigh following a process of holistic review, at the main entry points of 13 and 16, and in other years where places are available. Regular small groups open mornings are held and a wide range of academic and non-academic Scholarships are available.

CRANLEIGH
EX CULTU ROBUR

(Founded 1865)

Horseshoe Lane, Cranleigh, Surrey GU6 8QQ UK

Tel: +44 (0) 1483 273666

Fax: +44 (0) 1483 267398

Email: admissions@cranleigh.org

Website: www.cranleigh.org

Headmaster: Mr Martin Reader MA, MPhil, MBA

Appointed: September 2014

School type: Co-educational Boarding & Day

Age range of pupils: 7–18 (including Prep School)

No. of pupils enrolled as at 01/09/2017: 626

Boys: 398 ***Girls:*** 228 ***Sixth Form:*** 250

No. of boarders: 450

Fees per annum as at 01/09/2017:

Day: £29,985

Full Boarding: £36,615

Average class size: 20 (9 in Sixth Form)

Teacher/pupil ratio: 1:6

Durlston Court

"Pupils develop high levels of self-understanding, growing into confident, resilient young people who are prepared to take risks, and have huge determination to succeed." ISI, May 2017

Durlston Court Prep School is known for happy pupils, exceptional pastoral care, the breadth of opportunities and our excellent teaching and learning. We are a friendly, family school where the children and parents enjoy being part of a secure and happy community – the Durlston family.

Our Pre-Prep department (including Kindergarten) provides an outstanding foundation for learning within a nurturing and caring environment. Dedicated Pre-Prep facilities offer bright, spacious, indoor and outdoor learning areas. Our younger pupils also regularly visit other areas of the school to use specialist facilities and to be taught by our specialist teachers. Pre-Prep can often be found in 'The Den' – our Forest School, where the mud kitchen, art area and activities such as den building and stick whittling enhance our children's learning.

"The excellent outdoor facilities for learning..., allow many opportunities for quiet reflection and immersion in the natural world whilst learning." ISI, May 2017

Pupils at Durlston make full use of all of our impressive facilities and specialist teaching including our fully equipped Design and Technology Centre complete with 3D printers and laser cutter. We also offer various STEM related clubs from Engineering to Programming and we have 2 fully equipped IT suites. All pupils learn to play at least one musical instrument and are given regular opportunities to perform, helping them to develop their confidence. Our drama productions showcase talent but also provide opportunities for all pupils to be involved in a spectacular show including being part of the back stage technical team. Pupils also develop their creativity in the Art Room, Ceramics Studio and outdoors in our Art Terrace as well as further afield around our spacious grounds. From Year 3 all pupils have at least one hour of sport with daily lessons and weekly opportunities to compete in fixtures. Specialist coaching and teaching takes place across our extensive facilities. Additionally, we have over 50 activities and clubs on offer for pupils. There is something to suit everyone from our Tennis Academy to fencing, from construction to mindfulness.

"Pupils demonstrate high levels of success... in an extremely wide variety of activities including in the creative and performing arts and sport." ISI, May 2017

We are committed to promoting an all-round education and fully preparing our pupils for Senior School. Our academic achievements in terms of scholarships, entrance examinations and CE results speak for themselves. We are extremely proud of our pupils' academic success including 100% pass rate in Year 8 Common Entrance Examinations and we have a strong record of scholarship awards to senior schools in all areas including academics, sport, art and music demonstrating the all-round nature of a Durlston Education.

High expectations, both inside and outside the classroom, ensure pupils leave Durlston as well-rounded, independent and confident young people, equipped and prepared to engage and to succeed in the world of today and tomorrow.

✦
DURLSTON COURT
Preparatory School

(Founded 1903)

Becton Lane, Barton-on-Sea, New Milton, Hampshire BH25 7AQ UK

Tel: 01425 610010

Fax: 01425 622731

Email: secretary@durlstoncourt.co.uk

Website: www.durlstoncourt.co.uk

Head of School: Mr Richard May

Appointed: September 2015

School type: Coeducational Day

Age range of pupils: 2–13

No. of pupils enrolled as at 01/09/2017: 296

Boys: 165 ***Girls:*** 131

Fees per annum as at 01/09/2017:

Day: £3,540–£15,390

Average class size: 12-15

Teacher/pupil ratio: 1:4-1:15

DURLSTON COURT

Eagle House School

Eagle House is a coeducational, boarding and day Prep, Pre-Prep and Nursery located in Berkshire. The school's superb grounds and excellent facilities are the background to an experience where success, confidence and happiness are paramount. The school is proud of its academic record, preparing children for a host of top independent schools and boasting a diverse and robust curriculum.

Younger pupils follow the International Primary Curriculum and our older children have embarked on a new Humanities curriculum that links subjects through topics and themes. Great teaching, new technology and a focus on the basics mean that children make good progress and love to be in the classroom. Independent learning is a focus for all children and our Extended Project programme helps drive inquisitive minds.

Eagle House was recently recognised by The Week Magazine as having the best Prep School extra-curricular programme and we unashamedly offer lots as part of our Golden Eagle activities experience. Children benefit from a huge range of opportunities in sport, music, drama, art, outward bound and community programmes. Busy children are happy and fulfilled children and we like to think that all pupils are Learning for Life.

Learning for Life means that children benefit from the best all-round education. They can feel confident in the classroom, on the games field, on stage, in the concert hall and in the community. Everyone is given the chance to stretch themselves in every area. Challenge is an important part of growing up and at Eagle House we learn that success and failure are both positive experiences.

Bright learning environments, outdoor learning areas and wonderful sporting facilities are important but it is the community that shapes a young person. Through the excellent pastoral care and tutor system, coupled with a buddy structure, ensuring children have an older pupil to support them, Eagle House seeks to develop wellbeing from the youngest to the oldest.

Recognising how to be a positive influence within a community is also part of the Eagle House journey. Through our wonderful Learning for Life programme that teaches children about themselves and the wider community, we aim to make all our pupils responsible and independent as well as able to show empathy and understanding towards others. Time for reflection in chapel and assemblies also improves the way we look at the world and mindfulness sessions help us all take stock.

Boarding is a popular option and allows children to experience a varied evening programme of activities as well as being part of a vibrant and caring community. Boarding encourages independence but it is also great fun and whether full, weekly or flexi, boarders have the most wonderful time.

We often say that Eagle House children have the time of their lives and we firmly believe this. Learning for Life at Eagle House opens the doors to all sorts of opportunities and this results in children who are highly motivated and enthusiastic in all they do.

Eagle House buzzes with achievement and laughter – not a bad way to grow up!

Eagle House is a registered charity (No 309093) for the furtherance of education.

(Founded 1820)

Sandhurst, Berkshire GU47 8PH UK

Tel: 01344 772134

Email: info@eaglehouseschool.com

Website: www.eaglehouseschool.com

Headmaster: Mr A P N Barnard BA(Hons), PGCE

Appointed: September 2006

School type: Coeducational Day & Boarding

Age range of pupils: 3–13

No. of pupils enrolled as at 01/09/2017: 388

Boys: 220 ***Girls:*** 168

No. of boarders: 50

Fees per annum as at 01/09/2017:

Day: £11,235–£17,580

Full Boarding: £23,610

Average class size: 16

Teacher/pupil ratio: 1:8

Gordon's School

A non-selective state boarding school, Gordon's School was established in 1885 at the request of Queen Victoria and has since developed into one of the leading boarding schools in the UK. Situated in 50-acres of beautiful grounds with generous facilities, Gordon's School achieved World-class School status in 2016, was ranked one of the top-five best schools in both the Sunday Times and the Daily Telegraph in 2016 and was again judged to be 'outstanding' by Ofsted in 2017.

"There is an unstinting focus on the pursuit of excellence." Ofsted 2014

Academic

Officially listed as one of Britain's outstanding schools by Her Majesty's Chief Inspector, Gordon's School recognises that a good education is not just about outstanding examination results but a thorough preparation for life. The School provides opportunities and experiences for all young people to find their talents and interests, develop good character, become accomplished, and achieve across a range of disciplines and ultimately develop the confidence to go and make their mark in the world.

Great importance is placed on the quality of teaching in the classroom. Supported by talented, committed staff, Gordon's School is one of the top performing schools in the country, and has been for the last decade. However, the real judgement of Gordon's is the students. Visitors are struck by the friendliness, discipline and vibrancy throughout the School and by the family atmosphere, exemplified by the special rapport between staff and students. Students and staff model the School's five characteristics of courtesy, integrity, diligence, enthusiasm and resilience.

"Respect, courtesy and consideration for others are embedded in the culture of the school." Ofsted 2017

Extra-Curricular

The aim of any successful school must be to develop the whole person as well as stretching them academically. For this reason, sport and extra-curricular activities have always been very important at Gordon's, which is why the School offers an extensive range of traditional team games, and competitive and recreational activities as a vital part of the Gordon's curriculum. The School also runs a 'Good to Great' programme, which ensures that students are challenged in sport, creative arts, academic enrichment, leadership and outdoor pursuits.

"Residential boarders flourish and make exceptional academic, social and emotional progress." Ofsted 2017

Sixth Form

As well as a thriving Main School, Gordon's School also runs a growing Sixth Form. Students at Gordon's are expected to take every opportunity to ensure that they fulfil their academic potential and develop into confident, well-rounded young people, ready to take their place in the world. There are many opportunities available at Gordon's Sixth Form, from improving academic skills through qualified courses such as TEFL, Model United Nations and the Debating team, to social skills and life skills such as volunteering, societies, sports teams, first aid and cooking, there are plenty of options for those looking to boost their CV, add to their personal statement or just get involved.

"The Sixth Form is outstanding. Students make excellent progress and achieve high academic standards. They take advantage of a wide range of opportunities to develop leadership skills and the vast majority go on to secure places in higher education." Ofsted 2014

(Founded 1885)

West End, Woking, Surrey GU24 9PT UK

Tel: 01276 858084

Fax: 01276 855335

Email: registrar@gordons.surrey.sch.uk

Website: www.gordons.surrey.sch.uk

Head Teacher: Andrew Moss MEd

Appointed: September 2010

School type: Coeducational Boarding & Day

Age range of pupils: 11–18

No. of pupils enrolled as at 01/09/2017: 840

Boys: 430 ***Girls:*** 410 ***Sixth Form:*** 250

Fees per annum as at 01/09/2017:

Full Boarding: £15,135–£16,167

Average class size: 22

Teacher/pupil ratio: 1:12

Greenfields Independent Day & Boarding School

Greenfields Independent Day and Boarding School is an Independent Schools Association school with a Montessori-based Nursery, a Reception class (forming the Early Years Foundation Stage), an Infant and Junior School, a Senior School including Sixth Form and a long and short-term English as a Foreign Language unit. Fees start from £59 a week.

Situated in beautiful grounds, with its adventure playground backing into the Ashdown Forest itself, the school is a safe and inspirational place to learn.

What is Unique about Greenfields?

- The main difference between Greenfields and other schools is the unique teaching method it uses. This method (Study Technology) isolates the barriers preventing or hindering a child from learning and then provides precise tools to deal with them. Its use allows any child of any ability to learn anything.
- The school applies a strong moral code (The Way to Happiness) ensuring happy students and successful graduates.
- Greenfields delivers an independent education with exceptionally low fees for local public, whilst maintaining a high staff to student ratio
- We have small class sizes and can provide one-to-one assistance for students as needed.
- The good relationships between staff and students, and amongst the students themselves, are a notable feature of Greenfields School and are part of its strength.
- Greenfields offers a full educational solution from age 2 through to age 18, Nursery to A Levels, so that parents have a complete pathway for their child.
- We maintain a safe, bully-free and drug free environment.
- The school offers courses and internships in how to study, including the 'Study Skills for Life' and the 'Basic Study Manual' which give students the ability to become independent learners.
- We utilise Rossetta Stone based short and long term EFL courses for international students both during the summer holidays and throughout the year.
- We have an entire department called Qualifications to ensure that students are helped through each stage of their education with one-to-one assistance as needed.
- Annual assessments are provided by Cambridge International Examinations for quality control purposes and other formal and informal assessments to ensure that students are making progress within the school year.
- The school is 20 minutes from Gatwick airport, 50 minutes from London and 35 minutes from Brighton and the coast.
- The school is located on the edge of the Ashdown Forest in 6 acres of its own forest and fields with room for up to 50 boarders and 200 day students.
- As well as having access to the usual on site facilities, boarders and students have easy access to nearby shops and activities. These include swimming, horse riding, cycling, canoeing, archery, dancing, a rock school, cinema and many other indoor and outdoor activities of all kinds.

Greenfields respects every child and young person as an individual and aims to give them opportunities to explore and realise their potential in their development of academic, sporting, creative and social skills.

Our product is well educated, happy children who become competent and valuable adults.

(Founded 1981)

Priory Road, Forest Row, East Sussex RH18 5JD UK

Tel: +44 (0)1342 822189

Fax: +44 (0)1342 825289

Email: admissions@greenfieldsschool.com

Website: www.greenfieldsschool.com

Executive Head: Mr. Jeff Smith

Appointed: 2009

School type: Coeducational Boarding & Day

Religious Denomination: Non-denominational

Age range of pupils: 2–19

Average class size: 5-15

Teacher/pupil ratio: 1:6

Hurstpierpoint College

Extracts from The Good Schools Guide's review

"The only head we've come across where pupils gave an audible 'aaaah' when asked for their views: 'the best head; respectful of us as pupils; makes the effort and knows all our names; you can have a conversation with him'

"Pupils say the challenge grade system 'helps you get to where you want to be', and it certainly works, Hurst is in the top 10% nationally for value added.

"Parents choose Hurst because they feel it provides something more than an academic education: 'We want (them) to do well academically but not as an expression of everything else, we want them to be brought on as people'. Seen, then, as an holistic educational experience by parents.

"Pupils are well taught and achieve their academic potential', said a parent. 'It does its core purpose brilliantly', said another

Hurst constantly strives to be outstanding. Not just in everything we do but also in the manner in which we do it. The school is driven by a determination to enable each child to achieve, and continue to build upon, their personal bests throughout their school career in all aspects of school life.

Pupils are challenged to make the most of the talents that lie within them and, as importantly, the huge opportunities which are available to them during their time here.

We are ambitious for our pupils to achieve the best that they can in all that they do and we recognise and encourage both engagement and achievement.

We understand that the best possible academic grades are critical but, at the same time, the development of those key skills, qualities and values which are so important in life come perhaps more from engagement with life beyond the classroom.

Hurst provides teaching, mentoring and coaching of the highest order, a phenomenal range of facilities (that continue to improve year-on-year) and access to opportunities of every sort within its welcoming, warm and dynamic community. We make no secret of the fact that at Hurst we encourage, indeed expect, our pupils to fully engage whilst they are with us.

Genuine, sustained engagement opens the door to new worlds of opportunity. A real love of learning develops. Nurtured in a community stimulated by intelligent conversation and intellectual challenge, information grows into knowledge and matures into understanding, wisdom and self-knowledge.

Academically selective, but not aggressively so (and certainly not de-selective), the school has an excellent track record and the vast majority of pupils go on to Russell Group universities including Oxford, Cambridge, the various London Universities, as well as large numbers to Exeter, Bristol and Durham.

When we reflect upon the life of the College, we don't just focus on the great headline triumphs but on the degree to which all our children are truly engaged with Hurst life. I know that enabling our children to pursue and achieve their personal bests is how they develop into successful, independent and confident individuals with a good sense of themselves and the world around them, who will succeed in their lives whichever route they choose to take. This is the only outcome that does justice to both their abilities and talents and the faith placed in us by their parents.

Tim Manly
Headmaster

(Founded 1849)

College Lane, Hurstpierpoint, West Sussex BN6 9JS UK

Tel: 01273 833636

Fax: 01273 835257

Email: info@hppc.co.uk

Website: www.hppc.co.uk

Headmaster: Mr. T J Manly BA, MSc

School type: Coeducational Boarding & Day

Age range of pupils: 4–18

No. of pupils enrolled as at 01/09/2017: 1156

Fees per annum as at 01/09/2017:

Day: £8,790 (Prep)–£22,860 (Senior)

Weekly Boarding: £28,800

Flexi Boarding: £27,015

Kent College

'Success through a personalised learning experience'
Situated in a delightful location, overlooking the historic city of Canterbury. Kent College provides a challenging yet unfailingly supportive community for 3 to 18-year-olds that nurtures and develops an impressive range of talents and interests enabling every pupil to realise their full potential.

Kent College is part of the Methodist Schools Group, though it happily welcomes pupils of all faiths and none. It is renowned as a particularly friendly and welcoming school with a strong family feeling.

The high expectations of the school mean that pupils of all ages are given every opportunity and support to achieve academic excellence. The International Baccalaureate Diploma runs alongside A levels in the Sixth Form with results amongst the very best in the country. Timetabling is done at an individual level so that each child can specialise and receive accelerated learning opportunities when appropriate.

The School can proudly boast that almost all sixth formers go on to their first choice University, including Oxford and Cambridge. This academic strength reflects the small class sizes and the quality of the exceptionally well-qualified, enthusiastic and experienced teaching staff.

Boarding is available from the age of seven. Every child is given personal attention and supervision, and new arrivals are given special help to settle into their new home. Recent investment has brought seamless wireless internet connection to all the senior boarding houses. Students and parents benefit from flexibility as the school provides termly, weekly and occasional boarding. Easy access to London makes weekly boarding a particularly attractive option.

With the benefit of a floodlit all-weather pitch, used for hockey in the winter and tennis in the summer, as well as a superbly equipped Sports Hall and numerous pitches, Kent College teams make formidable competitors in any sport. Hockey is a particular strength, with regular representation in County and National squads.

Music and drama play a central role in the life of the school, with many performances each year. The Music Centre offers state of the art facilities for all aspects of the subject. The provision for Music Technology is now amongst the best in the country.

A huge range of extracurricular activities is available during lunch breaks, after school and at weekends. These opportunities are varied ranging from Duke of Edinburgh, to debating. The school even has its own farm and developing equine centre. Language exchanges and overseas trips play an important role in offering a diverse range of personal development opportunities.

Recent results for GCSE, A Level and the International Baccalaureate recognise Kent College as excellent. In 2016 Kent College was placed in the top ten schools in Kent for its A Level results and the most recent International Baccalaureate results place us close to the top of the rankings not just in the UK but globally.

KENT COLLEGE
CANTERBURY

(Founded 1885)

Whitstable Road, Canterbury, Kent CT2 9DT UK

Tel: 01227 763231

Fax: 01227 787450

Email: admissions@kentcollege.co.uk

Website: www.kentcollege.com

Executive Head Master: Dr D J Lamper

Appointed: September 2007

School type: Coeducational Day & Boarding

Religious Denomination: Methodist

Age range of pupils: 3–18

No. of pupils enrolled as at 01/09/2017: 702

Fees per annum as at 01/09/2017:

Day: £15,981–£17,691

Full Boarding: £32,748–£33,480

Average class size: 20 max

Teacher/pupil ratio: 1:8

King Edward VI School

King Edward VI School, Southampton, has been at the heart of the city for over 460 years and is one of the UK's leading independent 11-18 co-educational day schools.

With a reputation for academic excellence, the School boasts a thriving Sixth Form that produces consistently excellent A Level examination results ensuring students continue on to a range of competitive institutions, most to one of the UK's top 25 universities and, on average, approximately 10% of students proceed to Oxford or Cambridge. Results at GCSE and IGCSE level are also excellent, further consolidating King Edward's reputation for outstanding academic achievement.

Not only does King Edward's promote academic excellence, it also aims to foster in every pupil a sense of personal worth through a wide range of co-curricular activities, particularly with an active engagement in community work, so that every individual emerges as a fully responsible member of society. In the last year alone the student Charities Commission has raised over £27,000 for local and national charitable causes.

Each year students can be found taking part in excursions to worldwide destinations. A yearly charitable trip to South Africa allows Sixth Formers to work with disadvantaged children living in rural poverty, whilst other recent destinations have included Maine, USA for the annual ski trip, kayaking in the Swedish archipelagos, a Biology field trip in Ecuador and the Galapagos Islands, a cultural excursion to Morocco and a trekking expedition in the Himalayas. Language students regularly participate in the exchange programmes on offer to Germany, France and Spain as well as in cultural visits to schools in the USA and Prague. Closer to home the School also organises an annual summer camp to Swanage for local young carers, run by our Sixth Formers.

Sport and the arts are an integral part of school life. Students are given the opportunity to represent the School across the major team games as well as individual sports. Overseas tours, regular fixtures, tournaments and school events offer a competitive sporting environment and King Edward's boasts 33 acres of sports ground, a fully equipped gym and multiple all weather pitches. The Creative Arts Faculty offers an amazing array of facilities from recital rooms, a recording studio and music technology suite to a custom-built dance studio. A wonderful new theatre has just been built that has a capacity for 400 seats and provides a superb venue for our talented dramatists and musicians. An array of public performances throughout the year allow King Edward's performers to showcase their talents, whatever their ability level.

Students are actively encouraged to become involved in fund-raising and community work and take part in some of the 150 clubs and societies that are available outside of lesson time. King Edward's also runs a well-established Duke of Edinburgh Award Scheme that makes use of the school's Rural Studies Centre in Dartmoor.

King Edward's strives to ensure that all pupils reach and fulfil their full potential. A happy atmosphere amongst first-class teaching facilities provide exceptional academic stimulus alongside an extraordinary breadth of co-curricular opportunities. Seventeen bus routes extend throughout south Hampshire, allowing students from the New Forest, Salisbury, Winchester and east of Southampton easy and direct access to the School.

(Founded 1553)

Wilton Road, Southampton, Hampshire SO15 5UQ UK

Tel: 023 8070 4561

Fax: 023 8070 5937

Email: enquiries@kes.hants.sch.uk

Website: www.kes.hants.sch.uk

Head Master: Mr A J Thould MA(Oxon)

Appointed: April 2002

School type: Coeducational Day

Age range of pupils: 11–18

No. of pupils enrolled as at 01/09/2017: 970

Fees per annum as at 01/09/2017:

Day: £15,510

Average class size: 22

Teacher/pupil ratio: 1:10

Lanesborough

Lanesborough Prep School for boys is located in the centre of Guildford, and offers a superb range of facilities. A fabulous new Sports Hall has just been completed extending the range of sports available to the boys, it has a viewing gallery and extensive changing rooms.

The school is currently converting the previous gym into a bespoke performance space for drama and music.

The academic success of Lanesborough is renowned, with boys regularly achieving academic, music and sports scholarships to their chosen senior school. An average of 70% of Lanesborough boys go on to the RGS Guildford each year. Five of the top academic Scholarships to the RGS this year were awarded to Lanesborough boys. Three other academic scholarships were awarded. Four boys left with music scholarships, one with sport and one with art.

The superb music tradition is enhanced with the cathedral boy choristers all attending the school. Over 50 different clubs from Astronomy to Warhammer are on offer enabling the boys to develop a wide range of interests. However, the most important aspect for all staff is ensuring that the boys thrive, are happy and reach their full potential in a stimulating, fun and caring environment.

Lanesborough is about learning how to learn, not just what to learn, developing a range of interests and preparing the young men so that they are interesting and interested citizens, resilient and ready to take their place in our ever evolving world.

To fully appreciate Lanesborough you will need to visit and experience first-hand, all that is on offer.

Open Mornings are held in October and March – check the website for full details. Alternatively, parents can arrange an individual tour with the Head. Please call Mrs Francis, Admissions Secretary, on 01483 880489, admissions@lanesborough.surrey.sch.uk.

(Founded 1930)

Maori Road, Guildford, Surrey GU1 2EL UK

Tel: 01483 880489

Fax: 01483 880651

Email: admissions@lanesborough.surrey.sch.uk

Website: www.lanesborough.surrey.sch.uk

Head: Mrs Clare Turnbull BA(Hons) MEd

Appointed: Sept 2007

School type: Boys' Day

Age range of boys: 3–13

No. of pupils enrolled as at 01/09/2017: 350

Fees per annum as at 01/09/2017:

Day: £10,479–£14,688

Average class size: 16

Leighton Park School

At its core, a Leighton Park education focuses on the individual and the promise of choice. Our ethos informs an approach where students are able to follow their most impassioned interests, become active learners and strive to fulfil their potential.

Students benefit from an academically rigorous, broad and innovative curriculum. The sciences, mathematics and the creative arts, including music, film production and art, are particular strengths of the school.

This strength in breadth enables a focus on creative problem-solving and interdisciplinary approaches, encouraging students to analyse and put forward solutions to today's complex challenges, often supported by the school's impressive partnerships with universities, industry and cultural organisations, such as Cisco and Pinewood Studios. The success of our approach is demonstrated by 94% of our Sixth Formers achieving their first university choice last year.

Our cross-cutting skills programmes position students for success in a fast-changing world, where many of today's jobs will not exist in 30 years time. Central to the school's approach, we teach leadership, creative thinking and risk-taking, empowering students to be a force for good in the world and reflecting the school's Quaker ethos.

In Sixth Form, students can choose between the International Baccalaureate Diploma Programme (IB) or A Levels, and can opt to do four A Levels so that their choices are not limited so early in life. Among other accolades, the school is in the top five in the UK for small cohort IB results.

Our wrap-around provision, which welcomes day students from 7.30am to 9pm, offers all our pupils the time to discover and develop their greatest talents. Located just 35 minutes from London and Heathrow Airport, Leighton Park has a thriving boarding community, offering full, weekly and flexible options for students. Co-educational, the boarding houses are split roughly 50/50 boys and girls with each group having their own wings but sharing communal spaces. Students represent 44 countries, with strong UK representation. The five houses mix boarding and day students, creating vibrant communities.

The school's cross-cutting skills programmes position students for success in a fast-changing world, where many of today's jobs will not exist in 30 years' time. Central to the school's approach, we teach leadership, creative thinking and risk-taking, empowering students to be a force for good in the world and reflecting the school's Quaker ethos. The range of choice and the school's focus on the individual create a fun, supportive and nurturing programme.

Sport plays an important role in life at Leighton Park with many individual performers and teams reaching county and regional level in sports. The school's Advanced Performer Programme supports elite athletes. Music and creative media is a particular strength at Leighton Park, reflected by the school's status as a Yamaha European Centre of Excellence – the only one in the UK.

The quiet moments and the calm atmosphere of our 60 acre park, encourage students to collect their thoughts and reflect within a caring community, providing high academic standards, excellent pastoral care and a rich and diverse co-curricular programme of activities. All of this, and the focus on mutual respect, create a stable, unique and sustainable environment where children can live, learn and grow.

Leighton Park
School

(Founded 1890)

Shinfield Road, Reading, Berkshire RG2 7ED UK

Tel: +44 (0) 118 987 9600

Email: admissions@leightonpark.com

Website: www.leightonpark.com

Head: Nigel Williams BA(Bristol), MA(London), PGCE

Appointed: January 2013

School type: Co-educational Day & Boarding

Religious Denomination: Quaker

Age range of pupils: 11–18

No. of pupils enrolled as at 01/09/2017: 459

Fees per annum as at 01/09/2017:

Day: £17,358–£22,404

Weekly Boarding: £23,886–£30,051

Full Boarding: £27,162–£34,794

Average class size: 17

Teacher/pupil ratio: 1:8

Lord Wandsworth College

Lord Wandsworth College (LWC) is a highly successful, well-respected boarding and day school for children aged 11-18 on the north Hampshire/Surrey border. It offers a broad, well-balanced curriculum and an incredible range of sports, activities and co-curricular opportunities. The heart of the school sits within an idyllic 1200 acre site of leafy woodlands, rolling hills and beautiful landscapes. It is an extremely happy and strong community where pupils are challenged, cheered-on and supported by classmates, houseparents and teachers.

At LWC, there are five key pillars that inspire our pupils, leaving them with an inner self-confidence, but an outward modesty and resilience to make a positive difference in the world. We believe in character education, in championing the pupil voice, in good mental health and wellbeing, in challenging pupils and creating opportunities to make a difference to others.

Lord Wandsworth College is named after a wealthy London banker who, in 1912, left a generous bequest to educate orphaned children. This charitable spirit lives on today as the Lord Wandsworth Foundation offers a number of assisted places to children who have lost the support of one or both parents and who would benefit from an outstanding education in a caring, nurturing environment. All pupils are conscious of this, and a sense of inclusion and collective responsibility for the happiness of others is strong here. In fact, it is paramount.

Lord Wandsworth College offers full, weekly and flexi boarding (three nights a week). There are eight boarding houses, all run by caring houseparents who provide the main point of contact between school and home, organise house activities and social events and are supported by a team of compassionate tutors and matrons. Day pupils are fully integrated into the boarding house system.

Pupils find a wide range of subjects to challenge, engage and inspire them. The curriculum is taught by experienced teachers who create 'high challenge – low threat' learning environments and use a variety of techniques to bring learning to life. The school's goal is to develop a life-long love of learning. Pupils are encouraged to stretch themselves to an academic level two years ahead and urged to ask that extra question, discover new inter-relationships and share their knowledge.

The sporting facilities are outstanding and include two floodlit astroturfs, a 25 metre indoor swimming pool, tennis courts, 2 sports halls, squash courts, a climbing wall, netball courts, indoor and outdoor cricket nets, numerous cricket, rugby, hockey and football pitches, a grass athletics track and a cross-country course. Many pupils take advantage of the adventure training and leadership opportunities provided by the Combined Cadet Force and the Duke of Edinburgh Award scheme is also immensely popular.

Renowned for the high standard of its productions, the Music and Drama Centre provides opportunities for personal instruction, performance and exhibition in the 120 seat bespoke auditorium. Students are encouraged to get involved in all aspects of theatre production including acting, directing, set design, costume, make-up, lighting and sound. LWC also offers ballet, street dance and modern dance lessons and there are many vocal and instrumental groups including Concert Band, Chamber Orchestra, Senior Choir, Barbershop, Flautissimo, Classical Guitar and Sax Group.

Further information, including forthcoming Open Days, can be found at www.lordwandsworth.org.

LORD WANDSWORTH COLLEGE

A GREAT FOUNDATION

(Founded 1922)

Long Sutton, Hook, Hampshire RG29 1TB UK

Tel: 01256 862201

Fax: 01256 860363

Email: admissions@lordwandsworth.org

Website: www.lordwandsworth.org

Head of School: Mr Adam Williams

Appointed: September 2015

School type: Coeducational Boarding & Day

Religious Denomination: Non-denominational

Age range of pupils: 11–18 years

No. of pupils enrolled as at 01/09/2017: 600

Fees per annum as at 01/09/2017:

Day: £19,650–£22,575

Weekly Boarding: £27,225–£30,600

Full Boarding: £28,140–£32,100

Average class size: Approx 19

Teacher/pupil ratio: 1:9

Northbourne Park School

Northbourne Park School is a co-educational independent day and boarding school for children between the ages of Nursery and 13. Set in over 100 acres of beautiful park and woodland in rural Kent, the school is within easy reach from central London, Eurostar and Gatwick Airport. Northbourne Park School provides children with a first-class education focussing on the individual needs of every child, inspiring them to succeed across a wide range of learning experiences. We are a school that offers each child freedom and space, together with countless opportunities to grow in confidence and succeed.

Academic

From the Nursery and Pre-Prep right through to the Prep School, Northbourne Park School is an environment where each and every child can flourish. Pupils gain confidence in their learning and through inspirational teaching from dedicated staff, and adapt well to an engaging and stimulating curriculum with a real sense of achievement. We focus on individual needs and consistently achieve academic excellence, with many of our pupils gaining scholarships to prestigious Senior Schools. The school's unique Language Programme helps every child develop foreign languages in an integrated learning environment. The result is a clear advantage when they move on to Senior Schools.

Sport

We are passionate about sport and through an excellent sports programme the pupils develop key skills and learn the importance of teamwork and leadership. There are many opportunities to try a variety of sports from traditional sports to the more diverse such as archery and trampolining.

Creative Arts

We nurture a love for all the Arts. Many pupils learn one or more instruments in our purpose-built Music suite. They have the opportunity to take part in the choir, band, orchestra, string and brass groups performing regularly within the school and in the local area. Other opportunities include LAMDA lessons, regular drama productions and Public Speaking that ensure the pupils are articulate and confident in their performances. Artistic talents are encouraged through a range of media including sculpture, costume design, film-making on iMacs and pottery.

Community

Pupils are provided with a first-class level of pastoral care in a safe and nurturing environment with a real family atmosphere. Our welcoming boarding community provides a home-from-home environment and a continuous boarding service at weekends throughout the term. Boarders enjoy regular excursions and activities, and the accompanied services to London and Paris provide opportunities for weekends at home. Northbourne Park School holds Tier 4 Status for non-European pupils requiring visas under the UK Visa and Immigration Service scheme.

Extra Curricular

We provide the pupils with a fun and extensive programme of afternoon clubs that help develop their interests and skills in hobbies that can endure long into adult life. Love of the outdoors and respect for the environment begins in the Pre-Prep and develops through into the Prep School with fun physical adventures. Whether they are playing in the woods, camping out overnight or following our pioneering Outdoor Education Programme, children love Northbourne Park life.

The children are at the heart of everything we do and it is important to us that they learn with confidence and enjoy each and every day at school. All prospective pupils are welcome and we offer a wide range of scholarships.

Every day is an Open Day at Northbourne Park School, come and visit us!

(Founded 1936)

Betteshanger, Deal, Kent CT14 0NW UK

Tel: 01304 611215/218

Fax: 01304 619020

Email: admissions@northbournepark.com

Website: www.northbournepark.com

Headmaster: Mr Sebastian Rees BA(Hons), PGCE, NPQH

Appointed: September 2015

School type: Coeducational Day & Boarding

Age range of pupils: 3–13

No. of pupils enrolled as at 01/09/2017: 149

Boys: *90* ***Girls:*** *59*

No. of boarders: 45

Fees per annum as at 01/09/2016:

Day: £7,632–£16,326

Weekly Boarding: £20,376

Full Boarding: £23,673

Average class size: Av 15

Teacher/pupil ratio: 1:9

Pangbourne College

A distinctive school that puts huge emphasis on self-discipline, teamwork and leadership. Caring and supportive, Pangbourne buzzes with activity and encourages every pupil to have a go and get involved. – Good Schools Guide

The personal development of Pangbourne's students is outstanding, meeting the College's aim to develop the character of all students. This is supported by an excellent, broad curriculum which enables students to progress academically and supports the development of the whole individual. – ISI Inspection Report

Pangbourne is a place where the individual matters. We have a beautiful site and excellent facilities, but first and foremost this is a 'people place'. We are committed to the personal development of our pupils in the fullest sense. They are encouraged to work hard towards academic success and we celebrate the results they achieve. Just as important is the development of their characters: confidence and values, creative and physical skills and an appreciation of who they are and what they can contribute to the world.

We are proud of our outstanding pastoral care and we take an integrated approach to caring for each pupil. We are not complacent about the challenges which young people face and we are always seeking to improve the support which we can provide. Pangbournians are encouraged not only to challenge themselves and reach their potential, but also to be happy and fulfilled. The College offers a comprehensive co-curricular programme which enables pupils to find their niche and thrive as their specific abilities are recognised and developed.

Our Flag Values of Kindness, Selflessness, Moral Courage, Initiative, Industry, Resilience, and Integrity underpin all we do as a College. They are rooted in our Christian ethos and go a long way to prepare our pupils for life's challenges and the responsibilities of adulthood. Our aim is to equip Pangbournians with the strongest possible foundations for their future.

The College is set in 230 acres within an Area of Outstanding Natural Beauty and rural Berkshire countryside, yet within easy reach of excellent transport connections. We are just 10 minutes from Junction 12 of the M4 motorway, and on the mainline rail network between Oxford (30 minutes) and London Paddington (45 minutes). Daily school transport services are available from Newbury, Basingstoke, Wantage and, from 2018, Henley and surrounding area.

We offer entry at 11+, 13+ and 16+, and occasionally into other year groups if space permits. The only way to experience the authentic Pangbourne is to come and visit us, enjoy a tour of the College and speak to pupils and staff here. They will give you real insight into what Pangbourne is today.

Scholarships and Bursaries are available.

(Founded 1917)

Pangbourne, Reading, Berkshire RG8 8LA UK

Tel: 0118 984 2101

Fax: 0118 984 1239

Email: registrar@pangbourne.com

Website: www.pangbourne.com

Headmaster: Thomas J C Garnier

School type: Coeducational Boarding & Day

Age range of pupils: 11–18

No. of pupils enrolled as at 01/09/2017: 410

Boys: 267 ***Girls:*** 143 ***Sixth Form:*** 143

Fees per annum as at 01/09/2017:

Day: £17,055–£24,036

Full Boarding: £24,021–£33,996

Part Boarding: £21,408 – £30,246

Average class size:

15-20 up to Year 5 (smaller sets for A levels)

Teacher/pupil ratio: 1:7

Reddam House Berkshire

The Reddam House philosophy is unlike any other and with a worldwide reputation for academic, cultural and sporting excellence. Reddam House Berkshire is a majestic school, in a beautiful, secure setting at the heart of the 125-acre estate – a truly inspirational environment.

Our philosophy is designed around the individual, giving pupils a large amount of freedom in how their schooling is organized, with personalised supervision and guidance from Reddam House committed teachers. Because we cater for children from just three months old to 18 years, we can offer a unique, seamless education to all and lasting friendships. Our co-educational, non-denominational formula is designed to inspire pupils to attain their maximum potential in a nurturing, progressive and academic environment.

We carefully select our teachers, who are specialists in their field, to ensure pupils get the very best guidance and advice throughout their schooling: we create happy, well-rounded children who love school and the school experience. In addition to an extensive range of subjects at GCSE and A-level, the EPQ (Extended Project Qualification) course in the Sixth Form allows our young people to further develop their research and communication skills. Light and airy classrooms, equipped with the latest in technology, provide an enhanced learning environment.

Public speaking is a timetabled lesson in Middle School and pupils can take part in local competitions. Both Dance and Music are an integral part of the Reddam House experience, giving pupils the chance to work their way through graded examinations, further increasing their confidence. Our magnificent theatre, with seating for up to 350, puts pupils centre stage in a wide range of productions, from plays and musicals, to dance shows and debates. We have a large dance studio, two smaller studios and a music school with numerous practice rooms. All pupils are encouraged to learn at least one musical instrument, and we have a wide range of music and instrumental groups, from jazz and rock to string ensembles and a chamber choir.

While pupils are encouraged and pushed to reach their full potential, the primary aim is for pupils to enjoy their sport and to participate. Regular fixtures take place in Rugby, Hockey, Football, Cricket, Netball, Rounders, Swimming, Tennis, Basketball, Golf, Cross Country and Judo.

Our dedicated Gymnasium Centre, with its sprung floor, encourages our award-winning gymnasts, who are already recognised at national and international level. The Duke of Edinburgh award and the Combined Cadet Force (CCF) are also both popular options.

Class tutors are fine-tuned to respond to pupils' individual emotional needs while our senior students act as mentors to the younger pupils and lead by example. Our Student Voice reports to the Sixth Form Judiciary – elected by a whole school vote – which meets regularly with the Principal to convey pupils' comments and feedback.

Alongside our Extended Day Options, which offer supervision and meals from 7.30am – 8.30pm, we offer the full range of boarding options – flexi, weekly and full. We currently have two boarding houses with separate accommodation for boys and girls aged 11-18, with resident house-parents, tutors and a matron. All rooms have recently been refurbished to a high standard and single rooms are en-suite. There is a full programme of activities for pupils who stay with us at weekends, with cinema and theatre trips, visits to places of interest and, of course, shopping!

(Founded 2015)

Bearwood Road, Sindlesham, Wokingham, Berkshire RG41 5BG UK

Tel: 0118 974 8300

Fax: 0118 977 3186

Email: registrar@reddamhouse.org.uk

Website: reddamhouse.org.uk

Principal: Mrs Tammy Howard

School type: Coeducational Boarding & Day

Religious Denomination: Non-denominational

Age range of pupils: 3 months–18 years

No. of pupils enrolled as at 01/09/2017: 480

Fees per annum as at 01/09/2017:

Day: £9,885–£16,800

Weekly Boarding: £26,310–£30,330

Full Boarding: £27,855–£31,875

THREE MONTHS TO 18 YEARS
WE SHALL GIVE BACK
REDDAM House

Seaford College

Seaford College is a coeducational independent day and boarding school for pupils aged 7 to 18, situated amid 400 acres of picturesque parkland in West Sussex. The College, with its excellent amenities and outstanding panoramic views, offers an inspirational environment that nurtures academic excellence, sporting success and creative talent.

The college uses its resources to provide and enhance educational, cultural, spiritual and social opportunities so that students leave school as confident, articulate and well-rounded individuals.

Pupils in the Preparatory School at Seaford College share the superb facilities with the Senior School and enjoy a seamless education from 7 to 18. The Prep School prides itself on its friendly atmosphere.

Boarding is offered to students from the age of 10 and many pupils elect to board in order to take full advantage of the social, sporting and extracurricular activities on offer. The College offers full boarding, weekly and flexible boarding in order to meet the needs of pupils and their parents.

A new boys' boarding house, has individual and twin bedrooms opened in 2011. Girls board in the historic Mansion house.

Recent developments include a new music suite, which consists of individual teaching and practice rooms, a computer and keyboard room, a sound-proofed band practice room and outdoor concert arena.

A state-of-the-art maths and science block offers the latest technologies and facilities, while the College has long been recognised as a centre of excellence for art and design. A large exhibition gallery is incorporated into the purpose-built arts faculty.

Seaford College offers outstanding sports facilities, including an all-weather water-based Astroturf hockey pitch, golf course and driving range. Students regularly play at county level.

All the usual academic subjects are taught, with 24 subjects available at GCSE and 28 at A level. The college also offers preparation for the Cambridge Pre-U.

Overseas students are expected to study English as a foreign language and study for the International Language Testing System, which is a requirement for UK university entrance.

Seaford sees its Sixth Form very much as a transitional stage. They have their own social centre, which has facilities for individual study, a lounge area and several classrooms where subjects such as Economics, Business Studies and Media Studies are taught.

Sixth Form boarders have individual study bedrooms, as well as their own common room. Students are divided into small tutor groups, but most commonly meet on a 1-to-1 basis with their tutors to discuss aspects of their work and progress.

Many of Seaford's Sixth Formers go on to university or higher education – all are equipped with self-confidence, as well as a passion for life and a willingness to succeed.

Entry to the College is by test and Trial Day and, although intake is non-selective, expectations are high. If your child is talented and enthusiastic, the College offers a range of scholarships at 11+, 13+ and Sixth Form, including Academic Studies, Music, Art and Sport.

The college has its own dedicated learning support unit, catering for pupils with dyslexia, dyscalculia and dyspraxia.

Whatever their chosen path, Seaford College seeks to prepare young people for adult life so that they have the personal skills and confidence to make it a success. The school allows its pupils to achieve their potential and beyond, inspiring personal ambition and success so that personal ambitions are achieved inside and outside the classroom.

(Founded 1884)

Lavington Park, Petworth, West Sussex GU28 0NB UK

Tel: 01798 867392

Fax: 01798 867606

Email: headmasterpa@seaford.org

Website: www.seaford.org

Headmaster: J P Green MA BA

School type: Coeducational Boarding & Day

Age range of pupils: 7–18

No. of pupils enrolled as at 01/09/2017: 732

Boys: 508 ***Girls:*** 224 ***Sixth Form:*** 194

No. of boarders: 194

Fees per annum as at 01/09/2017:

Day: £10,020–£20,775

Weekly Boarding: £20,880–£28,140

Full Boarding: £32,130

Average class size: 15-20

Teacher/pupil ratio: 1:9

St Lawrence College

Educating boys and girls from the age of 3 to 18 years, this safe and caring school is set in 45 acres of spacious, stunning grounds which house beautiful old architecture combined with new modern builds and facilities. Founded in 1879, it is home to 600 day and boarding pupils from local, UK and international families and welcomes boarders from 7 years of age.

St Lawrence is a medium-sized school – small enough to ensure that individual pupils receive the attention and care they require, but large enough to provide outstanding facilities. Visitors to the school often remark on the excellent atmosphere within its walls, on the friendly familiarity that exists between staff and pupils, and on the politeness that they see around them. The school is very proud of the level and quality of care that the staff provide to all of its pupils, especially those who are boarders and for whom the school is their home.

In the Classroom

Academic standards are high across the school and an extensive choice of GCSEs and A-levels are offered, with an excellent success rate of pupils going on to their first choice university. Our policy for keeping class sizes small ensures that our teachers can look after the individual needs of each pupil, so that high-flyers gain their places at the top universities, and our less able pupils develop skills in areas which will serve them well in the future.

Outside the Classroom

Sporting facilities are exceptional, and expert coaching is provided at all levels in a variety of disciplines including rugby, netball, hockey and cricket. The magnificent sports centre houses a fitness suite, squash courts, climbing wall, dance studio and a large sports hall for badminton, basketball, etc.

Music and drama flourish, enhanced by the school's 500-seat theatre, and there are many opportunities for pupils to perform. All pupils benefit from an extensive activities programme which in the Senior School includes the CCF (Combined Cadet Force) and a thriving Duke of Edinburgh's Award Scheme, as well as chess, archery, golf, fencing, football, sailing, horse riding, swimming, table tennis, musical theatre and many more activities.

Boarding at St Lawrence

The school is a vibrant and exciting place with a strong sense of community and superb pastoral care. Boarding is central to the school's life and is one of our great strengths. A wide range of evening and weekend activities are provided for boarders and additional events and fun day trips are organised.

We try very hard to provide a 'home-from-home' for our boarding pupils, both in terms of comfort and atmosphere. In recent years, a massive programme of investment has created some truly remarkable facilities for our boarders, and all rooms are en-suite. We are proud to say that most visiting families comment that our boarding facilities are the finest they have ever seen!

Location

The self-contained campus is situated within easy walking distance of the historic seaside town of Ramsgate. It has excellent transport links to the continent, being near both Dover and the Channel Tunnel. London is only 75 minutes away by high-speed rail link to St Pancras International. Gatwick and Heathrow are under two hours away.

Do come and visit – you and your family will receive a very warm welcome.

ST LAWRENCE
COLLEGE

(Founded 1879)

Ramsgate, Kent CT11 7AE UK

Tel: 01843 572931

Fax: 01843 572901

Email: admissions@slcuk.com

Website: www.slcuk.com

Principal: Mr Antony Spencer

School type: Coeducational Boarding & Day

Age range of pupils: 3–18

No. of pupils enrolled as at 01/09/2017: 640

Boys: 340 ***Girls:*** 300 ***Sixth Form:*** 115

No. of boarders: 210

Fees per annum as at 01/09/2017:

Day: £7,470–£18,495

Full Boarding: £26,055–£34,635

Teacher/pupil ratio: 1:8

Main Reception

St Neot's School

St Neot's, founded in 1888 is a happy, vibrant community for boys and girls from 1 to 13 years. The school is situated on the border of Hampshire and Berkshire and is set in 70 acres of beautiful grounds and woodland.

The school's educational philosophy is to inspire children to develop a love of learning in a supportive and happy environment, where each individual is encouraged to achieve their full academic potential and beyond. Children are motivated to discover their full range of talents and to develop the passion to pursue them. They are given the opportunity to embrace challenge, think creatively, develop self-confidence and foster empathy towards others, preparing them both intellectually and emotionally for success in the 21st Century.

We aim to provide the highest standards in teaching and learning within a well rounded educational experience and St Neot's has a very strong record of success in achieving Scholarships and Awards to numerous Senior Schools.

St Neot's is committed to providing a World of Opportunity in every aspect of school life. Stimulating learning environments ensure that engaged pupils work towards the highest academic standards whilst also enjoying a breadth of experience in sport, music, art, drama and dance.

Emphasis is placed on developing independence, self confidence, curiosity and collaboration. Forest School and Outdoor Education programmes encourage children of all ages to develop these attributes, which are so vital in the modern world. The St Neot's journey culminates in the Years 7 and 8 leadership programme, which draws together a mix of skills through the core elements of the Prep Schools Baccalaureate (PSB).

Physical Education is a strength of the school and our new sports complex, comprising sports hall, 25m indoor swimming pool, all-weather astro, cricket nets, hard tennis and netball courts, significantly supplement our extensive playing fields. There is also an on-site mountain bike track and a traversing wall. Judo, dance and tennis are taught by specialist coaches and there are many after school clubs and activities covering a wide range of interests. Holiday Clubs run in all school breaks and offer a wealth of opportunities, both sporting and creative.

St Neot's holds a Gold Artsmark award, giving recognition to our achievements in art, music, drama and dance. A number of plays, concerts and recitals take place throughout the school year for all age groups, either in the school grounds or the Performing Arts Centre.

Open Mornings take place termly and details of these can be found on the school website – www.stneotsprep.co.uk. We would also be delighted to arrange an individual tour and a meeting with the Head. Please contact Admissions on 0118 9739650 – e-mail – admissions@stneotsprep.co.uk

ST NEOT'S
PREPARATORY SCHOOL

(Founded 1888)

St Neot's Road, Eversley, Hampshire RG27 0PN UK

Tel: 0118 9739650

Email: admissions@stneotsprep.co.uk

Website: www.stneotsprep.co.uk

Head of School: Mrs Deborah Henderson

Appointed: September 2015

School type: Co-educational Day, Preparatory

Age range of pupils: 1–13 years

No. of pupils enrolled as at 01/09/2017: 327

Boys: 183 ***Girls:*** 144

Fees per annum as at 01/09/2017:

Day: £4,896–£14,994

Average class size: 18

Teacher/pupil ratio: 1:8

St. Andrew's School

St. Andrew's School was founded in 1937 and is a respected and thriving coeducational prep school, of around 300 children. Set in 11 acres of grounds approximately half a mile from Woking town centre, the School seeks to create a nurturing and happy environment of trust and support in which all pupils are encouraged and enabled to develop their skills, talents, interests and potential to the full – intellectually, physically and spiritually.

At St. Andrew's children feel secure and confident and are highly motivated to perform to the best of their ability in all aspects of school life. They are competitive without losing sight of their responsibility to share and they are justifiably proud of their school and their own personal achievements. We also place great emphasis on consideration for others. Courtesy and mutual respect underpins the behaviour policy at St. Andrew's and we aim to teach children about patience, empathy and unselfishness, whilst encouraging them to use their time wisely in an independent and self-reliant manner.

St. Andrew's School prides itself in providing a broad based curriculum that focuses on enabling our children to enjoy a full range of subjects. Educating the whole child is central to our ethos and, whilst academic standards are high, there are also real opportunities to develop their skills in art, music and sport together with a fantastic programme of after school activities. This is supported by specialist teaching facilities for all subjects including science, ICT, music and art. In our latest ISI inspection (Jan 2016) the school was rated 'excellent' in all areas and, with the benefit of individual attention and specialist teachers in all areas of the curriculum, the children are able to reach their full potential in a happy, caring and supportive environment.

When it is time to move on to senior schools at the end of Year 8, the children are prepared for entrance and scholarship exams to a wide range of independent senior schools and the school provides guidance and advice to parents on the senior school choices that best suit each individual child.

St. Andrew's is very proud of its excellent on-site facilities including sports pitches, all weather sports surface, tennis courts, cricket nets and a swimming pool. We are very fortunate to enjoy the benefits of carefully designed school grounds that meet the needs of the children's physical and social development. Main school games are football, hockey, cricket, netball and rounders. Other activities include rugby, cross-country running, swimming, tennis and athletics.

Children can be supervised at school from 8am and, through our extensive after-school activities programme for Year 3 and above, until 6-6.30 pm most evenings during the week. An after-school club is available from 4pm to 6pm (chargeable) for Pre-Prep, Year 3 and Year 4 children.

Children are assessed for entry into Year 2 and above. The school has a number of scholarships and bursaries available.

Don't just take our word for it, come and visit the school to see for yourself! We have three open days, one per term, but you are also welcome to visit the school at other times. Please contact the Headmaster's PA (Registrar) for more information and to arrange a visit. We look forward to welcoming you.

(Founded 1937)

Church Hill House, Horsell, Woking, Surrey GU21 4QW UK

Tel: 01483 760943

Fax: 01483 740314

Email: admin@st-andrews.woking.sch.uk

Website: www.st-andrews.woking.sch.uk

Headmaster: Mr A Perks

Appointed: 2008

School type: Coeducational Day Preparatory

Age range of pupils: 3–13

No. of pupils enrolled as at 01/09/2017: 313

Boys: 206 ***Girls:*** 107

Fees per annum as at 01/09/2017:

Day: £3,690–£14,520

Teacher/pupil ratio: 1:10

Sutton Valence School

Although steeped in more than 440 years of history and tradition, Sutton Valence School is innovative and passionate about developing its curriculum to extend the learning of every child. It is something we do very well, being in the top two per cent of schools nationally for the academic value we add to all our students. In recent years, the School has gone from strength-to-strength. Examination grades are consistently improving and our value added score is the best it has ever been. We are seeing students flourish within their passions and being stretched as they take on new challenges. Parental feedback is overwhelmingly positive, as one parent put it: 'All schools promise the earth, Sutton Valence delivers'.

None of this is by chance; the School leadership team is focused on continuous improvement and innovation. Our four journeys (Academic, Enrichment, Community and Leadership and Service) create bespoke challenges for each child that grow strengths and address weaknesses. We stretch our students to surpass their expectations, not just in exams, but their whole education.

Sutton Valence firmly believes in the strength of its four Journeys, where academic pursuits are supported by exciting and challenging enrichment opportunities, transferable leadership skills and positive character traits are developed and the School community supports and encourages all to achieve their potential. No child is the same as another and, through our Journeys, we enable our students to find their niche; this not only helps individual self-confidence but also inspires the pupils to apply their passion and self-discipline to other areas of School life. As they mature, they will grow in their determination and self-esteem, leaving the School as confident, charming and capable, but not arrogant, young adults.

(Founded 1576)

Junior: North Street, Sutton Valence, Kent ME17 3HL UK

Senior: Church Road, Chart Sutton, Kent ME17 3RF

Junior Tel: 01622 845200

Senior Tel: 01622 842117

Email: enquiries@svs.org.uk

Website: www.svs.org.uk

Headmaster: Bruce Grindlay MA Cantab, MusB, FRCO, CHM

Appointed: September 2009

Head of Prep: Claire Corkran MEd, BEd(Hons) Cantab

School type: Coeducational Day & Boarding

Religious Denomination: Church of England

Age range of pupils: 11–18

No. of pupils enrolled as at 01/09/2017: 570

Fees per term as at 01/09/2017:

Junior Tuition: £5,280 (First Form) – £6,000 (Second Form)

Senior Tuition: £6,895

Full Boarding (plus tuition): £3,060 (Junior)– £3,845 (Senior)

Weekly Boarding (plus tuition): £2,670 (Junior,)– £3,090 (Senior)

Prep Fees: £2,900 (Nursery)– £4,455 (Year 6)

Average class size: 17

Teacher/pupil ratio: 1:9

Wellington College

Wellington College, founded in 1853, is arguably the UK's leading coeducational boarding and day school. Its pupils develop a unique identity inspired by intellectual curiosity, true independence, a generous and far-reaching inclusivity and the courage to be properly and unselfishly individual.

The College is celebrated for its achievements both in and out of the classroom and its sporting, artistic and dramatic provision are second to none. Stellar examination results, outstanding provision across all co-curricular areas, a raft of national accolades, and an exclusively 'excellent' 2014 ISI inspection report contribute to the College's national and international reputation.

Wellingtonians study GCSEs, followed by the IB Diploma or A-levels: whichever route they take, results are superb. In 2017 the average A-level outcome was AAA, and the College's IB average of 39 yet again made Wellington one of the UK's highest achieving boarding schools to offer the IB Diploma. Over the past four years, half of IB pupils have secured scores of above 40 and 15 have achieved a perfect 45, including four in 2017. 77 Wellingtonians have been offered places at Oxford or Cambridge over the past three years and over 20 pupils move on to US universities each year, many to Ivy League institutions.

The College has an outstanding reputation in sport and 31 different activities are offered at Wellington. National team and individual success this year came in Hockey, Rugby/Rugby 7s, Golf, Triathlon, Equestrian, Fencing, Real Tennis, Skiing, Chess, Rackets, Lacrosse, Girls' Football, Modern Pentathlon and Shooting: a staggering number of individuals gained International or National honours across 14 different sports. A relay team swam the English Channel for the fifth year in a row.

Performing Arts are equally strong. Music and Drama are stunning, with nearly two-thirds of pupils taking lessons in musical instruments or LAMDA. Recent achievements include: the Orchestra playing at LSO St Luke's, the Choir tour to Spain, an annual musical (this year was *Anything Goes*), contemporary Shakespeare productions and imaginative and inclusive junior plays. Dance enjoys a purpose-designed studio and two spectacular shows each year play to packed houses. It was no surprise that Wellington was awarded Artsmark Gold by the Arts Council. Clubs and societies range from Amnesty International to the fully co-ed Field Gun team, from WTV (Wellington's own television company) and its pupil-run Radio Station, Dukebox to a full range of more traditional pastimes such as Photography, Cooking and Model United Nations. Wellington's new 1,400-seater Performing Arts Centre will be completed later this year.

Leadership and service to others are also central to the College's core values: co-curricular activities include CCF, Duke of Edinburgh, and a pioneering Service Learning scheme, embedding academic study within community service projects. Wellington's family of schools include its prep school, Eagle House, four schools in China, and sponsored Primary and Secondary Academies in Wiltshire; schools in Thailand and Abu Dhabi will soon follow. Wellington was the first HMC school to be accredited as a Teaching School and now partners 18 local state schools. All of this provides pupils and staff with meaningful opportunities for partnership and service within the national and international communities.

Further information including details about Visitors' Days can be found on the website and the Admissions Office can be contacted on +44 (0)1344 444013.

WELLINGTON
COLLEGE

(Founded 1853)

Duke's Ride, Crowthorne, Berkshire RG45 7PU UK

Tel: +44 (0)1344 444000

Fax: +44 (0)1344 444002

Email: admissions@wellingtoncollege.org.uk

Website: www.wellingtoncollege.org.uk

Master: Mr Julian Thomas

Appointed: September 2015

Director of IB: Mr Richard Atherton

School type: Coeducational Boarding & Day

Religious Denomination: Church of England

Age range of pupils: 13–18

No. of pupils enrolled as at 01/09/2017: 1040

Boys: 635 ***Girls:*** 405 ***Sixth Form:*** 455

No. of boarders: 845

Fees per annum as at 01/09/2017:

Day: £27,930–£32,085

Full Boarding: £38,220

Average class size:

Lower + Middle = 20 Upper School = 12

Teacher/pupil ratio: 1:7

South-West

EF Academy Torbay

EF Academy International Boarding Schools prepares students for a global future with a superior secondary school education in the U.S. or UK. At EF Academy, we believe in every student's ability to succeed. We empower them to do so through our renowned curricula, as well as quality one-on-one relationships with teachers and mentors alike. With a student body made up of 75 different nationalities, multilingualism and intercultural exchange are built into every course, which helps distinguish our students' academic credentials to both university admissions officers and future employers.

The School

Our private high school is situated in a modern-day castle on a hill overlooking the sea and Torquay, a quiet town on England's sunny south coast. The art studio has large windows that face the sea – perfect for landscape study – and the state-of-the-art science labs are ideal for conducting experiments and research in class and with study groups. The community, made up of students, school staff and locals, has often been described as a family and our students feel very much at home in this encouraging, international learning environment.

Students live in on-campus residences with their classmates and house parents. House parents look after the students and ensure that they are safe and comfortable when they are not in class.

Academics

At EF Academy Torbay, students follow the IGCSE program in their first two years of secondary school and can choose from the IB Diploma or A-Level program in their last two years. They benefit from our small class sizes and the interactive learning styles our experienced teachers employ in their lessons.

Personal tutors provide one-on-one individualized support and guidance. Each student is assigned a personal tutor whose role is to monitor the student's academic progress and general welfare. Students are encouraged to nurture their talents and develop new skills and confidence. The guidance counselors support students in everything from managing homework and selecting the right courses, to helping them overcome homesickness or culture shock.

University Placement

EF Academy Torbay students have been accepted to universities such as Durham, Warwick and Exeter. They have also gone on to study Business at the University of Bath, ranked number one for Business in the UK, and Accounting and Finance at the University of Leeds, also ranked number one for that subject in the UK. Our dedicated university advisor works together with our students to help them explore program and career options, research universities in the UK, U.S. and their home country, and prepare for entrance exams and interviews.

Co-curricular Activities

Students at EF Academy Torbay have access to a wide range of co-curricular activities. From subject-specific academic groups and competitions to sports and arts, there is an option for every student. On weekends, students often enjoy exploring nearby Babbacombe Beach, sailing in the harbor or rock climbing with a guide. The school's enrichment coordinator also arranges teacher-led excursions for students on the weekends so they have the opportunity to experience the culture of the community and the country in which they are studying.

INTERNATIONAL
BOARDING SCHOOLS

Castle Road, Torquay, Devon TQ1 3BG UK

Tel: +41 (0) 43 430 4095

Email: iaeurope@ef.com

Website: www.ef.com/academy

Head of School: Mr. Mark Howe

School type: Coeducational Boarding

Age range of pupils: 14–19

No. of pupils enrolled as at 01/09/2017: 270

Fees per annum as at 01/09/2017:

IB Diploma/A-Levels: £24,450

IGCSE: £23,850

EF Academy

Exeter Cathedral School

Exeter Cathedral School is a leading independent day and boarding Prep School for girls and boys aged 2½-13.

Founded in the 12th century as a choir school, ECS now educates approximately 270 pupils. 36 of these are the boy and girl Choristers of Exeter Cathedral, who continue the centuries-old pattern of leading the daily sung worship in the Cathedral. Nowadays, we offer a fully-rounded Prep School education to pupils from a variety of backgrounds and with a range of talents and interests, whether they be sporting, academic, artistic or musical.

We have an enviable location (right in the heart of the city and yet nestled safely in the lee of the Cathedral); small class sizes, allowing us to really know each and every pupil as an individual; a proven track record of securing places and scholarships (academic, art, music, performing arts, sport) to a range of leading senior schools; and a firm commitment to being a forward-thinking Prep School with traditional values. We aim to offer an outstanding Prep School experience and are proud of our commitment to educating the 'whole child': we seek to do this by providing a nurturing, purposeful, exciting and gently-Christian environment in which each child is known as an individual, and in which each child is mindful of, and grateful for, those around them, and aware of the part that they and others play in building their community.

Our purpose-built Nursery building was opened in 2015 and is housed in our Pre-Prep Department in the Cathedral Close. Run by our specialist Head of Nursery and a team of Key Workers, the ECS Nursery offers a first-rate Nursery Education which encourages children to explore, to question, to discover and to build confidence. Children spend 2 years in our Nursery before moving across the playground into our Reception classes.

Our Pre-Prep is housed in a former Canonry in the Cathedral Close, nestled safely between the ancient city wall and the Bishop's Garden. Children transfer across the playground into Reception, before moving up to Year 1 and then Year 2. Our dedicated and highly-qualified staff, led by our Head of Pre-Prep, work with the children (c15 per class) and families to build independence, enquiry, curiosity and a genuine love of learning.

Our Prep School is located right next to the Cathedral: our main site is on Palace Gate and other departments are clustered together in the corner of the Cathedral Green. In the younger years, the core subjects are taught by Form Teachers and our creative curriculum is delivered by in-house specialists. Our senior pupils receive Common Entrance preparation from experienced subject specialists. At 13, pupils move on to a range of leading Senior Schools, many with scholarships and awards: in 2016, 100% of Year 8 pupils secured a place/scholarship at their first-choice senior school.

We expect high standards from our pupils and our staff, and we share a commitment to rigorous academic endeavour; outstanding pastoral care and individualized attention; an exciting range of extra-curricular opportunities; a world-class musical heritage; and to working with families to help each child flourish and thrive.

Above all, we are a school where *people* matter, and where staff and families work in partnership to help children acquire the right habits for life.

UT VOCE ITA VITA

(Founded 1179)

The Chantry, Palace Gate, Exeter, Devon EX1 1HX UK

Tel: 01392 255298

Email: admissions@exetercs.org

Website: www.exetercs.org

Headmaster: James Featherstone

Appointed: January 2016

School type: Co-educational Day & Boarding

Age range of pupils: 2½–13

No. of pupils enrolled as at 01/09/2017: 257

Boys: 131 ***Girls:*** 125

No. of boarders: 23

Fees per annum as at 01/09/2017:

Day: £6,915–£11,535

Full Boarding: £17,700–£18,735

Average class size: 15

Hazlegrove Prep School

Whether you are thinking of making the big move to the country or looking for a prep school where your children can experience a genuine childhood away from the hothouse pressures so prevalent in London and the South East, do come and visit us at Hazlegrove. Located in 200 acres of parkland just off the A303 in Somerset, we are committed to providing the very best all-round education to the boys and girls in our care.

In our rapidly changing and demanding world, it is vital that our children experience a breadth of opportunity that encourages them to be independent thinkers and confident problem-solvers so that they are ready to embrace whatever challenges lie ahead. At Hazlegrove we do this right from the start where even the very youngest pupils in the Nursery and Pre-Prep will enjoy specialist teaching for Forest School, Music, Drama, Tennis and Games whilst establishing the building blocks of English and Maths with experienced classroom teachers. As the children move up through the school, French, Latin and Mandarin are introduced as is Design Technology (including digital design and realisation), Food Technology and Outdoor Education which covers a myriad of activities from archery and kayaking to putting up tents and looking after animals on the mini-farm. Sport, Music and Drama all play a significant part with countless matches (from local to national level), concerts nearly every week and every child being involved in a major dramatic production every year. We want the stage to hold no fears whether they are presenting to peers or performing to a wider audience.

This wealth of opportunity does not come at the expense of academic endeavour and all pupils work towards the 13+ Common Entrance or Academic Scholarship so they move on, appropriately equipped, to a wide range of destinations from local schools to prestigious national institutions. The foundations of learning are firmly laid in the pre-prep. On joining the prep school (progression to which is automatic), the children will start moving around the school for subjects such as science and by the time they reach Year 6 (aged 10) they can expect to have specialist teaching for every subject. Setting and streaming ensure that all pupils are working at the appropriate level and a highly accredited learning support department is on hand to help those children who would benefit from a little extra help.

Fundamental to success is providing a caring, structured and secure environment where the children can focus their energy on being the best that they can be – not looking over their shoulders and worrying about what others think. The secret is not just in having very-well qualified staff who are inspirational teachers but them being the sort of people who can be excellent role-models and who can build strong relationships with your children. This applies not just to the classroom, but throughout all aspects of life from the thriving boarding houses via the tutoring system to the extensive extra-curricular program.

We want all our children to leave Hazlegrove having enjoyed a proper childhood as confident (not arrogant) individuals who are ready to make the most of the opportunities at their next schools – the fabulous feedback we get suggests we certainly achieve this. Do please come and meet us either by appointment or at one of our many open mornings – we would be delighted to meet you.

(Founded 1947)

Hazlegrove House, Sparkford, Somerset BA22 7JA UK

Tel: +44 (0)1963 442606

Email: admissions@hazlegrove.co.uk

Website: www.hazlegrove.co.uk

Headmaster: Mr R B Fenwick MA

Appointed: September 2002

School type: Coeducational Boarding & Day

Age range of pupils: 2–13

No. of pupils enrolled as at 01/09/2017: 355

Boys: 192 ***Girls:*** 163

No. of boarders: 95

Fees per term as at 01/09/2017:

Day: £2,843–£5,764 per term

Full Boarding: £6,686–£8,531 per term

Average class size: 14.5

Teacher/pupil ratio: 1:11

King's School

King's School, Plymouth, aces School Inspection Service report

Staff and students alike are celebrating at King's School & Nursery, in the Mannamead area of Plymouth, after the school passed its School Inspection Service (SIS) report with – quite literally – outstanding results across the board.

The independently run, co-educational school for children up to the age of 11 achieved an 'outstanding' rating (the highest available) in all categories across the SIS' comprehensive report, including: the quality of education; pupils' personal development; safeguarding pupils' welfare, health and safety; leadership, management and governance and the effectiveness of the Early Years' provision. The achievement is no mean feat for any school, and one that requires plenty of planning, organisation and an excellent team of teaching staff to ensure each and every pupil has every opportunity to reach and exceed their potential.

Itself an independent body, the SIS is a respected institution and one that exists to *"provide high-quality inspection of specific groups of independent schools, on behalf of the Department for Education (DfE)"*, effectively fulfilling the same role as Ofsted does for other organisations.

Speaking of the school's students in the report, Reporting Inspector Andrew Rickett said *"They make excellent progress in their learning and achieve standards that are at least in line with national averages and which are exceeded by a significant number of pupils"*.

King's School is no stranger to success. The South West school was founded back in 1989 and has gone from strength to strength ever since, having achieved the same excellent report from SIS back in 2013.

Founded on a core of strong Christian values, King's School takes pride in instilling a sense of care and respect for others in every child taught there, offering a friendly, family-focused environment for children to learn, grow, and of course, play. *"I believe that education should be a partnership between caring parents and a caring school"*, says Headteacher, Jane Lee. *"School and family life should be complementary, working to the same end and helping each child grow into a well-rounded person."*

By keeping class sizes under control, teachers are able to give each child the care and attention they deserve. The children are given the space they need to develop their own sense of self, creative and critical thinking and the discipline they'll need later on in life to become well-rounded adults – all in the comfort and safety of a warm, friendly and structured learning environment.

The school also boast an impressive plethora of extracurricular activities to develop the children's learning and social skills, from sports such as martial arts and fencing to creative endeavours such as street jazz, guitar and piano lessons.

Visit Website for open days throughout the year.

(Founded 1989)

Hartley Road, Mannamead, Plymouth, Devon PL3 5LW UK

Tel: 01752 771789

Fax: 01752 770826

Email: school.secretary@kingsschool-plymouth.co.uk

Website: www.kingsschool-plymouth.co.uk

Headteacher: Mrs Jane Lee

School type: Coeducational Day

Age range of pupils: 3–11

No. of pupils enrolled as at 01/09/2017: 142

Fees per annum as at 01/09/2017:

Day: £5,895–£7,440

Average class size: 15

PREFECT

Kingsley School

Welcome to Kingsley School

There are many reasons students could fall in love with Kingsley School, an independent co-educational boarding and day school located in Bideford on the banks of the River Torridge in North Devon.

One reason could be location – Kingsley is set in 25 acres of playfields and woodland, surrounded by stunning countryside, and just five minutes from popular surfing beaches. And another reason could be the school's strong academic tradition – at Kingsley every sixth form student typically goes on to university, including top-tier higher education institutes like Oxford and Cambridge.

But ultimately our students rate the opportunity to find their place, the exceptional support they receive and the welcome as the prime reasons they just can't see themselves going anywhere else but Kingsley.

Kingsley School is an inclusive day and boarding school where every child is important and is treated with dignity and respect. As a relatively small school of around 400 boys and girls, Kingsley's atmosphere is like that of a large family where everybody knows each other well.

The school's philosophy encourages personal qualities such as courage, generosity, honesty, imagination, tolerance and kindness. In addition, we develop the students' wider interests and skills in sport, music, art, and drama. Kingsley also has a national reputation for its Learning Development Centre which provides additional support for students with moderate learning needs. Overall, a Kingsley education develops the individual character and talents of each and every student both inside and outside the classroom.

Becoming part of the family: The boarding houses at Kingsley help form part of the family atmosphere at the school. Students live in three comfortable and well-equipped houses in the school's grounds; two for boys and one for girls. Each house has 30-40 students who are supervised by two teachers and their families who live in the houses as well.

Sport and Clubs: Sport includes traditional sports plus judo, handball and gymnastics squads competing at a National level. As part of the National Theatre Connections programme, the school drama cast performed at the Theatre Royal, Plymouth and the National Theatre, London this year. Popular extra-curricular clubs include the Duke of Edinburgh's Award Scheme, orchestra, computing, art, film making, choir and surfing.

Transport: we run an accompanied coach service to and from Heathrow Airport and Bristol Airport at the beginning and end of each term. Weekly boarding options with transport to London and the South East.

Headmaster Pete Last said: "As a parent, I know that choosing the right school can be daunting, but Kingsley is a place which really does recognise that each child has individual needs, with their own set of skills and talents that deserve to be developed. Smaller, more attentive classes with caring and supportive teachers gives the school a familial feel. I am proud of each and every student, their progress, support of one another and their outstanding personal achievements."

Do follow us on social media

Facebook: Kingsley School Bideford
Instagram: Kingsley School
Twitter: @KSBideford
Pinterest: Kingsley School
YouTube: Kingsley School Bideford
www.kingsleyschoolbideford.co.uk

(Founded 2009)

Northdown Road, Bideford, Devon EX39 3LY UK

Tel: 01237 426200

Fax: 01237 425981

Email: admissions@kingsleyschoolbideford.co.uk

Website: www.kingsleyschoolbideford.co.uk

Headmaster: Mr Pete Last

Appointed: January 2017

Head of the Prep School: Mr Andrew Trythall

School type: Coeducational Day & Boarding

Age range of pupils: 0–18

No. of pupils enrolled as at 01/09/2017: 395

No. of boarders: 100

Fees per term as at 01/09/2017:

Day: From £1,950 per term

Weekly Boarding: From £5,495 per term

Full Boarding: From £7,095 per term

Average class size: 14

Teacher/pupil ratio: 1:9

West Midlands

Denstone College

Achievement, confidence and happiness are central to the College philosophy, with pupils always encouraged to aim high and reach their full potential.

We offer a rounded education, where proper emphasis is placed on academic achievement, but where a wide range of other opportunities ensures that every individual finds and develops his or her own talents. Denstonians emerge with a degree of self-esteem and confidence that is only possible after years of opportunity and challenge, both academic and extracurricular. The College site of over 100 acres is located in magnificent countryside, yet is well served by road, rail and air. We welcome parents and their children to visit us and experience a taste of the Denstone education.

Three-school structure

At the heart of our approach to educating young people is the 'three-school structure'. Unusual in traditional independent schools, this is a structure that allows our three different age groups to live, work and socialise in their own unique areas. It is based on the fact that 18-year-olds and the under-13s have very different needs. The traditional house system runs happily alongside this structure, and all its best features remain. House loyalty and spirit are as strong as ever in competitions, sport, music and drama.

Facilities

In recent years the College has benefited from a £10m development programme, with a new Music School and additional classrooms opened in September 2010. Further extensive classroom facilities and the Adamson's sports complex were completed and opened in June 2012. Then in September 2013 the doors opened to a beautiful library which is at the heart of teaching and learning at Denstone.

In addition a brand new classroom block, housing Maths and Modern Foreign Languages has just been completed and will be in use by September 2017.

The day and boarding accommodation undergoes regular improvement and redecoration, and impressive language and IT teaching facilities have been developed, along with general classroom refurbishments to a high standard.

A large sports hall allows for a wide range of minority and unusual sports. Other recent improvements include a second Astroturf, and all weather cricket facilities.

Academic focus

Pupils are given every support and opportunity to realise their full academic potential, with progress being monitored closely through a highly developed system of tutors, reports and grade sheets. We provide a purposeful environment with skilled teachers, where high standards are expected and pupil/teacher ratios are very favourable.

Opportunities

A Denstone education gives students more choices and greater opportunities to expand their horizons. Frequent trips are a feature of our calendar, and a programme of more than 40 activities and an excellent record in the Duke of Edinburgh's Award Scheme also help to ensure that Denstonians are always busy. Our sporting history is outstanding with College teams county champions and national finalists many times over. We have a modern sports hall, swimming pool, two all-weather AstroTurfs, fives courts and an English Golf Union (EGU)-affiliated golf course.

"Being a Denstonian gives you more chances in life… there's no limit to what you can do." Sixth-former

(Founded 1868)

Uttoxeter, Staffordshire ST14 5HN UK

Tel: 01889 590484

Fax: 01889 590744

Email: admissions@denstonecollege.net

Website: www.denstonecollege.org

Headmaster: Mr David Derbyshire MSc, BA

Appointed: 1996

School type: Coeducational Boarding & Day

Age range of pupils: 11–18

No. of pupils enrolled as at 01/09/2017: 618

Boys: 368 ***Girls:*** 250 ***Sixth Form:*** 202

No. of boarders: 197

Fees per annum as at 01/09/2017:

Day: £12,693–£15,342

Weekly Boarding: £18,387–£20,679

Full Boarding: £18,387–£26,712

Average class size: Less than 20

Teacher/pupil ratio: 1:11

JOSH RUSSELL
CAPTAIN OF SCHOOL

King Edward VI High School for Girls

Founded in 1883, King Edward VI High School for Girls is one of the country's premier day schools, achieving outstanding GCSE and A Levels which place it consistently amongst the highest-performing day schools in the country. KEHS offers girls a richly varied and exciting education in a friendly, nurturing environment. It has the capacity to transform the lives of the bright, multi-talented girls who come here from an extraordinary range of backgrounds.

As a close-knit, caring community, KEHS is able to offer individual attention and support – whether a girl is a gifted mathematician, linguist or scientist, an accomplished musician or a talented sportswoman. As one parent put it: "KEHS does difference well", and our liberal, tolerant ethos and respect for diversity, allows students to flourish.

KEHS aims to support girls to become resilient, confident young women, prepared for the challenges of modern life in further education and employment. We believe KEHS offers the best possible preparation for university life and beyond, thanks to the academic rigour and the intellectual confidence instilled in our girls through the outstanding teaching and the wide range of experiences on offer.

Last year saw one of our most successful sets of results ever:

GCSE results 2016

- 75% A*
- 93% of grades were at A*/ A
- 40% of girls achieved 10 or more A*
- 68% achieved all A*/A

A Level results 2016

- 31% A*
- 76% A*/A
- 91.4% A*/B
- 74% of girls achieved 3 or more A Levels at A*/ A

The majority of girls join King Edward VI High School for Girls in the Thirds (Year 7). Each year around 96 girls join us from a wide variety of backgrounds and schools.

Entrance examinations for the Thirds (Year 7) take place the year before entry, at the beginning of October. Registration opens at Easter and closes two weeks before the entrance examination takes place.

Girls wishing to join the Sixth Form, are invited to apply in Year 11 between September and January. Most are invited to visit school and to attend an academic interview; we make conditional offers on the basis of the application and the interview.

Our Governors' Assisted Places Scheme aims to ensure that girls who would benefit from an education at KEHS can come to the school irrespective of parental income. The scheme is means-tested and parents wishing to apply for fee remission must complete and return a statement of income annually.

We also offer academic scholarships to recognise girls who excel in our 11+ entrance examinations and 16+ applications. These scholarships are independent of parental income, and can be combined with Assisted Places for exceptional candidates.

To understand what makes us so distinctive – the intellectual curiosity, the inspirational teaching and the excitement of so many bright, creative people working together – you need to experience it first-hand; meet our amazing girls and staff and see for yourself the unique blend of tradition and innovative thinking which lie at the heart of KEHS.

Further information is available at www.kehs.org.uk.

KING EDWARD VI
HIGH SCHOOL FOR GIRLS

(Founded 1883)

Edgbaston Park Road, Birmingham, West Midlands B15 2UB UK

Tel: 0121 472 1834

Fax: 0121 471 3808

Email: admissions@kehs.co.uk

Website: www.kehs.org.uk

Principal: Ms Ann Clark

Appointed: 2013

School type: Girls' Day

Age range of girls: 11–18

No. of pupils enrolled as at 01/09/2017: 577

Sixth Form: 164

Fees per annum as at 01/09/2017:

Day: £12,402

Average class size: 20

Teacher/pupil ratio: 1:12

King's High School for Girls

King's High is an independent GSA girls' school comprising up to 650 pupils, ages of 11 to 18 years. Judged 'Excellent' in all areas in our recent ISI inspection report, King's High has an enviable academic reputation coupled with an unusually wide range of supra-curricular activities.

Best of Both Worlds

We believe that our girls obtain the best of both worlds, being educated within a single-sex environment, whilst reaping co-educational benefits from our close links with Warwick School, our brother school in the Warwick Independent Schools Foundation. A range of optional co-curricular activities is on offer in conjunction with Warwick School, together with a Joint Activities Programme in the Sixth Form.

We strive to provide an exceptional educational environment, especially tailored to girls, where each girl will flourish, growing into a well-rounded, well-educated, confident, spirited and compassionate young woman. This was recognised in the ISI Report: *'Pupils' exceptional achievements cross a very wide range of academic, creative and sporting activities.'*

Outstanding teachers who inspire the girls in their subjects are key to achieving this. Class sizes vary by Key Stage, generally being smaller further up the school to reflect the more individual needs of girls as they approach public examinations. In 2017, for all independent girls' schools, King's was ranked 29th at GCSE and in 72nd at A Level.

King's High is situated in the heart of Warwick in a beautiful, historic setting. Our modern facilities are extensive, incorporating all that would be expected and much more. In January 2017, Dame Lynne Brindley, DBE opened our renovated Sixth Form Centre and Study area and our new Library and Innovation Centre, as collaborative, learning, study and research spaces.

Project One Campus

Building has commenced on 'Project One Campus', a £30 million development which will see King's High relocated to the Myton Road campus joining Warwick School and our sister school, Warwick Preparatory School, on the same site.

Our pupils will benefit from the new state-of the art buildings, playgrounds and playing fields, with a 4G sports pitch, connected by interlinking, tree-lined walkways and set amidst landscaped courtyards. The project includes a new King's High School building, a new music building for King's and Warwick Preparatory School, new play spaces for Warwick Prep, improvements and extension to the Bridge Sports Centre and a new shared Sixth Form Centre, including a first-class Careers Zone, with Warwick School.

Aspire, Achieve Enjoy

King's High is committed to providing an enjoyable, safe and stimulating environment in which girls will grow into confident and secure young women. We cater for a wide range of girls with individual skills, needs and interests, placing immense value on the importance of personal choice and happiness. In addition to the support of all members of staff, each pupil receives specific pastoral care from her form tutor and her Head of Key Stage, under the guidance of our Deputy Head (Pastoral) and the Head Master. Together with our Matron and our Well-Being Mentor, these members of staff deal with the key areas of health, day-to-day well-being and specific pastoral, academic and recreational guidance.

We respond to particular needs flexibly and positively, looking to fully support and develop each girl's life skills, as well as her talents.

Our School motto, "Aspire, Achieve, Enjoy," celebrates the enjoyment, fun and accomplishment our girls enjoy at King's.

(Founded 1879)

Smith Street, Warwick, Warwickshire CV34 4HJ UK

Tel: 01926 494485

Fax: 01926 403089

Email: enquiries@kingshighwarwick.co.uk

Website: www.kingshighwarwick.co.uk

Head Master: Mr Richard Nicholson MA (Oxon)

Appointed: September 2015

School type: Girls' Day

Age range of girls: 11–18 years

Average class size: Av 16

Teacher/pupil ratio: 1:9

Lucton School

Small classes, talented and committed teachers, a friendly atmosphere and a wonderful rural location combine to provide an outstanding, all-round educational experience at Lucton.

An Oxford University admissions tutor commented that the typical thing about Lucton students is that there is no typical student – they are very much individuals! What they do have in common is that they leave us confident in their abilities and strengths, ready to embrace opportunities and play their part.

They also achieve excellent results at A-level and GCSE and secure an impressive range of university places. The School is justly proud of its remarkable added-value scores and its ability to draw out the full potential of every individual.

A safe and secure location

Founded in 1708, the School is set in a safe, healthy location in 55 acres of beautiful Herefordshire countryside. There is a good mix of day pupils, weekly boarders and full boarders. Many team and individual sports are offered and boarders enjoy a wealth of weekend activities – sporting, cultural, social and just good fun – all included in the fees.

Senior boarders have individual rooms – although some younger ones prefer to share – and pastoral care at Lucton is second to none. Overseas students may use the School's free airport buses at the beginning and end of term.

Strong academic record

Offering a wide range of GCSE and A-level subjects, Lucton has a strong academic record and an established tradition of getting the best possible results from each pupil. We accept mixed ability students, yet over the last two years A-level results have averaged 80% A–C. In 2017 the A-level results were over 30% A* to A grades and all leavers have gained places at their first choice universities.

A unique feature is Lucton's 'Access to A-level' course, which also serves as a Pre-IB course, designed to provide overseas students with a grounding in a range of subjects and incorporating accelerated learning of English – ultimately preparing them for entry to the best courses at the best universities.

Excellent facilities

Facilities include junior and senior libraries, science laboratories, ICT rooms, a design and technology workshop, sports hall, tennis courts, indoor swimming pool, many games fields and Equestrian Centre. Senior students enjoy their own sixth-form centre, including library, IT suite, comfortable common room and quiet study area.

Admission can take place at any time of year by interview and assessment. The School offers discounts to Forces families.

In a previous boarding inspection, Lucton School was awarded 'Outstanding' for Equality and Diversity, an excellent reflection of how well boarders from all backgrounds are made welcome at Lucton. In the latest whole school inspection, along with many other categories, boarding was rated as 'Excellent'.

(Founded 1708)

Lucton, Herefordshire HR6 9PN UK

Tel: 01568 782000

Fax: 01568 782001

Email: admissions@luctonschool.org

Website: www.luctonschool.org

Headmistress: Mrs Gill Thorne MA

Appointed: 2003

School type: Coeducational Day & Boarding

Religious Denomination: Christian

Age range of pupils: 1–18

No. of pupils enrolled as at 01/09/2017: 330

No. of boarders: 92

Fees per term as at 01/09/2017:

Day: £3,205–£4,440 per term

Weekly Boarding: £7,205–£8,515 per term

Full Boarding: £9,295–£10,120 per term

Teacher/pupil ratio: 1:8

Mander Portman Woodward – Birmingham

MPW Birmingham was founded in 1980 with the goal of ensuring that students experience an education based on the Oxford and Cambridge tutorial system. This means that lessons are more relaxed and informal than a typical school, but are also academically stimulating and demanding. With fewer than ten students in any class, lessons are intensive but rewarding with plenty of opportunity for individual attention and personalised teaching.

MPW Birmingham guides students in their learning by encouraging them to focus on our model of success: aspiration, attitude, attendance, application and achievement. We help students obtain results that all too often they never thought were possible. With almost 30 subjects to choose from at A level and many at GCSE, MPW Birmingham provides a breadth of study opportunity that is unique for a small college. MPW helps students demystify the examination process and develop both the technical skills and academic knowledge needed to perform well under timed conditions. We offer all of our students the opportunity to sit weekly assessments enabling students to perfect examination technique.

We run a university support programme that values every student in equal measure regardless of aspiration; we treat all students as though they are elite. We prepare students for a range of courses including medicine, dentistry and Oxbridge and ensure that they are well equipped to cope with the demands of university life.

Students benefit from outstanding pastoral care with each student being allocated a Personal Tutor. This builds upon our core values of diligence, respect, tolerance and care. We expect our students to work hard but we also expect to provide more support to our students than they would receive at other schools. Our culture is one based on high expectations but one that is both nurturing and unpretentious. We run a non-compulsory enrichment programme in which many students participate, developing both sporting and cultural interests. There is no glass ceiling in MPW Birmingham and we strive to enable all students to reach their potential and use their talents without inhibition.

Our mission is to be one of the leading colleges of its type within the country, enabling students to develop confidence, maturity, knowledge and skills, turning academic aspirations into reality. MPW helps build the character of students enabling them to develop good self-discipline regarding work, intellectual curiosity and a sense of duty regarding community. Our best ambassadors are our students and we are rightly proud of what they achieve with us and what they go on to achieve afterwards. We change lives for the better and help bring about progress and success. Irrespective of where a student is starting from, MPW helps young people achieve special things.

M|P|W

Mander Portman Woodward

(Founded 1980)

17-18 Greenfield Crescent, Edgbaston, Birmingham, West Midlands B15 3AU UK

Tel: 0121 454 9637

Fax: 0121 454 6433

Email: birmingham@mpw.ac.uk

Website: www.mpw.ac.uk

Principal: Mr Mark Shingleton

School type: Coeducational Day

Age range of pupils: 14–19

Average class size: 8

Superdry
YORK NOTES ADVANCED
ANTONY AND CLEOPATRA
WILLIAM SHAKESPEARE

Packwood Haugh School

Founded in 1892, Packwood Haugh celebrates its 125th anniversary during the 2017-18 academic year. Over its long and illustrious history this co-educational, independent day and boarding prep school has earned a reputation for excellence in all areas – academic, sporting and in the arts. Success is reflected on the school's Honours Boards that list no fewer than 25 scholarship awards for the 2017 cohort alone, and by its proud record of 100% pass rate in Common Entrance every year in living memory. This year's scholarships include top academic awards to Winchester, Shrewsbury, Repton and Rugby as well as awards for music, sport and drama to many of the country's best independent senior schools.

Packwood is about more than academic success alone. Set in 65 acres of glorious Shropshire countryside in the heart of the country, the school's outstanding facilities and grounds enable the provision of a truly all-round education. With a focus on educating the whole child, the ethos at Packwood is to develop characteristics of grit, determination and endeavour that prepare pupils for future challenges at senior school and beyond. Pupils are encouraged to aim high and to work hard to fulfil their potential in everything they do. There is a strong sporting tradition and Packwood enjoys great success in a variety of team and individual sports at county, regional and national level. Furthermore, after their recent visit, the Independent Schools Inspectorate reported on 'particularly high standards in Music, Art and Drama' with many pupils enjoying extra clubs and one-to-one tuition, in addition to class lessons.

Alongside the wide-ranging, academically rigorous curriculum that inspires and challenges, Packwood offers countless opportunities and experiences to extend, enrich and broaden the children's development. As well as an excellent programme of extra-curricular activities, educational visits and trips both at home and overseas, and regular workshops and speakers at school, the school fields, gardens, woods and ponds provide the perfect environment for learning in the outdoors. In their time outside the classroom, the children develop a connection to and curiosity about the natural world and the awe and wonder it inspires.

Boarding at Packwood remains an enduringly popular option and was greatly praised by the ISI inspectors who reported that 'the quality of boarding provision and care is excellent'. Boarders thrive in the happy, supportive environment of their boarding houses where they 'develop key qualities such as tolerance, confidence and independence'. The boarders' weekends are full and busy with activities ranging from clay pigeon shooting and gymnastics to drama workshops and cupcake baking or even an impromptu go-kart race. The children themselves are unfailingly enthusiastic about everything available to them, and most importantly of all, about building friendships for life.

Headmaster, Clive Smith-Langridge, says, *"Our 125th anniversary is a wonderful opportunity to celebrate past successes but also to look forward to future developments. Packwood is thriving and continues to go from strength to strength. We are committed to providing the best possible education for our pupils in every way we can. The success we enjoy every year is testament to not only the dedication and professionalism of members of staff, but above all to the diligence and enthusiasm of the children. They flourish in the happy and positive environment at Packwood and invariably meet – and exceed – the high expectations we have of them."*

(Founded 1892)

Ruyton XI Towns, Shrewsbury, Shropshire SY4 1HX UK

Tel: 01939 260217

Fax: 01939 262077

Email: hm@packwood-haugh.co.uk

Website: www.packwood-haugh.co.uk

Headmaster: Clive Smith-Langridge BA (Hons), PGCE

Appointed: September 2012

School type: Coeducational Day & Boarding

Age range of pupils: 4–13

No. of pupils enrolled as at 01/09/2017: 216

Boys: 154 ***Girls:*** 62

No. of boarders: 92

Fees per annum as at 01/09/2017:

Day: £8,505–£17,685

Full Boarding: £22,635

Average class size: 13

Teacher/pupil ratio: 1:7

Shrewsbury School

Set in the heart of England Shrewsbury is a unique school in many ways. We are committed to strong academic standards and we believe in a vision of holistic education, as demonstrated through an incredible range of different activities and societies.

We are passionate about boarding not just being for convenience, but in providing the best opportunity for young men and women to develop real confidence and belief in themselves. We are fortunate to have one of the best locations of any school in the country, a most beautiful campus-style site on the edge of one of the most historic county towns in England.

Life at Shrewsbury is founded on a close partnership between staff, parents and pupils to promote the strength of family life, foster responsibility, and balance the claims of developing individuality with the needs of a vibrant community.

We believe our traditional values and time-honoured reputation is enhanced by a dynamic development plan designed to fully embrace the advantages of co-education. We are committed to providing an environment where young men and women can learn together on foundations of trust and mutual respect. We are confident that the future will be a more equal one and we support that historical evolution.

The celebration of individuals and individual talent is central to education at Shrewsbury – both in and beyond the classroom. In whatever sphere, a pupil will find a member of staff to support and encourage, enthuse and inspire him or her to exceed their expectations and meet the challenges that lie ahead with confidence and good judgement.

The results speak for themselves. Our 2016 leavers achieved another excellent year for A Level results with 80% of the exams awarded the top A*, A or B grades and 25% of all exams gaining the top A* grade.

We celebrated one of our best ever set of GCSE results, with a near record 70.8% of the exams awarded an A* or A grade and a record-breaking 43.8% of results achieving the top A* grade.

We want all our pupils, whatever their ability, to enjoy their life beyond the classroom, and Shrewsbury has a well-earned reputation for academic, musical and sporting excellence. We compete internationally in cricket and rowing, and we are one of the strongest schools in the country for football, cross-country running and fives; facilities and coaching for these and a host of other sports including tennis, fencing, lacrosse, hockey, rugby, and netball are excellent.

Our school plays and musicals have drawn praise at the Edinburgh Fringe Festival and in London. As one would expect from one of the strongest music departments in the country, the breadth and quality of music-making is remarkable, and a number of students win places at some of the top music colleges each year.

We also offer our pupils an extraordinary array of clubs, societies and other extra-curricular activities, many of which take place on a dedicated weekly activity afternoon. The majority are led by members of school staff. Shrewsbury is surrounded by glorious unspoilt countryside and the School makes the most of its easy access to the Shropshire Hills, the Welsh Marches and Snowdonia.

Above all, in the words of the motto of our youth club, based in inner-city Liverpool, 'People matter more than things'. You will find at Shrewsbury a community which is aiming for the stars in every respect. Come and visit our beautiful school and meet some of the people who make it such an inspirational place.

Shrewsbury School

(Founded 1552)

The Schools, Shrewsbury, Shropshire SY3 7BA UK

Tel: 01743 280552

Fax: 01743 243107

Email: admissions@shrewsbury.org.uk

Website: www.shrewsbury.org.uk

Headmaster: Mr Mark Turner MA

Appointed: 2010

School type: Coeducational Day & Boarding

Religious Denomination: Anglican

Age range of pupils: 13–18

No. of pupils enrolled as at 01/09/2017: 810

Boys: 586 ***Girls:*** 215 ***Sixth Form:*** 381

No. of boarders: 630

Fees per annum as at 01/09/2017:

Day: £24,390

Full Boarding: £35,040

Average class size: GCSE: 18; A level: 8

Teacher/pupil ratio: 1:9

West House School

Situated in the leafy oasis of the Calthorpe Estate, West House School has occupied the same site since its foundation in 1895. Since that time, the school has evolved significantly to become an independent preparatory school for boys aged 4-11 years, with a co-educational Early Years Department offering care and education for children aged from 12 months. West House is a member of The Independent Association of Preparatory Schools and, as such, upholds the requirement to provide a 'world class education'.

Set within five acres of beautiful grounds, less than two miles from Birmingham city centre, the school lies at the heart of a thriving community. Pupils of all ages benefit from two all-weather playing surfaces, a nature reserve and the multi-functional Duce Hall, providing indoor sporting and theatrical facilities. The school is also surrounded by many outstanding cultural and recreational amenities which enrich the lives of all pupils and allow them to explore and extend their talents in numerous curricular and extra-curricular pursuits.

West House is a non-denominational school, guided by Christian principles. It is divided into three departments – Prep (Years 3-6), Pre-Prep (Years 1 & 2) and the Early Years Foundation Stage (Nursery – Reception). From their earliest years, children are encouraged to adopt the core values of the school which are actively promoted throughout the working day and frequently form the focus of assemblies and PSHE lessons.

The school continues to boast a unique family atmosphere of which founding Headmaster, Arthur Perrott Cary Field, would have been proud. In the spirit of combining the best of its traditions with an education that prepares pupils for life in the middle part of the twenty first century, it remains determined to be at the forefront of innovation. This is reflected in the delivery of an ambitious curriculum which complements academic rigour with significant opportunities for pupils to explore personal interests in sport, art, music and drama.

Employing 45 full-time and part-time academic staff, many of whom are subject specialists, West House has grown considerably during the last five years to accommodate approximately 330 pupils, with 130 attending the EYFS Department.

Pupils are prepared for a wide range of senior schools, and standards at 11+ are consistently high, with most Year 6 boys transferring to local grammar schools, King Edward's School, Birmingham and Solihull School. A number of pupils are awarded academic and sporting scholarships and the school also enjoys outstanding success in academic challenges, quizzes and competitions at regional and national level.

Further details about the school can be found at www.westhouseprep.com

(Founded 1895)

24 St James's Road, Edgbaston, Birmingham, West Midlands B15 2NX UK

Tel: 0121 440 4097

Fax: 0121 440 5839

Email: secretary@westhouseprep.com

Website: www.westhouseprep.com

Headmaster: Mr Alistair M J Lyttle BA(Hons), PGCE, NPQH

School type: Boys' Day

Age range of boys: 1–11

Age range of girls: 1–4

No. of pupils enrolled as at 01/09/2017: 330

Fees per term as at 01/09/2017:

Day: £1,466–£3,795 per term

Average class size: 17 (two form entry)

Teacher/pupil ratio: 1:12

Wolverhampton Grammar School

Wolverhampton Grammar School is a selective, independent school, located to the west of Wolverhampton. Families from across the West Midlands, Staffordshire and Shropshire choose the school because of its excellent reputation and mission to deliver education that transforms lives as well as minds.

Founded in 1512, the school is an iconic local landmark and remains the top independent school in Wolverhampton. With over 500 years of exceptional education history, the school is still the first choice for parents who want approachability and a human dimension to education. Large enough to be able to offer an experience like no other and yet personal enough to adapt to suit the ambitions and interests of every child.

The school provides education with a personalised curriculum full of academic and extra-curricular opportunities. Providing this experience to boys and girls from Year 3 through to Year 13 (ages 7–18) with students coming from all kinds of backgrounds and cultures. Their knowledge and skills are diverse, and are a source of strength and richness to the school that partners with a range of local, national and international organisations.

The 23-acre school site blends stunning original architecture with creative, innovative learning spaces. Walk through the school and you will see how the Senior and Sixth Form buildings wrap around the Junior School; how superb grounds, a sports centre and pavilion provide the perfect showcase for sport and how the use of green and open spaces offer the ideal setting for the development of creative and critical thinkers.

The school accepts applications to the Junior, Senior School and Sixth Form throughout the year and there are a number of Scholarships and means-tested Bursaries available. As a selective, independent school all applicants (for Years 3–11) are asked to sit an assessment/entrance test relevant to their year of entry. Applicants to the Sixth Form are also invited to meet with the Head of Sixth Form. Students go on to achieve great things and have their pick of the best Russell Group and International Universities. The school also has a thriving worldwide alumni community of thousands in over 30 countries.

As the leading independent school in the area, demand for the school is high, it's therefore recommended that you contact the school as soon as possible to ensure you receive regular updates about open days and key application and assessment/entrance test dates.

The school actively encourages all applicants to visit and experience their approach to learning and it's famously welcoming atmosphere. To arrange a visit, taster or discover day or to register for an Open Day contact:

Jane Morris, Admissions Registrar, Wolverhampton Grammar School, Compton Road, Wolverhampton WV3 9RB tel: 01902 422939, email: jam@wgs-sch.net or visit the website www.wgs.org.uk for more details.

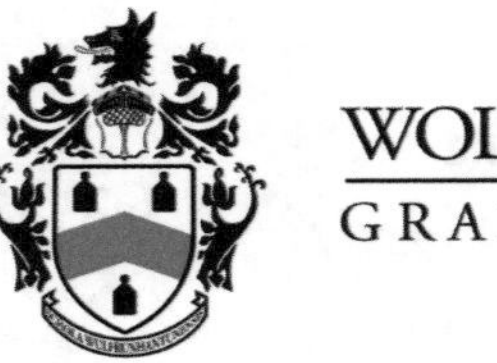

WOLVERHAMPTON
GRAMMAR SCHOOL

(Founded 1512)

Compton Road, Wolverhampton,
West Midlands WV3 9RB UK

Tel: 01902 421326

Email: wgs@wgs-sch.net

Website: www.wgs.org.uk

Head: Kathy Crewe-Read BSc

School type: Coeducational Selective Day

Age range of pupils: 7–18

No. of pupils enrolled as at 01/09/2017: 734

Boys: 427 ***Girls:*** 307 ***Sixth Form:*** 167

Fees per term as at 01/09/2017:

Day: £3,356–£4,421 per term

Average class size: 24 Max

Yorkshire & Humberside

Pocklington School

Pocklington School – inspired for life

Young people flourish in the supportive environment of Pocklington School, where specialist and innovative teaching from the ages of 3-18 helps each pupil achieve their full potential.

We are renowned for our emphasis on pastoral care as part of an excellent all-round education, with a focus on the individual, which produces confident, resourceful and capable young adults.

Pocklington School lies 12 miles east of York in a safe, rural setting on the edge of a small, friendly market town, on a 65-acre campus with good public transport links and its own minibus pick-up service.

The day and boarding school's extensive facilities include a 300-seat theatre, an indoor sports hall, conditioning room and swimming pool, plus 21 acres of grass sports pitches and two full-sized synthetic pitches.

Numerous co-curricular activities take place every day until 5pm, and each pupil is encouraged to pursue their own interests to help develop the depth of character and self-awareness to tackle life's challenges on their own terms.

Pocklington School was founded in 1514 and has remained true to its strong tradition of encouraging pupils to have the courage to take chances with learning and always remain true to themselves. Our motto Virtute et Veritate: With Courage and With Truth, reflects this.

Right through from Prep School, with its emphasis on nurturing children's natural curiosity, imagination and enthusiasm for learning, to the Sixth Form where independent thought is prized, our pupils are encouraged to be resilient, resourceful learners.

Lessons are planned around giving pupils the opportunity to evaluate and apply a solid foundation of learning, rather than simply acquiring and retaining facts.

We employ the best educational tools and appropriate new technology facilities to ensure youngsters are enthused and inspired by the world of knowledge available to them. The flexibility of learning platforms and the individual approach allows each pupil to progress at his or her pace, boosting their confidence and self-esteem so they often exceed their expectations.

Our new £2.5m Art and Design Technology Centre, opening in Autumn 2017, has every facility to encourage the pursuit of traditional arts and crafts, as well as provide cutting-edge equipment for digital and computer design, and manufacturing technology. The innovation and cross fertilisation of ideas the Centre promotes are increasingly valued in society today.

Sixth Form facilities include spacious communal areas, a study centre, and comprehensive library. Students are encouraged to work both collaboratively and independently as they begin to make the transition to university study and/or workplace success.

Full, flexible and casual boarding options are available, in boarding houses which create a home from home for both domestic and international students. A flexible range of opportunities allows them to create a balanced programme which not only fulfils their academic objectives, but also leaves time to explore new sporting, cultural and vocational activities to develop individual skills and strengths.

Recent former pupils who retain links with the school include Davis Cup winner Kyle Edmund, England rugby star Rob Webber and world-renowned concert pianist Alexandra Dariescu.

We aim to inspire our pupils for life, helping develop an inquiring mind and the self-respect they need to emerge as capable, adaptable and resilient young people ready to make a real contribution to society.

POCKLINGTON SCHOOL

Ages 3 to 18

(Founded 1514)

West Green, Pocklington, York,
North Yorkshire YO42 2NJ UK

Tel: 01759 321000

Fax: 01759 306366

Email: enquiry@pocklingtonschool.com

Website: www.pocklingtonschool.com

Headmaster: Mr Mark Ronan MA (Cantab)

Appointed: January 2008

School type: Coeducational Day & Boarding

Religious Denomination:
Christian ethos welcoming all faiths and none

Age range of pupils: 3–18

No. of pupils enrolled as at 06/06/2017: 773

Boys: 411 ***Girls:*** 362 ***Sixth Form:*** 171

No. of boarders: 87

Fees per annum as at 01/09/2017:

Day: £14,124

Weekly Boarding: £25,320

Full Boarding: £27,528

Average class size: 16

Teacher/pupil ratio: 1:16

Queen Ethelburga's Collegiate Foundation

Founded in 1912, Queen Ethelburga's Collegiate is a day and boarding school with 1500 pupils aged from 5 years to 18 years and from over 40 different countries. Set in 120 acres of beautiful North Yorkshire countryside, the campus has some of the most impressive study, boarding and leisure facilities in the independent school sector.

2016 saw QE celebrate its best ever A-Level results. Queen Ethelburga's College was ranked the top day and boarding school in the North of England, according to the Daily Telegraph 2016 League Table for percentage A*/A A levels and equivalent qualifications. It scored 85% which ranked it top in the North and the second UK day and boarding school overall.

The Faculty of Queen Ethelburga's, the Collegiate's other Sixth Form school, scored 81% with its percentage of A*/A A levels and equivalent qualifications in the Daily Telegraph table, placing it second in the North and fourth in the list of UK day and boarding schools.

Younger pupils study from the age of three years in Chapter House Preparatory School, starting with the Early Year Foundation Stage and child-led and adultled activities to foster their skills in reading, language and number work. By the time the children progress through Key Stage 1 and into Key Stage 2 they will be competent readers, with good verbal and writing skills and excellent number and data handling.

King's Magna Middle School takes pupils from age 10 years to 14 years. Here the transition is made from classbased teaching to specialist teaching, so that by Years 8 and 9, all subjects will be taught by specialist teachers. The curriculum is based on the National Curriculum, but extends beyond this with a comprehensive programme of sports and creative activities.

By Year 11 students will choose to attend the College, which offers a more traditional academic route of learning with GCSEs and A levels, or the Faculty, which offers GCSEs and A levels but also more vocational BTEC subjects such as performing arts, fashion or sports science.

For many students though, Queen Ethelburga's is more than a school, it is their home too, and the boarding facilities are simply exemplary. Student bedrooms and apartments are all air-conditioned and have their own en-suite facilities and for the older students, their own kitchen area. Each room has a direct dial telephone, satellite plasma television with timed gaming port and DVD player. House parents are on hand 24 hours a day to help with prep, heat up hot chocolate or to listen to career ideas.

We run a Cricket Academy which is being run in partnership with The Yorkshire County Cricket Club. This runs alongside our existing sporting academies – the Rugby Academy, supported by Leeds Rugby Academy and Foundation at Leeds Carnegie and the Netball Academy run by Yorkshire Jets. There will be further development of existing programmes in football, swimming, hockey and basketball, all will have the advantage of use of the facilities in our £30m Sports Village.

When homework is done, the new QE activity centre opens its doors. Complete with a go kart and speed skating track, assault course, climbing wall, 3D cinema, DJ and music area, game consoles and even a stunt bike track – there's something for everyone.

Queen Ethelburga's motto is about ambition and excellence – "to be the best that I can with the gifts that I have" – it is a school rich in talent and opportunities and well deserves such a maxim.

(Founded 1912)

Thorpe Underwood Hall, Ouseburn, York, North Yorkshire YO26 9SS UK

Tel: 01423 33 33 30

Email: info@qe.org

Website: www.qe.org

Principal: Steven Jandrell BA

Appointed: September 2006

School type: Coeducational Day & Boarding

Religious Denomination: Multi-Denominational

Age range of pupils: 3–19

No. of pupils enrolled as at 01/09/2017: 1550

Boys: 780 ***Girls:*** 770 ***Sixth Form:*** 595

No. of boarders: 1128

Average class size: 18

Teacher/pupil ratio: 1:10

The Froebelian School

The Froebelian School in Horsforth is a thriving and dynamic independent prep school, which places children at the very heart of all it strives to achieve. From the age of three, we seek to equip our boys and girls with a lifelong thirst for learning and the school continually achieves impressive levels of academic success; preparing our children for the next stage in their educational journey.

The Independent Schools Inspectorate report in 2017 judged The Froebelian School as 'excellent' for the quality of the pupils' achievements and the quality of pupils' personal development – this is the highest judgement available.

The inspectors accurately captured the essence of Froebelian and were struck by the children's high levels of academic performance, their attitudes to learning and the quality, breadth and depth of their personal development.

'The pupils' attitudes to learning are exceptional.' ISI Inspectorate 2017

We are passionate that all children enjoy a positive experience at school each and every day. Our aim is to provide a first class all-round education and committed pastoral care in which both the unique needs of our children as individuals are met and their talents can flourish in a caring, structured and secure environment. As a result, our children regularly secure a place at their first choice senior school and we enjoy an excellent scholarship success rate.

Welcoming around 180 pupils between the ages of 3 and 11, we set the highest standards and expectations and The Froebelian School is acknowledged as one of the North's leading independent prep schools. We have been placed consistently as the highest ranked school in the area in the prestigious Sunday Times Parent Power Survey.

Our children are bright, inquisitive individuals and we endeavour to cater for their unique abilities, interests and aspirations. This enables us to develop the whole child and we work hard to build solid foundations, which balance both the co-curricular and academic spheres of school life and honour our school motto – 'Giving a flying start to the citizens of tomorrow.'

The school offers outstanding opportunities, which promote growth in our children's personal and social development. We have built an excellent reputation for our co-curricular provision in sport, music, drama and technology. We foster our children's curiosity and imagination at every stage of school life and the children are nurtured and supported by an excellent staff: pupil ratio of 1:10.

Situated in Horsforth, a pleasant and vibrant suburb of Leeds near to the ring road, the school is easily accessible from most areas of Leeds, Bradford and Harrogate. Our site is very secure with a wooded area offering delightful views over the Aire valley.

In 2015, the Froebelian School opened a new nursery, First-Steps, which follows the school's ethos closely and offers younger children the opportunity to start realising their full potential at an earlier age. The private day nursery on New Road Side in Horsforth was given a judgment of 'outstanding' in each aspect of its first ever Ofsted inspection recently as well the overall verdict. It is open 51 weeks a year to all children.

'The leadership and management are inspirational.' Ofsted

At Froebelian the children and staff work harmoniously together creating a special place, with a uniquely happy atmosphere.

The school is an educational charity where ultimate responsibility rests with a School Council (governors). The day-to-day running of the school is delegated to the Headteacher, supported by a senior leadership team.

Visit www.froebelian.com to find out more

(Founded 1913)

Clarence Road, Horsforth, Leeds,
West Yorkshire LS18 4LB UK

Tel: 0113 2583047

Fax: 0113 2580173

Email: office@froebelian.co.uk

Website: www.froebelian.com

Head Teacher: Mrs Catherine Dodds BEd (Hons), PGCE

Appointed: 2015

School type: Coeducational Day

Age range of pupils: 3–11

No. of pupils enrolled as at 01/09/2017: 182

Boys: 93 ***Girls:*** 89

Fees per annum as at 01/09/2017:

Day: £4,980–£7,440

Teacher/pupil ratio: 1:10

Woodhouse Grove School

Woodhouse Grove was founded in 1812 and is a co-educational day and boarding school with 1060 pupils aged from 3 to 18 years.

An Independent Schools Inspectorate (ISI) inspection in March 2017 rated all aspects of Woodhouse Grove School as excellent. The Inspectors came away with very clear evidence of the attributes that we seek to promote, namely: Inspiration, Challenge and Grovian Values. Our outstanding academic and co-curricular programme was recognised and our aim to ensure that all our pupils reach their full potential was substantiated.

At Woodhouse Grove, we appreciate that every child is a unique individual and this is at the heart of everything we do. We aim to motivate pupils academically and beyond the classroom and to provide an educational environment designed to allow students to fully participate in school life.

We offer a rich, challenging and dynamic curriculum and want our students to ask questions of the world around them with an open mind; to have the character to listen to others, but also to stand up for their beliefs. We encourage our pupils to 'give back' to their community and we believe that this well-rounded, diverse approach is the key to building academic and personal confidence. Ultimately, our objective is to provide our students with the drive and aspiration to become the very best version of themselves that they can be.

Set in idyllic grounds near Leeds, the school is opposite Apperley Bridge train station and within four miles of Leeds Bradford Airport. We have high standards and an all-encompassing approach to education and our outstanding facilities reflect this. A recording studio, 230 seater theatre, sports halls, swimming pool and climbing wall are all within our 70 acre campus.

Our junior school, Brontë House enjoys its own facilities on a superb site situated half a mile from the Senior School, and includes our purpose built Early Years centre, Ashdown Lodge. Brontë is a busy and friendly place with the happiness and wellbeing of its pupils firmly at its heart. Our excellent academic curriculum is supported by enriching experiences in music, drama, art, outdoor education and sport. Our small class sizes allow us to focus on individuals and to instil a love of learning in each and every pupil. Children automatically transfer through to Woodhouse Grove at age 11.

Woodhouse Grove's holistic approach to education means that we offer a comprehensive range of co-curricular activities to run alongside our academic curriculum. Woodhouse Grove has a proud sporting heritage and we aim to nurture a love of sport in all of our students regardless of ability. Significant numbers of Grovians gain district, county, regional and international honours and pursue sporting careers at leading universities, professional sports clubs and scholarship opportunities in the USA.

We also have an extensive music and drama programme involving 30% of all pupils at the school, across a wide variety of clubs. School productions are held in our fully equipped theatre, offering both on stage and technical backstage opportunities to students from all age groups.

The diversity and richness of boarding at Woodhouse Grove School, coupled with our strong academic standards, attracts students from all over the world. Boarding is a thriving and integral part of our school life where students are enveloped in a caring family environment and are provided with stimulating and challenging experiences throughout the week and at weekends. They have access to all the school facilities as well as the chance to participate in specific boarding events, such as camping trips.

We welcome parents to visit Woodhouse Grove and Brontë House on our open days or at any time by prior arrangement. Dates and details are publicised on the school website or telephone for further information.

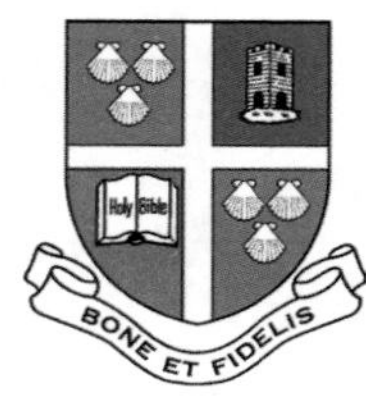

(Founded 1812)

Apperley Bridge, Bradford, West Yorkshire BD10 0NR UK

Tel: 0113 250 2477

Fax: 0113 250 5290

Email: amos.jl@woodhousegrove.co.uk

Website: www.woodhousegrove.co.uk

Headmaster: Mr James Lockwood MA

Appointed: 2016

School type: Coeducational Day & Boarding

Age range of pupils: 3–18

No. of pupils enrolled as at 01/09/2017: 1060

Fees per annum as at 01/09/2017:

Day: £8,790–£13,275

Full Boarding: £25,230–£26,985

Average class size: 20

Teacher/pupil ratio: 1:10

Scotland

Fettes College

Fettes College has over 5,000 Old Fettesians who remain in touch with us for one very compelling reason: being educated at Fettes was one of the most important and beneficial aspects of their lives.

Fettes is where their confidence was built, horizons broadened, talents nurtured and life-long friendships made. Where they achieved exam success, broke sporting records, were inspired by teachers and learnt the skills which would equip them for later life.

Fettes is where they were enthused, praised and encouraged to work hard and achieve the very best they could, while being surrounded by like-minded peers and caring staff.

To this day, a Fettes education is an incredible start to life.

The Individual

Our mission at Fettes is to develop broadly educated, confident and thoughtful individuals who are prepared for life after Fettes and all the opportunities and challenges it will bring. We are a community which believes in mutual support and co-operation and it is this happy, purposeful environment that encourages boys and girls to flourish and develop fully the skills and interests that they possess, whatever they may be.

24/7 Education

Fettes strongly believes in the benefits of boarding and the positive impact it has on the lives of our students – whether boarding or day. Being surrounded by supportive teachers and like-minded contemporaries gives our students the encouragement to try their very best in everything they undertake.

Care

The Care and Welfare of our students is fundamentally important to us as we know that a happy, supported child will flourish. Boarding houses are a vital part of boarding life, a caring community of students living together. A wealth of house activities cements the strong bond between housemates, younger pupils learn from older pupils and older pupils take responsibility to care for others.

Academics

Fettes is renowned around the world for the quality of education we provide which naturally includes superb academic results (GCSE, I-GCSEs , A Levels &IB). We provide the choice of curriculum simply because this ensures we play to the strengths of all of our students. We are by no means an academic hot house but we do believe that with expert tuition and encouragement, every student can maximise their academic potential.

Uncovering Talents

The skills and talents of each of our students is recognised and rewarded whether that be in the classroom, on the sports field, in the concert hall, on the stage or in the gallery. We are incredibly proud of the level and variety of achievement that our students achieve – a true reflection of an all-round education.

Proudly Scottish

Our location in the heart of Scotland's capital city provides a thrilling array of cultural facilities – world class galleries, theatres, and sporting venues while only a short drive away from the wonderful Scottish hills and countryside giving the freedom to sail, climb, walk, ski and cycle. We fully embrace all that Scotland has to offer and although the vast majority of our students come from the UK (75%), we have pupils from over 40 countries represented giving the Fettes community a unique mix of cultures, outlook and experiences. We very much prepare our students for life in a global society. With the core skills they learn, they are equipped to live, work and succeed anywhere in the world.

Fettes College

(Founded 1870)

Carrington Road, Edinburgh, EH4 1QX UK

Tel: +44 (0)131 332 2281

Email: enquiries@fettes.com

Website: www.fettes.com

Head of College: Mr Geoffrey Stanford

Appointed: 2017

Head of Prep: Mr Adam Edwards

School type: Coeducational Boarding & Day

Age range of pupils: 7–18

No. of pupils enrolled as at 01/09/2017: 770

Fees per annum as at 01/09/2017:

Day: £15,495 (Prep)–£26,790 (College)

Full Boarding: £24,210 (Prep)–£33,480 (College)

Average class size: 15

Teacher/pupil ratio: 1:8

Gordonstoun

As well as preparing students for exams, Gordonstoun prepares them for life.

The school's uniquely broad curriculum encourages every individual to fulfil their potential academically, but it does more than that. It encourages students to fulfil their potential as human beings. The school motto is 'Plus est en vous' – There is more in you. At Gordonstoun, this sense of possibility is presented to its students, every single day.

'It wasn't until we saw the curriculum and the schedule of what they would be doing each day that we truly understood the difference between Gordonstoun and other schools.' Current parent.

Although Gordonstoun is within striking distance of two international airports, the school's remarkable location on a 200 acre woodland estate by the Moray Coast in the North of Scotland provides the background for its world beating outdoor education programme. Gordonstoun was the birth place of both the Outward Bound Movement and the Duke of Edinburgh's Award, and expeditions to the Scottish Highlands or sail training on the School's 80ft Sailboat are an integral part of the school's day to day life. Students gain invaluable experience in being both leaders and team players and in having compassion and understanding for their fellows – and of themselves. Their outlook is broadened, their ability to consider the needs of others developed, and they gain resilience – life skills which can only complement the school's commitment to, and realisation of, academic excellence.

Active engagement in service to the local community also comprises a core part of Gordonstoun's 'working week', further expanding the students' sense of personal and social responsibility and building self-esteem. From Year 11 each student commits to one of the school's twelve services. These range from the Fire Service and Coastguards to Community Service and Technical support.

Gordonstoun follows the English GCSE and A level curriculum. With a staff/pupil ratio of 1:7 and every student's progress carefully overseen by their tutor, they go on Universities, Colleges and Art Schools all over the world – from Oxford and Cambridge, to Central St Martins, MIT or the Northern School of Music – to study a diverse range of subjects, from Latin to aeronautical engineering, from physics to drama and performance.

The students at Gordonstoun inhabit a community which is both balanced and internationally dynamic. Pupils aged 7-18 live and learn alongside fellow students from across the social, cultural and geographical board. And because Gordonstoun is one of the few remaining full boarding schools, it has a seven day programme which ensures that students are happily integrated and engaged. It also affords the opportunity to make full use of the comprehensive facilities on offer – which include an expansive sports centre, a drama and dance centre and music studios.

The uniquely all-round education on offer at Gordonstoun provides its students with the chance to develop intellectually, emotionally, physically and spiritually because Gordonstoun understands that the broader the experience the broader the mind.

In the words of a current parent:

"I send my children to Gordonstoun because I want them to have an excellent academic education. But I want them to have more than that. I want them to enter the ever changing world with a sense of possibility and optimism about themselves and their options. Gordonstoun's uniquely broad curriculum gives them the best possible chance of achieving that."

(Founded 1934)

Elgin, Moray IV30 5RF UK

Tel: 01343 837829

Fax: 01343 837808

Email: admissions@gordonstoun.org.uk

Website: www.gordonstoun.org.uk

Principal: Ms Lisa Kerr BA

Appointed: April 2017

School type: Coeducational Boarding & Day

Age range of pupils: 6–18

No. of pupils enrolled as at 01/09/2017: 521

Boys: 293 ***Girls:*** 228 ***Sixth Form:*** 211

Senior: 411

No. of boarders: 378

Fees per annum as at 01/09/2017:

Day: £13,842–£27,339

Weekly Boarding: £22,515 (Junior School only)

Full Boarding: £22,515–£36,909

Average class size: 12

Teacher/pupil ratio: 1:7

GORDONSTOUN
TS
K580

Lomond School

Lomond School is a co-educational independent school, for children aged 3 to 18 years, positioned in the elegant suburbs of the coastal town of Helensburgh located only 10 minutes from Loch Lomond and the Trossachs National Park. We make the most of our unique location by providing and encouraging participation in a wide range of opportunities for outdoor learning, sports and activities.

At Lomond School we believe passionately that education should be about supporting our young people to develop and grow, both academically and personally, as rounded individuals with strong values who are ultimately prepared to embark confidently and successfully on their life beyond Lomond School.

We uphold this commitment with six Guiding Principles which are delivered throughout our curriculum and co-curriculum. These include: Internationalism; Environmentalism; Adventure; Leadership; Lifelong Learning and Service. To find out more visit our website at www.lomondschool.com. Our focus is on preparing our students for their future by ensuring that they learn the skills necessary to be successful in the 21st century whilst developing the traditional values and qualities that they require to be responsible and active global citizens.

We provide small class sizes, an extensive programme of extra-curricular activities, attention to the individual and a strong record of academic achievement which opens the door to allow new experiences, skills and talents to be explored. All aspects of development are accorded importance, be they academic, musical, dramatic, sporting or in wider outdoor activities.

We were one of the first schools in the UK to integrate an ICT strategy which provides all our P6 to S6 students with their own personal iPad.

The Lomond Family

Our experienced pastoral care team ensures the welfare and onward progression of all of our students. Our young people are well known by staff and teachers and we see ourselves as a large family where any issues or problems are identified and dealt with promptly and effectively.

Extra-curricular and Outdoor Learning

Our location means that there is a particular emphasis on outdoor pursuits. The Duke of Edinburgh Award is, without doubt, a significant feature and we have enjoyed great success carrying out expeditions both locally and abroad. Many of our trips and excursions revolve around our passion for the outdoors and have included trekking in Morocco, canoeing in Norway and skiing in Austria.

We also build many cultural and educational trips into the school year with visits to Paris, Berlin, Brussels and Iceland, as well as Hockey and Rugby tours to South Africa or more locally. We support and encourage our young people to make the most of the opportunities available, recognising both the immediate and long-term benefits of the personal development these experiences and activities can offer.

Living at Lomond

Our boarding facility adds a distinctive dimension to the school; the mix of cultures and backgrounds enriches our curriculum and co-curriculum, supporting all of our pupils to develop their global awareness and understanding.

Our infrastructure boasts a mix of modern, purpose-built structure and characterful listed buildings, which make for an inspirational setting for our young people. We continually invest in our facilities and take a cutting-edge approach to every new project we initiate.

(Founded 1977)

10 Stafford Street, Helensburgh, Argyll & Bute G84 9JX UK

Tel: +44 (0)1436 672476

Fax: +44 (0)1436 678320

Email: admissions@lomondschool.com

Website: www.lomondschool.com

Principal: Mrs Johanna Urquhart

School type: Co-educational Day & Boarding

Age range of pupils: 3–18

No. of pupils enrolled as at 01/05/2017: 400

No. of boarders: 60

Fees per annum as at 01/07/2017:

Day: £8,310–£11,550

Full Boarding: £26,730

Queen Victoria School

Queen Victoria School is a coeducational and tri-Service boarding school fully funded by the Ministry of Defence to provide stability and continuity of education for the children of UK Armed Forces personnel who are Scottish, or who have served in Scotland or who have been members of a Scottish regiment.

All necessary expenses for each pupil are met by the Ministry of Defence, and we have a particular mission to care for those families who could not otherwise afford boarding education.

Because tuition and boarding costs, uniform, books, stationery and most other items of school expenditure are met by the Ministry of Defence, the financial contribution asked of parents is very small; currently it is £1,403 per annum. The contribution covers only non-essentials and helps to make boarding life more pleasant for the pupils; it allows us to provide newspapers and satellite TV in the houses, for example, as well as contributing towards the costs of transport for school outings. Service benevolent funds are very supportive of the school, and can assist those families who are unable to meet some or all of the parental contribution.

If your child comes to QVS (as we are known) he or she will be part of a pupil community made up entirely of the children of UK Armed Forces personnel. That sort of mutual understanding and support is invaluable, especially when parents are posted overseas or on long unaccompanied tours. All of our pupils have at least one actively serving parent when they enter the school.

Our main intake is into the Scottish system's Primary 7 year; there is no exact equivalent with the English system, but most of our P7 intake are aged ten or eleven when they join us. That said, there is a wide age range within the year groups. Many of our pupils have come from educationally disrupted backgrounds as they have moved from school to school and education system to education system, according to their families' postings.

After children whose parents have been killed or injured in Service, priority in admissions is given to children whose parents are likely to be posted frequently during their child's time at the school. We also try to allow siblings to attend QVS together.

Academically, the school regularly achieves pass rates at Standard Grade and Higher, which are well above the Scottish National Averages. We now follow the National 4, 5, Higher and Advanced Higher courses.

Games and outdoor activities are important parts of life at QVS. Rugby and hockey are the main sports, and the Duke of Edinburgh Award Scheme is pursued at all three levels: Bronze, Silver and Gold. We have a beautiful setting in some 45 acres of countryside on the edge of Dunblane, much of which is given over to games pitches and recreational areas.

The ceremonial aspects of school life are central to QVS. Marching as part of the school on one of our six Parade Sundays a year, and on Grand Day – the final day of the academic year – is one of the proudest moments of a Victorian's life (as well as that of his or her parents)! The Pipes, Drums and Dancers of QVS are internationally renowned, having played at tattoos both at home and abroad, most recently in the Basel Christmas Tattoo 2013 and The Royal Edinburgh Military Tattoo 2012.

Dunblane is on a main rail line to Glasgow and Edinburgh, and within easy driving distance of the majority of Forces bases in Scotland.

There is no substitute for visiting a school, meeting its pupils and staff and picking up the atmosphere. If you would like to know more before travelling to Dunblane to visit us, however, please request further information from the Admissions Secretary, Queen Victoria School, Dunblane FK15 0JY, or via our website **www.qvs.org.uk**.

(Founded 1908)

Dunblane, Perthshire FK15 0JY UK

Tel: 0131 310 2927

Fax: 0131 310 2926

Email: admissions@qvs.org.uk

Website: www.qvs.org.uk

Head: Donald Shaw BSc(Hons) PGCE

Appointed: August 2016

School type: Coeducational Boarding

Age range of pupils: 11–18

No. of pupils enrolled as at 01/09/2017: 267

Boys: 121 ***Girls:*** 146 ***Sixth Form:*** 30

Fees per annum as at 01/09/2017:

Full Boarding: £1,403

Wales

Llandovery College

AN OUTSTANDING INDEPENDENT SCHOOL SET IN THE HEART OF WALES

What Makes Llandovery College Special?

Llandovery College offers excellent facilities, first class teaching in small class sizes and a wide range of opportunities for intellectual, social and physical development. Our broad ability and inclusive school ensures that the learning needs of each pupil are catered for enabling them to reach and exceed their individual potential.

A Llandovery College education stand apart in the values and attitudes it engenders in its young men and women. Compassion, tolerance, kindness, integrity, generosity of spirit and good citizenship underpin a dedication to academic excellence.

Stunning Setting and Strong Sense of Community

Set within 45 acres of beautiful grounds in the picturesque Towy Valley there is a tangible sense of community and common purpose within the College. The House system brings boarders and day pupils together, promoting a strong sense of belonging and loyalty whilst forging deep bonds of friendship. Our pupils are well known by teachers and staff and we consider ourselves one large family.

Academic Success

The College boasts an enviable university entrance record with Oxbridge successes and a high proportion of pupils moving on to Russell Group universities. In addition, our pupils achieve an exceptionally high rate of acceptance to their first choice university.

Outstanding Opportunities

The College is renowned for its outstanding rugby heritage and achievements, producing world class rugby players such as Internationals and British & Irish Lions George North and Alun Wyn Jones.

The College's passion for sport is unrivalled and pupils have competed at regional, national and international levels in no less than 17 sports particularly excelling in fencing, equestrian and shooting. Facilities include a 9 hole golf course, fully equipped gym and extensive pitches.

Music and the performing arts also have an enviable reputation with the orchestra and choir performing to an exceptionally high standard both at home and overseas.

Co-Curricular Activities

An extensive co-curricular programme offers pupils the opportunity to explore new interests as well as develop expertise in existing passions. The College has a thriving Combined Cadet Force and one of the highest Duke of Edinburgh's Award Scheme achievement rates with almost every pupil working towards bronze, silver or gold awards.

Scholarships

Academic and special talent scholarships are available from Year 7 onwards.

"The pupils achieve excellent levels of personal development, feeling secure, safe and valued in the friendly, mutually trusting ethos which prevails throughout the school" – **ISI Report**

Contact

For more information or to visit Llandovery College please contact the Admissions Registrar Mrs Vicky Douch on 01550 723005 or admissions@llandoverycollege.com

(Founded 1847)

Queensway, Llandovery, Carmarthenshire SA20 0EE UK

Tel: +44 (0)1550 723005

Email: admissions@llandoverycollege.com

Website: www.llandoverycollege.com

Warden: Guy Ayling MA

Appointed: April 2012

School type: Co-educational Boarding & Day

Religious Denomination: Church in Wales

Age range of pupils: 4–18 years

No. of pupils enrolled as at 01/09/2017: 280

No. of boarders: 115

Fees per annum as at 01/09/2017:

Day: £8,205–£17,520

Full Boarding: £17,880–£26,460

Average class size: 10

Teacher/pupil ratio: 1:8

St John's College, Cardiff

St John's College has achieved an enviable reputation both in Wales and amongst the top independent schools in England as a centre of academic excellence, achieving the best A Level record in Wales over 17 years. We are also delighted to have been listed as the top academic school in Wales in The Sunday Times 'Parent Power', based on combined GCSE and A Level performance. The College's most recent Estyn Inspection Report graded the school 'Excellent' in all areas, including the enviable and seldom awarded 'Excellent' grade for quality of teaching. The report stated that, "The quality of teaching is an exceptional feature of the school's work." This year marks our 30th Anniversary and we remain committed to our aim of providing the best possible education for our girls and boys as they become young women and young men, embracing all that life has to offer with passion, commitment and integrity.

St John's has a distinguished record of success with University admissions. Specialist mentoring and one to one guidance are offered so that students are fully supported with their subject choices, UCAS personal statements, university choices and ultimately career paths. The school has an outstanding reputation for gaining places at first class universities. In 2017 the majority of our students, including a significant number with 4 A*/A grades, proceeded to Oxbridge and top Russell Group Universities.

Headmaster Mr Gareth Lloyd said: "This year nearly half the grades awarded were A* which is a truly outstanding achievement."

The school's strong, close-knit family community ensures that all pupils and students receive the care necessary to develop their full potential. Indeed, Estyn inspectors observed that "Throughout the school, there is a strong sense of collective purpose and a commitment to shared values and aims. The quality of teaching and learning has led to exceptional outcomes for pupils of all abilities" (Crown Copyright 2012).

Cathedral Choir & Music

The school is also proud of its outstanding musical reputation: a remarkable number of its most successful musicians are of diploma standard. The College's many instrumental ensembles include its award winning Concert Orchestra, which has been a finalist in the Welsh Proms Schools Competition and gives warmly received public concerts. As the Choir School to Cardiff Metropolitan Cathedral, St John's provides the boy and girl choristers for weekly services, two annual concerts at St David's Hall, and concert tours across continental Europe. Our Cathedral Choir has appeared in the Hollywood film 'One Chance', and sings annual broadcasts on BBC Radio 4. Most recent concert tours include Paris, Bruges and Madrid, and the Choir has performed in St Paul's Cathedral, Westminster Abbey and, most recently, with the choir of Gonville and Caius College, Cambridge.

Co-curricular Provision

Beyond the classroom, pupils of all ages benefit from extensive co-curricular provision, including an extended sports programme as well as regular sports and ski tours. In the field of performing arts, in recent years pupils have performed critically-acclaimed productions of *Twelfth Night*, *HMS Pinafore* and *The Sound of Music*. The College is also proud of its national success in Chess, Public Speaking, Debating, Poetry, Mathematics, Science, Engineering and Young Enterprise competitions. Inspectors commented that 'The range of extra-curricular activities, particularly the outstanding musical, choral and cultural opportunities, contributes significantly to pupils academic development and wellbeing' (Estyn Inspection Crown Copyright, 2012).

St John's College

College Green, Old St Mellons, Cardiff, Glamorgan CF3 5YX UK

Tel: 029 2077 8936

Fax: 029 2077 6182

Email: admin@stjohnscollegecardiff.co.uk

Website: www.stjohnscollegecardiff.com

Headteacher:
Gareth P Lloyd BA (Hons), MSc, FMusTCL (Cantab)

School type: Coeducational Day

Age range of pupils: 3–18

No. of pupils enrolled as at 01/09/2017: 525

Fees per annum as at 01/09/2017:

Day: £7,425–£13,629

Overseas

École Jeannine Manuel – Lille

École Jeannine Manuel Lille is a non-profit pre-K-12 coeducational school founded in 1992. As the sister school of École Jeannine Manuel Paris, they have the same educational project and the same mission: develop international understanding through bilingual (French/English) education. An associated UNESCO school, École Jeannine Manuel Lille is the only non-denominational independent school in Nord-Pas-de-Calais, with over 800 pupils representing 40 nationalities and every major cultural tradition. The school's academic excellence matches its diversity: École Jeannine Manuel Lille achieves excellent performances, both at the French Baccalaureate and the International Baccalaureate. The school is accredited by the French Ministry of Education, the International Baccalaureate Organization (IBO), the Council of International Schools (CIS) and the New England Association of Schools and Colleges (NEASC).

The campus of school extends over 3,5 hectares and includes a boarding house, a restaurant, two football fields, a multi-sport room, and high standard sports facilities and equipment. The boarding house welcomes this year 111 pupils from 6th to 12th grades.

Each year, École Jeannine Manuel Lille welcomes non-French speaking students. Over the years École Jeannine Manuel has developed a program to suit the needs of these students, for whom the emotional challenge of relocation is often as great than its academic challenge. Thanks to their French teachers and their methods, the students will be fluent in French in a few months.

The lower and middle school follow the French national curriculum with several exceptions: English is taught every day and, in middle school, experimental sciences, history and geography are taught in English. The curriculum is enriched at all levels, not only with a more advanced English language and literature curriculum, but also, for example, with Chinese language instruction (compulsory in grades 3-4-5), an integrated science programme in lower school, and independent research projects in middle school.

In upper school, tenth graders follow the French national curriculum, albeit taught 50% in French and 50% in English. In 11th grade, pupils choose between the French track (international option of the French baccalaureate (OIB)) and the International Baccalaureate Diploma Programme (IBDP). Approximately 25% of our pupils opt for the IBDP. (Please note that, since the IBDP does not receive any government subsidies, its tuition is three times the French track tuition.)

Admission

Although admission is competitive, every effort is made to reserve space for international applicants, including children of families who expect to remain in France for a limited period of time and wish to combine a cultural immersion in French education with the ability to re-enter their own school systems and excel.

(Founded 1954)

418 bis rue Albert Bailly, Marcq-en-Baroeul, 59700 France

Tel: +33 3 20 65 90 50

Fax: +33 3 20 98 06 41

Email: admissions-lille@ejm.net

Website: www.ecolejeanninemanuel.org

Head of School: Jérôme Giovendo

School type: Coeducational Day & Boarding

Age range of pupils: 4–18 years

No. of pupils enrolled as at 01/09/2017: 864

Fees per annum as at 01/09/2017:

Day: €4,752

Full Boarding: €12,995–€19,995

IB Classes: €8,962 – €16,495

Average class size: 25 (15 in IBDP)

École Jeannine Manuel – Paris

École Jeannine Manuel is a non-profit pre-K-12 coeducational school founded in 1954 with the mission to develop international understanding through bilingual (French/English) education. An associated UNESCO school, École Jeannine Manuel welcomes pupils representing 80 nationalities and every major cultural tradition. The school's academic excellence matches its diversity: École Jeannine Manuel is regularly ranked among the top French high schools (state and independent) for its overall academic performance (ranked first for five consecutive years). The school is accredited by the French Ministry of Education, the International Baccalaureate Organization (IBO), the Council of International Schools (CIS) and the New England Association of Schools and Colleges (NEASC).

Each year, École Jeannine Manuel welcomes more than one hundred new non-French speaking pupils who enroll in 'adaptation' classes where they follow a French immersion programme. A senior advisor follows them closely and, the following year, they join the mainstream where they continue to be supported with a special French programme involving three additional weekly hours of special French classes.

The lower and middle school follow the French national curriculum with several exceptions: English is taught every day and, in middle school, experimental sciences, history and geography are taught in English. The curriculum is enriched at all levels, not only with a more advanced English language and literature curriculum, but also, for example, with Chinese language instruction (compulsory in grades 3-4-5), an integrated science programme in lower school, and independent research projects in middle school.

In upper school, tenth graders follow the French national curriculum, albeit taught 50% in French and 50% in English. In 11th grade, pupils choose between the French track (international option of the French baccalaureate (OIB)) and the International Baccalaureate Diploma Programme (IBDP). Approximately 25% of our pupils opt for the IBDP. (Please note that, since the IBDP does not receive any government subsidies, its tuition is three times the French track tuition.)

Over the past three years, approximately 20% of our graduating class have gone to US colleges or universities, 48% chose the UK or Canada, 37% entered the French higher education system, and the balance pursued their education all over the world.

Admission

Although admission is competitive and applications typically exceed available spaces by a ratio of 7:1, every effort is made to reserve space for international applicants, including children of families who expect to remain in France for a limited period of time and wish to combine a cultural immersion in French education with the ability to re-enter their own school systems and excel.

(Founded 1954)

70 rue du Théâtre, Paris, 75015 France

Tel: +33 1 44 37 00 80

Fax: +33 1 45 79 06 66

Email: admissions@ejm.net

Website: www.ecolejeanninemanuel.org

Principal: Elisabeth Zéboulon

School type: Coeducational Day

Age range of pupils: 4–18 years

No. of pupils enrolled as at 01/09/2017: 2377

Fees per annum as at 01/09/2017:

Day: €5,847–€6,162

IB Classes: €19,485

Average class size:
25 (15 in adaptation classes and IBDP)

St. George's International School, Switzerland

Almost 100 years of academic excellence

Reflecting back on 90 years of exciting activity at St. George's International School, we can proudly say that we have successfully provided our students with the best international education in Switzerland while retaining the excellence of a British school.

Under an hour's drive from Geneva, our 12-acre campus is located in the residential suburb of Clarens, near Montreux, overlooking Lac Leman and the Alps. The high quality of our staff and the outstanding on-campus sports' facilities allow our students from 60 different nationalities to attain their academic potential while placing an emphasis on their physical skills and development.

Academia – *Levavi Oculos* ("I lift my eyes")

Our mission is to provide a global sense of excellence in education, reaching the perfect balance between intellectual stimulation, physical activity and the development of social skills. Our academic programmes give access to the world renowned IGCSE and IB Diploma examinations. They guarantee a solid learning base including mathematics, English, the sciences, foreign languages, humanities, sports and the arts preparing your children for a bright and strong academic future.

We aim to provide our students with a sense of initiative and the self confidence needed to help them become worldly, reliable, caring and responsible adults.

Boarders

St. George's has proved to be a 'home away from home' for thousands of young women and men giving them the chance to experience a unique way of life. Everything at the school is designed to help students adapt easily and quickly to their second home. In 2007 the school decided to open the boarding section to boys. We now welcome boys and girls from 11 to 18.

By enrolling your children at St. George's International School, you are giving them the chance to appreciate different cultures, instil in them the need for daily discipline, the values of respect, and monitor their development into mature caring achievers.

Summer Camp

Since the 1980s, St. George's International School Summer Camps have been a continued success, welcoming boys and girls aged 3 to 18 from over 30 countries throughout July and August. We provide our summer campers with a safe, happy, stimulating atmosphere in a beautiful environment. Campers are given the opportunity to improve their language skills while making friends from around the world. Excursions, sports and outdoor entertainment remain a major part of the programme to guarantee exciting lifelong memories.

ST. GEORGE'S INTERNATIONAL SCHOOL
SWITZERLAND

(Founded 1927)

Chemin de St. Georges 19,
CH-1815 Clarens/Montreux, Switzerland

Tel: +41 21 964 3411

Fax: +41 21 964 4932

Email: admissions@stgeorges.ch

Website: www.stgeorges.ch

Head of School: Mrs Jenny Aviss

School type: Coeducational Day & Boarding School

Age range of pupils: 1–19

No. of pupils enrolled as at 01/09/2017: 400

Fees per annum as at 01/09/2017:
Please enquire

ST. GEORGE'S SCHOOL IN
ST.

EF Academy New York

EF Academy International Boarding Schools prepares students for a global future with a superior secondary school education in the U.S. or UK. At EF Academy, we believe in every student's ability to succeed. We empower them to do so through our renowned curricula, as well as quality one-on-one relationships with teachers and mentors alike. Built into every course is an emphasis on multilingualism and intercultural exchange, which helps distinguish our students' academic credentials to both university admissions officers and future employers.

The School

Our private boarding school, which attracts students from 75 countries around the world, is located in upper New York State, approximately 40 minutes away from Manhattan. EF Academy's secure campus offers 100 acres of landscaped grounds, running trails and playing fields in the quiet suburban town of Thornwood. Theater students step into the spotlight in our beautiful auditorium where full-length plays are staged twice a year. Science labs equipped with state-of-the-art equipment and welcoming art studios not only enrich classwork, they also host science and art clubs after school and are available for students to use for independent study. Our students often complete their school day with physical activity in our fully equipped gym, dance studio, basketball court or off-road biking trails.

Students live in comfortable and secure on-campus dormitory accommodation. House parents and teachers provide support and mentorship around the clock, and ensure a safe "home away from home."

Academics

EF Academy New York is a four-year high school where students follow the IGCSE program in their first two years and either the IB Diploma or IB Certificate program in the last two years. Those who successfully complete their high school studies at EF Academy New York are awarded a nationally recognized New York State High School Diploma in addition to the other qualifications they earn. Instruction and guidance at EF Academy New York is highly personal. Students engage in interactive lessons in small classes led by inspiring teachers and they benefit from the individualized support they receive from dedicated counselors and university advisors who help them achieve their goals.

University Placement

EF Academy New York graduates have been accepted to top-ranked universities such as Harvard, Columbia University, University of Pennsylvania, High Point University and Rochester Institute of Technology, and other premiere business and engineering schools as well. Dedicated university guidance counselors work with students on a one-on-one basis to help them with everything from researching universities and writing college essays, to selecting a major that falls in line with their career goals. Students at EF Academy New York apply to universities in the U.S. as well as in the UK and in their home countries.

Co-curricular Activities

Universities look for well-rounded students who extend their learning beyond the classroom. Students at EF Academy New York have access to a wide range of co-curricular activities. From subject-specific academic groups and competitions to club and varsity sports, there is an option for every student. The school's activities coordinator also arranges teacher-led excursions for students on the weekends so they have many opportunities to explore Manhattan and the museums, musicals and sights the city is known for.

582 Columbus Avenue, Thornwood, NY 10594 USA

Tel: +1 914 495 6028

Email: iaadmissionsny@ef.com

Website: www.ef.edu/academy

Head of School: Dr. Brian Mahoney

School type: Coeducational Day & Boarding

Age range of pupils: 13–19

No. of pupils enrolled as at 01/09/2017: 800

Fees per annum as at 01/09/2017:

Grades 9 & 10 (IGCSE, High School Diploma): US$41,850

Grades 11 & 12: (IB, High School Diploma): US$47,250

MAIN
BUILDING

Geographical directory of schools

KEY TO SYMBOLS

- *Boys' school*
- *Girls' school*
- *International school*
- *Tutorial or sixth form college*
- *A levels*
- *Boarding accommodation*
- *Bursaries*
- *International Baccalaureate*
- *Learning support*
- *Entrance at 16+*
- *Vocational qualifications*
- *Independent Association of Preparatory Schools*
- *The Headmasters' & Headmistresses' Conference*
- *Independent Schools Association*
- *Girls' School Association*
- *Boarding Schools' Association*
- *Society of Heads*

Unless otherwise indicated, all schools are coeducational day schools. Single-sex and boarding schools will be indicated by the relevant icon.

Channel Islands

KEY TO SYMBOLS

- Boys' school
- Girls' school
- International school
- Tutorial or sixth form college
- A levels
- Boarding accommodation
- Bursaries
- International Baccalaureate
- Learning support
- Entrance at 16+
- Vocational qualifications
- Independent Association of Preparatory Schools
- The Headmasters' & Headmistresses' Conference
- Independent Schools Association
- Girls' School Association
- Boarding Schools' Association
- Society of Heads

Unless otherwise indicated, all schools are coeducational day schools. Single-sex and boarding schools will be indicated by the relevant icon.

Guernsey

Elizabeth College Junior School
Beechwood, Queen's Road, St Peter Port, Guernsey GY1 1PU
Tel: 01481 722123
Headteacher: Jim Walton
Age range: 2½–11
No. of pupils: 270
Fees: Day £9,375–£10,440

The Ladies' College
Les Gravees, St Peter Port, Guernsey GY1 1RW
Tel: 01481 721602
Principal: Mrs J Riches
Age range: G4–18
No. of pupils: 555 VIth100
Fees: Day £5,385–£5,964
(A) (16)

Jersey

Beaulieu Convent School
Wellington Road, St Helier, Jersey JE2 4RJ
Tel: 01534 731280
Headmaster: Mr C Beirne
Age range: G4–18
No. of pupils: 762 VIth127
Fees: Day £4,584
(A) (£) (16)

De La Salle College
Wellington Road, St Saviour, Jersey JE2 7TH
Tel: 01534 754100
Head of College: Mr Jason Turner
Age range: 4–18
No. of pupils: 762
Fees: Day £5,103
(A) (16)

FCJ Primary School
Deloraine Road, St Saviour, Jersey JE2 7XB
Tel: 01534 723063
Headmistress: Ms Maureen Doyle
Age range: 4–11
No. of pupils: 290
Fees: Day £2,820

Helvetia House School
14 Elizabeth Place, St Helier, Jersey JE2 3PN
Tel: 01534 724928
Headmistress: Mrs Ann Atkinson BA, DipEd
Age range: G4–11
No. of pupils: 82
Fees: Day £4,200

Jersey College For Girls
Le Mont Millais, St Saviour, Jersey JE2 7YB
Tel: 01534 516200

St George's Preparatory School
La Hague Manor, Rue de la Hague, St Peter, Jersey JE3 7DB
Tel: 01534 481593
Headmaster: Mr Cormac Timothy
Age range: 2–11
No. of pupils: 210
Fees: Day £4,890–£13,440
(£)

ST MICHAEL'S PREPARATORY SCHOOL
For further details see p. 44
La Rue de la Houguette, St Saviour, Jersey JE2 7UG
Tel: 01534 856904
Email: office@stmichaels.je
Website: www.stmichaels.je
Head of School: Mr Mike Rees
Age range: 3–14
No. of pupils: 309
Fees: Day £9,375–£14,475
(£)

Victoria College
Le Mont Millais, St Helier, Jersey JE1 4HT
Tel: 01534 638200
Headmaster: Mr Alun Watkins
Age range: B11–18
No. of pupils: 720 VIth200
Fees: Day £4,584
(A) (£) (16)

Victoria College Preparatory School
Pleasant Street, St Helier, Jersey JE2 4RR
Tel: 01534 723468
Headmaster: Russell Price BSc, MPhil
Age range: B7–11
No. of pupils: 300
Fees: Day £1,476

Central & West

KEY TO SYMBOLS

- Boys' school
- Girls' school
- International school
- Tutorial or sixth form college
- A levels
- Boarding accommodation
- Bursaries
- International Baccalaureate
- Learning support
- Entrance at 16+
- Vocational qualifications
- Independent Association of Preparatory Schools
- The Headmasters' & Headmistresses' Conference
- Independent Schools Association
- Girls' School Association
- Boarding Schools' Association
- Society of Heads

Unless otherwise indicated, all schools are coeducational day schools. Single-sex and boarding schools will be indicated by the relevant icon.

Bath & North-East Somerset

Bath Academy
27 Queen Square, Bath, Bath & North-East Somerset BA1 2HX
Tel: 01225 334577
Principal: Tim Naylor BA(Hons), MSc, PGCE
Age range: 14–19+
No. of pupils: 120
Fees: Day £23,700 FB £35,000

Downside School
Stratton-on-the-Fosse, Radstock, Bath, Bath & North-East Somerset BA3 4RJ
Tel: 01761 235103
Head Master: Dr J Whitehead
Age range: 11–18
No. of pupils: 350 VIth135
Fees: Day £14,937–£17,196 FB £23,559–£30,687

King Edward's Junior School
North Road, Bath, Bath & North-East Somerset BA2 6JA
Tel: 01225 464218
Head: Mr Greg Taylor
Age range: 7–11
No. of pupils: 182
Fees: Day £10,560

King Edward's Pre-Prep & Nursery School
Weston Lane, Bath, Bath & North-East Somerset BA1 4AQ
Tel: 01225 421681
Head: Ms. Jayne Gilbert
Age range: 3–7
No. of pupils: 107
Fees: Day £7,845–£9,525

KING EDWARD'S SENIOR SCHOOL
For further details see p. 52
North Road, Bath, Bath & North-East Somerset BA2 6HU
Tel: 01225 464313
Email: reception@kesbath.com
Website: www.kesbath.com
Head: Mr MJ Boden MA
Age range: 11–18
No. of pupils: 1085

Kingswood Preparatory School
College Road, Lansdown, Bath, Bath & North-East Somerset BA1 5SD
Tel: 01225 734460
Headmaster: Mr Marcus E Cornah
Age range: 3–11
No. of pupils: 335
Fees: Day £7,125–£8,250 WB £14,118 FB £16,806–£17,808

Kingswood School
Lansdown Lane, Bath, Bath & North-East Somerset BA1 5RG
Tel: 01225 734200
Age range: 3-11 (Prep)–11-18 (Senior)
No. of pupils: 642 VIth189
Fees: Day £9,789 WB £15,918–£19,722 FB £18,222–£21,828

MONKTON PREP SCHOOL
For further details see p. 54
Church Road, Combe Down, Bath, Bath & North-East Somerset BA2 7ET
Tel: +44 (0)1225 837912
Headmaster: Mr M Davis
Age range: 7–13 (boarding from 8)
No. of pupils: 240

MONKTON SENIOR SCHOOL
For further details see p. 54
Monkton Combe, Bath, Bath & North-East Somerset BA2 7HG
Tel: 01225 721133
Email: admissions@monkton.org.uk
Website: www.monkton.org.uk
Principal: Mr Chris Wheeler
Age range: 11–18

Prior Park College
Ralph Allen Drive, Bath, Bath & North-East Somerset BA2 5AH
Tel: 01225 831000
Head: Mr James Murphy-O'Connor
Age range: 11–18
No. of pupils: 580 VIth180
Fees: Day £11,736–£13,077 WB £18,687 FB £23,583

The Paragon School
Lyncombe House, Lyncombe Vale, Bath, Bath & North-East Somerset BA2 4LT
Tel: 01225 310837
Headmaster: Mr Titus Mills BA
Age range: 3–11
No. of pupils: 252
Fees: Day £5,835–£6,504

The Royal High School, Bath GDST
Lansdown Road, Bath, Bath & North-East Somerset BA1 5SZ
Tel: +44 (0)1225 313877
Head: Mrs Jo Duncan BA, MA
Age range: G3–18
No. of pupils: 640
Fees: Day £4,212 WB £8,105 FB £8,105

Bristol

Badminton Junior School
Westbury-on-Trym, Bristol BS9 3BA
Tel: 0117 905 5200
Head of the Junior School: Mrs E Davies
Age range: G3–11
No. of pupils: 130
Fees: Day £8,040–£10,830 FB £20,190–£21,240

Badminton School
Westbury-on-Trym, Bristol BS9 3BA
Tel: 0117 905 5271
Headmistress: Mrs Rebecca Tear BSc, MA, PGCE
Age range: G3–18
No. of pupils: 450
Fees: Day £8,490–£17,880 FB £213,000–£33,870

Bristol Grammar School
University Road, Bristol BS8 1SR
Tel: 0117 973 6006
Headmaster: R I Mackinnon
Age range: 4–18
No. of pupils: 1137 VIth288
Fees: Day £5,700–£10,590

Bristol Steiner School
Redland Hill House, Redland, Bristol BS6 6UX
Tel: 0117 933 9990
Age range: 3–16
No. of pupils: 213
Fees: Day £1,728–£4,800

Carmel Christian School
817A Bath Road, Brislington, Bristol BS4 5NL
Tel: 0117 977 5533
Headteacher: Mr David Owens
Age range: 5–16
No. of pupils: 28
Fees: Day £480–£720

Cleve House School
254 Wells Road, Knowle, Bristol BS4 2PN
Tel: 0117 9777218
Headmaster: Mr. Craig Wardle
Age range: 2–11
No. of pupils: 90
Fees: Day £6,075

Clifton College
32 College Road, Clifton, Bristol BS8 3JH
Tel: 0117 315 7000
Headmaster: Mr Mark J Moore
Age range: 3–18
No. of pupils: 1330 VIth280
Fees: Day £5,460–£16,245 WB £16,305–£21,645 FB £17,070–£24,075

Clifton College Preparatory School
The Avenue, Clifton, Bristol BS8 3HE
Tel: +44 (0)117 405 8396
Head of Preparatory School: Mr John Milne
Age range: 2–13
No. of pupils: 495
Fees: Day £12,465–£16,485 WB £15,465–£19,485 FB £21,420–£27,240

Clifton High School
College Road, Clifton, Bristol BS8 3JD
Tel: 0117 973 0201
Head: Dr Alison M Neill BSc, PhD, PGCE
Age range: 4–18
No. of pupils: 527
Fees: Day £7,605–£10,905 FB £19,605

Clifton Tutors Limited
31 Pembroke Road, Clifton, Bristol BS8 3BE
Tel: 0117 973 8376
Director of Studies: William P Shaw BA
Age range: 7–19

Colston's School
Stapleton, Bristol BS16 1BJ
Tel: 0117 965 5207
Headmaster: Peter Fraser
Age range: 3–18
No. of pupils: 581 VIth138
Fees: Day £5,160–£7,110 FB £15,045

Ecole Française de Bristol
Fonthill Centre, Stanton Road, Southmead, , Bristol BS10 5SJ
Tel: +44 (0) 117 9692410
Age range: 2–11

Fairfield School
Fairfield Way, Backwell, Bristol BS48 3PD
Tel: 01275 462743
Headmistress: Mrs Lesley Barton
Age range: 2–11
No. of pupils: 129
Fees: Day £2,480–£2,730

Gracefield Preparatory School
266 Overndale Road, Fishponds, Bristol BS16 2RG
Tel: 0117 956 7977
Headmistress: Mrs E Morgan
Age range: 4–11
No. of pupils: 90
Fees: Day £5,127

Queen Elizabeth's Hospital
Berkeley Place, Clifton, Bristol BS8 1JX
Tel: 0117 930 3040
Head: Mr Stephen Holliday MA (Cantab)
Age range: B7–18 G16–18
No. of pupils: 688
Fees: Day £8,793–£13,455

Redland High School for Girls
Redland Court, Redland, Bristol BS6 7EF
Tel: 0117 924 5796
Headmistress: Mrs Caroline Bateson BA(Hons)
Age range: G3–18
No. of pupils: 450 VIth90
Fees: Day £5,760–£9,600

Silverhill School
Swan Lane, Winterbourne, Bristol BS36 1RL
Tel: 01454 772156
Principal: Mr Julian Capper
Age range: 2–11
No. of pupils: 185
Fees: Day £4,800–£6,255

The Downs School
Wraxall, Bristol BS48 1PF
Tel: 01275 852008
Head: M A Gunn MA(Ed), BA, PGCE
Age range: 4–13
No. of pupils: 262

The Red Maids' Junior School
Grange Court Road, Westbury-on-Trym, Bristol BS9 4DP
Tel: 0117 962 9451
Headteacher: Mrs Lisa Brown BSc (Hons)
Age range: B3–7 G3–11

The Red Maids' Senior School
Westbury Road, Westbury-on-Trym, Bristol BS9 3AW
Tel: +44 (0)117 962 2641
Headmistress: Mrs Isabel Tobias BA (Hons)
Age range: G11–18

Tockington Manor School
Washingpool Hill Road, Tockington, Bristol BS32 4NY
Tel: 01454 613229
Headmaster: Mr Stephen Symonds
Age range: 2–14
No. of pupils: 250
Fees: Day £7,650–£12,510 FB £17,070

Torwood House School
8, 27-29 Durdham Park, Redland, Bristol BS6 6XE
Tel: 0117 9735620
Headmistress: Mrs D Seagrove
Age range: 0–11
No. of pupils: 70
Fees: Day £1,964–£2,049

Buckinghamshire

Akeley Wood School
Akeley Wood, Buckingham, Buckinghamshire MK18 5AE
Tel: 01280 814110
Headmaster: Dr Jerry Grundy BA, PhD
Age range: 12 months–18 years
No. of pupils: 833 VIth119
Fees: Day £7,185–£10,575

Ashfold School
Dorton House, Dorton, Aylesbury, Buckinghamshire HP18 9NG
Tel: 01844 238237
Headmaster: Mr M O M Chitty BSc
Age range: 3–13
No. of pupils: 280 VIth28
Fees: Day £7,320–£12,900 WB £15,084

Broughton Manor Preparatory School
Newport Road, Broughton, Milton Keynes, Buckinghamshire MK10 9AA
Tel: 01908 665234
Headmaster: Mr Ross Urquhart
Age range: 2 months–11 years
No. of pupils: 250
Fees: Day £9,600

Chesham Preparatory School
Two Dells Lane, Chesham, Buckinghamshire HP5 3QF
Tel: 01494 782619
Headmaster: Mr Michael Davies BA, PGCE
Age range: 3–13
No. of pupils: 392
Fees: Day £8,700–£12,300

Childfirst Day Nursery Aylesbury
Green End, off Rickford's Hill, Aylesbury, Buckinghamshire HP20 2SA
Tel: 01296 392516
Registrar: Mrs Carole Angood
Age range: 2 months–7 years
No. of pupils: 80
Fees: Day £6,276

Childfirst Pre School Aylesbury
35 Rickfords Hill, Aylesbury, Buckinghamshire HP20 2RT
Tel: 01296 433224

Crown House School
19 London Road, High Wycombe, Buckinghamshire HP11 1BJ
Tel: 01494 529927
Headmaster: Ben Kenyon
Age range: 4–11
No. of pupils: 120
Fees: Day £5,985–£6,570

Davenies School
Station Road, Beaconsfield, Buckinghamshire HP9 1AA
Tel: 01494 685400
Headmaster: C Rycroft
Age range: B4–13
No. of pupils: 323
Fees: Day £11,985–£16,200

Filgrave School
Filgrave Village, Newport Pagnell, Milton Keynes, Buckinghamshire MK16 9ET
Tel: 01234 711534
Headteacher: Mrs H Schofield BA(Hons), MA, PGCE
Age range: 2–7
No. of pupils: 27
Fees: Day £5,160

Gateway School
1 High Street, Great Missenden, Buckinghamshire HP16 9AA
Tel: 01494 862407
Headteacher: Mrs Sue LaFarge BA(Hons), PGCE
Age range: 2–11
No. of pupils: 355
Fees: Day £10,002

Godstowe Preparatory School
Shrubbery Road, High Wycombe, Buckinghamshire HP13 6PR
Tel: 01494 529273
Headmaster: Mr David Gainer
Age range: B3–7 G3–13
No. of pupils: 409
Fees: Day £8,505–£13,245 WB £19,455 FB £19,455

Griffin House School
Little Kimble, Aylesbury, Buckinghamshire HP17 0XP
Tel: 01844 346154
Headmaster: Mr Tim Walford
Age range: 3–11
No. of pupils: 100
Fees: Day £7,395–£7,695

High March School
23 Ledborough Lane, Beaconsfield, Buckinghamshire HP9 2PZ
Tel: 01494 675186
Headmistress: Mrs S J Clifford
Age range: G3–11
No. of pupils: 292
Fees: Day £5,265–£13,590

Milton Keynes Preparatory School
Tattenhoe Lane, Milton Keynes, Buckinghamshire MK3 7EG
Tel: 01908 642111
Heads of School: Mr C Bates & Mr S Driver
Age range: 3 months–11 years
No. of pupils: 500
Fees: Day £12,712–£14,700

Pipers Corner School
Pipers Lane, Great Kingshill, High Wycombe, Buckinghamshire HP15 6LP
Tel: 01494 718 255
Headmistress: Mrs H J Ness-Gifford BA(Hons), PGCE
Age range: G4–18
No. of pupils: VIth72
Fees: Day £7,230–£14,010 WB £18,750–£222,845 FB £18,990–£23,085

St Teresa's Catholic School & Nursery
Aylesbury Road, Princes Risborough, Buckinghamshire HP27 0JW
Tel: 01844 345005
Head: Mr Simon Detre
Age range: 3–11
No. of pupils: 132
Fees: Day £5,775–£7,308

Stowe School
Buckingham, Buckinghamshire MK18 5EH
Tel: 01280 818000
Headmaster: Dr Anthony Wallersteiner
Age range: 13–18
No. of pupils: 769 VIth318
Fees: Day £22,500 FB £30,975

Swanbourne House School
Swanbourne, Milton Keynes, Buckinghamshire MK17 0HZ
Tel: 01296 720264
Headmaster: Mr Simon Hitchings MA (Oxon)
Age range: 3–13
No. of pupils: 387
Fees: Day £1,227–£17,475 FB £22,275

The Beacon School
Chesham Bois, Amersham, Buckinghamshire HP6 5PF
Tel: 01494 433654
Headmaster: P Brewster BSc(Hons), PGCE
Age range: B3–13
No. of pupils: 470
Fees: Day £4,695–£13,200

The Grove Independent School
Redland Drive, Loughton, Milton Keynes, Buckinghamshire MK5 8HD
Tel: 01908 690590
Principal: Mrs Deborah Berkin
Age range: 3 months–13 years
No. of pupils: 210

The Webber Independent School
Soskin Drive, Stantonbury Fields, Milton Keynes, Buckinghamshire MK14 6DP
Tel: 01908 574740
Principal: Mrs Hilary Marsden
Age range: 3–18
No. of pupils: 300 VIth15
Fees: Day £3,894–£10,371

Thornton College
Thornton, Milton Keynes, Buckinghamshire MK17 0HJ
Tel: 01280 812610
Headmistress: Miss Agnes T Williams
Age range: B2–4+ G2–16
No. of pupils: 370
Fees: Day £6,300–£10,095 WB £10,500–£13,305 FB £13,305–£16,545

Walton Pre-Preparatory School & Nursery
The Old Rectory, Walton Drive, Milton Keynes, Buckinghamshire MK7 6BB
Tel: 01908 678403
Headmistress: Mrs M Ramsbotham CertEd
Age range: 2 months–7 years
No. of pupils: 120
Fees: Day £8,316

WYCOMBE ABBEY
For further details see p. 64
High Wycombe, Buckinghamshire HP11 1PE
Tel: +44 (0)1494 897008
Email: registrar@wycombeabbey.com
Website: www.wycombeabbey.com
Headmistress: Mrs Rhiannon J Wilkinson MA (Oxon) MEd
Age range: G11–18
No. of pupils: 611
Fees: Day £28,350 FB £37,800

Gloucestershire

Airthrie School
29 Christchurch Road, Cheltenham, Gloucestershire GL50 2NY
Tel: 01242 512837
Principal: Mrs A E Sullivan DipEd, DipIM, CertCounselling
Age range: 3–11
No. of pupils: 168
Fees: Day £5,280–£7,494

Al-Ashraf Secondary School for Girls
Sinope Street, off Widden Street, Gloucester, Gloucestershire GL1 4AW
Tel: 01452 300465
Head: Mufti Abdullah Patel
Age range: G11–16
No. of pupils: 67
Fees: Day £900–£1,000

Beaudesert Park School
Minchinhampton, Stroud, Gloucestershire GL6 9AF
Tel: 01453 832072
Headmaster: Mr J P R Womersley BA, PGCE
Age range: 3–13
No. of pupils: 430
Fees: Day £2,710–£5,310 WB £6,900

Berkhampstead School
Pittville Circus Road, Cheltenham, Gloucestershire GL52 2QA
Tel: 01242 523263
Head: R P Cross BSc(Hons)
Age range: 3–11
No. of pupils: 215
Fees: Day £2,793–£7,470

Bredon School
Pull Court, Bushley, Tewkesbury, Gloucestershire GL20 6AH
Tel: 01684 293156
Head Teacher: Mr Koen Claeys
Age range: 7–18

Cheltenham College
Bath Road, Cheltenham, Gloucestershire GL53 7LD
Tel: 01242 265600
Headmaster: Dr Alex Peterken
Age range: 13–18
No. of pupils: 650 VIth270
Fees: Day £25,350–£26,265 FB £33,795–£34,710

Cheltenham College Preparatory School
Thirlestaine Road, Cheltenham, Gloucestershire GL53 7AB
Tel: 01242 522697
Headmaster: Mr Jonathan Whybrow
Age range: 3–13
No. of pupils: 420
Fees: Day £2,421–£15,442 FB £5,424–£7,074

Cheltenham Ladies' College
Bayshill Road, Cheltenham, Gloucestershire GL50 3EP
Tel: +44 (0)1242 520691
Principal: Eve Jardine-Young MA
Age range: G11–18
No. of pupils: 850 VIth305
Fees: Day £23,040–£26,220 FB £34,320–£38,670

Dean Close Pre-Preparatory & Preparatory School
Lansdown Road, Cheltenham, Gloucestershire GL51 6QS
Tel: 01242 512217
Age range: 2+–13
No. of pupils: 292
Fees: Day £10,485–£15,852 FB £18,405–£23,310

Dean Close School
Shelburne Road, Cheltenham, Gloucestershire GL51 6HE
Tel: 01242 258044
Headmaster: Mr Bradley Salisbury MEd, PGCE
Age range: 13–18
No. of pupils: 482 VIth182
Fees: Day £22,671 FB £32,940

Dormer House School
High Street, Moreton-in-Marsh, Gloucestershire GL56 0AD
Tel: 01608 650758
Headmistress: Mrs Alison Thomas
Age range: 2–11
Fees: Day £7,425

Eastbrook College
7a Eastbrook Education Trust, Gloucester, Gloucestershire GL4 3DB
Tel: 01452 417722
Age range: 11–16
No. of pupils: 59

Focus School – Berkeley Campus
Wanswell, Berkeley, Gloucestershire GL13 9RS
Tel: 01453 511282
Headteacher: Mrs Lucy Sherrin
Age range: 7–18
No. of pupils: 100

Gloucestershire International School
Horton Road, Gloucester, Gloucestershire GL1 3PR
Tel: +44 (0) 1452 764248

Hatherop Castle School
Hatherop, Cirencester, Gloucestershire GL7 3NB
Tel: 01285 750206
Headmaster: P Easterbrook BEd
Age range: 2–13
No. of pupils: 190
Fees: Day £6,285–£10,455 FB £15,270–£16,110

Hopelands Preparatory School
38 Regent Street, Stonehouse, Gloucestershire GL10 2AD
Tel: 01453 822164
Headmistress: Mrs S Bradburn
Age range: 3–11
No. of pupils: 59
Fees: Day £4,479–£5,322

Kitebrook Preparatory School
Kitebrook House, Moreton-in-Marsh, Gloucestershire GL56 0RP
Tel: 01608 674350
Headmistress: Mrs Susan McLean
Age range: 3–13
No. of pupils: 180

Rendcomb College
Rendcomb, Cirencester, Gloucestershire GL7 7HA
Tel: 01285 831213
Headmaster: Mr R Jones BA(Hons), MEd
Age range: 3–18
No. of pupils: 371 VIth54
Fees: Day £5,205–£7,150 WB £7,480–£9,885 FB £7,480–£9,885

St Edward's Preparatory School
London Road, Charlton Kings, Cheltenham, Gloucestershire GL52 6NR
Tel: 01242 538900
Headmaster: Mr Stephen McKernan BA(Hons) MEd NPQH
Age range: 1–11
No. of pupils: 295
Fees: Day £7,095–£11,340

St Edward's School
Cirencester Road, Cheltenham, Gloucestershire GL53 8EY
Tel: 01242 538600
Head: Mrs P Clayfield BSc
Age range: 11–18
No. of pupils: 344 VIth105
Fees: Day £12,765–£15,435

The Acorn School
Church Street, Nailsworth, Gloucestershire GL6 0BP
Tel: 01453 836508
Headmaster: Mr Graeme E B Whiting
Age range: 3–19
No. of pupils: VIth30
Fees: Day £3,800–£6,000

The King's School
Gloucester, Gloucestershire GL1 2BG
Tel: 01452 337337
Headmaster: Alistair K J Macnaughton
Age range: 3–18
No. of pupils: VIth80
Fees: Day £5,985–£15,960

The Richard Pate School
Southern Road, Cheltenham, Gloucestershire GL53 9RP
Tel: 01242 522086
Headmaster: Mr Robert MacDonald
Age range: 3–11 years
No. of pupils: 300
Fees: Day £3,000–£9,360

Westonbirt Prep School
Westonbirt, Tetbury, Gloucestershire GL8 8QG
Tel: 01666 881400
Headmaster: Mr Sean Price
Age range: 3–11
Fees: Day £2,800–£3,750

WESTONBIRT SCHOOL
For further details see p. 62
Westonbirt, Tetbury, Gloucestershire GL8 8QG
Tel: 01666 881333
Email: enquiries@westonbirt.org
Website: www.westonbirt.org
Headmistress: Mrs Natasha Dangerfield
Age range: G11–18 years
Fees: Day £4,995 FB £9,750

Wycliffe Preparatory & Senior School
Bath Road, Stonehouse, Gloucestershire GL10 2JQ
Tel: 01453 822432
Senior School Head: Mr Nick Gregory BA, MEd
Age range: 2–18
No. of pupils: VIth178
Fees: Day £7,680–£18,990 FB £18,090–£31,785

Wynstones School
Whaddon Green, Gloucester, Gloucestershire GL4 0UF
Tel: 01452 429220
Chair of the College of Teachers: Marianna Law-Lindberg
Age range: 3–18
No. of pupils: VIth9
Fees: Day £4,956–£7,236 FB £4,835

North Somerset

Ashbrooke House School
9 Ellenborough Park North, Weston-Super-Mare, North Somerset BS23 1XH
Tel: 01934 629515
Headteacher: Karen Wallington
Age range: 3–11
Fees: Day £4,494–£5,277

Sidcot School
Oakridge Lane, Winscombe, North Somerset BS25 1PD
Tel: 01934 843102
Head: Iain Kilpatrick
Age range: 3–18
No. of pupils: 515 VIth170
Fees: Day £6,150–£14,250 FB £22,050–£27,750

Oxfordshire

Abacus College & Oxford Language Centre
Victory House, 116-120 London Road, Headington, Oxfordshire OX3 9AX
Tel: +44 (0)1865 240111
Principal: Dr Paul Quinn
Age range: 13–19+
No. of pupils: VIth90
Fees: Day £12,500–£14,500

Abingdon Preparatory School
Josca's House, Frilford, Abingdon, Oxfordshire OX13 5NX
Tel: 01865 391570
Headmaster: Mr C Hyde-Dunn
Age range: B4–13
No. of pupils: B250
Fees: Day £10,770–£14,805

Abingdon School
Park Road, Abingdon, Oxfordshire OX14 1DE
Tel: 01235 521563
Head: Michael Windsor
Age range: B11–18
No. of pupils: 1011
Fees: Day £19,275 WB £32,550 FB £38,970

Bellerbys College Oxford
Trajan House, Mill Street, Oxford, Oxfordshire OX2 0DJ
Tel: +44 (0)1865 263 400
Principal: Dr Charles Runacres
Age range: 15–25

Bloxham School
Bloxham, Banbury, Oxfordshire OX15 4PE
Tel: 01295 720222 or 724301
Headmaster: Mr Paul Sanderson
Age range: 11–18
No. of pupils: 431
Fees: Day £17,385–£24,630 WB £23,235 FB £32,445

Burford School
Cheltenham Road, Burford, Oxfordshire OX18 4PL
Tel: 01993 823303/823283
Headteacher: Mrs K Haig BA, MEd
Age range: 11–18
No. of pupils: 1156 VIth200
Fees: FB £9,600

Carfax College
25 Beaumont Street, Oxford, Oxfordshire OX1 2NP
Tel: +44 1865 200 676
Principal: Rupert Alesbury BA (Oxon.)

Carrdus School
Overthorpe Hall, Banbury, Oxfordshire OX17 2BS
Tel: 01295 263733
Head: Mr Edward Way
Age range: B3–8 G3–11
No. of pupils: 122
Fees: Day £1,125–£10,725

Chandlings
Bagley Wood, Kennington, Oxford, Oxfordshire OX1 5ND
Tel: 01865 730771
Head: Mrs Cath Burton-Green
Age range: 2–11
Fees: Day £9,540–£12,540

Cherwell College
Cantay House, Park End Street, Oxford, Oxfordshire OX1 1JD
Tel: 01865 242670
Principal: Andy Thompson MA(Cantab)
Age range: 15–21
No. of pupils: 150 VIth145
Fees: Day £15,000–£17,000 WB £22,000–£24,000 FB £23,000–£25,000

Childfirst Day Nursery Banbury
The Old Museum, 8 Horsefair, Banbury, Oxfordshire OX16 0AA
Tel: 01295 273743

Childfirst Day Nursery Bicester
32 Launton Road, Bicester, Oxfordshire OX26 6PY
Tel: 01869 323730
Headmistress: Miss J Fowler BA(Hons), QTS
Age range: 2 months–7 years
Fees: Day £7,500

Christ Church Cathedral School
3 Brewer Street, Oxford, Oxfordshire OX1 1QW
Tel: 01865 242561
Headmaster: Martin Bruce MA, BA, FCollP
Age range: B3–13 G3–4
No. of pupils: 159
Fees: Day £5,409–£12,123 FB £7,560

Cokethorpe School
Witney, Oxfordshire OX29 7PU
Tel: 01993 703921
Headmaster: Mr D Ettinger BA, MA, PGCE
Age range: 4–18
No. of pupils: 666 VIth133
Fees: Day £11,025–£15,974

Cothill House
Abingdon, Oxfordshire OX13 6JL
Tel: 01865 390800
Headmaster: Mr D M Bailey
Age range: B8–13
No. of pupils: 250
Fees: FB £24,300

Cranford House School
Moulsford, Wallingford, Oxfordshire OX10 9HT
Tel: 01491 651218
Age range: B3–11 G3–16
No. of pupils: 380
Fees: Day £10,500–£15,450

d'Overbroeck's
333 Banbury Road, Oxford, Oxfordshire OX2 7PL
Tel: 01865 310000
Principal: Mrs Emma-Kate Henry
Age range: 11–18
No. of pupils: 475 VIth263
Fees: Day £16,725–£23,025 FB £30,225–£36,225

Dragon School
Bardwell Road, Oxford, Oxfordshire OX2 6SS
Tel: 01865 315400
Head: Mr John R Baugh BEd
Age range: 4–13
No. of pupils: 844
Fees: Day £10,500–£18,690 FB £26,940

EF ACADEMY OXFORD
For further details see p. 50
Pullens Lane, Headington, Oxfordshire OX3 0DT
Tel: +41 (0) 43 430 4095
Email: iaeurope@ef.com
Website: www.ef.com/academy
Head of School: Dr. Paul Ellis
Age range: 16–19
No. of pupils: 160

Emmanuel Christian School
Sandford Road, Littlemore, Oxford, Oxfordshire OX4 4PU
Tel: 01865 395236
Principal: Mrs Natalie Duncan
Age range: 3–11
No. of pupils: 73
Fees: Day £5,040

Greene's Tutorial College
45 Pembroke Street, Oxford, Oxfordshire OX1 1BP
Tel: 01865 248308
Senior Tutor: Matthew Uffindell MA, DipEd
No. of pupils: 213 VIth160

Headington Preparatory School
26 London Road, Oxford, Oxfordshire OX3 7PB
Tel: +44 (0)1865 759400
Head: Mrs Jane Crouch BA (Hons) Keele, MA London
Age range: G3–11
No. of pupils: 250

Headington School
London Road, Oxford, Oxfordshire OX3 7TD
Tel: +44 (0)1865 759100
Headmistress: Mrs Caroline Jordan MA(Oxon)
Age range: G11–18
No. of pupils: 780
Fees: Day £7,002–£14,403 WB £19,287–£25,143 FB £20,937–£27,885

Kingham Hill School
Kingham, Chipping Norton, Oxfordshire OX7 6TH
Tel: 01608 658999
Age range: 11–18
No. of pupils: 310
Fees: Day £4,965–£5,680 WB £7,075–£8,695 FB £7,340–£9,490

King's School, Oxford
New Yatt Road, Witney, Oxford, Oxfordshire OX29 6TA
Tel: 01993 778463
Principal: Mr John Ellwood
Age range: 16+
No. of pupils: 140

Magdalen College School
Cowley Place, Oxford,
Oxfordshire OX4 1DZ
Tel: 01865 242191
Master: Dr Tim Hands
Age range: B7–18
No. of pupils: 669 VIth161
Fees: Day £8,018–£9,880

Moulsford Preparatory School
Moulsford, Wallingford,
Oxfordshire OX10 9HR
Tel: 01491 651438
Headmaster: Mr B Beardmore-Gray
Age range: B4–13
Fees: Day £9,840–£14,700 WB £18,450

New College School
2 Savile Road, Oxford,
Oxfordshire OX1 3UA
Tel: 01865 285 560
Headmaster: Mr N R Gullifer MA, FRSA
Age range: B4–13
No. of pupils: 160
Fees: Day £9,246–£14,949

Our Lady's Abingdon School
Radley Road, Abingdon,
Oxfordshire OX14 3PS
Tel: 01235 524658
Principal: Mr Stephen Oliver
Age range: 3–18
No. of pupils: VIth81
Fees: Day £8,079–£13,683

Oxford High School GDST
Belbroughton Road, Oxford,
Oxfordshire OX2 6XA
Tel: 01865 559888
Head: Mrs Judith Carlisle BA(Hons)
Age range: G4–18
No. of pupils: 900
Fees: Day £3,291–£4,808

Oxford Montessori School
Forest Farm, Elsfield, Oxford,
Oxfordshire OX3 9UW
Tel: 01865 358210
Principal: Judith Walker Mont Dip, NNEB
Age range: 5–10
No. of pupils: 169

OXFORD TUTORIAL COLLEGE
For further details see p. 56
12-13 King Edward Street,
Oxford, Oxfordshire OX1 4HT
Tel: +44 (0)1865 793333
Email: admissions@oxfordtutorialcollege.com
Website: www.oxfordtutorialcollege.com
Principal: Mr Mark Love
Age range: 15+
No. of pupils: 288

Radley College
Radley, Abingdon,
Oxfordshire OX14 2HR
Tel: 01235 543000
The Warden: Mr J S Moule
Age range: B13–18
No. of pupils: 688
Fees: FB £35,490

Rupert House School
90 Bell Street, Henley-on-Thames,
Oxfordshire RG9 2BN
Tel: 01491 574263
Headmistress: Mrs N J Gan MA(Ed), FRSA
Age range: B4–7 G4–11
No. of pupils: 214
Fees: Day £3,810–£9,150

Rye St Antony
Pullens Lane, Oxford,
Oxfordshire OX3 0BY
Tel: 01865 762802
Headmistress: Miss A M Jones BA, PGCE
Age range: B3–11 G3–18
No. of pupils: 400 VIth70
Fees: Day £9,360–£14,175 WB £19,410–£21,830 FB £20,550–£23,985

SHIPLAKE COLLEGE
For further details see p. 58
Henley-on-Thames,
Oxfordshire RG9 4BW
Tel: +44 (0)1189 402455
Email: registrar@shiplake.org.uk
Website: www.shiplake.org.uk
Headmaster: Mr A G S Davies BSc(St Andrews)
Age range: B11–18 G16–18
No. of pupils: 475 VIth192
Fees: Day £17,100–£21,480 WB £23,970–£29,970 FB £31,950

Sibford School
Sibford Ferris, Banbury,
Oxfordshire OX15 5QL
Tel: 01295 781200
Head of School: Toby Spence
No. of pupils: VIth840
Fees: Day £7,758–£12,453 WB £15,555–£22,530 FB £23,718–£24,195

St Clare's, Oxford
139 Banbury Road, Oxford,
Oxfordshire OX2 7AL
Tel: +44 (0)1865 552031
Principal: Mrs Paula Holloway BSc, PGCE, MSc(Oxon), DipPM
Age range: 15–19
No. of pupils: 270
Fees: Day £16,707 FB £34,990

St Edward's, Oxford
Woodstock Road, Oxford,
Oxfordshire OX2 7NN
Tel: +44 (0)1865 319200
Warden: Stephen Jones
Age range: 13–18
No. of pupils: 680
Fees: Day £9,515 FB £11,890

St Helen and St Katharine
Faringdon Road, Abingdon,
Oxfordshire OX14 1BE
Tel: 01235 520173
Headmistress: Mrs R Dougall BA MA
Age range: G9–18
No. of pupils: VIth170
Fees: Day £12,420

St Hugh's School
Carswell Manor, Faringdon,
Oxfordshire SN7 8PT
Tel: 01367 870700
Headmaster: A J P Nott BA(Hons), PGCE
Age range: 3–13
Fees: Day £10,530–£17,880 WB £20,025–£21,405

St John's Priory School
St John's Road, Banbury,
Oxfordshire OX16 5HX
Tel: 01295 259607
Headmaster: Paul Cawley-Wakefield
Age range: 3–11
Fees: Day £3,400–£8,130

St Mary's School
13 St Andrew's Road, Henley-on-Thames, Oxfordshire RG9 1HS
Tel: 01491 573118
Headmaster: Mr Rob Harmer (BA)Hons
Age range: 2–11
No. of pupils: 143
Fees: Day £3,320

Summer Fields
Mayfield Road, Oxford,
Oxfordshire OX2 7EN
Tel: 01865 454433
Headmaster: Mr David Faber MA(Oxon)
Age range: B7–13
No. of pupils: 256
Fees: Day £17,700 FB £22,857

The King's School, Witney
New Yatt Road, Witney,
Oxfordshire OX29 6TA
Tel: 01993 778463
Principal: Mr Steve Beegoo
Age range: 3–16
No. of pupils: 200
Fees: Day £4,536

The Manor Preparatory School
Faringdon Road, Abingdon,
Oxfordshire OX13 6LN
Tel: 01235 858458
Headmaster: Mr Piers Heyworth MA, PGCE
Age range: B2–7 years G2–11 years
No. of pupils: 375
Fees: Day £8,571–£14,400

THE UNICORN SCHOOL
For further details see p. 60
20 Marcham Road, Abingdon,
Oxfordshire OX14 1AA
Tel: 01235 530222
Email: info@unicornoxford.co.uk
Website: www.unicornoxford.co.uk
Headteacher: Mr. Andrew Day BEd (Hons)University of Wales (Cardiff)
Age range: 6–16 years
No. of pupils: 74
Fees: Day £19,500

Tudor Hall School
Wykham Park, Banbury, Oxfordshire OX16 9UR
Tel: 01295 263434
Headmistress: Miss Wendy Griffiths BSc
Age range: G11–18
No. of pupils: 332 VIth81
Fees: Day £6,865 FB £10,870

Windrush Valley School
The Green, London Lane, Ascott-under-Wychwood, Oxfordshire OX7 6AN
Tel: 01993 831793
Headmaster: Mr Alan Wood MEd, TCert, DipSpEd, ACP, FCollP
Age range: 3–11
No. of pupils: 125
Fees: Day £5,970

Wychwood School
74 Banbury Road, Oxford, Oxfordshire OX2 6JR
Tel: 01865 557976
Headmistress: Mrs A K Johnson BSc (Dunelm)
Age range: G11–18
No. of pupils: 120 VIth40
Fees: Day £14,700 WB £22,200 FB £23,400

West Berkshire

Brockhurst & Marlston House Schools
Hermitage, Newbury, West Berkshire RG18 9UL
Tel: 01635 200293
Joint Heads: Mr David Fleming & Mrs Caroline Riley
Age range: G3–13
No. of pupils: 275
Fees: Day £7,410–£12,450 WB £16,530 FB £16,530

Cheam School
Headley, Newbury, West Berkshire RG19 8LD
Tel: +44 (0)1635 268242
Headmaster: Mr Martin Harris
Age range: 3–13
No. of pupils: 407
Fees: Day £3,805–£6,655 FB £8,995

Downe House School
Hermitage Road, Cold Ash, Thatcham, West Berkshire RG18 9JJ
Tel: 01635 200286
Headmistress: Mrs E McKendrick BA(Liverpool)
Age range: G11–18
No. of pupils: VIth174
Fees: Day £25,440 FB £35,160

Horris Hill
Newtown, Newbury, West Berkshire RG20 9DJ
Tel: 01635 40594
Headmaster: Mr G F Tollit B.A.(Hons)
Age range: B8–13
No. of pupils: 120
Fees: Day £17,250 FB £23,250

Marlston House Preparatory School
Hermitage, Newbury, West Berkshire RG18 9UL
Tel: 01635 200293
Headmistress: Mrs Caroline Riley MA, BEd
Age range: G3–13
No. of pupils: 110
Fees: Day £7,410–£12,450 WB £16,530

Newbury Hall
Enborne Road, (corner of Rockingham Road), Newbury, West Berkshire RG14 6AD
Tel: +44 (0)1635 36879

St Gabriel's
Sandleford Priory, Newbury, West Berkshire RG20 9BD
Tel: 01635 555680
Principal: Mr Richard Smith MA (Hons), MEd, PGCE
Age range: B6 months–11 G6 months–18
No. of pupils: 469 VIth40
Fees: Day £10,308–£16,830

St Michael's School
Harts Lane, Burghclere, Newbury, West Berkshire RG20 9JW
Tel: 01635 278137
Headmaster: Rev. Fr. Patrick Summers
Age range: 5–18
No. of pupils: VIth5

The Cedars School
Church Road, Aldermaston, West Berkshire RG7 4LR
Tel: 0118 971 4251
Headteacher: Mrs Jane O'Halloran
Age range: 4–11
No. of pupils: 50
Fees: Day £8,250

Thorngrove School
The Mount, Highclere, Newbury, West Berkshire RG20 9PS
Tel: 01635 253172
Headmaster: Mr Adam King
Age range: 2–13
Fees: Day £11,070–£13,860

Wiltshire

Ashwicke Hall School – Bath, UK
Ashwicke Hall, Marshfield, Chippenham, Wiltshire SN14 8AG
Tel: +44 (0) 1225 891841
School Director: Mr J Nicholson
Age range: 10–18
No. of pupils: 150

Avondale School
High Street, Bulford, Salisbury, Wiltshire SP4 9DR
Tel: 01980 632387
Headmaster: Mr Stuart Watson
Age range: 3–11
Fees: Day £5,625–£5,685

Chafyn Grove School
33 Bourne Avenue, Salisbury, Wiltshire SP1 1LR
Tel: 01722 333423
Headmaster: Mr Simon Head
Age range: 3–13
No. of pupils: 265
Fees: Day £2,250–£5,430 FB £6,165–£7,500

DAUNTSEY'S SCHOOL
For further details see p. 48
High Street, West Lavington, Devizes, Wiltshire SN10 4HE
Tel: 01380 814500
Email: admissions@dauntseys.org
Website: www.dauntseys.org
Head Master: Mr Mark Lascelles
Age range: 11–18
No. of pupils: 820 VIth270
Fees: Day £18,450 FB £30,540

Emmaus School
School Lane, Staverton, Trowbridge, Wiltshire BA14 6NZ
Tel: 01225 782684
Head: Mrs M Wiltshire
Age range: 5–16
No. of pupils: 54
Fees: Day £2,900

Focus School – Wilton Campus
The Hollows, Wilton, Salisbury, Wiltshire SP2 0JE
Tel: 01722 741910
Age range: 11–18
No. of pupils: 100

Godolphin Preparatory School
Laverstock Road, Salisbury, Wiltshire SP1 2RB
Tel: 01722 430 652
Headmistress: Mrs P White BEd(Winchester)
Age range: G3–11
No. of pupils: 85
Fees: Day £5,535–£10,692

Heywood Prep
The Priory, Corsham, Wiltshire SN13 0AP
Tel: 01249 713379
Headmaster: Mr Guy Barrett BSc(Hons)
Age range: 2–11
No. of pupils: 140
Fees: Day £6,450–£7,410

Leehurst Swan Prep School
Campbell Road, Salisbury, Wiltshire SP1 3BQ
Tel: 01722 333094
Headmaster: Mr Roger Leake BSc (Hons), PGCE, CBiol, MSB
Age range: 6 weeks–16 years
Fees: Day £8,190–£13,770

Maranatha Christian School
Queenlaines Farm, Sevenhampton, Swindon, Wiltshire SN6 7SQ
Tel: 01793 762075
Headteacher: Mr Paul Medlock
Age range: 3–18
No. of pupils: 68
Fees: Day £1,935–£7,470

Marlborough College
Marlborough, Wiltshire SN8 1PA
Tel: 01672 892300
the Master: Mr Jonathan Leigh MA
Age range: 13–18
No. of pupils: 940 VIth408
Fees: FB £35,280

Meadowpark Nursery & Pre-Preparatory
Calcutt Street, Cricklade, Wiltshire SN6 6BA
Tel: 01793 752600
Headteacher: Mrs R Kular
Age range: 0–11
Fees: Day £4,900

Pinewood School
Bourton, Swindon, Wiltshire SN6 8HZ
Tel: 01793 782205
Headmaster: Mr P J Hoyland
Age range: 3–13
No. of pupils: 313
Fees: Day £6,485–£13,410 WB £13,800–£14,670 FB £14,310–£15,210

Prior Park Preparatory School
Calcutt Street, Cricklade, Wiltshire SN6 6BB
Tel: 01793 750275
Headteacher: M A Pearce
Age range: 3–13
No. of pupils: 240
Fees: Day £10,212–£12,804 FB £15,009–£17,898

Salisbury Cathedral School
The Old Palace, 1 The Close, Salisbury, Wiltshire SP1 2EQ
Tel: 01722 555300
Head Master: Mr Clive Marriott BEd MA
Age range: 3–13
No. of pupils: 200
Fees: Day £2,385–£4,535 FB £18,270

Sandroyd School
Rushmore, Tollard Royal, Salisbury, Wiltshire SP5 5QD
Tel: 01725 516264
Headmaster: Mr Alastair Speers
Age range: 5–13
No. of pupils: 225
Fees: Day £7,470–£17,505 FB £16,650–£20,940

South Hills School
Home Farm Road, Wilton, Salisbury, Wiltshire SP2 8PJ
Tel: 01722 744971
Principal: Mrs A Proctor
Age range: 3 months–7 Years

St Francis School
Marlborough Road, Pewsey, Wiltshire SN9 5NT
Tel: 01672 563228
Headmaster: Mr David Sibson
Age range: 2–13
Fees: Day £684–£12,216

St Margaret's Preparatory School
Curzon Street, Calne, Wiltshire SN11 0DF
Tel: 01249 857220
Headmistress: Mrs Karen Cordon
Age range: 3–11
No. of pupils: 200
Fees: Day £4,614–£12,600

St Mary's Calne
Curzon Street, Calne, Wiltshire SN11 0DF
Tel: 01249 857200
Headmistress: Dr Felicia Kirk BA(University of MD), MA, PhD(Brown University)
Age range: G11–18
No. of pupils: 348 VIth113
Fees: Day £27,150 FB £36,450

Stonar School
Cottles Park, Atworth, Melksham, Wiltshire SN12 8NT
Tel: 01225 701740
Head: Mr Toby Nutt
Age range: B2–11 G2–18
No. of pupils: 330 VIth46
Fees: Day £7,665–£14,895 WB £16,350–£19,050 FB £18,060–£26,880

The Godolphin School
Milford Hill, Salisbury, Wiltshire SP1 2RA
Tel: 01722 430509
Headmistress: Mrs Emma Hattersley
Age range: G11–18
No. of pupils: 340 VIth100
Fees: Day £18,528 FB £27,024

Warminster School
Church Street, Warminster, Wiltshire BA12 8PJ
Tel: +44 (0)1985 210160
Headmaster: Mr Mark Mortimer MBA BA
Age range: 3–18
No. of pupils: 550
Fees: Day £4,910 FB £10,195

East

KEY TO SYMBOLS

- *Boys' school*
- *Girls' school*
- *International school*
- *Tutorial or sixth form college*
- *A levels*
- *Boarding accommodation*
- *Bursaries*
- *International Baccalaureate*
- *Learning support*
- *Entrance at 16+*
- *Vocational qualifications*
- *Independent Association of Preparatory Schools*
- *The Headmasters' & Headmistresses' Conference*
- *Independent Schools Association*
- *Girls' School Association*
- *Boarding Schools' Association*
- *Society of Heads*

Unless otherwise indicated, all schools are coeducational day schools. Single-sex and boarding schools will be indicated by the relevant icon.

Bedfordshire

Bedford Girls' School
Cardington Road, Bedford, Bedfordshire MK42 0BX
Tel: 01234 361900
Headmistress: Miss Jo MacKenzie BSc, MSc
Age range: G7–18
No. of pupils: 1000
Fees: Day £7,602–£10,683

Bedford Modern School
Manton Lane, Bedford, Bedfordshire MK41 7NT
Tel: 01234 332500
Headmaster: Mr M Hall BA(Hons) MA
Age range: 7–18
No. of pupils: 1226
Fees: Day £9,273–£12,720

Bedford Preparatory School
De Parys Avenue, Bedford, Bedfordshire MK40 2TU
Tel: 01234 362271/362274
Headmaster: Mr C Godwin BSc, MA
Age range: B7–13
No. of pupils: 438
Fees: Day £9,312–£12,204 WB £14,694–£17,586 FB £15,414–£18,306

BEDFORD SCHOOL
For further details see p. 68
De Parys Avenue, Bedford, Bedfordshire MK40 2TU
Tel: +44 (0)1234 362216
Email: admissions@bedfordschool.org.uk
Website: www.bedfordschool.org.uk
Head Master: Mr James Hodgson BA
Age range: B7–18 years
No. of pupils: 1061
Fees: Day £11,973–£18,477 WB £20,310–£30,219 FB £21,309–£31,251

Focus School – Biggleswade Campus
The Oaks, Potton Road, Biggleswade, Bedfordshire SG18 0EP
Tel: 01767 602800
Age range: 7–18 years
No. of pupils: 75

Luton Pentecostal Church Christian Academy
15 Church Street, Luton, Bedfordshire LU1 3JE
Tel: 01582 412276
Principal: Pastor Chris Oakey
Age range: 3–13
No. of pupils: 56
Fees: Day £2,640

Orchard School & Nursery
High Gobion Road, Barton-le-Clay, Bedford, Bedfordshire MK45 4LT
Tel: 01582 882054
Headteacher: Mrs A Burton
Age range: 0–6
No. of pupils: 127

Pilgrims Pre-Preparatory School
Brickhill Drive, Bedford, Bedfordshire MK41 7QZ
Tel: 01234 369555
Head: Mrs J Webster BEd(Hons), EYPS
Age range: 3 months–8 years
No. of pupils: 385
Fees: Day £2,795–£7,590

Polam School
43-45 Lansdowne Road, Bedford, Bedfordshire MK40 2BU
Tel: 01234 261864
Head: Mrs Jessica Harris
Age range: 1–9
No. of pupils: 100
Fees: Day £8,145

Rabia Girls School
12-16 Portland Road, Luton, Bedfordshire LU4 8AX
Tel: 01582 493239
Headteacher: Mrs F Shaikh
Age range: G4–16
No. of pupils: 265

Rushmoor School
58-60 Shakespeare Road, Bedford, Bedfordshire MK40 2DL
Tel: 01234 352031
Headteacher: Ian Daniel BA, NPQH
Age range: B3–16 G3–11
Fees: Day £4,890–£8,985

Sceptre School
Ridgeway Avenue, Dunstable, Bedfordshire LU5 4QL
Tel: 01582 665676
Age range: 11–16
No. of pupils: 77

St Andrew's School
78 Kimbolton Road, Bedford, Bedfordshire MK40 2PA
Tel: 01234 267272
Headmistress: Mrs J E Marsland BPhil(Ed)
Age range: B3–9 G3–16
No. of pupils: 385
Fees: Day £5,205–£8,505

St George's School
28 Priory Road, Dunstable, Bedfordshire LU5 4HR
Tel: 01582 661471
Headmistress: Mrs Plater
Age range: 3–11
No. of pupils: 120
Fees: Day £4,020–£4,560

Cambridgeshire

Abbey College Cambridge
Homerton Gardens, Purbeck Road, Cambridge, Cambridgeshire CB2 8EB
Tel: 01223 578280
Principal: Dr Julian Davies
Age range: 13–21
No. of pupils: VIth370
Fees: Day £22,000 FB £39,000–£43,000

Bellerbys College Cambridge
Queens Campus, Bateman Street, Cambridge, Cambridgeshire CB2 1LU
Tel: +44 (0)1223 652 800
Principal: Mr Nicholas Waite
Age range: 15–25

Cambridge International School
Cherry Hinton Hall, Cherry Hinton Road, Cambridge, Cambridgeshire CB1 8DW
Tel: +44 (0)1223 416938
Age range: 3–18 years

Cambridge Seminars Tutorial College
Logic House, 143-147 Newmarket Road, Cambridge, Cambridgeshire CB5 8HA
Tel: 01223 313464
Principal: M R Minhas BSc, CEng
Age range: 16–20
Fees: Day £12,000

Cambridge Steiner School
Hinton Road, Fulbourn, Cambridge, Cambridgeshire CB21 5DZ
Tel: 01223 882727
Age range: 2 –11
No. of pupils: 100
Fees: Day £6,300

CATS Cambridge
13-15 Round Church Street, Cambridge, Cambridgeshire CB5 8AD
Tel: 01223 314431
Principal: Dr Craig Wilson
Age range: 14–19+

CCSS (Cambridge Centre for Sixth-form Studies)
4-5 Bene't Place, Lensfield Road, Cambridge, Cambridgeshire CB2 1EL
Tel: 01223 716890
Principal: Mr Stuart Nicholson MA(Oxon), MBA, PGCE, NPQH, CPhys
Age range: 15–21
Fees: Day £18,750–£23,655 FB £25,050–£37,200

Kimbolton School
Kimbolton, Huntingdon, Cambridgeshire PE28 0EA
Tel: 01480 860505
Headmaster: Jonathan Belbin BA
Age range: 4–18
No. of pupils: VIth170
Fees: Day £8,625–£13,425 FB £22,215

King's Acremont, King's Ely Nursery & Pre-Prep
30 Egremont Street, Ely, Cambridgeshire CB6 1AE
Tel: 01353 660702
Head: Lynda Brereton
Age range: 3–7
Fees: Day £7,563–£8,136

King's College School
West Road, Cambridge, Cambridgeshire CB3 9DN
Tel: 01223 365814
Headmaster: Mr Nicholas Robinson BA, PGCE, FRSA
Age range: 4–13
No. of pupils: 418
Fees: Day £10,755–£13,680 WB £21,300

KING'S ELY
For further details see p. 76
Ely, Cambridgeshire CB7 4DB
Tel: 01353 660700
Email: enquiries@kingsely.org
Website: www.kingsely.org
Principal: Mrs Susan Freestone MEd, GRSM, LRAM, ARCM, FRSA
Age range: 1–18
No. of pupils: 1025 VIth185
Fees: Day £13,830–£20,853 FB £22,053–£30,189

King's Ely Junior
Ely, Cambridgeshire CB7 4DB
Tel: 01353 660707
Head: Mr Richard Whymark
Age range: 7–13
No. of pupils: 345
Fees: Day £13,180–£14,382 FB £21,013–£22,181

Magdalene House Preparatory School
North Brink, Wisbech, Cambridgeshire PE13 1JX
Tel: 01945 586 780
Head: Mr Chris Moxon BA, PGCE
Age range: 4–11
No. of pupils: 180
Fees: Day £8,200

MANDER PORTMAN WOODWARD – CAMBRIDGE
For further details see p. 80
3-4 Brookside, Cambridge, Cambridgeshire CB2 1JE
Tel: 01223 350158
Email: cambridge@mpw.ac.uk
Website: www.mpw.ac.uk
Principal: Dr Markus Bernhardt
Age range: 15–19

Phoenix School Cambridge
Willow Tree, Twenty Pence Road, Wilburton, Ely, Cambridgeshire CB6 3PX
Tel: 01353 967581
Headteacher: Mrs Gill Cooke BEd (Hons)
Age range: 3–11
No. of pupils: 29

Sancton Wood School
2 St Paul's Road, Cambridge, Cambridgeshire CB1 2EZ
Tel: 01223 471703
Head Teacher: Mr Richard Settle
Age range: 3–16
No. of pupils: 193
Fees: Day £3,546–£11,337

St Andrew's Cambridge
2A Free School Lane, Cambridge, Cambridgeshire CB2 3QA
Tel: 01223 360040
Principal: Mrs A Collins
Age range: 14–20
No. of pupils: VIth130
Fees: FB £15,000–£17,000

ST FAITH'S
For further details see p. 88
Trumpington Road, Cambridge, Cambridgeshire CB2 8AG
Tel: 01223 352073
Email: admissions@stfaiths.co.uk
Website: www.stfaiths.co.uk
Headmaster: Mr N L Helliwell
Age range: 4–13
No. of pupils: 540
Fees: Day £11,865–£14,955

St John's College School
73 Grange Road, Cambridge, Cambridgeshire CB3 9AB
Tel: 01223 353532
Headmaster: Mr N. Chippington MA(Cantab), FRCO
Age range: 4–13
No. of pupils: 453
Fees: Day £11,391–£14,313 FB £22,602

St Mary's School
Bateman Street, Cambridge, Cambridgeshire CB2 1LY
Tel: 01223 353253
Headmistress: Ms Charlotte Avery
Age range: G4–18
No. of pupils: 619 VIth90
Fees: Day £15,324 WB £27,753 FB £32,241

Stephen Perse Foundation Junior School
St Eligius Street, Cambridge, Cambridgeshire CB2 1HX
Tel: 01223 346 140
Head: Miss K Milne
Age range: 7–11
No. of pupils: 135
Fees: Day £11,610

Stephen Perse Foundation Senior School
Union Road, Cambridge, Cambridgeshire CB2 1HF
Tel: 01223 454700
Principal: Miss P M Kelleher MA(Oxon), MA(Sussex)
Age range: 11–16 years
No. of pupils: VIth150
Fees: Day £15,405

Stephen Perse Pre-prep, Madingley
Cambridge Road, Madingley, Cambridge, Cambridgeshire CB23 8AH
Tel: 01954 210309
Head of Pre-prep: Mrs Sarah Holyoake
Age range: 3–7
No. of pupils: 60
Fees: Day £10,200

THE LEYS SCHOOL
For further details see p. 92
Trumpington Road, Cambridge, Cambridgeshire CB2 7AD
Tel: 01223 508900
Email: admissions@theleys.net
Website: www.theleys.net
Headmaster: Mr Martin Priestley
Age range: 11–18
No. of pupils: 565
Fees: Day £15,435–£21,390 FB £23,295–£31,965

The Perse Pelican Nursery and Pre-Preparatory School
Northwold House, 92 Glebe Road, Cambridge, Cambridgeshire CB1 7TD
Tel: 01223 403940
Headmistress: Mrs S C Waddington MA
Age range: 3–7
No. of pupils: 154
Fees: Day £11,640

The Perse Preparatory School
Trumpington Road, Cambridge, Cambridgeshire CB2 8EX
Tel: 01223 403920
Head: James Piper
Age range: 7–11

The Perse School
Hills Road, Cambridge, Cambridgeshire CB2 8QF
Tel: 01223 403800
Head: Mr E C Elliott
Age range: 11–18
No. of pupils: 851 VIth250
Fees: Day £13,263

The Peterborough School
Thorpe Road, Peterborough, Cambridgeshire PE3 6AP
Tel: 01733 343357
Headmaster: Mr A D Meadows BSc(Hons)
Age range: 6 weeks–18 years
No. of pupils: 430
Fees: Day £9,893–£14,121

Whitehall School
117 High Street, Somersham, Cambridgeshire PE28 3EH
Tel: 01487 840966
Principal: Rebecca Hutley
Age range: 3–11
No. of pupils: 109
Fees: Day £1,510–£1,953

Wisbech Grammar School
North Brink, Wisbech, Cambridgeshire PE13 1JX
Tel: 01945 583 631
Head: Mr Chris Staley BA, MBA
Age range: 11–18
No. of pupils: 410
Fees: Day £11,655

Essex

Alleyn Court Preparatory School
Wakering Road, Southend-on-Sea, Essex SS3 0PW
Tel: 01702 582553
Headmaster: Mr Gareth Davies BA(Hons), PGCE
Age range: 2–11
Fees: Day £2,607–£10,881

Brentwood Preparatory School
Middleton Hall Lane, Brentwood, Essex CM15 8EQ
Tel: 01277 243333
Headmaster: Mr Jason Whiskerd
Age range: 3–11
No. of pupils: 407
Fees: Day £6,957–£13,914

BRENTWOOD SCHOOL
For further details see p. 72
Middleton Hall Lane, Brentwood, Essex CM15 8EE
Tel: 01277 243243
Email: headmaster@brentwood.essex.sch.uk
Website: www.brentwoodschool.co.uk
Headmaster: Mr Ian Davies
Age range: 3–18
No. of pupils: 1529
Fees: Day £18,216 FB £35,700

Colchester High School
Wellesley Road, Colchester, Essex CO3 3HD
Tel: 01206 573389
Principal: David Young BA(Hons), PGCE
Age range: 2 –16
No. of pupils: 486
Fees: Day £3,300–£10,000

Coopersale Hall School
Flux's Lane, off Stewards Green Road, Epping, Essex CM16 7PE
Tel: 01992 577133
Headmistress: Miss Kaye Lovejoy
Age range: 2 –11
No. of pupils: 275
Fees: Day £3,645–£7,275

Dame Bradbury's School
Ashdon Road, Saffron Walden, Essex CB10 2AL
Tel: 01799 522348
Headmistress: Ms Tracy Handford
Age range: 3–11
No. of pupils: 254
Fees: Day £2,000–£10,950

Elm Green Preparatory School
Parsonage Lane, Little Baddow, Chelmsford, Essex CM3 4SU
Tel: 01245 225230
Principal: Ms Ann Milner
Age range: 4–11
No. of pupils: 220
Fees: Day £7,449

Felsted Preparatory School
Felsted, Great Dunmow, Essex CM6 3JL
Tel: 01371 822610
Headmistress: Mrs Jenny Burrett BA(Dunelm), MEd(Cantab), PGCE
Age range: 4–13
No. of pupils: 460
Fees: Day £6,390–£13,965 FB £17,850

Felsted School
Felsted, Great Dunmow, Essex CM6 3LL
Tel: +44 (0)1371 822608
Headmaster: Mr Chris Townsend
Age range: 13–18
No. of pupils: 522 VIth426
Fees: Day £22,485 WB £32,235 FB £34,275

Gosfield School
Cut Hedge Park, Halstead Road, Gosfield, Halstead, Essex CO9 1PF
Tel: 01787 474040
Principal: Dr Sarah Welch
Age range: 4–18
No. of pupils: VIth21
Fees: Day £4,740–£13,695 WB £15,465–£17,310 FB £17,985–£23,130

Great Warley School
Warley Street, Great Warley, Brentwood, Essex CM13 3LA
Tel: 01277 233288
Head: Mrs B Harding
Age range: 3–11
Fees: Day £2,250–£3,500

Heathcote School
Eves Corner, Danbury, Chelmsford, Essex CM3 4QB
Tel: 01245 223131
Head Teacher: Miss H Petersen
Age range: 2–11
Fees: Day £4,830–£7,245

Herington House School
1 Mount Avenue, Hutton, Brentwood, Essex CM13 2NS
Tel: 01277 211595
Principal: Mr R Dudley-Cooke
Age range: 3–11
No. of pupils: 129
Fees: Day £4,365–£8,670

Holmwood House Preparatory School
Chitts Hill, Lexden, Colchester, Essex CO3 9ST
Tel: 01206 574305
Headmaster: Alexander Mitchell
Age range: 4–13
No. of pupils: 302
Fees: Day £9,450–£16,695 WB £19,968–£21,183

Hutton Manor School
428 Rayleigh Road, Hutton, Brentwood, Essex CM13 1SD
Tel: 01277 245585
Head: Mr P Pryke
Age range: 3–11
Fees: Day £2,975–£3,995

Littlegarth School
Horkesley Park, Nayland, Colchester, Essex CO6 4JR
Tel: 01206 262332
Headmaster: Mr Peter H Jones
Age range: 2 –11 years
No. of pupils: 318
Fees: Day £2,700–£3,140

Maldon Court Preparatory School
Silver Street, Maldon, Essex CM9 4QE
Tel: 01621 853529
Headteacher: Mrs L Guest
Age range: 3–11
Fees: Day £7,305

New Hall School
The Avenue, Boreham, Chelmsford, Essex CM3 3HS
Tel: 01245 467588
Principal: Mrs Katherine Jeffrey MA, BA, PGCE, MA(Ed Mg), NPQH
Age range: Coed 3-11, Single 11-16, Coed 16–18
No. of pupils: 1180 VIth217
Fees: Day £9,432–£19,440 WB £19,038–£27,813 FB £21,033–£29,847

Oxford House School
2-4 Lexden Road, Colchester, Essex CO3 3NE
Tel: 01206 576686
Head Teacher: Mrs Sarah Leyshon
Age range: 2 –11
No. of pupils: 158

Saint Pierre School
16 Leigh Road, Leigh-on-Sea, Southend-on-Sea, Essex SS9 1LE
Tel: 01702 474164
Headmaster: Mr Chris Perkins
Age range: 2 –11+
Fees: Day £2,062–£6,186

St Anne's Preparatory School
New London Road, Chelmsford, Essex CM2 0AW
Tel: 01245 353488
Head: Mrs S Robson
Age range: 3–11
No. of pupils: 160
Fees: Day £6,300–£6,600

ST CEDD'S SCHOOL
For further details see p. 86
178a New London Road, Chelmsford, Essex CM2 0AR
Tel: 01245 392810
Email: info@stcedds.org.uk
Website: www.stcedds.org.uk
Head: Dr Pamela Edmonds
Age range: 3–11
No. of pupils: 400
Fees: Day £8,550–£10,110

St John's School
Stock Road, Billericay, Essex CM12 0AR
Tel: 01277 623070
Head Teacher: Mrs F Armour BEd(Hons)
Age range: 3–16
No. of pupils: 392
Fees: Day £4,470–£10,650

ST MARGARET'S PREPARATORY SCHOOL
For further details see p. 90
Gosfield Hall Park, Gosfield, Halstead, Essex CO9 1SE
Tel: 01787 472134
Email: admin@stmargaretsprep.com
Website: www.stmargaretsprep.com
Headmaster: Mr. Callum Douglas
Age range: 2–11
Fees: Day £9,315–£11,280

St Mary's School
Lexden Road, Colchester, Essex CO3 3RB
Tel: 01206 572544 Admissions: 01206 216420
Principal: Mrs H K Vipond MEd, BSc(Hons), NPQH
Age range: B3–4 G3–16
No. of pupils: 430
Fees: Day £7,464–£11,340

St Michael's Church Of England Preparatory School
198 Hadleigh Road, Leigh-on-Sea, Southend-on-Sea, Essex SS9 2LP
Tel: 01702 478719
Head: Steve Tompkins BSc(Hons), PGCE, MA, NPQH
Age range: 3–11
No. of pupils: 271
Fees: Day £3,510–£6,990

St Nicholas School
Hillingdon House, Hobbs Cross Road, Harlow, Essex CM17 0NJ
Tel: 01279 429910
Headmaster: Mr K M Knight BEd, MA, NPQH
Age range: 4–16
No. of pupils: 400
Fees: Day £7,470–£9,660

St Philomena's Catholic School
Hadleigh Road, Frinton-on-Sea, Essex CO13 9HQ
Tel: 01255 674492
Headmistress: Mrs B McKeown DipEd
Age range: 3–11
Fees: Day £5,670–£6,750

Thorpe Hall School
Wakering Road, Southend-on-Sea, Essex SS1 3RD
Tel: 01702 582340
Headmaster: Mr Andrew Hampton
Age range: 2–16 years
No. of pupils: 359
Fees: Day £7,695–£10,620

Trinity School
Brizes Park, Ongar Road, Kelvedon Hatch, Brentwood, Essex CM15 0DG
Tel: 01277 374123
Headmaster: Reverend M S B Reid BD
Age range: 4–18

Ursuline Preparatory School
Old Great Ropers, Great Ropers Lane, Warley, Brentwood, Essex CM13 3HR
Tel: 01277 227152
Headmistress: Mrs Pauline Wilson MSc
Age range: 3–11
Fees: Day £1,835–£3,425

Walden School
Mount Pleasant Road, Saffron Walden, Essex CB11 3EB
Tel: 01799 525351
Head: Ms Anna Chaudhri MA
Age range: 3–18
No. of pupils: 390 VIth50
Fees: Day £2,375–£5,305 WB £6,615–£7,690 FB £7,190–£8,590

Widford Lodge School
Widford Road, Chelmsford, Essex CM2 9AN
Tel: 01245 352581
Headmaster: Mr Simon Trowell
Age range: 2–11
Fees: Day £5,400–£7,050

Hertfordshire

Abbot's Hill School
Bunkers Lane, Hemel Hempstead, Hertfordshire HP3 8RP
Tel: 01442 240333
Headmistress: Mrs E Thomas BA (Hons), PGCE, NPQH
No. of pupils: 510
Fees: Day £10,050–£17,500

Aldenham School
Elstree, Hertfordshire WD6 3AJ
Tel: 01923 858122
Headmaster: Mr James C Fowler MA
Age range: 3–18
No. of pupils: 700
Fees: Day £15,291–£21,414 FB £21,099–£31,384

Aldwickbury School
Wheathampstead Road, Harpenden, Hertfordshire AL5 1AD
Tel: 01582 713022
Headmaster: Mr V W Hales
Age range: B4–13
No. of pupils: 330
Fees: Day £2,002–£3,012 WB £3,800–£3,884

Beechwood Park School
Markyate, St Albans, Hertfordshire AL3 8AW
Tel: 01582 840333
Headmaster: Mr E Balfour BA (Hons), PGCE
Age range: 3–13
No. of pupils: 535
Fees: Day £9,000–£15,225 WB £18,843

BERKHAMSTED SCHOOL
For further details see p. 70
Overton House, 131 High Street, Berkhamsted, Hertfordshire HP4 2DJ
Tel: 01442 358001
Email: admissions@berkhamstedschool.org
Website: www.berkhamstedschool.org
Principal: Mr Richard Backhouse MA(Cantab)
Age range: 3–18
No. of pupils: VIth405
Fees: Day £10,365–£20,250 WB £27,115 FB £32,255

Bhaktivedanta Manor School
Hilfield Lane, Aldenham, Watford, Hertfordshire WD25 8EZ
Tel: 01923 851000 Ext:241
Headteacher: Mrs. Wendy Harrison
Age range: 4–12
No. of pupils: 45
Fees: Day £1,680

Bishop's Stortford College
10 Maze Green Road, Bishop's Stortford, Hertfordshire CM23 2PJ
Tel: 01279 838575
Headmaster: Mr Jeremy Gladwin
Age range: 13–18
No. of pupils: VIth249
Fees: Day £18,915–£19,086 WB £27,183–£27,348 FB £28,950–£30,273

Bishop's Stortford College Prep School
Maze Green Road, Bishop's Stortford, Hertfordshire CM23 2PH
Tel: 01279 838607
Head of the Prep School: Mr Bill Toleman
Age range: 4–13
No. of pupils: 460
Fees: Day £13,500–£15,132 WB £20,010–£21,726 FB £20,226–£22,857

Charlotte House Preparatory School
88 The Drive, Rickmansworth, Hertfordshire WD3 4DU
Tel: 01923 772101
Head: Miss P Woodcock
Age range: G3–11
No. of pupils: 140
Fees: Day £6,900–£11,100

Duncombe School
4 Warren Park Road, Bengeo, Hertford, Hertfordshire SG14 3JA
Tel: 01992 414100
Headmaster: Mr Jeremy Phelan M.A. (Ed)
Age range: 2–11
No. of pupils: 325
Fees: Day £9,075–£12,585

Edge Grove School
Aldenham Village, Hertfordshire WD25 8NL
Tel: 01923 855724
Headmaster: Mr Ben Evans
Age range: 3–13
Fees: Day £11,100–£114,835 WB £15,870–£19,305 FB £15,870–£19,305

Egerton Rothesay School
Durrants Lane, Berkhamsted, Hertfordshire HP4 3UJ
Tel: 01442 865275
Headteacher: Mr Colin Parker BSc(Hons), Dip.Ed (Oxon), PGCE, C.Math MIMA
Age range: 6–19
No. of pupils: 166
Fees: Day £15,255–£21,711

Haberdashers' Aske's School
Butterfly Lane, Elstree, Borehamwood, Hertfordshire WD6 3AF
Tel: 020 8266 1700
Headmaster: Mr P B Hamilton MA
Age range: B5–18
No. of pupils: 1402 VIth310
Fees: Day £10,641–£14,103

Haberdashers' Aske's School for Girls
Aldenham Road, Elstree, Borehamwood, Hertfordshire WD6 3BT
Tel: 020 8266 2300
Headmistress: Miss Biddie A O'Connor MA (Oxon)
Age range: G4–18
No. of pupils: 1190
Fees: Day £14,199–£16,446

HAILEYBURY
For further details see p. 74
Haileybury, Hertford, Hertfordshire SG13 7NU
Tel: +44 (0)1992 706200
Email: admissions@haileybury.com
Website: www.haileybury.com
The Master: Mr Martin Collier MA BA PGCE
Age range: 11–18
No. of pupils: 804 VIth323
Fees: Day £16,455–£24,753 FB £20,796–£32,784

Haresfoot School
Chesham Road, Berkhamsted, Hertfordshire HP4 2SZ
Tel: 01442 872742
Principal: Mrs Carole Hawkins BA, PGCE
Age range: 0–11
Fees: Day £1,845–£7,770

Heath Mount School
Woodhall Park, Watton-at-Stone, Hertford, Hertfordshire SG14 3NG
Tel: 01920 830230
Headmaster: Mr C Gillam BEd(Hons)
Age range: 3–13
Fees: Day £6,480–£16,695 WB £17,690–£21,945

High Elms Manor School
High Elms Lane, Watford, Hertfordshire WD25 0JX
Tel: 01923 681 103
Headmistress: Mrs Sheila O'Neill MontDipDist, TCert, BA, AMI Dip
Age range: 2–11
No. of pupils: 100
Fees: Day £4,950–£11,400

Howe Green House School
Great Hallingbury, Bishop's Stortford, Hertfordshire CM22 7UF
Tel: 01279 657706
Age range: 2–11
Fees: Day £5,946–£9,444

Immanuel College
87/91 Elstree Road, Bushey, Hertfordshire WD23 4EB
Tel: 020 8950 0604
Headmaster: Mr Philip Skelker MA
Age range: 11–18
No. of pupils: 520 VIth127
Fees: Day £10,995

Kingshott
St Ippolyts, Hitchin, Hertfordshire SG4 7JX
Tel: 01462 432009
Headmaster: Mr Iain Gilmour
Age range: 3–13
No. of pupils: 372
Fees: Day £4,770–£10,350

Little Acorns Montessori School
Lincolnsfield Centre, Bushey Hall Drive, Bushey, Hertfordshire WD23 2ER
Tel: 01923 230705
Age range: 2–6
No. of pupils: 28
Fees: Day £2,120

Lochinver House School
Heath Road, Little Heath, Potters Bar, Hertfordshire EN6 1LW
Tel: 01707 653064
Headmaster: Ben Walker BA(Hons), PGCE, CELTA
Age range: B4–13
No. of pupils: 349
Fees: Day £9,000–£11,826

LOCKERS PARK
For further details see p. 78
Lockers Park Lane, Hemel Hempstead, Hertfordshire HP1 1TL
Tel: 01442 251712
Email: secretary@lockerspark.herts.sch.uk
Website: www.lockerspark.herts.sch.uk
Headmaster: Mr C R Wilson
Age range: B4–13 G4–7
No. of pupils: 170
Fees: Day £10,050–£16,530 FB £23,160

Longwood School
Bushey Hall Drive, Bushey, Hertfordshire WD23 2QG
Tel: 01923 253715
Head Teacher: Mrs Muriel Garman
Age range: 3–11
Fees: Day £4,590–£5,790

MANOR LODGE SCHOOL
For further details see p. 82
Rectory Lane, Ridge Hill, Shenley, Hertfordshire WD7 9BG
Tel: 01707 642424
Email: enquiries@manorlodgeschool.com
Website: www.manorlodgeschool.com
Headmaster: Mr G Dunn CertEd
Age range: 3–11
No. of pupils: 430
Fees: Day £10,650–£11,910

Merchant Taylors' Prep
Moor Farm, Sandy Lodge Road, Rickmansworth, Hertfordshire WD3 1LW
Tel: 01923 825648
Headmaster: Dr T D Lee BEd(Hons)
Age range: B4–13
No. of pupils: 300
Fees: Day £2,613–£9,414

Princess Helena College
Preston, Hitchin, Hertfordshire SG4 7RT
Tel: 01462 443888
Headmistress: Mrs Sue Wallace-Woodroffe
Age range: G11–18
No. of pupils: 194 VIth35
Fees: Day £15,585–£18,975 FB £22,185–£27,585

Queenswood
Shepherd's Way, Brookmans Park, Hatfield, Hertfordshire AL9 6NS
Tel: 01707 602500
Principal: Mrs P C Edgar BA(Hons)London, PGCE
Age range: G11–18
No. of pupils: 400 VIth120
Fees: Day £19,485–£21,825 FB £26,295–£28,665

Radlett Preparatory School
Kendal Hall, Watling Street, Radlett, Hertfordshire WD7 7LY
Tel: 01923 856812
Principal: Mr G White BEd (Hons)
Age range: 4–11
Fees: Day £9,180

Rudolf Steiner School
Langley Hill, Kings Langley, Hertfordshire WD4 9HG
Tel: 01923 262505
Age range: 3–19
No. of pupils: 405
Fees: Day £2,985–£7,800

Sherrardswood School
Lockleys, Welwyn, Hertfordshire AL6 0BJ
Tel: 01438 714282
Headmistress: Mrs L Corry
Age range: 2–18
No. of pupils: 357
Fees: Day £6,720–£12,750

St Albans High School for Girls
Townsend Avenue, St Albans, Hertfordshire AL1 3SJ
Tel: 01727 853800
Headmistress: Mrs Jenny Brown MA (Oxon)
Age range: G4–18
No. of pupils: 940 VIth170

St Albans School
Abbey Gateway, St Albans, Hertfordshire AL3 4HB
Tel: 01727 855521
Headmaster: Mr JWJ Gillespie MA(Cantab), FRSA
Age range: B11–18 G16–18
No. of pupils: 870
Fees: Day £17,238

St Albans Tutors
69 London Road, St Albans, Hertfordshire AL1 1LN
Tel: 01727 842348
Principals: Mr. A N Jemal & Mr Elvis Cotena
Age range: 15+
Fees: Day £3,400

St Christopher School
Barrington Road, Letchworth, Hertfordshire SG6 3JZ
Tel: 01462 650 850
Head: Richard Palmer
Age range: 3–18
No. of pupils: 511 VIth78
Fees: Day £3,375–£14,505 FB £15,600–£25,470

St Columba's College
King Harry Lane, St Albans,
Hertfordshire AL3 4AW
Tel: 01727 855185
Headmaster: David R Buxton
Age range: B4–18
No. of pupils: 860 VIth150
Fees: Day £8,235–£10,416

St Columba's College Prep School
King Harry Lane, St Albans,
Hertfordshire AL3 4AW
Tel: 01727 862616
Head of Prep: Mrs Ruth Loveman
Age range: B4–11
No. of pupils: 250
Fees: Day £9,702–£12,087

St Edmund's College & Prep School
Old Hall Green, Nr Ware,
Hertfordshire SG11 1DS
Tel: 01920 824247
Head: Paulo Durán BA MA
Age range: 3–18
No. of pupils: 799 VIth135
Fees: Day £9,465–£14,955 WB £19,830–£22,575 FB £21,855–£24,990

St Edmund's Prep
Old Hall Green, Ware,
Hertfordshire SG11 1DS
Tel: 01920 824239
Head: Mr Steven Cartwright BSc (Surrey)
Age range: 3–11
No. of pupils: 185
Fees: Day £8,484–£12,252

St Francis' College
Broadway, Letchworth Garden City, Hertfordshire SG6 3PJ
Tel: 01462 670511
Headmistress: Mrs B Goulding
Age range: G3–18
No. of pupils: 460 VIth75
Fees: Day £8,670–£13,830 WB £19,425–£22,875 FB £24,195–£27,645

St Hilda's
High Street, Bushey,
Hertfordshire WD23 3DA
Tel: 020 8950 1751
Headmistress: Miss Sarah-Jane Styles MA
Age range: B2–4 G2–11
Fees: Day £4,635–£8,685

St Hilda's School
28 Douglas Road, Harpenden,
Hertfordshire AL5 2ES
Tel: 01582 712307
Headmaster: Mr Dan Sayers
Age range: G3–11 years
No. of pupils: 144
Fees: Day £5,715–£9,975

St John's Preparatory School
The Ridgeway, Potters Bar,
Hertfordshire EN6 5QT
Tel: 01707 657294
Headmistress: Mrs C Tardios BA(Hons)
Age range: 4–11
No. of pupils: 184
Fees: Day £8,190–£8,730

St Joseph's In The Park
St Mary's Lane, Hertingfordbury,
Hertford, Hertfordshire SG14 2LX
Tel: 01992 513810
Age range: 3–11
No. of pupils: 150
Fees: Day £5,430–£16,011

St Margaret's School, Bushey
Merry Hill Road, Bushey,
Hertfordshire WD23 1DT
Tel: 020 8416 4400
Head: Mrs Rose Hardy MA(Oxon), MEd, FRSA
Age range: G4–18 years
No. of pupils: 450 VIth100
Fees: Day £14,730 WB £20,220–£23,670 FB £27,600

Stanborough School
Stanborough Park, Garston,
Watford, Hertfordshire WD25 9JT
Tel: 01923 673268
Head Teacher: Ms Lorraine Dixon
Age range: 3–19
No. of pupils: 300 VIth20
Fees: Day £3,660–£5,500 WB £12,834–£15,846

Stormont
The Causeway, Potters Bar,
Hertfordshire EN6 5HA
Tel: 01707 654037
Age range: G4–11
Fees: Day £10,215–£10,680

The Christian School (Takeley)
Dunmow Road, Brewers End,
Takeley, Bishop's Stortford,
Hertfordshire CM22 6QH
Tel: 01279 871182
Headmaster: M E Humphries
Age range: 5–16
Fees: Day £3,720

The King's School
Elmfield, Ambrose Lane, Harpenden,
Hertfordshire AL5 4DU
Tel: 01582 767566
Principal: Mr Clive John Case BA, HDE
Age range: 5–16
Fees: Day £6,960

The Purcell School, London
Aldenham Road, Bushey,
Hertfordshire WD23 2TS
Tel: 01923 331100
Headteacher: Mr. Stephen Yeo
Age range: 10–18
No. of pupils: 180

TRING PARK SCHOOL FOR THE PERFORMING ARTS
For further details see p. 94
Tring Park, Tring,
Hertfordshire HP23 5LX
Tel: 01442 824255
Email: info@tringpark.com
Website: www.tringpark.com
Principal: Mr Stefan Anderson MA, ARCM, ARCT
Age range: 8–19
No. of pupils: 335 VIth217
Fees: Day £14,070–£22,410 FB £23,715–£33,540

Westbrook Hay Prep School
London Road, Hemel Hempstead,
Hertfordshire HP1 2RF
Tel: 01442 256143
Headmaster: Keith D Young BEd(Hons)
Age range: 3–13
No. of pupils: 300
Fees: Day £9,780–£14,085

York House School
Redheath, Sarratt Road,
Croxley Green, Rickmansworth,
Hertfordshire WD3 4LW
Tel: 01923 772395
Headmaster: Jon Gray BA(Ed)
Age range: 3–13
No. of pupils: 240
Fees: Day £10,845

Norfolk

All Saints School
School Road, Lessingham,
Norwich, Norfolk NR12 0DJ
Tel: 01692 582083
Head teacher: P Wright
Age range: 7–16
Fees: Day £3,600–£5,400

Beeston Hall School
Beeston Regis, West Runton,
Cromer, Norfolk NR27 9NQ
Tel: 01263 837324
Headmaster: Mr R C Gainher BSc(Hons)
Age range: 7–13
Fees: Day £15,333 FB £20,709

Downham Preparatory School & Montessori Nursery
The Old Rectory, Stow Bardolph,
Kings Lynn, Norfolk PE34 3HT
Tel: 01366 388066
Headmistress: Mrs E Laffeaty-Sharpe MontDip
Age range: 2–11
No. of pupils: 170
Fees: Day £4,959–£6,702

Focus School – Swaffham Campus
Turbine Way, Swaffham,
Norfolk PE37 7XD
Tel: 01760 336939
Headteacher: Mr John Shanahan
Age range: 7–18
No. of pupils: 161 VIth29

Glebe House School
2 Cromer Road, Hunstanton,
Norfolk PE36 6HW
Tel: 01485 532809
Headmaster: Mr Crofts
Age range: 0–13
No. of pupils: 110
Fees: Day £7,200–£10,800 WB £9,180–£12,780

Gresham's Nursery and Pre-Prep School
Market Place, Holt, Norfolk NR25 6BB
Tel: 01263 714575
Headmistress: Mrs Sarah Hollingsworth
Age range: 2–7
No. of pupils: 90
Fees: Day £9,750–£10,470

Gresham's Prep School
Cromer Road, Holt, Norfolk NR25 6EY
Tel: 01263 714600
Headmaster: Mr J H W Quick BA, PGCE
Age range: 7–13
No. of pupils: 263

Gresham's Senior School
Cromer Road, Holt, Norfolk NR25 6EA
Tel: 01263 714 614
Headmaster: Mr Douglas Robb
Age range: 13–18
No. of pupils: 490

Hethersett Old Hall School
Hethersett, Norwich, Norfolk NR9 3DW
Tel: 01603 810390
Headmaster: Mr S Crump
Age range: B3–11 G3–18
No. of pupils: 200
Fees: Day £5,850–£12,450 WB £13,395–£17,850 FB £15,585–£23,175

Langley School
Langley Park, Loddon, Norwich, Norfolk NR14 6BJ
Tel: 01508 520210
Headmaster: Dominic Findlay
Age range: 10–18
No. of pupils: 461 VIth97
Fees: Day £12,555 WB £21,285 FB £25,515

Norwich High School for Girls GDST
95 Newmarket Road, Norwich, Norfolk NR2 2HU
Tel: 01603 453265
Headmaster: Mr J J Morrow BA(Oxon), MA
Age range: G3–18
No. of pupils: VIth120
Fees: Day £6,906–£11,031

Norwich School
70 The Close, Norwich, Norfolk NR1 4DD
Tel: 01603 728430
Head Master: Steffan D A Griffiths
Age range: 7–18
No. of pupils: 1065
Fees: Day £13,725–£15,060

Norwich Steiner School
Hospital Lane, Norwich, Norfolk NR1 2HW
Tel: 01603 611175
Headteacher: Mr Andrew Vestrini
Age range: 3–18
No. of pupils: 91
Fees: Day £2,419–£6,515

Notre Dame Preparatory School
147 Dereham Road, Norwich, Norfolk NR2 3TA
Tel: 01603 625593
Headmaster: Mr K O'Herlihy
Age range: 2–11
No. of pupils: 140
Fees: Day £810–£5,445

Riddlesworth Hall Preparatory School
Garboldisham, Diss, Norfolk IP22 2TA
Tel: 01953 681 246
Principal: Mrs Susan Hayes
Age range: 2–13
No. of pupils: 137
Fees: Day £10,470 WB £16,500 FB £17,535

Sacred Heart School
17 Mangate Street, Swaffham, Norfolk PE37 7QW
Tel: 01760 721330/724577
Headmistress: Sr Francis Ridler FDC, BEd(Hons), EYPS
Age range: 3–16 years
No. of pupils: 156
Fees: Day £7,935–£11,775 WB £16,845–£18,045 FB £21,825–£21,825

St Nicholas House Prep School & Nursery
46 Yarmouth Road, North Walsham, Norfolk NR28 9AT
Tel: 01692 403143
Headteacher: Mr Philip Oldroyd
Age range: 2–11
No. of pupils: 95
Fees: Day £5,380

Stretton School
West Lodge, Albemarle Road, Norwich, Norfolk NR2 2DF
Tel: 01603 451285
Principal: Mrs Y D Barnett
Age range: 1–8
No. of pupils: 80
Fees: Day £1,020–£7,500

Taverham Hall Preparatory School
Taverham, Norwich, Norfolk NR8 6HU
Tel: 01603 868206
Headmaster: Mr Mike A Crossley NPQH, BEd(Hons)
Age range: 2 –13
Fees: Day £9,975–£11,400 WB £17,775 FB £17,775

The New Eccles Hall School
Quidenham, Norwich, Norfolk NR16 2NZ
Tel: 01953 887217
Headmaster: Richard Allard
Age range: 7–18
No. of pupils: 150
Fees: Day £6,945–£11,370 FB £16,740–£19,785

Thetford Grammar School
Bridge Street, Thetford, Norfolk IP24 3AF
Tel: 01842 752840
Headmaster: Mr G J Price MA
Age range: 4–18
No. of pupils: 298 VIth20
Fees: Day £10,191–£12,327

Thorpe House Langley Preparatory School
7 Yarmouth Road, Norwich, Norfolk NR7 0EA
Tel: 01603 433055
Headmaster: Simon Marfleet
Age range: 2–11
No. of pupils: 144
Fees: Day £2,100–£2,540

Town Close House Preparatory School
14 Ipswich Road, Norwich, Norfolk NR2 2LR
Tel: 01603 620180
Headmaster: Mr Graeme Lowe BEd
Age range: 3–13
No. of pupils: 455
Fees: Day £7,080–£11,085

Suffolk

Barnardiston Hall Preparatory School
Barnardiston, Nr Haverhill, Suffolk CB9 7TG
Tel: 01440 786316
Headmaster: Lt Col K A Boulter MA(Cantab)
Age range: 6 months–13 years
No. of pupils: 220
Fees: Day £8,040–£13,395 WB £18,510 FB £20,085

Brookes Cambridge
Flempton Road, Risby, Bury St Edmunds, Suffolk IP28 6QJ
Tel: 01284 760531
Headteacher: Mrs C Beedham
Age range: 0–16
No. of pupils: 240
Fees: Day £4,800–£5,850

Culford Preparatory School
Culford, Bury St Edmunds, Suffolk IP28 6TX
Tel: 01284 385383
Headmaster: Mr Mike Schofield
Age range: 7–13
No. of pupils: 214
Fees: Day £9,795–£13,200 FB £18,780–£20,340

Culford Pre-Preparatory School
Fieldgate House, Bury St Edmunds, Suffolk IP28 6TX
Tel: 01284 385412
Headmistress: Mrs Sarah Preston BA
Age range: 3–7
Fees: Day £2,380–£8,745

Culford School
Culford, Bury St Edmunds, Suffolk IP28 6TX
Tel: 01284 728615
Headmaster: Mr J F Johnson-Munday MA, MBA
Age range: 3 3/4–18
No. of pupils: 650 VIth150
Fees: Day £17,340 FB £26,580–£27,990

Fairstead House School
Fordham Road, Newmarket, Suffolk CB8 7AA
Tel: 01638 662318
Head: Lynda Brereton
Age range: 3 months–11 years
No. of pupils: 118
Fees: Day £9,210–£9,930

Felixstowe International College
Maybush Lane, Felixstowe, Suffolk IP11 7NA
Tel: 01394 282388
Principal: Mrs J S Lee
Age range: 10–17
No. of pupils: 20
Fees: FB £19,500

Finborough School
The Hall, Great Finborough, Stowmarket, Suffolk IP14 3EF
Tel: 01449 773600
Principal: Mr J Sinclair
Age range: 2–18
No. of pupils: 226 VIth20
Fees: Day £5,220–£8,580 WB £10,860–£14,280 FB £13,200–£17,010

Framlingham College
College Road, Framlingham, Suffolk IP13 9EY
Tel: 01728 723789
Headmaster: Mr Paul Taylor BA(Hons)
Age range: 2–18
No. of pupils: 700
Fees: Day £8,172–£18,635 WB £23,931–£25,495 FB £28,981

Ipswich High School for Girls
Woolverstone, Ipswich, Suffolk IP9 1AZ
Tel: 01473 201058
Head of School: Ms Oona Carlin
Age range: G3–18
No. of pupils: 500 VIth40
Fees: Day £7,839–£13,374

Ipswich Preparatory School
3 Ivry Street, Ipswich, Suffolk IP1 3QW
Tel: 01473 282800
Headteacher: Mrs A H Childs
Age range: 3–11
No. of pupils: 311
Fees: Day £8,358–£9,201

Ipswich School
Henley Road, Ipswich, Suffolk IP1 3SG
Tel: 01473 408300
Headmaster: Mr Nicholas Weaver MA
Age range: 11–18
No. of pupils: 739 VIth218
Fees: Day £11,478–£12,582 WB £18,759–£21,099 FB £20,313–£23,289

Moreton Hall Preparatory School
Mount Road, Bury St Edmunds, Suffolk IP32 7BJ
Tel: 01284 753532
Headmaster: Mr Chris Moxon BA PGCE
Age range: 4–13
No. of pupils: 100
Fees: Day £8,145–£13,320 WB £18,195 FB £20,385

Old Buckenham Hall School
Brettenham, Ipswich, Suffolk IP7 7PH
Tel: 01449 740252
Headmaster: Mr J A Brett MA
Age range: 3–13
No. of pupils: 228
Fees: Day £15,300 WB £20,070 FB £20,070

ORWELL PARK SCHOOL
For further details see p. 84
Nacton, Ipswich, Suffolk IP10 0ER
Tel: 01473 659225
Email: admissions@orwellpark.org
Website: www.orwellpark.co.uk
Headmaster: Mr Adrian Brown MA(Cantab)
Age range: 2–13
No. of pupils: 301

Saint Felix School
Halesworth Road, Southwold, Suffolk IP18 6SD
Tel: 01502 722175
Headmaster: Mr. James Harrison
Age range: 2–18
No. of pupils: 312 VIth65
Fees: Day £6,900–£14,970 WB £16,440–£20,970 FB £21,630–£26,160

South Lee Preparatory School
Nowton Road, Bury St Edmunds, Suffolk IP33 2BT
Tel: 01284 754654
Headmaster: Mr Mervyn Watch BEd (Hons)
Age range: 2–13
Fees: Day £7,575–£9,375

St Joseph's College
Birkfield, Belstead Road, Ipswich, Suffolk IP2 9DR
Tel: 01473 690281
Principal: Mrs Danielle Clarke
Age range: 3–18
No. of pupils: 564
Fees: Day £5,310–£13,305 WB £21,945–£24,000 FB £22,980–£29,685

Stoke College
Stoke-by-Clare, Sudbury, Suffolk CO10 8JE
Tel: 01787 278141
Head: Mr Chris Lumb
Age range: 3–16
Fees: Day £6,732–£10,482 WB £14,586–£16,926

Summerhill School
Leiston, Suffolk IP16 4HY
Tel: 01728 830540
Principal: Mrs Zoe Readhead
Age range: 5–17
No. of pupils: 69
Fees: Day £5,100–£10,830 FB £11,319–£18,291

The Meadows Montessori School
32 Larchcroft Road, Ipswich, Suffolk IP1 6AR
Tel: 01473 233782
Headteacher: Ms Samantha Sims
Age range: 4–11
No. of pupils: 54

The Old School Henstead
Toad Row, Beccles, Suffolk NR34 7LG
Tel: 01502 741150
Head: Mr W J McKinney
Age range: 2–11
No. of pupils: 123
Fees: Day £6,600–£9,510

The Royal Hospital School
Holbrook, Ipswich, Suffolk IP9 2RX
Tel: +44 (0) 1473 326200
Headmaster: Mr Simon Lockyer
Age range: 11–18
No. of pupils: 700 VIth220
Fees: Day £12,792–£17,610 WB £21,624–£27,209 FB £21,624–£27,209

Woodbridge School
Marryott House, Burkitt Road, Woodbridge, Suffolk IP12 4JH
Tel: 01394 615000
Headmaster: Mr N P Tetley MA(Cantab), PGCE
Age range: 4–18
No. of pupils: 900 VIth104
Fees: Day £14,802–£16,020 FB £29,985

East Midlands

KEY TO SYMBOLS

- *Boys' school*
- *Girls' school*
- *International school*
- *Tutorial or sixth form college*
- *A levels*
- *Boarding accommodation*
- *Bursaries*
- *International Baccalaureate*
- *Learning support*
- *Entrance at 16+*
- *Vocational qualifications*
- *Independent Association of Preparatory Schools*
- *The Headmasters' & Headmistresses' Conference*
- *Independent Schools Association*
- *Girls' School Association*
- *Boarding Schools' Association*
- *Society of Heads*

Unless otherwise indicated, all schools are coeducational day schools. Single-sex and boarding schools will be indicated by the relevant icon.

Derbyshire

Barlborough Hall School
Barlborough, Chesterfield,
Derbyshire S43 4TJ
Tel: 01246 810511
Headteacher: Mrs Nic Boys
Age range: 3–11
No. of pupils: 198
Fees: Day £6,420–£8,553

Dame Catherine Harpur's School
Rose Lane, Ticknall, Derby,
Derbyshire DE73 7JW
Tel: 01332 862792
Head: Ms Whyte
Age range: 3–11
No. of pupils: 28
Fees: Day £3,375

Derby Grammar School
Rykneld Hall, Rykneld Road, Littleover,
Derby, Derbyshire DE23 4BX
Tel: 01332 523027
Headmaster: Mr Richard D Paine
Age range: B7–18 G16–18
No. of pupils: 298 VIth66
Fees: Day £7,779–£10,779

Derby High School
Hillsway, Littleover, Derby,
Derbyshire DE23 3DT
Tel: 01332 514267
Headmaster: Mr C T Callaghan
Age range: B3–11 G3–18
No. of pupils: 576 VIth74
Fees: Day £7,050–£9,510

Emmanuel School
Juniper Lodge, 43 Kedleston Road,
Derby, Derbyshire DE22 1FP
Tel: 01332 340505
Headteacher: Mrs C Pearson
Age range: 3–16
No. of pupils: 65
Fees: Day £1,698–£2,706

Foremarke Hall
Milton, Derby, Derbyshire DE65 6EJ
Tel: 01283 707100
Headmaster: Mr R Merriman
MA, BSc(Hons), FCollP
Age range: 3–13

Gateway Christian School
Moor Lane, Dale Abbey,
Ilkeston, Derbyshire DE7 4PP
Tel: 0115 9440609
Head Teacher: Mrs Corinna Walters
Age range: 3–11
No. of pupils: 31
Fees: Day £2,400

Michael House Steiner School
The Field, Shipley, Heanor,
Derbyshire DE75 7JH
Tel: 01773 718050
Age range: 3–16
No. of pupils: 150
Fees: Day £1,500–£4,200

MOUNT ST MARY'S COLLEGE
For further details see p. 98
Spinkhill, Derbyshire S21 3YL
Tel: 01246 433388
Email: admissions@msmcollege.com
Website: www.msmcollege.com
Headmaster: Dr Nicholas Cuddihy
Age range: 11–18

Normanton House Primary School
Normanton House, Village Street,
Derby, Derbyshire DE23 8DF
Tel: 01332 769333
Headteacher: Mr Nighat Sultana Khan
Age range: 5–10
No. of pupils: 97

Ockbrook School
The Settlement, Ockbrook,
Derby, Derbyshire DE72 3RJ
Tel: 01332 673532
Head: Mr Tom Brooksby
Age range: 2–18
No. of pupils: 409 VIth55
Fees: Day £2,820–£12,180 WB
£19,365–£20,370 FB £24,690–£25,215

Old Vicarage School
11 Church Lane, Darley Abbey,
Derby, Derbyshire DE22 1EW
Tel: 01332 557130
Headmaster: Mr M J Adshead
Age range: 3–13
No. of pupils: 95
Fees: Day £6,135–£6,810

Repton School
The Hall, Repton, Derbyshire DE65 6FH
Tel: 01283 559222
Head: Mr W M A Land MA
Age range: 13–18
No. of pupils: 653 VIth299
Fees: Day £25,242 FB £34,026

S. Anselm's School
Stanedge Road, Bakewell,
Derbyshire DE45 1DP
Tel: 01629 812734
Headmaster: Peter Phillips BA
(Hons), MA, PGCE (SPLD), NPQH
Age range: 3–13
No. of pupils: 215
Fees: Day £7,680–£14,940 FB £17,550

St Peter & St Paul School
Brambling House, Hady Hill,
Chesterfield, Derbyshire S41 0EF
Tel: 01246 278522
Headteacher: Mr Steven Horsley
Age range: 3 months–11 years
No. of pupils: 120
Fees: Day £8,658 WB £9,159

St Wystan's School
High Street, Repton,
Derbyshire DE65 6GE
Tel: 01283 703258
Head Teacher: Karan Hopkinson
Age range: 3–11
Fees: Day £8,000

Leicestershire

Al-Aqsa Schools Trust
The Wayne Way, Leicester,
Leicestershire LE5 4PP
Tel: 0116 2760953
Headteacher: Mrs Amina Wiltshire
Age range: 5–16
No. of pupils: 231

Ashby School
School House, Leicester Road, Ashby-de-la-Zouch, Leicestershire LE65 1DH
Tel: +44 (0) 1530 413759
Headteacher: Mr Eddie Green
Age range: B11–19
No. of pupils: 1643

Brooke House College
Leicester Road, Market Harborough,
Leicestershire LE16 7AU
Tel: 01858 462452
Principal: Mr G E I Williams
Age range: 14–20
No. of pupils: VIth73
Fees: FB £21,750

Brooke House Day School
Croft Road, Cosby, Leicester,
Leicestershire LE9 1SE
Tel: 0116 286 7372
Head: Mrs Joy Parker
Age range: 3–14

Darul Arqam Educational Institute
2 Overton Road, Leicester,
Leicestershire LE5 0JA
Tel: 0116 2741626
Headteacher: Mr Ahmed
Abdul Dadipatel
Age range: B5–16
No. of pupils: 75

Darul Uloom Leicester
119 Loughborough Road,
Leicester, Leicestershire LE4 5LN
Tel: 0116 2668922
Headteacher: Mr Haroon M. Makda
Age range: B11–25
Fees: Day £1,800 FB £2,700

Fairfield Preparatory School
Leicester Road, Loughborough,
Leicestershire LE11 2AE
Tel: 01509 215172
Headmaster: Mr A Earnshaw
BA Lancaster NPQH
Age range: 4–11
No. of pupils: 489

Grace Dieu Manor School
Grace Dieu, Thringstone,
Leicestershire LE67 5UG
Tel: 01530 222276
Headmaster: Mr Peter Fisher
Age range: 3–13
No. of pupils: 315
Fees: Day £7,935–£11,313

Jameah Girls Academy
49 Rolleston Street, Leicester,
Leicestershire LE5 3SD
Tel: 0116 262 7745
Headteacher: Mrs S Patel
Age range: G6–16
No. of pupils: 142

Leicester Grammar Junior School
London Road, Grea Glen,
Leicester, Leicestershire LE8 9FL
Tel: 0116 259 1950
Age range: 3–11
No. of pupils: 391

Leicester Grammar School
London Road, Great Glen,
Leicester, Leicestershire LE8 9FL
Tel: 0116 259 1900
Head & Chief Executive: C P M King MA
Age range: 10–18
No. of pupils: 704 VIth188
Fees: Day £7,905

Leicester High School for Girls
454 London Road, Leicester,
Leicestershire LE2 2PP
Tel: 0116 2705338
Headmaster: Mr Alan Whelpdale
Age range: G3–18
No. of pupils: 435 VIth60
Fees: Day £2,250–£3,100

Leicester International School
16-20 Beal Street, Leicester,
Leicestershire LE2 0AA
Tel: 0116 2515345
Principal: Mr N Hussein
Age range: 5–11
No. of pupils: 146

Leicester Islamic Academy
320 London Road, Leicester,
Leicestershire LE2 2PP
Tel: 0116 2705343
Principal: Dr M H Mukadam
FRSA, BEd(Hons), PhD
Age range: 3–16
Fees: Day £1,300–£1,400

Leicester Prep School
2 Albert Road, Leicester,
Leicestershire LE2 2AA
Tel: 0116 2707414
Headmaster: Christopher
J Cann MA(Oxon)
Age range: 3–11
No. of pupils: 130
Fees: Day £1,530–£5,820

Loughborough Grammar School
6 Burton Walks, Loughborough,
Leicestershire LE11 2DU
Tel: 01509 233233
Headmaster: Mr Duncan Byrne
Age range: B10–18
No. of pupils: 1010
Fees: Day £10,413 FB £19,356

Loughborough High School
Burton Walks, Loughborough,
Leicestershire LE11 2DU
Tel: 01509 212348
Headmistress: Mrs G Byrom
Age range: G11–18
No. of pupils: VIth170
Fees: Day £10,191

Manor House School
South Street, Ashby-de-la-Zouch,
Leicestershire LE65 1BR
Tel: 01530 412932
Headteacher: Mrs E A Scrine
Age range: 4–16
Fees: Day £4,302–£5,700

Our Lady's Convent School
Gray Street, Loughborough,
Leicestershire LE11 2DZ
Tel: 01509 263901
Headmaster: Dr Julian Murphy
Age range: B4–11 G4–18
No. of pupils: 224
Fees: Day £9,531–£11,637

Ratcliffe College
Fosse Way, Ratcliffe on the Wreake,
Leicester, Leicestershire LE7 4SG
Tel: 01509 817000
Headmaster: Mr J Reddin
BSc, MSc, NPQH
Age range: 3–18
No. of pupils: 831 VIth142
Fees: Day £8,850–£15,657 WB
£19,680–£22,026 FB £24,708–£28,728

St Crispin's School
6 St Mary's Road, Stoneygate,
Leicester, Leicestershire LE2 1XA
Tel: 0116 2707648
Head Master: Andrew Atkin
Age range: 2–16

Stoneygate School
6 London Road, Great Glen,
Leicester, Leicestershire LE8 9DJ
Tel: 0116 259 2282
Headmaster: Mr John H
Morris MA(Cantab)
Age range: 3–13
Fees: Day £4,800–£6,100

The Dixie Grammar School
Station Road, Market Bosworth,
Leicestershire CV13 0LE
Tel: 01455 292244
Headmaster: J Wood MA
Age range: 3–18
No. of pupils: 520 VIth71
Fees: Day £5,760–£7,920

Tiny Tots Pre-School & Primary
16-20 Beal Street, Leicester,
Leicestershire LE2 0AA
Tel: 0116 2515345
Principal: Mr N Hussein
Age range: 2 –11
No. of pupils: 104

Lincolnshire

Ayscoughfee Hall School
Welland Hall, London Road,
Spalding, Lincolnshire PE11 2TE
Tel: 01775 724733
Headmistress: Mrs Clare
Ogden BA(Hons), PGCE
Age range: 3–11
No. of pupils: 146
Fees: Day £4,080–£6,030

Bicker Preparatory School & Early Years
School Lane, Bicker, Boston,
Lincolnshire PE20 3DW
Tel: 01775 821786
Head Teacher: Mrs J Miles BA.PGCE
Age range: 3–11
No. of pupils: 74
Fees: Day £2,057–£5,655

Copthill Independent Day School
Barnack Road, Uffington,
Stamford, Lincolnshire PE9 3AD
Tel: 01780 757506
Headmaster: Mr J A Teesdale
BA(Hons), PGCE
Age range: 2–11
No. of pupils: 309
Fees: Day £8,370–£9,180

Dudley House School
1 Dudley Road, Grantham,
Lincolnshire NG31 9AA
Tel: 01476 400184
Headmistress: Mrs Jenny Johnson
Age range: 3–11
No. of pupils: 50
Fees: Day £4,545

Grantham Preparatory International School
Gorse Lane, Grantham, Lincolnshire NG31 7UF
Tel: +44 (0)1476 593293
Headmistress: Mrs K A Korcz
Age range: 3–11
No. of pupils: 136
Fees: Day £7,350–£8,970

Greenwich House School
106 High Holme Road, Louth, Lincolnshire LN11 0HE
Tel: 01507 609252
Headmistress: Mrs J Brindle
Age range: 9 months–11 years
No. of pupils: 50
Fees: Day £5,100

Handel House Preparatory School
Northolme Road, Gainsborough, Lincolnshire DN21 2JB
Tel: 01427 612426
Headmistress: Mrs Victoria Haigh
Age range: 2–11
Fees: Day £2,580–£3,075

Kirkstone House School
Main Street, Baston, Peterborough, Lincolnshire PE6 9PA
Tel: 01778 560350
Head: Mrs C Jones BSocSc
Age range: 5–16
No. of pupils: 234
Fees: Day £9,270–£11,412

Lincoln Minster School
Upper Lindum Street, Lincoln, Lincolnshire LN2 5RW
Tel: 01522 551300
Principal: Mr Clive Rickart
Age range: 21/2–18
No. of pupils: 840 VIth144
Fees: Day £6,510–£9,672 WB £14,289–£16,947 FB £15,417–£18,285

Regents Academy
Bliney House, Manby Park, Manby, Lincolnshire LN11 8UT
Tel: 01507 327859
Headteacher: Mrs D Rusling
Age range: 3–18
No. of pupils: 30
Fees: Day £2,448

St Hugh's School
Cromwell Avenue, Woodhall Spa, Lincolnshire LN10 6TQ
Tel: 01526 352169
Head: C Ward BEd(Hons)
Age range: 2–13
No. of pupils: 195
Fees: Day £7,452–£12,987 FB £18,381

Stamford Endowed Schools
Brazenose House, St Paul's Street, Stamford, Lincolnshire PE9 2BE
Tel: 01780 750310
Principal: Stephen C Roberts
Age range: 2–18
No. of pupils: 1634 VIth400
Fees: Day £8,262–£13,446 WB £17,355–£21,717 FB £19,146–£24,909

Stamford High School
St Martin's, Stamford, Lincolnshire PE9 2LL
Tel: 01780 428200
Principal: Mr S C Roberts
Age range: G11–18
No. of pupils: 633 VIth201
Fees: Day £12,252 WB £16,932–£19,488 FB £22,356

Stamford Junior School
Kettering Road, Stamford, Lincolnshire PE9 2LR
Tel: 01780 484400
Principal: Mr S C Roberts
Age range: 2–11
No. of pupils: 344
Fees: Day £8,580 WB £17,436 FB £17,544

Viking School
140 Church Road North, Skegness, Lincolnshire PE25 2QJ
Tel: 01754 765749
Principal: Mrs S J Barker
Age range: 3–11
No. of pupils: 100
Fees: Day £1,085

Witham Hall Preparatory School
Witham-on-the-Hill, Bourne, Lincolnshire PE10 0JJ
Tel: +44(0)1778 590222
Headmaster: Mr Charles Welch B.Ed (Hons)
Age range: 4–13
No. of pupils: 228
Fees: Day £6,645–£10,875 FB £14,850

Northamptonshire

Beachborough School
Westbury, Brackley, Northamptonshire NN13 5LB
Tel: 01280 700071
Headmaster: Mr Jeremy Banks BEd
Age range: 2–13
No. of pupils: 260
Fees: Day £570–£10,485

Bosworth Independent College
Nazareth House, Barrack Road, Northampton, Northamptonshire NN2 6AF
Tel: 01604 235090
Principal: Mr Michael W McQuin MEd
Age range: 14–University
No. of pupils: VIth250
Fees: Day £9,840 WB £18,925–£21,450 FB £19,975–£22,500

Childfirst Day Nursery Northampton
Moulton Lodge, Moulton Way North, Moulton, Northampton, Northamptonshire NN3 7RW
Tel: 01604 790440
Headmistress: Mrs Mary Heal BA(Hons)Ed
Age range: 2 months–7 years
Fees: Day £6,255

Laxton Junior School
East Road, Oundle, Peterborough, Northamptonshire PE8 4BX
Tel: 01832 277275
Head: Mr Mark Potter MEd BEd(Hons)
Age range: 4–11
No. of pupils: 260
Fees: Day £10,185–£11,175

Maidwell Hall
Maidwell, Northampton, Northamptonshire NN6 9JG
Tel: 01604 686234
Headmaster: Mr R A Lankester MA, PGCE
Age range: 7–13
No. of pupils: 124
Fees: Day £16,500 WB £25,350 FB £25,350

Northampton High School GDST
Newport Pagnell Road, Hardingstone, Northampton, Northamptonshire NN4 6UU
Tel: 01604 765765
Headmistress: Dr Helen Stringer DPhil, MA, PGCE
Age range: G3–18
No. of pupils: 649 VIth128
Fees: Day £9,981–£13,356

Oundle School
Oundle, Peterborough, Northamptonshire PE8 4GH
Tel: 01832 277 122
Head of School: Mrs Sarah Kerr-Dineen
Age range: 11–18
No. of pupils: 1107
Fees: Day £22,065 FB £34,440

Overstone Park School
Overstone Park, Overstone, Northampton, Northamptonshire NN6 0DT
Tel: 01604 643787
Principal: Mrs M F Brown BA(Hons), PGCE
Age range: 0–18
No. of pupils: 85
Fees: Day £2,267–£3,013

Pitsford School
Pitsford Hall, Pitsford, Northampton, Northamptonshire NN6 9AX
Tel: 01604 880306
Headmaster: N R Toone BSc, MInstP
Age range: 4–18
No. of pupils: VIth49
Fees: Day £8,223–£14,277

Quinton House School
Upton Hall, Upton, Northampton, Northamptonshire NN5 4UX
Tel: 01604 752050
Headteacher: Ms C Cozens
Age range: 2–18
No. of pupils: 455
Fees: Day £8,145–£11,520

Spratton Hall
Smith Street, Spratton, Northampton, Northamptonshire NN6 8HP
Tel: 01604 847292
Head Master: Mr Simon Clarke
Age range: 4–13
No. of pupils: 396
Fees: Day £9,600–£14,175

St Peter's Independent School
Lingswood Park, Blackthorn, Northampton, Northamptonshire NN3 8TA
Tel: 01604 411745
Head: Tim Cooper
Age range: 4–18
No. of pupils: 130
Fees: Day £3,600

St Peter's School
52 Headlands, Kettering, Northamptonshire NN15 6DJ
Tel: 01536 512066
Headmistress: Mrs Maria Chapman
Age range: 2 –11
No. of pupils: 161
Fees: Day £3,765–£6,795

Wellingborough School
Wellingborough, Northamptonshire NN8 2BX
Tel: 01933 222427
Headmaster: Mr G R Bowe MA
Age range: 3–18
No. of pupils: VIth145
Fees: Day £6,522–£11,004

Winchester House School
High Street, Brackley, Northamptonshire NN13 7AZ
Tel: 01280 702483
Head: Emma Goldsmith
Age range: 3–13
No. of pupils: 325
Fees: Day £690–£17,025
WB £17,820–£22,485

Nottinghamshire

Colston Bassett Preparatory School
School Lane, Colston bassett, Nottingham, Nottinghamshire NG12 3FD
Tel: 01949 81118
Headteacher: Mrs Julie Hunt
Age range: 4–11
Fees: Day £5,925

Coteswood House School
19 Thackeray's Lane, Woodthorpe, Nottingham, Nottinghamshire NG5 4HT
Tel: 0115 9676551
Head: Mrs S M Fernley
Age range: 3–11
No. of pupils: 40
Fees: Day £4,200

Hazel Hurst School
400 Westdale Lane, Mapperley, Nottingham, Nottinghamshire NG3 6DG
Tel: 0115 9606759
Headteacher: Mrs Rosemary Eadie
Age range: 2–8
Fees: Day £5,406–£6,024

Highfields School
London Road, Newark, Nottinghamshire NG24 3AL
Tel: 01636 704103
Headmaster: Mr R C R Thomson BEd (Hons) NPQH
Age range: 2–11
No. of pupils: 140
Fees: Day £8,970

Hollygirt School
Elm Avenue, Nottingham, Nottinghamshire NG3 4GF
Tel: 0115 958 0596
Headmistress: Mrs Pam Hutley BA(Hons), PGCE, MSc
Age range: 3–16
No. of pupils: 200
Fees: Day £8,550–£11,820

Iona School
310 Sneinton Dale, Nottingham, Nottinghamshire NG3 7DN
Tel: 01159 415295
Chair of College: Richard Moore
Age range: 3–11
Fees: Day £3,816

Jamia Al-Hudaa Residential College
Forest House, Berkeley Avenue, Mapperley Park, Nottingham, Nottinghamshire NG3 5TT
Tel: 0115 9690800
Principal: Raza ul-Haq Siakhvy
Age range: G5–19
No. of pupils: 224

Jubilee House Christian School
226 Nottingham Road, Eastwood, Nottinghamshire NG16 3GR
Tel: 01773 688100
Headteacher: Mrs J Marks
Age range: 3–16
No. of pupils: 70

Nottingham Girls' High School GDST
9 Arboretum Street, Nottingham, Nottinghamshire NG1 4JB
Tel: 0115 9417663
Headmistress: Mrs S M Gorham
Age range: G4–18
No. of pupils: 1117 VIth239
Fees: Day £6,978–£9,627

Nottingham High Infant and Junior School
Waverley Mount, Nottingham, Nottinghamshire NG7 4ED
Tel: 0115 845 2214
Headteacher: Mrs Clare Bruce
Age range: 4–11
No. of pupils: 180
Fees: Day £3,155–£3,670

Nottingham High School
Waverley Mount, Nottingham, Nottinghamshire NG7 4ED
Tel: 0115 9786056
Headmaster: Mr Kevin Fear BA
Age range: 4–18
No. of pupils: 1002
Fees: Day £9,465–£13,824

Nottingham Islamia School
30 Bentinck Road, Hyson Green, Nottingham, Nottinghamshire NG7 4AF
Tel: 0115 970 5858
Head: Dr Musharraf Hussain
Age range: 5–11

Plumtree School
Church Hill, Plumtree, Nottingham, Nottinghamshire NG12 5ND
Tel: 0115 937 5859
Head Teacher: Phil Simpson
Age range: 3–11
Fees: Day £5,250

Salterford House School
Salterford Lane, Calverton, Nottingham, Nottinghamshire NG14 6NZ
Tel: 0115 9652127
Headmistress: Mrs Marlene Venables CertEd
Age range: 2–11
No. of pupils: 124
Fees: Day £6,150

Saville House School
11 Church Street, Mansfield Woodhouse, Mansfield, Nottinghamshire NG19 8AH
Tel: 01623 625068
Head: Mrs S Hagues
Age range: 3–11
No. of pupils: 89
Fees: Day £4,125

St Joseph's School
33 Derby Road, Nottingham, Nottinghamshire NG1 5AW
Tel: 0115 9418356
Head Teacher: Mr Ashley Crawshaw
Age range: 1–11
Fees: Day £7,503

The Lammas School
Lammas Road, Sutton-in-Ashfield, Nottinghamshire NG17 2AD
Tel: 01623 516879
Head: Mrs P Sessions
Age range: 4–16
Fees: Day £5,125–£6,650

The Orchard School
South Leverton, Retford, Nottinghamshire DN22 0DJ
Tel: 01427 880395
Principal: Mrs S M Fox BA, PGCE
Age range: 5–16
No. of pupils: 150
Fees: Day £4,665–£7,425

Trent College
Derby Road, Long Eaton, Nottingham, Nottinghamshire NG10 4AD
Tel: 0115 8494949
Head: Mrs G Dixon BSc, MBA
Age range: 11–18
No. of pupils: 1117 VIth200
Fees: Day £7,200–£13,500 WB £16,305–£17,685 FB £19,020–£20,625
A £ 16·

Wellow House School
Wellow, Newark, Nottinghamshire NG22 0EA
Tel: 01623 861054
Headmaster: Peter Cook BEd(Hons)
Age range: 3–13
No. of pupils: 152
Fees: Day £7,500–£11,985 WB £13,845
£

Worksop College
Worksop, Nottinghamshire S80 3AP
Tel: 01909 537100
Headmaster: G W Horgan MA (Oxon)
Age range: 3–18
No. of pupils: 614 VIth141
Fees: Day £12,765–£17,865 FB £17,985–£28,365
A £ 16·

Worksop College Preparatory School, Ranby House
Retford, Nottinghamshire DN22 8HX
Tel: 01777 714387 (Admissions)
Headmaster: C S J Pritchard MA, BA(Hons), QTS
Age range: 3–11 years
No. of pupils: 190
Fees: Day £2,664–£4,338
£

Rutland

Brooke Priory School
Station Approach, Oakham, Rutland LE15 6QW
Tel: 01572 724778
Headmistress: Mrs E Bell BEd
Age range: 2–11
No. of pupils: 180
Fees: Day £8,655
£

Oakham School
Chapel Close, Oakham, Rutland LE15 6DT
Tel: 01572 758758
Headmaster: Mr Nigel M Lashbrook BA
Age range: 10–18
No. of pupils: VIth405
Fees: Day £16,650–£18,780 WB £21,450–£27,990 FB £25,350–£31,110
A £ IB 16·

Uppingham School
Uppingham, Rutland LE15 9QE
Tel: 01572 822216 Admissions: 01572 820611
Headmaster: Dr Richard Maloney
Age range: 13–18
No. of pupils: 798 VIth344
Fees: Day £8,435 FB £12,050
A £ 16·

Greater London

KEY TO SYMBOLS

- Boys' school
- Girls' school
- International school
- Tutorial or sixth form college
- A levels
- Boarding accommodation
- Bursaries
- International Baccalaureate
- Learning support
- Entrance at 16+
- Vocational qualifications
- Independent Association of Preparatory Schools
- The Headmasters' & Headmistresses' Conference
- Independent Schools Association
- Girls' School Association
- Boarding Schools' Association
- Society of Heads

Unless otherwise indicated, all schools are coeducational day schools. Single-sex and boarding schools will be indicated by the relevant icon.

Essex

Al-Noor Primary School
Newton Industrial Estate, Eastern Avenue, Chadwell Health, Romford, Essex RM6 5SD
Tel: 020 8597 7576
Head: Mrs Someera Butt
Age range: 4–10
No. of pupils: 175
Fees: Day £2,550–£2,750

AVON HOUSE PREPARATORY SCHOOL
For further details see p. 102
490 High Road, Woodford Green, Essex IG8 0PN
Tel: 020 8504 1749
Email: office@ahsprep.co.uk
Website: www.avonhouseschool.co.uk
Headteacher: Mrs Amanda Campbell
Age range: 3–11
No. of pupils: 230
Fees: Day £9,375–£10,290

Bancroft's School
High Road, Woodford Green, Essex IG8 0RF
Tel: 020 8505 4821
Head: Mr Simon Marshall MA, PGCE (Cantab), MA, MPhil (Oxon)
Age range: 7–18
No. of pupils: 1155 VIth261
A £ 16·

Beehive Preparatory School
233 Beehive Lane, Redbridge, Ilford, Essex IG4 5ED
Tel: 020 8550 3224
Headmaster: Mr C J Beasant BEd
Age range: 4–11
Fees: Day £4,900

Braeside School for Girls
130 High Road, Buckhurst Hill, Essex IG9 5SD
Tel: 020 8504 1133
Head Teacher: Mrs G Haddon BA(Hons), PGCE
Age range: G3–16
No. of pupils: 199
Fees: Day £5,175–£10,875

Chigwell School
High Road, Chigwell, Essex IG7 6QF
Tel: 020 8501 5700
Headmaster: Mr M E Punt MA, MSc
Age range: 4–18
No. of pupils: 915 VIth185
Fees: Day £10,200–£16,020 FB £26,730–£26,730
A £ 16·

Cranbrook College
Mansfield Road, Ilford, Essex IG1 3BD
Tel: 020 8554 1757
Executive Principal: Mr. David Morrison
Age range: B4–16
No. of pupils: 200
Fees: Day £6,405–£8,235
£

Eastcourt Independent School
1 Eastwood Road, Goodmayes, Ilford, Essex IG3 8UW
Tel: 020 8590 5472
Headmistress: Mrs Christine Redgrave BSc(Hons), DipEd, MEd
Age range: 3–11
Fees: Day £6,300

Gidea Park College
2 Balgores Lane, Gidea Park, Romford, Essex RM2 5JR
Tel: 01708 740381
Headmistress: Mrs Susan-Jayne Gooding BA
Age range: 3–11
No. of pupils: 177
Fees: Day £1,275–£2,500

Goodrington School
17 Walden Road, Hornchurch, Essex RM11 2JT
Tel: 01708 448349
Head Teacher: Mrs J R Ellenby
Age range: 3–11
Fees: Day £6,150

Guru Gobind Singh Khalsa College
Roding Lane, Chigwell, Essex IG7 6BQ
Tel: 020 8559 9160
Principal: Mr Amarjit Singh Toor BSc(Hons), BSc, BT
Age range: 3–17
Fees: Day £3,900

Ilford Grammar School
785 High Road, Seven Kings, Ilford, Essex IG3 8RW
Tel: 020 8599 8822
Headmistress: B P M Wiggs BSc(Hons), PGCE
Age range: 3–16
Fees: Day £5,250–£7,200

Immanuel School
Havering Grange Centre, Havering Road North, Romford, Essex RM1 4HR
Tel: 01708 764449
Principal: Miss Norcross
Age range: 3–16

Loyola Preparatory School
103 Palmerston Road, Buckhurst Hill, Essex IG9 5NH
Tel: 020 8504 7372
Headmaster: Mr P G M Nicholson CertEd, BEd(Hons)
Age range: B3–11
No. of pupils: 195
Fees: Day £8,820
£

Maytime Montessori Nursery – Cranbrook Road
341 Cranbrook Road, Ilford, Essex IG1 4UF
Tel: 020 8554 3079

Maytime Montessori Nursery – Eastwood Road
2 Eastwood Road, Goodmayes, Essex IG3 8XB
Tel: 020 8599 3744

Maytime Montessori Nursery – York Road
87 York Road, Ilford, Essex IG1 3AF
Tel: 020 8553 1524
Age range: 0–6

Oakfields Montessori School
Harwood Hall, Harwood Hall Lane, Corbets Tey, Essex RM14 2YG
Tel: 01708 220117
Headmistress: Mrs K Malandreniotis
Age range: 2–11
Fees: Day £2,508–£4,260

Oaklands School
8 Albion Hill, Loughton, Essex IG10 4RA
Tel: 020 8508 3517
Headmistress: Mrs Cheryl Macnair
Age range: B2–7 G2–11
No. of pupils: 243
Fees: Day £3,795–£7,650

Park School for Girls
20 Park Avenue, Ilford, Essex IG1 4RS
Tel: 020 8554 2466
Headmistress: Mrs N O'Brien BA
Age range: G7–18
No. of pupils: 230 VIth19
Fees: Day £4,755–£6,285
A 16·

Raphael Independent School
Park Lane, Hornchurch, Essex RM11 1XY
Tel: 01708 744735
Age range: 4–16
No. of pupils: 135
Fees: Day £5,200–£7,800

St Aubyn's School
Bunces Lane, Woodford Green, Essex IG8 9DU
Tel: 020 8504 1577
Headmaster: Mr Leonard Blom BEd(Hons) BA NPQH
Age range: 3–13
No. of pupils: 525
Fees: Day £5,190–£11,670
£

St Mary's Hare Park School & Nursery
South Drive, Gidea Park, Romford, Essex RM2 6HH
Tel: 01708 761220
Head Teacher: Mrs K Karwacinski
Age range: 2–11
No. of pupils: 180
Fees: Day £4,485

The Daiglen School
68 Palmerston Road, Buckhurst Hill, Essex IG9 5LG
Tel: 020 8504 7108
Headteacher: Mrs M Bradfield
Age range: 3–11
No. of pupils: 130
Fees: Day £6,360
£

The Ursuline Preparatory School Ilford
2-8 Coventry Road, Ilford, Essex IG1 4QR
Tel: 020 8518 4050
Headteacher: Mrs Lisa McCoy
Age range: G3–11
No. of pupils: 159
Fees: Day £5,697

Woodford Green Preparatory School
Glengall Road, Woodford Green, Essex IG8 0BZ
Tel: 020 8504 5045
Headmaster: Mr J P Wadge
Age range: 3–11
No. of pupils: 381
Fees: Day £3,140
£

Hertfordshire

LYONSDOWN SCHOOL
For further details see p. 112
3 Richmond Road, New Barnet, Barnet, Hertfordshire EN5 1SA
Tel: 020 8449 0225
Email: enquiries@lyonsdownschool.co.uk
Website: www.lyonsdownschool.co.uk
Head: Mr C Hammond BA (Hons) PGCE
Age range: B3–7 G3–11
No. of pupils: 185
Fees: Day £4,080–£10,200

Norfolk Lodge Montessori Nursery & Pre-Prep School
Dancers Hill Road, Barnet, Hertfordshire EN5 4RP
Tel: 020 8447 1565
Head Teacher: Mrs Mary Wales
Age range: 6 months–7 years
No. of pupils: 140
Fees: Day £2,200–£2,400

St Martha's School
Camlet Way, Hadley Wood, Barnet, Hertfordshire EN4 0NJ
Tel: 020 8449 6889
Headmaster: Mr Matthew Burke
Age range: G11–18
No. of pupils: 220 VIth40
Fees: Day £4,625

Susi Earnshaw Theatre School
68 High Street, Barnet, Hertfordshire EN5 5SJ
Tel: 020 8441 5010
Headteacher: Mr David Earnshaw
Age range: 11–16
No. of pupils: 60
Fees: Day £10,500

The Royal Masonic School for Girls
Rickmansworth Park, Rickmansworth, Hertfordshire WD3 4HF
Tel: 01923 773168
Headmaster: Mr Kevin Carson M.Phil (Cambridge)
Age range: G4–18
No. of pupils: 930 VIth165
Fees: Day £10,455–£15,915 WB £18,345–£25,935 FB £19,350–£28,140

Kent

Ashgrove School
116 Widmore Road, Bromley, Kent BR1 3BE
Tel: 020 8460 4143
Principal: Patricia Ash CertEd, BSc(Hons), PhD, CMath, FIMA
Age range: 4–11
Fees: Day £8,820

Babington House School
Grange Drive, Chislehurst, Kent BR7 5ES
Tel: 020 8467 5537
Headmaster: Mr Tim Lello MA, FRSA, NPQH
Age range: B3-11 & 16–18 G3–18
No. of pupils: 347

Benedict House Preparatory School
1-5 Victoria Road, Sidcup, Kent DA15 7HD
Tel: 020 8300 7206
Headmistress: Mrs Gemma Chikola
Age range: 3–11
Fees: Day £2,145–£2,395

Bickley Park School
24 Page Heath Lane, Bickley, Bromley, Kent BR1 2DS
Tel: 020 8467 2195
Headmaster: Mr Paul Ashley
Age range: B3–13 G3–4
No. of pupils: 370
Fees: Day £6,525–£11,925

Bishop Challoner School
228 Bromley Road, Shortlands, Bromley, Kent BR2 0BS
Tel: 020 8460 3546
Headteacher: Ms Paula Anderson
Age range: 3–18
No. of pupils: 412 VIth32
Fees: Day £6,441–£9,036

BREASIDE PREPARATORY SCHOOL
For further details see p. 104
41-43 Orchard Road, Bromley, Kent BR1 2PR
Tel: 020 8460 0916
Email: info@breaside.co.uk
Website: www.breaside.co.uk
Executive Principal: Mrs Karen A Nicholson B.Ed, NPQH, Dip EYs
Age range: 2½–11
No. of pupils: 365
Fees: Day £10,545–£12,285

Bromley High School GDST
Blackbrook Lane, Bickley, Bromley, Kent BR1 2TW
Tel: 020 8781 7000/1
Head: Mrs A M Drew BA(Hons), MBA (Dunelm)
Age range: G4–18
No. of pupils: 912 VIth125
Fees: Day £12,855–£15,942

Darul Uloom London
Foxbury Avenue, Perry Street, Chislehurst, Kent BR7 6SD
Tel: 020 8295 0637
Principal: Mufti Mustafa
Age range: B11–18
No. of pupils: 160
Fees: FB £2,400

FARRINGTONS SCHOOL
For further details see p. 106
Perry Street, Chislehurst, Kent BR7 6LR
Tel: 020 8467 0256
Email: admissions@farringtons.kent.sch.uk
Website: www.farringtons.org.uk
Head: Mrs Dorothy Nancekievill
Age range: 3–18
No. of pupils: 681 VIth94
Fees: Day £14,610 WB £28,830 FB £30,600

Merton Court Preparatory School
38 Knoll Road, Sidcup, Kent DA14 4QU
Tel: 020 8300 2112
Headmaster: Mr Dominic Price BEd, MBA
Age range: 3–11
Fees: Day £8,115–£8,910

St Christopher's The Hall School
49 Bromley Road, Beckenham, Kent BR3 5PA
Tel: 020 8650 2200
Headmaster: Mr A Velasco MEd, BH(Hons), PGCE
Age range: 3–11
No. of pupils: 305
Fees: Day £2,250–£6,630

St. David's Prep
Justin Hall, Beckenham Road, Kent BR4 0QS
Tel: 020 8777 5852
Principal: Mrs J Foulger
Age range: 4–11
No. of pupils: 155
Fees: Day £6,015–£6,165

West Lodge School
36 Station Road, Sidcup, Kent DA15 7DU
Tel: 020 8300 2489
Head Teacher: Mrs Susan Webb
Age range: 3–11
No. of pupils: 163
Fees: Day £5,205–£8,700

Wickham Court School
Schiller International, Layhams Road, West Wickham, Kent BR4 9HW
Tel: 020 8777 2942
Head: Mrs Barbara Hunter
Age range: 2–16
No. of pupils: 121
Fees: Day £4,481–£6,900

Middlesex

Acorn House College
39-47 High Street, Southall, Middlesex UB1 3HF
Tel: 020 8571 9900
Principal: Mr John Wilson
Age range: 13–19
No. of pupils: 121 VIth85
Fees: Day £5,200–£14,600

ACS Hillingdon International School
Hillingdon Court, 108 Vine Lane, Hillingdon, Uxbridge, Middlesex UB10 0BE
Tel: +44 (0) 1895 259 771
Age range: 4–18
No. of pupils: 520
Fees: Day £17,260–£23,110

Alpha Preparatory School
21 Hindes Road, Harrow, Middlesex HA1 1SH
Tel: 020 8427 1471
Head: C.J.W Trinidad BSc(Hons), PGCE
Age range: 3–11
No. of pupils: 170
Fees: Day £3,300–£10,590

Ashton House School
50-52 Eversley Crescent, Isleworth, Middlesex TW7 4LW
Tel: 020 8560 3902
Headteacher: Mrs M Grundberg MA, PGCE
Age range: 3–11
Fees: Day £9,300–£10,200

Athelstan House School
36 Percy Road, Hampton, Middlesex TW12 2LA
Tel: 020 8979 1045
Headmistress: Elsa Woolf
Age range: 3–7

Buckingham Preparatory School
458 Rayners Lane, Pinner, Middlesex HA5 5DT
Tel: 020 8866 2737
Headmaster: Mr L S Smith BA(Hons), MSc, LCP, PGDE, CertEd
Age range: B4–11
Fees: Day £7,560–£9,900

Buxlow Preparatory School
5/6 Castleton Gardens, Wembley, Middlesex HA9 7QJ
Tel: 020 8904 3615
Headmistress: Mrs Ann Baines
Age range: 4–11
Fees: Day £6,885

Edgware Jewish Girls – Beis Chinuch
Yeshurun Synagogue, Fernhurst Gardens, Edgware, Middlesex HA8 7PH
Tel: 020 8951 0239
Headteacher: Mr M Cohen
Age range: G3–7

Halliford School
Russell Road, Shepperton, Middlesex TW17 9HX
Tel: 01932 223593
Headmaster: Mr James Davies BMus
Age range: B11–18 G16–18
No. of pupils: 400
Fees: Day £15,285

Hampton Prep and Pre-Prep School
Gloucester Road, Hampton, Middlesex TW12 2UQ
Tel: 020 8979 1844
Headmaster: Mr Tim Smith
Age range: 3–11
Fees: Day £4,995–£11,580

Hampton School
Hanworth Road, Hampton, Middlesex TW12 3HD
Tel: 020 8979 9273
Headmaster: Mr Kevin Knibbs MA (Oxon)
Age range: B11–18
No. of pupils: 1200
Fees: Day £6,125

Harrow School
5 High Street, Harrow on the Hill, Middlesex HA1 3HT
Tel: 020 8872 8000
Head Master: Mr Jim Hawkins
Age range: B13–18
No. of pupils: 830 VIth320
Fees: FB £33,285

Holland House School
1 Broadhurst Avenue, Edgware, Middlesex HA8 8TP
Tel: 020 8958 6979
Headmistress: Mrs Irinia Tyk BA(Hons)
Age range: 4–11
Fees: Day £7,308

Jack and Jill School
30 Nightingale Road, Hampton, Middlesex TW12 3HX
Tel: 020 8979 3195
Principal: Miss K Papirnik BEd(Hons)
Age range: B2–5 G2–7
No. of pupils: 155
Fees: Day £2,409–£9,597

Kew House School
Kew House, 6 Capital Interchange Way, London, Middlesex TW8 0EX
Tel: 0208 742 2038
Headmaster: Mr Mark Hudson
Age range: 11–18
Fees: Day £18,924

Lady Nafisa Independent Secondary School for Girls
83A Sunbury Road, Feltham, Middlesex TW13 4PH
Tel: 020 8751 5610
Headteacher: Ms Fouzia Butt
Age range: G11–16

Menorah Grammar School
Abbots Road, Edgware, Middlesex HA8 0QS
Tel: 020 8906 9756
Headteacher: Rabbi A M Goldblatt
Age range: B11–17
No. of pupils: 203

Merchant Taylors' School
Sandy Lodge, Northwood, Middlesex HA6 2HT
Tel: 01923 820644
Head: Mr S J Everson MA (Cantab)
Age range: B11–18
No. of pupils: 865 VIth282
Fees: Day £16,660

Newland House School
Waldegrave Park, Twickenham, Middlesex TW1 4TQ
Tel: 020 8865 1305
Headmaster: Mr D A Alexander
Age range: B4–13 G4–11
No. of pupils: 425
Fees: Day £3,625–£4,055

North London Collegiate School
Canons, Canons Drive, Edgware, Middlesex HA8 7RJ
Tel: +44 (0)20 8952 0912
Headmistress: Mrs Bernice McCabe
Age range: G4–18
No. of pupils: 1080
Fees: Day £5,370–£6,354

Northwood College for Girls GDST
Maxwell Road, Northwood, Middlesex HA6 2YE
Tel: 01923 825446
Head Mistress: Miss Jacqualyn Pain MA, MA, MBA
Age range: G3–18
No. of pupils: 840 VIth100

Oak Heights
3 Red Lion Court, Alexandra Road, Hounslow, Middlesex TW3 1JS
Tel: 020 8577 1827
Head: Mr S Dhillon
Age range: 11–16
No. of pupils: 48
Fees: Day £6,000

Orley Farm School
South Hill Avenue, Harrow, Middlesex HA1 3NU
Tel: 020 8869 7600
Headmaster: Mr Tim Calvey
Age range: 4–13
No. of pupils: 497
Fees: Day £13,749–£15,861

Quainton Hall School & Nursery
91 Hindes Road, Harrow, Middlesex HA1 1RX
Tel: 020 8861 8861
Headmaster: S Ford BEd (Hons), UWE Bristol
Age range: B2 –13 G2 –11
Fees: Day £9,075–£9,975

Radnor House
Pope's Villa, Cross Deep, Twickenham, Middlesex TW1 4QG
Tel: 020 8891 6264

Reddiford School
36-38 Cecil Park, Pinner,
Middlesex HA5 5HH
Tel: 020 8866 0660
Headteacher: Mrs J Batt CertEd, NPQH
Age range: 3–11
No. of pupils: 320
Fees: Day £3,480–£8,340

Regent College
Sai House, 167 Imperial Drive,
Harrow, Middlesex HA2 7HD
Tel: 020 8966 9900
Principal: Mr Selva Pankaj MBA, FCMA
Age range: 11–19
No. of pupils: 167
Fees: Day £2,745–£12,995

Roxeth Mead School
Buckholt House, 25 Middle Road,
Harrow, Middlesex HA2 0HW
Tel: 020 8422 2092
Headmistress: Mrs A Isaacs
Age range: 3–7
No. of pupils: 54
Fees: Day £9,450

ST CATHERINE'S SCHOOL
For further details see p. 114
Cross Deep, Twickenham,
Middlesex TW1 4QJ
Tel: 020 8891 2898
Email: info@stcatherineschool.co.uk
Website:
www.stcatherineschool.co.uk
Headmistress: Sister Paula
Thomas BEd(Hons), MA
Age range: G3–18
No. of pupils: 430
Fees: Day £10,509–£14,517

St Christopher's School
71 Wembley Park Drive,
Wembley, Middlesex HA9 8HE
Tel: 020 8902 5069
Headteacher: Mr G. P. Musetti
Age range: 4–11
Fees: Day £8,400–£9,225

St Helen's College
Parkway, Hillingdon, Uxbridge,
Middlesex UB10 9JX
Tel: 01895 234371
Joint Headteachers: Mr D A
Crehan & Mrs G R Crehan
Age range: 3–11
No. of pupils: 351
Fees: Day £5,850–£10,695

St Helen's School
Eastbury Road, Northwood,
Middlesex HA6 3AS
Tel: +44 (0)1923 843210
Headmistress: Dr Mary Short BA, PhD
Age range: G3–18
No. of pupils: VIth165

St John's School
Potter Street Hill, Northwood,
Middlesex HA6 3QY
Tel: 020 8866 0067
Headmaster: Mr M S Robinson BSc
Age range: B3–13 years
No. of pupils: 350
Fees: Day £10,070–£14,600

St John's Senior School
North Lodge, The Ridgeway,
Enfield, Middlesex EN2 8BE
Tel: 020 8366 0035
Headmaster: Mr Andrew Tardios
LLB(Hons), BA(Hons), CertEd
Age range: 11–18 years
No. of pupils: 309 VIth95
Fees: Day £13,170

St Martin's School
40 Moor Park Road, Northwood,
Middlesex HA6 2DJ
Tel: 01923 825740
Headmaster: Mr D T
Tidmarsh BSc(Wales)
Age range: B3–13
No. of pupils: 400
Fees: Day £1,450–£4,066

Tashbar of Edgeware
47-49 Mowbray Road, Edgware,
Middlesex HA8 8JL
Tel: 020 8958 5162
Headteacher: Mr N Jaffe
Age range: B3–11
No. of pupils: 88

The Falcons Preparatory School for Boys
41 Few Foot Road, Richmond,
Middlesex TW9 2SS
Tel: 0844 225 2211
Headmaster: Mr Gordon Milne
Age range: B7–13
No. of pupils: 100
Fees: Day £12,660

The Hall Pre-Preparatory School & Nursery
The Grange Country House,
Rickmansworth Road, Northwood,
Middlesex HA6 2RB
Tel: 01923 822807
Headmistress: Mrs S M Goodwin
Age range: 1–7
Fees: Day £3,120–£10,350

The John Lyon School
Middle Road, Harrow on the
Hill, Middlesex HA2 0HN
Tel: 020 8515 9400
Head: Miss Katherine Haynes
BA, MEd, NPQH
Age range: B11–18
No. of pupils: 600
Fees: Day £5,544–£5,756

The Lady Eleanor Holles School
Hanworth Road, Hampton,
Middlesex TW12 3HF
Tel: 020 8979 1601
Head of School: Mrs Heather Hanbury
Age range: G7–18
No. of pupils: 875
Fees: Day £18,945

The Mall School
185 Hampton Road, Twickenham,
Middlesex TW2 5NQ
Tel: 0208 977 2523
Headmaster: Mr D C Price BSc, MA
Age range: B4–13
No. of pupils: 320
Fees: Day £10,281–£11,934

The Noam Primary School
8-10 Forty Avenue, Wembley,
Middlesex HA9 8JW
Tel: 020 8908 9491
Headteacher: Mrs Sarah Simmonds
Age range: 3–11
No. of pupils: 154

The St Michael Steiner School
Park Road, Hanworth Park,
London, Middlesex TW13 6PN
Tel: 0208 893 1299
Age range: 3–16 (17 from Jul 2014)
No. of pupils: 101
Fees: Day £5,800–£8,900

Twickenham Preparatory School
Beveree, 43 High Street, Hampton,
Middlesex TW12 2SA
Tel: 020 8979 6216
Head: Mr D Malam BA(Hons)
(Southampton), PGCE(Winchester)
Age range: B4–13 G4–11
No. of pupils: 272
Fees: Day £9,345–£10,110

Surrey

Al-Khair School
109-117 Cherry Orchard Road,
Croydon, Surrey CR0 6BE
Tel: 020 8662 8664
Headteacher: Mr Usman Qureshi
Age range: 5–16
No. of pupils: 126

Broomfield House School
Broomfield Road, Kew Gardens,
Richmond, Surrey TW9 3HS
Tel: 020 8940 3884
Head Teacher: Mr N O York
BA(Hons), MA, MPhil, FRSA
Age range: 3–11
No. of pupils: 160
Fees: Day £6,510–£13,140

Cambridge Tutors College
Water Tower Hill, Croydon,
Surrey CR0 5SX
Tel: 020 8688 5284/7363
Principal: Mr M Eagers
Age range: 15–19
No. of pupils: 215 VIth200
Fees: Day £19,800

Canbury School
Kingston Hill, Kingston upon
Thames, Surrey KT2 7LN
Tel: 020 8549 8622
Headmistress: Ms Louise Clancy
Age range: 11–16
No. of pupils: 65
Fees: Day £14,490

Collingwood School
3 Springfield Road, Wallington,
Surrey SM6 0BD
Tel: 020 8647 4607
Headmaster: Mr Chris Fenwick
Age range: 3–11
No. of pupils: 120
Fees: Day £3,600–£6,750

Croydon High School GDST
Old Farleigh Road, Selsdon, South Croydon, Surrey CR2 8YB
Tel: 020 8260 7500
Head of Junior School: Mrs Sophie Bradshaw
Age range: G3–18
No. of pupils: 580 VIth110

Cumnor House School
168 Pampisford Road, South Croydon, Surrey CR2 6DA
Tel: 020 8660 3445
Headmaster: Mr F Steadman M Ed Cert Ed
Age range: B2–13 G2–4
No. of pupils: 440
Fees: Day £3,350–£4,030

Cumnor House School – Treetops Nursery
91 Pampisford Road, South Croydon, Surrey CR2 6DH
Tel: +44 (0)20 8660 3445
Manager: Mrs Charlotte Figueira BEd(Hons)
Age range: 2–4
No. of pupils: 200
Fees: Day £1,370–£2,945

Cumnor House School for Girls
1 Woodcote Lane, Purley, Surrey CR8 3HB
Tel: 020 8660 3445
Headmaster: Mr Peter Kelly
Age range: G2–11
No. of pupils: 180
Fees: Day £2,945–£3,735

Date Valley School
Mitcham Court, Cricket Green, Mitcham, Surrey CR4 4LB
Tel: +44 (0)20 8648 4647
Headteacher: Mrs Razina Karim
Age range: 3–11
No. of pupils: 110
Fees: Day £1,869–£3,150

Educare Small School
12 Cowleaze Road, Kingston upon Thames, Surrey KT2 6DZ
Tel: 020 8547 0144
Head Teacher: Mrs E Steinthal
Age range: 3–11
No. of pupils: 46
Fees: Day £5,040

Elmhurst School
44-48 South Park Hill Rd, South Croydon, Surrey CR2 7DW
Tel: 020 8688 0661
Headmaster: Mr M J Apsley BA(Hons), PGCE
Age range: B4–11
No. of pupils: 207
Fees: Day £6,300–£7,545

Folly's End Christian School
Folly's End Church, 5-9 Surrey Street, Croydon, Surrey CR0 1RG
Tel: 020 8649 9121
Senior Leaders: Dave & Ze Markee
Age range: 3–11
Fees: Day £4,740

Holy Cross Preparatory School
George Road, Kingston upon Thames, Surrey KT2 7NU
Tel: 020 8942 0729
Headteacher: Mrs S Hair BEd(Hons)
Age range: G4–11
No. of pupils: 250
Fees: Day £9,960

Homefield Preparatory School
Western Road, Sutton, Surrey SM1 2TE
Tel: 0208 642 0965
Headmaster: Mr John Towers
Age range: B3–13
No. of pupils: 350
Fees: Day £2,045–£4,380

KEW COLLEGE
For further details see p. 108
24-26 Cumberland Road, Kew, Surrey TW9 3HQ
Tel: 020 8940 2039
Email: enquiries@kewcollege.com
Website: www.kewcollege.com
Headteacher: Mrs Marianne Austin BSc(Hons) MA(Hons) ACA PGCE
Age range: 3–11
No. of pupils: 296

Kew Green Preparatory School
Layton House, Ferry Lane, Kew Green, Richmond, Surrey TW9 3AF
Tel: 020 8948 5999
Headmaster: Mr J Peck
Age range: 4–11
No. of pupils: 260
Fees: Day £15,606

KING'S HOUSE SCHOOL
For further details see p. 110
68 King's Road, Richmond, Surrey TW10 6ES
Tel: 020 8940 1878
Email: schooloffice@kingshouseschool.org
Website: www.kingshouseschool.org
Head: Mr Mark Turner BA, PGCE, NPQH
Age range: B3–13 G3–4
No. of pupils: 460
Fees: Day £2,165–£5,120

Kingston Grammar School
70 London Rd, Kingston upon Thames, Surrey KT2 6PY
Tel: 020 8456 5875
Head: Mr Stephen Lehec
Age range: 11–18
No. of pupils: 820
Fees: Day £18,045

Laleham Lea School
29 Peaks Hill, Purley, Surrey CR8 3JJ
Tel: 020 8660 3351
Headteacher: Mrs J Staunton
Age range: 3–11
Fees: Day £2,128–£6,405

Maple House School
23 Parchmore Road, Thornton Heath, Surrey CR7 8LY
Tel: 020 8653 1827
Headteacher: Mrs Pauline Khoo
Age range: 5–10
No. of pupils: 97

Marymount International School London
George Road, Kingston upon Thames, Surrey KT2 7PE
Tel: +44 (0)20 8949 0571
Headmistress: Mrs Margaret Frazier
Age range: G11–18
No. of pupils: 250 VIth100
Fees: Day £20,015–£22,860 WB £34,365–£37,210 FB £36,030–£38,875

Oakwood Independent School
Godstone Road, Purley, Surrey CR8 2AN
Tel: 020 8668 8080
Headmaster: Mr Ciro Candia BA(Hons), PGCE
Age range: 3–11
No. of pupils: 176
Fees: Day £5,280–£7,644

Old Palace of John Whitgift School
Old Palace Road, Croydon, Surrey CR0 1AX
Tel: 020 8686 7347
Head: Mrs. C Jewell
Age range: B3 months–4 years G3 months–19 years
No. of pupils: 740 VIth120
Fees: Day £10,086–£13,497

Old Vicarage School
48 Richmond Hill, Richmond, Surrey TW10 6QX
Tel: 020 8940 0922
Headmistress: Mrs G D Linthwaite
Age range: G4–11
No. of pupils: 200
Fees: Day £4,380

Park Hill School
8 Queens Road, Kingston upon Thames, Surrey KT2 7SH
Tel: 020 8546 5496
Principal: Mrs Marie Christie
Age range: 2 –7
No. of pupils: 100
Fees: Day £4,320–£8,130

Reedham Park School
71A Old Lodge Lane, Purley, Surrey CR8 4DN
Tel: 020 8660 6357
Headteacher: Mrs Katie Shah
Age range: 4–11
No. of pupils: 122
Fees: Day £3,540–£4,110

Rokeby School
George Road, Kingston upon Thames, Surrey KT2 7PB
Tel: 020 8942 2247
Head: Mr J R Peck
Age range: B4–13
No. of pupils: 370
Fees: Day £3,974–£4,948

Royal Russell Junior School
Coombe Lane, Croydon, Surrey CR9 5BX
Tel: 020 8651 5884
Junior School Headmaster: Mr James C Thompson
Age range: 3–11
No. of pupils: 300
Fees: Day £3,660–£10,155

Royal Russell School
Coombe Lane, Croydon,
Surrey CR9 5BX
Tel: 020 8657 3669
Headmaster: Christopher Hutchinson
Age range: 11–18
No. of pupils: 590 VIth180
Fees: Day £15,285 FB £22,365–£30,240

Seaton House School
67 Banstead Road South,
Sutton, Surrey SM2 5LH
Tel: 020 8642 2332
Headmistress: Mrs Debbie Morrison
Higher Diploma in Education (RSA)
Age range: B3–5 G3–11
No. of pupils: 164
Fees: Day £2,187–£8,955

Shrewsbury House School
107 Ditton Road, Surbiton,
Surrey KT6 6RL
Tel: 020 8399 3066
Headmaster: Mr K Doble
BA, PDM, PGCE
Age range: B7–13
No. of pupils: 320
Fees: Day £13,680

St David's School
23/25 Woodcote Valley Road,
Purley, Surrey CR8 3AL
Tel: 020 8660 0723
Headmistress: Mrs Lindsay
Nash BEd(Hons)
Age range: 3–11
No. of pupils: 167
Fees: Day £2,985–£5,940

St James Senior Boys School
Church Road, Ashford, Surrey TW15 3DZ
Tel: 01784 266930
Headmaster: Mr David Brazier
Age range: B11–18
No. of pupils: 390 VIth65
Fees: Day £17,280

STAINES PREPARATORY SCHOOL
For further details see p. 116
3 Gresham Road, Staines upon
Thames, Surrey TW18 2BT
Tel: 01784 450909
Email: admissions@stainesprep.co.uk
Website: www.stainesprep.co.uk
Head of School: Ms Samantha
Sawyer B.Ed (Hons), M.Ed, NPQH
Age range: 3–11
No. of pupils: 377
Fees: Day £9,510–£11,055

Surbiton High School
13-15 Surbiton Crescent, Kingston
upon Thames, Surrey KT1 2JT
Tel: 020 8546 5245
Principal: Ann Haydon BSc(Hons)
Age range: G4–18
No. of pupils: 1210 VIth186
Fees: Day £6,390–£10,857

Sutton High School GDST
55 Cheam Road, Sutton,
Surrey SM1 2AX
Tel: 020 8642 0594
Headmistress: Mrs Katharine Crouch
Age range: G3–18
No. of pupils: 600 VIth60
Fees: Day £9,153–£15,450

The Cedars School
Coombe Road, Lloyd Park,
Croydon, Surrey CR0 5RD
Tel: 020 8185 7770
Headmaster: Robert Teague Bsc (Hons)
Age range: B11–18

The Royal Ballet School
White Lodge, Richmond,
Surrey TW10 5HR
Tel: 020 7836 8899
Director: Ms Gailene Stock AM
Age range: 11–19
No. of pupils: VIth80
Fees: Day £14,394–£18,946
FB £17,709–£25,588

The Study School
57 Thetford Road, New
Malden, Surrey KT3 5DP
Tel: 020 8942 0754
Age range: 3–11
No. of pupils: 134
Fees: Day £3,984–£8,973

Trinity School
Shirley Park, Croydon, Surrey CR9 7AT
Tel: 020 8656 9541
Headmaster: Alasdair
Kennedy MA (Cantab)
Age range: B10–18 G16–18
No. of pupils: 1007
Fees: Day £15,906

Unicorn School
238 Kew Road, Richmond,
Surrey TW9 3JX
Tel: 020 8948 3926
Headmaster: Mr Kit Thompson
Age range: 3–11
Fees: Day £6,000–£11,010

Westbury House
80 Westbury Road, New
Malden, Surrey KT3 5AS
Tel: 020 8942 5885
Age range: 3–11
Fees: Day £1,045–£2,507

Whitgift School
Haling Park, South Croydon,
Surrey CR2 6YT
Tel: +44 (0)20 8633 9935
Headmaster: Mr Christopher Ramsey
Age range: B10–18
No. of pupils: 1464
Fees: Day £17,340 WB £27,924 FB £33,396

D332

London

KEY TO SYMBOLS

- Boys' school
- Girls' school
- International school
- Tutorial or sixth form college
- A levels
- Boarding accommodation
- Bursaries
- International Baccalaureate
- Learning support
- Entrance at 16+
- Vocational qualifications
- Independent Association of Preparatory Schools
- The Headmasters' & Headmistresses' Conference
- Independent Schools Association
- Girls' School Association
- Boarding Schools' Association
- Society of Heads

Unless otherwise indicated, all schools are coeducational day schools. Single-sex and boarding schools will be indicated by the relevant icon.

Central London

CATS London
43-45 Bloomsbury Square,
London WC1A 2RA
Tel: 02078 411580
Principal: Mario Di Clemente
Age range: 15–24

Charterhouse Square School
40 Charterhouse Square,
London EC1M 6EA
Tel: 020 7600 3805
Age range: 3–11
No. of pupils: 196
Fees: Day £4,575

CITY OF LONDON SCHOOL
For further details see p. 124
Queen Victoria Street,
London EC4V 3AL
Tel: 020 3680 6300
Email: admissions@cityoflondonschool.org.uk
Website: www.cityoflondonschool.org.uk
Head: Mr A R Bird MSc
Age range: B10–18
No. of pupils: 930 VIth250
Fees: Day £16,731

City of London School for Girls
St Giles' Terrace, Barbican,
London EC2Y 8BB
Tel: 020 7847 5500
Headmistress: Mrs E Harrop
Age range: G7–18
No. of pupils: 725

Dallington School
8 Dallington Street, Islington,
London EC1V 0BW
Tel: 020 7251 2284
Headteacher: Mrs M C Hercules
Age range: 3–11
No. of pupils: 130
Fees: Day £9,978–£12,630

École Jeannine Manuel – London
43-45 Bedford Square, ,
London WC1B 3DN
Tel: 020 3829 5970
Principal: Pauline Prévot
Age range: 3–15 years
No. of pupils: 350
Fees: Day £16,890

Italia Conti Academy of Theatre Arts
Italia Conti House, 23 Goswell
Road, London EC1M 7AJ
Tel: 020 7608 0047
Principal: Anne Sheward
Age range: 10–21

ST PAUL'S CATHEDRAL SCHOOL
For further details see p. 148
2 New Change, London EC4M 9AD
Tel: 020 7248 5156
Email: admissions@spcs.london.sch.uk
Website: www.spcslondon.com
Headmaster: Mr Simon Larter-Evans BA (Hons), PGCE, FRSA
Age range: 4–13
No. of pupils: 248
Fees: Day £4,501–£4,855 FB £2,808

The College of Central London
Tower Bridge Business Centre, 46-48
East Smithfield, London E1W 1AW
Tel: +44 (0) 20 3667 7607
Principal: Nicolas Kailides
Fees: Day £3,300

The Lyceum
6 Paul Street, London EC2A 4JH
Tel: 020 7247 1588
Joint Headteachers: Mr Jeremy Rowe & Mrs Lynn Hannay
Age range: 4–11
No. of pupils: 100
Fees: Day £8,700–£13,800

Urdang Academy
The Old Finsbury Town Hall, Rosebery
Avenue, London EC1R 4RP
Tel: 020 7713 7710
Principal: Stephanie Pope ARAD (dip PDTC)
Age range: 10–16

East London

Al-Falah Primary School
48 Kenninghall Road,
Clapton, London E5 8BY
Tel: 020 8985 1059
Headteacher: Mr M A Hussain
Age range: 5–11
No. of pupils: 83
Fees: Day £1,600

Al-Mizan School
46 Whitechapel Road, London E1 1JX
Tel: 020 7650 3070
Head: Mr Ziaurr Ahman
Age range: B7–18
No. of pupils: 200 VIth13
Fees: Day £2,400

Azhar Academy
235A Romford Road, Forest
Gate, London E7 9HL
Tel: 020 8534 5959
Headteacher: Mrs R Rehman
Age range: G11–16
No. of pupils: 189

Beis Trana Girls' School
186 Upper Clapton Road,
London E5 9DH
Tel: 020 8815 8003
Age range: G3–16
No. of pupils: 270

Chingford House School
22 Marlborough Road, Waltham
Forest, London E4 9AL
Tel: 020 8527 2902; 07749 899 498
Head teacher: Helen McNulty
Age range: 0–5
Fees: Day £5,460–£8,320

Faraday School
Old Gate House, 7 Trinity Buoy
Wharf, London E14 0JW
Tel: 020 8965 7374
Executive Head Teacher: Mrs. S. Gillam
Age range: 4–11
No. of pupils: 105
Fees: Day £3,044

Forest School
College Place, Snaresbrook,
London E17 3PY
Tel: 020 8520 1744
Warden: Mr Anthony Faccinello
Age range: 4–18
No. of pupils: 1355 VIth260
Fees: Day £11,049–£16,335

Gatehouse School
Sewardstone Road, Victoria
Park, London E2 9JG
Tel: 020 8980 2978
Headmistress: Mrs Belinda Canham JP, BA(Hons), PGCE(Froebel)
Age range: 3–11
No. of pupils: 320
Fees: Day £6,920–£8,502

Grangewood Independent School
Chester Road, Forest
Gate, London E7 8QT
Tel: 020 8472 3552
Headteacher: Mrs B A Roberts B.Ed (Hons); PG Cert (SEN)
Age range: 2–11
No. of pupils: 71
Fees: Day £5,157–£6,750

Green Gables Montessori School
St George in the East Crypt West, 14
Cannon Street Road, London E1 0BH
Tel: 020 7488 2374
Head: Mrs V Hunt
Age range: 0–8
No. of pupils: 45
Fees: Day £740–£10,480

Hyland House School
Holcombe Road, Tottenham,
, London N17 9AD
Tel: 020 8520 4186
Head Teacher: Mrs Gina Abbequaye
Age range: 3–11
Fees: Day £2,520

London East Academy
46-80 Whitechapel Road,
London E1 1JX
Tel: 020 7650 3070
Headteacher: Musleh Faradhi
Age range: B11–18
No. of pupils: VIth18
Fees: Day £3,000

Lubavitch House School (Junior Boys)
135 Clapton Common, London E5 9AE
Tel: 020 8800 1044
Head: Rabbi D Golomb
Age range: B5–11
No. of pupils: 101
Fees: Day £520–£3,100

Madani Girls School
Myrdle Street, London E1 1HL
Tel: 020 7377 1992
Headteacher: Mrs F Liyawdeen
Age range: G11–18
No. of pupils: 248 VIth11
Fees: Day £1,900

Normanhurst School
68-74 Station Road, Chingford, London E4 7BA
Tel: 020 8529 4307
Headmistress: Mrs Claire Osborn
Age range: 2–16
No. of pupils: 250
Fees: Day £7,470–£11,235

Paragon Christian Academy
233-241 Glyn Road, London E5 0JP
Tel: 020 8985 1119
Headteacher: Mrs J A Lynch
Age range: 5–16
No. of pupils: 34

Pillar Box Montessori Nursery & Pre-Prep School
107 Bow Road, London E3 2AN
Tel: 020 8980 0700
Age range: 0–7
Fees: Day £250–£500

Promised Land Academy
St Cedds Hall, Webb Gardens, Plaistow, London E13 8SR
Tel: 0207 473 3229
Head: Mr A Coote
Age range: 4–16

Quwwat-ul Islam Girls School
16 Chaucer Road, Forest Gate, London E7 9NB
Tel: 020 8548 4736
Headteacher: Mrs B Khan
Age range: G4–11
No. of pupils: 150

River House Montessori School
3-4 Shadwell Pierhead, Glamis Road, London E1W 3TD
Tel: 020 7538 9886
Headmistress: Miss S Greenwood
Age range: 3–12
Fees: Day £2,700–£9,000

Snaresbrook Preparatory School
75 Woodford Road, South Woodford, London E18 2EA
Tel: 020 8989 2394
Age range: 3–11
No. of pupils: 164
Fees: Day £6,696–£8,952

St Joseph's Convent School For Girls
59 Cambridge Park, Wanstead, London E11 2PR
Tel: 020 8989 4700
Headteacher: Ms C Glover
Age range: G3–11
No. of pupils: 171
Fees: Day £5,355

Talmud Torah Machikei Hadass School
96-98 Clapton Common, London E5 9AL
Tel: 020 8800 6599
Headteacher: Rabbi C Silbiger
Age range: B4–11
No. of pupils: 271

Winston House Preparatory School
140 High Road, London E18 2QS
Tel: 020 8505 6565
Head Teacher: Mrs Marian Kemp
Age range: 3–11
Fees: Day £5,850–£7,050

North London

Annemount School
18 Holne Chase, Hampstead Garden Suburb, London N2 0QN
Tel: 020 8455 2132
Principal: Mrs G Maidment BA(Hons), MontDip
Age range: 2–7
No. of pupils: 100
Fees: Day £2,500–£4,500

Avenue Nursery & Pre-Preparatory School
2 Highgate Avenue, London N6 5RX
Tel: 020 8348 6815
Principal: Mrs. Mary Fysh
Age range: 3½–7½
No. of pupils: 79

Beis Chinuch Lebonos Girls School
Woodberry Down Centre, Woodberry Down, London N4 2SH
Tel: 020 88097 737
Headmistress: Mrs Bertha Schneck
Age range: G2–16
No. of pupils: 421

Beis Malka Girls School
93 Alkham Road, London N16 6XD
Tel: 020 8806 2070
Headmaster: M Dresdner
Age range: G5–16
No. of pupils: 339

Beis Rochel D'Satmar Girls School
51-57 Amhurst Park, London N16 5DL
Tel: 020 8800 9060
Headmistress: Mrs A Scher
Age range: G2–17
No. of pupils: 788

Bnois Jerusalem School
79-81 Amhurst Park, London N16 5DL
Tel: 020 8802 7470
Head: Mrs Sonnenschein
Age range: G3–16

Channing School
The Bank, Highgate, London N6 5HF
Tel: 020 8340 2328
Head: Mrs B M Elliott
Age range: G4–18
No. of pupils: 746 VIth108
Fees: Day £14,085–£15,255

Dwight School London
6 Friern Barnet Lane, London N11 3LX
Tel: +44 (0)20 8920 0637
Head: Mrs Alison Cobbin BA, Dip Ed, MBA
Age range: 3–18

Finchley & Acton Yochien School
6 Hendon Avenue, Finchley, London N3 1UE
Tel: 020 8343 2191
Headteacher: Mr Katsumasa Kitagaki
Age range: 2–6
No. of pupils: 145

Getters Talmud Torah
86 Amhurst Park, London N16 5AR
Tel: 020 8802 2512
Headteacher: Mr David Kahana
Age range: B4–11
No. of pupils: 171

Grange Park Preparatory School
13 The Chine, Grange Park, Winchmore Hill, London N21 2EA
Tel: 020 8360 1469
Headteacher: Miss F Rizzo
Age range: G4–11
No. of pupils: 90
Fees: Day £9,900

Greek Secondary School of London
Avenue Lodge, Bounds Green Road, London N22 7EU
Tel: 020 8881 9320
Headteacher: Antonia Valavani
Age range: 13–18
No. of pupils: 200

Highgate
North Road, Highgate, London N6 4AY
Tel: 020 8340 1524
Head Master: Mr A S Pettitt MA
Age range: 3–18
No. of pupils: 1541 VIth312
Fees: Day £15,135–£17,475

Highgate Junior School
Cholmeley House, 3 Bishopswood Road, London N6 4PL
Tel: 020 8340 9193
Principal: Mr S M James BA
Age range: 7–11
Fees: Day £10,695–£11,955

Highgate Pre-Preparatory School
7 Bishopswood Road, London N6 4PH
Tel: 020 8340 9196
Principal: Mrs Diane Hecht
Age range: 3–7
No. of pupils: 150
Fees: Day £17,640

Keble Prep
Wades Hill, Winchmore Hill, London N21 1BG
Tel: 020 8360 3359
Headmaster: Mr G. P. McCarthy
Age range: B4–13
Fees: Day £3,760–£4,670

Kerem School
Norrice Lea, London N2 0RE
Tel: 020 8455 0909
Acting Head Teacher: Miss Alyson Burns
Age range: 3–11
Fees: Day £8,250–£6,675

Lubavitch House School (Senior Girls)
107-115 Stamford Hill, Hackney, London N16 5RP
Tel: 020 8800 0022
Headmaster: Rabbi Shmuel Lew FRSA
Age range: G11–17
No. of pupils: 102
Fees: Day £3,900

Montessori House
5 Princes Avenue, Muswell Hill, London N10 3LS
Tel: 020 8444 4399
Head: Ms Lisa Christoforou
Age range: 6 months–7 years
No. of pupils: 100
Fees: Day £5,355–£9,450

Norfolk House School
10 Muswell Avenue, Muswell Hill, London N10 2EG
Tel: 020 8883 4584
Head Teacher: Ms Sam Habgood
Age range: 4–11
No. of pupils: 130
Fees: Day £9,855

North London Grammar School
110 Colindeep Lane, Hendon, London NW9 6HB
Tel: 0208 205 0052
Head Teacher: Hakan Gokce
Age range: 11–18
No. of pupils: VIth20
Fees: Day £7,500
(A) (£)

North London Muslim School
131-133 Fore Street, Edmonton, London N18 2XF
Tel: 020 8345 7008
Headteacher: Mr W Abdulla
Age range: 4–10
No. of pupils: 21

North London Rudolf Steiner School
1-3 The Campsbourne, London N8 7PN
Tel: 020 8341 3770
Age range: 2½–7
No. of pupils: 40

Palmers Green High School
Hoppers Road, Winchmore Hill, London N21 3LJ
Tel: 020 8886 1135
Headmistress: Mrs Christine Edmundson BMus(Hons), MBA, PGCE, LRAM, ARCM
Age range: G3–16
No. of pupils: 300
Fees: Day £5,985–£10,785
(£)

Pardes House Grammar School
Hendon Lane, Finchley, London N3 1SA
Tel: 020 8349 4222
Headteacher: Mr S Mallett
Age range: B10–16
No. of pupils: 222

Phoenix Academy
85 Bounces Road, Edmonton, London N9 8LD
Tel: 020 8887 6888
Headteacher: Mr A Hawkes
Age range: 11–16
No. of pupils: 19

Rosemary Works Independent School
1 Branch Place, London N1 5PH
Tel: 020 7739 3950
Head: Dorothy Davey
Age range: 3–11
No. of pupils: 104
Fees: Day £6,195

Salcombe Preparatory School
224-226 Chase Side, Southgate, , London N14 4PL
Tel: 020 8441 5356
Headmistress: Mrs Sarah-Jane Davies BA(Hons) QTS MEd
Age range: 4–11
No. of pupils: 236
Fees: Day £7,890
(£)

St Paul's Steiner School
1 St Paul's Road, Islington, London N1 2QH
Tel: 020 7226 4454
College of Teachers: College of Teachers
Age range: 2–14
No. of pupils: 136
(£)

Sunrise Nursery, Stoke Newington
1 Cazenove Road, Stoke Newington, Hackney, London N16 6PA
Tel: 020 8806 6279
Principal: Didi Ananda Manika

Sunrise Primary School
55 Coniston Road, Tottenham, London N17 0EX
Tel: 020 8806 6279 (Office); 020 8885 3354 (School)
Head: Mrs Mary-Anne Lovage MontDipEd, BA
Age range: 2–11
No. of pupils: 30
Fees: Day £5,343

Talmud Torah Bobov Primary School
87 Egerton Road, London N16 6UE
Tel: 020 8809 1025
Headmaster: Mr Eisen
Age range: B3–13
No. of pupils: 320

Talmud Torah Chaim Meirim School
26 Lampard Grove, London N16 6XB
Tel: 020 8806 0017
Principal: Rabbi S Hoffman
Age range: B6–13

Talmud Torah Yetev Lev School
111-115 Cazenove Road, London N16 6AX
Tel: 020 8806 3834
Headteacher: Mr J Stauber
Age range: B2–11
No. of pupils: 567

Tawhid Boys School
21 Cazenove Road, London N16 6PA
Tel: 020 8806 2999
Headteacher: Mr Usman Mapara
Age range: B10–15
No. of pupils: 115
Fees: Day £2,000

Tayyibah Girls School
88 Filey Avenue, Stamford Hill, London N16 6JJ
Tel: 020 8880 0085
Headmistress: Mrs N B Qureishi MSc
Age range: G5–15
No. of pupils: 270
Fees: Day £1,630
(A)

The Children's House Upper School
King Henry's Walk, London N1 4PB
Tel: 020 7249 6273
Headteacher: Mrs J Rothwell
Age range: 4–7
No. of pupils: 60
Fees: Day £3,250

The Gower School Montessori Nursery
18 North Road, Islington, London N7 9EY
Tel: 020 7700 2445
Principal: Miss Emma Gowers
Age range: 3 months–5 years
No. of pupils: 237

The Gower School Montessori Primary
10 Cynthia Street, Barnsbury, London N1 9JF
Tel: 020 7278 2020
Principal: Miss Emma Gowers
Age range: 4–11
No. of pupils: 237
Fees: Day £4,680–£19,129

TTTYY School
14 Heathland Road, London N16 5NH
Tel: 020 8802 1348
Headmaster: Mr S B Gluck
Age range: B2–13
No. of pupils: 187

Vita et Pax School
Priory Close, Southgate, London N14 4AT
Tel: 020 8449 8336
Headteacher: Miss Gillian Chumbley
Age range: 3–11
Fees: Day £6,150

Yesodey Hatorah School
2-4 Amhurst Park, London N16 5AE
Tel: 020 8826 5500
Headteacher: Rabbi Pinter
Age range: 3–16
No. of pupils: 920

North-West London

Abercorn School
38 Portland Place, London NW8 9XP
Tel: 020 7286 4785
High Mistress: Mrs Andrea Greystoke BA(Hons)
Age range: 2 –13
No. of pupils: 360
Fees: Day £7,245–£13,425

Al-Sadiq & Al-Zahra Schools
134 Salusbury Road, London NW6 6PF
Tel: 020 7372 7706
Headteacher: Dr M Movahedi
Age range: 4–16
No. of pupils: 389

Arnold House School
1 Loudoun Road, St John's Wood, London NW8 0LH
Tel: 020 7266 4840
Headmaster: Mr Vivian Thomas
Age range: B5–13
No. of pupils: 270
Fees: Day £5,878
(£)

Ayesha Community School
10A Montagu Road, Hendon, London NW4 3ES
Tel: 02034112660
Headteacher: Mr Shakil Ahmed
Age range: G4–18
Fees: Day £3,000
(A)

Beis Hamedrash Elyon
211 Golders Green Road, London NW11 9BY
Tel: 020 8201 8668
Headteacher: Mr C Steinhart
Age range: B11–14
No. of pupils: 45

Beis Soroh Schneirer
Arbiter House, Wilberforce Road, London NW9 6AT
Tel: 020 8343 1190
Head: Mrs R Weiss
Age range: G2–11
No. of pupils: 150

Belmont, Mill Hill Preparatory School
The Ridgeway, London NW7 4ED
Tel: 020 8906 7270
Headmaster: Mr Leon Roberts MA
Age range: 7–13
No. of pupils: 490
Fees: Day £5,685
£

Beth Jacob Grammar School for Girls
Stratford Road, Hendon, London NW4 2AT
Tel: 020 8203 4322
Headteacher: Mrs D Steinberg
Age range: G11–17
No. of pupils: 264

Brondesbury College for Boys
8 Brondesbury Park, London NW6 7BT
Tel: 020 8830 4522
Headteacher: Mr Dan Salahuddin Clifton
Age range: B11–16
No. of pupils: 93
£

College Francais Bilingue De Londres
87 Holmes Road, Kentish Town, , London NW5 3AX
Tel: +44 (0) 20 7993 7400
Principal: Mr François-Xavier Gabet
Age range: 5–15
No. of pupils: 210

DEVONSHIRE HOUSE PREPARATORY SCHOOL
For further details see p. 126
2 Arkwright Road, Hampstead, London NW3 6AE
Tel: 020 7435 1916
Email: enquiries@devonshirehouseprepschool.co.uk
Website: www.devonshirehouseschool.co.uk
Headmistress: Mrs S. Piper BA(Hons)
Age range: B 2½–13 G2½–11
No. of pupils: 650
Fees: Day £9,750–£17,865
£

Fine Arts College, Hampstead
24 Lambolle Place, Belsize Park, London NW3 4PG
Tel: 020 7586 0312
Co Principals: Candida Cave & Nicholas Cochrane
Age range: 13–19
No. of pupils: 115
Fees: Day £6,000–£15,600
16· A £ 16·

FRANCIS HOLLAND SCHOOL, REGENT'S PARK, NW1
For further details see p. 128
Clarence Gate, Ivor Place, Regent's Park, London NW1 6XR
Tel: 020 7723 0176
Email: registrar@fhs-nw1.org.uk
Website: www.fhs-nw1.org.uk
Head: Mr C B Fillingham MA (King's College London)
Age range: G11–18
No. of pupils: 495 VIth120
Fees: Day £19,260
A £ 16·

Golders Hill School
666 Finchley Road, London NW11 7NT
Tel: 020 8455 2589
Headmistress: Mrs A T Eglash BA(Hons)
Age range: 2–7
No. of pupils: 180
Fees: Day £831–£6,870

Goodwyn School
Hammers Lane, Mill Hill, London NW7 4DB
Tel: 020 8959 3756
Principal: Struan Robertson
Age range: 3–11
No. of pupils: 223
Fees: Day £9,645–£10,779

Grimsdell, Mill Hill Pre-Preparatory School
Winterstoke House, Wills Grove, Mill Hill, London NW7 1QR
Tel: 020 8959 6884
Head: Mrs Kate Simon BA, PGCE
Age range: 3–7
No. of pupils: 182
Fees: Day £1,971–£4,285

Hampstead Hill Pre-Prep & Nursery School
St Stephen's Hall, Pond Street, Hampstead, London NW3 2PP
Tel: 020 7435 6262
Principal: Mrs Andrea Taylor
Age range: B2–7+ G2–7+
Fees: Day £11,000–£14,000

HEATHSIDE PREPARATORY SCHOOL
For further details see p. 132
16 New End, Hampstead, London NW3 1JA
Tel: +44 (0)20 7794 5857
Email: admissions@heathsideprep.net
Website: www.heathsideprep.net
Headteacher: Ms Melissa Remus MSc
Age range: 2–13
No. of pupils: 370
Fees: Day £9,300–£14,250

Hendon Preparatory School
20 Tenterden Grove, Hendon, London NW4 1TD
Tel: 020 8203 7727
Age range: 2–13 years
No. of pupils: 165
Fees: Day £6,030–£13,455
£

Hereward House School
14 Strathray Gardens, London NW3 4NY
Tel: 020 7794 4820
Headmaster: Mr T W Burden
Age range: B4–13
No. of pupils: 170
Fees: Day £13,065–£14,205

International Community School
4 York Terrace East, Regents Park, London NW1 4PT
Tel: +44 20 7935 1206
Age range: 3–18
No. of pupils: 260
Fees: Day £16,650–£22,100
IB 16·

Islamia Girls' High School
129 Salusbury Road, London NW6 6PE
Tel: 020 7372 3472
Headteacher: Ms S Jabeen
Age range: G11–16 years
Fees: Day £6,900

L'Ile Aux Enfants
22 Vicar's Road, London NW5 4NL
Tel: 020 7267 7119
Headmistress: Mrs Chailleux
Age range: 3–11
No. of pupils: 192
Fees: Day £3,270

London Jewish Girls' High School
18 Raleigh Close, Hendon, London NW4 2TA
Tel: 020 8203 8618
Headteacher: Mr Joel Rabinowitz
Age range: G11–16

Lyndhurst House Prep School
24 Lyndhurst Gardens, Hampstead, London NW3 5NW
Tel: 020 7435 4936
Head of School: Mr Andrew Reid MA (Oxon)
Age range: B4–13
No. of pupils: 165
Fees: Day £5,735–£6,410

Maple Walk School
62A Crownhill Road, London NW10 4EB
Tel: 020 8963 3890
Head Teacher: Mrs S Gillam
Age range: 4–11
No. of pupils: 200
Fees: Day £2,957
£

Maria Montessori Institute
26 Lyndhurst Gardens, Hampstead, London NW3 5NW
Tel: 020 7435 3646
Director of Training & School: Mrs Lynne Lawrence BA, Mont Int Dip(AMI)
Age range: 18+
No. of pupils: 50
Fees: Day £7,100
16·

Maria Montessori School – Hampstead
26 Lyndhurst Gardens, Hampstead, London NW3 5NW
Tel: +44 (0)20 7435 3646
Director of School: Mrs L Lawrence
Age range: 2–11
No. of pupils: 60
Fees: Day £5,400

Mill Hill School
The Ridgeway, Mill Hill Village, London NW7 1QS
Tel: 020 8959 1176
Head: Dr Dominic Luckett
Age range: 13–18
No. of pupils: 689 VIth259
Fees: Day £13,860 FB £21,900

Naima Jewish Preparatory School
21 Andover Place, London NW6 5ED
Tel: 020 7328 2802
Headteacher: Mr Michael Cohen MA, NPQH
Age range: 3–11
Fees: Day £5,997–£7,470

Nancy Reuben Primary School
Finchley Lane, Hendon, London NW4 1DJ
Tel: 020 82025646
Head: D A David
Age range: 3–11
No. of pupils: 207

NORTH BRIDGE HOUSE NURSERY SCHOOL HAMPSTEAD
For further details see p. 140
33 Fitzjohns Avenue, London NW3 5JY
Tel: 020 7435 9641
Head: Mrs A Allsopp
Age range: 2 years 9 months–5 years
No. of pupils: 229
Fees: Day £3,225–£11,865

NORTH BRIDGE HOUSE PREPARATORY SCHOOL REGENT'S PARK
For further details see p. 140
1 Gloucester Avenue, London NW1 7AB
Tel: 020 7428 1520
Head: Brodie Bibby
Age range: 7–13
No. of pupils: 100
Fees: Day £16,290

NORTH BRIDGE HOUSE PRE-PREPARATORY SCHOOL HAMPSTEAD
For further details see p. 140
8 Netherhall Gardens, London NW3 5RR
Tel: 0207 267 6266
Head Teacher: Mrs J Hockley
Age range: 5–6
No. of pupils: 208
Fees: Day £14,700

NORTH BRIDGE HOUSE SENIOR SCHOOL & SIXTH FORM CANONBURY
For further details see p. 140
6-9 Canonbury Place, Islington, London N1 2NQ
Tel: 020 7267 6266
Head Teacher: Mrs G Masefield
Age range: 11–16
No. of pupils: 310
Fees: Day £14,985

NORTH BRIDGE HOUSE SENIOR SCHOOL HAMPSTEAD
For further details see p. 140
65 Rosslyn Hill, London NW3 5UD
Tel: 020 7428 1520
Email: admissionsenquiries@northbridgehouse.com
Website: www.northbridgehouse.com
Head of Nursery & Pre-Prep Schools: Mrs. Christine McLelland
Age range: 2 years 9 months–18 years
No. of pupils: 1350
Fees: Day £13,680–£18,555

OYH Primary School
Finchley Lane, Hendon, London NW4 1DJ
Tel: 020 8202 5646
Headteacher: D A David
Age range: 3–11
No. of pupils: 180

Rainbow Montessori School
13 Woodchurch Road, Hampstead, London NW6 3PL
Tel: 020 7328 8986
Head Mistress: Maggy Miller MontDip
Age range: 5–12
Fees: Day £3,250–£3,297

Saint Christina's R C Preparatory School
25 St Edmunds Terrace, Regent's Park, London NW8 7PY
Tel: 020 7722 8784
Headteacher: Mrs P Mortimer
Age range: B3–7 G3–11
No. of pupils: 224
Fees: Day £11,076

Sarum Hall
15 Eton Avenue, London NW3 3EL
Tel: 020 7794 2261
Headmistress: Mrs Christine Smith
Age range: G3–11
No. of pupils: 170
Fees: Day £6,048–£10,065

South Hampstead High School GDST
3 Maresfield Gardens, London NW3 5SS
Tel: 020 7435 2899
Headmistress: Mrs J E Stephen BSc
Age range: G4–18
No. of pupils: 852 VIth162
Fees: Day £9,342–£12,006

Southbank International School – Hampstead
16 Netherhall Gardens, London NW3 5TH
Tel: 020 7243 3803
Principal: Shirley Harwood
Age range: 3–11

St Anthony's School for Boys
90 Fitzjohn's Avenue, Hampstead, London NW3 6NP
Tel: 020 7431 1066
Headmaster: Mr Paul Keyte
Age range: B4–13
No. of pupils: 310

St Christopher's School
32 Belsize Lane, Hampstead, London NW3 5AE
Tel: 020 7435 1521
Head: Mrs S A West BA(Hons), PGCE, MA
Age range: G4–11
No. of pupils: 235
Fees: Day £12,450

St Johns Wood Pre-Preparatory School
St Johns Hall, Lords Roundabout, Prince Albert Road, London NW8 7NE
Tel: 020 7722 7149
Headmistress: Ms D Louskas
Age range: 3–7
No. of pupils: 70
Fees: Day £7,620–£12,090

St Margaret's School
18 Kidderpore Gardens, Hampstead, London NW3 7SR
Tel: 020 7435 2439
Principal: Mr M Webster BSc, PGCE
Age range: G4–16
No. of pupils: 156
Fees: Day £10,410–£12,060

St Martin's School
22 Goodwyn Avenue, Mill Hill, London NW7 3RG
Tel: 020 8959 1965
Head: Dr Jason Walak
Age range: 3–11
No. of pupils: 90
Fees: Day £6,750

St Mary's School Hampstead
47 Fitzjohn's Avenue, Hampstead, London NW3 6PG
Tel: 020 7435 1868
Head Teacher: Mrs Harriet Connor-Earl
Age range: B2 years 9 months–7 years G2 years 9 months–11 years
No. of pupils: 300
Fees: Day £7,305–£13,500

St Nicholas School
22 Salmon Street, London NW9 8PN
Tel: 020 8205 7153
Headmistress: Mrs Alyce Gregory CertEd
Age range: 5–11
No. of pupils: 80
Fees: Day £5,760

Swaminarayan School
260 Brentfield Road, Neasden, London NW10 8HE
Tel: 020 8965 8381
Headteacher: Nilesh Manani
Age range: 2–18
No. of pupils: 452 VIth36
Fees: Day £7,818–£10,707

The Academy School
3 Pilgrims Place, Rosslyn Hill, Hampstead, London NW3 1NG
Tel: 020 7435 6621
Headteacher: Mr Garth Evans
Age range: 6–14

The American School in London
One Waverley Place, London NW8 0NP
Tel: 020 7449 1221
Head: Mrs Coreen Hester
Age range: 4–18
No. of pupils: 1350
Fees: Day £21,950–£25,650

The Cavendish School
31 Inverness Street, Camden Town, London NW1 7HB
Tel: 020 7485 1958
Headmistress: Mrs T Dunbar BSc(Hons), PGCE, NPQH
Age range: G3–11
No. of pupils: 218
Fees: Day £11,550

The Hall School
23 Crossfield Road, Hampstead, London NW3 4NU
Tel: 020 7722 1700
Headmaster: Mr Chris Godwin
Age range: B4–13
No. of pupils: 440
Fees: Day £9,300–£11,400

The King Alfred School
Manor Wood, North End Road, London NW11 7HY
Tel: 020 8457 5200
Head: Robert Lobatto MA (Oxon)
Age range: 4–18
No. of pupils: 650 VIth100
Fees: Day £14,862–£17,916

The Mount, Mill Hill International
Milespit Hill, London NW7 2RX
Tel: +44 (0)20 3826 33
Head of School: Ms Sarah Bellotti
Age range: 13–17 years
No. of pupils: 67
Fees: Day £23,799 WB £33,618 FB £39,549

The Mulberry House School
7 Minster Road, West Hampstead, London NW2 3SD
Tel: 020 8452 7340
Headteacher: Ms Julie Kirwan
Age range: 2–8
No. of pupils: 184
Fees: Day £8,460–£15,698

The School of the Islamic Republic of Iran
100 Carlton Vale, London NW6 5HE
Tel: 020 7372 8051
Headteacher: Mr Farzad Farzan
Age range: 6–16
No. of pupils: 53

The Village School
2 Parkhill Road, Belsize Park, London NW3 2YN
Tel: 020 7485 4673
Headmistress: Miss C E F Gay BSc(Hons), PGCE
Age range: G3–11
No. of pupils: 106
Fees: Day £15,525

Torah Vodaas
Julian Headon House, West Hendon Broadway, London NW9 7AL
Tel: 02036704670
Age range: B2–11

Trevor-Roberts School
55-57 Eton Avenue, London NW3 3ET
Tel: 020 7586 1444
Headmaster: Simon Trevor-Roberts BA
Age range: 5–13
Fees: Day £12,270–£14,070

UCS Phoenix School
36 College Crescent, London NW3 5LF
Tel: 020 7722 4433
Headmistress: Dr Zoe Dunn
Age range: 3–7
No. of pupils: 100

University College School
Frognal, Hampstead, London NW3 6XH
Tel: 020 7435 2215
Headmaster: Mr M J Beard MA
Age range: B11–18
No. of pupils: 850 VIth300
Fees: Day £16,005

University College School (Junior)
11 Holly Hill, London NW3 6QN
Tel: 020 7435 3068
Headmaster: Mr Lewis Hayward MA (Oxon Lit. Hum), MA (OU, ED. Management), PGCE
Age range: B7–11
No. of pupils: 250
Fees: Day £5,105

Wentworth Tutorial College
6-10 Brentmead Place, London NW11 9LH
Tel: 020 8458 8524/5
Principal: Alan Davies BSc, MSc
Age range: 14–19
No. of pupils: 115

South-East London

Alleyn's School
Townley Road, Dulwich, London SE22 8SU
Tel: 020 8557 1500
Headmaster: Dr G Savage MA, PhD, FRSA
Age range: 4–18
No. of pupils: 1223 VIth291
Fees: Day £14,139–£16,587

Bellerbys College London
Bounty House, Greenwich, London SE8 3DE
Tel: +44 (0)208 694 7000
Principal: Ms Alison Baines
Age range: 15–19

Blackheath High School GDST
Vanbrugh Park, Blackheath, London SE3 7AG
Tel: 020 8853 2929
Head: Mrs Carol Chandler-Thompson BA (Hons) Exeter, PGCE Exeter
Age range: G3–18
No. of pupils: 780

Blackheath Preparatory School
4 St Germans Place, Blackheath, London SE3 0NJ
Tel: 020 8858 0692
Headmistress: Mrs P J Thompson
Age range: 3–11
No. of pupils: 396
Fees: Day £7,020–£11,745

Colfe's Preparatory School
Horn Park Lane, Lee, London SE12 8AW
Tel: 020 8463 8240
Head: Mrs Sarah Marsh
Age range: 3–11
No. of pupils: 355
Fees: Day £8,730–£10,134

Colfe's School
Horn Park Lane, Lee, London SE12 8AW
Tel: 020 8852 2283
Head: Mr R F Russell MA(Cantab)
Age range: 3–18
No. of pupils: 1120
Fees: Day £11,934–£16,110

Dulwich College
London SE21 7LD
Tel: 020 8693 3601
Master: Dr J A F Spence
Age range: B7–18
No. of pupils: 1589 VIth470
Fees: Day £18,231 WB £35,679 FB £38,052

Dulwich College Kindergarten & Infants School
Eller Bank, 87 College Road, London SE21 7HH
Tel: 020 8693 1538
Head: Mrs H M Friell
Age range: 3 months–7 years
No. of pupils: 251

Dulwich College Preparatory School
42 Alleyn Park, Dulwich, London SE21 7AA
Tel: 020 8766 5500
Headmaster: Mr M W Roulston MBE, MEd
Age range: B3–13 G3–5
No. of pupils: 817
Fees: Day £4,350–£13,542 WB £18,213–£19,662

Eltham College
Grove Park Road, Mottingham, London SE9 4QF
Tel: 0208 857 1455
Headmaster: Guy Sanderson
Age range: B7–18 G16–18
No. of pupils: 830 VIth220
Fees: Day £17,058

Greenwich Steiner School
Woodlands, 90 Mycenae Road, Blackheath, London SE3 7SE
Tel: 020 8858 4404
Age range: 3–14
No. of pupils: 180
Fees: Day £5,310–£8,004

Heath House Preparatory School
37 Wemyss Road, Blackheath, London SE3 0TG
Tel: 020 8297 1900
Head Teacher: Mrs Sophia Laslett CertEd PGDE
Age range: 3–11
No. of pupils: 115
Fees: Day £10,185–£13,785

Henriette Le Forestier Preparatory School
147 Central Hill, Upper Norwood, London SE19 1RS
Tel: +44 (0)20 8653 2169
Head Teacher: Mrs L Pollard
Age range: 2–11
Fees: Day £3,739–£9,003

Herne Hill School
The Old Vicarage, 127 Herne Hill, London SE24 9LY
Tel: 020 7274 6336
Headteacher: Mrs Ngaire Telford
Age range: 2–7
No. of pupils: 296
Fees: Day £5,550–£13,755

JAMES ALLEN'S GIRLS' SCHOOL
For further details see p. 134
144 East Dulwich Grove, Dulwich, London SE22 8TE
Tel: 020 8693 1181
Email: enquiries@jags.org.uk
Website: www.jags.org.uk
Head of School: Mrs Sally-Anne Huang MA, MSc
Age range: G4–18
No. of pupils: 1075

Kings Kids Christian School
New Testament Church of God, Bawtree Road, New Cross, London SE14 6ET
Tel: 020 8691 5813
Headteacher: Mrs M Okenwa
Age range: 5–11
No. of pupils: 36

London Christian School
40 Tabard Street, London SE1 4JU
Tel: 020 3130 6430
Headmistress: Miss Georgina Hale
Age range: 3–11
No. of pupils: 105
Fees: Day £7,725

Marathon Science School
1-9 Evelyn Street, Surrey Quays, London SE8 5RQ
Tel: +44 (0)20 7231 3232
Headteacher: Mr Uzeyir Onur
Age range: B11–16
No. of pupils: 67

Oakfield Preparatory School
125-128 Thurlow Park Road, West Dulwich, London SE21 8HP
Tel: 020 8670 4206
Age range: 2–11 years
No. of pupils: 420
Fees: Day £9,750

Octavia House School, Kennington
214b Kennington Road, London SE11 6AU
Tel: 020 3651 4396 (Option:3)
Executive Head: Mr James Waite

Octavia House School, Vauxhall
Vauxhall Primary School, Vauxhall Street, , London SE11 5LG
Tel: 02036 514396 (Option:1)
Executive Head: Mr James Waite
Age range: 5–14
No. of pupils: 65

Octavia House School, Walworth
Larcom House, Larcom Street, , London SE17 1RT
Tel: 02036 514396 (Option:2)
Executive Head: Mr James Waite

Riverston School
63-69 Eltham Road, Lee Green, London SE12 8UF
Tel: 020 8318 4327
Headmistress: Mrs S E Salathiel
Age range: 9 months–19 years
No. of pupils: 215

Rosemead Preparatory School, Dulwich
70 Thurlow Park Road, London SE21 8HZ
Tel: 020 8670 5865
Headmaster: Arthur Bray CertEd
Age range: 3–11
No. of pupils: 366
Fees: Day £10,272–£11,286

St Dunstan's College
Stanstead Road, London SE6 4TY
Tel: 020 8516 7200
Headmistress: Mrs J D Davies BSc
Age range: 3–18
No. of pupils: 870

St Olave's Preparatory School
106 Southwood Road, New Eltham, London SE9 3QS
Tel: 020 8294 8930
Headteacher: Miss Claire Holloway BEd, QTS
Age range: 3–11
No. of pupils: 220
Fees: Day £7,264–£11,610

Sydenham High School GDST
19 Westwood Hill, London SE26 6BL
Tel: 020 8557 7000
Headteacher: Kathryn Pullen MA
Age range: G4–18
No. of pupils: 630 VIth70
Fees: Day £11,466–£14,592

The Pointer School
19 Stratheden Road, Blackheath, London SE3 7TH
Tel: 020 8293 1331
Headmaster: Mr R J S Higgins MA, BEd, CertEd, FCollP
Age range: 3–11
No. of pupils: 370
Fees: Day £6,912–£13,782

The Villa Pre-Preparatory School & Nursery
54 Lyndhurst Grove, Peckham, London SE15 5AH
Tel: 020 7703 6216
Head Teacher: Emma Bryant
Age range: 2–7
No. of pupils: 210

South-West London

Abbey College – London
22 Grosvenor Gardens, Belgravia, London SW1W 0DH
Tel: 020 7824 7300
Principal: Mr Mark Love BEd
Age range: 14–19
No. of pupils: 150 VIth150
Fees: Day £5,950–£16,400 FB £30,200

Al-Muntada Islamic School
7 Bridges Place, Parsons Green, London SW6 4HW
Tel: 020 7471 8283
Headteacher: Salma Ullah
Age range: 4–11
No. of pupils: 165
Fees: Day £2,500

Al-Risalah Secondary School
145 Upper Tooting Road, London SW17 7TJ
Tel: 020 8767 6057
Headmaster: Nasir Qurashi
Age range: 3–16
No. of pupils: 250

Beechwood School
55 Leigham Court Road, Streatham, London SW16 2NJ
Tel: 020 8677 8778
Headmistress: Mrs M Marshall
Age range: 0–11
No. of pupils: 100
Fees: Day £6,726–£7,875

Bertrum House School
290 Balham High Road, London SW17 7AL
Tel: 020 8767 4051
Principal: Miss. Kirsty Pirrie
Age range: 2 –7
No. of pupils: 94
Fees: Day £1,630–£4,090

Broomwood Hall School
68-74 Nightingale Lane, London SW12 8NR
Tel: 020 8682 8830
Headmistress: Mrs Carole Jenkinson
Age range: B4–8 G4–13
No. of pupils: 670
Fees: Day £14,790–£18,165

CAMERON HOUSE
For further details see p. 122
4 The Vale, Chelsea, London SW3 6AH
Tel: 020 7352 4040
Email: izzy@cameronhouseschool.org
Website: www.cameronhouseschool.org
Acting Headmistress: Miss Mary-Anne Malloy BE (HDE)
Age range: 4–11
No. of pupils: 118
Fees: Day £17,925

Centre Academy London
92 St John's Hill, Battersea, London SW11 1SH
Tel: 020 7738 2344
Principal: Dr. Duncan Rollo BA, MA, PhD
Age range: 9–19
Fees: Day £27,600–£40,100

Chelsea Independent College
517-523 Fulham Road, London SW6 1HD
Tel: +44 (0) 20 7610 1114
Principal: Dr Martin Meenagh
Age range: 14–19
No. of pupils: 164

Collingham
23 Collingham Gardens, London SW5 0HL
Tel: 020 7244 7414
Principal: Mr G Hattee MA(Oxon), DipEd
Age range: 14–19
No. of pupils: VIth200
Fees: Day £4,140–£11,850

Dolphin School
106 Northcote Road, London SW11 6QW
Tel: 020 7924 3472
Principal: Mrs. N. Baldwin
Age range: 2½–11
No. of pupils: 317
Fees: Day £5,550–£12,375

Donhead
33 Edge Hill, London SW19 4NP
Tel: 020 8946 7000
Headmaster: Mr G C McGrath BA(Hons), PGCE, MBA(Ed)
Age range: B4–11
No. of pupils: 280
Fees: Day £7,800–£8,325

Eaton House Belgravia
3-5 Eaton Gate, London SW1W 9BA
Tel: 020 7730 9343
Head of School: Mrs Annabel Abbott
Age range: B4–8
Fees: Day £15,390

Eaton House The Manor Girls School
58 Clapham Common Northside, London SW4 9RU
Tel: 020 7924 6000
Head: Mrs Sarah Segrave
Age range: G4–11
Fees: Day £14,244

Eaton House The Manor Pre Prep School
58 Clapham Common Northside, London SW4 9RU
Tel: 020 7924 6000
Age range: B4–8
No. of pupils: 220
Fees: Day £14,244

Eaton House The Manor Prep School
58 Clapham Common Northside, London SW4 9RU
Tel: 020 7924 6000
Head: Mrs Sarah Segrave
Age range: B8–13
No. of pupils: 215
Fees: Day £18,090

Eaton House The Vale
2 Elvaston Place, London SW7 5QH
Tel: 020 7924 6000
Head: Mr Robin Greenwood
Age range: 3–11
Fees: Day £7,416–£14,670

Eaton Square School
79 Eccleston Square, London SW1V 1PP
Tel: 020 7931 9469
Headmaster: Mr Sebastian Hepher BEd(Hons)
Age range: 2 –13
No. of pupils: 529
Fees: Day £4,080–£19,785

Ecole Charles De Gaulle – Wix
Clapham Common North Side, London SW4 0AJ
Tel: +44 20 7738 0287
Headteacher: Mr Blanchard
Age range: 5–11
No. of pupils: 100

Ecole Marie D'Orliac
60 Clancarty Road, London SW6 3AA
Tel: +44 7736 020 58 63
Principal: Mr Olivier Rauch
Age range: 4–11
No. of pupils: 50

Emanuel School
Battersea Rise, London SW11 1HS
Tel: 020 8870 4171
Headmaster: Mr Mark Hanley-Browne
Age range: 10–18
No. of pupils: 890
Fees: Day £17,574

Eveline Day & Nursery Schools
14 Trinity Crescent, Upper Tooting, London SW17 7AE
Tel: 020 8672 4673
Headmistress: Ms Eveline Drut
Age range: 3 months–11 years
No. of pupils: 80
Fees: Day £11,059

Falkner House
19 Brechin Place, South Kensington, London SW7 4QB
Tel: 020 7373 4501
Headteacher: Mrs Anita Griggs BA(Hons), PGCE
Age range: B3–4 G3–11
Fees: Day £8,025–£16,050

Finton House School
171 Trinity Road, London SW17 7HL
Tel: 020 8682 0921
Head of School: Mr Ben Freeman
Age range: 4–11
No. of pupils: 321
Fees: Day £4,630–£4,850

FRANCIS HOLLAND SCHOOL, SLOANE SQUARE, SW1
For further details see p. 130
39 Graham Terrace, London SW1W 8JF
Tel: 020 7730 2971
Email: registrar@fhs-sw1.org.uk
Website: www.fhs-sw1.org.uk
Head: Mrs Lucy Elphinstone MA(Cantab)
Age range: G4–18
No. of pupils: 520 VIth70
Fees: Day £17,760–£20,085

Garden House School
Boys' School & Girls' School, Turk's Row, London SW3 4TW
Tel: 020 7730 1652
Boys Head: C Warland BA(Hons)
Age range: 3–11
No. of pupils: 449
Fees: Day £9,300–£15,885

Glendower School
86/87 Queen's Gate, London SW7 5JX
Tel: 020 7370 1927
Headmistress: Mrs Sarah Knollys BA, PGCE
Age range: G4–11+
No. of pupils: 206
Fees: Day £14,280

Hall School Wimbledon
Beavers Holt, Stroud Crescent, Putney Vale, London SW15 3EQ
Tel: 020 8788 2370
Headmaster: Timothy J Hobbs MA
Age range: 4–16
No. of pupils: 520
Fees: Day £9,999–£13,224

Hall School Wimbledon Senior School
17 The Downs, Wimbledon, London SW20 8HF
Tel: 020 8879 9200
Headmaster: Timothy J Hobbs MA
Age range: 11–16
No. of pupils: 520
Fees: Day £10,698–£14,151

Hill House International Junior School
17 Hans Place, Chelsea, London SW1X 0EP
Tel: 020 7584 1331
Principals: Richard, Janet, William & Edmund Townend
Age range: 4–13
No. of pupils: 870
Fees: Day £12,000–£16,000

Hornsby House School
Hearnville Road, Balham, London SW12 8RS
Tel: 020 8673 7573
Headmaster: Mr Edward Rees
Age range: 4–11
Fees: Day £12,375–£13,305

Hurlingham School
122 Putney Bridge Road, Putney, London SW15 2NQ
Tel: 020 8874 7186
Headteacher: Mr Jonathan Brough
Age range: 4–11
No. of pupils: 326
Fees: Day £15,540–£16,185

Ibstock Place School
Clarence Lane, London SW15 5PY
Tel: 020 8876 9991
Head: Mrs Anna Sylvester-Johnson BA(Hons), PGCE
Age range: 4–18
No. of pupils: 970
Fees: Day £4,995–£6,400
A £ 16

KENSINGTON PARK SCHOOL
For further details see p. 136
59 Queen's Gate, South Kensington, London SW7 5JP
Tel: +44 (0)20 7225 0577
Email: admissions@kps.co.uk
Website: www.kps.co.uk
Director of Education: Mr. Dick Jaine MA
Age range: 11–18
16 A

Kensington Prep School GDST
596 Fulham Road, London SW6 5PA
Tel: 0207 731 9300
Head: Mrs P Lynch MA (St Andrews) PGCE
Age range: G4–11
No. of pupils: 289
Fees: Day £11,103

King's College Junior School
Southside, Wimbledon Common, London SW19 4TT
Tel: 020 8255 5335
Headmaster: Dr. G A Silverlock
Age range: B7–13
No. of pupils: 460
£

King's College School
Southside, Wimbledon Common, London SW19 4TT
Tel: 020 8255 5300
Head Master: A D Halls MA
Age range: B11–18 G16–18
No. of pupils: 855 VIth396
Fees: Day £19,830
A £ IB 16

Knightsbridge School
67 Pont Street, Knightsbridge, London SW1X 0BD
Tel: 020 7590 9000
Head: Ms Shona Colaco MA, PGCE, MSB, CBiol
Age range: 3–13
No. of pupils: 400
Fees: Day £16,224–£17,265
£

L'Ecole de Battersea
Trott Street, Battersea, London SW11 3DS
Tel: 020 7371 8350
Principal: Mrs F Brisset
Age range: 3–11
No. of pupils: 260
Fees: Day £11,910–£12,060

L'Ecole des Petits
2 Hazlebury Road, Fulham, London SW6 2NB
Tel: 020 7371 8350
Principal: Mrs F Brisset
Age range: 3–6
No. of pupils: 132
Fees: Day £11,640–£11,940

Lion House School
The Old Methodist Hall, Gwendolen Avenue, London SW15 6EH
Tel: 020 8780 9446
Head: Miss H J Luard MontDip
Age range: 2–7
No. of pupils: 115

Lycée Français Charles de Gaulle
35 Cromwell Road, London SW7 2DG
Tel: 020 7584 6322
Head of School: Mr Olivier Rauch
Age range: 5–19
No. of pupils: 4000
A £ 16

Mander Portman Woodward – London
90-92 Queen's Gate, London SW7 5AB
Tel: 020 7835 1355
Principal: Mr John Southworth BSc MSc
Age range: 14–19
No. of pupils: 724
Fees: Day £8,651–£9,374
16 A £

More House School
22-24 Pont Street, Knightsbridge, London SW1X 0AA
Tel: 020 7235 2855
Headmistress: Mrs. Amanda Leach
Age range: G11–18
No. of pupils: 201
Fees: Day £17,850
A £ 16

NEWTON PREP
For further details see p. 138
149 Battersea Park Road, London SW8 4BX
Tel: 020 7720 4091
Email: admin@newtonprep.co.uk
Website: www.newtonprepschool.co.uk
Headmistress: Mrs Alison Fleming BA, MA Ed, PGCE
Age range: 3–13
No. of pupils: 647
Fees: Day £6,840–£18,930
£

Northcote Lodge School
26 Bolingbroke Grove, London SW11 6EL
Tel: 020 8682 8888
Headmaster: Mr Mark Smith
Age range: B8–13
No. of pupils: 244
Fees: Day £18,265

Oliver House Preparatory School
7 Nightingale Lane, London SW4 9AH
Tel: 020 8772 1911
Headteacher: Ms Maureen Fields
Age range: 2–13
No. of pupils: 144
Fees: Day £4,200–£9,300

Parkgate House School
80 Clapham Common North Side, London SW4 9SD
Tel: +44 (0)20 7350 2461
Principal: Miss Catherine Shanley
Age range: 2½–11 years
No. of pupils: 220
Fees: Day £5,550–£14,550

Parsons Green Prep School
1 Fulham Park Road, Fulham, London SW6 4LJ
Tel: 020 7371 9009
Headteacher: Ms. Helen Stavert
Age range: 4–11
No. of pupils: 200
Fees: Day £4,995–£5,395

PROSPECT HOUSE SCHOOL
For further details see p. 144
75 Putney Hill, London SW15 3NT
Tel: 020 8246 4897
Email: info@prospecths.org.uk
Website: www.prospecths.org.uk
Headmaster: Mr Michael Hodge BPED(Rhodes) QTS
Age range: 3–11
No. of pupils: 300
Fees: Day £8,520–£17,760
£

Putney High School GDST
35 Putney Hill, London SW15 6BH
Tel: 020 8788 4886
Headmistress: Mrs Suzie Longstaff BA, MA, PGCE
Age range: G4–18
No. of pupils: 976 VIth150
A £ 16

QUEEN'S GATE SCHOOL
For further details see p. 146
133 Queen's Gate, London SW7 5LE
Tel: 020 7589 3587
Email: registrar@queensgate.org.uk
Website: www.queensgate.org.uk
Principal: Mrs R M Kamaryc BA, MSc, PGCE
Age range: G4–18
No. of pupils: 533
A £ 16

Ravenstone Preparatory School
24 Elvaston Place, South Kensington, London SW7 5NL
Tel: 020 7225 3131
Age range: 2–11
No. of pupils: 110
Fees: Day £11,280–£16,875

Redcliffe School Trust Ltd
47 Redcliffe Gardens, Chelsea, London SW10 9JH
Tel: 020 7352 9247
Head: Mrs Susan Bourne BSc, PGCE
Age range: B3–8 G3–11
Fees: Day £14,610–£14,610
£

Sinclair House Preparatory School
59 Fulham High Street, Fulham, London SW6 3JJ
Tel: 0207 736 9182
Principal: Mrs Carlotta T M O'Sullivan
Age range: 2–13
No. of pupils: 120
Fees: Day £10,950

St Mary's Summerstown Montessori
46 Wimbledon Road, Tooting, London SW17 0UQ
Tel: 020 8947 7359
Head: Liz Maitland NNEB, RSH, MontDip
Age range: 18 months–5 years
No. of pupils: 30
Fees: Day £1,300

St Nicholas Preparatory School
23 Princes Gate, Kensington, London SW7 1PT
Tel: 020 7225 1277
Headmistress: Jill Walker
Age range: 3–11
No. of pupils: 280
Fees: Day £11,475–£13,110

St Paul's Juniors
St Paul's School, Lonsdale Road, London SW13 9JT
Tel: 020 8748 3461
Age range: B7–13
No. of pupils: 436
Fees: Day £18,771

St Paul's School
Lonsdale Road, Barnes, London SW13 9JT
Tel: 020 8748 9162
High Master: Prof Mark Bailey
Age range: B13–18
No. of pupils: 897
Fees: Day £19,674 FB £29,466
Ⓐ 16·

St Philip's School
6 Wetherby Place, London SW7 4NE
Tel: 020 7373 3944
Headmaster: H J Biggs-Davison MA(Cantab)
Age range: B7–13
No. of pupils: 110
Fees: Day £12,750

Streatham & Clapham High School GDST
42 Abbotswood Road, London SW16 1AW
Tel: 020 8677 8400
Headmaster: Dr Millan Sachania
Age range: B3–5 G3–18
No. of pupils: 603 VIth70
Fees: Day £5,886–£9,810
Ⓐ 16·

Sussex House School
68 Cadogan Square, Knightsbridge, London SW1X 0EA
Tel: 020 7584 1741
Headmaster: Mr N P Kaye MA(Cantab), ACP, FRSA
Age range: B8–13
No. of pupils: 182
Fees: Day £16,200

Swedish School
82 Lonsdale Road, London SW13 9JS
Tel: 020 8741 1751
Head of School: Ms. Annika Simonsson Bergqvist
Age range: 3–18
No. of pupils: 300 VIth145
Fees: Day £8,650–£9,200–£6,900
16·

Thames Christian College
Wye Street, Battersea, London SW11 2HB
Tel: 020 7228 3933
Executive Head: Stephen Holsgrove PhD
Age range: 11–16
No. of pupils: 120
Fees: Day £9,660

The Hampshire School, Chelsea
15 Manresa Road, Chelsea, London SW3 6NB
Tel: 020 7352 7077
Principal: Mr Donal Brennan
Age range: 3–13
No. of pupils: 300
Fees: Day £16,155–£17,100

The Harrodian School
Lonsdale Road, London SW13 9QN
Tel: 020 8748 6117
Headmaster: James R Hooke
Age range: 5–18
No. of pupils: 890 VIth95
Fees: Day £10,407–£15,219
Ⓐ 16·

The Laurels School
126 Atkins Road, Clapham, London SW12 0AN
Tel: 020 8674 7229
Headmistress: Linda Sanders BA Hons (Bristol), MA (Madrid)

The Merlin School
4 Carlton Drive, Putney Hill, London SW15 2BZ
Tel: 020 8788 2769
Principal: Mrs Kate Prest
Age range: 4–8
No. of pupils: 170

The Moat School
Bishops Avenue, Fulham, London SW6 6EG
Tel: 020 7610 9018
Head: Ms Clare King
Age range: 9–16
Fees: Day £28,800

The Montessori Pavilion – The Kindergarten School
Vine Road, Barnes, London SW13 0NE
Tel: 020 8878 9695
Age range: 3–8
No. of pupils: 50
Fees: Day £1,950–£3,600

The Norwegian School
28 Arterberry Road, Wimbledon, London SW20 8AH
Tel: 020 8947 6617
Head: Mr Geir Johansen
Age range: 3–16

The Roche School
11 Frogmore, London SW18 1HW
Tel: 020 8877 0823
Headmistress: Mrs V Adams BA(Hons), PGCE, MA
Age range: 2–11 years
No. of pupils: 239
Fees: Day £12,090–£13,050

The Rowans School
19 Drax Avenue, Wimbledon, London SW20 0EG
Tel: 020 8946 8220
Head Teacher: Mrs S Wingrove
Age range: 3–8
Fees: Day £5,460–£10,725

The Study Preparatory School
Wilberforce House, Camp Road, Wimbledon Common, London SW19 4UN
Tel: 020 8947 6969
Headmistress: Mrs Susan Pepper MA Oxon, PGCE
Age range: G4–11
No. of pupils: 315

The Waldorf School of South West London
PO Box 8541, London SW16 1ZB
Tel: 0208 772 3504
Age range: 3 –14
No. of pupils: 80
Fees: Day £4,515–£6,217

THE WHITE HOUSE PREPARATORY SCHOOL & WOODENTOPS KINDERGARTEN
For further details see p. 152
24 Thornton Road, London SW12 0LF
Tel: 020 8674 9514
Email: office@whitehouseschool.com
Website: www.whitehouseschool.com
Principal: Mrs. Mary McCahery
Age range: 2 –11
Fees: Day £4,436–£4,740

Thomas's Preparatory School – Battersea
28-40 Battersea High Street, London SW11 3JB
Tel: 020 7978 0900
Head: Ben V R Thomas MA
Age range: 4–13
No. of pupils: 547
Fees: Day £12,510–£18,330

Thomas's Preparatory School – Clapham
Broomwood Road, London SW11 6JZ
Tel: 020 7326 9300
Headmaster: Mr Philip Ward BEd(Hons)
Age range: 4–13
No. of pupils: 647
Fees: Day £15,846–£17,916

Thomas's Preparatory School – Fulham
Hugon Road, London SW6 3ES
Tel: 020 7751 8200
Head: Miss Annette Dobson BEd(Hons), PGCertDys
Age range: 4–11

Tower House School
188 Sheen Lane, London SW14 8LF
Tel: 020 8876 3323
Head: Mr Gregory Evans
Age range: B4–13
No. of pupils: 180
Fees: Day £11,073–£12,558

Ursuline Preparatory School
18 The Downs, London SW20 8HR
Tel: 020 8947 0859
Headmistress: Mrs Anne Farnish BA (Hons) MA, NPQH, PGCE
Age range: B3–4 G3–11
Fees: Day £5,886–£9,600

Wandsworth Preparatory School
The Old Library, 2 Allfarthing Lane, London SW18 2PQ
Tel: 0208 870 4133
Fees: Day £4,328

Westminster Abbey Choir School
Dean's Yard, London SW1P 3NY
Tel: 0207 654 4918
Headmaster: Jonathan Milton BEd
Age range: B8–13
No. of pupils: 35
Fees: FB £8,240

Westminster Cathedral Choir School
Ambrosden Avenue, London SW1P 1QH
Tel: 020 7798 9081
Headmaster: Mr Neil McLaughlan
Age range: B8–13
No. of pupils: 150
Fees: Day £13,656 FB £6,945

WESTMINSTER SCHOOL
For further details see p. 154
Little Dean's Yard, Westminster, London SW1P 3PF
Tel: 020 7963 1003
Email: registrar@westminster.org.uk
Website: www.westminster.org.uk
Headmaster: Mr Patrick Derham
Age range: B13–18 G16–18
No. of pupils: 744
Fees: Day £26,130–£28,566 FB £37,740

Westminster Tutors
86 Old Brompton Road, South Kensington, London SW7 3LQ
Tel: 020 7584 1288
Principal: Virginia Maguire BA, MA, MLitt
Age range: 14–mature
No. of pupils: VIth40
Fees: Day £7,700–£23,500

Westminster Under School
Adrian House, 27 Vincent Square, London SW1P 2NN
Tel: 020 7821 5788
Headteacher: Mrs E A Hill MA
Age range: B7–13
No. of pupils: 265
Fees: Day £14,676

Willington School
Worcester Road, Wimbledon, London SW19 7QQ
Tel: 020 8944 7020
Head: Mr Michael Chanter
Age range: B4–13
No. of pupils: 250
Fees: Day £9,345–£11,385

Wimbledon Common Preparatory
113 Ridgway, Wimbledon, London SW19 4TA
Tel: 020 8946 1001
Head Teacher: Mrs Tracey Buck
Age range: B4–8
No. of pupils: 160
Fees: Day £10,725

Wimbledon High School GDST
Mansel Road, Wimbledon, London SW19 4AB
Tel: 020 8971 0900
Headmistress: Mrs H Hanbury
Age range: G4–18
No. of pupils: 900 VIth155
Fees: Day £11,445–£15,024

West London

Albemarle Independent College
18 Dunraven Street, London W1K 7FE
Tel: 020 7409 7273
Co-Principals: Beverley Mellon & James Eytle
Age range: 16–19
No. of pupils: 160
Fees: Day £15,000–£18,000

Arts Educational Schools London Sixth Form
Cone Ripman House, 14 Bath Road, Chiswick, London W4 1LY
Tel: 020 8987 6666
Head Teacher: Mr Adrian Blake
Age range: 16–18
No. of pupils: 85
Fees: Day £14,190

Arts Educational Schools London Years 7-11
Cone Ripman House, 14 Bath Road, Chiswick, , London W4 1LY
Tel: 020 8987 6666
Head Teacher: Mr Adrian Blake
Age range: 11–16
No. of pupils: 141
Fees: Day £13,350

Ashbourne Independent Sixth Form College
17 Old Court Place, Kensington, London W8 4PL
Tel: 020 7937 3858
Principal: M J Kirby MSc, BApSc
Age range: 16–19
No. of pupils: 170
Fees: Day £19,725 FB £21,500

Ashbourne Middle School
17 Old Court Place, Kensington, London W8 4PL
Tel: 020 7937 3858
Principal: M J Kirby MSc, BApSc
Age range: 13–16
No. of pupils: VIth150
Fees: Day £14,725 FB £21,500

Avenue House School
70 The Avenue, Ealing, London W13 8LS
Tel: 020 8998 9981
Headteacher: Mr Sheppard
Age range: 3–11
No. of pupils: 135
Fees: Day £5,070–£8,670

Bales College
742 Harrow Road, Kensal Town, London W10 4AA
Tel: 020 8960 5899
Principal: William Moore
Age range: 11–19
No. of pupils: 90
Fees: Day £7,950–£8,550 FB £16,050

Barbara Speake Stage School
East Acton Lane, East Acton, London W3 7EG
Tel: 020 8743 1306
Headteacher: Mr David Speake BA (Hons)
Age range: 3–16
Fees: Day £8,700–£9,000

BASSETT HOUSE SCHOOL
For further details see p. 120
60 Bassett Road, London W10 6JP
Tel: 020 8969 0313
Email: info@bassetths.org.uk
Website: www.bassetths.org.uk
Headmistress: Mrs Philippa Cawthorne MA (Soton) PGCE Mont Cert
Age range: 3–11
No. of pupils: 190
Fees: Day £8,520–£17,760

Bute House Preparatory School for Girls
Bute House, Luxemburg Gardens, London W6 7EA
Tel: 020 7603 7381
Head: Mrs Helen Lowe
Age range: G4–11
No. of pupils: 306
Fees: Day £13,317

Chepstow House School
19 Pembridge Villas, London W11 3EP
Tel: 0207 243 0243
Headteacher: Angela Barr
Age range: 4–7

Chiswick & Bedford Park Prep School
Priory House, Priory Avenue, London W4 1TX
Tel: 020 8994 1804
Headmistress: Mrs C A Sunderland
Age range: B4–7+ G4–11
No. of pupils: 180
Fees: Day £8,850

Clifton Lodge
8 Mattock Lane, Ealing, London W5 5BG
Tel: 020 8579 3662
Head: Mr. Floyd Steadman
Age range: 3–13
No. of pupils: 146
Fees: Day £11,340–£12,405

Connaught House School
47 Connaught Square, London W2 2HL
Tel: 020 7262 8830
Principals: Mrs J A Hampton & Mr F Hampton MA, RCA
Age range: B4–8 G4–11
No. of pupils: 75
Fees: Day £13,200–£14,700

David Game College
31 Jewry Street, London EC3N 2ET
Tel: 020 7221 6665
Principal: D T P Game MA, MPhil
Age range: 14–19
No. of pupils: 200 VIth150
Fees: Day £12,000–£13,000

DLD College London
199 Westminster Bridge Road, London SE1 7FX
Tel: +44 (0)20 7935 8411
Principal: Ms. Rachel Borland MA
No. of pupils: 516
Fees: Day £18,000–£22,000 FB £15,000–£25,000

Durston House
12-14 Castlebar Road,
Ealing, London W5 2DR
Tel: 020 8991 6530
Headmaster: Mr Ian Kendrick MA, BEd(Hons)
Age range: B4–13
No. of pupils: 415
Fees: Day £9,810–£12,570

Ealing Independent College
83 New Broadway, Ealing,
London W5 5AL
Tel: 020 8579 6668
Principal: Dr Ian Moores
Age range: 13–22
No. of pupils: 100 VIth70
Fees: Day £3,865–£12,600

Ecole Francaise Jacques Prevert
59 Brook Green, London W6 7BE
Tel: 020 7602 6871
Principal: P Possenti
Age range: 4–11

Fulham Prep School
200 Greyhound Road, London W14 9SD
Tel: 020 7386 2444
Age range: 4–18
No. of pupils: 647
Fees: Day £16,335–£19,200

Great Beginnings Montessori School
The Welsh Church Hall, 82a Chiltern Street, Marylebone, London W1H 5JE
Tel: 020 7486 2276
Age range: 2–6
Fees: Day £1,095–£1,650

Greek Primary School of London
3 Pierrepoint Road, Acton,
London W3 9JR
Tel: 020 8992 6156
Age range: 1–11

Halcyon London International School
33 Seymour Place, , London W1H 5AU
Tel: +44 (0)20 7258 1169
Director: Mr Barry Mansfield
Age range: 11–18
No. of pupils: 130

Harvington School
20 Castlebar Road, Ealing,
London W5 2DS
Tel: 020 8997 1583
Headmistress: Mrs Anna Evans
Age range: B3–4 G3–11
No. of pupils: 140
Fees: Day £9,300–£12,120

Hawkesdown House School Kensington
27 Edge Street, Kensington,
London W8 7PN
Tel: 020 7727 9090
Headmistress: Mrs J A Mackay B.Ed
Age range: B3–8
No. of pupils: 141
Fees: Day £15,270–£17,565

Heathfield House School
Turnham Green Church Hall, Heathfield Gardens, Chiswick, London, London W4 4JU
Tel: 020 8994 3385
Headteacher: Mrs Goodsman
Age range: 4–11
Fees: Day £6,300–£6,900

Holland Park Pre Prep School and Day Nursery
5 & 9 Holland Road, Kensington,
London W14 8HJ
Tel: 020 7602 9066/020 7602 9266
Principal: Mrs Kitty Mason
Age range: 3 months–8 years
No. of pupils: 128
Fees: Day £4,650–£10,935

House Schools Group
42 Hartington Road, London W4 3TX
Tel: 020 8580 9626

Instituto Español Vicente Cañada Blanch
317 Portobello Road, London W10 5SZ
Tel: +44 (0) 20 8969 2664
Principal: Mr A Vitria
Age range: 4–19
No. of pupils: 405

International School of London (ISL) London
139 Gunnersbury Avenue,
Ealing, London W3 8LG
Tel: +44 (0)20 8992 5823
Middle & Lower School
Principal: Andrew Mitchell
Age range: 3–18 years
No. of pupils: 480
Fees: Day £18,000–£24,600

King Fahad Academy
Bromyard Avenue, Acton,
London W3 7HD
Tel: 020 8743 0131
Director: Dr Othman Alzamil
Age range: 3–19
No. of pupils: 510
Fees: Day £2,500–£4,500

La Petite Ecole Francais
73 Saint Charles Square,
London W10 6EJ
Tel: +44 208 960 1278
Principal: Ms A Stones
Age range: 2–6

Latymer Prep School
36 Upper Mall, Hammersmith,
London W6 9TA
Tel: 020 7993 0061
Principal: Ms Andrea Rutterford B.Ed (Hons)
Age range: 7–11
No. of pupils: 165
Fees: Day £16,860

Latymer Upper School
King Street, Hammersmith,
London W6 9LR
Tel: 020862 92024
Head: Mr D Goodhew MA(Oxon)
Age range: 11–18
No. of pupils: 1200
Fees: Day £18,510

Le Herisson
River Court Methodist Church, Rover Court Road, Hammersmith, London W6 9JT
Tel: 020 8563 7664
Head Teacher: C Behroozi
Age range: 2–6
Fees: Day £8,730–£8,970

L'Ecole Bilingue
St David's Welsh Church, St Mary's Terrace, London W2 1SJ
Tel: 020 7224 8427
Headteacher: Ms Veronique Ferreira
Age range: 3–11
No. of pupils: 68
Fees: Day £6,000–£6,600

Leiths School of Food & Wine
16-20 Wendell Road, Shepherd's Bush, London W12 9RT
Tel: 020 8749 6400
Managing Director: Camilla Schneideman
Age range: 17–99
No. of pupils: 96

Norland Place School
162-166 Holland Park Avenue,
London W11 4UH
Tel: 020 7603 9103
Headmaster: Mr Patrick Mattar MA
Age range: B4–8 years G4–11 years
Fees: Day £13,590–£16,389

Notting Hill & Ealing High School GDST
2 Cleveland Road, West Ealing, London W13 8AX
Tel: 020 8991 2165
Headmistress: Ms Lucinda Hunt
Age range: G4–18
No. of pupils: 903 VIth150
Fees: Day £12,849–£16,521

Notting Hill Preparatory School
95 Lancaster Road, London W11 1QQ
Tel: 020 7221 0727
Headmistress: Mrs Jane Cameron
Age range: 4–13
No. of pupils: 325
Fees: Day £6,100

One World Montessori Nursery & Pre-Prep
69-71 Brock Green, Hammersmith,
London W6 7BE
Tel: 020 7603 6065
Headteacher: Ms N Greer
Age range: 2–8
No. of pupils: 21

One World Preparatory School
10 Stanley Gardens, Acton,
London W3 7SZ
Tel: 020 87433300
Head: Ms Lisa Manser
Age range: 3–11
No. of pupils: 52
Fees: Day £3,000

ORCHARD HOUSE SCHOOL
For further details see p. 142
16 Newton Grove, Bedford Park, London W4 1LB
Tel: 020 8742 8544
Email: info@orchardhs.org.uk
Website: www.orchardhs.org.uk
Headmistress: Mrs Maria Edwards BEd(Beds) PGCE(Man) Mont Cert
Age range: 3–11
No. of pupils: 290
Fees: Day £8,520–£17,760

Pembridge Hall
18 Pembridge Square, London W2 4EH
Tel: 020 7229 0121
Headteacher: Mr Henry Keighley-Elstub
Age range: G4–11
No. of pupils: 413

Portland Place School
56-58 Portland Place, London W1B 1NJ
Tel: 0207 307 8700
Head: Mr Tim Cook
Age range: 11–18
No. of pupils: 300 VIth50
Fees: Day £12,522–£16,425

Queen's College
43-49 Harley Street, London W1G 8BT
Tel: 020 7291 7000
Head: Dr F M R Ramsey MA, DPhil(Oxon)
Age range: G11–18
No. of pupils: 360 VIth90

Ravenscourt Park Preparatory School
16 Ravenscourt Avenue, London W6 0SL
Tel: 020 8846 9153
Headmaster: Mr Carl Howes MA (Cantab), PGCE (Exeter)
Age range: 4–11
No. of pupils: 414
Fees: Day £16,215

Ravenstone Pre-Preparatory School
The Long Garden, St George's Fields, Albion Street, London W2 2AX
Tel: 020 7262 1190
Age range: 2–7
No. of pupils: 74
Fees: Day £11,280–£16,875

Ray Cochrane Beauty School
118 Baker Street, London W1U 6TT
Tel: 02033224738
Age range: 16–50
No. of pupils: 30
Fees: Day £2,195–£8,995

Southbank International School – Fitzrovia
17 Conway Street, London W1T 6BN
Tel: +44 2076 312600

Southbank International School – Kensington
36-38 Kensington Park Road, London W11 3BU
Tel: +44 (0)20 7243 3803
Interim Principal: Jonathan Coward
Age range: 3–18

Southbank International School – Westminster
63-65 Portland Place, London W1B 1QR
Tel: 020 7243 3803
Interim Principal: Siobhan McGrath
Age range: 11–18/19

St Augustine's Priory
Hillcrest Road, Ealing, London W5 2JL
Tel: 020 8997 2022
Headteacher: Mrs Sarah Raffray MA
Age range: B3–4 G3–18
No. of pupils: 460
Fees: Day £10,656–£15,162

St Benedict's School
54 Eaton Rise, Ealing, London W5 2ES
Tel: 020 8862 2000
Headmaster: Mr A Johnson BA
Age range: 3–18
No. of pupils: 1079 VIth210
Fees: Day £12,120–£15,300

St James Junior School
Earsby Street, London W14 8SH
Tel: 020 7348 1777
Headmistress: Mrs Catherine Thomlinson BA(Hons)
Age range: B4–11 G4–10
Fees: Day £10,650

St James Senior Girls' School
Earsby Street, London W14 8SH
Tel: 020 7348 1777
Headmistress: Mrs Sarah Labram BA
Age range: G11–18
No. of pupils: 295 VIth67
Fees: Day £18,330

St Paul's Girls' School
Brook Green, London W6 7BS
Tel: 020 7603 2288
High Mistress: Ms Clarissa Farr MA, PGCE
Age range: G11–18 years
No. of pupils: 740 VIth200
Fees: Day £21,918–£23,562

Sylvia Young Theatre School
1 Nutford Place, London W1M 5YZ
Tel: 020 7258 2330
Headteacher: Ms Frances Chave BSc, PGCE, NPQH
Age range: 10–16
Fees: Day £13,500–£13,800 WB £18,060–£18,360 FB £21,060–£21,360

Tabernacle School
32 St Anns Villas, Holland Park, London W11 4RS
Tel: 020 7602 6232
Headteacher: Mrs P Wilson
Age range: 3–16
Fees: Day £4,500

The Falcons School for Boys
2 Burnaby Gardens, Chiswick, London W4 3DT
Tel: 020 8747 8393
Headmaster: Mr Gordon Milne
Age range: B3–7
No. of pupils: 225
Fees: Day £3,875–£11,625

The Falcons School for Girls
15 Gunnersbury Avenue, Ealing, London W5 3XD
Tel: 020 8992 5189
Headteacher: Miss Joan McGillewie
Age range: G4–11
No. of pupils: 102
Fees: Day £3,625

The Godolphin and Latymer School
Iffley Road, Hammersmith, London W6 0PG
Tel: +44 (0)20 8741 1936
Head Mistress: Dr FMR Ramsey MA, DPhil (Oxon)
Age range: G11–18
No. of pupils: 824
Fees: Day £20,148

The Japanese School
87 Creffield Road, Acton, London W3 9PU
Tel: 020 8993 7145
Headteacher: Mrs Kiyoe Tsuruoka
Age range: 6–16
No. of pupils: 500

THE LLOYD WILLIAMSON SCHOOL
For further details see p. 150
12 Telford Road, London W10 5SH
Tel: 020 8962 0345
Email: admin@lws.org.uk
Website: www.lloydwilliamson.co.uk
Co-Principals: Ms Lucy Meyer & Mr Aaron Williams
Age range: 4 months–14 years (18 in 2019)
Fees: Day £13,560

Thomas's Preparatory School – Kensington
17-19 Cottesmore Gardens, London W8 5PR
Tel: 020 7361 6500
Headmistress: Miss Joanna Ebner MA, BEd(Hons)(Cantab), NPQH
Age range: 4–11
Fees: Day £14,505–£15,795

Wetherby Preparatory School
48 Bryanston Square, London W1H 2EA
Tel: 020 7535 3520
Headteacher: Mr Nick Baker
Age range: B8–13
No. of pupils: 192
Fees: Day £4,665

Wetherby Pre-Preparatory School
11 Pembridge Square, London W2 4ED
Tel: 020 7727 9581
Headmaster: Mr Mark Snell
Age range: B2½–8
No. of pupils: 340
Fees: Day £19,620

Young Dancers Academy
25 Bulwer Street, London W12 8AR
Tel: 020 8743 3856
Head: Mrs K Williams
Age range: 11–16
Fees: Day £10,500–£11,100

Ysgol Gymraeg Llundain London Welsh School
Hanwell Community Centre, Westcott Crescent, London W7 1PD
Tel: 020 8575 0237
Leadteacher: Miss Rachel Rawlins
Age range: 3–11
No. of pupils: 30
Fees: Day £1,950

North-East

KEY TO SYMBOLS

- *Boys' school*
- *Girls' school*
- *International school*
- *Tutorial or sixth form college*
- *A levels*
- *Boarding accommodation*
- *Bursaries*
- *International Baccalaureate*
- *Learning support*
- *Entrance at 16+*
- *Vocational qualifications*
- *Independent Association of Preparatory Schools*
- *The Headmasters' & Headmistresses' Conference*
- *Independent Schools Association*
- *Girls' School Association*
- *Boarding Schools' Association*
- *Society of Heads*

Unless otherwise indicated, all schools are coeducational day schools. Single-sex and boarding schools will be indicated by the relevant icon.

Durham

Barnard Castle Preparatory School
Westwick Road, Barnard Castle, Durham DL12 8UW
Tel: 01833 696032
Headmaster: C F Rycroft
Age range: 4–11
No. of pupils: 180
Fees: Day £7,671 FB £14,832

Barnard Castle Senior School
Barnard Castle, Durham DL12 8UN
Tel: 01833 690222
Headmaster: Alan D Stevens BA, MA
Age range: 11–18
No. of pupils: 570 VIth160
Fees: Day £10,980 FB £19,716

Bow, Durham School
South Road, Durham DH1 3LS
Tel: 0191 384 8233
Head of School: Mrs Sally Harrod BA, QTS
Age range: 3–11
No. of pupils: 155
Fees: Day £5,250–£10,821

Durham High School for Girls
Farewell Hall, Durham DH1 3TB
Tel: 0191 384 3226
Headmistress: Mrs Lynne Renwick
Age range: G3–18
No. of pupils: 421

DURHAM SCHOOL
For further details see p. 158
Durham City, Durham DH1 4SZ
Tel: +44 (0)191 386 4783
Email: admissions@durhamschool.co.uk
Website: www.durhamschool.co.uk
Headmaster: Mr K McLaughlin
Age range: 3–18
No. of pupils: 560 VIth156
Fees: Day £2,756–£5,331 WB £7,347–£8,786 FB £8,460–£9,846

Polam Hall School
Grange Road, Darlington, Durham DL1 5PA
Tel: 01325 463383
Headmaster: Mr J R Moreland MA (Oxon), PGCE (Oxford), NPQH
Age range: 4–19
No. of pupils: 182
Fees: Day £6,150–£8,550 WB £16,755–£16,755 FB £17,355–£17,355

The Chorister School
The College, Durham DH1 3EL
Tel: 0191 384 2935
Headmistress: Mrs Y F S Day
Age range: 3–13 years
No. of pupils: 214
Fees: Day £8,340–£11,235 WB £17,460 FB £10,170–£19,440

Northumberland

Longridge Towers School
Longridge Towers, Berwick-upon-Tweed, Northumberland TD15 2XH
Tel: 01289 307584
Headmaster: Mr T M Manning BSc
Age range: 3–18
No. of pupils: VIth46
Fees: Day £7,896–£12,336 WB £18,153–£19,506 FB £23,811–£25,128

Mowden Hall School
Newton, Stocksfield, Northumberland NE43 7TP
Tel: 01661 842147
Headmaster: Mr Ben Beardmore-Gray
Age range: 3–13
Fees: Day £7,920–£13,770 FB £17,790

Stockton-on-Tees

Red House School
36 The Green, Norton, Stockton-on-Tees TS20 1DX
Tel: 01642 553370
Headmaster: Mr Ken James LLB
Age range: 3–16
No. of pupils: 363
Fees: Day £6,810–£10,320

Teesside High School
The Avenue, Eaglescliffe, Stockton-on-Tees TS16 9AT
Tel: 01642 782095
Headmaster: Mr Thomas Packer BSc, MSc, FInstP
Age range: G3–18
No. of pupils: 390 VIth70

Yarm Preparatory School
Grammar School Lane, Yarm, Stockton-on-Tees TS15 9ES
Tel: 01642 781447
Headteacher: Mr Bill Sawyer
Age range: 3–11
No. of pupils: 360
Fees: Day £4,308–£8,859

Yarm School
The Friarage, Yarm, Stockton-on-Tees TS15 9EJ
Tel: 01642 786023
Headmaster: Mr D M Dunn BA
Age range: 3–18
No. of pupils: VIth200
Fees: Day £4,839–£11,940

Tyne & Wear

Argyle House School
19/20 Thornhill Park, Tunstall Road, Sunderland, Tyne & Wear SR2 7LA
Tel: 0191 510 0726
Headmaster: Mr C Johnson
Age range: 3–16
Fees: Day £6,645–£7,815

Dame Allan Junior School
Hunters Road, Spital Tongues, Newcastle upon Tyne, Tyne & Wear NE2 4NG
Tel: 0191 275 0608
Head: Mr A J Edge
Age range: 3–11
No. of pupils: 140
Fees: Day £6,345–£8,310

Dame Allan's Boys' School
Fowberry Crescent, Fenham, Newcastle upon Tyne, Tyne & Wear NE4 9YJ
Tel: 0191 275 0608
Principal: Dr John R Hind
Age range: B11–16
No. of pupils: 304
Fees: Day £10,317

Dame Allan's Girls' School
Fowberry Crescent, Fenham, Newcastle upon Tyne, Tyne & Wear NE4 9YJ
Tel: 0191 275 0708
Principal: Dr John R Hind
Age range: G11–16
No. of pupils: 225
Fees: Day £10,317

Dame Allan's Sixth Form
Fowberry Crescent, Fenham, Newcastle upon Tyne, Tyne & Wear NE4 9YJ
Tel: 0191 275 0608
Principal: J R Hind MA, MEd, PhD
Age range: 16–18
No. of pupils: 200
Fees: Day £10,317

Gateshead Jewish Boarding School
10 Rydal Street, Gateshead, Tyne & Wear NE8 1HG
Tel: 0191 477 1431
Principal: Rabbi M Kupetz
Age range: B10–16
No. of pupils: 105

Gateshead Jewish High School for Girls
6 Gladstone Terrace, Gateshead, Tyne & Wear NE8 4DY
Tel: 0191 4773471
Headteacher: Rabbi D Bowden
Age range: G11–16
No. of pupils: 132

Gateshead Jewish Primary School
18-20 Gladstone Terrace, Gateshead, Tyne & Wear NE8 4EA
Tel: 0191 477 2154 / 0191 478 5841
Headmasters: A Hammond & Y Spitzer
Age range: 5–11
No. of pupils: 446
Fees: Day £2,392–£3,016

Newcastle High School for Girls GDST
Tankerville Terrace, Jesmond, Newcastle upon Tyne, Tyne & Wear NE2 3BA
Tel: 0191 281 1768
Head: Mrs H J French MA, MEd, NPQH
Age range: G3–18
No. of pupils: G850 VIth200
Fees: Day £7,695–£12,036

Newcastle Preparatory School
6 Eslington Road, Jesmond, Newcastle upon Tyne, Tyne & Wear NE2 4RH
Tel: 0191 281 1769
Head Teacher: Mrs Margaret Coates
Age range: 3–11
No. of pupils: 273
Fees: Day £7,779–£8,742

Newcastle School for Boys
30 West Avenue, Gosforth, Newcastle upon Tyne, Tyne & Wear NE3 4ES
Tel: 0191 255 9300
Headmaster: Mr D J Tickner
Age range: B3–18
No. of pupils: 400
Fees: Day £6,900–£9,270

ROYAL GRAMMAR SCHOOL
For further details see p. 160
Eskdale Terrace, Newcastle upon Tyne, Tyne & Wear NE2 4DX
Tel: 0191 281 5711
Email: hm@rgs.newcastle.sch.uk
Website: www.rgs.newcastle.sch.uk
Headmaster: Mr John Fern
Age range: 7–18
No. of pupils: 1325 VIth341
Fees: Day £10,662–£12,657

Westfield School
Oakfield Road, Gosforth, Newcastle upon Tyne, Tyne & Wear NE3 4HS
Tel: 0191 255 3980
Headmistress: Mrs M Farndale BA(Hons)(Lon), PGCE(Oxon), FRSA
Age range: G3–18
No. of pupils: 315 VIth50
Fees: Day £1,372–£3,688

North-West

KEY TO SYMBOLS

- *Boys' school*
- *Girls' school*
- *International school*
- *Tutorial or sixth form college*
- *A levels*
- *Boarding accommodation*
- *Bursaries*
- *International Baccalaureate*
- *Learning support*
- *Entrance at 16+*
- *Vocational qualifications*
- *Independent Association of Preparatory Schools*
- *The Headmasters' & Headmistresses' Conference*
- *Independent Schools Association*
- *Girls' School Association*
- *Boarding Schools' Association*
- *Society of Heads*

Unless otherwise indicated, all schools are coeducational day schools. Single-sex and boarding schools will be indicated by the relevant icon.

Cheshire

Abbey Gate College
Saighton Grange, Saighton, Chester, Cheshire CH3 6EN
Tel: 01244 332077
Head: Mrs Tracy Pollard
Age range: 4–18
No. of pupils: 514 VIth92
Fees: Day £7,440–£10,875
A £ 16·

Abbey Gate Prep School
Clare Avenue, Hoole, Chester, Cheshire CH2 3HR
Tel: 01244 319649
Headteacher: Mrs Sally Ann Rhodes-Leader
Age range: 3–11
No. of pupils: 50
£

Alderley Edge School for Girls
Wilmslow Road, Alderley Edge, Cheshire SK9 7QE
Tel: 01625 583028
Headmistress: Mrs Susan Goff
Age range: G2–18
No. of pupils: 500 VIth60
Fees: Day £5,070–£9,201
A £ IB 16·

Beech Hall School
Beech Hall Drive, Tytherington, Macclesfield, Cheshire SK10 2EG
Tel: 01625 422192
Headmistress: Mrs G Yandell BA
Age range: 6 months–16 years
No. of pupils: 230
Fees: Day £6,285–£8,940
£

Bowdon Preparatory School for Girls
Ashley Road, Altrincham, Cheshire WA14 2LT
Tel: 0161 928 0678
Headmistress: Mrs J H Tan BA, DipEd
Age range: G3–11
No. of pupils: 200
Fees: Day £4,986

Brabyns Preparatory School
34-36 Arkwright Road, Marple, Stockport, Cheshire SK6 7DB
Tel: 0161 427 2395
Headteacher: Mr Lee Sanders
Age range: 2 –11
No. of pupils: 134
Fees: Day £1,313–£1,779
£

Cransley School
Belmont Hall, Great Budworth, Northwich, Cheshire CW9 6HN
Tel: 01606 891747
Head of School: Richard Pollock
Age range: 4–16
No. of pupils: 150
Fees: Day £2,440–£3,440
£

Greater Grace School of Christian Education
Church Lane, Backford, Chester, Cheshire CH2 4BE
Tel: 01244 851 797
Head Teacher: Mrs A Mulligan
Age range: 5–18
Fees: Day £1,900

GREEN MEADOW INDEPENDENT PRIMARY SCHOOL
For further details see p. 166
Robson Way, Lowton, Warrington, Cheshire WA3 2RD
Tel: 01942 671138
Email: greenmeadowteachers@gmail.com
Website: www.greenmeadowindependentprimaryschool.co.uk
Head: Mrs S Green
Age range: 4–11

Hale Preparatory School
Broomfield Lane, Hale, Cheshire WA15 9AS
Tel: 0161 928 2386
Headmaster: Mr J F Connor
Age range: 4–11
No. of pupils: 202
Fees: Day £7,110

Lady Barn House School
Schools Hill, Cheadle, Cheshire SK7 1JE
Tel: 0161 428 2912
Age range: 3–11
No. of pupils: 483
Fees: Day £7,782
£

Pownall Hall School
Carrwood Road, Pownall Park, Wilmslow, Cheshire SK9 5DW
Tel: 01625 523141
Headmaster: Mr David Goulbourn
Age range: 2–11
Fees: Day £2,475–£5,385

Terra Nova School
Jodrell Bank, Holmes Chapel, Crewe, Cheshire CW4 8BT
Tel: 01477 571251
Headmaster: Mr M Mitchell
Age range: 3–13
No. of pupils: 295
Fees: Day £4,050–£12,990
£

The Firs School
Newton Lane, Upton, Chester, Cheshire CH2 2HJ
Tel: 01244 322443
Head Teacher: Mrs L Davies
Age range: 3–11
No. of pupils: 172
Fees: Day £8,160
£

The Grange School
Bradburns Lane, Hartford, Northwich, Cheshire CW8 1LU
Tel: 01606 74007 or 77447
Headmaster: Mrs Deborah Leonard
Age range: 4–18
No. of pupils: 1185 VIth193
Fees: Day £7,080–£9,480
A £ 16·

The Hammond School
Mannings Lane, Chester, Cheshire CH2 4ES
Tel: 01244 305350
Principal: Ms Maggie Evans BA (Hons) MA, PGCE, NPQH, FRSA
Age range: 6–19
No. of pupils: 280
Fees: Day £8,055–£17,985 FB £21,240–£26,130
A £ 16·

The King's School
Wrexham Road, Chester, Cheshire CH4 7QL
Tel: 01244 689500
Headmaster: G J Hartley MA, MSc
Age range: 4–18
No. of pupils: 1080 VIth218
Fees: Day £8,988–£13,275
A £ 16·

The King's School
Cumberland Street, Macclesfield, Cheshire SK10 1DA
Tel: 01625 260000
Headmaster: Dr Simon Hyde
Age range: 3–18
No. of pupils: 1200 VIth250
Fees: Day £7,740–£10,770
A £ 16·

The Queen's School
City Walls Road, Chester, Cheshire CH1 2NN
Tel: 01244 312078
Headmistress: Mrs E S Clark
Age range: G4–18
No. of pupils: 610 VIth100
Fees: Day £7,455–£10,650
A £ 16·

The Ryleys School
Ryleys Lane, Alderley Edge, Cheshire SK9 7UY
Tel: 01625 583241
Headteacher: Claire Hamilton BSc(Hons), PGCE
Age range: 3–13
No. of pupils: 251
Fees: Day £9,261–£10,752
£

Wilmslow Preparatory School
Grove Avenue, Wilmslow, Cheshire SK9 5EG
Tel: 01625 524246
Headteacher: Mrs Helen Rigby
Age range: 3–11
No. of pupils: 117
Fees: Day £4,635–£10,365
£

Yorston Lodge School
18 St John's Road, Knutsford, Cheshire WA16 0DP
Tel: 01565 633177
Headmistress: Mrs J Dallimore BEd(Hons)
Age range: 3–11
Fees: Day £5,160

Cumbria

Austin Friars School
Etterby Scaur, Carlisle, Cumbria CA3 9PB
Tel: 01228 528042
Headmaster: Mr Christopher Lumb BSc, MEd
Age range: 3–18
No. of pupils: 507 VIth70
Fees: Day £4,470–£9,210
(A) (£) (16·)

Casterton, Sedbergh Preparatory School
Casterton, Carnforth, Cumbria LA6 2SG
Tel: 01524 279200
Headmaster: Mr Scott Carnochan BEd
Age range: 3–13
No. of pupils: 210
(£)

Hunter Hall School
Frenchfield, Penrith, Cumbria CA11 8UA
Tel: 01768 891291
Head Teacher: Mrs Donna Vinsome
Age range: 3–11
No. of pupils: 101
Fees: Day £7,101–£8,226
(£)

Lime House School
Holm Hill, Dalston, Carlisle, Cumbria CA5 7BX
Tel: 01228 710225
Headmaster: Mr N A Rice BA, CertEd, MA(EdMan)
Age range: 5–18
No. of pupils: 140 VIth28
Fees: Day £8,700–£10,500 WB £21,000–£24,000 FB £24,000–£27,225
(A) (£) (16·)

Sedbergh School
Sedbergh, Cumbria LA10 5HG
Tel: 015396 20535
Headmaster: Mr A Fleck MA
Age range: 3–18
No. of pupils: 500 VIth200
Fees: Day £22,950 FB £31,146
(A) (£) (16·)

Windermere Preparatory School
Ambleside Road, Windermere, Cumbria LA23 1AP
Tel: 015394 46164
Head: Mrs Rachael Thomas
Age range: 3–11
No. of pupils: 120
(£)

WINDERMERE SCHOOL
For further details see p. 174
Patterdale Road, Windermere, Cumbria LA23 1NW
Tel: 015394 46164
Email: ws@windermereschool.co.uk
Website: www.windermereschool.co.uk
Age range: 3–18
No. of pupils: 340
Fees: Day £17,250 WB £29,265 FB £30,420
(£) (IB) (16·)

Greater Manchester

Abbey College Manchester
5-7 Cheapside, King Street, Manchester, Greater Manchester M2 4WG
Tel: 0161 817 2700
Principal: Ms Liz Elam
Age range: 15–19
No. of pupils: 220 VIth175
Fees: Day £11,900
(16·) (A) (£) (16·)

Abbotsford Preparatory School
211 Flixton Road, Urmston, Manchester, Greater Manchester M41 5PR
Tel: 0161 748 3261
Head Teacher: Mrs Pamela Shiels
Age range: 3–11
No. of pupils: 106
Fees: Day £5,065–£5,469
(£)

Al Jamiah Al Islamiyyah (Bolton Darul Uloom)
Willows Lane, Bolton, Greater Manchester BL3 4HF
Tel: 01204 62622
Headmaster: Mr S J Haneef
Age range: B12–18
No. of pupils: 140
Fees: Day £750 FB £1,500
(A) (16·)

Altrincham Preparatory School
Marlborough Road, Bowdon, Altrincham, Greater Manchester WA14 2RR
Tel: 0161 928 3366
Headmaster: Mr Andrew C Potts
Age range: B3–11
No. of pupils: 310
Fees: Day £6,180–£6,840

Beech House School
184 Manchester Road, Rochdale, Greater Manchester OL11 4JQ
Tel: 01706 646309
Headmaster: K Sartain BSc(Hons), PGCE, DipSp, CBiol, FIBiol
Age range: 2–16
Fees: Day £3,945–£4,938

Beis Rochel School
1-7 Seymour Road, Crumpsall, Manchester, Greater Manchester M8 5BQ
Tel: 0161 795 1830
Headmistress: Mrs E Krausz
Age range: G3–16
No. of pupils: 200

Bnos Yisroel School
Foigel Esther Shine House, Leicester Road, Manchester, Greater Manchester M7 4DA
Tel: 0161 792 3896
Headmaster: Rabbi R Spitzer
Age range: G2–16
No. of pupils: 489

Bolton School (Boys' Division)
Chorley New Road, Bolton, Greater Manchester BL1 4PA
Tel: 01204 840201
Headmaster: Philip J Britton MBE
Age range: B7–18
No. of pupils: VIth210
Fees: Day £9,024–£11,280
(A) (£) (16·)

Bolton School (Girls' Division)
Chorley New Road, Bolton, Greater Manchester BL1 4PB
Tel: 01204 840201
Headmistress: Miss Sue Hincks MA(Oxon)
Age range: B0–7 G0–18
No. of pupils: VIth210
Fees: Day £9,024–£11,280
(A) (£) (16·)

Branwood Preparatory School
Stafford Road, Monton, Eccles, Manchester, Greater Manchester M30 9HN
Tel: 0161 789 1054
Head: Mrs C Follett NPQSL, MA, BEd(Hons), Dip
Age range: 3–11
No. of pupils: 156
Fees: Day £5,925

Bridgewater School
Drywood Hall, Worsley Road, Worsley, Manchester, Greater Manchester M28 2WQ
Tel: 0161 794 1463
Head Teacher: Mrs J A T Nairn CertEd(Distinction)
Age range: 3–18
No. of pupils: 467
Fees: Day £6,750–£9,000
(A) (£) (16·)

Bury Catholic Preparatory School
Arden House, Manchester Road, Bury, Greater Manchester BL9 9BH
Tel: 0161 764 2346
Headteacher: Mrs A C Dean
Age range: 3–11
Fees: Day £4,500
(£)

Bury Grammar School Boys
Tenterden Street, Bury, Greater Manchester BL9 0HN
Tel: 0161 797 2700
Headmaster: Mr R N Marshall MSc
Age range: B7–18
No. of pupils: 602 VIth92
Fees: Day £6,750–£9,084
(A) (£) (16·)

Bury Grammar School for Girls
Bridge Road, Bury, Greater Manchester BL9 0HH
Tel: 0161 696 8600
Headmistress: Mrs R S Georghiou
Age range: B4–7 G4–18
No. of pupils: VIth120
Fees: Day £6,750–£9,084
(A) (£) (16·)

Cheadle Hulme School
Claremont Road, Cheadle Hulme, Cheadle, Greater Manchester SK8 6EF
Tel: 0161 488 3345
Head: Ms Lucy Pearson B.A. (Oxon)
Age range: 4–18
No. of pupils: 1396 VIth254
Fees: Day £8,244–£11,412

CHETHAM'S SCHOOL OF MUSIC
For further details see p. 164
Long Millgate, Manchester, Greater Manchester M3 1SB
Tel: 0161 834 9644
Email: hello@chethams.com
Website: www.chethams.com
Age range: 8–18
No. of pupils: 299
Fees: Day £24,819 FB £32,031

Clarendon Cottage School
Ivy Bank House, Half Edge Lane, Eccles, Manchester, Greater Manchester M30 9BJ
Tel: 0161 950 7868
Headteacher: Mrs E L Howard
Age range: 3–11
No. of pupils: 81
Fees: Day £3,210–£3,840

Clevelands Preparatory School
425 Chorley New Road, Bolton, Greater Manchester BL1 5DH
Tel: 01204 843898
Headteacher: Mrs Lesley Parlane
Age range: 2–11
No. of pupils: 141
Fees: Day £6,240

Covenant Christian School
The Hawthorns, 48 Heaton Moor Road, Stockport, Greater Manchester SK4 4NX
Tel: 0161 432 3782
Head: Dr Roger Slack
Age range: 5–16
No. of pupils: 32

Darul Uloom Al Arabiya Al Islamiya
Holcombe Hall, Holcombe, Bury, Greater Manchester BL8 4NG
Tel: 01706 826106
Head: R Abdulla
Age range: B12–16
No. of pupils: 326

Etz Chaim School at The Belmont
89 Middleton Road, Crumpsall, Manchester, Greater Manchester M8 4JY
Tel: 0161 740 6800
Headteacher: Rabbi Eli Cohen
Age range: B11–16
No. of pupils: 98

Farrowdale House Preparatory School
Farrow Street, Shaw, Oldham, Greater Manchester OL2 7AD
Tel: 01706 844533
Headteacher: Miss Z. N. Campbell BA Hons PGCE
Age range: 3–11
No. of pupils: 90
Fees: Day £5,550–£6,267

Firwood Manor Preparatory School
Broadway, Chadderton, Oldham, Greater Manchester OL9 0AD
Tel: 0161 6206570
Headteacher: Mrs P M Wild
Age range: 2–11
Fees: Day £5,400

Forest Park School
Lauriston House, 27 Oakfield, Sale, Greater Manchester M33 6NB
Tel: 0161 973 4835
Headteacher: Mrs Helen Gee BEd(Hons)
Age range: 3–11
No. of pupils: 145
Fees: Day £4,515–£4,950

Forest Preparatory School
Moss Lane, Timperley, Altrincham, Greater Manchester WA15 6LJ
Tel: 0161 980 4075
Headmaster: Rick Hyde
Age range: 2–11
No. of pupils: 197
Fees: Day £1,940–£2,190

Grafton House Preparatory School
1 Warrington Street, Ashton-under-Lyne, Greater Manchester OL6 6XB
Tel: 0161 343 3015
Head: Mrs Pamela Oaks
Age range: 2–11
No. of pupils: 110

Greenbank Preparatory School
Heathbank Road, Cheadle Hulme, Cheadle, Greater Manchester SK8 6HU
Tel: 0161 485 3724
Headmistress: Mrs J L Lowe
Age range: 3–11
Fees: Day £7,095

Hulme Hall Grammar School
Beech Avenue, Stockport, Greater Manchester SK3 8HB
Headteacher: Miss Rachael Allen
Age range: 2–16
No. of pupils: 272
Fees: Day £7,800–£9,057

Jewish Senior Boys School
Hubert House, 4 Newhall Road, Salford, Greater Manchester M7 4EL
Tel: 0161 708 9175
Headmaster: Rabbi Joshua Michael Israel
Age range: B10–16

Kassim Darwish Grammar School for Boys
Hartley Hall, Alexandra Road South, Manchester, Greater Manchester M16 8NH
Tel: 0161 8607676
Headteacher: Mr Wahid Anwar
Age range: B11–16
No. of pupils: 170
Fees: Day £5,644

King of Kings School
142 Dantzic Street, Manchester, Greater Manchester M4 4DN
Tel: 0161 834 4214
Head Teacher: Mrs B Lewis
Age range: 3–18
No. of pupils: 29

Lighthouse Christian School
193 Ashley Lane, Moston, Manchester, Greater Manchester M9 4NQ
Tel: 0161 205 0957
Head: Mr A I Akinyele
Age range: 3–11
No. of pupils: 18
Fees: Day £2,880

Lord's Independent School
53 Manchester Road, Bolton, Greater Manchester BL2 1ES
Tel: 01204 523731
Headteacher: Mrs Anne Ainsworth
Age range: 11–16
No. of pupils: 83

Loreto Preparatory School
Dunham Road, Altrincham, Greater Manchester WA14 4GZ
Tel: 0161 928 8310
Headteacher: Mrs R A Hedger
Age range: B3–7 G3–11
No. of pupils: 163
Fees: Day £4,650

Madrasatul Imam Muhammad Zakariya
Keswick Street, Bolton, Greater Manchester BL1 8LX
Tel: 01204 384434
Headteacher: Mrs Amena Sader
Age range: G11–19
No. of pupils: 110

Manchester High School for Girls
Grangethorpe Road, Manchester, Greater Manchester M14 6HS
Tel: 0161 224 0447
Head Mistress: Mrs A C Hewitt
Age range: G4–18
No. of pupils: 936 VIth182
Fees: Day £8,133–£11,253

Manchester Islamic High School for Girls
55 High Lane, Chorlton Cum Hardy, Manchester, Greater Manchester M21 9FA
Tel: 0161 881 2127
Headmistress: Mrs Mona Mohamed
Age range: G11–16
No. of pupils: 235
Fees: Day £3,980

Manchester Junior Girls School
64 Upper Park Road, Salford, Greater Manchester M7 4JA
Tel: 0161 740 0566
Headmistress: Mrs Lieberman
Age range: G3–11
No. of pupils: 200

Manchester Muslim Preparatory School
551 Wilmslow Road, Withington, Manchester, Greater Manchester M20 4BA
Tel: 0161 445 5452
Head Teacher: Mrs N. Hameed BA Hons, NPQH
Age range: 3–11
No. of pupils: 186
Fees: Day £5,225–£5,500

Mechinoh L'Yeshivah
Shenstone House, 13 Upper Park Road, Salford, Greater Manchester M7 4HY
Tel: 0161 795 9275
The Head: Headmaster
Age range: B11–15
No. of pupils: 49

Monton Village School
Francis Street, Monton, Eccles, Manchester, Greater Manchester M30 9PR
Tel: 0161 789 0472
Head: Mrs K S McWilliams
Age range: 1–7
No. of pupils: 109

Moor Allerton School
131 Barlow Moor Road, West Didsbury, Manchester, Greater Manchester M20 2PW
Tel: 0161 445 4521
Age range: 3–11
Fees: Day £6,660–£7,185

Oldham Hulme Grammar School
Chamber Road, Oldham, Greater Manchester OL8 4BX
Tel: 0161 624 4497
Principal: Mr CJD Mairs
Age range: 2–18
No. of pupils: 766
Fees: Day £7,335–£10,035
A £ 16·

OYY Lubavitch Girls School
Beis Menachem, Park Lane, Salford, Greater Manchester M7 4JD
Tel: 0161 795 0002
Headmistress: Mrs J Hanson
Age range: 2–16
No. of pupils: 82

Prestwich Preparatory School
St Margaret's Building, 400 Bury Old Road, Prestwich, Manchester, Greater Manchester M25 1PZ
Tel: 0161 773 1223
Headmistress: Miss P Shiels
Age range: 2–11
No. of pupils: 122
Fees: Day £3,336

Ramillies Hall School
Cheadle Hulme, Cheadle, Greater Manchester SK8 7AJ
Tel: 0161 485 3804
Principal: Miss D M Patterson BA, PGCE & Mrs A L Poole
Age range: 0–16
No. of pupils: 166
Fees: Day £6,000–£8,550
£

Rochdale Girls' School and Boys' Branch
Greenbank Road, Rochdale, Greater Manchester OL12 0HZ
Tel: 01706 710184
Headteacher: Mrs Aishah Akhtar
Age range: G11–16
No. of pupils: 165
Fees: Day £1,600

Saddleworth School
High Street, Uppermill, Oldham, Greater Manchester OL3 6BU
Tel: 01457 872072
Headmistress: Mrs L K Hirst
Age range: 3–7

St Ambrose Preparatory School
Hale Barns, Altrincham, Greater Manchester WA15 0HE
Tel: 0161 903 9193
Headmaster: F J Driscoll
Age range: B3–11 G3–4
No. of pupils: 150
Fees: Day £6,195
£

St Bede's College
Alexandra Park Road, Manchester, Greater Manchester M16 8HX
Tel: 0161 226 3323
Headmaster: Mr Richard Robson
Age range: 11–19
Fees: Day £7,170
A £ 16·

Stella Maris Junior School
St Johns Road, Heaton Mersey, Stockport, Greater Manchester SK4 3BR
Tel: 0161 432 0532
Headteacher: Mrs N Johnson
Age range: 3–11
No. of pupils: 68
Fees: Day £7,488

Stockport Grammar School
Buxton Road, Stockport, Greater Manchester SK2 7AF
Tel: 0161 456 9000
Headmaster: Mr A H Chicken BA, MEd, FRSA
Age range: 3–18
No. of pupils: 1456 VIth240
Fees: Day £8,262–£10,710
A £ 16·

Tashbar School
20 Upper Park Road, Salford, Greater Manchester M7 4HL
Tel: 0161 7208254
Headteacher: Mr Pinczewski
Age range: B5–11
No. of pupils: 325

The Manchester Grammar School
Old Hall Lane, Fallowfield, Manchester, Greater Manchester M13 0XT
Tel: 0161 224 7201
High Master: Dr Martin Boulton
Age range: B7–18
Fees: Day £11,400
A £ IB 16·

Trinity Christian School
Birbeck Street, Stalybridge, Greater Manchester SK15 1SH
Tel: 0161 303 0674
Headteacher: Mr W Ross Evans
Age range: 3–16
Fees: Day £2,964–£4,146

Withington Girls' School
Wellington Road, Fallowfield, Manchester, Greater Manchester M14 6BL
Tel: 0161 224 1077
Headmistress: Mrs S J Haslam BA
Age range: G7–18
No. of pupils: 660 VIth150
Fees: Day £8,685–£11,685
A £ 16·

Yeshivah Ohr Torah School
28 Broom Lane, Salford, Greater Manchester M7 4FX
Tel: 0161 7921230
Headteacher: Rabbi Y Wind
Age range: B11–16
No. of pupils: 40

Isle of Man

King William's College
Castletown, Isle of Man IM9 1TP
Tel: +44 (0)1624 820400
Principal: Mr Joss Buchanan
Age range: 11–18
No. of pupils: 370
Fees: Day £4,999–£7,200
FB £8,249–£10,450
£ IB 16·

The Buchan School
West Hill, Castletown, Isle of Man IM9 1RD
Tel: 01624 820481
Headteacher: Mrs Alison Hope Hedley
Age range: 4–11
No. of pupils: 195
Fees: Day £2,849–£3,716
£

Lancashire

Abrar Academy
56 Garstang Road, Preston,
Lancashire PR1 1NA
Tel: 01772 82 87 32
Head: Mr A Esmail
Age range: 11–16

Al-Islah Schools
108 Audley Range, Blackburn,
Lancashire BB1 1TF
Tel: 01254 261573
Headteacher: Nizammuddin I Makda
Age range: 9–17
No. of pupils: 192

Arnold KEQMS (AKS)
Clifton Drive South, Lytham St
Annes, Lancashire FY8 1DT
Tel: 01253 784100
Headmaster: Mr. Mike Walton
BA, MA (Ed), PGCE, NPQH
Age range: 2–18
No. of pupils: 800 VIth165
Fees: Day £6,537–£8,541

Ashbridge Independent School
Lindle Lane, Hutton, Preston,
Lancashire PR4 4AQ
Tel: 01772 619900
Headteacher: Mrs H Sharples
Age range: 0–11
No. of pupils: 315
Fees: Day £6,318

Ghausia Girls' High School
1-3 Cross Street, Nelson,
Lancashire BB9 7EN
Tel: 01282 699214
Principal: Jamil Mohammed
Age range: G11–16
No. of pupils: 35
Fees: Day £1,000

Heathland School
Broadoak, Sandy Lane, Accrington,
Lancashire BB5 2AN
Tel: 01254 234284
Principal: Mrs J Harrison
BA(Hons), CertEd, FRSA
Age range: 4–16
Fees: Day £4,515

Highfield Priory School
58 Fulwood Row, Preston,
Lancashire PR2 5RW
Tel: 01772 709624
Headmaster: Mr Jeremy
Duke BSc (Hons)
Age range: 6 months–11 years
No. of pupils: 276
Fees: Day £7,315

Islamiyah School
Willow Street, Blackburn,
Lancashire BB1 5RQ
Tel: 01254 661 259
Headteacher: Mrs Zarina Seedat
Age range: G11–16
No. of pupils: 178

Jamea Al Kauthar
Ashton Road, Lancaster,
Lancashire LA1 5AJ
Tel: 01524 389898
Headteacher: Miss Ayesha Uddin
Age range: G11–16
No. of pupils: 392

Jamiatul-Ilm Wal-Huda UK School
15 Moss Street, Blackburn,
Lancashire BB1 5HW
Tel: 01254 673105
Headteacher: Mr A Ahmed
Age range: B11–16
No. of pupils: 348

Kingsfold Christian School
Moss Lane, Hesketh Bank,
Preston, Lancashire PR4 6AA
Tel: 01772 813824
Age range: 4–16

KIRKHAM GRAMMAR SCHOOL
For further details see p. 168
Ribby Road, Kirkham, Preston,
Lancashire PR4 2BH
Tel: 01772 684264
Email: info@kirkhamgrammar.co.uk
Website:
www.kirkhamgrammar.co.uk
Headmaster: Mr. Daniel Berry
Age range: 3–18
No. of pupils: 860 VIth180

Lancaster Steiner School
Lune Road, Lancaster,
Lancashire LA1 5QU
Tel: 01524 841351
Headteacher: Mrs Denise Randal
Age range: 0–14

Markazul Uloom
Park Lee Road, Blackburn,
Lancashire BB2 3NY
Tel: 01254 581569
Headteacher: Mr Nu'amaan Limbada
Age range: G11–19
Fees: Day £1,200 FB £2,700

Moorland School
Ribblesdale Avenue, Clitheroe,
Lancashire BB7 2JA
Tel: 01200 423833
Principal: Mr T Smith BSc(Hons), PGCE
Age range: 3 months–16 years
Fees: Day £4,650–£5,190 WB
£10,800–£12,750 FB £11,250–£13,500

Oakhill School and Nursery
Wiswell Lane, Whalley, Clitheroe,
Lancashire BB7 9AF
Tel: 01254 823546
Principal: Mrs Carmel Crouch
Age range: 0–16
No. of pupils: 330
Fees: Day £7,440–£11,574

Palm Tree School
Oakenhurst Road, Blackburn,
Lancashire BB2 1SN
Tel: 01254 264254
Headteacher: Mrs N Hameed
Age range: 3–11
Fees: Day £1,200

ROSSALL SCHOOL
For further details see p. 170
Broadway, Fleetwood,
Lancashire FY7 8JW
Tel: +44 (0)1253 774201
Email: admissions@rossall.org.uk
Website: www.rossallschool.org.uk
Head: Ms Elaine Purves
Age range: 2–18
No. of pupils: 600 VIth170
Fees: Day £7,830–£12,750
FB £20,100–£36,450

Scarisbrick Hall School
Southport Road, Scarisbrick,
Ormskirk, Lancashire L40 9RQ
Tel: 01704 841151
Headmaster: Mr J Shaw
Age range: 0–18
Fees: Day £5,000–£9,500

St Anne's College Grammar School
293 Clifton Drive South, Lytham
St Annes, Lancashire FY8 1HN
Tel: +44 (0)1253 725815
Principal: Mrs S M Welsby
Age range: 2–18
No. of pupils: VIth16
Fees: Day £4,900–£7,800
WB £5,200 FB £7,500

St Joseph's School, Park Hill
Park Hill, Padiham Road,
Burnley, Lancashire BB12 6TG
Tel: 01282 455622
Headmistress: Mrs Annette Robinson
Age range: 3–11
Fees: Day £5,600

St Pius X Preparatory School
Oak House, 200 Garstang Road,
Fulwood, Preston, Lancashire PR2 8RD
Tel: 01772 719937
Headmistress: Miss B M Banks MA
Age range: 2–11
No. of pupils: 260
Fees: Day £6,975–£7,325

STONYHURST COLLEGE
For further details see p. 172
Stonyhurst, Clitheroe,
Lancashire BB7 9PZ
Tel: 01254 827073
Email: admissions@stonyhurst.ac.uk
Website: www.stonyhurst.ac.uk
Headmaster: John Browne MA
Age range: 13–18
No. of pupils: 480 VIth240
Fees: Day £19,560 WB
£29,250 FB £34,110

Stonyhurst St Mary's Hall
Stonyhurst, Lancashire BB7 9PU
Tel: 01254 827073
Headmaster: Mr Ian Murphy
BA (Hons), PGCE Durham
Age range: 3–13
No. of pupils: 262
Fees: Day £8,370–£15,585
WB £20,325 FB £23,985

The Alternative School
The Old Library, Fern Lea Avenue,
Barnoldswick, Lancashire BB18 5DW
Tel: 01282 851800
Age range: 13–16

Westholme School
Meins Road, Blackburn,
Lancashire BB2 6QU
Tel: 01254 506070
Principal: Mrs Lynne Horner
BA(Hons), PGCE, DipEd
Age range: 3 months–18 years
No. of pupils: 792 VIth72
Fees: Day £7,200–£10,290

Merseyside

Auckland College
65-67 Parkfield Road, Wavertree, Liverpool, Merseyside L17 4LE
Tel: 0151 727 0083
Headmaster: Simon Parris
Age range: 0–18
No. of pupils: 172 VIth15
Fees: Day £5,656

Avalon Preparatory School
Caldy Road, West Kirby, Wirral, Merseyside CH48 2HE
Tel: 0151 625 6993
Age range: 2–11
No. of pupils: 178
Fees: Day £1,860–£5,205

Belvedere Preparatory School
23 Belvidere Road, Princes Park, Aigburth, Liverpool, Merseyside L8 3TF
Tel: 0151 471 1137
Age range: 3–11
No. of pupils: 180

Birkenhead School
The Lodge, 58 Beresford Road, Birkenhead, Merseyside CH43 2JD
Tel: 0151 652 4014
Headmaster: Mr David John Clark MA
Age range: 3 months–18 years
No. of pupils: VIth103
Fees: Day £6,645–£9,606

Carleton House Preparatory School
145 Menlove Avenue, Liverpool, Merseyside L18 3EE
Tel: 0151 722 0756
Head: Mr Peter Andrew
Age range: 4–11
No. of pupils: 145
Fees: Day £5,928

Christian Fellowship School
Overbury Street, Edge Hill, Liverpool, Merseyside L7 3HL
Tel: 0151 709 1642
Headteacher: Mr Richard Worsley
Age range: 4–16
No. of pupils: 136
Fees: Day £2,434–£4,867

Kingsmead School
Bertram Drive, Hoylake, Wirral, Merseyside CH47 0LL
Tel: 0151 632 3156
Headmaster: Mr M G Gibbons BComm, MSc, QTS
Age range: 3–16
Fees: Day £2,625–£9,105 WB £13,050–£15,345 FB £13,755–£16,050

Merchant Taylors' Boys' School
186 Liverpool Road, Crosby, Liverpool, Merseyside L23 0QP
Tel: 0151 928 3308
Headmaster: Mr D Cook MA
Age range: B7–18
No. of pupils: 727
Fees: Day £8,025–£10,734

Merchant Taylors' Girls' School
Liverpool Road, Crosby, Liverpool, Merseyside L23 5SP
Tel: 0151 924 3140
Headmistress: Mrs L A Robinson MEd, BA(Hons), NPQH
Age range: B4–7 G4–18
No. of pupils: 801
Fees: Day £7,944–£10,734

Prenton Preparatory School
Mount Pleasant, Oxton, Wirral, Merseyside CH43 5SY
Tel: 0151 652 3182
Head: Mr Jones
Age range: 2 –11
Fees: Day £4,650

Redcourt St Anselm's
Redcourt, Devonshire Place, Birkenhead, Merseyside CH43 1TX
Tel: 0151 652 5228
Age range: 3–11
No. of pupils: 320
Fees: Day £2,500–£3,000

Runnymede St Edward's School
North Drive, Sandfield Park, Liverpool, Merseyside L12 1LE
Tel: 0151 281 2300
Headmaster: Mr Bradley Slater
Age range: 3–11
No. of pupils: 270
Fees: Day £6,276–£6,617

St Mary's College
Everest Road, Crosby, Liverpool, Merseyside L23 5TW
Tel: 0151 924 3926
Principal: Mr Michael Kennedy Bsc, MA
No. of pupils: 880 VIth132
Fees: Day £7,208–£10,623

Streatham House School
Victoria Road West, Blundellsands, Liverpool, Merseyside L23 8UQ
Tel: 0151 924 1514
Executive Headteacher: Mrs Debby Rigby BA(Hons), PGCE, CertEd(Man)
Age range: B3 months–11 G3 months–16
Fees: Day £1,200

Tower College
Mill Lane, Rainhill, Prescot, Merseyside L35 6NE
Tel: 0151 426 4333
Principal: Miss R J Oxley NNEB, RSH
Age range: 3–16
No. of pupils: 486
Fees: Day £5,013–£5,895

South-East

KEY TO SYMBOLS

- *Boys' school*
- *Girls' school*
- *International school*
- *Tutorial or sixth form college*
- *A levels*
- *Boarding accommodation*
- *Bursaries*
- *International Baccalaureate*
- *Learning support*
- *Entrance at 16+*
- *Vocational qualifications*
- *Independent Association of Preparatory Schools*
- *The Headmasters' & Headmistresses' Conference*
- *Independent Schools Association*
- *Girls' School Association*
- *Boarding Schools' Association*
- *Society of Heads*

Unless otherwise indicated, all schools are coeducational day schools. Single-sex and boarding schools will be indicated by the relevant icon.

Berkshire

Alder Bridge School
Bridge House, Mill Lane, Padworth, Reading, Berkshire RG7 4JU
Tel: 0118 971 4471
Age range: 0–14 years
No. of pupils: 65
Fees: Day £3,354–£8,295

Bradfield College
Bradfield, Berkshire RG7 6AU
Tel: 0118 964 4516
Headmaster: Dr Christopher Stevens
Age range: 13–18
No. of pupils: 776
Fees: Day £28,224 FB £35,280
A £ IB 16·

Brigidine School Windsor
Queensmead, King's Road, Windsor, Berkshire SL4 2AX
Tel: 01753 863779
Headmistress: Mrs Elizabeth Robinson
Age range: B2–7 G3–18
No. of pupils: 300
Fees: Day £3,945–£11,865
A £ 16·

Caversham School
16 Peppard Road, Caversham, Reading, Berkshire RG4 8JZ
Tel: 01189 478 684
Head: Mrs Jacqueline Lawson
Age range: 4–11
No. of pupils: 60
Fees: Day £6,750

Claires Court Junior Boys
Maidenhead Thicket, Maidenhead, Berkshire SL6 3QE
Tel: 01628 327700
Head: J M E Spanswick
Age range: B4–11
No. of pupils: 248
Fees: Day £7,965–£13,860
£

Claires Court Nursery, Girls and Sixth Form
1 College Avenue, Maidenhead, Berkshire SL6 6AW
Tel: 01628 327700
Head: Mr Paul Bevis
Age range: B16–18 G3–18
No. of pupils: 495 VIth111
Fees: Day £5,715–£14,580
A £ 16·

Claires Court Senior Boys
Ray Mill Road East, Maidenhead, Berkshire SL6 8TE
Tel: 01628 327700
Headmaster: Mr J M Rayer BSc, PGCE
Age range: B11–16
No. of pupils: 335 VIth112
Fees: Day £13,860–£14,580
A £ 16·

Crosfields School
Shinfield, Reading, Berkshire RG2 9BL
Tel: 0118 987 1810
Headmaster: Mr J P Wansey
Age range: 3–13
No. of pupils: 510
Fees: Day £6,600–£10,710
£

Dolphin School
Waltham Road, Hurst, Reading, Berkshire RG10 0FR
Tel: 0118 934 1277
Head: Mr Tom Lewis
Age range: 3–13
Fees: Day £8,340–£11,190
£

EAGLE HOUSE SCHOOL
For further details see p. 190
Sandhurst, Berkshire GU47 8PH
Tel: 01344 772134
Email: info@eaglehouseschool.com
Website: www.eaglehouseschool.com
Headmaster: Mr A P N Barnard BA(Hons), PGCE
Age range: 3–13
No. of pupils: 388
Fees: Day £11,235–£17,580 FB £23,610
£

Elstree School
Woolhampton, Reading, Berkshire RG7 5TD
Tel: 0118 971 3302
Headmaster: Mr S Inglis
Age range: B3–13 G3–7
No. of pupils: 248
Fees: Day £17,775 FB £22,800
£

Eton College
Windsor, Berkshire SL4 6DW
Tel: 01753 671249
Head Master: Simon Henderson MA
Age range: B13–18
No. of pupils: 1300 VIth520
Fees: FB £33,270
A £ 16·

Eton End PNEU School
35 Eton Road, Datchet, Slough, Berkshire SL3 9AX
Tel: 01753 541075
Headmistress: Mrs V M Pilgerstorfer BA(Hons), PGCE
Age range: B3–7 G3–11
No. of pupils: 245
Fees: Day £5,850–£6,900

Heathfield School
London Road, Ascot, Berkshire SL5 8BQ
Tel: 01344 898342
Age range: G11–18
No. of pupils: 200
Fees: Day £6,900–£7,092 FB £11,125–£11,400
A £ 16·

Hemdean House School
Hemdean Road, Caversham, Reading, Berkshire RG4 7SD
Tel: 0118 947 2590
Headmistress: Mrs J Harris BSc
Age range: B3–11 G3–16
Fees: Day £5,280–£7,200
£

Herries Preparatory School
Dean Lane, Cookham Dean, Berkshire SL6 9BD
Tel: 01628 483350
Headmistress: Sophie Green
Age range: 3–11
Fees: Day £6,645–£8,985
£

Highfield Preparatory School
2 West Road, Maidenhead, Berkshire SL6 1PD
Tel: 01628 624918
Headteacher: Mrs Joanna Leach
Age range: B3–5 G3–11
Fees: Day £897–£10,110
£

Holme Grange School
Heathlands Road, Wokingham, Berkshire RG40 3AL
Tel: 0118 978 1566
Headteacher: Mrs Claire Robinson
Age range: 3–16 years
No. of pupils: 410
Fees: Day £9,690–£13,590
£

Hurst Lodge
Bagshot Road, Ascot, Berkshire SL5 9JU
Tel: 01344 622154
Principal: Ms Victoria Smit
Age range: 3–18
No. of pupils: 202 VIth13
Fees: Day £6,420–£25,200 WB £19,905–£34,005
A £ 16·

Lambrook School
Winkfield Row, Bracknell, Berkshire RG42 6LU
Tel: 01344 882717
Headmaster: Mr Jonathan Perry
Age range: 3–13
No. of pupils: 440
Fees: Day £9,078–£15,180 WB £16,803–£18,009 FB £17,433–£18,639
£

LEIGHTON PARK SCHOOL
For further details see p. 204
Shinfield Road, Reading, Berkshire RG2 7ED
Tel: +44 (0) 118 987 9600
Email: admissions@leightonpark.com
Website: www.leightonpark.com
Head: Nigel Williams BA(Bristol), MA(London), PGCE
Age range: 11–18
No. of pupils: 459
Fees: Day £17,358–£22,404 WB £23,886–£30,051 FB £27,162–£34,794
A £ IB 16·

Long Close School
Upton Court Road, Upton, Slough, Berkshire SL3 7LU
Tel: 01753 520095
Head: Mr Brendan Pavey
Age range: 2–16
No. of pupils: 335
Fees: Day £2,620–£4,545
£

Luckley House School
Luckley Road, Wokingham, Berkshire RG40 3EU
Tel: 0118 978 4175
Head: Mrs Jane Tudor
Age range: G11–18
No. of pupils: 230
Fees: Day £15,975 WB £25,908 FB £27,954
A £ 16·

Ludgrove
Wokingham, Berkshire RG40 3AB
Tel: 0118 978 9881
Age range: B8–13
No. of pupils: 190
£

LVS Ascot
London Road, Ascot, Berkshire SL5 8DR
Tel: 01344 882770
Headmistress: Mrs Christine Cunniffe BA (Hons), MMus, MBA
Age range: 4–18
No. of pupils: 817
Fees: Day £9,528–£18,261 FB £24,384–£32,085

Meadowbrook Montessori School
Malt Hill Road, Warfield, Bracknell, Berkshire RG42 6JQ
Tel: 01344 890869
Director of Education: Mrs S Gunn
Age range: 3–11
No. of pupils: 78
Fees: Day £10,200

Newbold School
Popeswood Road, Binfield, Bracknell, Berkshire RG42 4AH
Tel: 01344 421088
Headteacher: Mrs P Eastwood
Age range: 3–11
Fees: Day £3,000–£4,000

Our Lady's Preparatory School
The Avenue, Crowthorne, Wokingham, Berkshire RG45 6PB
Tel: 01344 773394
Headmistress: Mrs Helene Robinson
Age range: 3 months–11 years
No. of pupils: 100
Fees: Day £5,328–£10,464

Padworth College
Padworth, Reading, Berkshire RG7 4NR
Tel: 0118 983 2644
Principal: Mr John Aguilar
Age range: 13–19
No. of pupils: 116 VIth50
Fees: Day £14,250 FB £28,392

PANGBOURNE COLLEGE
For further details see p. 210
Pangbourne, Reading, Berkshire RG8 8LA
Tel: 0118 984 2101
Email: registrar@pangbourne.com
Website: www.pangbourne.com
Headmaster: Thomas J C Garnier
Age range: 11–18
No. of pupils: 410 VIth143
Fees: Day £17,055–£24,036 FB £24,021–£33,996

Papplewick School
Windsor Road, Ascot, Berkshire SL5 7LH
Tel: 01344 621488
Head: Mr T W Bunbury BA, PGCE
Age range: B6–13
No. of pupils: 195

Queen Anne's School
6 Henley Road, Caversham, Reading, Berkshire RG4 6DX
Tel: 0118 918 7300
Headmistress: Mrs Julia Harrington BA(Hons), PGCE, NPQH
Age range: G11–18
No. of pupils: 336 VIth100
Fees: Day £5,695 WB £7,545–£7,975 FB £8,395

Reading Blue Coat School
Holme Park, Sonning Lane, Sonning, Reading, Berkshire RG4 6SU
Tel: 0118 944 1005
Headmaster: Mr Jesse Elzinga
Age range: B11–18 G16–18
No. of pupils: 710 VIth230
Fees: Day £13,470

REDDAM HOUSE BERKSHIRE
For further details see p. 212
Bearwood Road, Sindlesham, Wokingham, Berkshire RG41 5BG
Tel: 0118 974 8300
Email: registrar@reddamhouse.org.uk
Website: reddamhouse.org.uk
Principal: Mrs Tammy Howard
Age range: 3 months–18 years
No. of pupils: 480
Fees: Day £9,885–£16,800 WB £26,310–£30,330 FB £27,855–£31,875

Redroofs School for the Performing Arts (Redroofs Theatre School)
26 Bath Road, Maidenhead, Berkshire SL6 4JT
Tel: 01628 674092
Principal: June Rose
Age range: 8–18
No. of pupils: 100
Fees: Day £4,000

St Andrew's School
Buckhold, Pangbourne, Reading, Berkshire RG8 8QA
Tel: 0118 974 4276
Headmaster: Dr D Livingstone BSc, PhD, NPQH
Age range: 3–13
Fees: Day £4,050–£14,280 WB £16,950

St Bernard's Preparatory School
Hawtrey Close, Slough, Berkshire SL1 1TB
Tel: 01753 521821
Head Teacher: Mr N Cheesman
Age range: 2–11
Fees: Day £2,580–£3,120

St Edward's School
64 Tilehurst Road, Reading, Berkshire RG30 2JH
Tel: 0118 957 4342
Principal: G W Mottram
Age range: B4–13
No. of pupils: 170
Fees: Day £6,660–£8,550

St George's Ascot
Wells Lane, Ascot, Berkshire SL5 7DZ
Tel: 01344 629920
Headmistress: Mrs Liz Hewer MA (Hons) (Cantab) PGCE
Age range: G11–18
No. of pupils: 280 VIth85
Fees: Day £20,250 WB £29,325–£30,375 FB £31,125

St George's School Windsor Castle
Windsor, Berkshire SL4 1QF
Tel: 01753 865553
Head Master: Mr C F McDade
Age range: 3–13
Fees: Day £8,493–£14,097 WB £18,723 FB £19,203

St John's Beaumont Preparatory School
Priest Hill, Old Windsor, Berkshire SL4 2JN
Tel: 01784 432428
Headmaster: Mr G E F Delaney BA(Hons), PGCE, MSc (Oxon)
Age range: B3–13
No. of pupils: 310
Fees: Day £7,140–£13,320 WB £17,520 FB £20,250

St Joseph's College
Upper Redlands Road, Reading, Berkshire RG1 5JT
Tel: 0118 966 1000
Headmaster: Mr Andrew Colpus
Age range: 3–18
No. of pupils: VIth46
Fees: Day £6,084–£10,401

St Mary's School Ascot
St Mary's Road, Ascot, Berkshire SL5 9JF
Tel: 01344 296614
Headmistress: Mrs Mary Breen BSc, MSc
Age range: G11–18
No. of pupils: 390 VIth120
Fees: Day £23,400 FB £32,850

St Piran's Preparatory School
Gringer Hill, Maidenhead, Berkshire SL6 7LZ
Tel: 01628 594302
Headmaster: Mr J A Carroll BA(Hons), BPhilEd, PGCE, NPQH
Age range: 3–11
Fees: Day £9,900–£14,550

Sunningdale School
Dry Arch Road, Sunningdale, Berkshire SL5 9PY
Tel: 01344 620159
Headmaster: T A C N Dawson MA, PGCE
Age range: B7–13
No. of pupils: 90
Fees: Day £13,950 FB £17,985

Teikyo School UK
Framewood Road, Wexham, Slough, Berkshire SL2 4QS
Tel: 01753 663711
Headmaster: A Watanabe BA
Age range: 16–18

The Abbey School
Kendrick Road, Reading, Berkshire RG1 5DZ
Tel: 0118 987 2256
Head: Mrs Rachel S E Dent
Age range: G3–18
No. of pupils: 1050
Fees: Day £15,720

The Deenway Montessori School
3-5 Sidmouth Street, Reading, Berkshire RG1 4QX
Tel: 0118 9574737
Headteacher: Mr M Karim
Age range: 3–11

The Marist Preparatory School
King's Road, Sunninghill, Ascot, Berkshire SL5 7PS
Tel: 01344 626137
Headteacher: J Finlayson
Age range: G2–11
No. of pupils: 225
Fees: Day £8,700–£9,360

The Marist Schools
King's Road, Sunninghill, Ascot, Berkshire SL5 7PS
Tel: 01344 624291
Head of Secondary School: Mr K McCloskey
Age range: G2–18
No. of pupils: 550 VIth60
Fees: Day £7,845–£10,695

The Oratory Preparatory School
Great Oaks, Goring Heath, Reading, Berkshire RG8 7SF
Tel: 0118 984 4511
Headmaster: Mr J J Smith BA, PGCE
Age range: 3–13
No. of pupils: 400
Fees: Day £3,425–£11,475 WB £14,565 FB £15,825

The Oratory School
Woodcote, Reading, Berkshire RG8 0PJ
Tel: 01491 683500
Head Master: Mr A J Wyles BSc(Hons), MEd, PGCE, FRGS
Age range: B11–18
No. of pupils: 380 VIth120
Fees: Day £23,250 FB £21,540–£31,950

The Vine Christian School
SORCF Christian Centre, Basingstoke Road, Three Mile Cross, Reading, Berkshire RG7 1AT
Tel: 0118 988 6464
Head: Mrs Joan Muirhead
Age range: 5–13
No. of pupils: 9

Upton House School
115 St Leonard's Road, Windsor, Berkshire SL4 3DF
Tel: 01753 862610
Headmistress: Mrs Madeleine Collins BA(Hons), PGCE(Oxford)
Age range: B2–7 G2–11
No. of pupils: 280

Waverley School
Waverley Way, Finchampstead, Wokingham, Berkshire RG40 4YD
Tel: 0118 973 1121
Principal: Mrs Jane Sculpher
Age range: 3–11
Fees: Day £3,300–£7,362

WELLINGTON COLLEGE
For further details see p. 224
Duke's Ride, Crowthorne, Berkshire RG45 7PU
Tel: +44 (0)1344 444000
Email: admissions@wellingtoncollege.org.uk
Website: www.wellingtoncollege.org.uk
Master: Mr Julian Thomas
Age range: 13–18
No. of pupils: 1040 VIth455
Fees: Day £27,930–£32,085 FB £38,220

Buckinghamshire

Caldicott
Crown Lane, Farnham Royal, Buckinghamshire SL2 3SL
Tel: 01753 649301
Headmaster: Mr S J G Doggart BA(Cantab)
Age range: B7–13
No. of pupils: 285 VIth55
Fees: Day £16,185–£18,057 FB £26,622

Dair House School
Bishops Blake, Beaconsfield Road, Farnham Royal, Buckinghamshire SL2 3BY
Tel: 01753 643964
Headmaster: Mr Terry Wintle BEd(Hons)
Age range: 3–11
No. of pupils: 125
Fees: Day £3,060–£4,100

Gayhurst School
Bull Lane, Gerrards Cross, Buckinghamshire SL9 8RJ
Tel: 01753 882690
Headmaster: A J Sims MA(Cantab)
Age range: B3–13 G3–13
Fees: Day £9,882–£12,555

Heatherton House School
Copperkins Lane, Chesham Bois, Amersham, Buckinghamshire HP6 5QB
Tel: 01494 726433
Headteacher: Mrs Debbie Isaachsen
Age range: B3–4 G3–11
Fees: Day £1,068–£12,330

Maltman's Green School
Maltman's Lane, Gerrards Cross, Buckinghamshire SL9 8RR
Tel: 01753 883022
Headmistress: Mrs Joanna Pardon MA, BSc(Hons), PGCE
Age range: G2–11
Fees: Day £10,200–£13,500

Sefton Park School
School Lane, Stoke Poges, Buckinghamshire SL2 4QA
Tel: 01753 662167
Headteacher: Mr Timothy Thorpe
Age range: 11–16
No. of pupils: 120

St Mary's School
94 Packhorse Road, Gerrards Cross, Buckinghamshire SL9 8JQ
Tel: 01753 883370
Headmistress: Mrs J A Ross BA(Hons), NPQH
Age range: G3–18
No. of pupils: 320 VIth38
Fees: Day £3,420–£12,155

Thorpe House School
Oval Way, Gerrards Cross, Buckinghamshire SL9 8QA
Tel: 01753 882474
Headmaster: Mr Terence Ayres
Age range: B3–16
Fees: Day £8,070–£15,570

East Sussex

Ashdown House School
Forest Row, East Sussex RH18 5JY
Tel: 01342 822574
Headmaster: Haydon Moore
Age range: 7–13
No. of pupils: 125
Fees: FB £23,250

Bartholomews Tutorial College
22-23 Prince Albert Street, Brighton, East Sussex BN1 1HF
Tel: 01273 205965/205141
Governor: W A Duncombe BSc
Age range: 16+
No. of pupils: 40 VIth25
Fees: Day £23,000 WB £28,000 FB £30,000

Battle Abbey School
Battle, East Sussex TN33 0AD
Tel: 01424 772385
Headmaster: Mr R C Clark BA(Hons), MA(Ed)
Age range: 2–18
No. of pupils: 286 VIth48
Fees: Day £6,630–£13,390 FB £23,190

Bede's School
The Dicker, Upper Dicker, Hailsham, East Sussex BN27 3QH
Tel: +44 (0)1323843252
Head: Dr Richard Maloney
Age range: 12½–18+
No. of pupils: 800 VIth295
Fees: Day £15,450 FB £25,725

Bellerbys College Brighton
1 Billinton Way, Brighton, East Sussex BN1 4LF
Tel: +44 (0)1273 339333
Principal: Mr Simon Mower
Age range: 13–18

Bricklehurst Manor Preparatory
Bardown Road, Stonegate, Wadhurst, East Sussex TN5 7EL
Tel: 01580 200448
Head Teacher: Mrs K Elliott
Age range: 3–11
No. of pupils: 117
Fees: Day £980–£11,460

Brighton & Hove High School GDST
Montpelier Road, Brighton, East Sussex BN1 3AT
Tel: 01273 280280
Head: Mrs Lorna Duggleby
Age range: G3–18
No. of pupils: 680 VIth70
Fees: Day £5,028–£8,898

Brighton & Hove Montessori School
67 Stanford Avenue, Brighton, East Sussex BN1 6FB
Tel: 01273 702485
Headteacher: Mrs Daisy Cockburn AMI, MontDip
Age range: 2–11
Fees: Day £1,400–£5,900

Brighton College
Eastern Road, Brighton, East Sussex BN2 0AL
Tel: 01273 704200
Head Master: Richard Cairns MA
Age range: 3–18
No. of pupils: 945 VIth340
Fees: Day £4,890–£18,675 WB £24,729–£25,884 FB £28,575–£30,141

Brighton Steiner School
John Howard House, Roedean Road, Brighton, East Sussex BN2 5RA
Tel: 01273 386300
Chair of the College of Teachers: Carrie Rawle
Age range: 3–16
Fees: Day £6,540

Buckswood School
Broomham Hall, Rye Road, Guestling, Hastings, East Sussex TN35 4LT
Tel: 01424 813 813
Headmaster: Mr Giles Sutton
Age range: 10–19
No. of pupils: 420

Buckswood St George's
Westwood House, 7-9 Holmesdale Gardens, Hastings, East Sussex TN34 1LY
Tel: 01424 813696
College Director: Ian Godfrey
Age range: B16–19 G16–20
No. of pupils: VIth50

Charters Ancaster College
Woodsgate Place, Gunters Lane, Bexhill-on-Sea, East Sussex TN39 4EB
Tel: 01424 216670
Headmistress: Mrs Miriam Black
Age range: 2–13
No. of pupils: 125
Fees: Day £5,325–£6,750

Claremont Preparatory & Nursery School
Ebdens Hill, Baldslow, St Leonards-on-Sea, East Sussex TN37 7PW
Tel: 01424 751555
Headmistress: Mrs Diane Durrant
Age range: 1–14
Fees: Day £5,000–£10,000

Claremont Senior & Sixth Form School
Bodiam, Nr Robertsbridge, East Sussex TN32 5UJ
Tel: 01580 830396
Headmaster: Mr. Giles Perrin

Darvell School
Darvell Bruderhof, Robertsbridge, East Sussex TN32 5DR
Tel: 01580 883300
Headteacher: Mr Arnold Meier
Age range: 4–16
No. of pupils: 121

Deepdene School
195 New Church Road, Hove, East Sussex BN3 4ED
Tel: 01273 418984
Heads: Mrs Nicola Gane & Miss Elizabeth Brown
Age range: 6 months–11 years
Fees: Day £1,800–£6,870

Dharma School
The White House, Ladies Mile Road, Patcham, Brighton, East Sussex BN1 8TB
Tel: 01273 502055
Headmaster: Kevin Fossey BEd
Age range: 3–11
Fees: Day £3,000

Didac School
16 Trinity Trees, Eastbourne, East Sussex BN21 3LE
Tel: +44 1323 417276
Age range: 16–18

Eastbourne College
Old Wish Road, Eastbourne, East Sussex BN21 4JX
Tel: 01323 452323 (Admissions)
Headmaster: Mr T Lawson MA(Oxon)
Age range: 13–18
No. of pupils: 628 VIth277
Fees: Day £22,260–£22,620 FB £33,930–£34,320

GREENFIELDS INDEPENDENT DAY & BOARDING SCHOOL
For further details see p. 194
Priory Road, Forest Row, East Sussex RH18 5JD
Tel: +44 (0)1342 822189
Email: admissions@greenfieldsschool.com
Website: www.greenfieldsschool.com
Executive Head: Mr. Jeff Smith
Age range: 2–19

Lancing College Preparatory School at Hove
The Droveway, Hove, East Sussex BN3 6LU
Tel: 01273 503452
Headmistress: Mrs Kirsty Keep BEd
Age range: 3–13
No. of pupils: 181
Fees: Day £3,765–£15,195

Lewes New School
Talbot Terrace, Lewes, East Sussex BN7 1RD
Tel: 01273 477074
Head of School: Linda Morris
Age range: 3–11
No. of pupils: 78
Fees: Day £7,374

Lewes Old Grammar School
High Street, Lewes, East Sussex BN7 1XS
Tel: 01273 472634
Headmaster: Mr Robert Blewitt
Age range: 3–18
No. of pupils: 463 VIth50
Fees: Day £5,550–£10,815

Mayfield School
The Old Palace, Mayfield, East Sussex TN20 6PH
Tel: +44 (0)1435 874600
Head: Ms Antonia Beary MA, Mphil (Cantab), PGCE
Age range: G11–18
No. of pupils: 365 VIth100
Fees: Day £19,650 FB £31,800

Michael Hall School
Kidbrooke Park, Priory Road, Forest Row, East Sussex RH18 5BG
Tel: 01342 822275
Age range: 3–19
Fees: Day £8,858–£12,180 FB £6,876–£7,876

Moira House Girls School
Upper Carlisle Road, Eastbourne, East Sussex BN20 7TE
Tel: 01323 644144
Headmaster: Mr James Sheridan MA, BSc
Age range: G0–18
No. of pupils: 289

Roedean School
Roedean Way, Brighton, East Sussex BN2 5RQ
Tel: 01273 667500
Headmaster: Mr. Oliver Bond BA(Essex), PGCE, NPQH
Age range: G11–18
No. of pupils: 492 VIth147
Fees: Day £15,495–£20,160 WB £27,675–£30,870 FB £29,880–£36,180

Sacred Heart School
Mayfield Lane, Durgates, Wadhurst, East Sussex TN5 6DQ
Tel: 01892 783414
Headteacher: Mrs H Blake BA(Hons), PGCE
Age range: 3–11
Fees: Day £2,235–£6,225

Skippers Hill Manor Prep School
Five Ashes, Mayfield, East Sussex TN20 6HR
Tel: 01825 830234
Headmaster: Mr M Hammond MA, BA, PGCE
Age range: 2–13
No. of pupils: 174
Fees: Day £7,920–£12,660

St Andrew's Prep
Meads, Eastbourne, East Sussex BN20 7RP
Tel: 01323 733203
Headmaster: Gareth Jones BA(Hons), PGCE
Age range: 9 months–13 years
Fees: Day £9,406–£16,350 FB £23,205

St Bede's Preparatory School
Duke's Drive, Eastbourne,
East Sussex BN20 7XL
Tel: 01323 734222
Head: Mr Nicholas Bevington
Age range: 3 months–13 years
No. of pupils: 395

St Christopher's School
33 New Church Road, Hove,
East Sussex BN3 4AD
Tel: 01273 735404
Headmaster: Mr Julian Withers
Age range: 4–13
Fees: Day £6,570–£8,688

The Drive Prep School
101 The Drive, Hove, East Sussex BN3 3JE
Tel: 01273 738444
Head Teacher: Mrs S Parkinson
CertEd, CertPerfArts
Age range: 7–16
Fees: Day £3,885–£7,500

Torah Academy
31 New Church Road, Hove,
East Sussex BN3 4AD
Tel: 01273 328675
Principal: P Efune
Age range: 4–11

Vinehall School
Robertsbridge, East Sussex TN32 5JL
Tel: 01580 880413
Headmaster: Richard Follett
Age range: 2–13
No. of pupils: 260
Fees: Day £8,913–£16,620
FB £19,545–£21,675

Windlesham School
190 Dyke Road, Brighton,
East Sussex BN1 5AA
Tel: 01273 553645
Headmistress: Mrs Aoife
Bennett-Odlum
Age range: 3–11
No. of pupils: 233
Fees: Day £5,100–£7,200

Hampshire

Alton Convent School
Anstey Lane, Alton,
Hampshire GU34 2NG
Tel: 01420 82070
Head: Graham Maher
Age range: B0–11 G0–18
No. of pupils: 563 VIth53
Fees: Day £8,655–£12,285

Ballard School
Fernhill Lane, New Milton,
Hampshire BH25 5SU
Tel: 01425 626900
Headmaster: Mr Alastair Reid
Age range: 18 months–16 years
No. of pupils: 500
Fees: Day £2,370–£4,265

Bedales School
Church Road, Steep, Petersfield,
Hampshire GU32 2DG
Tel: 01730 711733
Head: Keith Budge MA
Age range: 13–18
No. of pupils: 457
Fees: Day £9,272 FB £11,799

Boundary Oak School
Roche Court, Fareham,
Hampshire PO17 5BL
Tel: 01329 280955/820373
Head: Mrs Hazel Kellett
Age range: 2–13
No. of pupils: 120
Fees: Day £7,500–£12,510 WB
£5,370 FB £7,095–£19,605

Brockwood Park & Inwoods School
Brockwood Park, Bramdean,
Hampshire SO24 0LQ
Tel: +44 (0)1962 771744
Co-Principals: Mr Antonio Autor
& Dr Gopal Krishnamurthy
Age range: 4–19
No. of pupils: 88 VIth33
Fees: Day £5,800 FB £21,400

Brookham School
Highfield Lane, Liphook,
Hampshire GU30 7LQ
Tel: 01428 722005
Headteacher: Mrs Sophie Baber
Age range: 3–8
No. of pupils: 141
Fees: Day £10,125–£13,350

CHURCHER'S COLLEGE
For further details see p. 184
Petersfield, Hampshire GU31 4AS
Tel: 01730 263033
Email: admissions@
churcherscollege.com
Website:
www.churcherscollege.com
Headmaster: Mr Simon
Williams MA, BSc
Age range: 3–18 years
Fees: Day £9,675–£14,220

Daneshill School
Stratfield Turgis, Basingstoke,
Hampshire RG27 0AR
Tel: 01256 882707
Headmaster: S V Spencer
CertEd, DipPhysEd
Age range: 3–13
Fees: Day £3,900–£9,150

Ditcham Park School
Ditcham Park, Petersfield,
Hampshire GU31 5RN
Tel: 01730 825659
Headmaster: G Spawforth MA,MEd
Age range: 4–16
No. of pupils: 356
Fees: Day £8,262–£13,851

Dunhurst (Bedales Junior School)
Petersfield, Hampshire GU32 2DP
Tel: 01730 300200
Head of School: Colin Baty
Age range: 8–13
No. of pupils: 177
Fees: Day £5,500–£6,100
FB £7,223–£8,106

DURLSTON COURT
For further details see p. 188
Becton Lane, Barton-on-Sea, New
Milton, Hampshire BH25 7AQ
Tel: 01425 610010
Email: secretary@
durlstoncourt.co.uk
Website: www.durlstoncourt.co.uk
Age range: 2–13
No. of pupils: 296
Fees: Day £3,540–£15,390

Farleigh School
Red Rice, Andover,
Hampshire SP11 7PW
Tel: 01264 710766
Headmaster: Father Simon Everson
Age range: 3–13
Fees: Day £3,870–£14,085
FB £16,515–£18,345

Farnborough Hill
Farnborough Road, Farnborough,
Hampshire GU14 8AT
Tel: 01252 545197
Headmistress: Mrs A Neil
BA, MEd, PGCE
Age range: G11–18
No. of pupils: 563 VIth80
Fees: Day £12,120

Forres Sandle Manor
Fordingbridge, Hampshire SP6 1NS
Tel: 01425 653181
Headmaster: Mr M N Hartley BSc(Hons)
Age range: 3–13
No. of pupils: 264
Fees: Day £3,150–£14,205
WB £19,380 FB £19,380

Glenhurst School
16 Beechworth Road, Havant,
Hampshire PO9 1AX
Tel: 023 9248 4054
Principal: Mrs E M Haines
Age range: 3 months–8 years
Fees: Day £4,500

Hampshire Collegiate School
Embley Park, Romsey,
Hampshire SO51 6ZE
Tel: 01794 512206
Principal: Mrs Emma-Kate Henry
Age range: 2–18
No. of pupils: 683

Highfield School
Liphook, Hampshire GU30 7LQ
Tel: 01428 728000
Headmaster: Mr Philip Evitt MA
Age range: 8–13
Fees: Day £17,025–£19,575
FB £21,450–£23,550

KING EDWARD VI SCHOOL
For further details see p. 200
Wilton Road, Southampton,
Hampshire SO15 5UQ
Tel: 023 8070 4561
Email: enquiries@kes.hants.sch.uk
Website: www.kes.hants.sch.uk
Head Master: Mr A J
Thould MA(Oxon)
Age range: 11–18
No. of pupils: 970
Fees: Day £15,510

Kingscourt School
182 Five Heads Road, Catherington, Hampshire PO8 9NJ
Tel: 023 9259 3251
Head of School: Mr Jamie Lewis
Age range: 3–11
No. of pupils: 210
Fees: Day £2,856

LORD WANDSWORTH COLLEGE
For further details see p. 206
Long Sutton, Hook, Hampshire RG29 1TB
Tel: 01256 862201
Email: admissions@lordwandsworth.org
Website: www.lordwandsworth.org
Head of School: Mr Adam Williams
Age range: 11–18 years
No. of pupils: 600
Fees: Day £19,650–£22,575 WB £27,225–£30,600 FB £28,140–£32,100

Mayville High School
35/37 St Simon's Road, Southsea, Portsmouth, Hampshire PO5 2PE
Tel: 023 9273 4847
Headteacher: Mrs L Owens B.Ed
Age range: 6 months–16 years
No. of pupils: 479
Fees: Day £5,481–£8,040

Meoncross School
Burnt House Lane, Stubbington, Fareham, Hampshire PO14 2EF
Tel: 01329 662182
Headmistress: Mrs Sarah Ebery BSc (Hons), MEd
Age range: 2 –18
No. of pupils: 405
Fees: Day £7,365–£10,485

Moyles Court School
Moyles Court, Ringwood, Hampshire BH24 3NF
Tel: 01425 472856
Headmaster: Mr Dean
Age range: 3–16
Fees: Day £3,285–£4,650 FB £6,690–£7,740

New Forest Small School
1 Southampton Road, Lyndhurst, Hampshire SO43 7BU
Tel: 02380 284 415
Headteacher: Mr Nicholas Alp
Age range: 3–16

Norman Court
West Tytherley, Stockbridge, Hampshire SP5 1NH
Tel: 01980 322 322

Portsmouth High School GDST
Kent Road, Southsea, Portsmouth, Hampshire PO5 3EQ
Tel: 023 9282 6714
Headmistress: Mrs Jane Prescott BSc NPQH
Age range: G3–18
No. of pupils: 500
Fees: Day £2,722–£4,550

Prince's Mead School
Worthy Park House, Kings Worthy, Winchester, Hampshire SO21 1AN
Tel: 01962 888000
Headmistress: Miss Penelope Kirk
Age range: 4–11
No. of pupils: 270
Fees: Day £9,600–£14,640

Ringwood Waldorf School
Folly Farm Lane, Ashley, Ringwood, Hampshire BH24 2NN
Tel: 01425 472664
Age range: 3–18
No. of pupils: 235
Fees: Day £3,622–£7,825

Rookwood School
Weyhill Road, Andover, Hampshire SP10 3AL
Tel: 01264 325900
Headmistress: Mrs L Whetstone MA
Age range: 3–16
Fees: Day £7,770–£12,780 FB £19,545–£22,875

Salesian College
Reading Road, Farnborough, Hampshire GU14 6PA
Tel: 01252 893000
Headmaster: Mr P A Wilson BA(Hons), MA, CertEd
Age range: B11–18 G16–18
No. of pupils: 650 VIth140
Fees: Day £9,000

Sherborne House School
Lakewood Road, Chandlers Ford, Eastleigh, Hampshire SO53 1EU
Tel: 023 8025 2440
Head Teacher: Mrs Heather Hopson-Hill
Age range: 3–11
No. of pupils: 293
Fees: Day £1,044–£8,730

Sherfield School
Sherfield-on-Loddon, Hook, Hampshire RG27 0HU
Tel: +44 (0)1256 884 800
Headmaster: Mr Dick Jaine
Age range: 3 months–18 years
No. of pupils: 445 VIth16
Fees: Day £7,350–£13,890 FB £20,946

St John's College
Grove Road South, Southsea, Portsmouth, Hampshire PO5 3QW
Tel: 023 9281 5118
Headmaster: Mr Timothy Bayley
Age range: 2–18
No. of pupils: 600 VIth86
Fees: Day £9,225–£11,340 FB £24,450–£26,295

ST NEOT'S SCHOOL
For further details see p. 218
St Neot's Road, Eversley, Hampshire RG27 0PN
Tel: 0118 9739650
Email: admissions@stneotsprep.co.uk
Website: www.stneotsprep.co.uk
Head of School: Mrs Deborah Henderson
Age range: 1–13 years
No. of pupils: 327
Fees: Day £4,896–£14,994

St Nicholas' School
Redfields House, Redfields Lane, Church Crookham, Fleet, Hampshire GU52 0RF
Tel: 01252 850121
Headmistress: Mrs A V Whatmough BA, CertEd
Age range: B3–7 G3–16
No. of pupils: 370

St Swithun's Junior School
Alresford Road, Winchester, Hampshire SO21 1HA
Tel: 01962 835750
Headmistress: Mrs R Lyons-Smith BSc, PGCE, MBA
Age range: B3–7 G3–11
No. of pupils: 183
Fees: Day £1,655–£4,265

St Swithun's School
Alresford Road, Winchester, Hampshire SO21 1HA
Tel: 01962 835700
Headmistress: Jane Gandee MA(Cantab)
Age range: G11–18
No. of pupils: G525 VIth85
Fees: Day £17,640 FB £28,290

St Winifred's School
17-19 Winn Road, Southampton, Hampshire SO17 1EJ
Tel: 023 8055 7352
Head Teacher: Mr M Brogan BEd,CertSpNeeds
Age range: 3–11
Fees: Day £6,330

St. Mary's Independent School
57 Midanbury Lane, Bitterne Park, Southampton, Hampshire SO18 4DJ
Tel: 023 8067 1267
Age range: 3–16
No. of pupils: 470
Fees: Day £1,750–£2,350

Stockton House School
Stockton Avenue, Fleet, Hampshire GU51 4NS
Tel: 01252 616323
Early Years Manager: Mrs Jenny Bounds BA EYPS
Age range: 2–5
Fees: Day £25.50–£70

The Children's House and Grantham Farm Montessori School
Grantham Farm, Baughurst, Tadley, Hampshire RG26 5JS
Tel: 0118 981 5821
Head Teacher: Ms Emma Wetherley
Age range: 3–8

The Gregg School
Townhill Park House, Cutbush Lane, Southampton, Hampshire SO18 2GF
Tel: 023 8047 2133
Headteacher: Mrs S Sellers PGDip, MSc, BSc(Hons), NPQH, PGCE
Age range: 11–16
No. of pupils: 300
Fees: Day £11,970

The Grey House School
Mount Pleasant, Hartley Wintney,
Hampshire RG27 8PW
Tel: 01252 842353
Head: Mrs C E Allen BEd(Cantab)
Age range: 4–11+
Fees: Day £7,365–£8,994

The King's School
Lakesmere House, Allington Lane,
Fair Oak, Eastleigh, Southampton,
Hampshire SO50 7DB
Tel: 023 8060 0986
Age range: 3–16
No. of pupils: 256
Fees: Day £3,900–£6,840

The Pilgrims' School
3 The Close, Winchester,
Hampshire SO23 9LT
Tel: 01962 854189
Headmaster: Mr Tom Burden
Age range: B4–13
No. of pupils: 250
Fees: Day £18,150–£18,690 FB £23,580

The Portsmouth Grammar School
High Street, Portsmouth,
Hampshire PO1 2LN
Tel: +44 (0)23 9236 0036
Headmaster: Mr J E Priory MA
Age range: 2–18
No. of pupils: 1556 VIth336
Fees: Day £9,510–£14,817

The Stroud School
Highwood House, Highwood Lane,
Romsey, Hampshire SO51 9ZH
Tel: 01794 513231
Headmaster: Mr Joel Worrall
Age range: 3–13

The Westgate School
Cheriton Road, Winchester,
Hampshire SO22 5AZ
Tel: 01962 854757
Headteacher: Mr P Nicholson
Age range: 11–16
Fees: WB £7,380 FB £7,865

Twyford School
Twyford, Winchester,
Hampshire SO21 1NW
Tel: 01962 712269
Headmaster: Dr S J Bailey
BEd, PhD, FRSA
Age range: 3–13
Fees: Day £6,726–£18,570 WB £4,800

Walhampton
Walhampton, Lymington,
Hampshire SO41 5ZG
Tel: 01590 613 300
Headmaster: Mr Titus Mills
Age range: 2–13
No. of pupils: 353
Fees: Day £8,025–£15,555 FB £20,790

Wessex Tutors
44 Shirley Road, Southampton,
Hampshire SO15 3EU
Tel: 023 8033 4719
Principal: Mrs J E White BA(London)
Age range: 14–21
Fees: Day £800–£10,000

West Hill Park Preparatory School
Titchfield, Fareham,
Hampshire PO14 4BS
Tel: 01329 842356
Headmaster: A P Ramsay
BEd(Hons), MSc
Age range: 2–13
No. of pupils: 288
Fees: Day £8,985–£14,985
FB £13,785–£19,785

Winchester College
College Street, Winchester,
Hampshire SO23 9NA
Tel: 01962 621247
Headmaster: Dr. T R Hands
Age range: B13–18
No. of pupils: 690 VIth280
Fees: FB £36,678

Woodhill School, Botley
Brook Lane, Botley, Southampton,
Hampshire SO30 2ER
Tel: 01489 781112
Head Teacher: Mrs M Dacombe
Age range: 3–11
No. of pupils: 100
Fees: Day £2,199–£4,965

Yateley Manor School
51 Reading Road, Yateley,
Hampshire GU46 7UQ
Tel: 01252 405500
Headmaster: Mr R J Williams MA(Hons)
Edinburgh, PGCE Bedford
Age range: 3–13
No. of pupils: 453
Fees: Day £4,500–£12,150

Isle of Wight

Priory School
Beatrice Avenue, Whippingham,
Isle of Wight PO32 6LP
Tel: 01983 861222
Principal: Mr E J Matyjaszek
Age range: 5–18
Fees: Day £3,360–£7,200

Ryde School with Upper Chine
Queen's Road, Ryde, Isle
of Wight PO33 3BE
Tel: 01983 617970
Headmaster: Mr M. A. Waldron MA
Age range: 2½–18
No. of pupils: 742
Fees: Day £12,375 WB
£24,330 FB £27,255

Kent

Ashford School
East Hill, Ashford, Kent TN24 8PB
Tel: 01233 739030
Head: Mr M R Buchanan BSc(Hons),
CertEd, NPQH, CPhys
Age range: 3 months–18 years
No. of pupils: 835 VIth170
Fees: Day £8,400–£16,200
WB £28,500 FB £32,400

Beech Grove School
Beech Grove Bruderhof, Sandwich
Road, Nonington, Dover, Kent CT15 4HH
Tel: 01304 842980
Head: Mr Benjamin Shirky
Age range: 4–14
No. of pupils: 63

Beechwood Sacred Heart
12 Pembury Road, Tunbridge
Wells, Kent TN2 3QD
Tel: 01892 532747
Headmaster: Mr Aaron
Lennon BA(Hons)
Age range: 3–18
No. of pupils: 400 VIth70
Fees: Day £9,060–£15,936
WB £23,460 FB £26,460

Benenden School
Cranbrook, Kent TN17 4AA
Tel: 01580 240592
Headmistress: Mrs S Price
Age range: G11–18
No. of pupils: 550
Fees: FB £35,700

BETHANY SCHOOL
For further details see p. 180
Curtisden Green, Goudhurst, Cranbrook, Kent TN17 1LB
Tel: 01580 211273
Email: registrar@bethanyschool.org.uk
Website: www.bethanyschool.org.uk
Headmaster: Mr Francie Healy BSc, HDipEd, NPQH
Age range: 11–18 years
No. of pupils: 313 VIth98
Fees: Day £16,245–£17,925 WB £25,185–£27,825 FB £27,165–£30,585

Bronte School
Mayfield, 7 Pelham Road, Gravesend, Kent DA11 0HN
Tel: 01474 533805
Headmaster: Mr R Dyson
Age range: 4–11
No. of pupils: 120
Fees: Day £7,950

Bryony School
Marshall Road, Rainham, Gillingham, Kent ME8 0AJ
Tel: 01634 231511
Joint Head: Mr D Edmunds
Age range: 2–11
No. of pupils: 168
Fees: Day £5,862–£6,352

Canterbury Steiner School
Garlinge Green, Chartham, Canterbury, Kent CT4 5RU
Tel: 01227 738285
Age range: 3–18
Fees: Day £3,246–£4,405.50

CATS Canterbury
68 New Dover Road, Canterbury, Kent CT1 3LQ
Tel: +44 (0)1227866540
Principal: Mr. James Slocombe BSc(Hons), PGCE, QTS, MA, FRSA
Age range: 14–18
No. of pupils: 400

Chartfield School
45 Minster Road, Westgate on Sea, Kent CT8 8DA
Tel: 01843 831716
Head & Proprietor: Miss L P Shipley
Age range: 4–11
No. of pupils: 50
Fees: Day £2,580–£3,000

Cobham Hall School
Cobham, Kent DA12 3BL
Tel: 01474 823371
Headmistress: Dr Sandra Coates-Smith BSc, PhD
Age range: G11–18
No. of pupils: 180

Cranbrook School
Waterloo Road, Cranbrook, Kent TN17 3JD
Tel: 01580 711800
Head Teacher: Mr John Weeds
Age range: 13–18
No. of pupils: 757 VIth307
Fees: FB £14,648–£17,572

Derwent Lodge School for Girls
Somerhill, Tonbridge, Kent TN11 0NJ
Tel: 01732 352124
Head of School: Mrs Helen Hoffmann
Age range: G7–11
No. of pupils: 134
Fees: Day £12,675

Dover College
Effingham Crescent, Dover, Kent CT17 9RH
Tel: 01304 205969
Headmaster: Mr Gareth Doodes MA (Hons)
Age range: 3–18
No. of pupils: 301
Fees: Day £7,005 WB £19,590 FB £21,420

Dulwich Preparatory School
Coursehorn, Cranbrook, Kent TN17 3NP
Tel: 01580 712179
Headmaster: Mr Paul David BEd(Hons)
Age range: 3–13
No. of pupils: 535
Fees: Day £4,890–£14,400

Elliott Park School
18-20 Marina Drive, Minster, Sheerness, Kent ME12 2DP
Tel: 01795 873372
Head: Ms Colleen Hiller
Age range: 3–11
No. of pupils: 65
Fees: Day £5,025

Fosse Bank School
Mountains, Noble Tree Road, Hildenborough, Tonbridge, Kent TN11 8ND
Tel: 01732 834212
Headmistress: Mrs Lovatt-Young
Age range: 3–11
No. of pupils: 124
Fees: Day £1,560–£10,671

Gad's Hill School
Higham, Rochester, Medway, Kent ME3 7PA
Tel: 01474 822366
Headmaster: Mr D G Craggs BSc, MA, NPQH, FCollP, FRSA
Age range: 3–16
No. of pupils: 370
Fees: Day £6,000–£7,600

Haddon Dene School
57 Gladstone Road, Broadstairs, Kent CT10 2HY
Tel: 01843 861176
Head: Mrs E Rowe
Age range: 3–11
No. of pupils: 200
Fees: Day £4,950–£6,135

Hilden Grange School
62 Dry Hill Park Road, Tonbridge, Kent TN10 3BX
Tel: 01732 351169
Headmaster: Mr J Withers BA(Hons)
Age range: 3–13
Fees: Day £9,780–£12,950

Hilden Oaks School & Nursery
38 Dry Hill Park Road, Tonbridge, Kent TN10 3BU
Tel: 01732 353941
Head of School: Mrs. K J M Joiner
Fees: Day £8,985–£11,988

Holmewood House School
Langton Green, Tunbridge Wells, Kent TN3 0EB
Tel: 01892 860006
Headmaster: Mr J D B Marjoribanks BEd
Age range: 3–13
No. of pupils: 439
Fees: Day £2,160–£17,460 WB £20,640

KENT COLLEGE
For further details see p. 198
Whitstable Road, Canterbury, Kent CT2 9DT
Tel: 01227 763231
Email: admissions@kentcollege.co.uk
Website: www.kentcollege.com
Executive Head Master: Dr D J Lamper
Age range: 3–18
No. of pupils: 702
Fees: Day £15,981–£17,691 FB £32,748–£33,480

Kent College Junior School
Harbledown, Canterbury, Kent CT2 9AQ
Tel: 01227 762436
Headmaster: Mr Andrew Carter
Age range: 3–11
No. of pupils: 190
Fees: Day £9,939–£15,390 FB £24,375

Kent College Pembury
Old Church Road, Pembury, Tunbridge Wells, Kent TN2 4AX
Tel: +44 (0)1892 822006
Headmistress: Mrs Sally-Anne Huang MA(Oxon), MSc, PGCE
Age range: G3–18
No. of pupils: 650 VIth102
Fees: Day £7,887–£17,322 FB £21,471–£27,924

King's Preparatory School, Rochester
King Edward Road, Rochester, Medway, Kent ME1 1UB
Tel: 01634 888577
Headmaster: Mr R Overend
Age range: 8–13
No. of pupils: 210
Fees: Day £12,420–£14,100 FB £20,580

King's Pre-Preparatory School, Rochester
Chadlington House, Lockington Grove, Rochester, Kent ME1 1RH
Tel: 01634 888566
Headmistress: Mrs C Openshaw
Age range: 3–8
No. of pupils: 159
Fees: Day £9,570–£10,380

King's School, Rochester
Satis House, Boley Hill, Rochester, Kent ME1 1TE
Tel: 01634 888555
Principal: Mr J Walker
Age range: 13–18
No. of pupils: 260 VIth208
Fees: Day £6,070–£7,200 FB £9,860–£10,000

Linton Park School
3 Eccleston Road, Tovil, Maidstone, Kent ME17 4HT
Tel: 01622 740820
Headteacher: Mr C Allen
Age range: 7–18
No. of pupils: 134

Lorenden Preparatory School
Painter's Forstal, Faversham, Kent ME13 0EN
Tel: 01795 590030
Headmistress: Mrs R Simmonds
Age range: 3–11
No. of pupils: 100
Fees: Day £7,374–£10,680

Marlborough House School
High Street, Hawkhurst, Kent TN18 4PY
Tel: 01580 753555
Headmaster: Mr Martyn Ward
Age range: 2–13
No. of pupils: 334
Fees: Day £2,808–£14,700

Meredale Independent Primary School
Solomon Road, Rainham, Gillingham, Kent ME8 8EB
Tel: 01634 231405
Headteacher: Miss Michelle Ingledew
Age range: 3–11
No. of pupils: 53
Fees: Day £5,100

NORTHBOURNE PARK SCHOOL
For further details see p. 208
Betteshanger, Deal, Kent CT14 0NW
Tel: 01304 611215/218
Email: admissions@northbournepark.com
Website: www.northbournepark.com
Headmaster: Mr Sebastian Rees BA(Hons), PGCE, NPQH
Age range: 3–13
No. of pupils: 149
Fees: Day £7,632–£16,326 WB £20,376 FB £23,673

Radnor House, Sevenoaks
Combe Bank Drive, Sevenoaks, Kent TN14 6AE
Tel: 01959 563720
Head: Mr David Paton BComm (Hons) PGCE MA
Age range: 2½–18
No. of pupils: 250

Rochester Independent College
Star Hill, Rochester, Medway, Kent ME1 1XF
Tel: 01634 828115
Principals: Alistair Brownlow, Brian Pain, Pauline Bailey
Age range: 11–19
No. of pupils: 306 VIth233
Fees: Day £12,000–£16,500 WB £25,650–£27,300 FB £27,450–£29,100

Rose Hill School
Coniston Avenue, Tunbridge Wells, Kent TN4 9SY
Tel: 01892 525591
Headmaster: Mr D Westcombe BA, PGCE
Age range: 3–13
Fees: Day £3,040–£4,130

Russell House School
Station Road, Otford, Sevenoaks, Kent TN14 5QU
Tel: 01959 522352
Headmistress: Mrs Alison Cooke
Age range: 2–11
Fees: Day £4,650–£9,840

Sackville School
Tonbridge Rd, Hildenborough, Tonbridge, Kent TN11 9HN
Tel: 01732 838888
Headmaster: Mr Justin Foster-Gandey BSc (hons)
Age range: 11–18
No. of pupils: 184 VIth35
Fees: Day £13,620

Saint Ronan's School
Water Lane, Hawkhurst, Kent TN18 5DJ
Tel: 01580 752271
Headmaster: William Trelawny-Vernon BSc(Hons)
Age range: 3–13
No. of pupils: 300
Fees: Day £6,951–£11,892

Sevenoaks Preparatory School
Godden Green, Sevenoaks, Kent TN15 0JU
Tel: 01732 762336
Headmaster: Mr Luke Harrison
Age range: 2–13
No. of pupils: 388
Fees: Day £3,552–£11,910

Sevenoaks School
High Street, Sevenoaks, Kent TN13 1HU
Tel: +44 (0)1732 455133
Head: Dr Katy Ricks MA, DPhil
Age range: 11–18
No. of pupils: 1054 VIth423
Fees: Day £21,591–£24,516 FB £34,479–£37,404

Shernold School
Hill Place, Queens Avenue, Maidstone, Kent ME16 0ER
Tel: 01622 752868
Head Teacher: Ms. Sandra Dinsmore
Age range: 3–11
No. of pupils: 142
Fees: Day £3,525–£4,200

Solefield School
Solefield Road, Sevenoaks, Kent TN13 1PH
Tel: 01732 452142
Headmaster: Mr D A Philps BSc(Hons)
Age range: B4–13
No. of pupils: 180
Fees: Day £9,990–£12,060

Somerhill Pre-Prep
Somerhill, Five Oak Green Road, Tonbridge, Kent TN11 0NJ
Tel: 01732 352124
Headmistress: Mrs J Ruth Sorensen BEd(Hons), CertEd
Age range: 3–7
No. of pupils: 245

Spring Grove School
Harville Road, Wye, Ashford, Kent TN25 5EZ
Tel: 01233 812337
Headmaster: Mr Bill Jones
Age range: 2–11
No. of pupils: 194
Fees: Day £2,050–£3,125

St Andrew's School
24-28 Watts Avenue, Rochester, Medway, Kent ME1 1SA
Tel: 01634 843479
Principal: Mrs E Steinmann-Gilbert
Age range: 2–11
No. of pupils: 367
Fees: Day £6,672–£7,059

St Christopher's School
New Dover Road, Canterbury, Kent CT1 3DT
Tel: 01227 462960
The Master: Mr D Evans
Age range: 3–11
Fees: Day £7,600

St Edmund's Junior School
St Thomas Hill, Canterbury, Kent CT2 8HU
Tel: 01227 475600
Master: R G Bacon BA(Hons)(Durham)
Age range: 3–13
No. of pupils: 230
Fees: Day £6,969–£14,211 WB £18,969 FB £20,817

St Edmund's School
St Thomas' Hill, Canterbury, Kent CT2 8HU
Tel: 01227 475601
Head: Louise Moelwyn-Hughes
Age range: 3–18
No. of pupils: 535
Fees: Day £18,651 FB £29,781

St Faith's at Ash School
5 The Street, Ash, Canterbury, Kent CT3 2HH
Tel: 01304 813409
Headmaster: Mr Lawrence Groves
Age range: 2–11
No. of pupils: 225
Fees: Day £6,435–£8,100

St Joseph's Convent Prep School
46 Old Road East, Gravesend, Kent DA12 1NR
Tel: 01474 533012
Head Teacher: Mrs Carola Timney
Age range: 3–11
No. of pupils: 146
Fees: Day £6,655

ST LAWRENCE COLLEGE
For further details see p. 216
Ramsgate, Kent CT11 7AE
Tel: 01843 572931
Email: admissions@slcuk.com
Website: www.slcuk.com
Principal: Mr Antony Spencer
Age range: 3–18
No. of pupils: 640 VIth115
Fees: Day £7,470–£18,495 FB £26,055–£34,635

St Michael's Preparatory School
Otford Court, Otford,
Sevenoaks, Kent TN14 5SA
Tel: 01959 522137
Headteacher: Mrs Jill Aisher
Age range: 2–13
No. of pupils: 472
Fees: Day £2,064–£12,555

Steephill School
Off Castle Hill, Fawkham,
Longfield, Kent DA3 7BG
Tel: 01474 702107
Head: Mrs C Birtwell BSc, MBA, PGCE
Age range: 3–11
No. of pupils: 131
Fees: Day £6,860

Sutton Valence Preparatory School
Chart Sutton, Maidstone, Kent ME17 3RF
Tel: 01622 842117
Head: Miss C Corkran
Age range: 3–11
No. of pupils: 320
Fees: Day £8,700–£13,365

SUTTON VALENCE SCHOOL
For further details see p. 222
North Street, Sutton
Valence, Kent ME17 3HL
Tel: 01622 845200
Email: enquiries@svs.org.uk
Website: www.svs.org.uk
Headmaster: Bruce Grindlay MA
Cantab, MusB, FRCO, CHM
Age range: 11–18
No. of pupils: 570

The Granville School
2 Bradbourne Park Road,
Sevenoaks, Kent TN13 3LJ
Tel: 01732 453039
Headmistress: Mrs J Scott BEd(Cantab)
Age range: B3–4 G3–11
No. of pupils: 195
Fees: Day £5,184–£13,371

The Junior King's School, Canterbury
Milner Court, Sturry,
Canterbury, Kent CT2 0AY
Tel: 01227 714000
Headmaster: Mr Peter Wells BEd(Hons)
Age range: 3–13
Fees: Day £8,610–£14,610 FB £19,830

The King's School, Canterbury
The Precincts, Canterbury, Kent CT1 2ES
Tel: 01227 595501
Head: Mr P Roberts
Age range: 13–18
No. of pupils: 858 VIth385
Fees: Day £26,700 FB £35,295

The Mead School
16 Frant Road, Tunbridge
Wells, Kent TN2 5SN
Tel: 01892 525837
Headmistress: Mrs A
Culley CertEd(Oxon)
Age range: 3–11
No. of pupils: 188
Fees: Day £3,900–£9,945

The New Beacon School
Brittains Lane, Sevenoaks,
Kent TN13 2PB
Tel: 01732 452131
Headmaster: Mr M Piercy BA(Hons)
Age range: B4–13
No. of pupils: 400
Fees: Day £9,405–£12,135

Tonbridge School
Tonbridge, Kent TN9 1JP
Tel: 01732 365555
Headmaster: T H P Haynes
Age range: B13–18
No. of pupils: 785 VIth317
Fees: Day £27,216 FB £36,288

Walthamstow Hall Pre-Prep and Junior School
Sevenoaks, Kent TN13 3LD
Tel: 01732 451334
Headmistress: Mrs Jill
Milner MA(Oxford)
Age range: G2–11
No. of pupils: 218
Fees: Day £1,230–£9,990

Walthamstow Hall School
Sevenoaks, Kent TN13 3UL
Tel: 01732 451334
Headmistress: Mrs J Milner MA(Oxford)
Age range: G2–18
No. of pupils: 500 VIth80
Fees: Day £8,070–£13,710

Wellesley House
114 Ramsgate Road,
Broadstairs, Kent CT10 2DG
Tel: 01843 862991
Headmaster: Mr S T P O'Malley
MA(Hons), PGCE
Age range: 7–13
No. of pupils: 133
Fees: Day £14,985–£17,850 FB £22,575

Yardley Court
Somerhill, Five Oak Green Road,
Tonbridge, Kent TN11 0NJ
Tel: 01732 352124
Headmaster: J T Coakley
MA, BA(Hons), PGCE
Age range: B7–13
No. of pupils: 260
Fees: Day £13,150

Surrey

ABERDOUR SCHOOL
For further details see p. 178
Brighton Road, Burgh Heath,
Tadworth, Surrey KT20 6AJ
Tel: 01737 354119
Email: enquiries@
aberdourschool.co.uk
Website:
www.aberdourschool.co.uk
Headmaster: Mr S. D. Collins
Age range: 2–13 years
No. of pupils: 357
Fees: Day £1,350–£4,650

ACS Cobham International School
Heywood, Portsmouth Road,
Cobham, Surrey KT11 1BL
Tel: +44 (0) 1932 867251
Age range: 2–18
No. of pupils: 1460
Fees: Day £10,690–£25,050
FB £36,810–£39,310

ACS Egham International School
Woodlee, London Road,
Egham, Surrey TW20 0HS
Tel: +44 (0) 1784 430 800
Age range: 3–18
Fees: Day £7,080–£24,020

Aldro School
Shackleford, Godalming,
Surrey GU8 6AS
Tel: 01483 810266
Headmaster: Mr D W N
Aston BA(Hons), PGCE
Age range: B7–13
No. of pupils: 220
Fees: Day £14,610 FB £18,795

Amesbury
Hazel Grove, Hindhead,
Surrey GU26 6BL
Tel: 01428 604322
Headmaster: Mr Nigel Taylor MA
Age range: 2–13
No. of pupils: 360

Barfield School
Guildford Road, Runfold,
Farnham, Surrey GU10 1PB
Tel: 01252 782271
Head of School: James Reid
Age range: 2–13 years
No. of pupils: 170
Fees: Day £3,168–£13,620

Barrow Hills School
Roke Lane, Witley, Godalming,
Surrey GU8 5NY
Tel: +44 (0)1428 683639
Headmaster: Mr Sean Skehan
Age range: 2–13
No. of pupils: 230
Fees: Day £14,985

Belmont Preparatory School
Feldemore, Holmbury St Mary,
Dorking, Surrey RH5 6LQ
Tel: 01306 730852
Headmistress: Mrs Helen Skrine
BA, PGCE, NPQH, FRSA
Age range: 2–13
No. of pupils: 227
Fees: Day £6,120–£10,428 WB £15,345

Bishopsgate School
Bishopsgate Road, Englefield
Green, Egham, Surrey TW20 0YJ
Tel: 01784 432109
Headmaster: Mr Andrew
Cowell BEd, CPSE
Age range: 3–13
Fees: Day £4,500–£12,726

Bloo House School
The Lodge (Moore Place), Portsmouth Road, Esher, Surrey KT10 9LN
Tel: 01372 477113
Head of School: Ms Melissa Carter
Age range: 5–11
No. of pupils: 32
Fees: Day £5,200

Box Hill School
Old London Road, Mickleham, Dorking, Surrey RH5 6EA
Tel: 01372 373382
Headmaster: Mr Corydon Lowde
Age range: 11–18
No. of pupils: 425 VIth96
Fees: Day £16,140–£17,170 WB £24,600–£25,800 FB £29,970–£35,850

Bramley School
Chequers Lane, Walton-on-the-Hill, Tadworth, Surrey KT20 7ST
Tel: 01737 812004
Head of School: Ms Paula Burgess
Age range: G3–11
No. of pupils: 78
Fees: Day £5,355–£12,285

Caterham School
Harestone Valley, Caterham, Surrey CR3 6YA
Tel: 01883 343028
Head: Mr C. W. Jones MA(Cantab)
Age range: 11–18
No. of pupils: VIth321

Charterhouse
Godalming, Surrey GU7 2DX
Tel: +44 (0)1483 291501
Headmaster: Mr Andrew Turner BA, LLM
Age range: B13–18 G16–18
No. of pupils: 812

Chinthurst School
Tadworth Street, Tadworth, Surrey KT20 5QZ
Tel: 01737 812011
Head: Miss Catherine Trundle
Age range: B3–11
No. of pupils: 170
Fees: Day £1,650–£4,350

City of London Freemen's School
Ashtead Park, Ashtead, Surrey KT21 1ET
Tel: 01372 277933
Headmaster: Mr R Martin
Age range: 7–18
No. of pupils: 877 VIth213
Fees: Day £10,872–£14,598 FB £23,238

Claremont Fan Court School
Claremont Drive, Esher, Surrey KT10 9LY
Tel: 01372 467841
Head of Senior School: Mr Jonathan Insall-Reid
Age range: 2½–18
No. of pupils: 780
Fees: Day £4,995–£16,530

Coworth Flexlands School
Chertsey Road, Chobham, Woking, Surrey GU24 8TE
Tel: 01276 855707
Headmistress: Mrs Anne Sweeney
Age range: B2½–7 G2½–11
No. of pupils: 150
Fees: Day £8,250–£12,825

Cranleigh Preparatory School
Horseshoe Lane, Cranleigh, Surrey GU6 8QH
Tel: 01483 274199
Headmaster: Mr M T Wilson BSc
Age range: 7–13
No. of pupils: 290
Fees: Day £11,385 FB £14,025

CRANLEIGH SCHOOL
For further details see p. 186
Horseshoe Lane, Cranleigh, Surrey GU6 8QQ
Tel: +44 (0) 1483 273666
Email: admissions@cranleigh.org
Website: www.cranleigh.org
Headmaster: Mr Martin Reader MA, MPhil, MBA
Age range: 7–18 (including Prep School)
No. of pupils: 626 VIth250
Fees: Day £29,985 FB £36,615

Cranmore School
Epsom Road, West Horsley, Surrey KT24 6AT
Tel: 01483 280340
Headmaster: Mr Michael Connolly BSc, BA, MA, MEd
Age range: 2½–13
No. of pupils: 479
Fees: Day £11,850

Danes Hill School
Leatherhead Road, Oxshott, Surrey KT22 0JG
Tel: 01372 842509
Headmaster: Mr W Murdock BA
Age range: 3–13
No. of pupils: 872
Fees: Day £6,405–£17,745

Danesfield Manor School
Rydens Avenue, Walton-on-Thames, Surrey KT12 3JB
Tel: 01932 220930
Principal: Mrs Helen Chalmers
Age range: 2–11
No. of pupils: 170
Fees: Day £8,400

Downsend School
1 Leatherhead Road, Leatherhead, Surrey KT22 8TJ
Tel: 01372 372197
Headmaster: Mr Ian Thorpe
Age range: 2–13
No. of pupils: 740
Fees: Day £13,455

Downsend School
Ashtead Lodge, 22 Oakfield Road, Ashtead, Surrey KT21 2RE
Tel: 01372 385439
Head Teacher: Mrs K Barrett
Age range: 2–6
No. of pupils: 66
Fees: Day £2,190–£8,250

Downsend School
Epsom Lodge, 6 Norman Avenue, Epsom, Surrey KT17 3AB
Tel: 01372 385438
Head Teacher: Miss J Birchall
Age range: 2–6
No. of pupils: 110
Fees: Day £2,325–£11,640

Downsend School
Leatherhead Lodge, Epsom Road, Leatherhead, Surrey KT22 8ST
Tel: 01372 372123
Headteacher: Mrs Gill Brooks
Age range: 2 –6
Fees: Day £6,780–£8,250

Drayton House School
35 Austen Road, Guildford, Surrey GU1 3NP
Tel: 01483 504707
Headmistress: Mrs J Tyson-Jones Froebel Cert.Ed. London University
Age range: 3 months–7 years
Fees: Day £4,420–£12,500

Duke of Kent School
Peaslake Road, Ewhurst, Surrey GU6 7NS
Tel: 01483 277313
Head: Mrs Judith Fremont-Barnes
Age range: 3–16
No. of pupils: 234
Fees: Day £4,860–£14,130 WB £13,350–£16,770 FB £15,735–£18,855

Dunottar School
High Trees Road, Reigate, Surrey RH2 7EL
Tel: 01737 761945
Head of School: Mr Mark Tottman
Age range: 11–18
No. of pupils: 319
Fees: Day £15,492

Edgeborough
Frensham, Farnham, Surrey GU10 3AH
Tel: 01252 792495
Headmaster: Mr C J Davies BA
Age range: 2–13
No. of pupils: 285
Fees: Day £9,105–£14,850 WB £16,752–£18,282

Emberhurst School
94 Ember Lane, Esher, Surrey KT10 8EN
Tel: 020 8398 2933
Headmistress: Mrs P Chadwick BEd
Age range: 2 +–7+
No. of pupils: 70
Fees: Day £2,265–£6,495

Epsom College
Epsom, Surrey KT17 4JQ
Tel: 01372 821000
Headmaster: Mr Jay A Piggot MA
Age range: 13–18
No. of pupils: 730
Fees: Day £21,255 FB £31,098

Essendene Lodge School
Essendene Road, Caterham, Surrey CR3 5PB
Tel: 01883 348349
Head Teacher: Mrs J Wermig
Age range: 2–11
No. of pupils: 153
Fees: Day £2,775–£5,550

Ewell Castle School
Church Street, Ewell, Epsom, Surrey KT17 2AW
Tel: 020 8393 1413
Principal: Peter Harris
Age range: B3–18 G3-11–16-18
No. of pupils: 531
Fees: Day £6,750–£13,020

Feltonfleet School
Cobham, Surrey KT11 1DR
Tel: 01932 862264
Headmaster: P C Ward
Age range: 3–13
No. of pupils: 356
Fees: Day £7,680–£11,250 WB £15,750

Focus School – Hindhead Campus
Tilford Road, Hindhead, Surrey GU26 6SJ
Tel: 01428 601800
Head: Mr S Hardy
Age range: 8–18
No. of pupils: 90

Frensham Heights
Rowledge, Farnham, Surrey GU10 4EA
Tel: 01252 792561
Headmaster: Mr Andrew Fisher BA, MEd, FRSA
Age range: 3–18
No. of pupils: 497 VIth105
Fees: Day £5,205–£15,300 FB £19,485–£22,680

Glenesk School
Ockham Road North, East Horsley, Surrey KT24 6NS
Tel: 01483 282329
Headmistress: Mrs S Christie-Hall
Age range: 2–7
Fees: Day £1,350–£8,112

GORDON'S SCHOOL
For further details see p. 192
West End, Woking, Surrey GU24 9PT
Tel: 01276 858084
Email: registrar@gordons.surrey.sch.uk
Website: www.gordons.surrey.sch.uk
Head Teacher: Andrew Moss MEd
Age range: 11–18
No. of pupils: 840 VIth250
Fees: FB £15,135–£16,167

Greenfield
Brooklyn Road, Woking, Surrey GU22 7TP
Tel: 01483 772525
Headmistress: Mrs Tania Botting BEd
Age range: 3–11
No. of pupils: 179
Fees: Day £4,284–£9,450

Guildford High School
London Road, Guildford, Surrey GU1 1SJ
Tel: 01483 561440
Headmistress: Mrs F J Boulton BSc, MA
Age range: G4–18
No. of pupils: 980 VIth160
Fees: Day £10,176–£16,512

Hall Grove School
London Road, Bagshot, Surrey GU19 5HZ
Tel: 01276 473059
Headmaster: Mr A R Graham BSc, PGCE
Age range: 3–13
Fees: Day £8,880–£12,480

Halstead Preparatory School
Woodham Rise, Woking, Surrey GU21 4EE
Tel: 01483 772682
Headmistress: Mrs P Austin
Age range: G3–11
No. of pupils: 220
Fees: Day £2,673–£12,162

Hampton Court House
Hampton Court Road, East Molesey, Surrey KT8 9BS
Tel: 020 8943 0889
Headmaster: Mr Guy Holloway
Age range: 3–16
No. of pupils: VIth20
Fees: Day £7,842–£10,017

Hawley Place School
Fernhill Road, Blackwater, Camberley, Surrey GU17 9HU
Tel: 01276 32028
Age range: B2–11 G2–16
No. of pupils: 370
Fees: Day £4,446–£11,400

Hazelwood School
Wolf's Hill, Limpsfield, Oxted, Surrey RH8 0QU
Tel: 01883 712194
Head: Mrs Maxine Shaw
Age range: 2–13
No. of pupils: 399
Fees: Day £3,585–£11,100

Hoe Bridge School
Hoe Place, Old Woking Road, Woking, Surrey GU22 8JE
Tel: 01483 760018 & 01483 772194
Head: Mr N Arkell BSc
Age range: 2–14
Fees: Day £5,355–£14,080

Hurtwood House
Holmbury St Mary, Dorking, Surrey RH5 6NU
Tel: 01483 279000
Principal: Mr Cosmo Jackson
Age range: 16–18
No. of pupils: 300
Fees: FB £30,600–£35,100

International School of London (ISL) Surrey
Old Woking Road, Woking, Surrey GU22 8HY
Tel: +44 (0)1483 750409
Campus Principal & Head of Secondary: Richard Parker
Age range: 2–18 years
No. of pupils: 252
Fees: Day £17,700–£21,900

King Edward's Witley
Godalming, Surrey GU8 5SG
Tel: +44 (0)1428 686700
Headmaster: Mr John Attwater MA
Age range: 11–18
No. of pupils: 410 VIth185
Fees: Day £19,950 FB £29,595

Kingswood House School
56 West Hill, Epsom, Surrey KT19 8LG
Tel: 01372 723590
Headmaster: Mr Peter Brooks MA, BEd(Hons)
Age range: B3–16 G3–7
No. of pupils: 202

LANESBOROUGH
For further details see p. 202
Maori Road, Guildford, Surrey GU1 2EL
Tel: 01483 880489
Email: admissions@lanesborough.surrey.sch.uk
Website: www.lanesborough.surrey.sch.uk
Head: Mrs Clare Turnbull BA(Hons) MEd
Age range: B3–13
No. of pupils: 350
Fees: Day £10,479–£14,688

Lingfield College
Racecourse Road, Lingfield, Surrey RH7 6PH
Tel: 01342 833176
Headmaster: Mr R Bool
Age range: 2–18
No. of pupils: 935
Fees: Day £11,250–£14,600

Longacre School
Hullbrook Lane, Shamley Green, Guildford, Surrey GU5 0NQ
Tel: 01483 893225
Head of School: Mrs Alexia Bolton
Age range: 2–11
No. of pupils: 273

Lyndhurst School
36 The Avenue, Camberley, Surrey GU15 3NE
Tel: 01276 22895
Head: Mr A Rudkin BEd(Hons)
Age range: 2–11
Fees: Day £9,690–£11,655

Manor House School
Manor House Lane, Little Bookham, Leatherhead, Surrey KT23 4EN
Tel: 01372 458538
Headmistress: Tracey Fantham
Age range: G2–16
No. of pupils: 360
Fees: Day £750–£4,070

Micklefield School
10/12 Somers Road, Reigate, Surrey RH2 9DU
Tel: 01737 242615
Headmistress: Mrs L Rose BEd(Hons), CertEd, Dip PC
Age range: 3–11
No. of pupils: 272
Fees: Day £2,565–£9,030

Milbourne Lodge School
Arbrook Lane, Esher, Surrey KT10 9EG
Tel: 01372 462737
Head: Mrs Judy Waite
Age range: 4–13
No. of pupils: 255
Fees: Day £11,325–£14,085

Notre Dame School
Cobham, Surrey KT11 1HA
Tel: 01932 869990
Head of Seniors: Mrs Anna King MEd, MA (Cantab), PGCE
Age range: 2–18
No. of pupils: 600

Oakhyrst Grange School
160 Stanstead Road, Caterham, Surrey CR3 6AF
Tel: 01883 343344
Headmaster: Mr A Gear
Age range: 4–11
No. of pupils: 142
Fees: Day £1,107–£2,450

Parkside School
The Manor, Stoke d'Abernon, Cobham, Surrey KT11 3PX
Tel: 01932 862749
Headmaster: Mr David Aylward BEd(Hons), MA
Age range: B2–13 G2–4
No. of pupils: 382
Fees: Day £1,089–£13,350

Prior's Field
Priorsfield Road, Godalming, Surrey GU7 2RH
Tel: 01483 810551
Age range: G11–18
No. of pupils: 450
Fees: Day £15,855 FB £25,575

Priory Preparatory School
Bolters Lane, Banstead, Surrey SM7 2AJ
Tel: 01737 366920
Headmaster: Graham D Malcom MA, BEd, FRSA
Age range: B2–13
No. of pupils: 200
Fees: Day £4,650–£10,350

Reed's School
Sandy Lane, Cobham, Surrey KT11 2ES
Tel: 01932 869001
Headmaster: Mr Mark Hoskins BA MA MSc
Age range: B11–18 G16–18
No. of pupils: 650 VIth230
Fees: Day £16,938–£21,184 FB £22,582–£28,023

Reigate Grammar School
Reigate Road, Reigate, Surrey RH2 0QS
Tel: 01737 222231
Headmaster: Mr Shaun Fenton MA (Oxon) MEd (Oxon)
Age range: 11–18
No. of pupils: 969 VIth262
Fees: Day £17,460

Reigate St Mary's Prep & Choir School
Chart Lane, Reigate, Surrey RH2 7RN
Tel: 01737 244880
Headmaster: Mr Marcus Culverwell MA
Age range: 3–11
No. of pupils: 280

Ripley Court School
Rose Lane, Ripley, Surrey GU23 6NE
Tel: 01483 225217
Headmaster: Mr A J Gough
Age range: 3–13
No. of pupils: 281
Fees: Day £8,985–£13,680

Rowan Preparatory School
6 Fitzalan Road, Claygate, Surrey KT10 0LX
Tel: 01372 462627
Headmistress: Mrs Susan Clarke BEd, NPQH
Age range: G2–11
No. of pupils: 317
Fees: Day £10,551–£13,998

Royal Alexandra and Albert School
Gatton Park, Reigate, Surrey RH2 0TD
Tel: 01737 649 000
Headmaster: Mr Mark Dixon
Age range: 7–18 years
No. of pupils: 1000 VIth200
Fees: Day £5,358 WB £14,355 FB £14,355

Royal Grammar School, Guildford
High Street, Guildford, Surrey GU1 3BB
Tel: 01483 880600
Headmaster: Dr J M Cox BSc, PhD
Age range: B11–18
No. of pupils: 940
Fees: Day £17,595

Rydes Hill Preparatory School
Rydes Hill House, Aldershot Road, Guildford, Surrey GU2 8BP
Tel: 01483 563160
Headmistress: Mrs Stephanie Bell MA(Oxon)
Age range: B3–7 G3–11
No. of pupils: 200
Fees: Day £897–£3,771

Shrewsbury Lodge School
22 Milbourne Lane, Esher, Surrey KT10 9EA
Tel: 01372 462781
Head: Mr James Tilly BA (Hons), QTS
Age range: 3–7
Fees: Day £2,655–£4,232

Sir William Perkins's School
Guildford Road, Chertsey, Surrey KT16 9BN
Tel: 01932 574900
Head: Mr C Muller
Age range: G11–18 years
No. of pupils: 605 VIth140
Fees: Day £14,163

St Catherine's School
Bramley, Guildford, Surrey GU5 0DF
Tel: 01483 893363
Headmistress: Mrs A M Phillips MA(Cantab)
Age range: G4–18
No. of pupils: 900
Fees: Day £7,695–£15,660 FB £25,770

St Christopher's School
6 Downs Road, Epsom, Surrey KT18 5HE
Tel: 01372 721807
Headteacher: Mrs A C Thackray MA, BA(Hons)
Age range: 3–7
No. of pupils: 137
Fees: Day £1,250–£2,450

St Edmund's School
Portsmouth Road, Hindhead, Surrey GU26 6BH
Tel: 01428 604808
Headmaster: Mr A J Walliker MA(Cantab), MBA, PGCE
Age range: 2–13
Fees: Day £2,160–£13,842

St George's College
Weybridge Road, Addlestone, Weybridge, Surrey KT15 2QS
Tel: 01932 839300
Headmaster: Mr Joe Peake
Age range: 11–18
No. of pupils: 909 VIth250
Fees: Day £15,120–£17,235

St George's Junior School
Thames Street, Weybridge, Surrey KT13 8NL
Tel: 01932 839400
Head Master: Mr Antony Hudson MA (CANTAB), PGCE, NPQH
Age range: 3–11 years
No. of pupils: 644
Fees: Day £4,980–£12,915

St Hilary's School
Holloway Hill, Godalming, Surrey GU7 1RZ
Tel: 01483 416551
Headmistress: Mrs Jane Whittingham BEdCert, ProfPracSpLD
Age range: B2–7 G2–11
No. of pupils: 250
Fees: Day £9,705–£14,280

St Ives School
Three Gates Lane, Haslemere, Surrey GU27 2ES
Tel: 01428 643734
Headteacher: Mrs S E Cattaneo CertEd
Age range: B3–4 G3–11
No. of pupils: 149
Fees: Day £6,600–£9,225

St John's School
Epsom Road, Leatherhead,
Surrey KT22 8SP
Tel: 01372 373000
Head of School: Mrs Rowena Cole
Age range: 11–18
No. of pupils: 761
Fees: Day £23,580 WB £29,790

St Teresa's Effingham (Preparatory School)
Effingham, Surrey RH5 6ST
Tel: 01372 453456
Headmaster: Mr. Mike Farmer
Age range: B2–4 G2–11
No. of pupils: 100
Fees: Day £735–£11,235
WB £19,845 FB £21,780

St Teresa's Effingham (Senior School)
Beech Avenue, Effingham,
Surrey RH5 6ST
Tel: 01372 452037
Head: Mr Michael Farmer
Age range: G2–18
No. of pupils: 450 VIth90
Fees: Day £14,190–£14,730 WB
£22,800–£23,340 FB £22,800–£23,340

ST. ANDREW'S SCHOOL
For further details see p. 220
Church Hill House, Horsell,
Woking, Surrey GU21 4QW
Tel: 01483 760943
Email: admin@st-andrews.woking.sch.uk
Website: www.st-andrews.woking.sch.uk
Headmaster: Mr A Perks
Age range: 3–13
No. of pupils: 313
Fees: Day £3,690–£14,520

Surbiton Preparatory School
3 Avenue Elmers, Surbiton,
Surrey KT6 4SP
Tel: 020 8390 6640
Head of Surbiton High, Junior Girls' & Bo: Ms C Bufton BA(Hons)
Age range: B4–11
No. of pupils: 135
Fees: Day £6,783–£9,246

TASIS The American School in England
Coldharbour Lane, Thorpe,
Surrey TW20 8TE
Tel: +44 (0)1932 582316
Interim Head of School: Mr Bryan Nixon
Age range: 3–18
No. of pupils: 650
Fees: Day £10,900–£23,190 FB £41,870

The Hawthorns School
Pendell Court, Bletchingley,
Redhill, Surrey RH1 4QJ
Tel: 01883 743048
Headmaster: Mr A E Floyd
BSc(Hons), PGCE
Age range: 2–13
No. of pupils: 535
Fees: Day £1,920–£12,600

The Royal School, Haslemere
Farnham Lane, Haslemere,
Surrey GU27 1HQ
Tel: 01428 603052
Principal: Mrs Anne Lynch
BA, PGCE, FRSA
Age range: B6 weeks–16
years G6 weeks–18 years
No. of pupils: 507
Fees: Day £9,531–£17,193 WB
£24,819–£25,446 FB £28,380–£29,007

Tormead School
27 Cranley Road, Guildford,
Surrey GU1 2JD
Tel: 01483 575101
Headmistress: Mrs Christina Foord
Age range: G4–18
No. of pupils: 760 VIth120
Fees: Day £5,520–£11,565

Warlingham Park School
Chelsham Common,
Warlingham, Surrey CR6 9PB
Tel: 01883 626844
Headmaster: Mr M R Donald BSc
Age range: 3–11
No. of pupils: 96
Fees: Day £4,110–£8,310

Weston Green School
Weston Green Road, Thames
Ditton, Surrey KT7 0JN
Tel: 020 8398 2778
Head: Mrs Lucia Harvey CertEd
Age range: 4–8
Fees: Day £4,574–£7,800

Westward Preparatory School
47 Hersham Road, Walton-on-Thames, Surrey KT12 1LE
Tel: 01932 220911
Headmistress: Mrs P Robertson CertEd
Age range: 3–12
No. of pupils: 140
Fees: Day £4,560–£5,655

Woldingham School
Marden Park, Woldingham,
Surrey CR3 7YA
Tel: 01883 349431
Headmistress: Mrs Jayne
Triffitt MA(Oxon)
Age range: G11–18
No. of pupils: 530 VIth150
Fees: Day £23,700 FB £28,410

Woodcote House School
Snows Ride, Windlesham,
Surrey GU20 6PF
Tel: 01276 472115
Headmaster: Mr Henry Knight
Age range: B7–13
No. of pupils: 100
Fees: Day £14,025 FB £18,900

Yehudi Menuhin School
Stoke Road, Stoke d'Abernon,
Cobham, Surrey KT11 3QQ
Tel: 01932 864739
Headmaster: Dr. Richard J
Hillier MA(Cantab), PhD
Age range: 7–19
No. of pupils: 80 VIth36
Fees: FB £41,928

West Sussex

Ardingly College
College Road, Ardingly, Haywards
Heath, West Sussex RH17 6SQ
Tel: +44 (0)1444 893320
Headmaster: Mr Ben Figgis
Age range: 13–18
No. of pupils: 559
Fees: Day £22,380–£23,610
FB £30,480–£32,130

Ardingly College Preparatory School
Haywards Heath, West Sussex RH17 6SQ
Tel: 01444 893200
Headmaster: Mr Chris Calvey BEd
Age range: 2 –13
Fees: Day £5,925–£13,950

Ashton Park School
Brinsbury Campus East, Stane
Street, North Heath, Pulborough,
West Sussex RH20 1DJ
Tel: 01798 875836
Head: Mr G Holding
Age range: 11–16
No. of pupils: 66

Brambletye
Brambletye, East Grinstead,
West Sussex RH19 3PD
Tel: 01342 321004
Headmaster: Will Brooks
Age range: 2 –13
No. of pupils: 280
Fees: Day £7,260–£19,635
FB £23,400–£23,940

Burgess Hill Girls
Keymer Road, Burgess Hill,
West Sussex RH15 0EG
Tel: 01444 241050
Head: Mrs Kathryn Bell
BSc (Hons), PGCE
Age range: B2½–4 G2½–18
No. of pupils: 550 VIth87
Fees: Day £7,350–£16,950
FB £27,300–£30,450

CHRIST'S HOSPITAL
For further details see p. 182
Horsham, West Sussex RH13 0LJ
Tel: 01403 211293
Email: enquiries@christs-hospital.org.uk
Website: www.christs-hospital.org.uk
Headmaster: Mr Simon Reid
Age range: 11–18
No. of pupils: 900
Fees: Day £16,950–£21,330 FB £32,790

Conifers School
Egmont Road, Midhurst,
West Sussex GU29 9BG
Tel: 01730 813243
Headmistress: Mrs Emma Smyth
Age range: 2–13
No. of pupils: 104
Fees: Day £6,030–£8,400

Copthorne Prep School
Effingham Lane, Copthorne,
West Sussex RH10 3HR
Tel: 01342 712311
Headmaster: Mr Chris Jones
Age range: 2–13
No. of pupils: 340
Fees: Day £2,860–£4,980 WB £5,650

Cottesmore School
Buchan Hill, Pease Pottage,
West Sussex RH11 9AU
Tel: 01293 520648
Head: T F Rogerson
Age range: 4–13
No. of pupils: 150
Fees: Day £4,800–£12,600
WB £16,875 FB £18,750

Cumnor House Sussex
London Road, Danehill, Haywards
Heath, West Sussex RH17 7HT
Tel: 01825 792 006
Headmaster: Christian Heinrich
Age range: 2–13
No. of pupils: 385
Fees: Day £8,025–£18,795 FB £22,365

Dorset House School
The Manor, Church Lane, Bury,
Pulborough, West Sussex RH20 1PB
Tel: 01798 831456
Headmaster: R C M Brown MA, PGCE
Age range: 3–13
No. of pupils: 135
Fees: Day £7,290–£14,595
WB £15,810–£17,685

Farlington School
Strood Park, Horsham,
West Sussex RH12 3PN
Tel: 01403 282573
Headmistress: Ms Louise
Higson BSc, PGCE
Age range: G3–18
No. of pupils: 300
Fees: Day £5,660 WB £9,170 FB £9,600

Great Ballard School
Eartham, Chichester, West
Sussex PO18 0LR
Tel: 01243 814236
Head: Mr Richard Evans
Age range: 2–13
No. of pupils: 125
Fees: Day £7,800–£14,550
WB £15,450 FB £21,000

Great Walstead School
East Mascalls Lane, Lindfield,
Haywards Heath, West Sussex RH16 2QL
Tel: 01444 483528
Headmaster: Mr C Baty
NPQH, BEd(Waikato NZ)
Age range: 2½–13
No. of pupils: 465
Fees: Day £7,695–£14,835

Handcross Park School
Handcross, Haywards Heath,
West Sussex RH17 6HF
Tel: 01444 400526
Headmaster: Mr Richard Brown
Age range: 2–13
No. of pupils: 339
Fees: Day £3,060–£6,040
FB £5,090–£7,720

HURSTPIERPOINT COLLEGE
For further details see p. 196
College Lane, Hurstpierpoint,
West Sussex BN6 9JS
Tel: 01273 833636
Email: info@hppc.co.uk
Website: www.hppc.co.uk
Headmaster: Mr. T J Manly BA, MSc
Age range: 4–18
No. of pupils: 1156
Fees: Day £8,790–£22,860
WB £28,800

Hurstpierpoint College Prep School
Hurstpierpoint, West Sussex BN6 9JS
Tel: 01273 834975
Head: Mr I D Pattison BSc
Age range: 4–13
No. of pupils: 360

Lancing College
Lancing, West Sussex BN15 0RW
Tel: 01273 465805
Head Master: Mr Dominic T Oliver MPhil
Age range: 13–18
No. of pupils: 550 VIth255
Fees: Day £7,710 FB £10,970

Lancing College Preparatory School at Worthing
Broadwater Road, Worthing,
West Sussex BN14 8HU
Tel: 01903 201123
Head: Mrs Heather Beeby
Age range: 2–13
No. of pupils: 165
Fees: Day £765–£10,380

Oakwood Preparatory School
Chichester, West Sussex PO18 9AN
Tel: 01243 575209
Headteacher: Mrs Clare Bradbury
Age range: 2½–11
No. of pupils: 260
Fees: Day £1,600–£4,565

Our Lady of Sion School
Gratwicke Road, Worthing,
West Sussex BN11 4BL
Tel: 01903 204063
Headmaster: Mr M Scullion MA, BEd
Age range: 2–18
No. of pupils: 528 VIth55
Fees: Day £5,715–£9,150

Pennthorpe School
Church Street, Horsham,
West Sussex RH12 3HJ
Tel: 01403 822391
Headmaster: Mr Matthew
King BA(Hons)
Age range: 2–13
No. of pupils: 362
Fees: Day £1,392–£12,690

Rikkyo School in England
Guildford Road, Rudgwick,
Horsham, West Sussex RH12 3BE
Tel: 01403 822107
Headmaster: Mr Roger Munechika
Age range: 10–18
No. of pupils: 116
Fees: FB £15,000–£21,600

SEAFORD COLLEGE
For further details see p. 214
Lavington Park, Petworth,
West Sussex GU28 0NB
Tel: 01798 867392
Email: headmasterpa@seaford.org
Website: www.seaford.org
Headmaster: J P Green MA BA
Age range: 7–18
No. of pupils: 732 VIth194
Fees: Day £10,020–£20,775 WB
£20,880–£28,140 FB £32,130

Shoreham College
St Julians Lane, Shoreham-by-Sea, West Sussex BN43 6YW
Tel: 01273 592681
Headmaster: Mr R Taylor-West
Age range: 3–16 years
No. of pupils: 375
Fees: Day £8,550–£13,350

Slindon College
Slindon House, Slindon, Arundel,
West Sussex BN18 0RH
Tel: 01243 814320
Headmaster: Mr D Quick
Age range: B8–18
No. of pupils: 80 VIth17
Fees: Day £6,900 WB £9,845 FB £9,845

Sompting Abbotts Preparatory School for Boys and Girls
Church Lane, Sompting,
West Sussex BN15 0AZ
Tel: 01903 235960
Principal: Mrs P M Sinclair
Age range: 2–13
No. of pupils: 185
Fees: Day £7,860–£10,095

Steyning Grammar School
Shooting Field, Steyning,
West Sussex BN44 3RX
Tel: +44 (0)1903 814555
Headteacher: Mr Nick Wergan
Age range: 11–18
No. of pupils: 1975
Fees: WB £9,060 FB £10,725
A £ IB 16·

The Prebendal School
52-55 West Street, Chichester,
West Sussex PO19 1RT
Tel: 01243 772220
Headteacher: Mrs L Salmond Smith
Age range: 3–13
No. of pupils: 181
Fees: Day £7,695–£14,610
WB £18,930 FB £20,100
£

The Towers Convent School
Convent of the Blessed Sacrement,
Henfield Road, Upper Beeding,
Steyning, West Sussex BN44 3TF
Tel: 01903 812185
Headmistress: Mrs Clare Trelfa
Age range: B2–8 G2–16
No. of pupils: 320
Fees: Day £7,320–£10,200
£

Westbourne House School
Shopwyke, Chichester,
West Sussex PO20 2BH
Tel: 01243 782739
Headmaster: Mr Martin Barker
Age range: 21/2–13 years
No. of pupils: 420
Fees: Day £9,960–£17,160 FB £20,940
£

Willow Tree Montessori School
Charlwood House, Charlwood
Road, Lowfield Heath, Crawley,
West Sussex RH11 0QA
Tel: 01293 820721
Headmistress: Mrs G Kerfante MontDip
Age range: 1–8
Fees: Day £2,310–£2,700

Windlesham House School
Washington, Pulborough,
West Sussex RH20 4AY
Tel: 01903 874700
Headmaster: Mr Richard
Foster BEd(Hons)
Age range: 4–13
No. of pupils: 350
£

Worth School
Paddockhurst Road, Turners Hill,
Crawley, West Sussex RH10 4SD
Tel: +44 (0)1342 710200
Head Master: Gino Carminati MA, FRSA
Age range: 11–18
No. of pupils: 580 VIth222
Fees: Day £20,235 FB £27,849
A £ IB 16·

D376

South-West

KEY TO SYMBOLS

- *Boys' school*
- *Girls' school*
- *International school*
- *Tutorial or sixth form college*
- *A levels*
- *Boarding accommodation*
- *Bursaries*
- *International Baccalaureate*
- *Learning support*
- *Entrance at 16+*
- *Vocational qualifications*
- *Independent Association of Preparatory Schools*
- *The Headmasters' & Headmistresses' Conference*
- *Independent Schools Association*
- *Girls' School Association*
- *Boarding Schools' Association*
- *Society of Heads*

Unless otherwise indicated, all schools are coeducational day schools. Single-sex and boarding schools will be indicated by the relevant icon.

Cornwall

Polwhele House School
Truro, Cornwall TR4 9AE
Tel: 01872 273011
Headmaster: Mr Alex McCullough
Age range: 3–13
No. of pupils: 100
Fees: Day £1,350–£10,845
WB £10,929–£14,865

Roselyon School
St Blazey Road, Par, Cornwall PL24 2HZ
Tel: 01726 812110
Head Teacher: Hilary Mann
Age range: 2–11
No. of pupils: 103
Fees: Day £628–£8,625

St Joseph's School
15 St Stephen's Hill, Launceston, Cornwall PL15 8HN
Tel: 01566 772580
Head Teacher: Mrs Sue Rowe
Age range: 3–16
No. of pupils: 226
Fees: Day £4,566–£8,475

St Petroc's School
Ocean View Road, Bude, Cornwall EX23 8NJ
Tel: 01288 352876
Headmaster: Mr Hilton
Age range: 0–11
Fees: Day £4,950–£7,335

St Piran's School
Trelissick Road, Hayle, Cornwall TR27 4HY
Tel: 01736 752612
Headteacher: Mrs Carol de Labat BEd(Hons), CertEd
Age range: 3–16
Fees: Day £2,823–£12,480

The Valley Nursery
Trevowah Road, Crantock, Newquay, Cornwall TR8 5RU
Tel: 01637 830680
Principal: Mrs Gail P Wilson
Age range: 3 months–5 years
Fees: Day £1,098–£2,700

Truro High School for Girls
Falmouth Road, Truro, Cornwall TR1 2HU
Tel: 01872 272830
Head: Caroline Pascoe
Age range: B3–5 G3–18
No. of pupils: 432 VIth60
Fees: Day £7,254–£10,890 WB £19,755–£20,460 FB £19,998–£20,703

Truro School
Trennick Lane, Truro, Cornwall TR1 1TH
Tel: 01872 272763
Headmaster: Mr A S Gordon-Brown BCom, MSc, CA (SA)
Age range: 3–18
No. of pupils: 780 VIth210

Devon

Abbey School
Hampton Court, St Marychurch, Torquay, Devon TQ1 4PR
Tel: 01803 327868
Principal: Mrs S J Greinig
Age range: 0–11
Fees: Day £673.20–£7,200

Blundell's Preparatory School
Milestones House, Blundell's Road, Tiverton, Devon EX16 4NA
Tel: 01884 252393
Head Master: Mr Andrew Southgate BA Ed (Hons)
Age range: 2½–11
No. of pupils: 220
Fees: Day £1,658–£11,100

Blundell's School
Tiverton, Devon EX16 4DN
Tel: 01884 252543
Head: Mrs N Huggett
Age range: 11–18
No. of pupils: 600 VIth205
Fees: Day £12,870–£20,385 WB £19,635–£27,915 FB £21,690–£31,755

Bramdean School
Richmond Lodge, Homefield Road, Heavitree, Exeter, Devon EX1 2QR
Tel: 01392 273387
Head: D Stoneman NAHT
Age range: 3–18
No. of pupils: 180 VIth12
Fees: Day £4,740–£7,875

EF ACADEMY TORBAY
For further details see p. 228
Castle Road, Torquay, Devon TQ1 3BG
Tel: +41 (0) 43 430 4095
Email: iaeurope@ef.com
Website: www.ef.com/academy
Head of School: Mr. Mark Howe
Age range: 14–19
No. of pupils: 270

EXETER CATHEDRAL SCHOOL
For further details see p. 230
The Chantry, Palace Gate, Exeter, Devon EX1 1HX
Tel: 01392 255298
Email: admissions@exetercs.org
Website: www.exetercs.org
Headmaster: James Featherstone
Age range: 2½–13
No. of pupils: 257
Fees: Day £6,915–£11,535 FB £17,700–£18,735

Exeter School
Victoria Park Road, Exeter, Devon EX2 4NS
Tel: 01392 273679
Headmaster: Mr R Griffin
Age range: 7–18
No. of pupils: 923 VIth218
Fees: Day £10,695–£11,865

Exeter Tutorial College
44/46 Magdalen Road, Exeter, Devon EX2 4TE
Tel: 01392 278101
Principal: K D Jack BA, DipEd
Age range: 16+
No. of pupils: 75
Fees: Day £1,500–£8,500

Fletewood School
88 North Road East, Plymouth, Devon PL4 6AN
Tel: 01752 663782
Headteacher: Mrs R Gray
Age range: 3–11
No. of pupils: 70
Fees: Day £4,425

KING'S SCHOOL
For further details see p. 234
Hartley Road, Mannamead, Plymouth, Devon PL3 5LW
Tel: 01752 771789
Email: school.secretary@kingsschool-plymouth.co.uk
Website: www.kingsschool-plymouth.co.uk
Headteacher: Mrs Jane Lee
Age range: 3–11
No. of pupils: 142
Fees: Day £5,895–£7,440

KINGSLEY SCHOOL
For further details see p. 236
Northdown Road, Bideford, Devon EX39 3LY
Tel: 01237 426200
Email: admissions@kingsleyschoolbideford.co.uk
Website: www.kingsleyschoolbideford.co.uk
Headmaster: Mr Pete Last
Age range: 0–18
No. of pupils: 395
Fees: Day £1,950 WB £5,495 FB £7,095

Magdalen Court School
Mulberry House, Victoria Park Road, Exeter, Devon EX2 4NU
Tel: 01392 494919
Head: Mr Jeremy Bushrod
Age range: 0–18+
No. of pupils: 150 VIth20
Fees: Day £1,800–£8,250

Mount Kelly
Parkwood Road, Tavistock, Devon PL19 0HZ
Tel: +44 (0)1822 813100
Head Master: Mr. Mark Semmence
Age range: 3–18
No. of pupils: 600
Fees: Day £6,900–£16,710 WB £15,510–£27,150 FB £17,250–£29,100

Park School
Park Road, Dartington, Totnes, Devon TQ9 6EQ
Tel: 01803 864588
Teacher-in-charge: Amanda Bellamy
Age range: 3–12
Fees: Day £4,518–£6,738

Plymouth College
Ford Park, Plymouth, Devon PL4 6RN
Tel: +44 (0)1752 505100
Headmaster: Mr. Jonathan Standen
Age range: 3–18
No. of pupils: 501 VIth163
Fees: Day £12,645–£14,970 FB £25,245–£28,920

Plymouth College Preparatory School
St Dunstan's Abbey, The Millfields, Plymouth, Devon PL1 3JL
Tel: 01752 201352
Headmaster: Chris Gatherer
Age range: 3–11
No. of pupils: 310
Fees: Day £1,867–£6,000

Sands School
Greylands, 48 East Street, Ashburton, Devon TQ13 7AX
Tel: 01364 653666
Administrator: Sean Bellamy MA(Cantab), PGCE
Age range: 11–17
Fees: Day £8,289–£9,210

Shebbear College
Shebbear, Beaworthy, Devon EX21 5HJ
Tel: 01409 282000
Headmaster: Mr S. D. Weale MA (Oxon)
Age range: 3–18
No. of pupils: 350 VIth54
Fees: Day £7,185–£11,400 WB £12,390–£17,190 FB £15,990–£22,245

South Devon Steiner School
Hood Manor, Buckfastleigh Road, Dartington, Totnes, Devon TQ9 6AB
Tel: 01803 762528
Education Manager: Ms Gillian Mills
Age range: 3–16
No. of pupils: 307
Fees: Day £2,397–£3,978

St Christopher's Preparatory School
Mount Barton, Staverton, Devon TQ9 6PF
Tel: 01803 762202
Headmistress: Victoria Kennington
Age range: 3–11
No. of pupils: 100
Fees: Day £3,600–£5,565

St John's International School
Broadway, Sidmouth, Devon EX10 8RG
Tel: 01395 513984
Headmaster: Mr Mike Burgess
Age range: 2–18
No. of pupils: 200
Fees: Day £6,495–£10,215 WB £12,141 FB £15,570–£19,200

St Peter's School
Harefield, Lympstone, Exmouth, Devon EX8 5AU
Tel: 01395 272148
Headmaster: N Neeson NPQH, BEd(Hons)
Age range: 3–13
No. of pupils: 275
Fees: Day £6,042–£10,350 WB £15,580

St Wilfrid's School
25-29 St David's Hill, Exeter, Devon EX4 4DA
Tel: 01392 276171
Headmistress: Mrs Alexandra E M MacDonald-Dent DPhyEd
Age range: 5–16
Fees: Day £2,085–£3,060

Stover School
Newton Abbot, Devon TQ12 6QG
Tel: 01626 354505
Principal: Mrs Sue Bradley BSc, CBiol, MSB
Age range: 3–18
No. of pupils: 423 VIth67
Fees: Day £6,879–£10,695 WB £15,183–£21,894 FB £16,575–£20,850

The Maynard School
Denmark Road, Exeter, Devon EX1 1SJ
Tel: 01392 273417
Headmistress: Ms B Hughes
Age range: G7–18
No. of pupils: VIth80
Fees: Day £8,790–£10,992

The New School
The Avenue, Exminster, Exeter, Devon EX6 8AT
Tel: 01392 496122
Headmistress: Miss M Taylor BA(Hons), PGCE
Age range: 3–7
No. of pupils: 61
Fees: Day £690–£5,430

Tower House School
Fisher Street, Paignton, Devon TQ4 5EW
Tel: 01803 557077
Headteacher: Mrs A Jordan BA, HDE
Age range: 2–16
Fees: Day £6,552–£9,576

Trinity School
Buckeridge Road, Teignmouth, Devon TQ14 8LY
Tel: 01626 774138
Headmaster: Mr Lawrence Coen
Age range: 4–11
No. of pupils: 110

West Buckland School
Barnstaple, Devon EX32 0SX
Tel: 01598 760281
Headmaster: J Vick MA(Cantab)
Age range: 3–18
No. of pupils: VIth135
Fees: Day £2,280–£4,250 WB £6,760–£7,880 FB £6,760–£7,880

Dorset

Bournemouth Collegiate School
St Osmunds Road, Parkstone, Poole, Dorset BH14 9JY
Tel: 01202 436 550
Head Teacher: Mrs Mercer
Age range: 2 –16
No. of pupils: 301
Fees: Day £2,925–£9,225

Bryanston School
Blandford Forum, Dorset DT11 0PX
Tel: 01258 484633
Head: Ms S J Thomas
Age range: 13–18
No. of pupils: 681
Fees: Day £29,229 FB £35,646

Buckholme Towers School & Nursery
18 Commercial Road, Lower Parkstone, Poole, Dorset BH14 0JW
Tel: 01202 742871
Headteacher: Mr Iain Robertson
Age range: 3–11
No. of pupils: 106
Fees: Day £6,030–£8,100

Canford School
Canford Magna, Wimborne, Dorset BH21 3AD
Tel: 01202 841254
Headmaster: B A M Vessey MA, MBA
Age range: 13–18
No. of pupils: 640 VIth257
Fees: Day £7,954 FB £10,374

Castle Court School
Knoll Lane, Corfe Mullen, Wimborne, Dorset BH21 3RF
Tel: 01202 694438
Headmaster: Mr Richard Stevenson
Age range: 2–13
No. of pupils: 307
Fees: Day £1,350–£12,945

Clayesmore Preparatory School
Iwerne Minster, Blandford Forum, Dorset DT11 8PH
Tel: 01747 813155
Head of School: Mr William Dunlop
Age range: 3–13
No. of pupils: 230
Fees: Day £12,630–£17,910 FB £16,860–£23,970

Clayesmore School
Iwerne Minster, Blandford Forum, Dorset DT11 8LL
Tel: 01747 812122
Headmaster: Mr M G Cooke
Age range: 13–18
No. of pupils: VIth180
Fees: Day £24,180 FB £30,837

Dumpton School
Deans Grove House, Deans Grove, Wimborne, Dorset BH21 7AF
Tel: 01202 883818
Headmaster: Mr A W Browning BSc (Hons), PGCE, MA(Ed), CChem MRSC
Age range: 2–13
No. of pupils: 340
Fees: Day £8,265–£14,808

Hanford School
Child Okeford, Blandford, Dorset DT11 8HN
Tel: 01258 860219
Headmaster: Mr Rory Johnston
Age range: G7–13
No. of pupils: 100
Fees: Day £5,800 FB £7,050

Knighton House School and The Orchard Pre-prep
Durweston, Blandford Forum, Dorset DT11 0PY
Tel: 01258 452065
Age range: B3–7 G3–13
No. of pupils: 140
Fees: Day £2,325–£4,260 FB £7,200

Leweston Preparatory School
Leweston, Sherborne, Dorset DT9 6EN
Tel: 01963 210790
Headteacher: Mrs M Allen
Age range: 2–11
No. of pupils: 84
Fees: Day £7,485–£10,695 WB £13,695 FB £15,855

Leweston School
Senior School, Sherborne, Dorset DT9 6EN
Tel: 01963 210691
Head: Mrs K Reynolds MA(Oxon), PGCE
Age range: G11–18
No. of pupils: 240 VIth70

Milton Abbey School
Blandford Forum, Dorset DT11 0BZ
Tel: 01258 880484
Headmaster: Mr Magnus Bashaarat
Age range: 13–18
No. of pupils: 229
Fees: Day £16,485 FB £32,070

Park School
45-49 Queens Park, South Drive, Bournemouth, Dorset BH8 9BJ
Tel: 01202 396640
Headmaster: Mr Andrew D. Edwards
Age range: 2–11
No. of pupils: 387
Fees: Day £6,045–£8,400

Port Regis
Motcombe Park, Shaftesbury, Dorset SP7 9QA
Tel: 01747 857800
Headmaster: B H Dunhill BA(Hons) (London), PGCE(Sussex)
Age range: 3–13
No. of pupils: 324
Fees: Day £6,300–£15,105 WB £19,395 FB £19,395

Sherborne Girls
Bradford Road, Sherborne, Dorset DT9 3QN
Tel: +44 (0)1935 818224
Headmistress: Mrs J Dwyer BEd (Hons)
Age range: G11–18
No. of pupils: 460
Fees: Day £18,945–£23,310 FB £25,890–£32,085

Sherborne International
Newell Grange, Newell, Sherborne, Dorset DT9 4EZ
Tel: 01935 814743
Principal: Mr Tim Waters MA (Oxon), MSc (Oxon)
Age range: 11–17
No. of pupils: 147

Sherborne Preparatory School
Acreman Street, Sherborne, Dorset DT9 3NY
Tel: 01935 812097
Headmaster: Mr Nick Folland Bsc (Hons), MIAPS, MISI
Age range: 2–13
No. of pupils: 258
Fees: Day £7,305–£13,515 WB £18,495–£19,350 FB £18,495–£19,350

Sherborne School
Abbey Road, Sherborne, Dorset DT9 3AP
Tel: +44 (0)1935 812249
Headmaster: Dr Dominic Luckett BA, DPhil, FRSA,FHA
Age range: B13–18
No. of pupils: 596 VIth210
Fees: Day £24,525 FB £30,300

St Martin's School
15 Stokewood Road, Bournemouth, Dorset BH3 7NA
Tel: 01202 292011
Headteacher: Laura Richards
Age range: 4–11 years
No. of pupils: 100
Fees: Day £4,485–£6,996

St Mary's School
Shaftesbury, Dorset SP7 9LP
Tel: 01747 852416
Head of School: Mary Arnal
Age range: G9–18
No. of pupils: 220
Fees: Day £15,750–£20,250 FB £19,500–£30,555

St Thomas Garnet's School
Parkwood Road, Boscombe, Bournemouth, Dorset BH5 2BH
Tel: 01202 420172
Headteacher: Mrs Sarah Breeze
Age range: 3–11
Fees: Day £5,580–£7,800

Sunninghill Preparatory School
South Court, South Walks, Dorchester, Dorset DT1 1EB
Tel: 01305 262306
Headmaster: Mr Andrew Roberts-Wray BA(Hons) Dunelm, PGCE
Age range: 3–13

Talbot Heath
Rothesay Road, Bournemouth, Dorset BH4 9NJ
Tel: 01202 761881
Head: Mrs A Holloway MA, PGCE
Age range: G3–18
Fees: Day £13,857 WB £23,397 FB £24,546

Talbot House Preparatory School
8 Firs Glen Road, Bournemouth, Dorset BH9 2LR
Tel: 01202 510348
Headteacher: Mrs Emma Haworth
Age range: 3–11
Fees: Day £1,182–£2,279

Yarrells Preparatory School
Yarrells House, Upton, Poole, Dorset BH16 5EU
Tel: 01202 622229
Headmistress: Mrs Charlotte Oosthizen
Age range: 2–13
No. of pupils: 212
Fees: Day £1,642–£3,365

Somerset

All Hallows Preparatory School
Cranmore Hall, Shepton Mallet, Somerset BA4 4SF
Tel: 01749 881600
Head: Ms A M Lee MA,BA,LTCL,PGCE
Age range: 3–13
No. of pupils: 300

Bruton School for Girls
Sunny Hill, Bruton, Somerset BA10 0NT
Tel: 01749 814400
Headmistress: Mrs Nicola Botterill
Age range: G2–18
No. of pupils: 250
Fees: Day £6,690–£14,031 FB £17,067–£25,554

Chard School
Fore Street, Chard, Somerset TA20 1QA
Tel: 01460 63234
Head of School: Mrs Sarah Graham
Age range: 0–11
No. of pupils: 100
Fees: Day £6,258–£7,359

HAZLEGROVE PREP SCHOOL
For further details see p. 232
Hazlegrove House, Sparkford, Somerset BA22 7JA
Tel: +44 (0)1963 442606
Email: admissions@hazlegrove.co.uk
Website: www.hazlegrove.co.uk
Headmaster: Mr R B Fenwick MA
Age range: 2 –13
No. of pupils: 355
Fees: Day £2,843–£5,764 FB £6,686–£8,531

King's Bruton
The Plox, Bruton, Somerset BA10 0ED
Tel: 01749 814200
Headmaster: Mr I S Wilmshurst MA
Age range: 13–18
No. of pupils: 330

King's College
Taunton, Somerset TA1 3LA
Tel: 01823 328204
Headmaster: R R Biggs
Age range: 2–13
No. of pupils: 440 VIth180
Fees: Day £7,335–£15,675 FB £17,430–£22,665

King's Hall School
Kingston Road, Taunton, Somerset TA2 8AA
Tel: 01823 285920
Headmaster: Mr Justin Chippendale
Age range: 3–13
Fees: Day £4,350–£11,520 FB £13,110–£17,040

Millfield Preparatory School
Edgarley Hall, Glastonbury, Somerset BA6 8LD
Tel: 01458 832446
Headmistress: Mrs S Shayler
Age range: 2–13
No. of pupils: 360
Fees: Day £10,500–£18,120 WB £27,495 FB £27,495

Millfield School
Street, Somerset BA16 0YD
Tel: 01458 442 291/296
Headmaster: Craig A Considine
Age range: 13–18
No. of pupils: 1245
Fees: Day £24,810 FB £36,945

Perrott Hill
North Perrott, Crewkerne, Somerset TA18 7SL
Tel: 01460 72051
Headteacher: Mr Tim Butcher
Age range: 3–13
No. of pupils: 204
Fees: Day £5,265–£13,755 WB £14,835 FB £18,345

Queen's College
Trull Road, Taunton, Somerset TA1 4QS
Tel: 01823 272559
Headmaster: Mr Christopher J Alcock BSc, FRSG, FRSA
Age range: 3–18
No. of pupils: 784 VIth150
Fees: Day £5,250–£14,700 FB £10,605–£23,400

Springmead Preparatory School & Nursery
Castle Corner, Beckington, Frome, Somerset BA11 6TA
Tel: 01373 831555
Principal: Ms Madeleine Taylor
Age range: 2–11
No. of pupils: 105
Fees: Day £5,445–£6,051

Sunny Hill Prep School
Sunny Hill, Bruton, Somerset BA10 0NT
Tel: 01749 814 427
Head: Mrs Helen Snow BEd
Age range: B2–7 G2–11
No. of pupils: 68
Fees: Day £4,650–£9,600 WB £15,750–£16,050 FB £16,905–£17,205

Taunton Preparatory School
Staplegrove Road, Taunton, Somerset TA2 6AE
Tel: 01823 703305
Headmaster: Duncan Sinclair
Age range: 0–13
No. of pupils: 418
Fees: Day £7,920–£14,925 WB £11,010–£19,170 FB £13,770–£23,955

Taunton School
Staplegrove Road, Taunton, Somerset TA2 6AD
Tel: +44 (0)1823 703703
Headmaster: Mr. Lee Glaser
Age range: 13–18
No. of pupils: 520 VIth240
Fees: Day £6,275 FB £10,700

The Park School
The Park, Yeovil, Somerset BA20 1DH
Tel: 01935 423514
Head: Mrs J Huntington ARAM GRSM LRAM CPSEd
Age range: 3–18+
No. of pupils: VIth30
Fees: Day £4,350–£8,640 WB £14,385–£15,405 FB £15,750–£17,550

Wellington Prep School
South Street, Wellington, Somerset TA21 8NT
Tel: 01823 668700
Headmaster: Adam Gibson
Age range: 3–11
Fees: Day £5,685–£10,350 WB £16,521 FB £21,036

Wellington School
South Street, Wellington, Somerset TA21 8NT
Tel: 01823 668800
Headmaster: Henry Price MA (Oxon)
Age range: 3–18
No. of pupils: VIth165
Fees: Day £12,459–£13,659 FB £25,668–£28,185

Wells Cathedral Junior School
8 New Street, Wells, Somerset BA5 2LQ
Tel: 01749 834400
Headteacher: Mr N M Wilson BA, PGCE
Age range: 3–11
No. of pupils: 150
Fees: Day £6,054–£11,265 WB £15,951 FB £19,545

Wells Cathedral School
The Liberty, Wells, Somerset BA5 2ST
Tel: 01749 834200
Head: Mrs Elizabeth Cairncross
Age range: 3–18
No. of pupils: 752
Fees: Day £6,999–£17,223 FB £23,196–£28,824

D382

West Midlands

KEY TO SYMBOLS

- *Boys' school*
- *Girls' school*
- *International school*
- *Tutorial or sixth form college*
- *A levels*
- *Boarding accommodation*
- *Bursaries*
- *International Baccalaureate*
- *Learning support*
- *Entrance at 16+*
- *Vocational qualifications*
- *Independent Association of Preparatory Schools*
- *The Headmasters' & Headmistresses' Conference*
- *Independent Schools Association*
- *Girls' School Association*
- *Boarding Schools' Association*
- *Society of Heads*

Unless otherwise indicated, all schools are coeducational day schools. Single-sex and boarding schools will be indicated by the relevant icon.

Herefordshire

Hereford Cathedral Junior School
28 Castle Street, Hereford, Herefordshire HR1 2NW
Tel: 01432 363511
Headmaster: Mr T C Wheeler MA, BA, PGCE
Age range: 3–11
Fees: Day £7,200–£8,937

Hereford Cathedral School
The Old Deanery, The Cathedral Close, Hereford, Herefordshire HR1 2NG
Tel: 01432 363522
Headmaster: Mr Paul Smith
Age range: 3–18
No. of pupils: 535 VIth130

LUCTON SCHOOL
For further details see p. 246
Lucton, Herefordshire HR6 9PN
Tel: 01568 782000
Email: admissions@luctonschool.org
Website: www.luctonschool.org
Headmistress: Mrs Gill Thorne MA
Age range: 1–18
No. of pupils: 330
Fees: Day £3,205–£4,440 WB £7,205–£8,515 FB £9,295–£10,120

Shropshire

Adcote School for Girls
Little Ness, Shrewsbury, Shropshire SY4 2JY
Tel: 01939 260202
Headmistress: Mrs Diane Browne
Age range: G7–18
No. of pupils: 220
Fees: Day £9,141–£14,838 WB £17,263–£24,754 FB £19,618–£27,097

Bedstone College
Bedstone, Bucknell, Shropshire SY7 0BG
Tel: 01547 530303
Headmaster: Mr David Gajadharsingh
Age range: 4–18
No. of pupils: 230
Fees: Day £10,500–£14,505 WB £13,600–£20,650 FB £17,295–£26,265

Birchfield School
Albrighton, Wolverhampton, Shropshire WV7 3AF
Tel: 01902 372534
Headmaster: Mr H Myott
Age range: B4–13 G4–12
No. of pupils: 145
Fees: Day £5,995–£12,420 WB £17,565

Castle House School
Chetwynd End, Newport, Shropshire TF10 7JE
Tel: 01952 567600
Headmaster: Mr Mark Crewe-Read BSc Econ, PGCE
Age range: 2–11
No. of pupils: 87
Fees: Day £7,095–£8,445

Concord College
Acton Burnell Hall, Shrewsbury, Shropshire SY5 7PF
Tel: 01694 731631
Principal: N G Hawkins MA(Cantab), PGCE
Age range: 13–19
No. of pupils: 521 VIth343
Fees: Day £12,810 FB £34,200

Ellesmere College
Ellesmere, Shropshire SY12 9AB
Tel: 01691 622321
Head: Mr B J Wignall MA, FRSA, MCMI
Age range: 7–18
No. of pupils: VIth161
Fees: Day £9,756–£15,975 WB £20,079–£20,646 FB £21,564–£26,955

Moor Park
Ludlow, Shropshire SY8 4DZ
Tel: 01584 872342
Headmaster: Mr Charles G O'B Minogue
Age range: 3–13 years
No. of pupils: 227
Fees: Day £7,140–£15,930 FB £19,560–£23,475

Moreton First
Weston Rhyn, Oswestry, Shropshire SY11 3EW
Tel: 01691 776028
Head: Mrs Catherine Ford M.A., B.Sc.
Age range: 6 months–11 years
No. of pupils: 119
Fees: Day £9,225–£13,020 FB £21,270

Oswestry School
Upper Brook Street, Oswestry, Shropshire SY11 2TL
Tel: 01691 655711
Headmaster: Mr Julian Noad BEng
Age range: 4–19
No. of pupils: VIth92
Fees: Day £8,160–£14,700 WB £21,390–£25,920 FB £24,570–£30,750

PACKWOOD HAUGH SCHOOL
For further details see p. 250
Ruyton XI Towns, Shrewsbury, Shropshire SY4 1HX
Tel: 01939 260217
Email: hm@packwood-haugh.co.uk
Website: www.packwood-haugh.co.uk
Headmaster: Clive Smith-Langridge BA (Hons), PGCE
Age range: 4–13
No. of pupils: 216
Fees: Day £8,505–£17,685 FB £22,635

Prestfelde Preparatory School
London Road, Shrewsbury, Shropshire SY2 6NZ
Tel: 01743 245400
Head of School: Mrs F Orchard
Age range: 3–13
No. of pupils: 300
Fees: Day £4,935–£15,060 WB £18,900

Shrewsbury High School GDST
32 Town Walls, Shrewsbury, Shropshire SY1 1TN
Tel: 01743 494000
Headmaster: Mr M Getty BA(Hons), NPQH
Age range: B3–13 G3–18
No. of pupils: VIth120
Fees: Day £8,049–£11,082

SHREWSBURY SCHOOL
For further details see p. 252
The Schools, Shrewsbury, Shropshire SY3 7BA
Tel: 01743 280552
Email: admissions@shrewsbury.org.uk
Website: www.shrewsbury.org.uk
Headmaster: Mr Mark Turner MA
Age range: 13–18
No. of pupils: 810 VIth381
Fees: Day £24,390 FB £35,040

St Winefride's Convent School
Belmont, Shrewsbury, Shropshire SY1 1TE
Tel: 01743 369883
Headmistress: Sister M Felicity CertEd, BA(Hons)
Age range: 3–11
No. of pupils: 179
Fees: Day £4,355–£4,380

The Old Hall School
Stanley Road, Wellington, Shropshire TF1 3LB
Tel: 01952 223117
Headmaster: Martin Stott
Age range: 4–11
No. of pupils: 239
Fees: Day £7,605–£11,775

White House School
Heath Road, Whitchurch, Shropshire SY13 2AA
Tel: 01948 662730
Headmistress: Mrs H M Clarke
Age range: 3–11
Fees: Day £3,900

Wrekin College
Wellington, Shropshire TF1 3BH
Tel: 01952 265600
Headmaster: Mr Tim Firth
Age range: 11–18
No. of pupils: 415 VIth140
Fees: Day £13,695–£16,590 WB £19,740–£23,340 FB £24,780–£29,790

Staffordshire

Abbots Bromley School
High Street, Abbots Bromley, Rugeley, Staffordshire WS15 3BW
Tel: 01283 840232
Executive Head: Mrs Victoria Musgrave BA M Ed
Age range: B3-11 & 15–18 G3–18
No. of pupils: 198
Fees: Day £4,518–£15,357 WB £17,040–£21,552 FB £20,904–£25,725

Abbotsholme School
Rocester, Uttoxeter, Staffordshire ST14 5BS
Tel: 01889 590217
Headmaster: Mr Steve Fairclough
Age range: 2–18
No. of pupils: 310 VIth55
Fees: Day £8,490–£20,715 WB £16,545–£25,470 FB £22,625–£30,420

Chase Grammar School
Lyncroft House, St John's Road, Cannock, Staffordshire WS11 0UR
Tel: 01543 501800
Principal: Dr Paul Silverwood MA(Cantab), MSc, PhD, QTS, CChem
Age range: 2–19
No. of pupils: 300 VIth100
Fees: Day £5,352–£11,581 WB £21,210–£21,210 FB £24,150–£30,300

Chase Grammar School International Study Centre
Lyncroft House, St John's Road, Cannock, Staffordshire WS11 0UR
Tel: 01543 501800
Principal: Mr M D Ellse MA, CPhys, MInstP
Age range: 11–18
No. of pupils: 102
Fees: Day £2,832–£9,744

Copsewood Primary School
Verulam Road, Stafford, Staffordshire ST16 3EA
Tel: 01785 258482
Head: Mr J Spicer
Age range: 7–11
No. of pupils: 20

DENSTONE COLLEGE
For further details see p. 240
Uttoxeter, Staffordshire ST14 5HN
Tel: 01889 590484
Email: admissions@denstonecollege.net
Website: www.denstonecollege.org
Headmaster: Mr David Derbyshire MSc, BA
Age range: 11–18
No. of pupils: 618 VIth202
Fees: Day £12,693–£15,342 WB £18,387–£20,679 FB £18,387–£26,712

Denstone College Preparatory School
Smallwood Manor, Uttoxeter, Staffordshire ST14 8NS
Tel: 01889 562083
Headmaster: Mr Jerry Gear
Age range: 2–11
No. of pupils: 162
Fees: Day £3,115–£3,995

Edenhurst Preparatory School
Westlands Avenue, Newcastle-under-Lyme, Staffordshire ST5 2PU
Tel: 01782 619348
Headmaster: N H F Copestick BSc, CertEd
Age range: 3 months–11 years
Fees: Day £7,780–£9,335

Lichfield Cathedral School
The Palace, The Close, Lichfield, Staffordshire WS13 7LH
Tel: 01543 306170
Head: Mrs Susan E Hannam BA (Hons) MA PGCE
Age range: 3–18 years
No. of pupils: 426
Fees: Day £1,795–£5,960

Maple Hayes Dyslexia School
Abnalls Lane, Lichfield, Staffordshire WS13 8BL
Tel: 01543 264387
Principal: Dr E N Brown MSc, BA, MINS, MSCMe, AFBPsS, CPsychol, FRSA, CSci
Age range: 7–17
No. of pupils: 118
Fees: Day £14,760–£19,725

Newcastle-under-Lyme School
Mount Pleasant, Newcastle-under-Lyme, Staffordshire ST5 1DB
Tel: 01782 631197
Headmaster: D M Williamson BA MA
Age range: 3–18
No. of pupils: 879 VIth152
Fees: Day £8,382–£11,514

St Bede's School
Bishton Hall, Wolseley Bridge, Stafford, Staffordshire ST17 0XN
Tel: 01889 881277
Headmaster: Mr Charlie Northcote
Age range: 3–13
No. of pupils: 75
Fees: Day £6,000–£9,900 WB £12,000 FB £12,000

St Dominic's Priory School Stone
21 Station Road, Stone, Staffordshire ST15 8EN
Tel: +44 (0)1785 814181
Headteacher: Mrs Patricia Adamson
Age range: B3 months–11 G3 months–18
No. of pupils: 320 VIth40
Fees: Day £6,522–£10,242

St Joseph's Preparatory School
London Road, Trent Vale, Stoke-on-Trent, Staffordshire ST4 5NT
Tel: 01782 417533
Head: Mrs S D Hutchinson
Age range: 3–11
Fees: Day £1,460–£1,930

St. Dominic's Brewood
32 Bargate Street, Brewood, Staffordshire ST19 9BA
Tel: 01902 850248
Headteacher: Mr Peter McNabb BSc Hons, PGCE
Age range: B2–11 years G2–18 years
No. of pupils: 198 VIth31
Fees: Day £6,015–£12,000 FB £21,500–£21,500

Stafford Grammar School
Burton Manor, Stafford, Staffordshire ST18 9AT
Tel: 01785 249752
Headmaster: Mr M R Darley BA
Age range: 11–18
No. of pupils: 330 VIth96
Fees: Day £12,117

Yarlet School
Yarlet, Stafford, Staffordshire ST18 9SU
Tel: 01785 286568
Headmaster: Mr I Raybould BEd(Hons)
Age range: 2–13
No. of pupils: 169
Fees: Day £2,305–£3,865

Warwickshire

Arnold Lodge School
15-17 Kenilworth Road, Leamington Spa, Warwickshire CV32 5TW
Tel: 01926 778050
Headmaster: David Williams
Age range: 3–16
No. of pupils: 252
Fees: Day £6,960–£9,540

Bilton Grange
Dunchurch, Rugby, Warwickshire CV22 6QU
Tel: 01788 810217
Headmaster: Mr Alex Osiatynski MA Oxon PGCE
Age range: 4–13
No. of pupils: 321

Crackley Hall School
St Joseph's Park, Kenilworth, Warwickshire CV8 2FT
Tel: 01926 514444
Headmaster: Mr R Duigan
Age range: 2–11
No. of pupils: 233
Fees: Day £7,836–£8,274

Emscote House School
46 Warwick Place, Leamington Spa, Warwickshire CV32 5DE
Tel: 01926 425067
Headmistress: Mrs G J Andrews CertEd, BEd
Age range: 2 –8
No. of pupils: 47
Fees: Day £6,450

Jamia Islamia Islamic Studies Centre
Watling Street, Nuneaton, Warwickshire CV11 6BE
Tel: 024 7664 1333
Headteacher: Mr Tauqir Ishaq
Age range: B11–21
No. of pupils: 61
Fees: FB £4,550–£5,400

KING'S HIGH SCHOOL FOR GIRLS
For further details see p. 244
Smith Street, Warwick, Warwickshire CV34 4HJ
Tel: 01926 494485
Email: enquiries@kingshighwarwick.co.uk
Website: www.kingshighwarwick.co.uk
Head Master: Mr Richard Nicholson MA (Oxon)
Age range: G11–18 years

Milverton House School
Holman Way, Park Street, Attleborough, Warwickshire CV11 4EL
Tel: 024 7664 1722
Head Teacher: Mr O Pipe
Age range: 0–11
No. of pupils: 275
Fees: Day £3,400–£3,800

Princethorpe College
Leamington Road, Princethorpe, Rugby, Warwickshire CV23 9PX
Tel: 01926 634200
Headmaster: Mr E D Hester
Age range: 11–18
No. of pupils: 817 VIth184
Fees: Day £9,723

Rugby School
Rugby, Warwickshire CV22 5EH
Tel: +44 (0)1788 556274
Headmaster: P R A Green
Age range: 11–18
No. of pupils: 804 VIth366
Fees: Day £20,094 FB £32,025

Stratford Preparatory School
Church House, Old Town, Stratford-upon-Avon, Warwickshire CV37 6BG
Tel: 01789 297993
Headmaster: Mr N Musk MA, BA(Jt Hons), PGCE
Age range: 2–11
Fees: Day £6,600–£10,650

The Crescent School
Bawnmore Road, Bilton, Rugby, Warwickshire CV22 7QH
Tel: 01788 521595
Headteacher: Mr Huw Marshall
Age range: 4–11
No. of pupils: 137
Fees: Day £6,990–£7,560

The Croft Preparatory School
Alveston Hill, Loxley Road, Stratford-upon-Avon, Warwickshire CV37 7RL
Tel: 01789 293795
Headmaster: Mr Marcus Cook
Age range: 2–11
No. of pupils: 425
Fees: Day £1,560–£10,800

The Kingsley School
Beauchamp Avenue, Leamington Spa, Warwickshire CV32 5RD
Tel: 01926 425127
Headteacher: Ms Heather Owens
Age range: B3–11 G3–18
No. of pupils: 333 VIth61
Fees: Day £10,035–£12,555

Twycross House Pre-Preparatory School
The Hollies, The Green, Atherstone, Warwickshire CV9 3PQ
Tel: 01827 880725
Joint Heads: Mr S D Assinder BA & Mrs R T Assinder BEd
Age range: 4–8
Fees: Day £6,000

Twycross House School
Main Road, Twycross, Atherstone, Warwickshire CV9 3QA
Tel: 01827 880651
Headmaster: Mr S D Assinder
Age range: 8–18
Fees: Day £5,775–£6,750

Warwick Preparatory School
Bridge Field, Banbury Road, Warwick, Warwickshire CV34 6PL
Tel: 01926 491545
Headmaster: Mr M Turner BA(Hons), PCGE, NPQH
Age range: B3–7 G3–11
No. of pupils: 438
Fees: Day £3,393–£8,670

Warwick School
Myton Road, Warwick, Warwickshire CV34 6PP
Tel: 01926 776400
Head Master: Mr A R Lock MA (Oxon)
Age range: B7–18
No. of pupils: 1214 VIth249
Fees: Day £8,505–£10,935 WB £21,870 FB £23,337

West Midlands

Abu Bakr Girls School
154-160 Wednesbury Road, Palfrey, Walsall, West Midlands WS1 4JJ
Tel: 01922 626829
Head: Mr Mohammad Luqman
Age range: G11–15

Al Huda Girls School
74-76 Washwood Heath Road, Saltley, Birmingham, West Midlands B8 1RD
Tel: 0121 328 8999
Headmistress: Mrs Y Jawaid
Age range: G11–17
No. of pupils: 87

Al-Ameen Primary School
Stanfield House, 447 Warwick Way, Birmingham, West Midlands B11 2JR
Tel: 0121 706 3322
Officer in Charge: Mrs Shefa Malik
Age range: 3–11
No. of pupils: 22

Al-Burhan Grammar School
28A George Street, Balsall Heath, Birmingham, West Midlands B12 9RG
Tel: 0121 4405454
Head: Dr Mohammad Nasrullah
Age range: G11–16
No. of pupils: 80
Fees: Day £3,000

Al-Furqan Community College
Reddings Lane, Tyseley, Birmingham, West Midlands B11 3EY
Tel: 0121 777 8666
Principal: Mr Amjad Ahmed BSc, PGCE
Age range: G11–16
Fees: Day £5,400

Al-Hijrah School
Cherrywood Centre, Burbidge Road, Bordesley Green, Birmingham, West Midlands B9 4US
Tel: 0121 7737979
Headteacher: Mohammad Abdul Karim Saqib
Age range: 5–10
No. of pupils: 306

Al-Hira School
99-103 Clifton Road, Balsall Heath, Birmingham, West Midlands B12 8SR
Tel: 0121 4426775
Headteacher: S N Ul Hussan
Age range: B10–16
No. of pupils: 72

Archway Academy
86 Watery Lane Middleway, Bordesley, Birmingham, West Midlands B9 4HN
Tel: 0121 772 7772
Executive Managing Director: Jim Ryan
Age range: 14–19

Bablake Junior School
Coundon Road, Coventry, West Midlands CV1 4AU
Tel: 024 7627 1260
Headmaster: Mr N Price
Age range: 3–11
Fees: Day £8,334

Bablake PrePrep
8 Park Road, Coventry, West Midlands CV1 2LH
Tel: 024 7622 1677
Head of Pre Prep: Mrs T Horton
Age range: 3–8
Fees: Day £6,654

Bablake School
Coundon Road, Coventry, West Midlands CV1 4AU
Tel: 024 7627 1200
Headmaster: Mr J W Watson MA
Age range: 11–18
Fees: Day £10,980

Birchfield Independent Girls' School
Beacon House, 30 Beacon Hill, Aston, Birmingham, West Midlands B6 6JU
Tel: 0121 327 7707
Head: Mr Anwar Teladia
Age range: G11–17
No. of pupils: 150 VIth100
Fees: Day £1,050

Birmingham Muslim School
Bisley Works, Golden Hillock Road, Sparkbrook, Birmingham, West Midlands B11 2PY
Tel: 0121 7668129
Principal: Ms A Abdrabba
Age range: 4–10
No. of pupils: 90

Childfirst Day Nursery Solihull
Cooks Lane, Kingshurst, Solihull, West Midlands B37 6NZ
Tel: 0121 788 8148

Copsewood School
168-170 Roland Avenue, Holbrooks, Coventry, West Midlands CV6 4LX
Tel: 024 7668 0680
Headteacher: Mr A R G Shedden
Age range: 11–16
No. of pupils: 77

Coventry Muslim School
643 Foleshill Road, Coventry, West Midlands CV6 5JQ
Tel: 024 7626 1803
Head: Mrs Ashique
Age range: G5–16
No. of pupils: 97
Fees: Day £1,300

Darul Uloom Islamic High School
521 Coventry Road, Small Heath, Birmingham, West Midlands B10 0LL
Tel: 0121 772 6408
Principal: Dr Asm Abdur Rahim
Age range: B11–16
No. of pupils: 70

Edgbaston High School for Girls
Westbourne Road, Edgbaston, Birmingham, West Midlands B15 3TS
Tel: 0121 454 5831
Head: Dr Ruth A Weeks BSc, PhD
Age range: G2–18
No. of pupils: 950 VIth104
Fees: Day £6,501–£10,005

Elmfield Rudolf Steiner School
14 Love Lane, Stourbridge, West Midlands DY8 2EA
Tel: 01384 394633
College of Teachers: Education Admin
Age range: 3–17
No. of pupils: VIth100
Fees: Day £3,240–£6,290

Elmhurst School for Dance
249 Bristol Road, Edgbaston, Birmingham, West Midlands B5 7UH
Tel: 0121 472 6655
Principal: Jessica Ward BA(Hons), NPQH
Age range: 11–19
No. of pupils: VIth69
Fees: Day £18,378–£19,047 FB £23,556–£25,395

Emmanuel School (Walsall)
36 Wolverhampton Road, Walsall, West Midlands WS2 8PR
Tel: 01922 635810
Head Teacher: Mr Jonathan Swain BA PGCE
Age range: 3–16
No. of pupils: 82
Fees: Day £558–£7,200

Eversfield Preparatory School
Warwick Road, Solihull, West Midlands B91 1AT
Tel: 0121 705 0354
Headmaster: Mr R A Yates BA, PGCE, LPSH
Age range: 2–11
Fees: Day £4,337–£9,066

Green Heath School
43-51 Whitmore Road, Small Heath, Birmingham, West Midlands B10 0NR
Tel: 0121 213 1171
Age range: 11–19

Hallfield School
Church Road, Edgbaston, Birmingham, West Midlands B15 3SJ
Tel: 0121 454 1496
Headmaster: Mr Roger Outwin-Flinders
Age range: 3 months–11
No. of pupils: 570

Hamd House Preparatory School
730 Bordesley Green, Birmingham, West Midlands B9 5PQ
Tel: +44 (0) 121 771 3030
Headteacher: Mr S Ali
Age range: 3–11
No. of pupils: 206

Highclare School
10 Sutton Road, Erdington, Birmingham, West Midlands B23 6QL
Tel: 0121 373 7400
Head: Dr Richard Luker
Age range: B1–12 G1–18
No. of pupils: 638 VIth28
Fees: Day £3,990–£9,330

Hydesville Tower School
25 Broadway North, Walsall, West Midlands WS1 2QG
Tel: 01922 624374
Acting Headteachers: Mrs Gill Whitehouse & Miss Kam Nijjar
Age range: 3–16
No. of pupils: 293
Fees: Day £8,355–£12,105

Jamia Islamia Birmingham Islamic College
Fallows Road, Sparkbrook, Birmingham, West Midlands B11 1PL
Tel: 0121 7726400
Headteacher: Mohammed Govalia
Age range: 11–16
No. of pupils: 111

KING EDWARD VI HIGH SCHOOL FOR GIRLS
For further details see p. 242
Edgbaston Park Road, Birmingham, West Midlands B15 2UB
Tel: 0121 472 1834
Email: admissions@kehs.co.uk
Website: www.kehs.org.uk
Principal: Ms Ann Clark
Age range: G11–18
No. of pupils: 577 VIth164
Fees: Day £12,402

King Edward's School
Edgbaston Park Road, Birmingham, West Midlands B15 2UA
Tel: 0121 472 1672
Chief Master: Dr. Mark Fenton MA MSc
Age range: B11–18
No. of pupils: 856 VIth213
Fees: Day £12,375

King Henry VIII Preparatory School
Kenilworth Road, Coventry, West Midlands CV3 6PT
Tel: 024 7627 1307
Headteacher: Mrs Gillian Bowser BA (QTS Hons), NPQH
Age range: 3–11
Fees: Day £8,334–£8,880

King Henry VIII School
Warwick Road, Coventry, West Midlands CV3 6AQ
Tel: 024 7627 1111
Headmaster: Mr J Slack MA Ed
Age range: 11–18
No. of pupils: 724 VIth210
Fees: Day £10,200

Kingswood School
St James Place, Shirley, Solihull, West Midlands B90 2BA
Tel: 0121 744 7883
Headmaster: Mr Rob Luckham BSc(Hons), PGCE
Age range: 3–11
No. of pupils: 89

Lambs Christian School
113 Soho Hill, Hockley, Birmingham, West Midlands B19 1AY
Tel: 0121 5543790
Headteacher: Mrs Patricia Ekhuenelo
Age range: 3–11
No. of pupils: 43

MANDER PORTMAN WOODWARD – BIRMINGHAM
For further details see p. 248
17-18 Greenfield Crescent, Edgbaston, Birmingham, West Midlands B15 3AU
Tel: 0121 454 9637
Email: birmingham@mpw.ac.uk
Website: www.mpw.ac.uk
Principal: Mr Mark Shingleton
Age range: 14–19

Mayfield Preparatory School
Sutton Road, Walsall, West Midlands WS1 2PD
Tel: 01922 624107
Headmaster: Mr Matthew Draper
Age range: 2–11
No. of pupils: 213
Fees: Day £4,860–£8,100

Newbridge Preparatory School
51 Newbridge Crescent, Tettenhall, Wolverhampton, West Midlands WV6 0LH
Tel: 01902 751088
Headmistress: Mrs Sarah Fisher
Age range: B3–4 G3–11
No. of pupils: 148
Fees: Day £4,215–£6,408

Norfolk House School
4 Norfolk Road, Edgbaston, Birmingham, West Midlands B15 3PS
Tel: 0121 454 7021
Headmistress: Mrs Sarah Morris BA (Hons), PGCE
Age range: 3–11
No. of pupils: 146
Fees: Day £6,420–£8,391

Palfrey Girls School
72 Queen Mary Street, Palfrey, Walsall, West Midlands WS1 4AB
Tel: 01922 625510
Headteacher: Mrs Jane Collins
Age range: G11–16
No. of pupils: 169
Fees: Day £1,100

Pattison College
86-90 Binley Road, Coventry, West Midlands CV3 1FQ
Tel: 024 7645 5031
Principal: Mrs E.A.P. McConnell B.Ed. (Hons)
Age range: 3–16
No. of pupils: 110 VIth16
Fees: Day £6,141–£8,115

Priory School
39 Sir Harry's Road, Edgbaston, Birmingham, West Midlands B15 2UR
Tel: 0121 440 4103
Headmaster: Mr J Cramb
Age range: 6 months–18 years
No. of pupils: 438 VIth23
Fees: Day £2,705–£4,085
(A) (£) (16)

Rosslyn School
1597 Stratford Road, Hall Green, Birmingham, West Midlands B28 9JB
Tel: 0121 744 2743
Principal: Mrs Jane Scott
Age range: 2–11
Fees: Day £2,000–£3,900

Ruckleigh School
17 Lode Lane, Solihull, West Midlands B91 2AB
Tel: 0121 705 2773
Headmistress: Mrs Barbara Forster
Age range: 3–11
Fees: Day £2,549–£7,404

Saint Martin's School
Malvern Hall, Brueton Avenue, Solihull, West Midlands B91 3EN
Tel: 0121 705 1265
Headmistress: Mrs J Carwithen BSc, MA, PGCE
Age range: G3–18
No. of pupils: 430 VIth40
Fees: Day £7,335–£10,095
(A) (£) (16)

Salafi Independent School
472 Coventry Road, Birmingham, West Midlands B10 0UG
Tel: 0121 7724567
Headteacher: Abdul Moxin
Age range: 5–11
No. of pupils: 159

Solihull School
Warwick Road, Solihull, West Midlands B91 3DJ
Tel: 0121 705 0958
Headmaster: Mr David E J J Lloyd
Age range: 7–18
No. of pupils: 1013 VIth279
Fees: Day £8,673–£10,590
(A) (£) (16)

Sporting Edge Independent School
St George's Church Centre, Bridge Street West, Newtown, Birmingham, West Midlands B19 2YX
Tel: 0121 333 7325
Head: Mr S C McCullough
Age range: 14–16
No. of pupils: 19

St George's School, Edgbaston
31 Calthorpe Road, Birmingham, West Midlands B15 1RX
Tel: 0121 625 0398
Head of School: Mr Gary Neal BEd (Hons)
Age range: 2–18
No. of pupils: 368 VIth48
Fees: Day £4,965–£9,765
(A) (£) (16)

Tettenhall College
Wood Road, Tettenhall, Wolverhampton, West Midlands WV6 8QX
Tel: 01902 751119
Head: Mr D C Williams
Age range: 2–18
No. of pupils: VIth66
Fees: Day £7,002–£13,284 WB £15,156–£20,541 FB £19,044–£25,518
(A) (£) (16)

The Birmingham Theatre School
The Old Rep Theatre, Station Street, Birmingham, West Midlands B5 4DY
Tel: 0121 440 1665
Principal: C Rozanski BA(Hons)
Age range: 5–65
Fees: Day £4,100
(£) (16)

The Blue Coat School
Somerset Road, Edgbaston, Birmingham, West Midlands B17 0HR
Tel: 0121 410 6800
Headmaster: Mr N G Neeson
Age range: 2–11
Fees: Day £3,798–£11,898
(£)

The Royal School Wolverhampton
Penn Road, Wolverhampton, West Midlands WV3 0EG
Tel: +44 (0)1902 341230

The Shrubbery School
Walmley Ash Road, Walmley, Sutton Coldfield, West Midlands B76 1HY
Tel: 0121 351 1582
Head Teacher: Hilary Atkins
Age range: 3–11
Fees: Day £1,542–£3,093

WEST HOUSE SCHOOL
For further details see p. 254
24 St James's Road, Edgbaston, Birmingham, West Midlands B15 2NX
Tel: 0121 440 4097
Email: secretary@westhouseprep.com
Website: www.westhouseprep.com
Headmaster: Mr Alistair M J Lyttle BA(Hons), PGCE, NPQH
Age range: B1–11 G1–4
No. of pupils: 330
Fees: Day £1,466–£3,795
(£)

WOLVERHAMPTON GRAMMAR SCHOOL
For further details see p. 256
Compton Road, Wolverhampton, West Midlands WV3 9RB
Tel: 01902 421326
Email: wgs@wgs-sch.net
Website: www.wgs.org.uk
Head: Kathy Crewe-Read BSc
Age range: 7–18
No. of pupils: 734 VIth167
Fees: Day £3,356–£4,421
(A) (£) (16)

Woodstock Girls' School
11-15 Woodstock Road, Moseley, Birmingham, West Midlands B13 9BB
Tel: 0121 4496690
Headteacher: Mrs Na'zihah Ahmed-Atif
Age range: G11–16
No. of pupils: 123

Worcestershire

Abberley Hall
Abberley Hall, Worcester, Worcestershire WR6 6DD
Tel: 01299 896275
Headmaster: Mr Will Lockett
Age range: 2–13
Fees: Day £7,200–£15,495 FB £19,440
(£)

Bowbrook House School
Peopleton, Pershore, Worcestershire WR10 2EE
Tel: 01905 841242
Headteacher: Mr C D Allen BSc(Hons)
Age range: 3–16
Fees: Day £3,480–£6,450
(£)

Bromsgrove Preparatory School
Old Station Road, Bromsgrove, Worcestershire B60 2BU
Tel: 01527 579600
Headmaster: P Lee-Smith
Age range: 7–13
Fees: Day £7,860–£10,245 WB £10,260–£13,245 FB £15,600–£19,350
(£)

Bromsgrove Pre-preparatory & Nursery School
Avoncroft House, Hanbury Road, Bromsgrove, Worcestershire B60 4JS
Tel: 01527 873007
Headmistress: Mrs Susan Pickering BPhil(Ed), CertEd
Age range: 2–7
Fees: Day £2,490–£4,800

Bromsgrove School
Worcester Road, Bromsgrove, Worcestershire B61 7DU
Tel: +44 (0)1527 579679
Headmaster: Peter Clague
Age range: 7–18
No. of pupils: 1300 VIth374
Fees: Day £15,420 FB £22,650–£33,855
(A) (£) (IB) (16)

Cambian New Elizabethan School
Quarry Bank, Hartlebury, Kidderminster, Worcestershire DY11 7TE
Tel: 0800 138 1184
Headteacher: Craig Moreton BA (Hons), PGCE, NPQH
Age range: 7–19
No. of pupils: 21
Fees: Day £3,000–£7,500

Dodderhill School
Crutch Lane, Droitwich, Worcestershire WR9 0BE
Tel: 01905 778290
Headmistress: Mrs C H M Awston
Age range: B3–9 G3–16
No. of pupils: 220
Fees: Day £7,500–£9,750

Heathfield Knoll School
Wolverley Road, Wolverley, Nr. Kidderminster, Worcestershire DY10 3QE
Tel: 01562 850204
Head of School: Mr. L. G. Collins B.Sc.(Hons), M.A.,P.G.C.E.
Age range: 3 months–16 years
No. of pupils: 231
Fees: Day £6,795–£11,265

King's College Saint Michaels
Oldwood Road, Tenbury Wells, Worcestershire WR15 8PH
Tel: 01584 811300
Headteacher: Mrs Nicola Walker
Age range: 14–18
No. of pupils: 115
Fees: FB £25,995

King's Hawford
Hawford Lock Lane, Claines, Worcester, Worcestershire WR3 7SE
Tel: 01905 451292
Headmaster: Mr J Turner
Age range: 2–11
No. of pupils: 330
Fees: Day £5,150–£9,585

King's St Alban's School
Mill Street, Worcester, Worcestershire WR1 2NJ
Tel: 01905 354906
Headmaster: Mr R Chapman
Age range: 4–11
No. of pupils: 216
Fees: Day £5,904–£10,305

King's Worcester
5 College Green, Worcester, Worcestershire WR1 2LL
Tel: 01905 721700
Headmaster: Mr Matthew Armstrong MA
Age range: 11–18
No. of pupils: 935 VIth270
Fees: Day £10,506

Madinatul Uloom Islamic College
Butts Lane, Stone, Kidderminster, Worcestershire DY10 4BH
Tel: 01562 66894
The Head: Head
Age range: B11–24
No. of pupils: 200

Madresfield Early Years Centre
Hayswood Farm, Madresfield, Malvern, Worcestershire WR13 5AA
Tel: 01684 574378
Head: Mrs A Bennett M.B.E.
Age range: 1–5
No. of pupils: 216
Fees: Day £5,800–£6,500

Malvern College
College Road, Malvern, Worcestershire WR14 3DF
Tel: 01684 581500
Headmaster: Antony R Clark
Age range: 13–18
No. of pupils: 655 VIth320
Fees: Day £7,747 FB £11,687–£12,096

Malvern St James
Avenue Road, Great Malvern, Worcestershire WR14 3BA
Tel: 01684 892288
Head Teacher: Mrs Olivera Raraty BA PGCE
Age range: G4–18
No. of pupils: 450
Fees: Day £7,980–£18,465 WB £17,985–£30,345 FB £19,980–£33,150

Moffats School
Kinlet Hall, Kinlet, Bewdley, Worcestershire DY12 3AY
Tel: 01299 841230
Head: Mrs R McCarthy MA (Oxon)
Age range: 3–13
No. of pupils: 60
Fees: Day £7,020–£10,860 FB £26,000

RGS Springfield
Springfield, Britannia Square, Worcester, Worcestershire WR1 3DL
Tel: 01905 24999
Headmistress: Laura Brown
Age range: 2–11
Fees: Day £2,484–£3,822

RGS The Grange
Grange Lane, Claines, Worcester, Worcestershire WR3 7RR
Tel: 01905 451205
Headmaster: Mr Gareth Hughes
Age range: 2–11
No. of pupils: 350
Fees: Day £2,590–£3,984

River School
Oakfield House, Droitwich Road, Worcester, Worcestershire WR3 7ST
Tel: 01905 457047
Principal: Mr Richard Wood
Age range: 5–16
Fees: Day £4,140

The Downs Malvern
Colwall, Malvern, Worcestershire WR13 6EY
Tel: 01684 544100
Headmaster: Mr Alastair Cook
Age range: 3–13
Fees: Day £5,793–£13,908 FB £13,968–£18,408

The Elms
Colwall, Malvern, Worcestershire WR13 6EF
Tel: 01684 540344
Headmaster: Mr A J L Thomas
Age range: 3–13
No. of pupils: 200
Fees: Day £6,720–£17,052 FB £17,880–£18,870

The Knoll School
33 Manor Avenue, Kidderminster, Worcestershire DY11 6EA
Tel: 01562 822622
Age range: 3 months–11 years
No. of pupils: 125
Fees: Day £1,796–£2,731

The Royal Grammar School Worcester
Upper Tything, Worcester, Worcestershire WR1 1HP
Tel: 01905 613391
Headmaster: Mr John Pitt
Age range: 12–18
No. of pupils: VIth215
Fees: Day £3,798

Winterfold House
Chaddesley Corbett, Kidderminster, Worcestershire DY10 4PL
Tel: 01562 777234
Headmaster: Mr W Ibbetson-Price BA, MA, NPQH
Age range: 6 weeks–13 years
Fees: Day £6,360–£10,680

Yorkshire & Humberside

KEY TO SYMBOLS

- *Boys' school*
- *Girls' school*
- *International school*
- *Tutorial or sixth form college*
- *A levels*
- *Boarding accommodation*
- *Bursaries*
- *International Baccalaureate*
- *Learning support*
- *Entrance at 16+*
- *Vocational qualifications*
- *Independent Association of Preparatory Schools*
- *The Headmasters' & Headmistresses' Conference*
- *Independent Schools Association*
- *Girls' School Association*
- *Boarding Schools' Association*
- *Society of Heads*

Unless otherwise indicated, all schools are coeducational day schools. Single-sex and boarding schools will be indicated by the relevant icon.

East Riding of Yorkshire

Froebel House School
5 Marlborough Avenue, Kingston upon Hull, East Riding of Yorkshire HU5 3JP
Tel: 01482 342272
Headmistress: Mrs L A Roberts CertEd, BA(Ed)
Age range: 4–11
No. of pupils: 131
Fees: Day £4,473

Hessle Mount School
Jenny Brough Lane, Hessle, East Riding of Yorkshire HU13 0JZ
Tel: 01482 643371
Headmistress: Mrs C Cutting
Age range: 3–8
No. of pupils: 155
Fees: Day £3,300–£3,525

Hull Collegiate School
Tranby Croft, Anlaby, Kingston upon Hull, East Riding of Yorkshire HU10 7EH
Tel: 01482 657016
Headteacher: Mrs Rebecca Glover
Age range: 3–18
No. of pupils: 650
Fees: Day £4,890–£11,229

Hymers College
Hymers Avenue, Kingston upon Hull, East Riding of Yorkshire HU3 1LW
Tel: 01482 343555
Headmaster: Mr D Elstone
Age range: 8–18
No. of pupils: 977 VIth215
Fees: Day £7,443–£8,946

North Yorkshire

Ampleforth College
York, North Yorkshire YO62 4ER
Tel: 01439 766000
Headmaster: Fr Wulstan Peterburs OSB BA, PhD
Age range: 13–18
No. of pupils: VIth255
Fees: Day £23,223 FB £33,390

Ashville College
Green Lane, Harrogate, North Yorkshire HG2 9JP
Tel: 01423 566358
Headmaster: Mr D M Lauder
Age range: 3–18
No. of pupils: 892 VIth170
Fees: Day £77,950–£13,800 FB £17,295–£27,750

Aysgarth School
Newton le Willows, Bedale, North Yorkshire DL8 1TF
Tel: 01677 450240
No. of pupils: 200
Fees: Day £5,865 WB £880–£1,165 FB £7,635

Bootham Junior School
Rawcliffe Lane, York, North Yorkshire YO30 6NP
Tel: 01904 655021
Head: Mrs Helen Todd
Age range: 3–11
Fees: Day £6,390–£9,285

Bootham School
York, North Yorkshire YO30 7BU
Tel: 01904 623261
Headmaster: Chris Jeffery BA, FRSA
Age range: 11–18
No. of pupils: 480 VIth172
Fees: Day £15,885–£17,520 WB £17,970–£26,430 FB £17,970–£30,510

Botton Village School
Danby, Whitby, North Yorkshire YO21 2NJ
Tel: 01287 661 206
Age range: 4–14

Brackenfield School
128 Duchy Road, Harrogate, North Yorkshire HG1 2HE
Tel: 01423 508558
Headteacher: Ms Patricia Sowa
Age range: 2–11
No. of pupils: 179
Fees: Day £2,065–£2,230

Chapter House Preparatory School
Thorpe Underwood Hall, Ouseburn, York, North Yorkshire YO26 9SZ
Tel: 01423 333330
Head Teacher: Mrs Karen Kilkenny BSc
Age range: 3–10
No. of pupils: 122
Fees: Day £4,518–£6,144 FB £20,250–£20,904

Clifton School and Nursery
York, North Yorkshire YO30 6AB
Tel: 01904 527361
Head: Philip Hardy BA (Hons) PGCE
Age range: 3–8
No. of pupils: 199
Fees: Day £7,200–£7,620

Cundall Manor School
Helperby, York, North Yorkshire YO61 2RW
Tel: 01423 360200
Joint Heads: Mrs Amanda Kirby BA (Hons) PGCE, NPQH & Mr John Sample BSc (Hons) PGCE
Age range: 2–16
No. of pupils: 350
Fees: Day £8,985–£14,415 WB £18,975

Fyling Hall School
Robin Hood's Bay, Whitby, North Yorkshire YO22 4QD
Tel: 01947 880353
Headmaster: Mr. Steven Allen
Age range: 4–18
No. of pupils: VIth54
Fees: Day £6,552–£8,736 WB £15,288–£17,784 FB £15,912–£19,032

Giggleswick Junior School
Mill Lane, Giggleswick, Settle, North Yorkshire BD24 0DG
Tel: 01729 893100
Headmaster: Mr. James Mundell
Age range: 3–11 (boarding from 9)
No. of pupils: 75
Fees: Day £3,912 FB £6,515

Giggleswick School
Giggleswick, Settle, North Yorkshire BD24 0DE
Tel: 01729 893000
Head: Mr. Mark Brotherton
Age range: 13–18
No. of pupils: 320 VIth145
Fees: Day £14,730 FB £20,970

Harrogate Ladies' College
Clarence Drive, Harrogate, North Yorkshire HG1 2QG
Tel: 01423 504543
Principal: Mrs Sylvia Brett
Age range: G11–18
No. of pupils: 300
Fees: Day £14,370 FB £24,360–£30,855

Highfield Prep School
Clarence Drive, Harrogate, North Yorkshire HG1 2QG
Tel: 01423 504 543
Headmistress: Rachel Colbourn
Age range: 4–10
No. of pupils: 216
Fees: Day £6,090–£6,600

Pocklington Prep School
West Green, Pocklington, York, North Yorkshire YO42 2NH
Tel: 01759 321228
Headmaster: Mr I D Wright BSc(Hons), PGCE, NPQH
Age range: 3–11
No. of pupils: 225
Fees: Day £7,275–£11,412 WB £19,923 FB £21,462

POCKLINGTON SCHOOL
For further details see p. 260
West Green, Pocklington, York, North Yorkshire YO42 2NJ
Tel: 01759 321000
Email: enquiry@pocklingtonschool.com
Website: www.pocklingtonschool.com
Headmaster: Mr Mark Ronan MA (Cantab)
Age range: 3–18
No. of pupils: 773 VIth171
Fees: Day £14,124 WB £25,320 FB £27,528

QUEEN ETHELBURGA'S COLLEGIATE FOUNDATION
For further details see p. 262
Thorpe Underwood Hall, Ouseburn, York, North Yorkshire YO26 9SS
Tel: 01423 33 33 30
Email: info@qe.org
Website: www.qe.org
Principal: Steven Jandrell BA
Age range: 3–19
No. of pupils: 1550 VIth595

Queen Margaret's School
Escrick Park, York, North Yorkshire YO19 6EU
Tel: 01904 727600
Head of School: Mrs Jessica Miles
Age range: G11–18
No. of pupils: 302 VIth120
Fees: Day £19,590 FB £29,850

Queen Mary's School
Baldersby Park, Topcliffe, Thirsk, North Yorkshire YO7 3BZ
Tel: 01845 575000
PA to Head: Mrs Amanda Stringer
Age range: B3–8 G3–16
No. of pupils: 235
Fees: Day £5,445–£13,050 FB £14,400–£16,995

Read School
Drax, Selby, North Yorkshire YO8 8NL
Tel: 01757 618248
Headmaster: J A Sweetman BSc, PhD
Age range: 3–18
No. of pupils: VIth36
Fees: Day £6,480–£9,180 WB £15,447–£17,748 FB £17,295–£19,800

Scarborough College
Filey Road, Scarborough, North Yorkshire YO11 3BA
Tel: +44 (0)1723 360620
Headmaster: Charles Ellison
Age range: 3–18
No. of pupils: 339
Fees: Day £6,819–£13,883 FB £19,785–£25,548

St Martins Ampleforth
Gilling Castle, Gilling East, York, North Yorkshire YO62 4HP
Tel: 01439 766600
Headmaster: Dr D Moses
Age range: 3–13 years
No. of pupils: 155
Fees: Day £8,079–£14,973 FB £22,527

St Olave's School
Clifton, York, North Yorkshire YO30 6AB
Tel: 01904 527416
The Master: Mr A Falconer
Age range: 8–13
No. of pupils: 355
Fees: Day £11,580–£14,010 FB £22,265–£24,540

St Peter's School
Clifton, York, North Yorkshire YO30 6AB
Tel: 01904 527300
Head Master: Mr L Winkley MA(Oxon), MEd(OU)
Age range: 13–18
No. of pupils: 375 VIth231
Fees: Day £16,560 FB £27,375

Terrington Hall
Terrington, York, North Yorkshire YO60 6PR
Tel: 01653 648227
Headmaster: Mr. Stephen Mulryne B.Ed (Hons) Liverpool
Age range: 3–13
No. of pupils: 150

The Minster School
Deangate, York, North Yorkshire YO1 7JA
Tel: 0844 939 0000
Headmaster: Mr A Donaldson
Age range: 3–13
Fees: Day £4,674–£7,188

The Mount School, York
Dalton Terrace, York, North Yorkshire YO24 4DD
Tel: 01904 667500
Principal: Adrienne Richmond
Age range: G11–18

Tregelles
Junior Department, The Mount School, Dalton Terrace, York, North Yorkshire YO24 4DD
Tel: 01904 667513
Head: Mr Martyn Andrews BSc(Hons), PGCE
Age range: 3–11
Fees: Day £1,710–£2,280

Wharfedale Montessori School
Bolton Abbey, Skipton, North Yorkshire BD23 6AN
Tel: 01756 710452
Headmistress/Principal: Mrs Jane Lord
Age range: 2–12
Fees: Day £6,225

York Steiner School
Danesmead, Fulford Cross, York, North Yorkshire YO10 4PB
Tel: 01904 654983
Administrator: Maurice Dobie
Age range: 3–14
No. of pupils: 197
Fees: Day £728–£4,800

North-East Lincolnshire

Montessori School
Station Road, Stallingborough, North-East Lincolnshire DN41 8AJ
Tel: 01472 886000
Headteacher: Ms Theresa Ellerby
Age range: 4–11
No. of pupils: 21

St James' School
22 Bargate, Grimsby, North-East Lincolnshire DN34 4SY
Tel: 01472 503260
Headmaster: Dr J Price
Age range: 2–18
No. of pupils: 238 VIth25
Fees: Day £4,605–£11,067 WB £11,775–£17,367 FB £13,125–£18,717

St Martin's Preparatory School
63 Bargate, Grimsby, North-East Lincolnshire DN34 5AA
Tel: 01472 878907
Headmaster: Mr S Thompson BEd
Age range: 2–11
Fees: Day £5,520–£6,420

South Yorkshire

Al-Mahad-Al-Islam School
1 Industry Road, Sheffield, South Yorkshire S9 5FP
Tel: 0114 242 3138
Headteacher: Mrs F Messoul
Age range: G11–17
No. of pupils: 70

Ashdell Preparatory School
266 Fulwood Road, Sheffield, South Yorkshire S10 3BL
Tel: 0114 266 3835
Headteacher: Mrs Anne Camm
Age range: B3–4 G3–11
No. of pupils: 130
Fees: Day £8,985–£9,600

Bethany School
Finlay Street, Sheffield, South Yorkshire S3 7PS
Tel: 0114 272 6994
Headteacher: K Walze
Age range: 4–16
No. of pupils: 76

Birkdale School
Oakholme Road, Sheffield, South Yorkshire S10 3DH
Tel: 0114 2668409
Head Master: Dr Paul Owen
Age range: B4–18 G16–18
No. of pupils: VIth200
Fees: Day £7,716–£11,052

Elsworth House School
Rother Way, Hellerby Estate, Rotherham, South Yorkshire S66 8QN
Tel: 01709 533770
Headteacher: Mr F McCabe
Age range: 11–16
No. of pupils: 40

Handsworth Christian School
231 Handsworth Road, Handsworth, Sheffield, South Yorkshire S13 9BJ
Tel: 0114 2430276
Headteacher: Mrs Pauline Elizabeth Arnott
Age range: 4–16
No. of pupils: 148
Fees: Day £2,340

Hill House School
6th Avenue, Auckley, Doncaster, South Yorkshire DN9 3GG
Tel: +44 (0)1302 776300
Principal: David Holland
Age range: 2 3–16
Fees: Day £6,150–£879

Hope House School Barnsley
Hope House, Blucher Street, Barnsley, South Yorkshire S70 1AP
Tel: 01226 211011
Headteacher: Mr G J Barnes
Age range: 4–16
No. of pupils: 79
Fees: Day £3,300–£4,980
£

Mylnhurst Preparatory School & Nursery
Button Hill, Woodholm Road, Ecclesall, Sheffield, South Yorkshire S11 9HJ
Tel: 0114 2361411
Headmaster: Christopher Emmott BSc(Hons), PGCE
Age range: 3–11
No. of pupils: 185
Fees: Day £7,575

Sheffield High School GDST
10 Rutland Park, Sheffield, South Yorkshire S10 2PE
Tel: 0114 266 0324
Headmistress: Mrs Dunsford BA
Age range: G4–18
No. of pupils: 1020
Fees: Day £6,912–£9,531
A £ 16·

Sycamore Hall Preparatory School
1 Hall Flat Lane, Balby, Doncaster, South Yorkshire DN4 8PT
Tel: 01302 856800
Headmistress: Miss J Spencer
Age range: 3–11
Fees: Day £1,650

Westbourne School
Westbourne Road, Sheffield, South Yorkshire S10 2QT
Tel: 0114 2660374
Headmaster: Mr John B Hicks MEd
Age range: 4–16
No. of pupils: 338
Fees: Day £2,550–£3,590
£

West Yorkshire

Ackworth School
Pontefract Road, Ackworth, nr. Pontefract, West Yorkshire WF7 7LT
Tel: 01977 611401
Head: Mr. Anton Maree BA Rhodes (HDE)
Age range: 3–18
No. of pupils: 490
Fees: Day £7,800–£13,185 FB £25,005
A £ 16·

Al Mu'min Primary School
Clifton St, Bradford, West Yorkshire BD8 7DA
Tel: 01274 488593
Headteacher: Mr M M Azam
Age range: 3–10
No. of pupils: 102

Al-Furqan Preparatory School
Drill Hall House, Bath Street, Dewsbury, West Yorkshire WF13 2JR
Tel: 01924 453 661
Headteacher: Mr Ahmad Farook Raja
Age range: 5–11
No. of pupils: 139

Bradford Christian School
Livingstone Road, Bolton Woods, Bradford, West Yorkshire BD2 1BT
Tel: 01274 532649
Headmaster: P J Moon BEd(Hons)
Age range: 4–16
Fees: Day £1,236–£2,532

Bradford Grammar School
Keighley Road, Bradford, West Yorkshire BD9 4JP
Tel: 01274 542492
Headmaster: Mr Kevin Riley BA, MEd
Age range: 6–18
No. of pupils: VIth266
A £ 16·

Bronte House School
Apperley Bridge, Bradford, West Yorkshire BD10 0NR
Tel: 0113 2502811
Headmaster: Simon W Dunn
Age range: 2–11
No. of pupils: 340
Fees: Day £8,790–£11,640 WB £17,000 FB £18,000
£

Crystal Gardens
38-40 Greaves Street, Bradford, West Yorkshire BD5 7PE
Tel: 01274 575400
Headteacher: Muhammad Abdur Raqeeb
Age range: 5–11
No. of pupils: 20

Dale House Independent School
Ruby Street, Carlinghow, Batley, West Yorkshire WF17 8HL
Tel: 01924 422215
Headmistress: Mrs S M G Fletcher BA, CertEd
Age range: 2–11
No. of pupils: 100
£

Darul Uloom Dawatul Imaan
Harry Street, Off Wakefield Road, Bradford, West Yorkshire BD4 9PH
Tel: 01274 402233
Principal: Mr Mohamed Bilal Lorgat
Age range: B11–13
No. of pupils: 112

Eternal Light Secondary School
Christopher Street, Off Little Horton Lane, Bradford, West Yorkshire BD5 9DH
Tel: 01274 501597
Headteacher: Mr Yusuf Collector
Age range: B11–15
No. of pupils: 91

Focus School – York Campus
Bishopthorpe Road, York, West Yorkshire YO23 2QA
Tel: 01904 663 300
Headteacher: Ms Barbara Plumtree-Varley
Age range: 7–18
No. of pupils: 44

Fulneck School
Fulneck, Pudsey, Leeds, West Yorkshire LS28 8DS
Tel: 0113 257 0235
Principal: Mrs Deborah Newman
Age range: 3–19
No. of pupils: 440 VIth67
Fees: Day £6,210–£11,010 WB £15,390–£18,585 FB £16,725–£20,700
A £ 16·

Gateways School
Harewood, Leeds, West Yorkshire LS17 9LE
Tel: 0113 2886345
Headmistress: Dr Tracy Johnson
Age range: B2–11 G2–18
No. of pupils: 394 VIth48
Fees: Day £7,620–£12,720
A £ 16·

Ghyll Royd School and Pre-School
Greystone Manor, Ilkley Road, Burley in Wharfedale, West Yorkshire LS29 7HW
Tel: 01943 865575
Headteacher: Mr David Martin BA MA PGCE
Age range: 2–11
No. of pupils: 110
Fees: Day £2,850–£3,100
£

Hipperholme Grammar Junior School
45 Wakefield Road, Lightcliffe, Halifax, West Yorkshire HX3 8AQ
Tel: 01422 201330
Headteacher: Mrs Louise Reynolds
Age range: 3–11
No. of pupils: 131
Fees: Day £3,250–£7,845
£

Hipperholme Grammar School
Bramley Lane, Hipperholme, Halifax, West Yorkshire HX3 8JE
Tel: 01422 202256
Headmaster: Mr Jack D Williams BSc
Age range: 3–18
No. of pupils: VIth30
Fees: Day £8,799–£10,995
Ⓐ £ 16·

Huddersfield Grammar School
Royds Mount, Luck Lane, Marsh, Huddersfield, West Yorkshire HD1 4QX
Tel: 01484 424549
Headmaster: Mr Tim Hoyle
Age range: 3–16
No. of pupils: 510
Fees: Day £7,878–£9,664
£

Institute of Islamic Education
South Street, Savile Town, Dewsbury, West Yorkshire WF12 9NG
Tel: 01924 485712/01924 455762
Principal: Moulana Saeed Patel
Age range: B12–16
No. of pupils: 184

Islamia Girls High School
2 Thornton Lodge Road, Thornton Lodge, Huddersfield, West Yorkshire HD1 3JQ
Tel: 01484 518 817
Head: Mrs Samira El-Turabi
Age range: G11–16
Fees: Day £1,300

Islamic Tarbiyah Preparatory School
Ambler Street, Bradford, West Yorkshire BD8 8AW
Tel: 01274 490462
Headteacher: Mr S A Nawaz
Age range: 5–10
No. of pupils: 123

Jaamiatul Imaam Muhammad Zakaria School
Thornton View Road, Clayton, Bradford, West Yorkshire BD14 6JX
Tel: 01274 882007
Headteacher: Mrs Z Hajee
Age range: G11–16
No. of pupils: 416

Lady Lane Park School & Nursery
Lady Lane, Bingley, West Yorkshire BD16 4AP
Tel: 01274 551168
Headmistress: Mrs Gill Wilson
Age range: 2–11
No. of pupils: 150
Fees: Day £7,554

Leeds Menorah School
393 Street Lane, Leeds, West Yorkshire LS17 6HQ
Tel: 0113 268 3390
Headteacher: Rabbi J Refson
Age range: 5–16
No. of pupils: 55

M A Institute
Lumb Lane, Bradford, West Yorkshire BD8 7RZ
Tel: 01274 395454
Age range: B11–16
No. of pupils: 68

Madni Muslim Girls High School
Thornie Bank, Off Scarborough St, Savile Town, Dewsbury, West Yorkshire WF12 9AX
Tel: 01924 520720
Headmistress: Mrs S A Mirza
Age range: G3–18
No. of pupils: 250
Ⓐ

Mill Cottage Montessori School
Wakefield Road, Brighouse, West Yorkshire HD6 4HA
Tel: 01484 400500
Principal: Ailsa Nevile
Age range: 0–11

Moorfield School
Wharfedale Lodge, 11 Ben Rhydding Road, Ilkley, West Yorkshire LS29 8RL
Tel: 01943 607285
Headmistress: Mrs Jessica Crossley
Age range: 2–11
Fees: Day £8,139
£

Moorlands School
Foxhill, Weetwood Lane, Leeds, West Yorkshire LS16 5PF
Tel: 0113 2785286
Headteacher: Miss J Atkinson
Age range: 2–11
No. of pupils: 149
Fees: Day £7,491–£8,379
£

Mount School
3 Binham Road, Edgerton, Huddersfield, West Yorkshire HD2 2AP
Tel: 01484 426432
Headteacher: Janet Brook
Age range: 3–11
Fees: Day £6,075

Netherleigh & Rossefield School
Parsons Road, Heaton, Bradford, West Yorkshire BD9 4AY
Tel: 01274 543162
Headteacher: Richard McIntosh
Age range: 2–11
No. of pupils: 141
Fees: Day £6,495
£

New Horizon Community School
Newton Hill House, Newton Hill Road, Leeds, West Yorkshire LS7 4JE
Tel: 0113 262 4001
Head: Hena Salim Hashmi
Age range: G11–16
No. of pupils: 87
Fees: Day £1,500

Olive Secondary School
Byron Street, Bradford, West Yorkshire BD3 0AD
Tel: +44+ (0)1274 725005 / +44 (0)1274 725013
Headteacher: Mr Amjad Mohammed
Age range: 11–18
No. of pupils: 115
Fees: Day £1,500

Paradise Primary School
1 Bretton Street, Dewsbury, West Yorkshire WF12 9BB
Tel: 01924 439803
Headteacher: Mrs Hafsa Patel
Age range: 2–11
No. of pupils: 217

Queen Elizabeth Grammar School (Junior School)
158 Northgate, Wakefield, West Yorkshire WF1 3QY
Tel: 01924 373821
Head: Mrs L A Gray
Age range: B7–11
No. of pupils: 261
Fees: Day £6,207–£6,558
£

Queen Elizabeth Grammar School (Senior School)
154 Northgate, Wakefield, West Yorkshire WF1 3QY
Tel: 01924 373943
Headmaster: David Craig
Age range: B11–18
No. of pupils: 677
Fees: Day £7,080
Ⓐ £ 16·

Queenswood School
Queen Street, Morley, Leeds, West Yorkshire LS27 9EB
Tel: 0113 2534033
Headteacher: Mrs J A Tanner MMus, BA, FTCL, ARCO
Age range: 4–11
Fees: Day £3,885–£4,275

Rastrick Independent School
Ogden Lane, Rastrick, Brighouse, West Yorkshire HD6 3HF
Tel: 01484 400344
Headmistress: Mrs S A Vaughey
Age range: 0–16
No. of pupils: 200
Fees: Day £5,985–£8,760
Ⓐ £ 16·

Richmond House School
170 Otley Road, Leeds, West Yorkshire LS16 5LG
Tel: 0113 2752670
Headteacher: Mrs Helen Stiles
Age range: 3–11
No. of pupils: 219
Fees: Day £5,544–£9,255
£

Rishworth School
Rishworth, Halifax, West Yorkshire HX6 4QA
Tel: 01422 822217
Headmaster: Mr. A S Gloag
Age range: 3–18
No. of pupils: 600 VIth90
Fees: Day £4,905–£9,585 WB £15,285–£16,725 FB £16,830–£18,360
Ⓐ £ 16·

Silcoates School
Wrenthorpe, Wakefield, West Yorkshire WF2 0PD
Tel: 01924 291614
Headmaster: Darryl S Wideman
Age range: 7–18
No. of pupils: 768
Fees: Day £6,618–£11,181
Ⓐ £ 16·

St Hilda's School
Dovecote Lane, Horbury, Wakefield, West Yorkshire WF4 6BB
Tel: 01924 260706
Headmistress: Mrs J L Sharpe
Age range: B0–7 G0–11
No. of pupils: 127
Fees: Day £4,722–£4,944

Sunny Hill House School
Wrenthorpe Lane, Wrenthorpe, Wakefield, West Yorkshire WF2 0QB
Tel: 01924 291717
Headmistress: Mrs H K Cushing CertEd, MA
Age range: 2–7
No. of pupils: 116
Fees: Day £5,256

The Branch Christian School
Dewsbury Revival Centre, West Park Street, Dewsbury, West Yorkshire WF13 4LA
Tel: +44 (0)1924 452511
Headteacher: R Ward
Age range: 3–16
No. of pupils: 26

THE FROEBELIAN SCHOOL
For further details see p. 264
Clarence Road, Horsforth, Leeds, West Yorkshire LS18 4LB
Tel: 0113 2583047
Email: office@froebelian.co.uk
Website: www.froebelian.com
Head Teacher: Mrs Catherine Dodds BEd (Hons), PGCE
Age range: 3–11
No. of pupils: 182
Fees: Day £4,980–£7,440

The Gleddings School
Birdcage Lane, Savile Park, Halifax, West Yorkshire HX3 0JB
Tel: 01422 354605
School Director: Mrs P J Wilson CBE
Age range: 3–11
No. of pupils: 191
Fees: Day £3,555–£5,910

The Grammar School at Leeds
Alwoodley Gates, Harrogate Road, Leeds, West Yorkshire LS17 8GS
Tel: 0113 2291552
Principal and CEO: Mr Michael Gibbons
Age range: 3–18
No. of pupils: 2120 VIth418
Fees: Day £7,723–£11,282

Wakefield Girls' High School (Junior School)
2 St John's Square, Wakefield, West Yorkshire WF1 2QX
Tel: 01924 374577
Headmistress: Daphne Cawthorne BEd
Age range: B3–7 G3–11
No. of pupils: 493
Fees: Day £6,609–£7,212

Wakefield Girls' High School (Senior School)
Wentworth Street, Wakefield, West Yorkshire WF1 2QS
Tel: 01924 372490
Headmistress: Gillian Wallwork BA(Hons,) PGCE
Age range: G11–18
No. of pupils: 715
Fees: Day £9,996

Wakefield Independent School
The Nostell Centre, Doncaster Road, Nostell, Wakefield, West Yorkshire WF4 1QG
Tel: 01924 865757
Headmistress: Mrs K E Caryl
Age range: 21/2–16
No. of pupils: 190
Fees: Day £4,590–£6,375

West Cliffe Montessori School & Nursery
33, Barlow Road, access Belgrave Road, Keighley, West Yorkshire BD21 2TA
Tel: 01535 609797
Principal: Mrs T Bisby
Age range: 0–8
No. of pupils: 42

Westville House Preparatory School
Carter's Lane, Middleton, Ilkley, West Yorkshire LS29 0DQ
Tel: 01943 608053
Headteacher: Mrs R James BSc(Hons), PGCE
Age range: 3–11
Fees: Day £4,545–£7,875

WOODHOUSE GROVE SCHOOL
For further details see p. 266
Apperley Bridge, Bradford, West Yorkshire BD10 0NR
Tel: 0113 250 2477
Email: amos.jl@woodhousegrove.co.uk
Website: www.woodhousegrove.co.uk
Headmaster: Mr James Lockwood MA
Age range: 3–18
No. of pupils: 1060
Fees: Day £8,790–£13,275 FB £25,230–£26,985

Northern Ireland

KEY TO SYMBOLS

- *Boys' school*
- *Girls' school*
- *International school*
- *Tutorial or sixth form college*
- *A levels*
- *Boarding accommodation*
- *Bursaries*
- *International Baccalaureate*
- *Learning support*
- *Entrance at 16+*
- *Vocational qualifications*
- *Independent Association of Preparatory Schools*
- *The Headmasters' & Headmistresses' Conference*
- *Independent Schools Association*
- *Girls' School Association*
- *Boarding Schools' Association*
- *Society of Heads*

Unless otherwise indicated, all schools are coeducational day schools. Single-sex and boarding schools will be indicated by the relevant icon.

County Antrim

Belfast Royal Academy
7 Cliftonville Road, Belfast, County Antrim BT14 6JL
Tel: 028 9074 0423
Headmaster: Mr J M G Dickson MA
Age range: 11–18
No. of pupils: VIth382
Fees: Day £140

Campbell College
Belfast, County Antrim BT4 2ND
Tel: 028 9076 3076
Headmaster: Mr Robert Robinson
Age range: B11–18
No. of pupils: 896 VIth200
Fees: Day £2,200 FB £10,951–£15,111

Campbell College Junior School
Belmont Road, Belfast, County Antrim BT4 2ND
Tel: 028 9076 3076
Head: Mrs H M Rowan
Age range: B3–11 G3–4
Fees: Day £3,484–£3,740

Hunterhouse College
Finaghy, Belfast, County Antrim BT10 0LE
Tel: 028 9061 2293
Principal: Mr A Gibson MA, DipEd, PQH
Age range: G11–18
No. of pupils: 710 VIth180
Fees: Day £320

Inchmarlo
Cranmore Park, Belfast, County Antrim BT9 6JR
Tel: 028 9038 1454

Methodist College
1 Malone Road, Belfast, County Antrim BT9 6BY
Tel: 028 9020 5205
Principal: J Scott W Naismith
Age range: 4–19
No. of pupils: 2307 VIth548
Fees: Day £130–£3,425

Royal Belfast Academical Institution
College Square East, Belfast, County Antrim BT1 6DL
Tel: 028 9024 0461
Principal: Miss J A Williamson MA(Oxon), NPQH
Age range: B4–18
No. of pupils: 1290 VIth275
Fees: Day £940–£4,140

St Mary's Christian Brothers Grammar School
Glen Road, Belfast, County Antrim BT11 8NR
Tel: 028 9029 4000
Headmaster: Mr. John Martin
Age range: B12–18
No. of pupils: 112

Victoria College Belfast
Cranmore Park, Belfast, County Antrim BT9 6JA
Tel: 028 9066 1506
Principal: Ms Patricia Slevin
Age range: G5–18
No. of pupils: 1070 VIth224
Fees: Day £432 WB £10,500 FB £10,500–£17,100

County Armagh

The Royal School
College Hill, Armagh, County Armagh BT61 9DH
Tel: 02837 522807
Headmaster: P Crute MA, BA, PGCE
Age range: 11–18
No. of pupils: 654 VIth157
Fees: Day £110–£163 WB £4,165–£6,365 FB £6,365–£10,165

County Down

Bangor Grammar School
Gransha Road, Bangor, County Down BT19 7QU
Tel: 028 91 473734
Principal: Mrs E P Huddleson B.Ed., M.SSc., PQH(NI)
Age range: B3–18
No. of pupils: 900 VIth220
Fees: Day £80–£450

Holywood Steiner School
34 Croft Road, Holywood, County Down BT18 0PR
Tel: 028 9042 8029
Chairperson of the School Management Team: Julie Higgins
Age range: 2 years 10 months–17 years
No. of pupils: 110
Fees: Day £4,008–£4,512

Rockport School
Craigavad, Holywood, County Down BT18 0DD
Tel: 028 9042 8372
Headmaster: Mr George Vance
Age range: 3–18
No. of pupils: 200
Fees: Day £5,640–£12,360 WB £12,720–£16,470 FB £16,770–£20,460

County Londonderry

Coleraine Academical Institution
Castlerock Road, Coleraine, County Londonderry BT51 3LA
Tel: 028 7034 4331
Headmaster: Dr D R J Carruthers
Age range: B11–18
No. of pupils: 711 VIth144
Fees: Day £140

County Tyrone

The Royal School Dungannon
2 Ranfurly Road, Dungannon, County Tyrone BT71 6EG
Tel: 028 8772 2710
Headmaster: Dr David Burnett
Age range: 11–18
No. of pupils: 648 VIth105
Fees: Day £70–£150 WB £7,800–£7,800 FB £10,050–£19,850

Scotland

KEY TO SYMBOLS

- *Boys' school*
- *Girls' school*
- *International school*
- *Tutorial or sixth form college*
- *A levels*
- *Boarding accommodation*
- *Bursaries*
- *International Baccalaureate*
- *Learning support*
- *Entrance at 16+*
- *Vocational qualifications*
- *Independent Association of Preparatory Schools*
- *The Headmasters' & Headmistresses' Conference*
- *Independent Schools Association*
- *Girls' School Association*
- *Boarding Schools' Association*
- *Society of Heads*

Unless otherwise indicated, all schools are coeducational day schools. Single-sex and boarding schools will be indicated by the relevant icon.

Aberdeen

Albyn School
17-23 Queen's Road,
Aberdeen AB15 4PB
Tel: 01224 322408
Headmaster: Ian E Long
AKC, PhD, FRGS, FRSA
Age range: B2–14 G2–18
No. of pupils: 675 VIth57
Fees: Day £3,500–£9,785

Robert Gordon's College
Schoolhill, Aberdeen AB10 1FE
Tel: 01224 646346
Head of College: Mr Hugh
Ouston MA, DipEd
Age range: 4–18
No. of pupils: 1573 VIth350
Fees: Day £5,949–£9,264

St Margaret's School for Girls
17 Albyn Place, Aberdeen AB10 1RU
Tel: 01224 584466
Headmistress: Miss A Tomlinson
MTheol (Hons), PGCE
Age range: B3–5 years G3–18 years
No. of pupils: 380 VIth34
Fees: Day £7,685–£12,174

Aberdeenshire

The International School of Aberdeen
Pitfodels House, North Deeside
Road, Pitfodels, Cults, Aberdeen,
Aberdeenshire AB15 9PN
Tel: 01224 730300
Director: Dr D A Hovde
Age range: 3–18
No. of pupils: VIth64
Fees: Day £18,235–£20,420

Angus

Lathallan School
Brotherton Castle, Johnshaven,
Montrose, Angus DD10 0HN
Tel: 01561 362220
Headmaster: Mr R Toley
No. of pupils: 220
Fees: Day £10,230–£17,670 WB
£4,234–£4,326 FB £6,555–£6,555

Argyll & Bute

LOMOND SCHOOL
For further details see p. 274
10 Stafford Street, Helensburgh,
Argyll & Bute G84 9JX
Tel: +44 (0)1436 672476
Email: admissions@lomondschool.com
Website: www.lomondschool.com
Principal: Mrs Johanna Urquhart
Age range: 3–18
No. of pupils: 400
Fees: Day £8,310–£11,550 FB £26,730

Borders

St Mary's Prep School
Abbey Park, Melrose, Borders TD6 9LN
Tel: 01896 822517
Headmaster: Mr Liam Harvey
Age range: 2–13
Fees: Day £8,700–£11,550 WB £14,250

Clackmannanshire

Dollar Academy
Dollar, Clackmannanshire FK14 7DU
Tel: 01259 742511
Rector: Mr David Knapman Mphil
Age range: 5–18
No. of pupils: 1200 VIth142
Fees: Day £7,974–£10,665 WB
£20,637–£23,328 FB £21,978–£24,669

Dundee

High School of Dundee
Euclid Crescent, Dundee DD1 1HU
Tel: 01382 202921
Rector: Dr John Halliday
Age range: 3–18
No. of pupils: 1067 VIth102
Fees: Day £8,499–£12,063

East Lothian

Belhaven Hill
Dunbar, East Lothian EH42 1NN
Tel: 01368 862785
Headmaster: Mr. Henry Knight
Age range: 8–13
No. of pupils: 122
Fees: Day £14,325 FB £20,655

Loretto Junior School
North Esk Lodge, 1 North High Street,
Musselburgh, East Lothian EH21 6JA
Tel: 0131 653 4570
Headmaster: Richard Selley BEd
Age range: 3–12
No. of pupils: 200
Fees: Day £6,210–£11,550
FB £13,500–£15,000

Loretto School
Linkfield Road, Musselburgh,
East Lothian EH21 7RE
Tel: 0131 653 4455
Headmaster: Dr Graham
Hawley BSc, PhD
Age range: 0–18
No. of pupils: 610 VIth189
Fees: Day £8,550–£21,750
FB £17,700–£31,950

The Compass School
West Road, Haddington,
East Lothian EH41 3RD
Tel: 01620 822642
Headmaster: Mr Mark Becher
MA(Hons), PGCE
Age range: 4–12
No. of pupils: 120
Fees: Day £6,685–£7,755

Edinburgh

Basil Paterson Tutorial College
66 Queen Street, Edinburgh EH2 4NA
Tel: 0131 225 3802
Principal: David Van Den Bergh
Age range: 16+
No. of pupils: 40 VIth35
Fees: Day £3,440–£21,440 WB £140

Cargilfield School
45 Gamekeeper's Road,
Edinburgh EH4 1PU
Tel: 0131 336 2207
Headmaster: Mr. Robert Taylor
Age range: 3–13
No. of pupils: 325
Fees: Day £4,080–£11,850
WB £14,400 FB £15,000

Clifton Hall
Newbridge, Edinburgh EH28 8LQ
Tel: 0131 333 1359
Headmaster: Mr R Grant
Age range: 3–18
No. of pupils: 299 VIth8
Fees: Day £1,500–£9,500

Edinburgh Steiner School
60 Spylaw Road, Edinburgh EH10 5BR
Tel: 0131 337 3410
Age range: 3–18
Fees: Day £3,756–£7,860

FETTES COLLEGE
For further details see p. 270
Carrington Road,
Edinburgh EH4 1QX
Tel: +44 (0)131 332 2281
Email: enquiries@fettes.com
Website: www.fettes.com
Head of College: Mr Geoffrey Stanford
Age range: 7–18
No. of pupils: 770
Fees: Day £15,495–£26,790 FB £24,210–£33,480
(A) (£) (IB) (16)

Fettes College Preparatory School
East Fettes Avenue, Edinburgh EH4 1QZ
Tel: 0131 332 2976
Headmaster: Mr A A Edwards
Age range: 7–13
No. of pupils: 169
Fees: Day £11,331 FB £17,739
(A) (£) (IB)

George Heriot's School
Lauriston Place, Edinburgh EH3 9EQ
Tel: 0131 229 7263
Principal: Mr Gareth E Doodes MA
Age range: 4–18
No. of pupils: 1641 VIth352
Fees: Day £6,867–£10,299
(£) (16)

George Watson's College
Colinton Road, Edinburgh EH10 5EG
Tel: 0131 446 6000
Principal: Mr Melvyn Roffe
Age range: 3–18
No. of pupils: 2362
Fees: Day £4,491–£11,577
(A) (£) (IB) (16)

Merchiston Castle School
294 Colinton Road, Edinburgh EH13 0PU
Tel: 0131 312 2201
Headmaster: Mr A R Hunter BA
Age range: B7–18
No. of pupils: 450
Fees: Day £14,595–£23,505 FB £20,280–£31,650
(A) (£) (16)

St George's School for Girls
Garscube Terrace, Edinburgh EH12 6BG
Tel: 0131 311 8000
Head: Mrs Alex Hems BA(Hons) Oxon
Age range: B2–5 years G2–18 years
No. of pupils: 815 VIth170
Fees: Day £7,980–£12,960 FB £27,090
(A) (£) (16)

St Mary's Music School
Coates Hall, 25 Grosvenor Crescent, Edinburgh EH12 5EL
Tel: 0131 538 7766
Headteacher: Dr Kenneth Taylor BSc Hons, PhD, PGCE, PG Dip
Age range: 9–19
No. of pupils: VIth13
(A) (16)

Stewart's Melville College
Queensferry Road, Edinburgh EH4 3EZ
Tel: 0131 311 1000
Principal: Mr J N D Gray BA
Age range: B11–18 G16–18
No. of pupils: 864
Fees: Day £9,096 FB £18,249
(£) (16)

The Edinburgh Academy
42 Henderson Row, Edinburgh EH3 5BL
Tel: 0131 556 4603
Rector: Marco Longmore
Age range: 2–18
No. of pupils: 992 VIth93
Fees: Day £8,860–£14,960
(A) (£) (16)

The Mary Erskine & Stewart's Melville Junior School
Queensferry Road, Edinburgh EH4 3EZ
Tel: 0131 311 1111
Headmaster: Mr Bryan Lewis
Age range: 3–11
No. of pupils: 1218
Fees: Day £5,574–£7,218 WB £14,628–£14,814 FB £15,051–£15,237
(£)

The Mary Erskine School
Ravelston, Edinburgh EH4 3NT
Tel: 0131 347 5700
Headmaster: Mr J N D Gray BA
Age range: B16–18 G11–18
Fees: Day £9,096 FB £18,249
(£) (16)

Wallace College
12 George IV Bridge, Edinburgh EH1 1EE
Tel: 0131 220 3634
Age range: 14–19
Fees: Day £1,410–£6,900 FB £4,070–£9,590
(16) (A)

Fife

Osborne House School
Orchard Croft, West Port, Dysart, Fife KY1 2TD
Tel: 01592 651461
Headteacher: Miss Eunice Cameron
Age range: 10–17
Fees: Day £7,800

St Leonards School
St Andrews, Fife KY16 9QJ
Tel: 01334 472126
Head of School: Dr Michael Carslaw
Age range: 5–1 8
No. of pupils: 510
Fees: Day £13,137 FB £32,040
(£) (IB) (16)

Glasgow

Belmont House School
Sandringham Avenue, Newton Mearns, Glasgow G77 5DU
Tel: 0141 639 2922
Principal: Mr Melvyn D Shanks BSc, DipEd, MInstP, CPhys, SQH
Age range: 3–18
No. of pupils: 300
Fees: Day £5,976–£11,316
(£) (16)

Craigholme School
72 St Andrews Drive, Pollokshields, Glasgow G41 4HS
Tel: 0141 427 0375
Principal: Ms Gillian C K Stobo BSc, MSc, DipEd
Age range: B3–5 G3–18
No. of pupils: 442 VIth30
Fees: Day £4,137–£9,735
(£) (16)

Fernhill School
Fernbrae Avenue, Burnside, Rutherglen, Glasgow G73 4SG
Tel: 0141 634 2674
Headteacher: Mrs Jacqueline Sexton BSc, PGCE
Age range: B4–11 G4–18
No. of pupils: 300 VIth16
Fees: Day £7,470–£8,976
(£) (16)

Hutchesons' Grammar School
21 Beaton Road, Glasgow G41 4NW
Tel: 0141 423 2933
Rector: Mr Colin Gambles BSc (Hons) PGCE
Age range: 5–18
No. of pupils: 1242 VIth139
Fees: Day £9,098–£11,304
(A) (£) (16)

St Aloysius' College
45 Hill Street, Glasgow G3 6RJ
Tel: 0141 332 3190
Headmaster: Mr J E Stoer BA
Age range: 3–18
No. of pupils: 1289 VIth81
Fees: Day £6,804–£9,009
(A) (£) (16)

The Glasgow Academy
Colebrooke Street, Kelvinbridge, Glasgow G12 8HE
Tel: 0141 334 8558
Rector: Mr Peter Brodie MA, MA(Ed)
Age range: 3–18
No. of pupils: 1148 VIth221
Fees: Day £3,255–£9,645
(£) (16)

The Glasgow Academy Dairsie
54 Newlands Road, Newlands, Glasgow G43 2JG
Tel: 0141 632 0736
Headmistress: Mrs Shona McKnight
Age range: 3–9
No. of pupils: 74
Fees: Day £2,730–£5,505

The Glasgow Academy, Milngavie
Mugdock Road, Milngavie, Glasgow G62 8NP
Tel: +44 (0)1419 563758
Fees: Day £3,540–£8,025

The High School of Glasgow
637 Crow Road, Glasgow G13 1PL
Tel: 0141 954 9628
Rector: John O'Neill
Age range: 3–18
No. of pupils: 1022 VIth97
Fees: Day £4,125–£11,919
(£) (16)

The Kelvinside Academy
33 Kirklee Road, Glasgow G12 0SW
Tel: 0141 357 3376
Rector: Mrs Lesley Douglas
Age range: 3–18
No. of pupils: 640 VIth73
Fees: Day £2,313–£8,895
(A) (£) (16)

Moray

Drumduan School
Clovenside Road, Forres, Moray IV36 2RD
Tel: + 44 (0)1309 676300
Principal Teacher: Krzysztof Zajaczkowski
Age range: 3–16

GORDONSTOUN
For further details see p. 272
Elgin, Moray IV30 5RF
Tel: 01343 837829
Email: admissions@gordonstoun.org.uk
Website: www.gordonstoun.org.uk
Principal: Ms Lisa Kerr BA
Age range: 6–18
No. of pupils: 521 VIth211
Fees: Day £13,842–£27,339 WB £22,515 FB £22,515–£36,909

Perth & Kinross

Ardvreck School
Gwydyr Road, Crieff, Perth & Kinross PH7 4EX
Tel: 01764 653112
Headmaster: Mr Dan Davey
Age range: 4–13
Fees: Day £13,484 FB £20,280

Craigclowan Preparatory School
Edinburgh Road, Perth, Perth & Kinross PH2 8PS
Tel: 01738 626310
Head of School: John Gilmour
Age range: 3–13
No. of pupils: 245
Fees: Day £11,820

Glenalmond College, Perth
Glenalmond, Perth, Perth & Kinross PH1 3RY
Tel: 01738 842000
Warden: Elaine Logan
Age range: 12–18
No. of pupils: 400 VIth175
Fees: Day £16,470–£21,954 FB £24,147–£32,229

Kilgraston School
Bridge of Earn, Perth, Perth & Kinross PH2 9BQ
Tel: 01738 812257
Head: Mrs Dorothy MacGinty
Age range: G5–18
No. of pupils: 260
Fees: Day £3,385–£5,490 FB £7,165–£9,380

Morrison's Academy
Crieff, Perth & Kinross PH7 3AN
Tel: 01764 653885
Principal: Mr Gareth Warren BSc (Hons)
Age range: 3–18
No. of pupils: VIth47
Fees: Day £8,127–£12,300

Strathallan School
Forgandenny, Perth, Perth & Kinross PH2 9EG
Tel: 01738 812546
Headmaster: Mr B K Thompson MA(Oxon)
Age range: 9–18
No. of pupils: 557 VIth195
Fees: Day £12,930–£19,710 FB £20,718–£29,046

Perthshire

QUEEN VICTORIA SCHOOL
For further details see p. 276
Dunblane, Perthshire FK15 0JY
Tel: 0131 310 2927
Email: admissions@qvs.org.uk
Website: www.qvs.org.uk
Head: Donald Shaw BSc(Hons) PGCE
Age range: 11–18
No. of pupils: 267 VIth30
Fees: FB £1,403

Renfrewshire

Cedars School of Excellence
31 Ardgowan Square, Greenock, Renfrewshire PA16 8NJ
Tel: 01475 723905
Headteacher: Mrs Alison Speirs
Age range: 5–16
No. of pupils: 95
Fees: Day £3,400–£5,000

St Columba's School
Duchal Road, Kilmacolm, Renfrewshire PA13 4AU
Tel: 01505 872238
Head of School: Mrs Andrea Y Angus BSc
Age range: 3–18
No. of pupils: 701 VIth125
Fees: Day £2,975–£11,690

South Ayrshire

Wellington School
Carleton Turrets, Ayr, South Ayrshire KA7 2XH
Tel: 01292 269321
Head: Mr R M Parlour BSc(Hons), BA, PGCE(Oxon), MMBA, FIAP, FRSA
Age range: 3–18
No. of pupils: VIth45
Fees: Day £5,304–£10,407

South Lanarkshire

Hamilton College
Bothwell Road, Hamilton, South Lanarkshire ML3 0AY
Tel: 01698 282700
Principal: Ms Margaret Clarke
Age range: 3–18
No. of pupils: VIth49
Fees: Day £6,450–£8,574

Stirling

Beaconhurst School
52 Kenilworth Road, Bridge of Allan, Stirling FK9 4RR
Tel: 01786 832146
Headmaster: Mr Iain Kilpatrick BA, MEd, FRSA
Age range: 3–18
No. of pupils: 403
Fees: Day £6,474–£8,706

Wales

KEY TO SYMBOLS

- *Boys' school*
- *Girls' school*
- *International school*
- *Tutorial or sixth form college*
- *A levels*
- *Boarding accommodation*
- *Bursaries*
- *International Baccalaureate*
- *Learning support*
- *Entrance at 16+*
- *Vocational qualifications*
- *Independent Association of Preparatory Schools*
- *The Headmasters' & Headmistresses' Conference*
- *Independent Schools Association*
- *Girls' School Association*
- *Boarding Schools' Association*
- *Society of Heads*

Unless otherwise indicated, all schools are coeducational day schools. Single-sex and boarding schools will be indicated by the relevant icon.

Carmarthenshire

LLANDOVERY COLLEGE
For further details see p. 280
Queensway, Llandovery, Carmarthenshire SA20 0EE
Tel: +44 (0)1550 723005
Email: admissions@llandoverycollege.com
Website: www.llandoverycollege.com
Warden: Guy Ayling MA
Age range: 4–18 years
No. of pupils: 280
Fees: Day £8,205–£17,520 FB £17,880–£26,460
(A) (£) (16)

St Michael's School
Bryn, Llanelli, Carmarthenshire SA14 9TU
Tel: 01554 820325
Age range: 3–18
No. of pupils: 420 VIth80
Fees: Day £4,179–£7,968 FB £18,250
(A) (16)

Clwyd

Rydal Penrhos Preparatory School
Pwllycrochan Avenue, Colwyn Bay, Clwyd LL29 7BP
Tel: 01492 530381
Headmaster: Mr Roger McDuff
Age range: 2 –11
No. of pupils: 180
Fees: Day £7,155–£9,540

St David's College
Gloddaeth Hall, Llandudno, Clwyd LL30 1RD
Tel: 01492 875974
Headmaster: Mr Stuart Hay
Age range: 9–19
No. of pupils: 254 VIth77
Fees: Day £10,425–£15,210
(A) (£) (16)

Conwy

Rydal Penrhos School
Pwllycrochan Avenue, Colwyn Bay, Conwy LL29 7BT
Tel: +44 (0)1492 530155
Acting Headmaster: Mr Roger McDuff
Age range: 2 –18
No. of pupils: 530
Fees: Day £7,020–£15,825 WB £19,500–£21,825 FB £25,590–£31,515
(A) (£) (IB) (16)

Denbighshire

Fairholme School
The Mount, Mount Road, St Asaph, Denbighshire LL17 0DH
Tel: 01745 583505
Principal: Mrs E Perkins MA(Oxon)
Age range: 3–11
No. of pupils: 110
Fees: Day £6,000–£6,600

Ruthin School
Ruthin, Denbighshire LL15 1EE
Tel: 01824 702543
Headmaster: Mr T J Belfield
Age range: 3–18
No. of pupils: 240 VIth41
Fees: Day £5,550–£10,320 WB £13,965 FB £16,755
(A) (£) (16)

Glamorgan

Cardiff Sixth Form College
1-3 Trinity Court, 21-27 Newport Road, , Glamorgan CF24 0AA
Tel: +44 (0)29 2049 3121
Principal: Mr Gareth Collier
Fees: Day £15,500 FB £28,900–£45,500

Ffynone House School
36 St James's Crescent, Swansea, Glamorgan SA1 6DR
Tel: 01792 464967
Headteacher: Mrs Nicola Walker BSc(Hons), PGCE, MBA, NPQH
Age range: 11–18
No. of pupils: VIth25
Fees: Day £8,655
(A) (£) (16)

Howell's School, Llandaff GDST
Cardiff Road, Llandaff, Cardiff, Glamorgan CF5 2YD
Tel: 029 2056 2019
Principal: Mrs Sally Davis BSc
Age range: 16–18 G3–18
No. of pupils: 780
Fees: Day £7,829–£13,317
(A) (£) (16)

Kings Monkton School
6 West Grove, Cardiff, Glamorgan CF24 3XL
Tel: 02920 482854
Principal: Mr Paul Norton
Age range: 3–18
No. of pupils: 250
Fees: Day £2,650–£4,600
(A) (16)

Oakleigh House School
38 Penlan Crescent, Uplands, Swansea, Glamorgan SA2 0RL
Tel: 01792 298537
Headmistress: Mrs R Ferriman BA(Hons)Ed, MEd
Age range: 2–11
Fees: Day £5,550–£6,570
(£)

St Clare's School
Newton, Porthcawl, Glamorgan CF36 5NR
Tel: 01656 782509
Head of School: Mr S Antwis
Age range: 3–18
No. of pupils: 298 VIth45
Fees: Day £5,685–£9,885
(A) (16)

ST JOHN'S COLLEGE, CARDIFF
For further details see p. 282
College Green, Old St Mellons, Cardiff, Glamorgan CF3 5YX
Tel: 029 2077 8936
Email: admin@stjohnscollegecardiff.co.uk
Website: www.stjohnscollegecardiff.com
Headteacher: Gareth P Lloyd BA (Hons), MSc, FMusTCL (Cantab)
Age range: 3–18
No. of pupils: 525
Fees: Day £7,425–£13,629
(A) (£) (16)

The Cardiff Academy
40-41 The Parade, Cardiff, Glamorgan CF24 3AB
Tel: 029 2040 9630
Principal: Dr S R Wilson
Age range: 14–18
No. of pupils: 51 VIth44
Fees: Day £9,000
(A)

The Cathedral School, Llandaff
Llandaff, Cardiff, Glamorgan CF5 2YH
Tel: 029 2056 3179
Headmaster: Mr P L Gray MA(Cantab), ARCO, PGCE
Age range: 3–16
Fees: Day £5,625–£8,175
(£)

Westbourne School
Hickman Road, Penarth, Glamorgan CF64 2AJ
Tel: 029 2070 5705
Age range: 3–18
No. of pupils: 162
Fees: Day £6,450–£11,700 FB £23,350–£25,850
(£) (IB) (16)

Gwynedd

St Gerard's School
Ffriddoedd Road, Bangor, Gwynedd LL57 2EL
Tel: 01248 351656
Headteacher: Miss Anne Parkinson BA(Hons)
Age range: 3–18
No. of pupils: VIth25
Fees: Day £5,790–£8,760
A £ 16+

Monmouthshire

Haberdashers' Agincourt School
Dixton Lane, Monmouth, Monmouthshire NP25 3SY
Tel: 01600 713970
Head: Mrs E Thomas
Age range: 3–7
No. of pupils: 124
Fees: Day £2,574–£4,134

Haberdashers' Monmouth School for Girls
Hereford Road, Monmouth, Monmouthshire NP25 5XT
Tel: 01600 711104
Head: Mrs H Davy MA(Oxon)
Age range: G7–18
No. of pupils: 582 VIth156
Fees: Day £9,537–£12,141
FB £18,171–£23,112
A £ 16+

Monmouth School
Almshouse Street, Monmouth, Monmouthshire NP25 3XP
Tel: 01600 710433
Headmaster: Dr. Andrew J Daniel BSc, MEd, PhD
Age range: B7–18
No. of pupils: 649 VIth183
Fees: Day £10,149–£14,427
FB £18,999–£27,801
A £ 16+

Rougemont School
Llantarnam Hall, Malpas Road, Newport, Monmouthshire NP20 6QB
Tel: 01633 820800
Headmaster: Mr Robert Carnevale
Age range: 3–18
No. of pupils: 700 VIth111
Fees: Day £5,880–£9,240
A £ 16+

St John's-on-the-Hill
Tutshill, Chepstow, Monmouthshire NP16 7LE
Tel: 01291 622045
Headmaster: Mr N Folland BSc
Age range: 3 months–13 years
No. of pupils: 362
Fees: Day £7,005–£11,565
WB £16,275 FB £16,275
£

Pembrokeshire

Nant-y-Cwm Steiner School
Llanycefn, Clunderwen, Pembrokeshire SA66 7QJ
Tel: 01437 563 640
Age range: 0–14

Redhill Preparatory School
The Garth, St David's Road, Haverfordwest, Pembrokeshire SA61 2UR
Tel: 01437 762472
Principal: Mrs Lovegrove
Age range: 0–11
Fees: Day £4,950–£5,100
£

Powys

Christ College
Brecon, Powys LD3 8AF
Tel: 01874 615440
Head: Mrs E Taylor MA(Oxon)
Age range: 7–18
No. of pupils: 347 VIth135
Fees: Day £13,275–£15,870
FB £18,270–£24,510
A £ 16+

Vale of Glamorgan

UWC Atlantic College
St Donat's Castle, St Donat's, Llantwit Major, Vale of Glamorgan CF61 1WF
Tel: +44 (0)1446 799000
Principal: John Walmsley
Age range: 15–19
No. of pupils: 367
Fees: FB £28,105
£ IB 16+

Examinations and qualifications

Common Entrance

What is Common Entrance?

The Common Entrance examinations are used in UK independent schools (and some independent schools overseas) for transfer from junior to senior schools at the ages of 11+ and 13+. They were first introduced in 1904 and are internationally recognised as being a rigorous form of assessment following a thorough course of study. The examinations are produced by the Independent Schools Examinations Board and backed by HMC (Headmasters' and Headmistresses' Conference), GSA (Girls' Schools Association), and IAPS (Independent Association of Prep Schools) which together represent the leading independent schools in the UK, and many overseas.

Common Entrance is not a public examination as, for example, GCSE, and candidates may normally be entered only in one of the following circumstances:

a) they have been offered a place at a senior school subject to their passing the examination, or

b) they are entered as a 'trial run', in which case the papers are marked by the junior school concerned

Candidates normally take the examination in their own junior or preparatory schools, either in the UK or overseas.

How does Common Entrance fit into the progression to GCSEs?

Rapid changes in education nationally and internationally have resulted in regular reviews of the syllabuses for all the Common Entrance examinations. Reviews of the National Curriculum, in particular, have brought about a number of changes, with the Board wishing to ensure that it continues to set high standards. It is also a guiding principle that Common Entrance should be part of the natural progression from 11- 16, and not a diversion from it.

Common Entrance at 11+

At 11+, the examination consists of papers in English, mathematics and science. It is designed so that it can be taken by candidates either from independent preparatory schools or by candidates from schools in the maintained sector or overseas who have had no special preparation. The examination is normally taken in January for entrance to senior schools in the following September.

Common Entrance at 13+

At 13+, most candidates come from independent preparatory schools. The compulsory subjects are English, mathematics and science. Papers in French, geography, German, Classical Greek, history, Latin, religious studies and Spanish are also available and candidates usually offer as many subjects as they can. In most subjects, papers are available at more than one level to cater for candidates of different abilities. There are three examination sessions each year, with the majority of candidates sitting in the summer prior to entry to their senior schools in September.

Marking and grading

The papers are set centrally but the answers are marked by the senior school for which a candidate is entered. Mark schemes are provided by the Board but senior schools are free to set their own grade boundaries. Results are available within two weeks of the examinations taking place.

Pre-Testing and the ISEB Common Pre-Tests

A number of senior independent schools 'pre-test' pupils for entry, prior to them taking their main entrance examinations at a later date. Usually, these pre-tests take place when a pupil is in Year 6 or Year 7 of his or her junior school and will then be going on to sit Common Entrance in Year 8. The tests are designed to assess a pupil's academic potential and suitability for a particular senior school so that the child, the parents and the school know well in advance whether he/ she is going to be offered a place at the school, subject to a satisfactory performance in the entrance examinations. The tests enable senior schools which are heavily oversubscribed to manage their lists and help to ensure that pupils are not entered for examinations in which they are unlikely to be successful. In short, it reduces uncertainty for all concerned.

Pre-tests may be written specifically for the senior school for which the candidate is entered but a growing number of schools are choosing to use the Common Pre-Tests provided by the Independent Schools Examinations Board. These online tests are usually taken in the candidate's own junior school and one of their main advantages is that a pupil need sit the tests only once, with the results then made available to any senior school which wishes to use them. The multiple-choice tests cover verbal reasoning, non- verbal reasoning, English and mathematics, with the results standardised according to the pupil's age when they are taken. Further information is available on the ISEB website at www.iseb.co.uk.

Parents are advised to check the entrance requirements for senior schools to see if their child will be required to sit a pre-test.

Further information

Details of the Common Entrance examinations and how to register candidates are available on the ISEB website www.iseb.co.uk. Copies of past papers and a wide range of textbooks and other resources can be purchased from Galore Park Publishing Ltd at www. galorepark.co.uk. Support materials are also available from Hodder Education and other publishers; see the Resources section of the ISEB website for details.

Independent Schools Examinations Board Suite 3,
Endeavour House,
Crow Arch Lane,
Ringwood, Hampshire BH24 1HP

Telephone: 01425 470555
Email: enquiries@iseb.co.uk
Web: www.iseb.co.uk

7+ Entrance Exams

What is the 7+?

The 7+ is the descriptive name given to the entrance exams set by an increasing number of independent schools for pupils wishing to gain admission into their Year 3.

7+ entrance exams may be simply for admission into a selective preparatory school, which will then prepare the child for Common Entrance exams to gain a place at senior school. Alternatively, the 7+ can be a route into a school with both prep and senior departments, therefore often effectively bypassing the 11+ or 13+ Common Entrance exams.

The Independent Schools Examinations Board provides Common Entrance examinations and assessments for pupils seeking entry to independent senior schools at 11+ and 13+, but there is as yet no equivalent for the 7+. The testing is largely undertaken by the individual schools, although some schools might commission test from external agencies. Many schools in the incredibly competitive London area offer entrance exams at 7+ and some, such as Haberdasher's Aske's Boys' School, share specimen papers on their website to clarify what 7+ children will face.

Who sits the 7+?

The 7+ is sat by Year 2 children, who may be moving from a state primary school or a stand-alone pre-prep school to an independent prep school (although many prep schools now have their own pre-prep department, with a cohort of children poised to pass into Year 3 there).

Registration for 7+ entrance exams usually closes in the November of Year 2, with the exams then sat in January or February, for entry that September.

How is the 7+ assessed?

Written exam content will be primarily English and maths based, whilst spelling, dictation, mental arithmetic and more creative skills may be assessed verbally on a one-to-one basis. Group exercises are also sometimes used to look at a child's initiative and their ability to work with others.

Schools will not only be looking for academic potential, but also good citizens and a mixture of personalities to produce a well-rounded year group. For this reason, children are often asked to attend an interview. Some schools interview all candidates, whilst others may call back a limited number with good test results. They will be looking for a child's ability to look an adult in the eye and think on their feet, but also simply to show some spark and personality.

After the assessments, children will be told if they have been successful in gaining a firm place, or a place on a waiting list.

Further Information

As the 7+ is not centrally regulated, it is best for parents to seek accurate admissions and testing information direct from the schools in which they are interested. In addition to a school's facilities and ethos, choosing a school for admission at 7+ will probably also involve whether the school has a senior department and if not, the prep school's record in gaining its students places at target senior schools.

Experienced educational consultants may be able to help parents decide which independent prep school is best suited for their child, based on their personality, senior school ambitions and academic potential. Many parents enlist the help of tutors to prepare children for the 7+, if only to reduce the fear of the unknown in these very young children. This is achieved by teaching them the required curriculum, what to expect on their test and interview days, and giving them the opportunity to practice tackling the type of assessments they will face.

Prep School Baccalaureate

The Prep School Baccalaureate (PSB) is a framework of study for children in junior and preparatory schools that was introduced in 2012, and focuses on the active development and assessment of 6 core skills: Communication, Collaboration, Leadership, Independence, Reviewing and improving and Thinking and Learning. Member schools promote the core skills across all areas of school life, and provide guidance for pupils in progressing these skills, which are seen as essential for developing capable and balanced adults, able to make the most of the opportunities of a fast-changing world. A strong but appropriate knowledge base compliments this, with the use of focused tutoring, pastoral care and Well Being programmes.

Schools do not work to a prescribed curriculum and the emphasis is upon promoting an independent approach which works for each individual school. There are subject INSET days for PSB school staff annually and these are supported by senior school colleagues, to ensure that work done in PSB schools compliments the demands of education at higher levels.

The PSB is a whole school initiative from Early Years to either Year 6 or Year 8, at which point the certificate is awarded at the time of matriculation to senior schools. An additional PSB Year 9 framework is being developed together with international membership.

The development of skills is now recognised as essential by the Independent Schools Inspectorate (ISI), and recent ISI reports on PSB schools highlight the excellent contribution the PSB has in schools achieving excellence.

Assessment

The PSB has a 10 point scale for all subjects studied with a compulsory spine covering: English, Maths, Science, Modern Languages, The Humanities, Art, Design Technology, Music, Sport and PE with each pupil additionally completing a cross curricular project. Optional subjects are agreed with schools but these must be supported by a scheme of work clearly identifying appropriate core skills which are assessed on a 5 point scale. There are distinction levels on both scales and the 10 point scale cross references both ISEB and National Curriculum assessment levels.

Pupils moving on to senior school do so via individual senior school pre-testing arrangements, the award of the PSB certificate, core ISEB papers or a combination of the above.

Membership categories

Partner membership is available to schools developing the PSB with support given from existing schools and the Communications director.

Full membership entitles schools to use the PSB matriculation certificate and join the PSB committee as voting members.

Affiliated membership is for schools that have developed their own skills based approach, in line with PSB principles; staff can participate in all training opportunities and the Heads of Affiliated Schools join committee meetings as non-voting guests.

Membership of the above categories is dependent upon strong ISI reports, the development of a skills based curriculum, with skills clearly identified in schemes of work and excellent teaching.

Associate membership is for senior schools that actively support the PSB in providing staff for subject meetings, hosting meetings, conferences and committee meetings and offer a valuable perspective on the demands of GCSE, A Level and the International Baccalaureate.

Further details

The PSB is an entirely independent charity overseen by a Board of Trustees who have expertise in both primary and secondary education. Details of the PSB can be found on the website – psbacc.org – together with contact details for the Communications Director who can provide further details on request.

General Certificate of Secondary Education (GCSE)

What are the GCSE qualifications?

GCSE qualifications were first introduced in 1986 and are the principal means of assessment at Key Stage 4 across a range of academic subject areas. They command respect and have status not only in the UK but worldwide.

Main features of the GCSE

There are four unitary awarding organisations for GCSEs in England (see 'Awarding organisations and examination dates' section, p425). WJEC and CCEA also offer GCSE qualifications in Wales and Northern Ireland. Each examining group designs its own specifications but they are required to conform to set criteria. For some aspects of the qualification system, the exam boards adopt common ways of working. When the exam boards work together in this way they generally do so through the Joint Council of Qualifications (JCQ). The award of a grade is intended to indicate that a candidate has met the required level of skills, knowledge and understanding.

GCSEs are in the process of reform. New GCSEs in English literature, English language and maths were first taught in September 2015, with first results in summer 2017. Assessment in these reformed GCSEs consists primarily of formal examinations taken at the end of the student's two-year course. Other types of assessment, non-exam assessment (NEA), is used where there are skills and knowledge which cannot be assessed through exams. Ofqual have set the percentage of the total marks that will come from NEA.

Ofqual says there will be new, more demanding content, which has been developed by the government and the exam boards. Courses will be designed for two years of study (linear assessment) and no longer divided into different modules.

Exams can only be split into 'foundation tier' and 'higher tier' if one exam paper does not give all students the opportunity to show their knowledge and their abilities. Resit opportunities will only be available each November in English language and maths.

New GCSEs taught from September 2016: ancient languages, art and design, biology, chemistry, citizenship studies, computer science, combined science, dance, drama, food preparation and nutrition, history, geography, modern foreign languages (French, German, Spanish), music, physics, physical education, religious studies.

New GCSEs taught from September 2017: ancient history, astronomy, business, classical civilisation, design and technology, economics, electronics, engineering, film studies, geology, media studies, psychology, sociology, statistics, other (minority) foreign languages e.g. Italian, Polish.

Grading

The basic principle that exam boards follow when setting grade boundaries is that if the group of students (the cohort) taking a qualification in one year is of similar ability to the cohort in the previous year then the overall results (outcomes) should be comparable.

The reformed exams taken in summer 2017 were the first to show a new grading system, with the A* to G grades being phased out.

The new grading system is 9 to 1, with 9 being the top grade. Ofqual says this allows greater differentiation between students. It expects that broadly the same proportion of students will achieve a grade 4 and above as currently achieve a grade C and above, that broadly the same proportion of students will achieve a grade 7 and above as currently achieve a grade A and above. The bottom of grade 1 will be aligned with the bottom of grade G, grade 5 will be awarded to around the top third of students gaining the equivalent of a grade C and bottom third of a grade B. Grade 9 will be set using the tailored approach formula in the first award.

Grades 2, 3, 5 and 6 will be awarded arithmetically

so that the grade boundaries are equally spaced in terms of marks from neighbouring grades.

The government's definition of a 'good pass' will be set at grade 5 for reformed GCSEs. A grade 4 will continue to be a level 2 achievement. The DfE does not expect employers, colleges or universities to raise the bar to a grade 5 if a grade 4 would meet their requirements.

Can anyone take GCSE qualifications?

GCSEs are intended mainly for 16-year-old pupils, but are open to anyone of any age, whether studying full-time or part-time at a school, college or privately. There are no formal entry requirements.

Students normally study up to ten subjects over a two-year period. Short course GCSEs are available in some subjects (including ICT and religious studies) – these include half the content of a full GCSE, so two short course GCSEs are equivalent to one full GCSE.

The English Baccalaureate

The English Baccalaureate (EBacc) is a school performance measure. It allows people to see how many pupils get a grade C or above (current grading) in the core academic subjects at Key Stage 4 in any government-funded school.

The DfE introduced the EBacc measure in 2010. In June 2015, it announced its intention that all pupils who start year 7 in September 2015 take the EBacc subjects when they reach their GCSEs in 2020.

Progress 8 and Attainment 8

Progress 8 aims to capture the progress a pupil makes from the end of primary school to the end of secondary school. It is a type of value added measure, which means that pupils' results are compared to the actual achievements of other pupils with the same prior attainment.

The new performance measures are designed to encourage schools to offer a broad and balanced curriculum with a focus on an academic core at Key Stage 4, and reward schools for the teaching of all their pupils, measuring performance across 8 qualifications. Every increase in every grade a pupil achieves will attract additional points in the performance tables.

Progress 8 will be calculated for individual pupils solely in order to calculate a school's Progress 8 score, and there will be no need for schools to share individual Progress 8 scores with their pupils. Schools should continue to focus on which qualifications are most suitable for individual pupils, as the grades pupils achieve will help them reach their goals for the next stage of their education or training

Attainment 8 will measure the achievement of a pupil across 8 qualifications including mathematics (double weighted) and English (double weighted), 3 further qualifications that count in the English Baccalaureate (EBacc) measure and 3 further qualifications that can be GCSE qualifications (including EBacc subjects) or any other non-GCSE qualification on the DfE approved list.

General Certificate of Education (GCE) Advanced level (A level)

Typically, A level qualifications are studied over a two-year period. There are no lower or upper age limits. Schools and colleges usually expect students aged 16-18 to have obtained grades A*-C (grade 5 in the new criteria) in five subjects at GCSE level before taking an advanced level course. This requirement may vary between centres and according to which specific subjects are to be studied. Mature students may be assessed on different criteria as to their suitability to embark on the course.

GCE Qualifications

AS level and A level qualifications are being reformed. The new subjects are being introduced gradually, with the first wave being taught from September 2015. Subjects that have not been reformed will no longer be available for teaching from September 2018.

GCE qualifications are available at two levels. The Advanced Subsidiary (AS) is the two-or three-unit General Certificate of Education (GCE). The A level is the four- or six-unit GCE. Nearly 70 titles are available, covering a wide range of subject areas, including humanities, sciences, language, business, arts, mathematics and technology.

One of the major reforms is that AS level results will no longer count towards an A level (they previously counted for 50%). The two qualifications will be linear, with AS assessments typically taking place after one year and A levels after two.

New-style AS and A levels were first taught from September 2015 for: art and design, biology, business studies, chemistry, computer studies, economics, English language, English language and literature, English literature, history, physics, psychology, and sociology.

Subjects first taught from September 2016 include: ancient languages such as Latin or Greek, dance, drama (theatre studies), geography, modern languages such as Spanish or French, music, physical education, religious studies.

Those introduced for first teaching from September 2017: accounting, design and technology, music technology, history of art, environmental science, philosophy, maths, further maths, archaeology, accounting, electronics, ancient history, law, classical civilisation, film studies, media studies, politics, geology, statistics, Chinese, Italian, Russian. In 2018 Biblical Hebrew, Modern Hebrew & languages such as Bengali, Polish and Urdu will be available for first teaching.

Some GCE AS and A levels, particularly the practical ones, contain a proportion of coursework. All GCE A levels contain in one or more of the units an assessment that tests students' understanding of the whole specification (synoptic assessment). GCE AS are graded A-E and A levels are graded A*-E.

Overall the amount of coursework at A level has been reduced in the reforms. In some subjects, such as the sciences, practical work will not contribute to the final

A level but will be reported separately in a certificate of endorsement. In the sciences, students will do at least eight practical activities (16 for combined sciences), covering apparatus and techniques. Exam questions about practical work will make up at least 15% of the total marks for the qualification and students will be assessed on their knowledge, skills and understanding of practical work.

Cambridge International AS & A Level

Cambridge International AS & A Level is an internationally benchmarked qualification, taught in over 130 countries worldwide. It is typically for learners aged 16 to 19 years who need advanced study to prepare for university. It was created specifically for an international audience and the content has been devised to suit the wide variety of schools worldwide and avoid any cultural bias.

Cambridge International A Level is typically a two-year course, and Cambridge International AS Level is typically one year. Some subjects can be started as a Cambridge International AS Level and extended to a Cambridge International A Level. Students can either follow a broad course of study, or specialise in one particular subject area.

Learners use Cambridge International AS & A Levels to gain places at leading universities worldwide, including the UK, Ireland, USA, Canada, Australia, New Zealand, India, Singapore, Egypt, Jordan, South Africa, the Netherlands, Germany and Spain. In places such as the US and Canada, good grades in carefully chosen Cambridge International A Level subjects can result in up to one year of university course credit.

Assessment options:

Cambridge International AS & A Levels have a linear structure with exams at the end of the course. Students can choose from a range of assessment options:

Option 1: take Cambridge International AS Levels only. The Cambridge International AS Level syllabus content is half a Cambridge International A Level.

Option 2: staged assessment, which means taking the Cambridge International AS Level in one exam session and the Cambridge International A Level at a later session. However, this route is not possible in all subjects.

Option 3: take all Cambridge International A Level papers in the same examination session, usually at the end of the course.

Grades and subjects

Cambridge International A Levels are graded from A* to E. Cambridge International AS Levels are graded from A to E.

Subjects: available in 55 subjects including accounting, Afrikaans, Afrikaans – first language (AS only), Afrikaans language (AS only), applied information and communication technology, Arabic, Arabic language (AS only), art and design, biology, business, chemistry, Chinese, Chinese language (AS only), classical studies, computing, design and technology, design and textiles, divinity, economics, English language, English literature, environmental management, food studies, French, French language (AS only), French literature (AS only), general paper, geography, German, German language (AS only), Global Perspectives & Research, Hindi, Hindi language (AS only), Hindi literature (AS only), Hinduism, history, Islamic studies, Japanese language (AS only), English language and literature (AS only), law, Marathi, Marathi language (AS only), marine science, mathematics, further mathematics, media studies, music, physical education, physical science, physics, Portuguese, Portuguese language (AS only), Portuguese literature (AS only), psychology, sociology, Spanish, Spanish first language (AS only), Spanish language (AS only), Spanish literature (AS only), Tamil, Tamil language (AS only), Telugu, Telugu language (AS only), thinking skills, travel and tourism, Urdu, Urdu language (AS only), Urdu Pakistan.

Website: www.cie.org.uk/alevel

Cambridge International GCSE (IGCSE)

Cambridge IGCSE is the world's most popular international qualification for 14 to16 year olds. It develops skills in creative thinking, enquiry and problem solving, in preparation for the next stage in a student's education. Cambridge IGCSE is taken in over 145 countries, and is widely recognised by employers and higher education institutions worldwide.

Cambridge IGCSE is graded from A*-G. In the UK, Cambridge IGCSE is accepted as equivalent to the GCSE. It can be used as preparation for Cambridge International A & AS Levels, UK A and AS levels, IB or AP and in some instances entry into university. Cambridge IGCSE First Language English and Cambridge IGCSE English Language qualifications are recognised by a significant number of UK universities as evidence of competence in the language for university entrance.

Subjects: available in over 70 subjects including accounting, Afrikaans – first language, Afrikaans – second language, agriculture, Arabic – first language, Arabic – foreign language, art and design, Baha Indonesia, Bangladesh studies, biology, business studies, chemistry, child development, Chinese – first language, Chinese – second language, Chinese (Mandarin) – foreign language, computer studies, Czech – first language, design and technology, development studies, drama, Dutch – first language, Dutch – foreign language, economics, English – first language, English – literature, English – second language, enterprise, environmental management, food and nutrition, French – first language, French – foreign language, geography, German – first language, German – foreign language, global perspectives, Greek – foreign language, Hindi as a second language, Italian – foreign language, history, India studies, Indonesian – foreign language, information and communication technology, IsiZulu as a second language, Japanese – first language,

Japanese – foreign language, Kazakh as a second language, Korean (first language), Latin, Malay – foreign language, mathematics, mathematics – additional, international mathematics, music, Pakistan studies, physical education, physical science, physics, Portuguese – first language, Portuguese – foreign language, religious studies, Russian – first language, science – combined, sciences – co-ordinated (double), sociology, Spanish – first language, Spanish – foreign language, Spanish – literature, Thai – first language, travel and tourism, Turkish – first language, Urdu – second language, world literature.

Website: www.cie.org.uk/igcse

Cambridge Pre-U

Cambridge Pre-U is a post-16 qualification that equips students with the skills they need to succeed at university. Developed with universities, it was first introduced in UK schools in September 2008. It is now taught in 170 schools, including some schools outside the UK.

Cambridge Pre-U is a linear course, with exams taken at the end of two years. It encourages the development of well-informed, open and independent-minded individuals; promotes deep understanding through subject specialisation, with a depth and rigour appropriate to progression to higher education; and develops skills in independent research valued by universities.

Assessment

Cambridge Pre-U Principal Subjects are examined at the end of two years. Cambridge Pre-U Short Courses are available in some subjects and are typically examined at the end of one year. Students can study a combination of A Levels and Principal Subjects.

In order to gain the Cambridge Pre-U Diploma, students must study at least three Cambridge Pre-U Principal Subjects (up to two A Levels can be substituted for Principal Subjects) and Cambridge Pre-U Global Perspectives & Research (GPR). Cambridge Pre-U GPR includes an extended project in the second year, developing skills in research and critical thinking.

Grades and subjects

Cambridge Pre-U reports achievement on a scale of nine grades, with Distinction 1 being the highest grade and Pass 3 the lowest grade.

Subjects: available in 25 subjects including art and design, biology, business and management, chemistry, drama and theatre, economics, literature in English, French, further mathematics, geography, German, global perspectives and research, classical Greek, history, Italian, art history, Latin, Mandarin Chinese, mathematics, music, philosophy and theology, physics, psychology, Russian, Spanish.

Website: www.cie.org.uk/cambridgepreu

Edexcel International GCSEs

Pearson's Edexcel International GCSEs are academic qualifications aimed at learners aged 14 to 16. They're equivalent to a UK General Certificate of Secondary Education (GCSE), and are the main requirement for Level 3 studies, including progression to GCE AS or A levels, BTECs or employment. International GCSEs are linear qualifications, meaning that students take all of the exams at the end of the course. They are available at Level 1 (grades D-G) and Level 2 (grades A*-C). There are currently more than 100,000 learners studying Edexcel International GCSEs, in countries throughout Asia, Africa, Europe, the Middle East and Latin America. Developed by subject specialists and reviewed regularly, many of Pearson's Edexcel International GCSEs include specific international content to make them relevant to students worldwide.

Pearson's Edexcel International GCSEs were initially developed for international schools. They have since become popular among independent schools in the UK, but are not approved for use in UK state schools. If you're a UK state school, you may be interested in offering Pearson's Edexcel Level 1/Level 2 Certificates. These qualifications are based on the Edexcel International GCSE specifications but currently count towards national performance measures and are eligible for funding in UK state schools until 2016.

International GCSEs are offered in over 40 subjects. Subject areas include: Art and Design, Business & Economics, **English**, **Humanities**, Information and Communication Technology, **Languages, Mathematics, Sciences**. *Note that the subject areas highlighted in bold are also available as part of the Edexcel Certificate qualification suite.*

Free Standing Maths Qualifications (FSMQ)

Aimed at those students wishing to acquire further qualifications in maths, specifically additional mathematics and foundations of advanced mathematics (MEI).

Further UCAS points can be earned upon completion of the advanced FSMQ in additional mathematics, whereas the higher FSMQ in foundations of advanced mathematics is designed for those not yet ready to take AS/A level GCE mathematics.

For further details see the AQA or OCR website.

AQA Certificate in Mathematical Studies (Core Maths)

This new Level 3 qualification has been available from September 2015. It is designed for students who achieved a Grade 4 or above at GCSE and want to continue studying Maths. The qualification carries UCAS points equivalent to an AS level qualification

Scottish qualifications

Information supplied by Scottish Qualifications Authority

In Scotland, qualifications are awarded by the Scottish Qualifications Authority (SQA), the national accreditation and awarding body. A variety of qualifications are offered in Scotland's schools. These include:

- National Qualifications (including National Units, National Courses and Group Awards)
- Wider Achievement Awards
- Skills for Work Courses
- Scottish Baccalaureates

National Qualifications (NQ)

SQA has designed and developed new National Qualifications to support Curriculum for Excellence (CfE). The National Qualifications – National 1, National 2, National 3, National 4 and National 5 – have been available in schools since August 2013.

The new qualifications help young people to demonstrate the knowledge, understanding and skills they have developed at school or college and enable them to prepare for further learning, training and employment.

National Units

National Units are the building blocks of National Courses and Group Awards. They are also qualifications in their own right, and are normally designed to take 40 hours of teaching to complete. Over 3,500 National Units are available, including National 1 Units, which are stand-alone qualifications.

National Courses

National Courses are available at a number of levels including National 2, National 3, National 4, National 5, Higher and Advanced Higher.

Skills for Work Courses

Skills for Work courses encourage school pupils to become familiar with the world of work. They involve a strong element of learning through involvement in practical and vocational activities and develop knowledge, skills and experience that are related to employment. They are available at a number of levels and are often delivered in partnership with schools and colleges.

Awards

Awards provide young people with the opportunity to have the skills that they may have gained in environments outwith the classroom recognised. A variety of different Awards are offered at a number of levels and cover subjects including leadership, employability and enterprise. These awards are designed to recognise the life, learning and work skills that learners gain from partaking in different activities for example sports, volunteering and fundraising.

Scottish Baccalaureates

Scottish Baccalaureates consist of a coherent group of Higher and Advanced Higher qualifications and, uniquely, an interdisciplinary project selected by the candidate in one of four broad topics – languages, science, expressive arts or social studies. The interdisciplinary project is marked at Advanced Higher level and provides candidates with a platform to apply their knowledge in a realistic context. Aimed at high-achieving sixth year candidates, the Scottish Baccalaureate encourages personalised, in-depth study and interdisciplinary learning in their final year of secondary school.

For more information on SQA and its portfolio of qualifications, visit www.sqa.org.uk or follow us on Twitter @sqanews

Additional and Alternative

AQA Baccalaureate

The AQA Baccalaureate is awarded to students who achieve at least three A levels (minimum grade E or 2/3), a broader study AS level subject and the EPQ, plus they must undertake a minimum of 100 hours of 'enrichment activities'.

This is a complete curriculum programme, which adds a broader range of study, and includes the Extended Project Qualification (EPQ).

This qualification is built on familiar subjects, so it can be tailored to fit in with existing curricula. It includes extracurricular activities and encourages a series of 'enrichment activities' covering personal qualities, perseverance, leadership, independence, time management, commitment and communication.

The AQA Bacc is accepted by universities; offers are based on the component parts of the diploma, with students receiving their AQA certificate alongside their A level, AS level and EPQ certificates.

Cambridge Primary

Cambridge Primary is typically for learners aged 5 to 11 years. It develops learner skills and understanding through the primary years in English, mathematics and science. The flexible curriculum frameworks include optional assessment tools to help schools monitor learners' progress and give detailed feedback to parents. At the end of Cambridge Primary, schools can enter students for Cambridge Primary Checkpoint tests which are marked in Cambridge.
Website: www.cie.org.uk/primary

Cambridge ICT Starters introduces learners, typically aged 5 to 14 years, to the key ICT applications they need to achieve computer literacy and to understand the impact of technology on our daily lives. It can be taught and assessed in English or Spanish.

Cambridge Secondary 1

Cambridge Secondary 1 is typically for learners aged 11 to 14 years. It develops learner skills and understanding in English, English as a second language, mathematics and science for the first three years of secondary education, and includes assessment tools. At the end of Cambridge Secondary 1, schools can enter students for Cambridge Secondary 1 Checkpoint tests which are marked in Cambridge and provide an external international benchmark for student performance.
Website: www.cie.org.uk/cambridgesecondary1

European Baccalaureate (EB)

Not to be confused with the International Baccalaureate (IB) or the French Baccalaureate, this certificate is available in European schools and recognised in all EU countries.

To obtain the baccalaureate, a student must obtain a minimum score of 60%, which is made up from: course-work, oral participation in class and tests (40%); five written examinations (36%) – mother-tongue, first foreign language and maths are compulsory for all candidates; four oral examinations (24%) – mother tongue and first foreign language are compulsory (history or geography may also be compulsory here, dependant on whether the candidate has taken a written examination in these subjects).

Throughout the EU the syllabus and examinations necessary to achieve the EB are identical. The only exception to this rule is the syllabus for the mother tongue language. The EB has been specifically designed to meet, at the very least, the minimum qualification requirements of each member state.

Study for the EB begins at nursery stage (age 4) and progresses through primary (age six) and on into secondary school (age 12).

Syllabus

Languages: Bulgarian, Czech, Danish, Dutch, English, Estonian, Finnish, Finnish as a second national language, French, German, Greek, Hungarian, Irish, Italian, Latvian, Lithuanian, Maltese, Polish, Portuguese, Romanian, Slovak, Slovenian, Spanish, Swedish, Swedish for Finnish pupils.

Literary: art education, non-confessional ethics, geography, ancient Greek, history, human sciences, Latin, music, philosophy, physical education.

Sciences: biology, chemistry, economics, ICT, integrated science, mathematics, physics.

For more information, contact:
Office of the Secretary-General of the European Schools, c/o European Commission, Rue Joseph II, 30-2ème étage, B-1049 Brussels, Belgium
Tel: +32 2295 3745; Fax: +32 2298 6298
Website: www.eursc.eu

The International Baccalaureate (IB)

The International Baccalaureate (IB) offers four challenging and high quality educational programmes for a worldwide community of schools, aiming to develop internationally minded people who, recognizing their common humanity and shared guardianship of the planet, help to create a better, more peaceful world.

The IB works with schools around the world (both state and privately funded) that share the commitment to international education to deliver these programmes.

Schools that have achieved the high standards required for authorization to offer one or more of the IB programmes are known as IB World Schools. There are over half a million students attending more than 4500 IB World Schools in 153 countries and this number is growing annually.

The Primary Years, Middle Years and Diploma Programmes share a common philosophy and common characteristics. They develop the whole student, helping students to grow intellectually, socially, aesthetically and culturally. They provide a broad and balanced education that includes science and the humanities, languages and mathematics, technology and the arts. The programmes teach students to think critically, and encourage them to draw connections between areas of knowledge and to use problem-solving techniques and concepts from many disciplines. They instil in students a sense of responsibility towards others and towards the environment. Lastly, and perhaps most importantly, the programmes give students an awareness and understanding of their own culture and of other cultures, values and ways of life.

A fourth programme called the IB Career Related Certificate (IBCC) became available to IB World Schools from September 2012. All IB programmes include:

- a written curriculum or curriculum framework;
- student assessment appropriate to the age range;
- professional development and networking opportunities for teachers;
- support, authorization and programme evaluation for the school.

The IB Primary Years Programme

The IB Primary Years Programme (PYP), for students aged three to 12, focuses on the development of the whole child as an inquirer, both in the classroom and in the world outside. It is a framework consisting of five essential elements (concepts, knowledge, skills, attitude, action) and guided by six trans-disciplinary themes of global significance, explored using knowledge and skills derived from six subject areas (language, social studies, mathematics, science and technology, arts, and personal, social and physical education) with a powerful emphasis on inquiry-based learning.

The most significant and distinctive feature of the PYP is the six trans-disciplinary themes. These themes are about issues that have meaning for, and are important to, all of us. The programme offers a balance between learning about or through the subject areas, and learning beyond them. The six themes of global significance create a trans-disciplinary framework that allows students to 'step up' beyond the confines of learning within subject areas:

- Who we are.
- Where we are in place and time.
- How we express ourselves.
- How the world works.
- How we organize ourselves.
- Sharing the planet.

The PYP exhibition is the culminating activity of the programme. It requires students to analyse and propose solutions to real-world issues, drawing on what they have learned through the programme. Evidence of student development and records of PYP exhibitions are reviewed by the IB as part of the programme evaluation process.

Assessment is an important part of each unit of inquiry as it both enhances learning and provides opportunities for students to reflect on what they know, understand and can do. The teacher's feedback to the students provides the guidance, the tools and the incentive for them to become more competent, more skilful and better at understanding how to learn.

The IB Middle Years Programme (MYP)

The Middle Years Programme (MYP), for students aged 11 to 16, comprises eight subject groups:

- Language acquisition
- Language and literature
- Individuals and societies
- Sciences
- Mathematics
- Arts
- Physical and health education
- Design

The MYP requires at least 50 hours of teaching time for each subject group in each year of the programme. In years 4 and 5, students have the option to take courses from six of the eight subject groups within certain limits, to provide greater flexibility in meeting local requirements and individual student learning needs.

Each year, students in the MYP also engage in at least one collaboratively planned interdisciplinary unit that involves at least two subject groups.

MYP students also complete a long-term project, where they decide what they want to learn about, identify what they already know, discovering what they will need to know to complete the project, and create a proposal or criteria for completing it

The MYP aims to help students develop their personal understanding, their emerging sense of self and their responsibility in their community.

The MYP allows schools to continue to meet state, provincial or national legal requirements for students with access needs. Schools must develop an inclusion/special educational needs (SEN) policy that explains assessment access arrangements, classroom accommodations and curriculum modification that meet individual student learning needs.

The IB Diploma Programme (IBDP)

The IB Diploma Programme, for students aged 16 to 19, is an academically challenging and motivating curriculum of international education that prepares students for success at university and in life beyond studies.

DP students choose at least one course from six subject groups, thus ensuring depth and breadth of knowledge and experience in languages, social studies, the experimental sciences, mathematics, and the arts. With more than 35 courses to choose from, students have the flexibility to further explore and learn subjects that meet their interest. Out of the six courses required, at least three and not more than four must be taken at higher level (240 teaching hours), the others at standard level (150 teaching hours). Students can take examinations in English, French or Spanish.

In addition, three unique components of the programme – the DP core – aim to broaden students' educational experience and challenge them to apply their knowledge and skills. The DP core – the extended essay (EE), theory of knowledge (TOK) and creativity, activity, service (CAS) – are compulsory and central to the philosophy of the programme.

The IB uses both external and internal assessment to measure student performance in the DP. Student results are determined by performance against set standards, not by each student's position in the overall rank order. DP assessment is unique in the way that it measures the extent to which students have mastered advanced academic skills not what they have memorized. DP assessment also encourages an international outlook and intercultural skills, wherever appropriate.

The IB diploma is awarded to students who gain at least 24 points out of a possible 45 points, subject to certain minimum levels of performance across the whole programme and to satisfactory participation in the creativity, activity, and service requirement.

Recognized and respected by leading universities globally, the DP encourages students to be knowledgeable, inquiring, caring and compassionate, and to develop intercultural understanding, open-mindedness and the attitudes necessary to respect and evaluate a range of viewpoints.

The IB Career Related Programme (IBCP)

The IB Career-related Programme, for students aged 16 to 19, offers an innovative educational framework that combines academic studies with career-related learning. Through the CP, students develop the competencies they need to succeed in the 21st century. More importantly, they have the opportunity to engage with a rigorous study programme that genuinely interests them while gaining transferable and lifelong skills that prepares them to pursue higher education, apprenticeships or direct employment.

CP students complete four core components – language development, personal and professional skills, service learning and a reflective project – in order to receive the International Baccalaureate Career-related Programme Certificate. Designed to enhance critical thinking and intercultural understanding, the CP core helps students develop the communication and personal skills, as well as intellectual habits required for lifelong learning.

Schools that choose to offer the CP can create their own distinctive version of the programme and select career pathways that suit their students and local community needs. The IB works with a variety of CRS providers around the world and schools seeking to develop career pathways with professional communities can benefit from our existing collaborations. All CRS providers undergo a rigorous curriculum evaluation to ensure that their courses align with the CP pedagogy and meet IB quality standards. The flexibility to meet the needs, backgrounds and contexts of learners allows CP schools to offer an education that is relevant and meaningful to their students.

Launched in 2012, there are more than 140 CP schools in over 23 countries to date. Many schools with the IB Diploma Programme (DP) and the Middle Years Programme (MYP) have chosen the CP as an alternative IB pathway to offer students. CP schools often report that the programme has helped them raise student aspiration, increase student engagement and retention and encouraged learners to take responsibility for their own actions, helping them foster high levels of self-esteem through meaningful achievements.

For more information on IB programmes, visit: www.ibo.org
Africa, Europe, Middle East Global Centre, Churchillplein 6, The Hague, 2517JW, The Netherlands
Tel: +31 (0)70 352 6233

Pearson Edexcel Mathematics Awards

Pearson's Edexcel Mathematics Awards are small, stand-alone qualifications designed to help students to develop and demonstrate proficiency in different areas of mathematics. These Awards enable students to focus on understanding key concepts and techniques, and are available across three subjects, including: Number and Measure (Levels 1 and 2), Algebra (Levels 2 and 3) and Statistical Methods (Levels 1, 2 and 3). The level 1 Award in Number and Measure is now also an approved stepping stone qualification for the 16-18 maths condition of funding

Designed to build students' confidence and fluency; the Awards can fit into the existing programme of delivery for mathematics in schools and colleges, prepare students for GCSE and/or GCE Mathematics, and to support further study in other subjects, training or the workplace. They offer a choice of levels to match students' abilities, with clear progression between the levels. These small, 60-70 guided learning hour qualifications are assessed through one written paper per level. Each qualification is funded and approved for pre-16 and 16-18 year old students in England and in schools and colleges in Wales.

Welsh Baccalaureate

The Welsh Baccalaureate was introduced to provide learners with a rounded educational experience. It enriches and incorporates existing general and vocational qualifications and is designed to prepare learners for higher education and employment. This qualification is administered by WJEC for all centres in Wales.

From 2015, a revised more rigorous Welsh Baccalaureate has been introduced based on a Skills Challenge Certificate and Supporting qualifications.

Skills Challenge Certificate

The primary aim of the Skills Challenge Certificate is to enable learners to develop and demonstrate an understanding of and proficiency in essential and employability skills: Communication, Numeracy, Digital Literacy, Planning and Organisation, Creativity and Innovation, Critical Thinking and Problem Solving, and Personal Effectiveness. The emphasis is on applied and purposeful learning and to provide opportunities for assessment in a range of real life context through three Challenge Briefs and an Individual Project.

The Skills Challenge Certificate is equivalent to one GCSE at Foundation and National levels and one GCE A Level at Advanced Level.

Supporting qualifications

The Supporting Qualifications include two mandatory GCSEs of English Language or Welsh Language together with Mathematics or Mathematics-Numeracy. Additional Supporting qualifications are selected by the student and can include a mixture of general and vocational qualifications.

Projects

Extended Project Qualification (EPQ)

AQA, OCR, Pearson and WJEC offer the Extended Project Qualification, which is a qualification aimed at developing a student's research and independent learning skills. The EPQ can be taken as a stand-alone qualification, and it is equivalent to half an A level in UCAS points (but only a third of performance points). It is also possible to take the EPQ as part of the AQA Baccalaureate.

Students complete a research based written report and may produce an artefact or a practical science experiment as part of their project

Entry level and basic skills

Entry Level Qualifications

If you want to take GCSE or NVQ level 1 but have not yet reached the standard required, then entry level qualifications are for you as they are designed to get you started on the qualifications ladder.

Entry level qualifications are available in a wide range of areas. You can take an entry level certificate in most subjects where a similar GCSE exists. There are also vocational entry level qualifications – some in specific areas like retail or catering and others where you can take units in different work-related subjects to get a taster of a number of career areas. There are also entry level certificates in life skills and the basic skills of literacy and numeracy.

Anyone can take an entry level qualification – your school or college will help you decide which qualification is right for you.

Entry level qualifications are flexible programmes so the time it takes to complete will vary according to where you study and how long you need to take the qualification.

Subjects available: art and design, computer science, english, geography, history, latin, mathematics, physical education and science

Essential Skills Wales

A new suite of Essential Skills Wales qualifications were introduced for first teaching from 2015. The suite includes qualifications in Application of Number, Communication and Digital Literacy which replace the legacy Essential Skills Wales qualifications. A fourth qualification, Essential Employability Skills replaces the three Wider Key Skills and encompasses Critical Thinking and Problem Solving, Planning and Organisation, Creativity and Innovation and Personal Effectiveness

The qualifications are available from Entry Level to Level 3 and are offered as standalone qualifications available to post-14 learners in a wide range of settings. Essential Application of Number Skills and Essential Communication Skills also contribute to the Foundation and National Post-16 Welsh Baccalaureate qualifications.

Essential Skills Wales are offered by four awarding organisations: Agored Cymru, City & Guilds, Pearson and WJEC.

Functional Skills

Functional Skills are qualifications in English, maths and ICT that equip learners with the basic practical skills required in everyday life, education and the workplace. They are available at Entry 1 through to Level 2. Functional Skills are identified as funded 'stepping stone' qualifications to English and maths GCSE for post-16 learners who haven't previously achieved a grade D in these subjects. There are

part of apprenticeship completion requirements.

Vocational qualifications

AQA Technical Awards

AQA's new suite of Technical Awards are practical, vocational level 1/2 qualifications for 14-16 year olds to take alongside GCSEs. First teaching will be in September 2017.

Technical Awards provide an introduction to life and work within a range of vocational areas, equipping learners with the practical, transferable skills and core knowledge needed to progress to further general or vocational study, including level 3 qualifications, employment or apprenticeships.

There are nine individual qualifications: Children's Learning and Development, Fashion and Textiles, Food and Catering, Health and Social Care, IT, Materials Technology, Performing Arts, Sport and Visual Communication. A STEM Technical Award was introduced in September 2017.

Learners are assessed on doing rather than knowing through the project-based internal assessments, where they can apply their knowledge to practical tasks. Assignments will vary according to the subject, but activities range from designing and making a working product or prototype; making a short film; planning and putting on a performance, or presenting to others. There are two internally assessed units worth 30% each, and an externally assessed exam worth 40%.

AQA Tech-levels

Level 3 technical qualifications have been designed in collaboration with employers and professional bodies. They're aimed at learners aged over 16 wanting to progress into a specific sector through apprenticeships, further study or employment. There are 16 individual qualifications within IT, Engineering, Business and Entertainment Technology. These vary in size of qualification.

Transferable skills have been contextualised explicitly within each qualification and are a mandatory part of the qualification outcome.

Learners are assessed through a combination of examinations, internally and externally assessed assignments.

AQA Applied General Level 3

Applied General qualifications are available in Business and Science and are a practical introduction to these subjects, they are a real alternative to A-level support progression to further study or employment aimed at students aged 16 to 19.

Developed together with teachers, schools, colleges and higher education institutions, they help learners to develop knowledge and skills.

A mixture of assessment types means learners can apply their knowledge in a practical way. An integrated approach creates a realistic and relevant qualification for learners.

BTECs

BTEC Level 2 First qualifications

ie BTEC Level 2 Diplomas, BTEC Level 2 Extended Certificates, BTEC Level 2 Certificates and BTEC Level 2 Award.

BTEC Firsts are Level 2 introductory work-related programmes covering a wide range of vocational areas including business, engineering, information technology, health and social care, media, travel and tourism, and public services.

Programmes may be taken full or part-time. They are practical programmes that provide a foundation for the knowledge and skills you will need in work. Alternatively, you can progress onto a BTEC National qualification, Applied GCE A level or equivalent.

There are no formal entry requirements and they can be studied alongside GCSEs. Subjects available: agriculture; animal care; applied science; art and design; business; children's care, learning and development; construction; countryside and the environment; engineering; fish husbandry; floristry; health and social care; horse care; horticulture; hospitality; IT; land-based technology; business; creative media production; music; performing arts; public services; sport; travel and tourism; and vehicle technology.

BTEC Foundation Diploma in Art and Design (QCF)

For those students preparing to go on to higher education within the field of art and design. This diploma is recognised as one of the best courses of its type in the UK, and is used in preparation for degree programmes. Units offered include researching, recording and responding in art and design, media experimentation, personal experimental studies, and a final major project.

BTEC Nationals

ie BTEC Level 3 Extended Diplomas (QCF), BTEC Level 3 Diplomas (QCF), BTEC Level 3 Subsidiary Diplomas (QCF), BTEC Level 3 Certificates (QCF)

BTEC National programmes are long-established vocational programmes. They are practical programmes that are highly valued by employers. They enable you to gain the knowledge and skills that you will need in work, or give you the choice to progress on to a BTEC Higher National, a Foundation Degree or a degree programme.

BTEC Nationals, which hold UCAS points cover a range of vocationally specialist sectors including child care, children's play, learning and development, construction, art and design, aeronautical engineering, electrical/electronic engineering, IT, business, creative and media production, performing arts, public services, sport, sport and exercise sciences and applied science. The programmes may be taken full- or part-time, and can be taken in conjunction with NVQs and/or functional skills units at an appropriate level.

There are no formal entry requirements, but if you have any of the following you are likely to be at the right level to study a BTEC national qualification.

- a BTEC Level 2 First qualification
- GCSEs – at grades A* to C in several subjects
- Relevant work experience

There are also very specialist BTEC Nationals, such as pharmaceutical science and blacksmithing and metalworking.

BTEC Higher Nationals

Known as HNDs and HNCs – ie BTEC Level 5 HND Diplomas (QCF) and BTEC Level 4 HNC Diplomas (QCF)

BTEC HNDs and HNCs are further and higher education qualifications that offer a balance of education and vocational training. They are available in a wide range of work-related areas such as graphic design, business, health and social care, computing and systems development, manufacturing engineering, hospitality management, and public services.

Pearson is introducing a new suite of subjects between 2016 and 2018, to match growing demand. For full information on the subjects, visit: www.ocr.org.uk/qualifications/by-type/entry-level/entry-level-2016/

BTEC higher national courses combine study with hands-on work experience during your course. Once completed, you can use the skills you learn to begin your career, or continue on to a related degree course.

HNDs are often taken as a full-time course over two years but can also be followed part-time in some cases.

HNCs are often for people who are working and take two years to complete on a part-time study basis by day release, evenings, or a combination of the two. Some HNC courses are done on a full-time basis.

There are no formal entry requirements, but if you have any of the following you are likely to be at the right academic level:

- at least one A level
- a BTEC Level 3 National qualification
- level 3 NVQ

BTEC specialist and professional qualifications

These qualifications are designed to prepare students for specific and specialist work activities. These are split into two distinct groups:

- Specialist qualifications (entry to level 3)
- Professional qualifications (levels 4 to 7)

Cambridge Nationals

Cambridge Nationals, the updated version of OCR Nationals, are vocationally-related qualifications that take an engaging, practical and inspiring approach to learning and assessment.

They are industry-relevant, geared to key sector requirements and very popular with schools and colleges because they suit such a broad range of learning styles and abilities.

Cambridge Nationals are available in business, child development, engineering, health and social care, ICT, science, sport, and creative iMedia. Available as joint Level 1 and 2 qualifications, the updated Nationals are aimed at students aged 14 to 16 in full-time study.

Cambridge Technicals

OCR's Cambridge Technicals are practical and flexible vocationally-related qualifications, offering students in-depth study in a wide range of subjects, including business, health and social care, IT, sport, art and design, digital media, science, performing arts and engineering.

Cambridge Technicals are aimed at young people aged 16 to 19 who have completed Key Stage 4 of their education and want to study in a more practical, work-related way.

Cambridge Technicals are available at Level 2 and Level 3, and carry UCAS points at Level 3.

NVQs

NVQs reward those who demonstrate skills gained at work. They relate to particular jobs and are usefully taken while you are working. Within reason, NVQs do not have to be completed in a specified amount of time. They can be taken by full-time employees or by school and college students with a work placement or part-time job that enables them to develop the appropriate skills. There are no age limits and no special entry requirements.

NVQs are organised into levels, based on the competencies required. Levels 1-3 are the levels most applicable to learners within the 14-19 phase. Achievement of level 4 within this age group will be rare. See the OCR website for further information.

Occupational Studies (Northern Ireland)

Targeted at learners working towards and at level 1 and 2 in Key Stage 4 within the Northern Ireland curriculum. For further information see the CCEA website.

OCR Vocational Qualifications

These are available at different levels and different sizes. Levels 1-3 are the levels most applicable to learners within the 14-19 phase. The different sizes are indicated with the use of Award, Certificate and Diploma in the qualification title and indicate the number of hours it typically takes to complete the qualification.

Vocational Qualifications are assessed according to each individual specification, but may include practical assessments and/or marked assessments. They are designed to provide evidence of a student's relevant skills and knowledge in their chosen subject. These qualifications can be used for employment or as a path towards further education.

See the OCR website for further details.

See the OCR website for further details.

WJEC Vocational Qualifications

WJEC's suite of vocational qualifications relate directly to the world of work, across a range of jobs, industries and professions.

The Vocational Awards and Certificates are designed primarily for 14-18 year old learners in a school or college environment and can be delivered alongside GCSEs as part of the Key Stage 4 curriculum. They are designed to offer exciting and interesting experiences that focus learning for 14-18 year-old learners through applied learning. The qualifications are devised around a 'plan, do, review' approach to learning, where learners are introduced to a concept, carry out activities and review outcomes and learning.

Vocational Awards and Certificates are characterised by:

- Clearly structured content and straightforward assessment criteria
- Regular teacher training courses
- Excellent support network including teacher guides and digital resources
- Direct access to your WJEC subject specialist

Available in the following nine subject areas, our Vocational Awards provide learners with a broad introduction to a vocational sector and support them to progress to further study or training.

- Constructing the Built Environment
- Creative and Media
- Designing the Built Environment
- Engineering
- Hospitality and Catering
- Planning and Maintaining the Built Environment
- Retail Business
- Sport
- Tourism

Vocational Certificates provide learners with an opportunity to extend their learning and focus on additional areas within a sector. Vocational Certificates are available in:

- Creative and Media
- Retail Business
- Sport
- Tourism

Awarding organisations and examination dates

Awarding organisations and examination dates

In England there are four awarding organisations, each offering GCSE, including Applied GCSEs, A level and Applied A levels (Eduqas offers only reformed qualifications in England, whereas WJEC offers in England, Wales, Northern Ireland and independent regions). There are separate awarding organisations in Wales (WJEC) and Northern Ireland (CCEA). The awarding organisation in Scotland (SQA) offers equivalent qualifications.

This information was supplied by the awarding bodies and was accurate at the time of going to press. It is intended as a general guide only for candidates in the United Kingdom. Dates are subject to variation and should be confirmed with the awarding organisation concerned.

AQA

Qualifications offered:
GCSE
AS and A level
Tech-levels
FCSE
FSMQ
Entry Level Certificate (ELC)
Foundation and Higher Projects
Extended Project Qualification (EPQ)
AQA Baccalaureate
AQA Level 3 Certificates and Extended Certificates
Functional Skills
Preparation for Working Life
Tech Awards

Other assessment schemes:
Unit Award Scheme (UAS)
L1/L2 Tech Awards

Examination dates for summer 2018: 7 May – 22 June

Contact:
Email: eos@aqa.org.uk
Website: www.aqa.org.uk
Tel: 0800 197 7162 (8am–5pm Monday to Friday)
+44 161 696 5995 (Outside the UK)

Devas Street, Manchester M15 6EX
Stag Hill House, Guildford, Surrey GU2 7XJ
31-33 Windsor House, Cornwall Road, Harrogate, HG1 2PW

CCEA – Council for the Curriculum, Examinations and Assessment

Qualifications offered:
GCSE
GCE AS/A2 level
Key Skills (Levels 1-4)
Entry Level Qualifications
Essential Skills (Levels 1,2 & Entry Level)
Occupational Studies (Levels 1 & 2)
QCF Qualifications
Applied GCSE, GCE and QCF Level 1 and 2 qualifications

Examination dates for summer 2017: 1 May – 25 June

Contact:
Email: info@ccea.org.uk
Website: www.ccea.org.uk

29 Clarendon Road, Clarendon Dock, Belfast, BT1 3BG
Tel: (028) 9026 1200

Eduqas

Eduqas, part of WJEC, offers Ofqual reformed GCSEs, AS and A levels to secondary schools and colleges. Our qualifications are available in England, Channel Islands, Isle of Man, Northern Ireland and to the independent sector in Wales (restrictions may apply).

Qualifications offered:
GCSE (9-1)
AS
A-level
Level 3

Examination dates for summer 2018: 14 May – 29 June

Contact:
Email:info@eduqas.co.uk
Website: www.eduqas.co.uk

Eduqas (WJEC CBAC Ltd),
245 Western Avenue, Cardiff, CF5 2YX
Telephone: 029 2026 5465

IB – International Baccalaureate

Qualification offered:
IB Diploma
IB Career-related Certificate

Contact:
www.ibo.org

Examination dates for summer 2018: 26 April – 18 May

IB Global Centre, The Hague, Churchillplein 6, 2517 JW, The Hague, The Netherlands

Tel: +31 70 352 60 00

OCR – Oxford Cambridge and RSA Examinations

Qualifications offered by OCR or sister awarding organisation Cambridge International Examinations, include:
GCSE
GCE AS/A level
IGCSE
Extended Project
Cambridge Pre-U
Cambridge Nationals
Cambridge Technicals
Functional Skills
FSMQ – Free Standing Maths Qualification
NVQ

Examination dates for summer 2018: 14 May to 22 June

Contact:
Website: www.ocr.org.uk (or www.cie.org.uk)

OCR Head Office, 1 Hills Road, Cambridge CB1 2EU
Tel: 01223 553998

Pearson

Qualifications offered:
Pearson's qualifications are offered in the UK but are also available through their international centres across the world. They include:
DiDA, CiDA, AiDA
GCE A levels
GCSEs
Adult Literacy and Numeracy
Functional Skills
Foundation Learning
International GCSEs
Key Skills
ESOL (Skills for Life)
BTEC Customised Qualifications
BTEC Foundation Diploma in Art & Design
BTEC Nationals
BTEC Higher National Certificates and Higher National Diplomas (HNC/HND)
BTEC Firsts
BTEC Specialist qualifications
BTEC Professional qualifications
BTEC WorkSkills
NVQs
Project qualifications

Examination dates for summer 2018: 14 May – 29 June

Contact:
190 High Holborn, London WC1V 7BH

See website for specific contact details: www.edexcel.com

SQA – Scottish Qualifications Authority

Qualifications offered:
National Qualifications: National 2, National 3, National 4 and National 5; Higher; Advanced Higher.
Higher National Qualifications: Higher National Certificate (HNC); Higher National Diploma (HND).
Vocational Qualifications: Scottish Vocational Qualifications (SVQ).

Examination dates for summer 2018: 30 April – 4 June

Contact:
Email: customer@sqa.org.uk
Website: www.sqa.org.uk

Glasgow – The Optima Building, 58 Robertson Street, Glasgow, G2 8DQ

Dalkeith – Lowden, 24 Wester Shawfair, Dalkeith, Midlothian, EH22 1FD

WJEC

With over 65 years' experience in delivering qualifications, WJEC is the largest provider in Wales and a leading provider in England and Northern Ireland.

Qualifications offered:
GCSE
GCE A/AS
Functional Skills
Entry Level
Welsh Baccalaureate Qualifications
Essential Skills Wales
Wider Key Skills
Project Qualifications Principal Learning
Other general qualifications such as Level 1 and Level 2 Awards and Certificates including English Language, English Literature, Latin Language, Latin Language & Roman Civilisation and Latin Literature
QCF Qualifications

Examination dates for summer 2018: 14 May – 29 June

Contact:
Email: info@wjec.co.uk
Website: www.wjec.co.uk

245 Western Avenue, Cardiff, CF5 2YX
Tel: 029 2026 5000

Educational organisations

Educational organisations

Artsmark

Arts Council England's Artsmark was set up in 2001, and rounds are held annually.
All schools in England can apply for an Artsmark – primary, middle, secondary, special and pupil referral units, maintained and independent – on a voluntary basis. An Artsmark award is made to schools showing commitment to the full range of arts – music, dance, drama and art and design.
Tel: 0845 300 6200/ 0161 934 4317
Email: artsmark@artscouncil.org.uk
Website: www.artsmark.org.uk

Association for the Education and Guardianship of International Students (AEGIS)

AEGIS brings together schools and guardianship organisations to promote the welfare of international students. AEGIS provides accreditation for all reputable guardianship organisations.
AEGIS, The Wheelhouse, Bond's Mill Estate, Bristol Road, Stonehouse, Gloucestershire GL10 3RF.
Tel: 01453 821293
Email: info@aegisuk.net
Website: www.aegisuk.net

The Association of American Study Abroad Programmes (AASAP)

Established in 1991 to represent American study programmes in the UK.
Contact: Kalyn Franke, AASAP/UK,
University of Maryland in London, Connaught Hall,
36-45 Tavistock Square, London WC1H 9EX
Tel: 020 7756 8350
Email: info@aasapuk.org
Website: www.aasapuk.org

The Association of British Riding Schools (ABRS)

An independent body of proprietors and principals of riding establishments, aiming to look after their interests and those of the riding public and to raise standards of management, instruction and animal welfare.
Association of British Riding Schools, Unite 8, Bramble Hill Farm, Five Oakes Road, Slinfold, Horsham, Sussex RH13 0RL.
Tel: 01403 790294
Email: office@abrs-info.org
Website: www.abrs-info.org

Association of Colleges (AOC)

Created in 1996 to promote the interest of further education colleges in England and Wales.
2-5 Stedham Place, London WC1A 1HU
Tel: 0207 034 9900
Fax: 0207 034 9950
Email: enquiries@aoc.co.uk
Website: www.aoc.co.uk

Association of Governing Bodies of Independent Schools (AGBIS)

AGBIS supports and advises governing bodies of schools in the independent sector on all aspects of governance.
(Registered charity No. 1108756)
Association of Governing Bodies of Independent Schools, 3 Codicote Road, Welwyn, Hertfordshire AL6 9LY
Tel: 01438 840730
Fax: 0560 3432632
Email: admin@agbis.org.uk
Website: www.agbis.org.uk

Association of Employment and Learning Providers (AELP)

AELP's purpose is to influence the education and training agenda. They are the voice of independent learning providers throughout England.
Association of Employment and Learning Providers,
2nd Floor, 9 Apex Court, Bradley Stoke, Bristol, BS32 4JT
Tel: 0117 986 5389
Email: enquiries@aelp.org.uk
Website: www.aelp.org.uk

The Association of School and Colleges Leaders (ASCL)

Formerly the Secondary Heads Association, the ASCL is a professional association for secondary school and college leaders.
130 Regent Road, Leicester LE1 7PG
Tel: 0116 299 1122
Fax: 0116 299 1123
Email: info@ascl.org.uk
Website: www.ascl.org.uk

Boarding Schools' Association (BSA)

For information on the BSA see editorial on page 35

The British Accreditation Council for Independent Further and Higher Education (BAC)

The British Accreditation Council (BAC) has now been the principal accrediting body for the independent further and higher education and training sector for nearly 30 years. BAC-accredited institutions in the UK now number more than 300, offering everything from website design to yoga to equine dentistry, as well as more standard qualifications in subjects such as business, IT, management and law. As well as our accreditation of institutions offering traditional teaching, BAC has developed a new accreditation scheme for providers offering online, distance and blended learning. Some students may also look to study outside UK at one of the institutions holding BAC international accreditation.
Ground Floor, 14 Devonshire Square, London, EC2M 4YT
Tel: 0300 330 1400
Email: info@the-bac.org
Website: www.the-bac.org

The British Association for Early Childhood Education (BAECE)

Promotes quality provision for all children from birth to eight in whatever setting they are placed. Publishes booklets and organises conferences for those interested in early years education and care. (Registered charity Nos. 313082; SCO39472)
54 Clarendon Road, Watford, WD17 1DU
Tel: 01923 438 04
Email: office@early-education.org.uk
Website: www.early-education.org.uk

The Choir Schools' Association (CSA)

Represents 44 schools attached to cathedrals, churches and college chapels, which educate cathedral and collegiate choristers.
CSA Information Officer, Village Farm, The Street, Market Weston, Diss, Norfolk IP22 2NZ
Tel: 01359 221333
Email: info@choirschools.org.uk
Website: www.choirschools.org.uk

The Council for Independent Education (CIFE)

CIFE is the professional association for independent sixth form and tutorial colleges accredited by the British Accreditation Council for Independent Further and Higher Education (BAC), the Independent Schools Council or the DfE (Ofsted). Member colleges specialise in preparing students for GCSE and A level (AS and A2) in particular and university entrance in general.
The aim of the association is to provide a forum for the exchange of information and ideas, and for the promotion of best practice, and to safeguard adherence to strict standards of professional conduct and ethical propriety.
Further information can be obtained from CIFE:
Tel: 0208 767 8666
Email: enquiries@cife.org.uk
Website: www.cife.org.uk

Council of British International Schools (COBIS)

COBIS is a membership association of British schools of quality worldwide and is committed to a stringent process of quality assurance for all its member schools. COBIS is a member of the Independent Schools Council (ISC) of the United Kingdom.
COBIS, 55-56 Russell Square, Bloomsbury,
London WC1B 4HP
Tel: 020 3826 7190
Email: executive.director@cobis.org.uk
Website: www.cobis.org.uk

Council of International Schools (CIS)

CIS is a not-for-profit organisation committed to supporting its member schools and colleges in achieving and delivering the highest standards of international education. CIS provides accreditation to schools, teacher and leader recruitment and best practice development. CIS Higher Education assists member colleges and universities in recruiting a diverse profile of qualified international students.
Schipholweg 113, 2316 XC Leiden, The Netherlands.
Tel: +31 71 524 3300
Email: info@cois.org
Website: www.cois.org

Dyslexia Action (DA)

A registered, educational charity (No. 268502), which has established teaching and assessment centres and conducts teacher-training throughout the UK. The aim of the institute is to help people with dyslexia of all ages to overcome their difficulties in learning to read, write and spell and to achieve their potential.
Dyslexia Action Training and Guild, Centurion House, London Road, Staines-upon-Thames TW18 4AX
Tel: 01784 222 304
Website: www.dyslexiaaction.org.uk

European Association for International Education (EAIE)

A not-for-profit organisation aiming for internationalisation in higher education in Europe. It has a membership of over 1800.
PO Box 11189, 1001 GD Amsterdam, The Netherlands
Tel: +31 20 344 5100
Fax: +31 20 344 5119
Email: info@eaie.org
Website: www.eaie.org

ECIS (European Collaborative for International Schools)

ECIS is a membership organisation which provides services to support professional development, good governance and leadership in international schools.
Fourth Floor, 146 Buckingham Palace Road,
London, SW1W 9TR
Tel: 020 7824 7040
Email: ecis@ecis.org
Website: www.ecis.org

The Girls' Day School Trust (GDST)

The Girls' Day School Trust (GDST) is one of the largest, longest-established and most successful groups of independent schools in the UK, with 4000 staff and over 20,000 students between the ages of three and 18.
As a charity that owns and runs a family of 26 schools in England and Wales, it reinvests all its income into its schools for the benefit of the pupils. With a long history of pioneering innovation in the education of girls, the GDST now also educates boys in some of its schools, and has two coeducational sixth form colleges. (Registered charity No. 306983)
100 Rochester Row, London SWIP 1JP
Tel: 020 7393 6666
Email: info@wes.gdst.net
Website: www.gdst.net

Girls' Schools Association (GSA)

For information on the GSA see editorial on page 36

The Headmasters' and Headmistresses' Conference (HMC)

For information on the HMC see editorial on page 37

Human Scale Education (HSE)

An educational reform movement aiming for small education communities based on democracy, fairness and respect. (Registered charity No. 1000400)
Email: contact@hse.org.uk
Website: www.hse.org.uk

The Independent Association of Prep Schools (IAPS)

For further information about IAPS see editorial on page 34

The Independent Schools Association (ISA)

For further information about ISA see editorial on page 35

The Independent Schools' Bursars Association (ISBA)

Exists to support and advance financial and operational performance in independent schools. The ISBA is a charitable company limited by guarantee. (Company No. 6410037; registered charity No. 1121757.)
Bluett House, Unit 11-12 Manor Farm, Cliddesden, Basingstoke, Hampshire RG25 2JB
Tel: 01256 330369
Fax: 01256 330376
Email: office@theisba.org.uk
Website: www.theisba.org.uk

The Independent Schools Council (ISC)

The Independent Schools Council exists to promote choice, diversity and excellence in education; the development of talent at all levels of ability; and the widening of opportunity for children from all backgrounds to achieve their potential. Its 1280 member schools educate more than 500,000 children at all levels of ability and from all socio-economic classes. Nearly a third of children in ISC schools receive help with fees. The Governing Council of ISC contains representatives from each of the eight ISC constituent associations listed below. See also page 40.

Members:
Association of Governing Bodies of Independent Schools (AGBIS)
Council of British International Schools (COBIS)
Girls' Schools Association (GSA)
Headmasters' and Headmistresses' Conference (HMC)
Independent Association of Prep Schools (IAPS)
Independent Schools Association (ISA)
Independent Schools Bursars' Association (ISBA)
The Society of Heads
The council also has close relations with the BSA and the SCIS.
First Floor, 27 Queen Anne's Gate,
London, SW1H 9BU
Tel: 020 7766 7070
Fax: 020 7766 7071
Email: research@isc.co.uk
Website: www.isc.co.uk

The Independent Schools Examinations Board (ISEB)

Details of the Common Entrance examinations are obtainable from:
Independent Schools Examinations Board,
Endeavour House, Crow Arch Lane, Ringwood BH24 1HP
Tel: 01425 470555
Email: enquiries@iseb.co.uk
Website: www.iseb.co.uk
Copies of past papers can be purchased from Galore Publishing Ltd: www.galorepark.co.uk

The Inspiring Futures Foundation (IFF)

The IFF provides careers education and guidance to schools and students. Professional support and training is available to school staff and our Futurewise programme provides individual, web-based, support for students and their parents. Career/subject insight courses, gap-year fairs and an information service are additional elements of the service.
Tel: 01491 820381
Email: helpline@inspiringfutures.org.uk
Website: www.inspiringfutures.org.uk

International Baccalaureate (IB)

For full information about the IB see full entry on page 416

International Schools Theatre Association (ISTA)

International body of teachers and students of theatre, run by teachers for teachers. Registered charity No. 1050103.
3 Omega Offices, 14 Coinagehall St,
Helston, Cornwall TR13 8EB
Tel: 01326 560398
Email: office@ista.co.uk
Website: www.ista.co.uk

Maria Montessori Institute (MMI)

Authorised by the Association Montessori Internationale (AMI) to run their training course in the UK. Further information is available from:
26 Lyndhurst Gardens, Hampstead, London NW3 5NW
Tel: 020 7435 3646
Email: info@mariamontessori.org
Website: www.mariamontessori.org

The National Association of Independent Schools & Non-Maintained Schools (NASS)

A membership organisation working with and for special schools in the voluntary and private sectors within the UK. Registered charity No. 1083632.
PO Box 705, York YO30 6WW
Tel/Fax: 01904 624446
Email: krippon@nasschools.org.uk
Website: www.nasschools.org.uk

National Day Nurseries Association (NDNA)

A national charity (No. 1078275) that aims to promote quality in early years.
NDNA, National Early Years Enterprise Centre,
Longbow Close, Huddersfield, West Yorkshire HD2 1GQ
Tel: 01484 407070
Fax: 01484 407060
Email: info@ndna.org.uk
Website: www.ndna.org.uk

NDNA Cymru, Office 2, Crown House, 11 Well Street,
Ruthin, Denbighshire LL15 1AE
Tel: 01824 707823;
Fax: 01824 707824;
Email: wales@ndna.org.uk

NDNA Scotland, The Mansfield Traquair Centre,
15 Mansfield Place, Edinburgh EH3 6BB
Tel: 0131 516 6967
Email: scotland@ndna.org.uk

National Foundation for Educational Research (NFER)

NFER is the UK's largest independent provider of research, assessment and information services for education, training and children's services. Its clients include UK government departments and agencies at both national and local levels. NFER is a not-for-profit organisation and a registered charity No. 313392.
Head Office, The Mere, Upton Park,
Slough, Berkshire SL1 2DQ
Tel: 01753 574123
Fax: 01753 691632
Email: enquiries@nfer.ac.uk
Website: www.nfer.ac.uk

Potential Plus UK

Potential Plus UK is an independent charity that supports the social, emotional and learning needs of children with high learning potential of all ages and backgrounds. Registered charity No. 313182.
Challenge House, Sherwood Drive, Bletchley, Milton Keynes, Buckinghamshire MK3 6DP
Tel: 01908 646433
Email: amazingchildren@potentialplusuk.org
Website: www.potentialplusuk.org

Round Square

An international group of schools formed in 1967 following the principles of Dr Kurt Hahn, the founder of Salem School in Germany, and Gordonstoun in Scotland. The Round Square, named after Gordonstoun's 17th century circular building in the centre of the school, now has more than 100 member schools. Registered charity No. 327117.
Round Square, Swan House, Madeira Walk, Windsor SL41EU
Tel: 01474 709843
Website: www.roundsquare.org

Royal National Children's Foundation

In December 2010, Joint Educational Trust and the Royal Wanstead Children's Foundation merged to form this new Foundation. For further information contact:
Sandy Lane, Cobham, Surrey KT11 2ES
Tel: 01932 868622
Fax: 01932 866420
Email: admin@rncf.org.uk
Website: www.rncf.org.uk

School Fees Independent Advice (SFIA)

For further information about SFIA, see editorial page 32

Schools Music Association of Great Britain (SMA)

The SMA is a national 'voice' for music in education. It is now part of the Incorporated Society of Musicians (Registered charity No. 313646)
Website: www.schoolsmusic.org.uk

Scottish Council of Independent Schools (SCIS)

Representing more than 70 independent, fee-paying schools in Scotland, the Scottish Council of Independent Schools (SCIS) is the foremost authority on independent schools in Scotland and offers impartial information, advice and guidance to parents. Registered charity No. SC01803. They can be contacted at:
61 Dublin Street, Edinburgh EH3 6NL
Tel: 0131 556 2316
Email: info@scis.org.uk
Website: www.scis.org.uk

Society of Education Consultants (SEC)

The Society is a professional membership organisation that supports management consultants who specialise in education and children's services. The society's membership includes consultants who work as individuals, in partnerships or in association with larger consultancies.
SEC, Bellamy House, 13 West Street, Cromer NR27 9HZ
Tel: 0330 323 0457
Email: administration@sec.org.uk
Website: www.sec.org.uk

The Society of Heads

For full information see editorial on page 40

The State Boarding Schools' Association (SBSA)

For full information about the SBSA see editorial on page 35

Steiner Waldorf Schools Fellowship (SWSF)

Representing Steiner education in the UK and Ireland, the SWSF has member schools and early years centres in addition to interest groups and other affiliated organisations. Member schools offer education for children within the normal range of ability, aged three to 18.
(Registered charity No. 295104)
Steiner Waldorf Schools Fellowship® Ltd, Suite 1, 3rd Floor, Copthall House, 1 New Road, Stourbridge, West Midlands, DY8 1PH
Tel: 01384 374116
Email: admin@steinerwaldorf.org
Website: www.steinerwaldorf.org.uk

Support and Training in Prep Schools (SATIPS)

SATIPS aims to support teachers in the independent and maintained sectors of education. (Registered charity No. 313699)
West Routengill, Walden, West Burton, Leyburn,
North Yorkshire, DL1 4LF
Tel: 07584 862263
Email: gensec@satips.org
Website: www.satips.org

The Tutors' Association

The Tutors' Association is the professional body for tutoring and wider supplementary education sector in the UK. Launched three years ago it now has over 500 members. Of these 150 are Corporate Members representing some 20,000 tutors throughout the UK.
Tel: +44 (0)1628 890130
Fax: +44 (0)1628 890131
Email: info@thetutorsassociation.org.uk
Website: www.tutor.co.uk

UCAS (Universities and Colleges Admissions Service)

UCAS is the organisation responsible for managing applications to higher education courses in England, Scotland, Wales and Northern Ireland. (Registered charity Nos. 1024741 and SCO38598)
Rosehill, New Barn Lane,
Cheltenham, Gloucestershire GL52 3LZ
Tel: 0371 468 0 468
Website: www.ucas.com

UKCISA – The Council for International Student Affairs

UKCISA is the UK's national advisory body serving the interests of international students and those who work with them. (Registered charity No. 1095294)
Website: www.ukcisa.org.uk

United World Colleges (UWC)

UWC was founded in 1962 and their philosophy is based on the ideas of Dr Kurt Hahn (see Round Square Schools). Registered charity No. 313690.
The United World Colleges (International),
Second Floor, 17-21 Emerald Street,
London WC1N 3QN
Tel: 020 7269 7800
Fax: 020 7405 4374
Email: info@uwcio.uwc.org
Website: www.uwc.org

World-Wide Education Service of CfBT Education Trust (WES)

A leading independent service which provides home education courses worldwide.
Waverley House, Penton,
Carlisle, Cumbria CA6 5QU
Tel: 01228 577123
Email: office@weshome.com
Website: www.weshome.com

Glossary

ACETS Awards and Certificates in Education
AEA Advanced Extension Award
AEB Associated Examining Board for the General Certificate of Education
AEGIS Association for the Education and Guardianship of International Students
AGBIS Association of Governing Bodies of Independent Schools
AHIS Association of Heads of Independent Schools
AJIS Association of Junior Independent Schools
ALP Association of Learning Providers
ANTC The Association of Nursery Training Colleges
AOC Association of Colleges
AP Advanced Placement
ASCL Association of School & College Leaders
ASL Additional and Specialist Learning
ATI The Association of Tutors Incorporated
AQA Assessment and Qualification Alliance/Northern Examinations and Assessment Board
BA Bachelor of Arts
BAC British Accreditation Council for Independent Further and Higher Education
BAECE The British Association for Early Childhood Education
BD Bachelor of Divinity
BEA Boarding Educational Alliance
BEd Bachelor of Education
BLitt Bachelor of Letters
BPrimEd Bachelor of Primary Education
BSA Boarding Schools' Association
BSc Bachelor of Science
BTEC Range of work-related, practical programmes leading to qualifications equivalent to GCSEs and A levels awarded by Edexcel
Cantab Cambridge University
CATSC Catholic Association of Teachers in Schools and Colleges
CCEA Council for the Curriculum, Examination and Assessment
CDT Craft, Design and Technology
CE Common Entrance Examination
CEAS Children's Education Advisory Service
CertEd Certificate of Education
CIE Cambridge International Examinations
CIFE Conference for Independent Education
CIS Council of International Schools
CISC Catholic Independent Schools' Conference
CLAIT Computer Literacy and Information Technology
CNED Centre National d'enseignement (National Centre of long distance learning)
COBIS Council of British International)

CSA	The Choir Schools' Association
CST	The Christian Schools' Trust
DfE	Department for Education (formerly DfES and DCFS)
DipEd	Diploma of Education
DipTchng	Diploma of Teaching
EAIE	European Association for International Education
ECIS	European Council of International Schools
EdD	Doctor of Education
Edexcel	GCSE Examining group, incorporating Business and Technology Education Council (BTEC) and University of London Examinations and Assessment Council (ULEAC)
EFL	English as a Foreign Language
ELAS	Educational Law Association
EPQ	Extended Project qualification
ESL	English as a Second Language
FCoT	Fellow of the College of Teachers (TESOL)
FEFC	Further Education Funding Council
FRSA	Fellow of the Royal Society of Arts
FSMQ	Free-Standing Mathematics Qualification
GCE	General Certificate of Education
GCSE	General Certificate of Secondary Education
GDST	Girls' Day School Trust
GNVQ	General National Vocational Qualifications
GOML	Graded Objectives in Modern Languages
GSA	Girls' Schools Association
GSVQ	General Scottish Vocational Qualifications
HMC	Headmasters' and Headmistresses' Conference
HMCJ	Headmasters' and Headmistresses' Conference Junior Schools
HNC	Higher National Certificate
HND	Higher National Diploma
IAPS	Independent Association of Prep Schools
IB	International Baccalaureate
ICT	Information and Communication Technology
IFF	Inspiring Futures Foundation (formerly ISCO)
IGCSE	International General Certificate of Secondary Education
INSET	In service training
ISA	Independent Schools Association
ISBA	Independent Schools' Bursars' Association
ISCis	Independent Schools Council information service
ISC	Independent Schools Council
ISEB	Independent Schools Examination Board
ISST	International Schools Sports Tournament
ISTA	International Schools Theatre Association
ITEC	International Examination Council
JET	Joint Educational Trust
LA	Local Authority
LISA	London International Schools Association
MA	Master of Arts
MCIL	Member of the Chartered Institute of Linguists
MEd	Master of Education
MIoD	Member of the Institute of Directors
MLitt	Master of Letters
MSc	Master of Science
MusD	Doctor of Music
MYP	Middle Years Programme
NABSS	National Association of British Schools in Spain
NAGC	National Association for Gifted Children
NAHT	National Association of Head Teachers
NAIS	National Association of Independent Schools
NASS	National Association of Independent Schools & Non-maintained Special Schools
NDNA	National Day Nurseries Association
NEASC	New England Association of Schools and Colleges
NFER	National Federation of Educational Research
NPA	National Progression Award
NQ	National Qualification
NQF	National Qualifications Framework
NQT	Newly Qualified Teacher
NVQ	National Vocational Qualifications
OCR	Oxford, Cambridge and RSA Examinations
OLA	Online Language Assessment for Modern Languages
Oxon	Oxford
PGCE	Post Graduate Certificate in Education
PhD	Doctor of Philosophy
PL	Principal Learning
PNEU	Parents' National Education Union
PYP	Primary Years Programme
QCA	Qualifications and Curriculum Authority
QCF	Qualifications and Credit Framework
RSIS	The Round Square Schools
SAT	Scholastic Aptitude Test
SATIPS	Support & Training in Prep Schools/Society of Assistant Teachers in Prep Schools
SBSA	State Boarding Schools Association
SCE	Service Children's Education
SCIS	Scottish Council of Independent Schools
SCQF	Scottish Credit and Qualifications Framework
SEC	The Society of Educational Consultants
SEN	Special Educational Needs
SFCF	Sixth Form Colleges' Forum
SFIA	School Fees Insurance Agency Limited
SFIAET	SFIA Educational Trust
SMA	Schools Music Association
SoH	The Society of Heads
SQA	Scottish Qualifications Authority
STEP	Second Term Entrance Paper (Cambridge)
SVQ	Scottish Vocational Qualifications
SWSF	Steiner Waldorf Schools Fellowship
TABS	The Association of Boarding Schools
TISCA	The Independent Schools Christian Alliance
TOEFL	Test of English as a Foreign Language
UCAS	Universities and Colleges Admissions Service for the UK
UCST	United Church Schools Trust
UKLA	UK Literacy Association
UKCISA	The UK Council for International Education
UWC	United World Colleges
WISC	World International Studies Committee
WJEC	Welsh Joint Education Committee
WSSA	Welsh Secondary Schools Association

Index

286
288
292
290

A

B

C

D

Y

C016536907